Playfair Football Who's Who

JACK ROLLIN

First published in 1999
by HEADLINE BOOK PUBLISHING

10 9 8 7 6 5 4 3 2 1

Front cover photographs
Top, left to right: Rio Ferdinand (West Ham United) – *ASP;*
Andrei Kanchelskis (Rangers) – *Empics;*
Roy Keane (Manchester United) – *ASP;*
Emile Heskey (Leicester City) – *Colorsport*
Centre: Shay Given (Newcastle United) – *Action Images*
Bottom, left to right: Tony Adams (Arsenal) – *Action Images;*
Dion Dublin (Aston Villa) – *Empics*
Back cover photographs
Top: David Ginola (Tottenham Hotspur);
bottom: Tor Andre Flo (Chelsea) – both *Empics*

ISBN 0 7472 6135 0

Typeset by Wearset, Boldon, Tyne and Wear

Printed and bound in Great Britain by
Caledonian International, Glasgow

HEADLINE BOOK PUBLISHING
A division of the Hodder Headline Group
338 Euston Road
London NW1 3BH

www.headline.co.uk
www.hodderheadline.com

THE AUTHOR

Jack Rollin was a soccer columnist for the *Sunday Telegraph* for twenty-one years, worked on BBC's *Match of the Day*, has written and compiled more than sixty books including twenty-seven editions of *Rothmans Football Yearbook*. He is the soccer consultant to the *Encyclopaedia Britannica*.

The British Library's *A Football Compendium* said: 'Jack Rollin's classic *Soccer at War 1939–45* provides an extremely comprehensive account of one of the lesser known eras of soccer's rich history.'

In 1975 he won the Designers and Art Directors Association Silver Award for the outstanding specialist feature of the year, the *Radio Times World Cup Special*.

PREFACE

The third edition of *Playfair Football Who's Who* contains career details of all players who appeared during the 1998–99 season in the FA Carling Premiership, Nationwide Football League and Bank of Scotland Scottish Premier League, plus Hibernian, the club promoted from the Scottish League First Division. The book also includes players in England who were contracted to clubs in the four English divisions who did not make appearances. Players' information includes date and place of birth, height and weight where known, playing position, League appearances and goals scored, source and main honours achieved. Appearances include those made as a substitute. Players with foreign clubs who have an asterisk * beside the team name indicates that club was outside its leading division that season.

The author would like to thank Glenda Rollin for her much valued contribution, Alan Elliott for Scottish League information and Gavin Willacy for England Schoolboy International details. The author also wishes to acknowledge the co-operation of Mike Foster and Jonathan Hargreaves of the FA Premier League, and Debbie Birch, Louise Standing and Andrea Stock of the Football League. Once again a special mention for Lorraine Jerram of Headline Book Publishing, whose invaluable input and support was much appreciated.

The Football League welcome Cheltenham Town to the Third Division in 1999–2000. The club's Nationwide Conference appearances and goals can be found on page 442 and there is a Stop Press for summer transfers on pages 441 and 442.

FOREWORD

The third edition of *Playfair Football Who's Who*, by Jack Rollin, maintains the long tradition of excellent football books produced by Headline, publishers of *Rothmans Football Yearbook* and *Playfair Football Annual*.

It is a difficult task these days to keep up to date with the changing face of personnel at clubs with the ever-increasing cosmopolitan nature of the game and Jack Rollin is to be congratulated on achieving this task successfully. There are precise details of professional players in England, Wales and Scotland which can be found by quick and easy alphabetical reference and the book provides all the information necessary for a football factfinder and devotees of fantasy football.

Playfair Football Who's Who will prove an invaluable help to all administrators, managers, soccer writers and supporters of football throughout the United Kingdom and will occupy a prominent place on my desk and I do not hesitate to recommend it.

Gordon Taylor,

Chief Executive, The Professional Footballers' Association

ABBEY, Nathan — Goalkeeper

H: 6 1 W: 11 13 b.Islington 11-7-78

Source: Trainee.

Season	Club	Appearances	Goals
1995–96	Luton T	0	0
1996–97	Luton T	0	0
1997–98	Luton T	0	0
1998–99	Luton T	2	0
Total:		**2**	**0**

ABLETT, Gary — Defender

H: 6 2 W: 11 04 b.Liverpool 19-11-65

Source: Apprentice. *Honours:* England Under-21, B.

Season	Club	Appearances	Goals
1983–84	Liverpool	0	0
1984–85	Liverpool	0	0
1984–85	Derby Co (loan)	6	0
1985–86	Liverpool	0	0
1986–87	Hull C (loan)	5	0
1986–87	Liverpool	5	1
1987–88	Liverpool	17	0
1988–89	Liverpool	35	0
1989–90	Liverpool	15	0
1990–91	Liverpool	23	0
1991–92	Liverpool	14	0
1991–92	Everton	17	1
1992–93	Everton	40	0
1993–94	Everton	32	1
1994–95	Everton	26	3
1995–96	Everton	13	0
1995–96	Sheffield U (loan)	12	0
1996–97	Birmingham C	42	1
1997–98	Birmingham C	36	0
1998–99	Birmingham C	26	0
Total:		**364**	**7**

ABOU, Samassi — Forward

H: 6 1 W: 12 08 b.Gagnoa 4-4-73

Season	Club	Appearances	Goals
1996–97	Cannes	27	4
1997–98	Cannes	10	1
1997–98	West Ham U	19	5
1998–99	West Ham U	3	0
1998–99	Ipswich T (loan)	5	1
Total:		**64**	**11**

ABRAHAMS, Paul — Forward

H: 5 10 W: 11 00 b.Colchester 31-10-73

Source: Trainee.

Season	Club	Appearances	Goals
1991–92	Colchester U	0	0
1992–93	Colchester U	23	6
1993–94	Colchester U	4	0
1994–95	Colchester U	28	2
1994–95	Brentford	10	3
1995–96	Brentford	17	3
1995–96	Colchester U (loan)	8	2
1996–97	Brentford	8	2
1996–97	Colchester U	29	7
1997–98	Colchester U	25	7
1998–99	Colchester U	27	2
Total:		**179**	**34**

ACHTERBERG, John — Goalkeeper

H: 6 1 W: 13 00 b.Utrecht 8-7-71

Source: VV RUC, Utrecht.

Season	Club	Appearances	Goals
1993–94	NAC	1	0
1994–95	NAC	2	0
1995–96	NAC	6	0
1996–97	Eindhoven	32	0
From Utrecht.			
1998–99	Tranmere R	24	0
Total:		**65**	**0**

ADAM, Stephane — Forward

H: 5 11 W: 12 00 b.Lille 15-5-69

Source: Creteil, Amiens.

Season	Club	Appearances	Goals
1995–96	Metz	19	1
1996–97	Metz	21	3
1997–98	Hearts	30	8
1998–99	Hearts	29	10
Total:		**99**	**22**

ADAMCZUK, Dariusz — Midfield

H: 5 10 W: 12 00 b.Stettin 20-10-69

Source: Eintracht Frankfurt.

Season	Club	Appearances	Goals
1993–94	Dundee	11	1
From Pogon Stettin			
1995–96	Dundee	13	0
1996–97	Dundee	30	1
1997–98	Dundee	34	1
1998–99	Dundee	26	6
Total:		**114**	**9**

ADAMS, Derek — Midfield

H: 5 10 W: 11 12 b.Aberdeen 25-6-75

Source: Aberdeen.

Season	Club	Appearances	Goals
1994–95	Burnley	0	0
1995–96	Burnley	2	0
1996–97	Ross Co	34	22
1997–98	Ross Co	34	16
1998–99	Motherwell	26	3
Total:		**96**	**41**

ADAMS, Kieran — Midfield

H: 5 11 W: 11 06 b.St Ives 20-10-77

Source: Trainee.

Season	Club	Appearances	Goals
1994–95	Barnet	4	0

1995–96	Barnet	1	0
1996–97	Barnet	3	0
1997–98	Barnet	11	1
1998–99	Barnet	0	0
Total:		**19**	**1**

ADAMS, Neil — Midfield

H: 5 9 W: 11 04 b.Stoke 23-11-65

Source: Local. *Honours:* England Under-21.

1985–86	Stoke C	32	4
1986–87	Everton	12	0
1987–88	Everton	8	0
1988–89	Everton	0	0
1988–89	Oldham Ath (loan)	9	0
1989–90	Oldham Ath	27	4
1990–91	Oldham Ath	31	6
1991–92	Oldham Ath	26	4
1992–93	Oldham Ath	32	9
1993–94	Oldham Ath	13	0
1993–94	Norwich C	14	0
1994–95	Norwich C	33	3
1995–96	Norwich C	42	2
1996–97	Norwich C	45	13
1997–98	Norwich C	30	4
1998–99	Norwich C	18	3
Total:		**372**	**52**

ADAMS, Tony — Defender

H: 6 3 W: 13 11 b.London 10-10-66

Source: Apprentice. *Honours:* England Youth, Under-21, B, 57 full caps, 4 goals.

1983–84	Arsenal	3	0
1984–85	Arsenal	16	0
1985–86	Arsenal	10	0
1986–87	Arsenal	42	6
1987–88	Arsenal	39	2
1988–89	Arsenal	36	4
1989–90	Arsenal	38	5
1990–91	Arsenal	30	1
1991–92	Arsenal	35	2
1992–93	Arsenal	35	0
1993–94	Arsenal	35	0
1994–95	Arsenal	27	3
1995–96	Arsenal	21	1
1996–97	Arsenal	28	3
1997–98	Arsenal	26	3
1998–99	Arsenal	26	1
Total:		**447**	**31**

ADAMSON, Christopher — Goalkeeper

H: 5 11 W: 11 00 b.Ashington 4-11-78

Source: Trainee.

1997–98	WBA	3	0
1998–99	WBA	0	0
1998–99	Mansfield T (loan)	2	0
Total:		**5**	**0**

ADCOCK, Tony — Forward

H: 5 11 W: 11 11 b.Bethnal Green 27-3-63

Source: Apprentice.

1980–81	Colchester U	1	0
1981–82	Colchester U	40	5
1982–83	Colchester U	30	17
1983–84	Colchester U	43	26
1984–85	Colchester U	28	24
1985–86	Colchester U	33	15
1986–87	Colchester U	35	11
1987–88	Manchester C	15	5
1987–88	Northampton T	18	10
1988–89	Northampton T	46	17
1989–90	Northampton T	8	3
1989–90	Bradford C	28	5
1990–91	Bradford C	10	1
1990–91	Northampton T	21	3
1991–92	Northampton T	14	7
1991–92	Peterborough U	24	7
1992–93	Peterborough U	45	16
1993–94	Peterborough U	42	12
1994–95	Luton T	2	0
1995–96	Colchester U	41	12
1996–97	Colchester U	36	11
1997–98	Colchester U	25	5
1998–99	Colchester U	6	0
Total:		**591**	**212**

ADEBOLA, Dele — Forward

H: 6 3 W: 12 08 b.Lagos 23-6-75

Source: Trainee.

1992–93	Crewe Alex	6	0
1993–94	Crewe Alex	0	0
1994–95	Crewe Alex	30	8
1995–96	Crewe Alex	29	8
1996–97	Crewe Alex	32	16
1997–98	Crewe Alex	27	7
1997–98	Birmingham C	17	7
1998–99	Birmingham C	39	13
Total:		**180**	**59**

AGGREY, Jimmy — Defender

H: 6 3 W: 13 06 b.London 26-10-78

Source: Chelsea Trainee.

1997–98	Fulham	0	0
1998–99	Torquay U	25	0
Total:		**25**	**0**

AGNEW, Paul — Defender

H: 5 9 W: 10 07 b.Lisburn 15-8-65

Source: Cliftonville. *Honours:* Northern Ireland Schools, Youth, Under-23.

1983–84	Grimsby T	1	0
1984–85	Grimsby T	12	0
1985–86	Grimsby T	16	0
1986–87	Grimsby T	29	0
1987–88	Grimsby T	38	1
1988–89	Grimsby T	34	0
1989–90	Grimsby T	24	2
1990–91	Grimsby T	7	0
1991–92	Grimsby T	24	0
1992–93	Grimsby T	23	0
1993–94	Grimsby T	23	0
1994–95	Grimsby T	10	0
1994–95	WBA	14	1
1995–96	WBA	3	0
1996–97	WBA	22	0
1997–98	Swansea C	7	0
1998–99	Swansea C	0	0
Total:		**287**	**4**

AGNEW, Steve — Midfield

H: 5 10 W: 10 06 b.Shipley 9-11-65

Source: Apprentice.

1983–84	Barnsley	1	0
1984–85	Barnsley	10	1
1985–86	Barnsley	2	0
1986–87	Barnsley	33	0
1987–88	Barnsley	25	6
1988–89	Barnsley	39	6
1989–90	Barnsley	46	8
1990–91	Barnsley	38	8
1991–92	Blackburn R	2	0
1992–93	Blackburn R	0	0
1992–93	Portsmouth (loan)	5	0
1992–93	Leicester C	9	1
1993–94	Leicester C	36	3
1994–95	Leicester C	11	0
1994–95	Sunderland	16	2
1995–96	Sunderland	29	5
1996–97	Sunderland	15	2
1997–98	Sunderland	3	0
1998–99	York C	20	2
Total:		**340**	**44**

AGOGO, Manuel — Midfield

H: 5 9 W: 11 07 b.Accra 1-8-79

Source: Willesden.

1996–97	Sheffield W	0	0
1997–98	Sheffield W	1	0
1998–99	Sheffield W	1	0
Total:		**2**	**0**

AGYEMANG, Patrick — Forward

H: 6 1 W: 12 00 b.London 29-9-80

Source: Trainee.

1998–99	Wimbledon	0	0

AINSWORTH, Gareth — Midfield

H: 5 8 W: 13 02 b.Blackburn 10-5-73

Source: Blackburn R Trainee.

1991–92	Preston NE	5	0
1992–93	Cambridge U	4	1
1992–93	Preston NE	26	0
1993–94	Preston NE	38	11
1994–95	Preston NE	16	1
1995–96	Preston NE	2	0
1995–96	Lincoln C	31	12
1996–97	Lincoln C	46	22
1997–98	Lincoln C	6	3
1997–98	Port Vale	40	5
1998–99	Port Vale	15	5
1998–99	Wimbledon	8	0
Total:		**237**	**60**

AISTON, Sam — Forward

H: 6 0 W: 12 01 b.Newcastle 21-11-76

Source: Newcastle U Trainee. *Honours:* England Schools.

1995–96	Sunderland	14	0
1996–97	Sunderland	2	0
1996–97	Chester C (loan)	14	0
1997–98	Sunderland	3	0
1998–99	Sunderland	1	0
1998–99	Chester C (loan)	11	0
Total:		**45**	**0**

AKINBIYI, Ade — Forward

H: 6 1 W: 13 09 b.Hackney 10-10-74

Source: Trainee.

1992–93	Norwich C	0	0
1993–94	Norwich C	2	0
1993–94	Hereford U (loan)	4	2
1994–95	Norwich C	13	0
1994–95	Brighton & HA (loan)	7	4
1995–96	Norwich C	22	3
1996–97	Norwich C	12	0
1996–97	Gillingham	19	7
1997–98	Gillingham	44	21
1998–99	Bristol C	44	19
Total:		**167**	**56**

ALBERT, Philippe — Defender

H: 6 3 W: 12 04 b.Bouillon 10-8-67

Honours: Belgium 40 full caps, 5 goals.

1987–88	Charleroi	32	5
1988–89	Charleroi	33	2
1989–90	Mechelen	22	0
1990–91	Mechelen	32	3
1991–92	Mechelen	33	2
1992–93	Anderlecht	25	5
1993–94	Anderlecht	25	4
1994–95	Newcastle U	17	2
1995–96	Newcastle U	23	4
1996–97	Newcastle U	27	2
1997–98	Newcastle U	23	0
1998–99	Newcastle U	6	0
1998–99	Fulham (loan)	13	2
Total:		**311**	**31**

ALBERTZ, Jorg — Midfield

H: 6 2 W: 13 05 b.Moenchengladbach 29-1-71

Honours: Germany 2 full caps.

1990–91	Fortuna Dusseldorf	12	1
1991–92	Fortuna Dusseldorf	11	0
1992–93	Fortuna Dusseldorf	35	3
1993–94	Hamburg	31	4
1994–95	Hamburg	34	9
1995–96	Hamburg	34	9
1996–97	Rangers	32	10
1997–98	Rangers	31	10
1998–99	Rangers	34	11
Total:		**254**	**57**

ALCIDE, Colin — Forward

H: 6 2 W: 13 11 b.Huddersfield 14-4-72

Source: Emley.

1995–96	Lincoln C	27	6
1996–97	Lincoln C	42	7
1997–98	Lincoln C	29	12
1998–99	Lincoln C	23	1
1998–99	Hull C	17	3
Total:		**138**	**29**

ALDRIDGE, Martin — Forward

H: 5 11 W: 12 02 b.Northampton 4-12-74

Source: Trainee.

1991–92	Northampton T	5	0
1992–93	Northampton T	9	2
1993–94	Northampton T	29	8
1994–95	Northampton T	27	7
1995–96	Northampton T	0	0
1995–96	Oxford U	18	9
1996–97	Oxford U	30	8
1997–98	Oxford U	24	2
1997–98	Southend U (loan)	11	1
1998–99	Blackpool	22	7
Total:		**175**	**44**

ALEXANDER, Gary — Forward

b.South London 15-8-79

Source: Trainee.

1998–99	West Ham U	0	0

ALEXANDER, Graham — Defender

H: 5 10 W: 12 02 b.Coventry 10-10-71

Source: Trainee.

1989–90	Scunthorpe U	0	0
1990–91	Scunthorpe U	1	0
1991–92	Scunthorpe U	36	5
1992–93	Scunthorpe U	41	5
1993–94	Scunthorpe U	41	4
1994–95	Scunthorpe U	40	4
1995–96	Luton T	37	1
1996–97	Luton T	45	2
1997–98	Luton T	39	8
1998–99	Luton T	29	4
1998–99	Preston NE	10	0
Total:		**319**	**33**

ALEXANDERSSON, Niclas — Midfield

H: 6 2 W: 11 07 b.Halmstad 29-12-71

Honours: Sweden 34 full caps, 3 goals.

1990	Halmstad	22	2
1991	Halmstad	16	3
1992	Halmstad	0	0
1993	Halmstad	25	4
1994	Halmstad	25	4
1995	Halmstad	26	5
1996	IFK Gothenburg	26	7
1997	IFK Gothenburg	26	6
1997–98	Sheffield W	6	0
1998–99	Sheffield W	32	3
Total:		**204**	**34**

ALJOFREE, Hasney — Defender

H: 6 0 W: 12 03 b.Manchester 11-7-78

Source: Trainee.

1996–97	Bolton W	0	0
1997–98	Bolton W	2	0
1998–99	Bolton W	4	0
Total:		**6**	**0**

ALLAN, Derek — Defender

H: 5 11 W: 12 05 b.Irvine 24-12-74

Source: Ayr U BC.

1992–93	Ayr U	5	0
1992–93	Southampton	1	0
1993–94	Southampton	0	0
1994–95	Southampton	0	0
1995–96	Southampton	0	0
1995–96	Brighton & HA (loan)	8	0
1996–97	Brighton & HA	31	0
1997–98	Brighton & HA	19	1
1998–99	Brighton & HA	22	1
Total:		**86**	**2**

ALLARDYCE, Craig — Defender

H: 6 2 W: 14 00 b.Bolton 9-6-75

Source: Trainee.

1992–93	Preston NE	1	0
1993–94	Preston NE	0	0
1994–95	Blackpool	0	0
1995–96	Blackpool	1	0
From Chorley.			
1997–98	Chesterfield	1	0
1998–99	Peterborough U	4	0
1998–99	Mansfield T	6	0
Total:		**13**	**0**

ALLEN, Alex — Defender

H: 6 0 W: 11 12 b.Doncaster 12-2-80

Source: Trainee.

1996–97	Norwich C	0	0
1997–98	Norwich C	0	0
1998–99	Norwich C	0	0

ALLEN, Bradley — Forward

H: 5 7 W: 10 07 b.Harold Wood 13-9-71

Source: School. *Honours:* England Youth, Under-21.

1988–89	QPR	1	0
1989–90	QPR	0	0
1990–91	QPR	10	2
1991–92	QPR	11	5
1992–93	QPR	25	10
1993–94	QPR	21	7
1994–95	QPR	5	2
1995–96	QPR	8	1
1995–96	Charlton Ath	10	3
1996–97	Charlton Ath	18	4
1997–98	Charlton Ath	12	2
1998–99	Charlton Ath	0	0
1998–99	Colchester U (loan)	4	1
Total:		**125**	**37**

ALLEN, Chris — Midfield

H: 5 11 W: 12 04 b.Oxford 18-11-72

Source: Trainee. *Honours:* England Under-21.

1990–91	Oxford U	0	0
1991–92	Oxford U	14	1
1992–93	Oxford U	31	3
1993–94	Oxford U	45	3
1994–95	Oxford U	36	2
1995–96	Oxford U	24	3
1995–96	Nottingham F (loan)	3	1
1996–97	Nottingham F	24	0
1997–98	Nottingham F	1	0
1997–98	Luton T (loan)	14	1
1998–99	Nottingham F	0	0
1998–99	Cardiff C (loan)	4	0
1998–99	Port Vale	5	1
Total:		**201**	**15**

ALLEN, Graham — Defender

H: 6 0 W: 12 00 b.Bolton 8-4-77

Source: Trainee. *Honours:* England Youth.

1994–95	Everton	0	0
1995–96	Everton	0	0
1996–97	Everton	1	0
1997–98	Everton	5	0
1998–99	Everton	0	0
1998–99	Tranmere R	41	5
Total:		**47**	**5**

ALLEN, Lee — Forward

H: 5 10 W: 10 08 b.Islington 12-3-79

1997–98	Leicester C	0	0
1998–99	Leicester C	0	0

ALLEN, Martin — Midfield

H: 5 11 W: 12 06 b.Reading 14-8-65

Source: School. *Honours:* England Youth, Under-21, B, Football League.

1983–84	QPR	0	0
1984–85	QPR	5	0
1985–86	QPR	31	3
1986–87	QPR	32	5
1987–88	QPR	38	4
1988–89	QPR	28	4
1989–90	QPR	2	0
1989–90	West Ham U	39	9
1990–91	West Ham U	40	3
1991–92	West Ham U	19	0
1992–93	West Ham U	34	4
1993–94	West Ham U	26	6
1994–95	West Ham U	29	2

1995–96	West Ham U	3	1
1995–96	Portsmouth	27	4
1996–97	Portsmouth	4	0
1997–98	Portsmouth	14	0
1997–98	Southend U (loan)	5	0
1998–99	Portsmouth	0	0
Total:		**376**	**45**

ALLEN, Rory — Forward

H: 5 11 W: 11 02 b.Beckenham 17-10-77

Source: Trainee. *Honours:* England Under-21.

1995–96	Tottenham H	0	0
1996–97	Tottenham H	12	2
1997–98	Tottenham H	4	0
1997–98	Luton T (loan)	8	6
1998–99	Tottenham H	5	0
Total:		**29**	**8**

ALLISON, Wayne — Forward

H: 6 0 W: 14 07 b.Huddersfield 16-10-68

1986–87	Halifax T	8	4
1987–88	Halifax T	35	4
1988–89	Halifax T	41	15
1989–90	Watford	7	0
1990–91	Bristol C	37	6
1991–92	Bristol C	43	10
1992–93	Bristol C	39	4
1993–94	Bristol C	39	15
1994–95	Bristol C	37	13
1995–96	Swindon T	44	17
1996–97	Swindon T	41	11
1997–98	Swindon T	16	3
1997–98	Huddersfield T	27	6
1998–99	Huddersfield T	44	9
Total:		**458**	**117**

ALLMAN, Anthony — Defender

H: 5 9 W: 10 07 b.Sidcup 14-12-80

Source: Trainee. *Honours:* England Schools.

1997–98	Charlton Ath	0	0
1998–99	Charlton Ath	0	0

ALLOTT, Mark — Forward

H: 5 11 W: 10 12 b.Middleton 16-3-78

Source: Trainee.

1995–96	Oldham Ath	0	0
1996–97	Oldham Ath	5	1
1997–98	Oldham Ath	22	2
1998–99	Oldham Ath	41	7
Total:		**68**	**10**

ALLOU, Bernard — Midfield

H: 5 8 W: 11 00 b.Cocody 19-6-75

1994–95	Paris St Germain	7	3
1995–96	Paris St Germain	19	0
1996–97	Paris St Germain	12	0
1997–98	Paris St Germain	3	0
From Grampas 8.			
1998–99	Nottingham F	2	0
Total:		**43**	**3**

ALLSOPP, Danny — Forward

H: 6 0 W: 12 08 b.Melbourne 10-8-78

Source: Port Melbourne.

1998–99	Manchester C	24	4
Total:		**24**	**4**

ALOISI, John — Forward

H: 6 1 W: 12 06 b.Adelaide 5-2-76

Source: Cremonese.

1996–97	Cremonese	26	2
1997–98	Portsmouth	38	12
1998–99	Portsmouth	22	13
1998–99	Coventry C	16	5
Total:		**102**	**32**

ALSAKER, Paul — Midfield

H: 5 9 W: 10 10 b.Bergen 6-11-73

Source: Flora Tallin.

1998–99	Stockport Co	1	0
Total:		**1**	**0**

ALSFORD, Julian — Defender

H: 6 2 W: 13 07 b.Poole 24-12-72

Source: Trainee.

1991–92	Watford	0	0
1992–93	Watford	5	0
1993–94	Watford	8	1
1994–95	Chester C	35	0
1995–96	Chester C	24	0
1996–97	Chester C	43	2
1997–98	Chester C	39	4
1997–98	Dundee U	3	0
1998–99	Chester C	10	1
1998–99	Barnet (loan)	9	1
Total:		**176**	**9**

ALSOP, Julian — Forward

H: 6 5 W: 14 08 b.Nuneaton 28-5-73

Source: Nuneaton, VS Rugby, RC Warwick, Tamworth, Halesowen T.

1996–97	Bristol R	16	3
1997–98	Bristol R	17	1
1997–98	Swansea C	12	3
1998–99	Swansea C	41	10
Total:		**86**	**17**

AMATO, Gabriel — Forward

H: 6 1 W: 13 00 b.Mar del Plata 22-10-70

1993–94	Huracan	15	6
1993–94	River Plate	9	0
1994–95	River Plate	24	5
1995–96	River Plate	34	8
1996–97	Hercules	36	2
1997–98	Mallorca	35	13
1998–99	Rangers	20	6
Total:		**173**	**40**

AMEOBI, Foluwashola — Forward

H: 6 2 W: 12 00 b.Zaria 12-10-81

Source: Trainee.

1998–99	Newcastle U	0	0

AMORUSO, Lorenzo — Defender

H: 6 2 W: 13 10 b.Bari 28-6-71

1988–89	Bari	3	0
1989–90	Bari	3	0
1990–91	Bari	5	1
1991–92	Bari	0	0
1991–92	Mantova	13	1
1992–93	Bari	0	0
1992–93	Pescavo	19	1
1993–94	Bari	37	3
1994–95	Bari	27	4
1995–96	Fiorentina	31	2
1996–97	Fiorentina	23	1
1997–98	Rangers	4	0
1998–99	Rangers	33	1
Total:		**198**	**14**

AMPADU, Kwame — Midfield

H: 5 10 W: 11 10 b.Bradford 20-12-70

Source: Belvedere, Trainee. *Honours:* Eire Youth, Under-21.

1988–89	Arsenal	0	0
1989–90	Arsenal	2	0
1990–91	Arsenal	0	0
1990–91	Plymouth Arg (loan)	6	1
1990–91	WBA (loan)	7	1
1991–92	WBA	21	3
1992–93	WBA	10	0
1993–94	WBA	11	0
1993–94	Swansea C	13	0
1994–95	Swansea C	44	6
1995–96	Swansea C	43	2
1996–97	Swansea C	29	4
1997–98	Swansea C	18	0
1998–99	Leyton Orient	29	1
Total:		**233**	**18**

AMSALEM, David — Defender

H: 6 1 W: 12 01 b.Israel 4-9-71

Honours: Israel 26 full caps.

1994–95	Hapoel Tel Aviv	27	4
1995–96	Beitar Jerusalem	28	3
1996–97	Beitar Jerusalem	29	2
1997–98	Beitar Jerusalem	28	0
1998–99	Crystal Palace	10	0
Total:		**122**	**9**

ANDERSEN, Braastrup — Goalkeeper

b.Slagelse 26-3-76

1993–94	Lyngby	3	0
1994–95	Lyngby	7	0
1995–96	Lyngby	33	0
1996–97	Lyngby	29	0
1997–98	Lyngby	32	0
1998–99	Lyngby	16	0
1998–99	Bristol C	10	0
Total:		**130**	**0**

ANDERSEN, Soren — Forward

H: 5 11 W: 12 06 b.Denmark 31-1-70

Honours: Denmark 7 full caps.

1991–92	Vejle	29	11
1992–93	Vejle	30	11
1993–94	Aarhus	12	11
1994–95	Rayo Vallecano	10	1
1995	Norrkoping	10	4
1995–96	Aalborg	11	7
1996–97	Aalborg	29	14
1997–98	Aalborg	27	9
1998–99	Bristol C	39	10
Total:		**197**	**78**

ANDERSON, Derek — Defender

H: 6 0 W: 11 00 b.Paisley 15-5-72

Source: Kilwinning Rangers.

1993–94	Kilmarnock	0	0
1994–95	Kilmarnock	20	0
1995–96	Kilmarnock	28	0
1996–97	Kilmarnock	17	0
1997–98	Kilmarnock	1	0
1997–98	Ayr U	12	1
1998–99	Hibernian	6	0
Total:		**84**	**1**

ANDERSON, Iain — Forward

H: 5 8 W: 9 07 b.Glasgow 23-7-77

Source: X-Form. *Honours:* Scotland Under-21.

1994–95	Dundee	10	1
1995–96	Dundee	17	0
1996–97	Dundee	35	5
1997–98	Dundee	36	6
1998–99	Dundee	28	3
Total:		**126**	**15**

ANDERSON, Ijah — Defender

H: 5 8 W: 10 06 b.Hackney 30-12-75

Source: Tottenham H Trainee.

1994–95	Southend U	0	0
1995–96	Brentford	25	2
1996–97	Brentford	46	1
1997–98	Brentford	17	0
1998–99	Brentford	38	1
Total:		**126**	**4**

ANDERSON, Russell — Defender

H: 5 11 W: 10 09 b.Aberdeen 25-10-78

Source: Dyce Juniors. *Honours:* Scotland Under-21.

1996–97	Aberdeen	14	0
1997–98	Aberdeen	26	0
1998–99	Aberdeen	16	0
Total:		**56**	**0**

ANDERSSON, Anders — Midfield

H: 5 9 W: 11 09 b.Tomelilla 15-3-74

Honours: Sweden 9 full caps, 1 goal.

1991	Malmo	1	0
1992	Malmo	28	3
1993	Malmo	19	4
1994	Malmo	19	2
1995	Malmo	23	3
1996	Malmo	23	5
1997	Malmo	13	2
1997–98	Blackburn R	4	0
1998–99	Blackburn R	0	0
Total:		**130**	**19**

ANDERSSON, Andreas — Forward

H: 6 1 W: 12 01 b.Osterhoninge 10-4-74

Source: Hova. *Honours:* Sweden 23 full caps, 5 goals.

1993	Tidaholm	9	6
1994	Degerfors	14	3
1995	Degerfors	26	13
1996	IFK Gothenburg	26	19
1997	IFK Gothenburg	13	13
1997–98	AC Milan	13	1
1997–98	Newcastle U	12	2
1998–99	Newcastle U	15	2
Total:		**128**	**59**

ANDERTON, Darren — Forward

H: 6 1 W: 12 05 b.Southampton 3-3-72

Source: Trainee. *Honours:* England Youth, Under-21, B, 27 full caps, 7 goals.

1989–90	Portsmouth	0	0
1990–91	Portsmouth	20	0
1991–92	Portsmouth	42	7
1992–93	Tottenham H	34	6
1993–94	Tottenham H	37	6
1994–95	Tottenham H	37	5
1995–96	Tottenham H	8	2
1996–97	Tottenham H	16	3
1997–98	Tottenham H	15	0
1998–99	Tottenham H	32	3
Total:		**241**	**32**

ANDREASSON, Marcus — Defender

H: 6 4 W: 13 02 b.Liberia 13-7-78

1997	Osters	8	0
1998	Osters	4	0
1998–99	Bristol R	5	0
Total:		**17**	**0**

ANDREASSON, Svein — Midfield

b.Hadsel 3-7-68

1998	Lillestrom	15	4
1998–99	Portsmouth	2	0
Total:		**17**	**4**

ANDREWS, Ben — Defender

H: 6 1 W: 12 13 b.Burton-on-Trent 18-11-80

Source: Trainee.

1997–98	Brighton & HA	3	0
1998–99	Brighton & HA	1	0
Total:		**4**	**0**

ANDREWS, Bradley — Midfield

H: 5 11 W: 10 12 b.Bristol 8-12-79

Source: Trainee.

1998–99	Norwich C	0	0
1998–99	Bristol R	3	0
Total:		**3**	**0**

ANDREWS, Ian — Goalkeeper

H: 6 2 W: 14 01 b.Nottingham 1-12-64

Source: Apprentice. *Honours:* England Youth, Under-21.

1982–83	Leicester C	0	0
1983–84	Leicester C	2	0
1983–84	Swindon T (loan)	1	0
1984–85	Leicester C	31	0
1985–86	Leicester C	39	0
1986–87	Leicester C	42	0
1987–88	Leicester C	12	0
1988–89	Celtic	5	0
1988–89	Leeds U (loan)	1	0
1989–90	Celtic	0	0
1989–90	Southampton	3	0
1990–91	Southampton	1	0
1991–92	Southampton	1	0
1992–93	Southampton	0	0
1993–94	Southampton	5	0
1994–95	Southampton	0	0
1994–95	Bournemouth	38	0
1995–96	Bournemouth	26	0
1996–97	Bournemouth	0	0
1996–97	Leicester C (loan)	0	0
1997–98	Leicester C	0	0
1998–99	Leicester C	0	0
Total:		**207**	**0**

ANDREWS, Keith — Midfield

H: 5 11 W: 11 05 b.Dublin 13-9-80

Source: Trainee.

1997–98	Wolverhampton W	0	0
1998–99	Wolverhampton W	0	0

ANDREWS, Wayne — Forward

H: 5 10 W: 11 09 b.Paddington 25-11-77

Source: Trainee.

1995–96	Watford	1	0
1996–97	Watford	25	4
1997–98	Watford	2	0
1998–99	Watford	0	0
1998–99	Cambridge U (loan)	2	0
1998–99	Peterborough U (loan)	10	5
Total:		**40**	**9**

ANELKA, Nicolas — Forward

H: 5 11 W: 12 03 b.Versailles 14-3-79

Honours: France Youth, Under-21, 9 full caps, 3 goals.

1995–96	Paris St Germain	2	0
1996–97	Paris St Germain	8	1
1996–97	Arsenal	4	0
1997–98	Arsenal	26	6
1998–99	Arsenal	35	17
Total:		**75**	**24**

ANGEL, Mark — Midfield

H: 5 8 W: 11 02 b.Newcastle 23-8-75

Source: Trainee.

1993–94	Sunderland	0	0
1994–95	Sunderland	0	0
1995–96	Oxford U	27	1
1996–97	Oxford U	24	2
1997–98	Oxford U	22	1
1998–99	WBA	22	1
Total:		**95**	**5**

ANGELL, Brett — Forward

H: 6 2 W: 13 10 b.Marlborough 20-8-68

Source: Portsmouth, Cheltenham T.

1987–88	Derby Co	0	0
1988–89	Stockport Co	26	5
1989–90	Stockport Co	44	23
1990–91	Southend U	42	15
1991–92	Southend U	43	21
1992–93	Southend U	13	5
1993–94	Southend U	5	4
1993–94	Everton (loan)	1	0
1993–94	Southend U	12	2
1993–94	Everton	15	1
1994–95	Everton	4	0
1994–95	Sunderland	8	0
1995–96	Sunderland	2	0
1995–96	Sheffield U (loan)	6	2
1995–96	WBA (loan)	3	0
1996–97	Sunderland	0	0
1996–97	Stockport Co	34	15
1997–98	Stockport Co	45	18
1998–99	Stockport Co	42	17
Total:		**345**	**128**

ANNAND, Edward — Forward

H: 5 11 W: 11 01 b.Glasgow 24-3-73

Source: Sligo R.

1995–96	Clyde	35	21
1996–97	Clyde	29	21
1996–97	Dundee	5	2
1997–98	Dundee	34	12
1998–99	Dundee	29	9
Total:		**132**	**65**

ANNONI, Enrico — Defender

H: 5 10 W: 13 00 b.Gloussand 10-7-66

1982–83	Seregno	27	0
1983–84	Como	2	0
1984–85	Como	0	0
1985–86	Sambened	28	3
1986–87	Sambened	32	1
1987–88	Como	28	1
1988–89	Como	33	1
1989–90	Como	34	0
1990–91	Torino	22	1
1991–92	Torino	29	1
1992–93	Torino	25	0
1993–94	Torino	27	0
1994–95	Torino	24	0
1995–96	Roma	23	0
1996–97	Roma	12	0
1996–97	Celtic	3	0
1997–98	Celtic	20	0
1998–99	Celtic	14	0
Total:		**383**	**8**

ANSAH, Andy — Forward

H: 5 7 W: 10 07 b.Lewisham 19-3-69

Source: Crystal Palace.

1988–89	Brentford	7	2
1989–90	Brentford	1	0
1989–90	Southend U	7	1
1990–91	Southend U	40	9
1991–92	Southend U	40	9
1992–93	Southend U	30	7
1993–94	Southend U	27	7
1994–95	Southend U	9	0
1994–95	Brentford (loan)	3	1
1995–96	Southend U	4	0
1995–96	Brentford (loan)	6	1
1995–96	Peterborough U	2	1
1995–96	Gillingham	2	0
1996–97	Leyton Orient	2	0
1997–98	Leyton Orient	0	0
1997–98	Brighton & HA	14	3
1998–99	Brighton & HA	11	0
Total:		**205**	**41**

ANSELIN, Cedric — Midfield

H: 5 7 W: 11 00 b.Lens 24-7-77

1995–96	Bordeaux	3	0
1996–97	Bordeaux	5	0
1997–98	Lille	14	1
1998–99	Bordeaux	1	0
1998–99	Norwich C	7	1
Total:		**30**	**2**

ANTHONY, Graham — Midfield

H: 5 7 W: 11 02 b.South Shields 9-8-75

Source: Trainee.

1993–94	Sheffield U	0	0
1994–95	Sheffield U	1	0
1995–96	Sheffield U	0	0
1995–96	Scarborough (loan)	2	0
1996–97	Sheffield U	2	0
1996–97	Swindon T	3	0
1997–98	Plymouth Arg	5	0
1997–98	Carlisle U	25	3
1998–99	Carlisle U	26	0
Total:		**64**	**3**

ANTHROBUS, Steve — Forward

H: 6 2 W: 12 06 b.Lewisham 10-11-68

1986–87	Millwall	0	0
1987–88	Millwall	3	0
1988–89	Millwall	3	0
1989–90	Millwall	15	4
1989–90	Southend U (loan)	0	0
1989–90	Wimbledon	10	0
1990–91	Wimbledon	3	0
1991–92	Wimbledon	10	0
1992–93	Wimbledon	5	0
1993–94	Wimbledon	0	0
1993–94	Peterborough U (loan)	2	0
1994–95	Wimbledon	0	0
1994–95	Chester C (loan)	7	0
1995–96	Shrewsbury T	39	10
1996–97	Shrewsbury T	33	6
1996–97	Crewe Alex	10	0
1997–98	Crewe Alex	30	6
1998–99	Crewe Alex	21	3
Total:		**191**	**29**

APPLEBY, Matty — Defender

H: 5 10 W: 11 08 b.Middlesbrough 16-4-72

Source: Trainee.

1989–90	Newcastle U	0	0
1990–91	Newcastle U	1	0
1991–92	Newcastle U	18	0
1992–93	Newcastle U	0	0

1993–94	Newcastle U	1	0
1993–94	Darlington (loan)	10	1
1994–95	Darlington	36	1
1995–96	Darlington	43	6
1996–97	Barnsley	35	0
1997–98	Barnsley	15	0
1998–99	Barnsley	34	0
Total:		**193**	**8**

APPLEBY, Ritchie — Midfield

H: 5 9 W: 11 03 b.Stockton 18-9-75

Source: Trainee. *Honours:* England Youth.

1993–94	Newcastle U	0	0
1994–95	Newcastle U	0	0
1994–95	Darlington (loan)	0	0
1995–96	Ipswich T	3	0
1996–97	Swansea C	11	1
1997–98	Swansea C	35	3
1998–99	Swansea C	39	3
Total:		**88**	**7**

APPLETON, Michael — Midfield

H: 5 8 W: 11 00 b.Salford 4-12-75

Source: Trainee.

1994–95	Manchester U	0	0
1995–96	Manchester U	0	0
1995–96	Lincoln C (loan)	4	0
1996–97	Manchester U	0	0
1996–97	Grimsby T (loan)	10	3
1997–98	Preston NE	38	2
1998–99	Preston NE	25	2
Total:		**77**	**7**

ARBER, Mark — Defender

H: 6 1 W: 12 11 b.Johannesburg 8-10-77

Source: Trainee.

1995–96	Tottenham H	0	0
1996–97	Tottenham H	0	0
1997–98	Tottenham H	0	0
1998–99	Tottenham H	0	0
1998–99	Barnet	35	2
Total:		**35**	**2**

ARDLEY, Neal — Midfield

H: 5 11 W: 11 09 b.Epsom 1-9-72

Source: Trainee. *Honours:* England Under-21.

1990–91	Wimbledon	1	0
1991–92	Wimbledon	8	0
1992–93	Wimbledon	26	4
1993–94	Wimbledon	16	1
1994–95	Wimbledon	14	1
1995–96	Wimbledon	6	0
1996–97	Wimbledon	34	2
1997–98	Wimbledon	34	2
1998–99	Wimbledon	23	0
Total:		**162**	**10**

ARENDSE, Andre — Goalkeeper

H: 6 4 W: 11 05 b.Cape Town 27-6-67

Source: Cape Town S. *Honours:* South Africa 27 full caps.

1997–98	Fulham	6	0
1998–99	Fulham	0	0
Total:		**6**	**0**

ARMSTRONG, Alun — Forward

H: 6 0 W: 13 08 b.Gateshead 22-2-75

Source: School.

1993–94	Newcastle U	0	0
1994–95	Stockport Co	45	14
1995–96	Stockport Co	46	13
1996–97	Stockport Co	39	9
1997–98	Stockport Co	29	12
1997–98	Middlesbrough	11	7
1998–99	Middlesbrough	6	1
Total:		**176**	**56**

ARMSTRONG, Chris — Forward

H: 6 0 W: 12 10 b.Newcastle 19-6-71

Source: Llay Welfare. *Honours:* England B.

1988–89	Wrexham	0	0
1989–90	Wrexham	22	3
1990–91	Wrexham	38	10
1991–92	Millwall	25	4
1992–93	Millwall	3	1
1992–93	Crystal Palace	35	15
1993–94	Crystal Palace	43	22
1994–95	Crystal Palace	40	8
1995–96	Tottenham H	36	15
1996–97	Tottenham H	12	5
1997–98	Tottenham H	19	5
1998–99	Tottenham H	34	7
Total:		**307**	**95**

ARMSTRONG, Craig — Defender

H: 5 11 W: 12 10 b.South Shields 23-5-75

Source: Trainee.

1992–93	Nottingham F	0	0
1993–94	Nottingham F	0	0
1994–95	Nottingham F	0	0
1994–95	Burnley (loan)	4	0
1995–96	Nottingham F	0	0
1995–96	Bristol R (loan)	14	0
1996–97	Nottingham F	0	0
1996–97	Gillingham (loan)	10	0
1996–97	Watford (loan)	15	0

1997–98	Nottingham F	18	0
1998–99	Nottingham F	22	0
1998–99	Huddersfield T	13	1
Total:		**96**	**1**

ARMSTRONG, Dean — Midfield

H: 5 8 W: 9 13 b.Chiswick 7-9-79

Source: Trainee.

1998–99	Cambridge U	0	0

ARMSTRONG, Gordon — Defender

H: 6 0 W: 13 04 b.Newcastle 15-7-67

Source: Apprentice.

1984–85	Sunderland	4	0
1985–86	Sunderland	14	2
1986–87	Sunderland	41	5
1987–88	Sunderland	37	5
1988–89	Sunderland	45	8
1989–90	Sunderland	46	8
1990–91	Sunderland	35	6
1991–92	Sunderland	40	10
1992–93	Sunderland	45	3
1993–94	Sunderland	26	2
1994–95	Sunderland	15	1
1995–96	Sunderland	1	0
1995–96	Bristol C (loan)	6	0
1995–96	Northampton T (loan)	4	1
1996–97	Bury	32	2
1997–98	Bury	37	2
1998–99	Bury	2	0
1998–99	Burnley	40	2
Total:		**470**	**57**

ARMSTRONG, Ian — Forward

b.Fazackerley 16-11-81

Source: Trainee. *Honours:* England Schools, Youth.

1998–99	Liverpool	0	0

ARMSTRONG, Paul — Midfield

H: 5 10 W: 10 09 b.Dublin 5-10-78

Source: Trainee. *Honours:* Eire Under-21.

1997–98	Brighton & HA	20	0
1998–99	Brighton & HA	28	2
Total:		**48**	**2**

ARNISON, Paul — Defender

H: 5 10 W: 10 12 b.Hartlepool 18-9-77

Source: Trainee.

1995–96	Newcastle U	0	0
1996–97	Newcastle U	0	0
1997–98	Newcastle U	0	0
1998–99	Newcastle U	0	0

ARNOTT, Andy — Midfield

H: 6 0 W: 12 02 b.Chatham 18-10-73

Source: Trainee.

1990–91	Gillingham	0	0
1991–92	Gillingham	19	2
1992–93	Gillingham	15	6
1992–93	Manchester U (loan)	0	0
1993–94	Gillingham	10	2
1994–95	Gillingham	28	2
1995–96	Gillingham	1	0
1995–96	Leyton Orient	19	3
1996–97	Leyton Orient	31	3
1997–98	Fulham	1	0
1998–99	Fulham	0	0
1998–99	Brighton & HA	27	2
Total:		**151**	**20**

ARPHEXAD, Pegguy — Goalkeeper

H: 6 2 W: 13 07 b.Abymes 18-5-73

Source: Brest.

1994–95	Lens	0	0
1995–96	Lens	3	0
1996–97	Lens	0	0
1997–98	Leicester C	6	0
1998–99	Leicester C	4	0
Total:		**13**	**0**

ASABA, Carl — Forward

H: 6 2 W: 13 00 b.London 28-1-73

Source: Dulwich Hamlet.

1994–95	Brentford	0	0
1994–95	Colchester U (loan)	12	2
1995–96	Brentford	10	2
1996–97	Brentford	44	23
1997–98	Reading	32	8
1998–99	Reading	1	0
1998–99	Gillingham	41	20
Total:		**140**	**55**

ASHBEE, Ian — Midfield

H: 6 1 W: 13 04 b.Birmingham 6-9-76

Source: Trainee. *Honours:* England Youth.

1994–95	Derby Co	1	0
1995–96	Derby Co	0	0
1996–97	Derby Co	0	0
1996–97	Cambridge U	18	0
1997–98	Cambridge U	27	1
1998–99	Cambridge U	31	4
Total:		**77**	**5**

ASHBY, Barry — Defender

H: 6 2 W: 13 08 b.London 2-11-70

Source: Trainee.

1988–89	Watford	0	0
1989–90	Watford	18	1
1990–91	Watford	23	0
1991–92	Watford	21	0
1992–93	Watford	35	0
1993–94	Watford	17	2
1993–94	Brentford	8	1
1994–95	Brentford	40	1
1995–96	Brentford	33	1
1996–97	Brentford	40	1
1997–98	Gillingham	43	0
1998–99	Gillingham	38	1
Total:		**316**	**8**

ASHCROFT, Lee — Forward

H: 5 9 W: 12 00 b.Preston 7-9-72

Source: Trainee. *Honours:* England Under-21.

1990–91	Preston NE	14	1
1991–92	Preston NE	38	5
1992–93	Preston NE	39	7
1993–94	WBA	21	3
1994–95	WBA	38	10
1995–96	WBA	26	4
1995–96	Notts Co (loan)	6	0
1996–97	WBA	5	0
1996–97	Preston NE	27	8
1997–98	Preston NE	37	14
1998–99	Preston NE	0	0
1998–99	Grimsby T	27	3
Total:		**278**	**55**

ASHLEY, Neil — Midfield

H: 5 10 W: 10 10 b.Chesterfield 16-9-80

Source: Nottingham F Trainee.

1997–98	Leicester C	0	0
1998–99	Leicester C	0	0

ASHTON, Jon — Defender

H: 6 0 W: 13 00 b.Plymouth 4-8-79

Source: Trainee.

1997–98	Plymouth Arg	0	0
1998–99	Plymouth Arg	26	0
Total:		**26**	**0**

ASHTON, Lee — Midfield

b.Yeovil 8-11-79

Source: Trainee.

1998–99	Bristol C	0	0

ASKEY, John — Forward

H: 6 0 W: 12 02 b.Stoke 4-11-64

Source: Port Vale.

1997–98	Macclesfield T	39	6
1998–99	Macclesfield T	38	4
Total:		**77**	**10**

ASPIN, Neil — Defender

H: 6 0 W: 13 02 b.Gateshead 12-4-65

Source: Apprentice.

1981–82	Leeds U	1	0
1982–83	Leeds U	15	0
1983–84	Leeds U	21	1
1984–85	Leeds U	32	1
1985–86	Leeds U	38	2
1986–87	Leeds U	41	1
1987–88	Leeds U	26	0
1988–89	Leeds U	33	0
1989–90	Port Vale	42	0
1990–91	Port Vale	41	1
1991–92	Port Vale	42	0
1992–93	Port Vale	35	0
1993–94	Port Vale	40	1
1994–95	Port Vale	37	0
1995–96	Port Vale	22	1
1996–97	Port Vale	33	0
1997–98	Port Vale	26	0
1998–99	Port Vale	30	0
Total:		**555**	**8**

ASPINALL, Warren — Midfield

H: 5 9 W: 11 12 b.Wigan 13-9-67

Source: Apprentice. *Honours:* England Youth.

1984–85	Wigan Ath	10	1
1985–86	Wigan Ath	0	0
1985–86	Everton	1	0
1985–86	Wigan Ath (loan)	41	21
1986–87	Everton	6	0
1986–87	Aston Villa	12	3
1987–88	Aston Villa	32	11
1988–89	Portsmouth	40	11
1989–90	Portsmouth	3	0
1990–91	Portsmouth	33	4
1991–92	Portsmouth	24	4
1992–93	Portsmouth	27	2
1993–94	Portsmouth	5	0
1993–94	Swansea C (loan)	5	0
1993–94	Bournemouth	24	5
1994–95	Bournemouth	9	4
1994–95	Carlisle U (loan)	7	1
1995–96	Carlisle U	42	6
1996–97	Carlisle U	40	5
1997–98	Carlisle U	18	0

1997–98	Brentford	24	3
1998–99	Brentford	19	2
1998–99	Colchester U	15	3
Total:		**437**	**86**

ATHERTON, Peter — Defender

H: 5 11 W: 13 13 b.Wigan 6-4-70

Source: Trainee. *Honours:* England Schools, Under-21.

1987–88	Wigan Ath	16	0
1988–89	Wigan Ath	40	1
1989–90	Wigan Ath	46	0
1990–91	Wigan Ath	46	0
1991–92	Wigan Ath	1	0
1991–92	Coventry C	35	0
1992–93	Coventry C	39	0
1993–94	Coventry C	40	0
1994–95	Sheffield W	41	1
1995–96	Sheffield W	36	0
1996–97	Sheffield W	37	2
1997–98	Sheffield W	27	3
1998–99	Sheffield W	38	2
Total:		**442**	**9**

ATKINS, Mark — Midfield

H: 6 1 W: 12 00 b.Doncaster 14-8-68

Honours: England Schools.

1986–87	Scunthorpe U	26	0
1987–88	Scunthorpe U	22	2
1988–89	Blackburn R	46	6
1989–90	Blackburn R	41	7
1990–91	Blackburn R	42	4
1991–92	Blackburn R	44	6
1992–93	Blackburn R	31	5
1993–94	Blackburn R	15	1
1994–95	Blackburn R	34	6
1995–96	Blackburn R	4	0
1995–96	Wolverhampton W	32	3
1996–97	Wolverhampton W	45	4
1997–98	Wolverhampton W	34	2
1998–99	Wolverhampton W	15	0
Total:		**431**	**46**

ATKINSON, Brian — Midfield

H: 5 10 W: 12 10 b.Darlington 19-1-71

Source: Trainee. *Honours:* England Under-21.

1988–89	Sunderland	3	0
1989–90	Sunderland	13	0
1990–91	Sunderland	6	0
1991–92	Sunderland	30	2
1992–93	Sunderland	36	2
1993–94	Sunderland	29	0
1994–95	Sunderland	17	0
1995–96	Sunderland	7	0
1995–96	Carlisle U (loan)	2	0
1996–97	Darlington	30	3
1997–98	Darlington	32	1
1998–99	Darlington	43	2
Total:		**248**	**10**

ATKINSON, Graeme — Defender

H: 5 8 W: 11 05 b.Hull 11-11-71

Source: Trainee.

1989–90	Hull C	13	1
1990–91	Hull C	16	0
1991–92	Hull C	25	8
1992–93	Hull C	46	6
1993–94	Hull C	40	7
1994–95	Hull C	9	1
1994–95	Preston NE	15	1
1995–96	Preston NE	44	5
1996–97	Preston NE	17	0
1997–98	Preston NE	3	0
1997–98	Rochdale (loan)	6	0
1997–98	Brighton & HA	9	0
1998–99	Brighton & HA	7	0
1998–99	Scunthorpe U	1	0
1998–99	Scarborough	15	1
Total:		**266**	**30**

ATKINSON, Paddy — Defender

H: 5 10 W: 11 06 b.Singapore 22-5-70

Source: Sheffield U Trainee.

1988–89	Hartlepool U	13	3
1989–90	Hartlepool U	8	0
From Workington.			
1995–96	York C	22	0
1996–97	York C	14	0
1997–98	York C	5	0
1998–99	Scarborough	27	0
Total:		**89**	**3**

ATZENI, Allessandro — Midfield

b.Italy 1-1-80

1997–98	Fiorentina	2	0
1998–99	Southampton	0	0
Total:		**2**	**0**

AUGUSTINE, Steve — Forward

H: 6 0 W: 13 07 b.Hammersmith 13-12-78

1997–98	Luton T	0	0
1998–99	Luton T	0	0

AUSTIN, Dean — Defender

H: 5 11 W: 11 11 b.Hemel Hempstead 26-4-70

Source: St. *Honours:* Albans C.

1989–90	Southend U	7	0
1990–91	Southend U	44	0
1991–92	Southend U	45	2
1992–93	Tottenham H	34	0
1993–94	Tottenham H	23	0
1994–95	Tottenham H	24	0
1995–96	Tottenham H	28	0
1996–97	Tottenham H	15	0
1997–98	Tottenham H	0	0
1998–99	Crystal Palace	20	1
Total:		**240**	**3**

AUSTIN, Kevin — Defender

H: 6 1 W: 14 00 b.Hackney 12-2-73

Source: Saffron Walden.

1993–94	Leyton Orient	30	0
1994–95	Leyton Orient	39	2
1995–96	Leyton Orient	40	1
1996–97	Lincoln C	44	1
1997–98	Lincoln C	46	0
1998–99	Lincoln C	39	1
Total:		**238**	**5**

AVDIU, Kemajl — Midfield

H: 5 10 W: 12 08 b.Yugoslavia 22-12-76

Source: Esbjerg.

1998–99	Bury	6	1
1998–99	Partick T (loan)	6	1
Total:		**12**	**2**

AWFORD, Andy — Defender

H: 5 9 W: 11 02 b.Worcester 14-7-72

Source: Worcester C. *Honours:* England Schools, Youth, Under-21, Football League.

1988–89	Portsmouth	4	0
1989–90	Portsmouth	0	0
1990–91	Portsmouth	14	0
1991–92	Portsmouth	45	0
1992–93	Portsmouth	44	0
1993–94	Portsmouth	35	0
1994–95	Portsmouth	4	0
1995–96	Portsmouth	18	1
1996–97	Portsmouth	39	0
1997–98	Portsmouth	39	0
1998–99	Portsmouth	35	1
Total:		**277**	**2**

AYORINDE, Sam — Forward

H: 6 0 W: 12 07 b.Lagos 20-10-74

Source: Stade Tunisien, Sturm Graz.

1995–96	Leyton Orient	1	0
1996–97	Leyton Orient	12	2
1997–98	Leyton Orient	0	0
1998–99	Leyton Orient	0	0
Total:		**13**	**2**

AYRES, James — Defender

H: 6 3 W: 13 00 b.Luton 18-9-80

Source: Trainee.

1998–99	Luton T	0	0

BAARDSEN, Espen — Goalkeeper

H: 6 5 W: 13 03 b.San Rafael 7-12-77

Source: San Francisco All Blacks. *Honours:* USA Youth, Norway Under-21, 3 full caps.

1996–97	Tottenham H	2	0
1997–98	Tottenham H	9	0
1998–99	Tottenham H	12	0
Total:		**23**	**0**

BABAYARO, Celestine — Defender

H: 5 9 W: 10 12 b.Kaduna 29-8-78

Honours: Nigeria 9 full caps.

1994–95	Anderlecht	22	0
1995–96	Anderlecht	28	5
1996–97	Anderlecht	25	3
1997–98	Chelsea	8	0
1998–99	Chelsea	28	3
Total:		**111**	**11**

BABB, Phil — Defender

H: 6 0 W: 12 03 b.Lambeth 30-11-70

Source: Trainee. *Honours:* Eire B, 29 full caps.

1988–89	Millwall	0	0
1989–90	Millwall	0	0
1990–91	Bradford C	34	10
1991–92	Bradford C	46	4
1992–93	Coventry C	34	0
1993–94	Coventry C	40	3
1994–95	Coventry C	3	0
1994–95	Liverpool	34	0
1995–96	Liverpool	28	0
1996–97	Liverpool	22	1
1997–98	Liverpool	19	0
1998–99	Liverpool	25	0
Total:		**285**	**18**

BACQUE, Herve — Forward

b.Bordeaux 13-7-76

Source: Monaco.

1998–99	Luton T	7	0
1998–99	Motherwell	1	0
Total:		**8**	**0**

BADDELEY, Lee — Defender

H: 6 1 W: 12 07 b.Cardiff 2-7-74

Source: Trainee. *Honours:* Wales Under-21.

1990–91	Cardiff C	2	0
1991–92	Cardiff C	18	0
1992–93	Cardiff C	8	0
1993–94	Cardiff C	30	0
1994–95	Cardiff C	36	1
1995–96	Cardiff C	30	0
1996–97	Cardiff C	9	0
1996–97	Exeter C	11	0
1997–98	Exeter C	32	1
1998–99	Exeter C	23	0
Total:		**199**	**2**

BADMAN, Mark — Midfield

b.Bath 21-12-79

Source: Trainee.

1998–99	Bristol C	0	0

BAGAN, David — Midfield

H: 5 6 W: 9 07 b.Irvine 26-4-77

Source: Troon Juniors. *Honours:* Scotland Under-21.

1995–96	Kilmarnock	0	0
1996–97	Kilmarnock	17	0
1997–98	Kilmarnock	7	0
1998–99	Kilmarnock	5	0
Total:		**29**	**0**

BAGSHAW, Neil — Defender

H: 6 2 W: 12 08 b.Doncaster 24-12-79

Source: Trainee.

1998–99	Rotherham U	0	0

BAGSHAW, Paul — Midfield

H: 5 10 W: 12 02 b.Sheffield 29-5-79

Source: Trainee.

1997–98	Barnsley	0	0
1998–99	Barnsley	1	0
1998–99	Carlisle U (loan)	9	0
Total:		**10**	**0**

BAIANO, Francesco — Forward

H: 5 6 W: 10 07 b.Naples 24-2-68

1985–86	Napoli	4	0
1986–87	Empoli	26	2
1987–88	Napoli	1	0
1987–88	Parma	25	4
1988–89	Empoli	38	14
1989–90	Avellino	32	6
1990–91	Foggia	36	22
1991–92	Foggia	33	16
1992–93	Fiorentina	31	10
1993–94	Fiorentina	11	4
1994–95	Fiorentina	27	2
1995–96	Fiorentina	28	11
1996–97	Fiorentina	21	2
1997–98	Derby Co	33	12
1998–99	Derby Co	22	4
Total:		**368**	**109**

BAILEY, Alan — Forward

H: 5 11 W: 12 03 b.Macclesfield 1-11-78

Source: Trainee.

1997–98	Manchester C	0	0
1998–99	Manchester C	0	0
1998–99	Macclesfield T (loan)	10	1
Total:		**10**	**1**

BAILEY, Dennis — Forward

H: 5 10 W: 11 08 b.Lambeth 13-11-65

Source: Fulham, Farnborough T.

1987–88	Crystal Palace	5	1
1988–89	Crystal Palace	0	0
1988–89	Bristol R (loan)	17	9
1989–90	Birmingham C	43	18
1990–91	Birmingham C	32	5
1990–91	Bristol R (loan)	6	1
1991–92	QPR	24	9
1992–93	QPR	15	1
1993–94	QPR	0	0
1993–94	Charlton Ath (loan)	4	0
1993–94	Watford (loan)	8	4
1994–95	QPR	0	0
1994–95	Brentford (loan)	6	3
1995–96	Gillingham	45	8
1996–97	Gillingham	30	2
1997–98	Gillingham	13	1

1997–98	Lincoln C	5	1
1998–99	Lincoln C	0	0
Total:		**253**	**63**

BAILEY, John — Midfield

H: 5 8 W: 10 02 b.London 6-5-69

Source: Enfield.

1995–96	Bournemouth	44	4
1996–97	Bournemouth	40	1
1997–98	Bournemouth	32	1
1998–99	Bournemouth	32	0
Total:		**148**	**6**

BAILEY, Mark — Midfield

H: 5 9 W: 11 11 b.Stoke 12-8-76

Source: Trainee.

1994–95	Stoke C	0	0
1995–96	Stoke C	0	0
1996–97	Stoke C	0	0
1996–97	Rochdale	15	0
1997–98	Rochdale	33	0
1998–99	Rochdale	19	1
Total:		**67**	**1**

BAIRD, Andy — Defender

H: 5 0 W: 11 13 b.East Kilbride 18-1-79

Source: Trainee.

1997–98	Wycombe W	2	0
1998–99	Wycombe W	28	6
Total:		**30**	**6**

BAKALLI, Adrian — Midfield

b.Brussels 22-11-76

Source: Molenbeek.

1998–99	Watford	0	0

BAKAYOKO, Ibrahima — Forward

b.Seguela 31-12-76

Source: Stade Abidjan.

1995–96	Montpellier	14	0
1996–97	Montpellier	27	13
1997–98	Montpellier	28	7
1998–99	Montpellier	7	4
1998–99	Everton	23	4
Total:		**99**	**28**

BAKER, Joe — Forward

H: 5 8 W: 10 07 b.London 9-4-77

Source: Charlton Ath Trainee.

1994–95	Leyton Orient	0	0
1995–96	Leyton Orient	20	0
1996–97	Leyton Orient	20	0
1997–98	Leyton Orient	31	3
1998–99	Leyton Orient	4	0
Total:		**75**	**3**

BAKER, Martin — Defender

H: 6 0 W: 10 12 b.Govan 8-6-74

Source: St Mirren BC.

1992–93	St Mirren	29	0
1993–94	St Mirren	38	1
1994–95	St Mirren	26	2
1995–96	St Mirren	26	0
1996–97	St Mirren	31	0
1997–98	Kilmarnock	19	0
1998–99	Kilmarnock	23	0
Total:		**192**	**3**

BAKER, Matthew — Goalkeeper

H: 6 0 W: 12 08 b.Claro 18-12-79

Source: Trainee.

1998–99	Hull C	0	0

BAKER, Paul — Forward

H: 6 2 W: 14 04 b.Newcastle 5-1-63

Source: Bishop Auckland.

1984–85	Southampton	0	0
1985–86	Carlisle U	35	2
1986–87	Carlisle U	36	9
1987–88	Hartlepool U	39	19
1988–89	Hartlepool U	40	7
1989–90	Hartlepool U	43	16
1990–91	Hartlepool U	46	12
1991–92	Hartlepool U	29	13
1992–93	Motherwell	9	1
1992–93	Gillingham	21	6
1993–94	Gillingham	33	8
1994–95	Gillingham	8	2
1994–95	York C	30	13
1995–96	York C	18	5
1995–96	Torquay U	20	4
1996–97	Torquay U	10	4
1996–97	Scunthorpe U	21	9
1996–97	Hartlepool U	6	2
1997–98	Hartlepool U	16	5
1998–99	Hartlepool U	13	2
Total:		**473**	**139**

BAKER, Steve — Defender

H: 6 0 W: 12 06 b.Pontefract 8-9-78

Honours: Eire Under-21.

1997–98	Middlesbrough	6	0
1998–99	Middlesbrough	2	0
Total:		**8**	**0**

BAKKE, Morten — Midfield

b.Gonefoff 16-12-68

Source: Molde.

1998–99	Wimbledon	0	0

BALDACCHINO, Ryan — Forward

H: 5 9 W: 12 03 b.Leicester 13-1-81

Source: Trainee.

1998–99	Blackburn R	0	0

BALDRY, Simon — Midfield

H: 5 11 W: 12 00 b.Huddersfield 12-2-76

Source: Trainee.

1993–94	Huddersfield T	10	2
1994–95	Huddersfield T	11	0
1995–96	Huddersfield T	14	0
1996–97	Huddersfield T	7	0
1997–98	Huddersfield T	11	1
1998–99	Huddersfield T	13	0
1998–99	Bury (loan)	5	0
Total:		**71**	**3**

BALL, Kevin — Midfield

H: 5 9 W: 11 06 b.Hastings 12-11-64

Source: Apprentice.

1983–84	Portsmouth	1	0
1984–85	Portsmouth	0	0
1985–86	Portsmouth	9	0
1986–87	Portsmouth	16	0
1987–88	Portsmouth	29	1
1988–89	Portsmouth	14	1
1989–90	Portsmouth	36	2
1990–91	Sunderland	33	3
1991–92	Sunderland	33	1
1992–93	Sunderland	43	3
1993–94	Sunderland	36	0
1994–95	Sunderland	42	2
1995–96	Sunderland	36	4
1996–97	Sunderland	32	3
1997–98	Sunderland	31	3
1998–99	Sunderland	42	2
Total:		**433**	**25**

BALL, Michael — Midfield

H: 6 1 W: 11 09 b.Liverpool 2-10-79

Source: Trainee. *Honours:* England Schools, Youth, Under-21.

1996–97	Everton	5	0
1997–98	Everton	25	1
1998–99	Everton	37	3
Total:		**67**	**4**

BALMER, Stuart — Defender

H: 6 0 W: 12 11 b.Falkirk 20-9-69

Source: Celtic BC.

1987–88	Celtic	0	0
1988–89	Celtic	0	0
1989–90	Celtic	0	0
1990–91	Charlton Ath	24	0
1991–92	Charlton Ath	18	0
1992–93	Charlton Ath	45	2
1993–94	Charlton Ath	31	1
1994–95	Charlton Ath	29	2
1995–96	Charlton Ath	32	1
1996–97	Charlton Ath	32	2
1997–98	Charlton Ath	16	0
1998–99	Charlton Ath	0	0
1998–99	Wigan Ath	36	1
Total:		**263**	**9**

BANGER, Nicky — Forward

H: 5 8 W: 11 10 b.Southampton 25-2-71

Source: Trainee.

1988–89	Southampton	0	0
1989–90	Southampton	0	0
1990–91	Southampton	6	0
1991–92	Southampton	4	0
1992–93	Southampton	27	6
1993–94	Southampton	14	0
1994–95	Southampton	4	2
1994–95	Oldham Ath	28	3
1995–96	Oldham Ath	13	2
1996–97	Oldham Ath	23	5
1997–98	Oxford U	28	3
1998–99	Oxford U	32	5
Total:		**179**	**26**

BANKOLE, Ademola — Goalkeeper

H: 6 3 W: 12 08 b.Lagos 9-9-69

Source: Leyton Orient.

1996–97	Crewe Alex	3	0
1997–98	Crewe Alex	3	0
1998–99	QPR	0	0
Total:		**6**	**0**

BANKS, Steve — Goalkeeper

H: 5 11 W: 12 04 b.Hillingdon 9-2-72

Source: Trainee.

1991–92	West Ham U	0	0
1992–93	West Ham U	0	0
1993–94	Gillingham	29	0
1994–95	Gillingham	38	0
1995–96	Blackpool	24	0
1996–97	Blackpool	46	0
1997–98	Blackpool	45	0
1998–99	Blackpool	35	0
1998–99	Bolton W	9	0
Total:		**226**	**0**

BANNERMAN, Scott — Forward

H: 5 6 W: 10 04 b.Edinburgh 21-3-79

Source: Hutchison Vale BC.

1995–96	Hibernian	0	0
1996–97	Hibernian	0	0
1997–98	Hibernian	1	0
1998–99	Hibernian	12	0
Total:		**13**	**0**

BARACLOUGH, Ian — Defender

H: 6 1 W: 12 02 b.Leicester 4-12-70

Source: Trainee.

1988–89	Leicester C	0	0
1989–90	Leicester C	0	0
1989–90	Wigan Ath (loan)	9	2
1990–91	Leicester C	0	0
1990–91	Grimsby T (loan)	4	0
1991–92	Grimsby T	0	0
1992–93	Grimsby T	1	0
1992–93	Lincoln C	36	5
1993–94	Lincoln C	37	5
1994–95	Mansfield T	36	3
1995–96	Mansfield T	11	2
1995–96	Notts Co	35	2
1996–97	Notts Co	38	2
1997–98	Notts Co	38	6
1997–98	QPR	8	0
1998–99	QPR	43	1
Total:		**296**	**28**

BARCLAY, Dominic — Forward

H: 6 0 W: 11 10 b.Bristol 5-9-76

Source: Trainee.

1993–94	Bristol C	2	0
1994–95	Bristol C	0	0
1995–96	Bristol C	2	0
1996–97	Bristol C	0	0
1997–98	Bristol C	8	0
1998–99	Macclesfield T	9	1
Total:		**21**	**1**

BARDSLEY, David — Defender

H: 5 10 W: 11 07 b.Manchester 11-9-64

Source: Apprentice. *Honours:* England Youth, 2 full caps.

1981–82	Blackpool	1	0
1982–83	Blackpool	28	0
1983–84	Blackpool	16	0
1983–84	Watford	25	0
1984–85	Watford	17	0
1985–86	Watford	13	2
1986–87	Watford	41	5
1987–88	Watford	4	0
1987–88	Oxford U	34	1
1988–89	Oxford U	37	6
1989–90	Oxford U	3	0
1989–90	QPR	31	1
1990–91	QPR	38	0
1991–92	QPR	41	0
1992–93	QPR	40	3
1993–94	QPR	32	0
1994–95	QPR	30	0
1995–96	QPR	29	0
1996–97	QPR	0	0
1997–98	QPR	12	0
1998–99	Blackpool	29	0
Total:		**501**	**18**

BARKER, Christopher — Defender

H: 6 0 W: 11 08 b.Sheffield 2-3-80

Source: Alfreton.

1998–99	Barnsley	0	0

BARKER, Richard — Forward

H: 6 0 W: 14 03 b.Sheffield 30-5-75

Source: Trainee. *Honours:* England Schools.

1993–94	Sheffield W	0	0
1994–95	Sheffield W	0	0
1995–96	Sheffield W	0	0
1995–96	Doncaster R (loan)	6	0
1996–97	Sheffield W	0	0
From Linfield			
1997–98	Brighton & HA	17	2
1998–99	Brighton & HA	43	10
Total:		**66**	**12**

BARKER, Simon — Midfield

H: 5 8 W: 11 07 b.Farnworth 4-11-64

Source: Apprentice. *Honours:* England Under-21.

1982–83	Blackburn R	0	0
1983–84	Blackburn R	28	3

1984–85	Blackburn R	38	2
1985–86	Blackburn R	41	10
1986–87	Blackburn R	42	11
1987–88	Blackburn R	33	9
1988–89	QPR	25	1
1989–90	QPR	28	3
1990–91	QPR	35	1
1991–92	QPR	34	6
1992–93	QPR	25	1
1993–94	QPR	37	5
1994–95	QPR	37	4
1995–96	QPR	33	5
1996–97	QPR	38	4
1997–98	QPR	23	3
1998–99	QPR	0	0
1998–99	Port Vale	27	2
Total:		**524**	**70**

BARLOW, Andy — Defender

H: 5 8 W: 11 12 b.Oldham 24-11-65

1984–85	Oldham Ath	33	0
1985–86	Oldham Ath	26	0
1986–87	Oldham Ath	29	2
1987–88	Oldham Ath	26	0
1988–89	Oldham Ath	15	0
1989–90	Oldham Ath	44	1
1990–91	Oldham Ath	46	0
1991–92	Oldham Ath	28	2
1992–93	Oldham Ath	6	0
1993–94	Oldham Ath	6	0
1993–94	Bradford C (loan)	2	0
1994–95	Oldham Ath	2	0
1995–96	Blackpool	34	1
1996–97	Blackpool	46	1
1997–98	Rochdale	38	0
1998–99	Rochdale	29	1
Total:		**410**	**8**

BARLOW, Martin — Midfield

H: 5 7 W: 10 03 b.Barnstable 25-6-71

Source: Trainee.

1988–89	Plymouth Arg	1	0
1989–90	Plymouth Arg	1	0
1990–91	Plymouth Arg	30	1
1991–92	Plymouth Arg	28	3
1992–93	Plymouth Arg	24	1
1993–94	Plymouth Arg	26	2
1994–95	Plymouth Arg	42	2
1995–96	Plymouth Arg	28	5
1996–97	Plymouth Arg	40	1
1997–98	Plymouth Arg	42	4
1998–99	Plymouth Arg	45	5
Total:		**307**	**24**

BARLOW, Stuart — Forward

H: 5 10 W: 11 01 b.Liverpool 16-7-68

Source: School.

1990–91	Everton	2	0
1991–92	Everton	7	0
1991–92	Rotherham U (loan)	0	0
1992–93	Everton	26	5
1993–94	Everton	22	3
1994–95	Everton	11	2
1995–96	Everton	3	0
1995–96	Oldham Ath	26	7
1996–97	Oldham Ath	35	12
1997–98	Oldham Ath	32	12
1997–98	Wigan Ath	9	3
1998–99	Wigan Ath	41	19
Total:		**214**	**63**

BARMBY, Nick — Forward

H: 5 6 W: 11 04 b.Hull 11-2-74

Source: Trainee. *Honours:* England Schools, Youth, Under-21, B, 10 full caps, 3 goals.

1991–92	Tottenham H	0	0
1992–93	Tottenham H	22	6
1993–94	Tottenham H	27	5
1994–95	Tottenham H	38	9
1995–96	Middlesbrough	32	7
1996–97	Middlesbrough	10	1
1996–97	Everton	25	4
1997–98	Everton	30	2
1998–99	Everton	24	3
Total:		**208**	**37**

BARNARD, Darren — Defender

H: 5 9 W: 12 03 b.Rinteln 30-11-71

Source: Wokingham T. *Honours:* England Schools, Wales 6 full caps.

1990–91	Chelsea	0	0
1991–92	Chelsea	4	0
1992–93	Chelsea	13	1
1993–94	Chelsea	12	1
1994–95	Chelsea	0	0
1994–95	Reading (loan)	4	0
1995–96	Chelsea	0	0
1995–96	Bristol C	34	4
1996–97	Bristol C	44	11
1997–98	Barnsley	35	2
1998–99	Barnsley	26	4
Total:		**172**	**23**

BARNARD, Mark — Defender

H: 5 11 W: 11 10 b.Sheffield 27-11-75

Source: Trainee.

1994–95	Rotherham U	0	0

1995–96	Darlington	37	3
1996–97	Darlington	37	0
1997–98	Darlington	36	0
1998–99	Darlington	33	1
Total:		**143**	**4**

BARNARD, Richard — Goalkeeper

b.Frimley 27-12-80

Source: Trainee.

1998–99	Millwall	0	0

BARNES, John — Midfield

H: 5 11 W: 12 07 b.Jamaica 7-11-63

Source: Sudbury Court. *Honours:* England Under-21, 79 full caps, 11 goals.

1981–82	Watford	36	13
1982–83	Watford	42	10
1983–84	Watford	39	11
1984–85	Watford	40	12
1985–86	Watford	39	9
1986–87	Watford	37	10
1987–88	Liverpool	38	15
1988–89	Liverpool	33	8
1989–90	Liverpool	34	22
1990–91	Liverpool	35	16
1991–92	Liverpool	12	1
1992–93	Liverpool	27	5
1993–94	Liverpool	26	3
1994–95	Liverpool	38	7
1995–96	Liverpool	36	3
1996–97	Liverpool	35	4
1997–98	Newcastle U	26	6
1998–99	Newcastle U	1	0
1998–99	Charlton Ath	12	0
Total:		**586**	**155**

BARNES, Kevin — Forward

H: 6 0 W: 12 05 b.Fleetwood 12-9-75

Source: Lancaster C.

1998–99	Blackpool	4	0

BARNES, Paul — Forward

H: 5 11 W: 13 00 b.Leeds 16-11-67

Source: Apprentice.

1985–86	Notts Co	14	4
1986–87	Notts Co	0	0
1987–88	Notts Co	11	2
1988–89	Notts Co	15	7
1989–90	Notts Co	13	1
1989–90	Stoke C	5	0
1990–91	Stoke C	6	0
1990–91	Chesterfield (loan)	1	0
1991–92	Stoke C	13	3
1992–93	York C	40	21
1993–94	York C	42	24
1994–95	York C	36	16
1995–96	York C	30	15
1995–96	Birmingham C	15	7
1996–97	Birmingham C	0	0
1996–97	Burnley	40	24
1997–98	Burnley	25	6
1997–98	Huddersfield T	15	1
1998–99	Huddersfield T	15	1
1998–99	Bury	8	0
Total:		**344**	**132**

BARNES, Phil — Goalkeeper

H: 6 1 W: 11 01 b.Rotherham 2-3-79

Source: Trainee.

1996–97	Rotherham U	2	0
1997–98	Blackpool	1	0
1998–99	Blackpool	1	0
Total:		**4**	**0**

BARNES, Steve — Midfield

H: 5 4 W: 10 09 b.Harrow 5-1-76

Source: Welling U.

1995–96	Birmingham C	3	0
1996–97	Birmingham C	0	0
1997–98	Birmingham C	0	0
1997–98	Brighton & HA (loan)	12	0
1998–99	Birmingham C	0	0
1998–99	Barnet	12	0
Total:		**27**	**0**

BARNESS, Anthony — Defender

H: 5 11 W: 12 01 b.Lewisham 25-3-73

Source: Trainee.

1990–91	Charlton Ath	0	0
1991–92	Charlton Ath	22	1
1992–93	Charlton Ath	5	0
1992–93	Chelsea	2	0
1993–94	Chelsea	0	0
1993–94	Middlesbrough (loan)	0	0
1994–95	Chelsea	12	0
1995–96	Chelsea	0	0
1995–96	Southend U (loan)	5	0
1996–97	Charlton Ath	45	2
1997–98	Charlton Ath	29	1
1998–99	Charlton Ath	3	0
Total:		**123**	**4**

BARNETT, Christopher — Midfield

H: 5 11 W: 12 00 b.Derby 20-12-78

Source: Trainee.

1996–97	Coventry C	0	0

1997–98	Coventry C	0	0
1998–99	Coventry C	0	0

BARNETT, Dave — Defender

H: 6 1 W: 12 08 b.Birmingham 16-4-67

Source: Windsor & Eton.

1988–89	Colchester U	20	0
1989–90	WBA	0	0
1990–91	Walsall	5	0
From Kidderminster H			
1991–92	Barnet	4	0
1992–93	Barnet	36	2
1993–94	Barnet	19	1
1993–94	Birmingham C	9	0
1994–95	Birmingham C	31	0
1995–96	Birmingham C	0	0
1996–97	Birmingham C	6	0
1997–98	Dunfermline Ath	21	1
1997–98	Port Vale	9	1
1998–99	Port Vale	27	0
Total:		**187**	**5**

BARNETT, Jason — Defender

H: 5 9 W: 10 10 b.Shrewsbury 21-4-76

Source: Trainee.

1994–95	Wolverhampton W	0	0
1995–96	Wolverhampton W	0	0
1995–96	Lincoln C	32	2
1996–97	Lincoln C	36	0
1997–98	Lincoln C	33	0
1998–99	Lincoln C	29	1
Total:		**130**	**3**

BARR, Billy — Defender

H: 5 11 W: 11 02 b.Halifax 21-1-69

Source: Trainee.

1987–88	Halifax T	30	0
1988–89	Halifax T	43	4
1989–90	Halifax T	23	2
1990–91	Halifax T	37	1
1991–92	Halifax T	35	3
1992–93	Halifax T	28	3
From Halifax T			
1994–95	Crewe Alex	34	2
1995–96	Crewe Alex	17	0
1996–97	Crewe Alex	34	5
1997–98	Carlisle U	39	3
1998–99	Carlisle U	23	0
Total:		**343**	**23**

BARRAS, Tony — Defender

H: 6 0 W: 13 00 b.Stockton 29-3-71

Source: Trainee.

1988–89	Hartlepool U	3	0
1989–90	Hartlepool U	9	0
1990–91	Stockport Co	40	0
1991–92	Stockport Co	42	5
1992–93	Stockport Co	14	0
1993–94	Stockport Co	3	0
1993–94	Rotherham U (loan)	5	1
1994–95	York C	31	1
1995–96	York C	32	3
1996–97	York C	46	1
1997–98	York C	38	6
1998–99	York C	24	0
1998–99	Reading	6	1
Total:		**293**	**18**

BARRETT, Adam — Midfield

b.Dagenham 29-11-79

1998–99	Plymouth Arg	1	0
Total:		**1**	**0**

BARRETT, Earl — Defender

H: 5 10 W: 11 02 b.Rochdale 28-4-67

Source: Apprentice. *Honours:* England Under-21, B, 3 full caps.

1984–85	Manchester C	0	0
1985–86	Manchester C	1	0
1985–86	Chester C (loan)	12	0
1986–87	Manchester C	2	0
1987–88	Manchester C	0	0
1987–88	Oldham Ath	18	0
1988–89	Oldham Ath	44	0
1989–90	Oldham Ath	46	2
1990–91	Oldham Ath	46	3
1991–92	Oldham Ath	29	2
1991–92	Aston Villa	13	0
1992–93	Aston Villa	42	1
1993–94	Aston Villa	39	0
1994–95	Aston Villa	25	0
1994–95	Everton	17	0
1995–96	Everton	8	0
1996–97	Everton	36	0
1997–98	Everton	13	0
1997–98	Sheffield U (loan)	5	0
1997–98	Sheffield W	10	0
1998–99	Sheffield W	5	0
Total:		**411**	**8**

BARRETT, Graham — Forward

b.Dublin 6-10-81

Source: Trainee. *Honours:* Eire Schools, Youth.

1998–99	Arsenal	0	0

BARRETT, Paul — Midfield

H: 5 9 W: 11 04 b.Newcastle 13-4-78

Source: Trainee.

1996–97	Newcastle U	0	0
1997–98	Newcastle U	0	0
1998–99	Newcastle U	0	0
1998–99	Wrexham	10	0
Total:		**10**	**0**

BARRETT, Scott — Goalkeeper

H: 5 11 W: 13 00 b.Ilkeston 2-4-63

Source: Ilkeston T.

1984–85	Wolverhampton W	4	0
1985–86	Wolverhampton W	21	0
1986–87	Wolverhampton W	5	0
1987–88	Stoke C	27	0
1988–89	Stoke C	17	0
1989–90	Stoke C	7	0
1989–90	Colchester U (loan)	13	0
1989–90	Stockport Co (loan)	10	0
1990–91	Colchester U	0	0
1991–92	Colchester U	0	0
1992–93	Gillingham	34	0
1993–94	Gillingham	13	0
1994–95	Gillingham	4	0
1995–96	Cambridge U	31	0
1996–97	Cambridge U	45	0
1997–98	Cambridge U	43	0
1998–99	Cambridge U	0	0
1998–99	Leyton Orient	20	0
Total:		**294**	**0**

BARRICK, Dean — Defender

H: 5 8 W: 12 00 b.Hemsworth 30-9-69

Source: Trainee.

1987–88	Sheffield W	0	0
1988–89	Sheffield W	8	2
1989–90	Sheffield W	3	0
1990–91	Sheffield W	0	0
1990–91	Rotherham U	19	2
1991–92	Rotherham U	34	1
1992–93	Rotherham U	46	4
1993–94	Cambridge U	44	1
1994–95	Cambridge U	44	1
1995–96	Cambridge U	3	1
1995–96	Preston NE	40	0
1996–97	Preston NE	36	0
1997–98	Preston NE	33	1
1998–99	Bury	20	1
Total:		**330**	**14**

BARRON, Michael — Defender

H: 5 11 W: 11 06 b.Lumley 22-12-74

Source: Trainee.

1992–93	Middlesbrough	0	0
1993–94	Middlesbrough	2	0
1994–95	Middlesbrough	0	0
1995–96	Middlesbrough	1	0
1996–97	Middlesbrough	0	0
1996–97	Hartlepool U (loan)	16	0
1997–98	Hartlepool U	33	0
1998–99	Hartlepool U	38	1
Total:		**90**	**1**

BARRY, Gareth — Defender

H: 5 11 W: 12 06 b.Hastings 23-2-81

Source: Trainee. *Honours:* England Youth, Under-21.

1997–98	Aston Villa	2	0
1998–99	Aston Villa	32	2
Total:		**34**	**2**

BART-WILLIAMS, Chris — Midfield

H: 5 11 W: 12 07 b.Freetown 16-6-74

Source: Trainee. *Honours:* England Youth, Under-21.

1990–91	Leyton Orient	21	2
1991–92	Leyton Orient	15	0
1991–92	Sheffield W	15	0
1992–93	Sheffield W	34	6
1993–94	Sheffield W	37	8
1994–95	Sheffield W	38	2
1995–96	Nottingham F	33	0
1996–97	Nottingham F	16	1
1997–98	Nottingham F	33	4
1998–99	Nottingham F	24	3
Total:		**266**	**26**

BARTLEY, Danny — Forward

b.Lincoln 11-9-79

Source: Trainee.

1998–99	West Ham U	0	0

BARTON, Warren — Defender

H: 5 11 W: 12 00 b.Stoke Newington 19-3-69

Source: Leytonstone/Ilford. *Honours:* England B, 3 full caps.

1989–90	Maidstone U	42	0

1990–91	Wimbledon	37	3
1991–92	Wimbledon	42	1
1992–93	Wimbledon	23	2
1993–94	Wimbledon	39	2
1994–95	Wimbledon	39	2
1995–96	Newcastle U	31	0
1996–97	Newcastle U	18	1
1997–98	Newcastle U	23	3
1998–99	Newcastle U	24	0
Total:		**318**	**14**

BARTRAM, Vince — Goalkeeper

H: 6 2 W: 13 04 b.Birmingham 8-8-68

Source: Local.

1985–86	Wolverhampton W	0	0
1986–87	Wolverhampton W	1	0
1987–88	Wolverhampton W	0	0
1988–89	Wolverhampton W	0	0
1989–90	Wolverhampton W	0	0
1989–90	Blackpool (loan)	9	0
1990–91	Wolverhampton W	4	0
1990–91	WBA (loan)	0	0
1991–92	Bournemouth	46	0
1992–93	Bournemouth	45	0
1993–94	Bournemouth	41	0
1994–95	Arsenal	11	0
1995–96	Arsenal	0	0
1996–97	Arsenal	0	0
1996–97	Wolverhampton W (loan)	0	0
1997–98	Arsenal	0	0
1997–98	Huddersfield T (loan)	12	0
1997–98	Gillingham	9	0
1998–99	Gillingham	44	0
Total:		**222**	**0**

BARWOOD, Danny — Forward

H: 5 9 W: 11 00 b.Caerphilly 25-2-81

Source: Trainee.

1997–98	Swansea C	3	1
1998–99	Swansea C	0	0
Total:		**3**	**1**

BASFORD, Luke — Defender

H: 5 6 W: 9 02 b.Lambeth 6-1-80

Source: Trainee.

1997–98	Bristol R	7	0
1998–99	Bristol R	9	0
Total:		**16**	**0**

BASHAM, Mike — Defender

H: 6 2 W: 13 09 b.Barking 27-9-73

Source: Trainee. *Honours:* England Schools.

1992–93	West Ham U	0	0
1993–94	West Ham U	0	0
1993–94	Colchester U (loan)	1	0
1993–94	Swansea C	5	0
1994–95	Swansea C	13	0
1995–96	Swansea C	11	1
1995–96	Peterborough U	14	1
1996–97	Peterborough U	5	0
1997–98	Barnet	20	1
1998–99	Barnet	32	1
Total:		**101**	**4**

BASHAM, Steve — Forward

H: 5 11 W: 12 04 b.Southampton 2-12-77

Source: Trainee.

1996–97	Southampton	6	0
1997–98	Southampton	9	0
1997–98	Wrexham (loan)	5	0
1998–99	Southampton	4	1
1998–99	Preston NE (loan)	17	10
Total:		**41**	**11**

BASS, David — Midfield

H: 5 11 W: 12 03 b.Frimley 29-11-74

Source: Trainee.

1991–92	Reading	3	0
1992–93	Reading	5	0
1993–94	Reading	1	0
1994–95	Reading	0	0
1995–96	Reading	0	0
1996–97	Reading	2	0
1997–98	Rotherham U	18	0
1998–99	Rotherham U	0	0
1998–99	Carlisle U	9	0
Total:		**38**	**0**

BASS, Jonathan — Defender

H: 6 0 W: 12 02 b.Weston-Super-Mare 1-1-76

Source: Trainee. *Honours:* England Schools.

1994–95	Birmingham C	0	0
1995–96	Birmingham C	5	0
1996–97	Birmingham C	13	0
1996–97	Carlisle U (loan)	3	0
1997–98	Birmingham C	30	0
1998–99	Birmingham C	11	0
Total:		**62**	**0**

BASSINDER, Gavin — Defender

H: 5 8 W: 11 01 b.Mexborough 24-9-79

Source: Trainee.

1997–98	Barnsley	0	0
1998–99	Barnsley	0	0

BASTOW, Darren — Midfield

b.Torquay 22-12-81

Source: Trainee.

1998–99	Plymouth Arg	29	2
Total:		**29**	**2**

BATE, Christopher — Midfield

b.Derby 30-1-81

Source: Trainee.

1998–99	Derby Co	0	0

BATER, Geraint — Defender

H: 5 8 W: 10 08 b.Bristol 26-7-80

1998–99	Bristol R	0	0

BATES, Jamie — Defender

H: 5 11 W: 14 06 b.Croydon 24-2-68

Source: Trainee.

1986–87	Brentford	24	1
1987–88	Brentford	23	1
1988–89	Brentford	36	1
1989–90	Brentford	15	0
1990–91	Brentford	32	2
1991–92	Brentford	42	1
1992–93	Brentford	24	0
1993–94	Brentford	45	2
1994–95	Brentford	38	2
1995–96	Brentford	36	4
1996–97	Brentford	37	2
1997–98	Brentford	40	1
1998–99	Brentford	27	1
1998–99	Wycombe W	9	0
Total:		**428**	**18**

BATTERSBY, Richard — Midfield

H: 5 8 W: 10 03 b.York 13-6-79

Source: Trainee.

1998–99	Oldham Ath	0	0

BATTERSBY, Tony — Forward

H: 6 0 W: 12 09 b.Doncaster 30-8-75

Source: Trainee.

1993–94	Sheffield U	0	0
1994–95	Sheffield U	0	0
1994–95	Southend U (loan)	8	1
1995–96	Sheffield U	10	1
1995–96	Notts Co	21	7
1996–97	Notts Co	18	1
1996–97	Bury (loan)	11	2
1997–98	Bury	37	6
1998–99	Bury	0	0
1998–99	Lincoln C	39	7
Total:		**144**	**25**

BATTY, David — Midfield

H: 5 8 W: 11 10 b.Leeds 2-12-68

Source: Trainee. *Honours:* England Under-21, B, 40 full caps.

1987–88	Leeds U	23	1
1988–89	Leeds U	30	0
1989–90	Leeds U	42	0
1990–91	Leeds U	37	0
1991–92	Leeds U	40	2
1992–93	Leeds U	30	1
1993–94	Leeds U	9	0
1993–94	Blackburn R	26	0
1994–95	Blackburn R	5	0
1995–96	Blackburn R	23	1
1995–96	Newcastle U	11	1
1996–97	Newcastle U	32	1
1997–98	Newcastle U	32	1
1998–99	Newcastle U	8	0
1998–99	Leeds U	10	0
Total:		**358**	**8**

BAYES, Ashley — Goalkeeper

H: 6 1 W: 13 05 b.Lincoln 19-4-72

Source: Trainee.

1989–90	Brentford	1	0
1990–91	Brentford	0	0
1991–92	Brentford	1	0
1992–93	Brentford	2	0
1993–94	Torquay U	32	0
1994–95	Torquay U	37	0
1995–96	Torquay U	28	0
1996–97	Exeter C	41	0
1997–98	Exeter C	45	0
1998–99	Exeter C	41	0
Total:		**228**	**0**

BAYLISS, Dave — Defender

H: 5 11 W: 12 00 b.Liverpool 8-6-76

Source: Trainee.

1994–95	Rochdale	1	0
1995–96	Rochdale	28	0
1996–97	Rochdale	24	0
1997–98	Rochdale	29	2
1998–99	Rochdale	25	1
Total:		**107**	**3**

BAYNE, Graham — Forward

H: 6 1 W: 12 07 b.Kirkcaldy 22-8-79

Source: Newburgh.

1997–98	Dundee	2	0
1998–99	Dundee	2	0
Total:		**4**	**0**

BAZELEY, Darren — Defender

H: 5 10 W: 12 00 b.Northampton 5-10-72

Source: Trainee. *Honours:* England Under-21.

1989–90	Watford	1	0
1990–91	Watford	7	0
1991–92	Watford	34	6
1992–93	Watford	22	1
1993–94	Watford	10	1
1994–95	Watford	28	4
1995–96	Watford	41	1
1996–97	Watford	41	3
1997–98	Watford	16	3
1998–99	Watford	40	2
Total:		**240**	**21**

BAZELYA, Eammon — Forward

H: 5 9 W: 11 00 b.London 25-10-78

Source: Trainee.

1996–97	Scarborough	0	0
1997–98	Scarborough	0	0
1998–99	Scarborough	0	0

BEADLE, Peter — Forward

H: 6 1 W: 13 07 b.Lambeth 13-5-72

Source: Trainee.

1988–89	Gillingham	2	0
1989–90	Gillingham	10	2
1990–91	Gillingham	22	7
1991–92	Gillingham	33	5
1992–93	Tottenham H	0	0
1992–93	Bournemouth (loan)	9	2
1993–94	Tottenham H	0	0
1993–94	Southend U (loan)	8	1
1994–95	Tottenham H	0	0
1994–95	Watford	20	1
1995–96	Watford	3	0
1995–96	Bristol R	27	12
1996–97	Bristol R	42	12
1997–98	Bristol R	40	15
1998–99	Port Vale	23	6
1998–99	Notts Co	14	3
Total:		**253**	**66**

BEAGRIE, Peter — Forward

H: 5 8 W: 12 00 b.Middlesbrough 28-11-65

Source: Local. *Honours:* England Under-21, B.

1983–84	Middlesbrough	0	0
1984–85	Middlesbrough	7	1
1985–86	Middlesbrough	26	1
1986–87	Sheffield U	41	9
1987–88	Sheffield U	43	2
1988–89	Stoke C	41	7
1989–90	Stoke C	13	0
1989–90	Everton	19	0
1990–91	Everton	17	2
1991–92	Everton	27	3
1991–92	Sunderland (loan)	5	1
1992–93	Everton	22	3
1993–94	Everton	29	3
1993–94	Manchester C	9	1
1994–95	Manchester C	37	2
1995–96	Manchester C	5	0
1996–97	Manchester C	1	0
1997–98	Bradford C	34	0
1997–98	Everton (loan)	6	0
1998–99	Bradford C	43	12
Total:		**425**	**47**

BEALE, Michael — Midfield

H: 6 1 W: 11 06 b.Sidcup 4-9-80

Source: Trainee.

1998–99	Charlton Ath	0	0

BEALL, Billy — Midfield

H: 5 6 W: 12 00 b.Enfield 4-12-77

Source: Trainee.

1995–96	Cambridge U	15	4
1996–97	Cambridge U	36	2
1997–98	Cambridge U	30	1
1998–99	Cambridge U	0	0
1998–99	Leyton Orient	23	2
Total:		**104**	**9**

BEARD, Mark — Midfield

H: 5 10 W: 10 12 b.Roehampton 8-10-74

Source: Trainee.

1992–93	Millwall	0	0
1993–94	Millwall	14	1
1994–95	Millwall	31	1
1995–96	Sheffield U	20	0
1996–97	Sheffield U	16	0
1997–98	Sheffield U	2	0
1997–98	Southend U (loan)	8	0
1998–99	Southend U	37	0
Total:		**128**	**2**

BEARDSLEY, Peter — Midfield

H: 5 8 W: 13 00 b.Newcastle 18-1-61

Source: Wallsend BC. *Honours:* England B, 59 full caps. Football League.

1979–80	Carlisle U	39	8
1980–81	Carlisle U	43	10
1981–82	Carlisle U	22	4
From Vancouver Whitecaps			
1982–83	Manchester U	0	0
From Vancouver Whitecaps			
1983–84	Newcastle U	35	20
1984–85	Newcastle U	38	17
1985–86	Newcastle U	42	19
1986–87	Newcastle U	32	5
1987–88	Liverpool	38	15
1988–89	Liverpool	37	10
1989–90	Liverpool	29	10
1990–91	Liverpool	27	11
1991–92	Everton	42	15
1992–93	Everton	39	10
1993–94	Newcastle U	35	21
1994–95	Newcastle U	34	12
1995–96	Newcastle U	35	8
1996–97	Newcastle U	25	5
1997–98	Newcastle U	0	0
1997–98	Bolton W	17	2
1997–98	Manchester C (loan)	6	0
1997–98	Fulham (loan)	8	1
1998–99	Bolton W	0	0
1998–99	Fulham (loan)	13	3
1998–99	Hartlepool U	22	2
Total:		**658**	**208**

BEARDSMORE, Russell — Midfield

H: 5 8 W: 10 04 b.Wigan 28-10-69

Source: Apprentice. *Honours:* England Under-21.

1986–87	Manchester U	0	0
1987–88	Manchester U	0	0
1988–89	Manchester U	23	2
1989–90	Manchester U	21	2
1990–91	Manchester U	12	0
1991–92	Manchester U	0	0
1991–92	Blackburn R (loan)	2	0
1992–93	Manchester U	0	0
1993–94	Bournemouth	24	0
1994–95	Bournemouth	43	3
1995–96	Bournemouth	44	0
1996–97	Bournemouth	38	0
1997–98	Bournemouth	29	1
1998–99	Bournemouth	0	0
Total:		**236**	**8**

BEASANT, Dave — Goalkeeper

H: 6 4 W: 14 02 b.Willesden 20-3-59

Source: Edgware T. *Honours:* England B, 2 full caps.

1979–80	Wimbledon	2	0
1980–81	Wimbledon	34	0
1981–82	Wimbledon	46	0
1982–83	Wimbledon	46	0
1983–84	Wimbledon	46	0
1984–85	Wimbledon	42	0
1985–86	Wimbledon	42	0
1986–87	Wimbledon	42	0
1987–88	Wimbledon	40	0
1988–89	Newcastle U	20	0
1988–89	Chelsea	22	0
1989–90	Chelsea	38	0
1990–91	Chelsea	35	0
1991–92	Chelsea	21	0
1992–93	Chelsea	17	0
1992–93	Grimsby T (loan)	6	0
1992–93	Wolverhampton W (loan)	4	0
1993–94	Chelsea	0	0
1993–94	Southampton	25	0
1994–95	Southampton	13	0
1995–96	Southampton	36	0
1996–97	Southampton	14	0
1997–98	Southampton	0	0
1997–98	Nottingham F	41	0
1998–99	Nottingham F	26	0
Total:		**658**	**0**

BEATTIE, Damien — Goalkeeper

H: 6 1 W: 13 00 b.Melbourne 24-10-78

Source: Moorrabbin.

1998–99	Notts Co	0	0

BEATTIE, James — Forward

H: 6 0 W: 13 03 b.Lancaster 27-2-78

Source: Trainee. *Honours:* England Under-21.

1994–95	Blackburn R	0	0
1995–96	Blackburn R	0	0
1996–97	Blackburn R	1	0
1997–98	Blackburn R	3	0
1998–99	Southampton	35	5
Total:		**39**	**5**

BEAUCHAMP, Joey — Midfield

H: 5 10 W: 12 07 b.Oxford 13-3-71

Source: Trainee.

1988–89	Oxford U	1	0
1989–90	Oxford U	3	0
1990–91	Oxford U	4	0
1991–92	Oxford U	27	7
1991–92	Swansea C (loan)	5	2
1992–93	Oxford U	44	7
1993–94	Oxford U	45	6
1994–95	West Ham U	0	0
1994–95	Swindon T	42	3
1995–96	Swindon T	3	0
1995–96	Oxford U	32	7
1996–97	Oxford U	45	7
1997–98	Oxford U	44	13
1998–99	Oxford U	37	4
Total:		**332**	**56**

BEAUMONT, Chris — Midfield

H: 5 11 W: 11 12 b.Sheffield 5-12-65

Source: Denaby U.

1988–89	Rochdale	34	7
1989–90	Stockport Co	22	5
1990–91	Stockport Co	45	15
1991–92	Stockport Co	34	2
1992–93	Stockport Co	44	14
1993–94	Stockport Co	32	1
1994–95	Stockport Co	38	2
1995–96	Stockport Co	43	0
1996–97	Chesterfield	33	1
1997–98	Chesterfield	39	1
1998–99	Chesterfield	39	2
Total:		**403**	**50**

BEAVERS, Paul — Forward

H: 6 0 W: 12 05 b.Blackpool 2-10-78

Source: Trainee.

1996–97	Sunderland	0	0
1997–98	Sunderland	0	0
1998–99	Sunderland	0	0
1998–99	Shrewsbury T (loan)	2	0
1998–99	Oldham Ath (loan)	7	2
Total:		**9**	**2**

BECK, Mikkel — Forward

H: 6 1 W: 13 05 b.Aarhus 4-5-73

Source: Kolding. *Honours:* Denmark 16 full caps, 3 goals.

1992–93	B 1909	13	2
1993–94	Fortuna Cologne	32	8
1994–95	Fortuna Cologne	19	11
1995–96	Fortuna Cologne	28	7
1996–97	Middlesbrough	25	5
1997–98	Middlesbrough	39	14
1998–99	Middlesbrough	27	5
1998–99	Derby Co	7	1
Total:		**190**	**53**

BECKETT, Luke — Forward

H: 5 11 W: 11 06 b.Sheffield 25-11-76

Source: Trainee.

1995–96	Barnsley	0	0
1996–97	Barnsley	0	0
1997–98	Barnsley	0	0
1998–99	Chester C	28	11
Total:		**28**	**11**

BECKHAM, David — Midfield

H: 6 0 W: 11 09 b.Leytonstone 2-5-75

Source: Trainee. *Honours:* England Youth, Under-21, 23 full caps, 1 goal.

1992–93	Manchester U	0	0
1993–94	Manchester U	0	0
1994–95	Manchester U	4	0
1994–95	Preston NE (loan)	5	2
1995–96	Manchester U	33	7
1996–97	Manchester U	36	7
1997–98	Manchester U	37	9
1998–99	Manchester U	34	6
Total:		**149**	**31**

BEDEAU, Anthony — Forward

H: 5 10 W: 11 00 b.Hammersmith 24-3-79

Source: Trainee.

1995–96	Torquay U	4	0
1996–97	Torquay U	8	1
1997–98	Torquay U	34	5
1998–99	Torquay U	36	9
Total:		**82**	**15**

BEECH, Chris — Midfield

H: 5 9 W: 11 03 b.Blackpool 16-9-74

Source: Trainee.

1992–93	Blackpool	1	0
1993–94	Blackpool	35	2
1994–95	Blackpool	28	2
1995–96	Blackpool	18	0
1996–97	Hartlepool U	42	7
1997–98	Hartlepool U	36	6
1998–99	Hartlepool U	16	9
1998–99	Huddersfield T	17	2
Total:		**193**	**28**

BEECH, Chris — Defender

H: 5 9 W: 12 09 b.Congleton 5-11-75

Source: Trainee. *Honours:* England Schools, Youth.

1992–93	Manchester C	0	0
1993–94	Manchester C	0	0
1994–95	Manchester C	0	0
1995–96	Manchester C	0	0
1996–97	Manchester C	0	0
1997–98	Cardiff C	46	1
1998–99	Rotherham U	24	0
Total:		**70**	**1**

BEENEY, Mark — Goalkeeper

H: 6 4 W: 14 10 b.Pembury 30-12-67

1986–87	Gillingham	2	0
1987–88	Maidstone U	0	0
1988–89	Maidstone U	0	0
1989–90	Maidstone U	33	0
1989–90	Aldershot (loan)	7	0
1990–91	Maidstone U	17	0
1990–91	Brighton & HA	2	0
1991–92	Brighton & HA	25	0
1992–93	Brighton & HA	42	0
1992–93	Leeds U	1	0
1993–94	Leeds U	22	0
1994–95	Leeds U	0	0
1995–96	Leeds U	10	0
1996–97	Leeds U	1	0
1997–98	Leeds U	1	0
1998–99	Leeds U	0	0
Total:		**163**	**0**

BEESLEY, Paul — Defender

H: 6 1 W: 12 06 b.Liverpool 21-7-65

Source: Marine.

1984–85	Wigan Ath	2	0
1985–86	Wigan Ath	17	0
1986–87	Wigan Ath	39	0
1987–88	Wigan Ath	42	1
1988–89	Wigan Ath	44	2
1989–90	Wigan Ath	11	0
1989–90	Leyton Orient	32	1
1990–91	Sheffield U	37	1
1991–92	Sheffield U	40	2
1992–93	Sheffield U	39	2
1993–94	Sheffield U	25	0
1994–95	Sheffield U	27	2
1995–96	Leeds U	10	0
1996–97	Leeds U	12	0
1996–97	Manchester C	6	0
1997–98	Manchester C	7	0
1997–98	Port Vale (loan)	5	0
1997–98	WBA (loan)	8	0
1998–99	Port Vale	35	3
Total:		**438**	**14**

BEETON, Alan — Defender

H: 5 11 W: 11 13 b.Watford 4-10-78

Source: Trainee.

1997–98	Wycombe W	20	0
1998–99	Wycombe W	16	0
Total:		**36**	**0**

BEHARALL, David — Defender

H: 6 0 W: 11 07 b.Newcastle 8-3-79

Source: Trainee.

1997–98	Newcastle U	0	0
1998–99	Newcastle U	4	0
Total:		**4**	**0**

BELL, Mickey — Defender

H: 5 8 W: 11 13 b.Newcastle 15-11-71

Source: Trainee.

1989–90	Northampton T	6	0
1990–91	Northampton T	28	0
1991–92	Northampton T	30	4
1992–93	Northampton T	39	5
1993–94	Northampton T	38	0
1994–95	Northampton T	12	1
1994–95	Wycombe W	31	3
1995–96	Wycombe W	41	1
1996–97	Wycombe W	46	2
1997–98	Bristol C	44	10
1998–99	Bristol C	33	5
Total:		**348**	**31**

BELLAMY, Craig — Forward

H: 5 8 W: 10 05 b.Cardiff 13-1-79

Source: Trainee. *Honours:* Wales Under-21, 7 full caps, 2 goals.

1996–97	Norwich C	3	0
1997–98	Norwich C	36	13
1998–99	Norwich C	40	17
Total:		**79**	**30**

BENALI, Francis — Midfield

H: 5 9 W: 11 03 b.Southampton 30-12-68

Source: Apprentice. *Honours:* England Schools.

1986–87	Southampton	0	0
1987–88	Southampton	0	0
1988–89	Southampton	7	0
1989–90	Southampton	27	0
1990–91	Southampton	12	0
1991–92	Southampton	22	0

1992–93	Southampton	33	0
1993–94	Southampton	37	0
1994–95	Southampton	35	0
1995–96	Southampton	29	0
1996–97	Southampton	18	0
1997–98	Southampton	33	1
1998–99	Southampton	23	0
Total:		**276**	**1**

BENJAMIN, Trevor — Forward

H: 6 2 W: 13 07 b.Kettering 8-2-79

Source: Trainee.

1995–96	Cambridge U	5	0
1996–97	Cambridge U	7	1
1997–98	Cambridge U	25	4
1998–99	Cambridge U	42	10
Total:		**79**	**15**

BENNETT, Frankie — Forward

H: 5 7 W: 12 10 b.Birmingham 13-1-69

Source: Halesowen T.

1992–93	Southampton	0	0
1993–94	Southampton	8	1
1994–95	Southampton	0	0
1995–96	Southampton	11	0
1996–97	Southampton	0	0
1996–97	Shrewsbury T (loan)	4	3
1996–97	Bristol R	11	1
1997–98	Bristol R	19	2
1998–99	Bristol R	4	1
Total:		**57**	**8**

BENNETT, Gary — Defender

H: 6 2 W: 12 01 b.Manchester 4-12-61

Source: Amateur.

1979–80	Manchester C	0	0
1980–81	Manchester C	0	0
1981–82	Cardiff C	19	1
1982–83	Cardiff C	36	8
1983–84	Cardiff C	32	2
1984–85	Sunderland	37	3
1985–86	Sunderland	28	3
1986–87	Sunderland	41	4
1987–88	Sunderland	38	2
1988–89	Sunderland	40	3
1989–90	Sunderland	36	3
1990–91	Sunderland	37	2
1991–92	Sunderland	39	3
1992–93	Sunderland	15	0
1993–94	Sunderland	38	0
1994–95	Sunderland	20	0
1995–96	Sunderland	0	0
1995–96	Carlisle U	26	5
1996–97	Scarborough	46	9
1997–98	Scarborough	42	9
1998–99	Darlington	29	4
Total:		**599**	**61**

BENNETT, Gary — Forward

H: 5 11 W: 12 00 b.Kirby 20-9-62

Source: Kirby T.

1984–85	Wigan Ath	20	3
1985–86	Chester C	43	13
1986–87	Chester C	33	13
1987–88	Chester C	43	10
1988–89	Chester C	7	0
1988–89	Southend U	17	2
1989–90	Southend U	25	4
1989–90	Chester C	8	1
1990–91	Chester C	30	3
1991–92	Chester C	42	11
1992–93	Wrexham	35	16
1993–94	Wrexham	41	32
1994–95	Wrexham	45	29
1995–96	Tranmere R	29	9
1995–96	Preston NE	8	1
1996–97	Preston NE	16	3
1996–97	Wrexham	15	5
1997–98	Chester C	41	12
1998–99	Chester C	7	1
Total:		**505**	**168**

BENNETT, Ian — Goalkeeper

H: 6 0 W: 12 10 b.Worksop 10-10-71

Source: Newcastle U Trainee.

1991–92	Peterborough U	7	0
1992–93	Peterborough U	46	0
1993–94	Peterborough U	19	0
1993–94	Birmingham C	22	0
1994–95	Birmingham C	46	0
1995–96	Birmingham C	24	0
1996–97	Birmingham C	40	0
1997–98	Birmingham C	45	0
1998–99	Birmingham C	10	0
Total:		**259**	**0**

BENNETT, Mickey — Midfield

H: 5 10 W: 11 11 b.Camberwell 22-7-69

Source: Apprentice. *Honours:* England Youth.

1986–87	Charlton Ath	2	0
1987–88	Charlton Ath	16	1
1988–89	Charlton Ath	11	0
1989–90	Charlton Ath	6	1
1989–90	Wimbledon	7	1
1990–91	Wimbledon	6	0
1991–92	Wimbledon	5	1
1992–93	Brentford	38	4
1993–94	Brentford	8	0

1993–94	Charlton Ath	10	1
1994–95	Charlton Ath	14	0
1994–95	Millwall	0	0
1995–96	Millwall	2	0
1996–97	Cardiff C	14	1
From Cambridge C.			
1997–98	Leyton Orient	2	0
1998–99	Brighton & HA	38	0
Total:		**179**	**10**

BENNETT, Neil — Goalkeeper

H: 6 1 W: 11 13 b.Dewsbury 29-10-80

Source: Trainee.

1998–99	Sheffield W	0	0

BENNETT, Tom — Midfield

H: 5 11 W: 11 08 b.Falkirk 12-12-69

Source: Trainee.

1987–88	Aston Villa	0	0
1988–89	Wolverhampton W	2	0
1989–90	Wolverhampton W	30	0
1990–91	Wolverhampton W	26	0
1991–92	Wolverhampton W	38	2
1992–93	Wolverhampton W	1	0
1993–94	Wolverhampton W	10	0
1994–95	Wolverhampton W	8	0
1995–96	Stockport Co	24	1
1996–97	Stockport Co	43	3
1997–98	Stockport Co	27	1
1998–99	Stockport Co	7	0
Total:		**216**	**7**

BENT, Junior — Forward

H: 5 5 W: 10 06 b.Huddersfield 1-3-70

Source: Trainee.

1987–88	Huddersfield T	7	0
1988–89	Huddersfield T	22	5
1989–90	Huddersfield T	7	1
1989–90	Burnley (loan)	9	3
1989–90	Bristol C	1	0
1990–91	Bristol C	20	2
1991–92	Bristol C	17	2
1991–92	Stoke C (loan)	1	0
1992–93	Bristol C	20	3
1993–94	Bristol C	20	2
1994–95	Bristol C	41	6
1995–96	Bristol C	40	2
1996–97	Bristol C	22	3
1996–97	Shrewsbury T (loan)	6	0
1997–98	Bristol C	2	0
1997–98	Blackpool	36	3
1998–99	Blackpool	39	1
Total:		**310**	**33**

BENT, Marcus — Forward

H: 6 2 W: 12 04 b.Hammersmith 19-5-78

Source: Trainee. *Honours:* England Under-21.

1995–96	Brentford	12	1
1996–97	Brentford	34	3
1997–98	Brentford	24	4
1997–98	Crystal Palace	16	5
1998–99	Crystal Palace	12	0
1998–99	Port Vale	15	0
Total:		**113**	**13**

BERESFORD, David — Forward

H: 5 5 W: 11 00 b.Manchester 11-11-76

Source: Trainee. *Honours:* England Schools, Youth.

1993–94	Oldham Ath	1	0
1994–95	Oldham Ath	2	0
1995–96	Oldham Ath	28	2
1995–96	Swansea C (loan)	6	0
1996–97	Oldham Ath	33	0
1996–97	Huddersfield T	6	1
1997–98	Huddersfield T	8	0
1998–99	Huddersfield T	19	2
Total:		**103**	**5**

BERESFORD, John — Midfield

H: 5 7 W: 12 00 b.Sheffield 4-9-66

Source: Apprentice. *Honours:* England Schools, Youth, B.

1983–84	Manchester C	0	0
1984–85	Manchester C	0	0
1985–86	Manchester C	0	0
1986–87	Barnsley	27	1
1987–88	Barnsley	34	3
1988–89	Barnsley	27	1
1988–89	Portsmouth	2	0
1989–90	Portsmouth	28	0
1990–91	Portsmouth	42	2
1991–92	Portsmouth	35	6
1992–93	Newcastle U	42	1
1993–94	Newcastle U	34	0
1994–95	Newcastle U	33	0
1995–96	Newcastle U	33	0
1996–97	Newcastle U	19	0
1997–98	Newcastle U	18	2
1997–98	Southampton	10	0
1998–99	Southampton	4	0
Total:		**388**	**16**

BERESFORD, Marlon — Goalkeeper

H: 6 1 W: 13 08 b.Lincoln 2-6-69

Source: Trainee.

1987–88	Sheffield W	0	0
1988–89	Sheffield W	0	0
1989–90	Sheffield W	0	0

1989–90	Bury (loan)	1	0
1989–90	Ipswich T (loan)	0	0
1990–91	Sheffield W	0	0
1990–91	Northampton T (loan)	13	0
1990–91	Crewe Alex (loan)	3	0
1991–92	Sheffield W	0	0
1991–92	Northampton T (loan)	15	0
1992–93	Burnley	44	0
1993–94	Burnley	46	0
1994–95	Burnley	40	0
1995–96	Burnley	36	0
1996–97	Burnley	40	0
1997–98	Burnley	34	0
1997–98	Middlesbrough	3	0
1998–99	Middlesbrough	4	0
Total:		**279**	**0**

BERG, Henning — Defender

H: 6 0 W: 12 01 b.Eidsvoll 1-9-69

Source: Lillestrom. *Honours:* Norway Under-21, 61 full caps, 6 goals.

1992–93	Blackburn R	4	0
1993–94	Blackburn R	41	1
1994–95	Blackburn R	40	1
1995–96	Blackburn R	38	0
1996–97	Blackburn R	36	2
1997–98	Manchester U	27	1
1998–99	Manchester U	16	0
Total:		**202**	**5**

BERGER, Patrik — Midfield

H: 6 1 W: 12 06 b.Prague 10-11-73

Honours: Czech Republic 34 full caps, 16 goals.

1991–92	Slavia Prague	20	3
1992–93	Slavia Prague	29	10
1993–94	Slavia Prague	12	4
1994–95	Slavia Prague	28	7
1995–96	Borussia Dortmund	25	4
1996–97	Liverpool	23	6
1997–98	Liverpool	22	3
1998–99	Liverpool	32	7
Total:		**191**	**44**

BERGKAMP, Dennis — Forward

H: 6 0 W: 12 05 b.Amsterdam 18-5-69

Honours: Holland 68 full caps, 36 goals.

1986–87	Ajax	14	2
1987–88	Ajax	25	5
1988–89	Ajax	30	13
1989–90	Ajax	25	8
1990–91	Ajax	33	25
1991–92	Ajax	30	24
1992–93	Ajax	28	26
1993–94	Internazionale	31	8
1994–95	Internazionale	21	3
1995–96	Arsenal	33	11
1996–97	Arsenal	29	12
1997–98	Arsenal	28	16
1998–99	Arsenal	29	12
Total:		**356**	**165**

BERGSSON, Gudni — Defender

H: 6 1 W: 12 03 b.Reykjavik 21-7-65

Source: Valur. *Honours:* Iceland Youth, Under-21, 75 full caps, 1 goal.

1988–89	Tottenham H	8	0
1989–90	Tottenham H	18	0
1990–91	Tottenham H	12	1
1991–92	Tottenham H	28	1
1992–93	Tottenham H	5	0
1993–94	Tottenham H	0	0
1994–95	Bolton W	8	0
1995–96	Bolton W	34	4
1996–97	Bolton W	33	3
1997–98	Bolton W	35	2
1998–99	Bolton W	17	0
Total:		**198**	**11**

BERKLEY, Austin — Midfield

H: 5 9 W: 10 10 b.Gravesend 28-1-73

Source: Trainee.

1990–91	Gillingham	0	0
1991–92	Gillingham	3	0
1992–93	Swindon T	0	0
1993–94	Swindon T	0	0
1994–95	Swindon T	1	0
1995–96	Shrewsbury T	38	1
1996–97	Shrewsbury T	24	0
1997–98	Shrewsbury T	36	3
1998–99	Shrewsbury T	41	8
Total:		**143**	**12**

BERKOVIC, Eyal — Midfield

H: 5 7 W: 10 02 b.Haifa 2-4-72

Honours: Israel 54 full caps, 6 goals.

1992–93	Maccabi Haifa	32	7
1993–94	Maccabi Haifa	38	10
1994–95	Maccabi Haifa	29	5
1995–96	Maccabi Haifa	29	3
1996–97	Southampton	28	4
1997–98	West Ham U	35	7
1998–99	West Ham U	30	3
Total:		**221**	**39**

BERNAL, Andy — Defender

H: 5 10 W: 12 05 b.Canberra 16-7-66

Source: Sporting Gijon. *Honours:* Australia full caps.

1992–93	Ipswich T	9	0

1993–94	Ipswich T	0	0
From Sydney Olympic			
1994–95	Reading	33	0
1995–96	Reading	34	2
1996–97	Reading	41	0
1997–98	Reading	34	0
1998–99	Reading	22	0
Total:		**173**	**2**

BERNARD, Curtis — Forward

H: 5 7 W: 12 00 b.Leeds 3-7-80

Source: Trainee.

1997–98	Barnsley	0	0
1998–99	Barnsley	0	0

BERNARD, Paul — Midfield

H: 5 11 W: 11 08 b.Edinburgh 30-12-72

Source: Trainee. *Honours:* Scotland Under-21, 2 full caps.

1990–91	Oldham Ath	2	1
1991–92	Oldham Ath	21	5
1992–93	Oldham Ath	33	4
1993–94	Oldham Ath	32	5
1994–95	Oldham Ath	17	2
1995–96	Oldham Ath	7	1
1995–96	Aberdeen	31	1
1996–97	Aberdeen	14	0
1997–98	Aberdeen	17	0
1998–99	Aberdeen	9	1
Total:		**183**	**20**

BERNTSEN, Robin — Forward

b.Tromso 10-7-70

Source: Tromso.

1998–99	Port Vale	1	0
Total:		**1**	**0**

BERRY, Trevor — Midfield

H: 5 6 W: 11 00 b.Haslemere 1-8-74

Source: Bournemouth.

1991–92	Aston Villa	0	0
1992–93	Aston Villa	0	0
1993–94	Aston Villa	0	0
1994–95	Aston Villa	0	0
1995–96	Aston Villa	0	0
1995–96	Rotherham U	36	7
1996–97	Rotherham U	30	4
1997–98	Rotherham U	42	3
1998–99	Rotherham U	18	2
Total:		**126**	**16**

BERTHE, Mohamed — Midfield

H: 6 2 W: 15 02 b.Conakry 12-9-72

Source: Gaz Ajaccio.

1997–98	West Ham U	0	0
1998–99	Bournemouth	15	2
1998–99	Hearts	1	0
Total:		**16**	**2**

BERTI, Nicola — Midfield

H: 6 1 W: 12 02 b.Salsomaggiore Terme 14-4-67

Honours: Italy 39 full caps, 3 goals.

1982–83	Parma	1	0
1983–84	Parma	0	0
1984–85	Parma	27	0
1985–86	Fiorentina	28	3
1986–87	Fiorentina	27	4
1987–88	Fiorentina	25	1
1988–89	Internazionale	32	7
1989–90	Internazionale	29	5
1990–91	Internazionale	30	4
1991–92	Internazionale	30	1
1992–93	Internazionale	32	4
1993–94	Internazionale	9	2
1994–95	Internazionale	30	5
1995–96	Internazionale	10	0
1996–97	Internazionale	23	1
1997–98	Internazionale	4	0
1997–98	Tottenham H	17	3
1998–99	Tottenham H	4	0
Total:		**358**	**40**

BEST, Russell — Midfield

b.Nottingham 1-9-79

1998–99	Manchester U	0	0

BESWETHERICK, John — Defender

H: 5 11 W: 11 04 b.Liverpool 15-1-78

Source: Trainee.

1996–97	Plymouth Arg	0	0
1997–98	Plymouth Arg	2	0
1998–99	Plymouth Arg	22	0
Total:		**24**	**0**

BETSY, Kevin — Forward

H: 6 1 W: 11 12 b.Seychelles 20-3-78

Source: Woking.

1998–99	Fulham	7	1
Total:		**7**	**1**

BETT, Baldur — Midfield

H: 5 8 W: 11 07 b.Reykjavik 12-4-80

Source: Hermes.

1998–99	Aberdeen	1	0
Total:		**1**	**0**

BETTERTON, Anthony — Midfield

b.Swindon 24-10-79

Source: Trainee.

1998–99	Bristol C	0	0

BETTNEY, Chris — Forward

H: 5 10 W: 11 00 b.Chesterfield 27-10-77

Source: Trainee.

1995–96	Sheffield U	0	0
1996–97	Sheffield U	1	0
1997–98	Sheffield U	0	0
1997–98	Hull C (loan)	30	1
1998–99	Sheffield U	0	0
Total:		**31**	**1**

BETTNEY, Scott — Defender

H: 5 9 W: 12 06 b.Hull 12-3-80

Source: Trainee.

1998–99	Sheffield W	0	0

BETTS, Robert — Midfield

H: 5 10 W: 11 00 b.Doncaster 21-12-81

Source: School.

1997–98	Doncaster R	3	0
1998–99	Coventry C	0	0
Total:		**3**	**0**

BETTS, Simon — Defender

H: 5 7 W: 11 06 b.Middlesbrough 3-3-73

Source: Trainee.

1991–92	Ipswich T	0	0
1992–93	Scarborough	0	0
1992–93	Colchester U	23	0
1993–94	Colchester U	33	1
1994–95	Colchester U	35	2
1995–96	Colchester U	45	5
1996–97	Colchester U	10	1
1997–98	Colchester U	17	0
1998–99	Colchester U	28	2
Total:		**191**	**11**

BEVAN, Scott — Goalkeeper

H: 6 6 W: 15 03 b.Southampton 16-9-79

Source: Trainee.

1997–98	Southampton	0	0
1998–99	Southampton	0	0

BIBBO, Sal — Goalkeeper

H: 6 2 W: 14 00 b.Basingstoke 24-8-74

Source: Bournemouth.

1993–94	Sheffield U	0	0
1994–95	Sheffield U	0	0
1994–95	Chesterfield (loan)	1	0
1995–96	Sheffield U	0	0
1996–97	Reading	5	0
1997–98	Reading	2	0
1998–99	Millwall	0	0
Total:		**8**	**0**

BIGNOT, Marcus — Defender

H: 5 9 W: 11 00 b.Birmingham 28-8-74

Source: Kidderminster H.

1997–98	Crewe Alex	42	0
1998–99	Crewe Alex	26	0
Total:		**68**	**0**

BILIC, Slaven — Defender

H: 6 3 W: 14 03 b.Split 11-9-68

Honours: Croatia 42 full caps, 3 goal.

1988–89	Hajduk Split	3	2
1989–90	Hajduk Split	27	3
1990–91	Hajduk Split	32	2
1991–92	Hajduk Split	20	1
1992–93	Hajduk Split	27	5
1993–94	Karlsruhe	26	2
1994–95	Karlsruhe	28	3
1995–96	West Ham U	13	0
1996–97	West Ham U	35	2
1997–98	Everton	24	0
1998–99	Everton	4	0
Total:		**239**	**20**

BILLINGTON, David — Defender

H: 5 7 W: 10 07 b.Oxford 15-10-80

Source: Trainee.

1996–97	Peterborough U	5	0
1996–97	Sheffield W	0	0
1997–98	Sheffield W	0	0
1998–99	Sheffield W	0	0
Total:		**5**	**0**

BILLY, Chris — Defender

H: 5 11 W: 12 06 b.Huddersfield 2-1-71

Source: Trainee.

1991–92	Huddersfield T	10	2
1992–93	Huddersfield T	13	0
1993–94	Huddersfield T	34	0
1994–95	Huddersfield T	37	2
1995–96	Plymouth Arg	32	4
1996–97	Plymouth Arg	45	3
1997–98	Plymouth Arg	41	2
1998–99	Notts Co	6	0
1998–99	Bury	37	0
Total:		**255**	**13**

BIMSON, Stuart — Defender

H: 5 11 W: 11 08 b.Liverpool 29-9-69

Source: Macclesfield T.

1994–95	Bury	19	0
1995–96	Bury	16	0
1996–97	Bury	1	0
1996–97	Lincoln C	15	1
1997–98	Lincoln C	12	0
1998–99	Lincoln C	31	2
Total:		**94**	**3**

BINGHAM, Michael — Goalkeeper

H: 6 0 W: 12 05 b.Preston 21-5-81

Source: Trainee. *Honours:* England Schools.

1998–99	Blackburn R	0	0

BIRCH, Gary — Midfield

b.Birmingham 8-10-81

Source: Trainee.

1998–99	Walsall	0	0

BIRCH, Paul — Midfield

H: 5 6 W: 10 04 b.West Bromwich 20-11-62

Source: Apprentice.

1980–81	Aston Villa	0	0
1981–82	Aston Villa	0	0
1982–83	Aston Villa	0	0
1983–84	Aston Villa	22	2
1984–85	Aston Villa	25	3
1985–86	Aston Villa	27	2
1986–87	Aston Villa	29	3
1987–88	Aston Villa	38	6
1988–89	Aston Villa	12	0
1989–90	Aston Villa	12	0
1990–91	Aston Villa	8	0
1990–91	Wolverhampton W	20	2
1991–92	Wolverhampton W	45	8
1992–93	Wolverhampton W	28	3
1993–94	Wolverhampton W	32	1
1994–95	Wolverhampton W	10	1
1995–96	Wolverhampton W	7	0
1995–96	Preston NE (loan)	11	2
1996–97	Doncaster R	27	2
1996–97	Exeter C	2	0
1997–98	Exeter C	33	5
1998–99	Exeter C	0	0
Total:		**388**	**40**

BIRCHAM, Marc — Defender

H: 5 10 W: 10 12 b.Wembley 11-5-78

Source: Trainee. *Honours:* Canada full caps.

1996–97	Millwall	6	0
1997–98	Millwall	4	0
1998–99	Millwall	28	0
Total:		**38**	**0**

BIRD, Tony — Forward

H: 5 11 W: 12 10 b.Cardiff 1-9-74

Source: Trainee. *Honours:* Wales Under-21.

1991–92	Cardiff C	0	0
1992–93	Cardiff C	9	1
1993–94	Cardiff C	35	5
1994–95	Cardiff C	19	4
1995–96	Cardiff C	12	3
From Barry T			
1997–98	Swansea C	41	14
1998–99	Swansea C	29	3
Total:		**145**	**30**

BISHOP, Charlie — Defender

H: 6 0 W: 13 07 b.Nottingham 16-2-68

Source: Stoke C Apprentice.

1986–87	Watford	0	0
1987–88	Bury	17	0
1988–89	Bury	38	3
1989–90	Bury	30	1
1990–91	Bury	29	2
1991–92	Barnsley	28	0
1992–93	Barnsley	43	0
1993–94	Barnsley	38	1
1994–95	Barnsley	8	0
1995–96	Barnsley	13	0
1995–96	Preston NE (loan)	4	0
1995–96	Burnley (loan)	9	0
1996–97	Wigan Ath	21	0
1997–98	Wigan Ath	7	0
1997–98	Northampton T	7	0
1998–99	Northampton T	4	0
Total:		**296**	**7**

BISHOP, Ian — Midfield

H: 5 10 W: 12 00 b.Liverpool 29-5-65

Source: Apprentice. *Honours:* England B.

1983–84	Everton	1	0
1983–84	Crewe Alex (loan)	4	0
1984–85	Everton	0	0
1984–85	Carlisle U	30	2
1985–86	Carlisle U	36	6
1986–87	Carlisle U	42	3
1987–88	Carlisle U	24	3
1988–89	Bournemouth	44	2
1989–90	Manchester C	19	2
1989–90	West Ham U	17	2
1990–91	West Ham U	40	4
1991–92	West Ham U	41	1
1992–93	West Ham U	22	1
1993–94	West Ham U	36	1
1994–95	West Ham U	31	1
1995–96	West Ham U	35	1
1996–97	West Ham U	29	1
1997–98	West Ham U	3	0
1997–98	Manchester C	6	0
1998–99	Manchester C	25	0
Total:		**485**	**30**

BJORNEBYE, Stig Inge — Defender

H: 5 10 W: 11 09 b.Elverum 11-12-69

Honours: Norway 70 full caps, 1 goal.

1988	Strammen	19	0
1989	Kongsvinger	21	2
1990	Kongsvinger	20	0
1991	Kongsvinger	21	1
1992	Rosenborg	21	3
1992–93	Liverpool	11	0
1993–94	Liverpool	9	0
1994–95	Liverpool	31	0
1995–96	Liverpool	2	0
1996–97	Liverpool	38	2
1997–98	Liverpool	25	0
1998–99	Liverpool	23	0
Total:		**241**	**8**

BLACK, Kingsley — Midfield

H: 5 10 W: 12 00 b.Luton 22-6-68

Source: School. *Honours:* England Schools, Northern Ireland Under-21, 30 full caps, 1 goal.

1986–87	Luton T	0	0
1987–88	Luton T	13	0
1988–89	Luton T	37	8
1989–90	Luton T	36	11
1990–91	Luton T	37	7
1991–92	Luton T	4	0
1991–92	Nottingham F	25	4
1992–93	Nottingham F	24	5
1993–94	Nottingham F	37	3
1994–95	Nottingham F	10	2
1994–95	Sheffield U (loan)	11	2
1995–96	Nottingham F	2	0
1995–96	Millwall (loan)	3	1
1996–97	Grimsby T	24	0
1997–98	Grimsby T	39	2
1998–99	Grimsby T	42	4
Total:		**344**	**49**

BLACK, Michael — Midfield

H: 5 8 W: 11 08 b.Chigwell 6-10-76

Source: Trainee. *Honours:* England Schools.

1995–96	Arsenal	0	0
1996–97	Arsenal	0	0
1997–98	Arsenal	0	0
1997–98	Millwall (loan)	13	2
1998–99	Arsenal	0	0
Total:		**13**	**2**

BLACK, Tommy — Midfield

b.Chigwell 26-11-79

Source: Trainee.

1998–99	Arsenal	0	0

BLACKMORE, Clayton — Midfield

H: 5 7 W: 12 01 b.Neath 23-9-64

Source: Apprentice. *Honours:* Wales Schools, Youth, Under-21, 39 full caps, 1 goal.

1982–83	Manchester U	0	0
1983–84	Manchester U	1	0
1984–85	Manchester U	1	0
1985–86	Manchester U	12	3
1986–87	Manchester U	12	1
1987–88	Manchester U	22	3
1988–89	Manchester U	28	3
1989–90	Manchester U	28	2
1990–91	Manchester U	35	4
1991–92	Manchester U	33	3
1992–93	Manchester U	14	0
1993–94	Manchester U	0	0
1994–95	Middlesbrough	30	2
1995–96	Middlesbrough	5	0
1996–97	Middlesbrough	16	2
1996–97	Bristol C (loan)	5	1
1997–98	Middlesbrough	2	0
1998–99	Middlesbrough	0	0
1998–99	Barnsley	7	0
Total:		**251**	**24**

BLACKWELL, Dean — Defender

H: 6 1 W: 12 10 b.Camden 5-12-69

Source: Trainee. *Honours:* England Under-21.

1988–89	Wimbledon	0	0

1989–90	Wimbledon	3	0
1989–90	Plymouth Arg (loan)	7	0
1990–91	Wimbledon	35	0
1991–92	Wimbledon	4	1
1992–93	Wimbledon	24	0
1993–94	Wimbledon	18	0
1994–95	Wimbledon	0	0
1995–96	Wimbledon	8	0
1996–97	Wimbledon	27	0
1997–98	Wimbledon	35	0
1998–99	Wimbledon	28	0
Total:		**189**	**1**

BLACKWOOD, Michael — Forward

H: 5 10 W: 11 07 b.Birmingham 30-9-79

Source: Trainee.

1998–99	Aston Villa	0	0

BLAKE, Dean — Midfield

H: 5 8 W: 10 01 b.Portsmouth 20-2-80

Source: Trainee.

1997–98	Southampton	0	0
1998–99	Southampton	0	0

BLAKE, Mark — Defender

H: 6 0 W: 12 06 b.Portsmouth 17-12-67

Source: Apprentice. *Honours:* England Youth.

1985–86	Southampton	1	0
1986–87	Southampton	8	1
1987–88	Southampton	6	1
1988–89	Southampton	3	0
1989–90	Southampton	0	0
1989–90	Colchester U (loan)	4	1
1989–90	Shrewsbury T (loan)	10	0
1990–91	Shrewsbury T	46	2
1991–92	Shrewsbury T	39	0
1992–93	Shrewsbury T	32	1
1993–94	Shrewsbury T	15	0
1994–95	Fulham	35	3
1995–96	Fulham	38	5
1996–97	Fulham	41	7
1997–98	Fulham	26	2
1998–99	Fulham	0	0
Total:		**304**	**23**

BLAKE, Marvin — Midfield

b.Leicester 22-8-79

Source: Trainee.

1998–99	WBA	0	0

BLAKE, Nathan — Forward

H: 6 0 W: 12 08 b.Cardiff 27-1-72

Source: Chelsea Trainee. *Honours:* Wales B, Under-21, 11 full caps, 2 goals.

1989–90	Cardiff C	6	0
1990–91	Cardiff C	40	4
1991–92	Cardiff C	31	6
1992–93	Cardiff C	34	11
1993–94	Cardiff C	20	14
1993–94	Sheffield U	12	5
1994–95	Sheffield U	35	17
1995–96	Sheffield U	22	12
1995–96	Bolton W	18	1
1996–97	Bolton W	42	19
1997–98	Bolton W	35	12
1998–99	Bolton W	12	6
1998–99	Blackburn R	11	3
Total:		**318**	**110**

BLAKE, Noel — Defender

H: 6 2 W: 14 02 b.Jamaica 12-1-62

Source: Walsall Amateur, Sutton Coldfield T.

1979–80	Aston Villa	3	0
1980–81	Aston Villa	0	0
1981–82	Aston Villa	1	0
1981–82	Shrewsbury T (loan)	6	0
1982–83	Aston Villa	0	0
1982–83	Birmingham C	37	3
1983–84	Birmingham C	39	2
1984–85	Portsmouth	42	3
1985–86	Portsmouth	42	4
1986–87	Portsmouth	41	3
1987–88	Portsmouth	19	0
1988–89	Leeds U	44	4
1989–90	Leeds U	7	0
1989–90	Stoke C	18	0
1990–91	Stoke C	44	3
1991–92	Stoke C	13	0
1991–92	Bradford C (loan)	6	0
1992–93	Bradford C	32	3
1993–94	Bradford C	7	0
1993–94	Dundee	23	2
1994–95	Dundee	31	0
1995–96	Exeter C	44	2
1996–97	Exeter C	46	6
1997–98	Exeter C	38	1
1998–99	Exeter C	7	0
Total:		**590**	**36**

BLAKE, Robbie — Forward

H: 5 8 W: 11 00 b.Middlesbrough 4-3-76

Source: Trainee.

1994–95	Darlington	9	0
1995–96	Darlington	29	11
1996–97	Darlington	30	10

1996–97	Bradford C	5	0
1997–98	Bradford C	34	8
1998–99	Bradford C	39	16
Total:		**146**	**45**

BLAMEY, Nathan — Defender

H: 5 10 W: 11 05 b.Plymouth 10-6-77

Source: Trainee.

1995–96	Southampton	0	0
1996–97	Southampton	0	0
1996–97	Shrewsbury T	6	0
1997–98	Shrewsbury T	9	1
1998–99	Shrewsbury T	0	0
Total:		**15**	**1**

BLATHERWICK, Steve — Defender

H: 6 1 W: 15 00 b.Nottingham 20-9-73

Source: Notts Co.

1992–93	Nottingham F	0	0
1993–94	Nottingham F	3	0
1993–94	Wycombe W (loan)	2	0
1994–95	Nottingham F	0	0
1995–96	Nottingham F	0	0
1995–96	Hereford U (loan)	10	1
1996–97	Nottingham F	7	0
1996–97	Reading (loan)	7	0
1997–98	Burnley	21	0
1998–99	Burnley	3	0
1998–99	Chesterfield	14	1
Total:		**67**	**2**

BLINKER, Regi — Forward

H: 5 8 W: 11 07 b.Surinam 2-6-69

Honours: Holland 3 full caps.

1986–87	Feyenoord	26	1
1987–88	Feyenoord	24	2
1988–89	Feyenoord	1	0
1988–89	Den Bosch	25	6
1989–90	Feyenoord	31	2
1990–91	Feyenoord	26	1
1991–92	Feyenoord	28	5
1992–93	Feyenoord	30	13
1993–94	Feyenoord	29	9
1994–95	Feyenoord	30	8
1995–96	Feyenoord	13	4
1995–96	Sheffield W	9	2
1996–97	Sheffield W	33	1
1997–98	Celtic	16	1
1998–99	Celtic	15	4
Total:		**336**	**59**

BLOMQVIST, Jesper — Forward

H: 5 9 W: 11 03 b.Tavelsjo 5-2-74

Honours: Sweden 29 full caps.

1992	Umea	27	6
1993	Umea	11	2
1993	IFK Gothenburg	6	1
1994	IFK Gothenburg	24	8
1995	IFK Gothenburg	18	3
1996	IFK Gothenburg	23	7
1996–97	AC Milan	19	1
1997–98	AC Milan	1	0
1997–98	Parma	28	1
1998–99	Manchester U	25	1
Total:		**182**	**30**

BLOOMER, Matthew — Defender

H: 6 0 W: 12 00 b.Cleethorpes 3-11-78

Source: Trainee.

1997–98	Grimsby T	0	0
1998–99	Grimsby T	4	0
Total:		**4**	**0**

BLUNT, Jason — Midfield

H: 5 8 W: 10 01 b.Penzance 16-8-77

Source: Trainee. *Honours:* England Youth.

1994–95	Leeds U	0	0
1995–96	Leeds U	3	0
1996–97	Leeds U	1	0
1997–98	Leeds U	0	0
1998–99	Blackpool	2	0
Total:		**6**	**0**

BOA MORTE, Luis — Forward

H: 5 10 W: 11 05 b.Lisbon 4-8-77

Source: Sporting Lisbon, Lourihanense (loan). *Honours:* Portugal Under-21.

1997–98	Arsenal	15	0
1998–99	Arsenal	8	0
Total:		**23**	**0**

BOARDMAN, John — Defender

b.Liverpool 6-9-80

Source: Trainee.

1998–99	Liverpool	0	0

BOATENG, Daniel — Midfield

b.London 14-11-80

Source: Arsenal Trainee.

1998–99	Leicester C	0	0

BOATENG, George — Midfield

H: 5 9 W: 10 12 b.Nkawkaw 5-9-75

1994–95	Excelsior	9	0
1995–96	Feyenoord	24	1
1996–97	Feyenoord	26	0
1997–98	Feyenoord	18	0
1997–98	Coventry C	14	1
1998–99	Coventry C	33	4
Total:		**124**	**6**

BODIN, Paul — Defender

H: 6 0 W: 12 06 b.Cardiff 13-9-64

Source: Chelsea Amateur. *Honours:* Wales Youth, Under-21, 23 full caps, 3 goals.

1981–82	Newport Co	0	0
1982–83	Cardiff C	31	0
1983–84	Cardiff C	26	3
From Bath C			
1987–88	Newport Co	6	1
1987–88	Swindon T	5	1
1988–89	Swindon T	16	1
1989–90	Swindon T	41	5
1990–91	Swindon T	31	2
1990–91	Crystal Palace	5	0
1991–92	Crystal Palace	4	0
1991–92	Newcastle U (loan)	6	0
1991–92	Swindon T	21	2
1992–93	Swindon T	35	11
1993–94	Swindon T	32	7
1994–95	Swindon T	25	6
1995–96	Swindon T	33	2
1996–97	Reading	37	1
1997–98	Reading	4	0
1997–98	Wycombe W (loan)	5	0
1998–99	Reading	0	0
Total:		**363**	**42**

BODLEY, Mick — Defender

H: 6 1 W: 13 01 b.Hayes 14-9-67

Source: Apprentice.

1985–86	Chelsea	0	0
1986–87	Chelsea	0	0
1987–88	Chelsea	6	1
1988–89	Chelsea	0	0
1988–89	Northampton T	20	0
1989–90	Northampton T	0	0
1990–91	Barnet	0	0
1991–92	Barnet	36	1
1992–93	Barnet	33	2
1993–94	Southend U	16	1
1994–95	Southend U	12	0
1994–95	Gillingham (loan)	7	0
1994–95	Birmingham C (loan)	3	0
1995–96	Southend U	39	1
1996–97	Peterborough U	31	0
1997–98	Peterborough U	31	1
1998–99	Peterborough U	24	0
Total:		**258**	**7**

BOERE, Jeroen — Forward

H: 6 3 W: 13 02 b.Arnheim 18-11-67

Source: Go Ahead.

1993–94	West Ham U	4	0
1993–94	Portsmouth (loan)	5	0
1994–95	West Ham U	20	6
1994–95	WBA (loan)	5	0
1995–96	West Ham U	1	0
1995–96	Crystal Palace	8	1
1995–96	Southend U	6	2
1996–97	Southend U	36	9
1997–98	Southend U	31	14
1998–99	Southend U	0	0
Total:		**116**	**32**

BOERTIEN, Paul — Defender

H: 5 10 W: 11 11 b.Carlisle 21-1-79

Source: Trainee.

1996–97	Carlisle U	0	0
1997–98	Carlisle U	9	0
1998–99	Carlisle U	8	1
1998–99	Derby Co	1	0
Total:		**18**	**1**

BOGIE, Ian — Midfield

H: 5 7 W: 11 10 b.Newcastle 6-12-67

Source: Apprentice. *Honours:* England Schools.

1985–86	Newcastle U	0	0
1986–87	Newcastle U	1	0
1987–88	Newcastle U	7	0
1988–89	Newcastle U	6	0
1988–89	Preston NE	13	1
1989–90	Preston NE	35	3
1990–91	Preston NE	31	8
1991–92	Millwall	25	0
1992–93	Millwall	22	0
1993–94	Millwall	4	1
1993–94	Leyton Orient	34	3
1994–95	Leyton Orient	31	2
1994–95	Port Vale	9	2
1995–96	Port Vale	32	3
1996–97	Port Vale	31	1
1997–98	Port Vale	38	1
1998–99	Port Vale	35	2
Total:		**354**	**27**

BOHINEN, Lars — Midfield

H: 6 1 W: 13 00 b.Vadso 8-9-69

Source: Young Boys. *Honours:* Norway 49 full caps, 10 goals.

1988	Valerengen	15	2
1989	Valerengen	18	3
1990	Viking	10	0
1990–91	Young Boys	22	4
1991–92	Young Boys	34	2
1992–93	Young Boys	2	0
1993–94	Nottingham F	23	1
1994–95	Nottingham F	34	6
1995–96	Nottingham F	7	0
1995–96	Blackburn R	19	4
1996–97	Blackburn R	23	2
1997–98	Blackburn R	16	1
1997–98	Derby Co	9	1
1998–99	Derby Co	32	0
Total:		**264**	**26**

BOKOTO, Mommainais — Forward

H: 5 11 W: 11 13 b.France 20-10-74

Source: Maria Aalter.

1996–97	Bristol C	0	0
1997–98	Bristol C	0	0
1998–99	Bristol R	0	0

BOLAND, Willie — Midfield

H: 5 9 W: 11 02 b.Ennis 6-8-75

Source: Trainee. *Honours:* Eire Youth, Under-21.

1992–93	Coventry C	1	0
1993–94	Coventry C	27	0
1994–95	Coventry C	12	0
1995–96	Coventry C	3	0
1996–97	Coventry C	1	0
1997–98	Coventry C	19	0
1998–99	Coventry C	0	0
Total:		**63**	**0**

BOLDER, Adam — Midfield

H: 5 9 W: 10 08 b.Hull 25-10-80

Source: Trainee.

1998–99	Hull C	1	0
Total:		**1**	**0**

BOLI, Roger — Forward

H: 5 8 W: 10 12 b.Adjame 26-9-65

Source: Romainville, Auxerre, Lille.

1991–92	Lens	33	4
1992–93	Lens	30	3
1993–94	Lens	35	20
1994–95	Lens	38	9
1995–96	Lens	28	4
1996–97	Le Havre	26	4
1997–98	Walsall	41	12
1998–99	Walsall	0	0
1998–99	Dundee U	3	0
1998–99	Bournemouth	6	0
Total:		**240**	**56**

BOLLAN, Gary — Midfield

H: 5 11 W: 12 12 b.Dundee 24-3-73

Source: Celtic BC. *Honours:* Scotland Under-21.

1987–88	Celtic	0	0
1988–89	Celtic	0	0
1989–90	Celtic	0	0
1990–91	Dundee U	2	0
1991–92	Dundee U	10	1
1992–93	Dundee U	15	3
1993–94	Dundee U	12	0
1994–95	Dundee U	7	0
1994–95	Rangers	6	0
1995–96	Rangers	4	0
1996–97	Rangers	0	0
1997–98	Rangers	1	0
1998–99	St Johnstone	33	4
Total:		**90**	**8**

BOLLAND, Paul — Midfield

H: 5 10 W: 10 12 b.Bradford 23-12-79

Source: Trainee.

1997–98	Bradford C	10	0
1998–99	Bradford C	2	0
1998–99	Notts Co	13	0
Total:		**25**	**0**

BONALAIR, Thierry — Defender

H: 5 9 W: 10 08 b.Paris 14-6-66

1987–88	Nantes	13	0
1988–89	Nantes	35	1
1989–90	Nantes	31	0
1990–91	Nantes	35	0
1991–92	Nantes	31	1
1992–93	Auxerre	25	1
1993–94	Lille	34	3
1994–95	Lille	35	2
1995–96	Neuchatel Xamax	34	3
1996–97	Neuchatel Xamax	34	6
1997–98	Nottingham F	31	2
1998–99	Nottingham F	28	1
Total:		**366**	**20**

BONNER, Mark — Midfield

H: 5 8 W: 11 00 b.Ormskirk 7-6-74

Source: Trainee.

1991–92	Blackpool	3	0
1992–93	Blackpool	15	0
1993–94	Blackpool	40	7
1994–95	Blackpool	17	0
1995–96	Blackpool	42	3
1996–97	Blackpool	29	1
1997–98	Blackpool	32	3
1998–99	Cardiff C	25	1
1998–99	Hull C (loan)	1	1
Total:		**204**	**16**

BONNOT, Alexandre — Midfield

b.Boissy 31-7-73

Source: Angers.

1998–99	Watford	4	0
Total:		**4**	**0**

BOOTH, Andy — Forward

H: 6 1 W: 13 00 b.Huddersfield 6-12-73

Source: Trainee. *Honours:* England Under-21.

1991–92	Huddersfield T	3	0
1992–93	Huddersfield T	5	2
1993–94	Huddersfield T	26	10
1994–95	Huddersfield T	46	26
1995–96	Huddersfield T	43	16
1996–97	Sheffield W	35	10
1997–98	Sheffield W	23	7
1998–99	Sheffield W	34	6
Total:		**215**	**77**

BOOTHROYD, Aidy — Defender

H: 5 9 W: 11 07 b.Bradford 8-2-71

Source: Trainee.

1989–90	Huddersfield T	10	0
1990–91	Bristol R	3	0
1991–92	Bristol R	13	0
1992–93	Hearts	4	0
1993–94	Hearts	0	0
1993–94	Mansfield T	23	1
1994–95	Mansfield T	36	0
1995–96	Mansfield T	43	2
1996–97	Peterborough U	26	1
1997–98	Peterborough U	0	0
1998–99	Peterborough U	0	0
Total:		**158**	**4**

BOOTY, Martyn — Defender

H: 5 9 W: 12 06 b.Kirby Muxloe 30-5-71

Source: Trainee.

1991–92	Coventry C	3	0
1992–93	Coventry C	0	0
1993–94	Coventry C	2	0
1993–94	Crewe Alex	31	1
1994–95	Crewe Alex	44	2
1995–96	Crewe Alex	21	2
1995–96	Reading	17	1
1996–97	Reading	14	0
1997–98	Reading	25	0
1998–99	Reading	8	0
1998–99	Southend U	20	0
Total:		**185**	**6**

BORBOKIS, Vassilis — Defender

H: 5 9 W: 12 02 b.Serres 10-2-69

Honours: Greece 2 full caps.

1992–93	Apollon	29	2
1993–94	AEK Athens	24	2
1994–95	AEK Athens	11	1
1995–96	AEK Athens	24	2
1996–97	AEK Athens	27	4
1997–98	Sheffield U	36	2
1998–99	Sheffield U	19	2
1998–99	Derby Co	4	0
Total:		**174**	**15**

BORG, John — Midfield

H: 5 7 W: 10 07 b.Salford 22-2-80

Source: Trainee.

1997–98	Doncaster R	1	0
1998–99	Bury	0	0
Total:		**1**	**0**

BORROWS, Brian — Defender

H: 5 10 W: 11 12 b.Liverpool 20-12-60

Source: Amateur. *Honours:* England B.

1979–80	Everton	0	0
1980–81	Everton	0	0
1981–82	Everton	15	0
1982–83	Everton	12	0
1982–83	Bolton W	9	0
1983–84	Bolton W	44	0
1984–85	Bolton W	42	0
1985–86	Coventry C	41	0
1986–87	Coventry C	41	1
1987–88	Coventry C	33	0
1988–89	Coventry C	38	1
1989–90	Coventry C	37	1
1990–91	Coventry C	38	6
1991–92	Coventry C	35	0

1992–93	Coventry C	38	2
1993–94	Coventry C	29	0
1993–94	Bristol C (loan)	6	0
1994–95	Coventry C	35	0
1995–96	Coventry C	21	0
1996–97	Coventry C	23	0
1997–98	Coventry C	0	0
1997–98	Swindon T	40	0
1998–99	Swindon T	40	0
Total:		**617**	**11**

BORTOLAZZI, Mario — Midfield

H: 5 9 W: 11 04 b.Verona 10-1-65

1980–81	Mantova	1	0
1981–82	Mantova	21	0
1982–83	Mantova	5	0
1982–83	Fiorentina	2	0
1983–84	Fiorentina	1	0
1984–85	Fiorentina	8	0
1985–86	AC Milan	7	0
1986–87	Parma	34	7
1987–88	AC Milan	13	1
1988–89	Verona	33	4
1989–90	Atalanta	20	2
1990–91	Genoa	31	1
1991–92	Genoa	32	4
1992–93	Genoa	31	1
1993–94	Genoa	32	0
1994–95	Genoa	31	1
1995–96	Genoa	36	3
1996–97	Genoa	32	2
1997–98	Genoa	25	4
1998–99	WBA	35	2
Total:		**430**	**32**

BOS, Gijsbert — Forward

H: 6 4 W: 12 09 b.Spakenburg 22-2-73

Source: Ijsselmeervogels. *Honours:*

1995–96	Lincoln C	11	5
1996–97	Lincoln C	23	1
1997–98	Rotherham U	16	4
1997–98	Walsall (loan)	0	0
1998–99	Rotherham U	2	0
Total:		**52**	**10**

BOSHELL, Daniel — Midfield

b.Bradford 30-5-81

Source: Trainee.

1998–99	Oldham Ath	0	0

BOSNICH, Mark — Goalkeeper

H: 6 1 W: 14 07 b.Fairfield 13-1-72

Source: Croatia Sydney. *Honours:* Australia full caps.

1989–90	Manchester U	1	0
1990–91	Manchester U	2	0
1991–92	Aston Villa	1	0
1992–93	Aston Villa	17	0
1993–94	Aston Villa	28	0
1994–95	Aston Villa	30	0
1995–96	Aston Villa	38	1
1996–97	Aston Villa	20	0
1997–98	Aston Villa	30	0
1998–99	Aston Villa	15	0
Total:		**182**	**1**

BOTTIGLIERI, Emiliob — Midfield

H: 5 8 W: 11 06 b.Port Hardy 13-4-79

Source: Metro Ford.

1997–98	Hibernian	0	0
1998–99	Hibernian	1	0
1998–99	Albion R	10	1
Total:		**11**	**1**

BOULD, Steve — Defender

H: 6 4 W: 14 02 b.Stoke 16-11-62

Source: Apprentice. *Honours:* England 2 full caps.

1980–81	Stoke C	0	0
1981–82	Stoke C	2	0
1982–83	Stoke C	14	0
1982–83	Torquay U (loan)	9	0
1983–84	Stoke C	38	2
1984–85	Stoke C	38	3
1985–86	Stoke C	33	0
1986–87	Stoke C	28	1
1987–88	Stoke C	30	0
1988–89	Arsenal	30	2
1989–90	Arsenal	19	0
1990–91	Arsenal	38	0
1991–92	Arsenal	25	1
1992–93	Arsenal	24	1
1993–94	Arsenal	25	1
1994–95	Arsenal	31	0
1995–96	Arsenal	19	0
1996–97	Arsenal	33	0
1997–98	Arsenal	24	0
1998–99	Arsenal	19	0
Total:		**479**	**11**

BOUND, Matthew — Defender

H: 6 2 W: 14 00 b.Bradford-on-Avon 9-11-72

Source: Trainee.

1990–91	Southampton	1	0
1991–92	Southampton	0	0

1992–93	Southampton	3	0
1993–94	Southampton	1	0
1993–94	Hull C (loan)	7	1
1994–95	Southampton	0	0
1994–95	Stockport Co	14	0
1995–96	Stockport Co	26	5
1995–96	Lincoln C (loan)	4	0
1996–97	Stockport Co	4	0
1997–98	Stockport Co	0	0
1997–98	Swansea C	28	0
1998–99	Swansea C	45	2
Total:		**133**	**8**

BOWEN, Jason — Midfield

H: 5 8 W: 11 02 b.Merthyr 24-8-72

Source: Trainee. *Honours:* Wales Youth, Under-21, 2 full caps.

1990–91	Swansea C	3	0
1991–92	Swansea C	11	0
1992–93	Swansea C	38	10
1993–94	Swansea C	41	11
1994–95	Swansea C	31	5
1995–96	Birmingham C	23	4
1996–97	Birmingham C	25	3
1997–98	Birmingham C	0	0
1997–98	Southampton (loan)	3	0
1997–98	Reading	14	1
1998–99	Reading	1	0
1998–99	Cardiff C	17	2
Total:		**207**	**36**

BOWEN, Mark — Defender

H: 5 8 W: 11 11 b.Neath 7-12-63

Source: Apprentice. *Honours:* Wales Schools, Youth, Under-21, 41 full caps, 3 goals.

1981–82	Tottenham H	0	0
1982–83	Tottenham H	0	0
1983–84	Tottenham H	7	0
1984–85	Tottenham H	6	0
1985–86	Tottenham H	2	1
1986–87	Tottenham H	2	1
1987–88	Norwich C	24	1
1988–89	Norwich C	35	2
1989–90	Norwich C	38	7
1990–91	Norwich C	37	1
1991–92	Norwich C	36	3
1992–93	Norwich C	42	1
1993–94	Norwich C	41	5
1994–95	Norwich C	36	2
1995–96	Norwich C	31	2
1996–97	West Ham U	17	1
From Shimizu.			
1997–98	Charlton Ath	36	0
1998–99	Charlton Ath	6	0
Total:		**396**	**27**

BOWER, Mark — Defender

H: 5 10 W: 10 11 b.Bradford 23-1-80

Source: Trainee.

1997–98	Bradford C	3	0
1998–99	Bradford C	0	0
Total:		**3**	**0**

BOWES, Terry — Midfield

H: 5 9 W: 11 00 b.London 13-9-79

Source: Arsenal Trainee.

1998–99	Ipswich T	0	0

BOWLING, Ian — Goalkeeper

H: 6 3 W: 13 11 b.Sheffield 27-7-65

Source: Gainsborough T.

1988–89	Lincoln C	8	0
1989–90	Lincoln C	0	0
1989–90	Hartlepool U (loan)	1	0
1990–91	Lincoln C	16	0
1991–92	Lincoln C	20	0
1992–93	Lincoln C	15	0
1992–93	Bradford C (loan)	7	0
1993–94	Bradford C	23	0
1994–95	Bradford C	6	0
1995–96	Mansfield T	44	0
1996–97	Mansfield T	46	0
1997–98	Mansfield T	33	0
1998–99	Mansfield T	37	0
Total:		**256**	**0**

BOWMAN, Rob — Defender

H: 6 1 W: 12 10 b.Durham 21-11-75

Source: Trainee. *Honours:* England Youth.

1992–93	Leeds U	4	0
1993–94	Leeds U	0	0
1994–95	Leeds U	0	0
1995–96	Leeds U	3	0
1996–97	Leeds U	0	0
1996–97	Rotherham U	13	0
1997–98	Carlisle U	7	1
1998–99	Carlisle U	24	1
Total:		**51**	**2**

BOWRY, Bobby — Midfield

H: 5 9 W: 10 08 b.Croydon 19-5-71

1991–92	Crystal Palace	0	0
1992–93	Crystal Palace	11	1
1993–94	Crystal Palace	21	0
1994–95	Crystal Palace	18	0
1995–96	Millwall	38	2

1996–97	Millwall	28	1
1997–98	Millwall	43	2
1998–99	Millwall	25	0
Total:		**184**	**6**

BOWYER, Lee — Midfield

H: 5 9 W: 10 09 b.London 3-1-77

Source: Trainee. *Honours:* England Youth, Under-21.

1993–94	Charlton Ath	0	0
1994–95	Charlton Ath	5	0
1995–96	Charlton Ath	41	8
1996–97	Leeds U	32	4
1997–98	Leeds U	25	3
1998–99	Leeds U	35	9
Total:		**138**	**24**

BOXALL, Danny — Defender

H: 5 8 W: 10 05 b.Croydon 24-8-77

Source: Trainee. *Honours:* Eire Under-21.

1994–95	Crystal Palace	0	0
1995–96	Crystal Palace	1	0
1996–97	Crystal Palace	6	0
1997–98	Crystal Palace	1	0
1997–98	Oldham Ath (loan)	18	0
1998–99	Brentford	38	1
Total:		**64**	**1**

BOYACK, Steven — Midfield

H: 5 10 W: 10 07 b.Edinburgh 4-9-76

Source: Rangers BC. *Honours:* Scotland Under-21.

1996–97	Rangers	1	0
1997–98	Rangers	0	0
1997–98	Hull C (loan)	12	3
1998–99	Rangers	0	0
1998–99	Dundee	8	2
Total:		**21**	**5**

BOYCE, Emmerson — Defender

H: 5 11 W: 11 02 b.Aylesbury 24-9-79

Source: Trainee.

1997–98	Luton T	0	0
1998–99	Luton T	1	0
Total:		**1**	**0**

BOYCE, Mark — Defender

H: 5 7 W: 10 00 b.Hammersmith 11-8-80

Source: Trainee.

1998–99	Watford	0	0

BOYD, Mark — Midfield

H: 5 9 W: 11 02 b.Carlisle 22-10-81

Source: Trainee.

1998–99	Newcastle U	0	0

BOYD, Tom — Defender

H: 5 11 W: 11 04 b.Glasgow 24-11-65

Source: 'S' Form. *Honours:* Scotland Youth, Under-21 B, 65 full caps, 1 goal.

1983–84	Motherwell	13	0
1984–85	Motherwell	36	0
1985–86	Motherwell	31	0
1986–87	Motherwell	31	0
1987–88	Motherwell	42	2
1988–89	Motherwell	36	1
1989–90	Motherwell	33	1
1990–91	Motherwell	30	2
1991–92	Chelsea	23	0
1991–92	Celtic	13	1
1992–93	Celtic	42	0
1993–94	Celtic	38	0
1994–95	Celtic	35	1
1995–96	Celtic	34	0
1996–97	Celtic	31	0
1997–98	Celtic	33	0
1998–99	Celtic	31	0
Total:		**532**	**8**

BOYLAN, Lee — Forward

b.Witham 2-9-78

Source: Trainee.

1996–97	West Ham U	1	0
1997–98	West Ham U	0	0
1998–99	West Ham U	0	0
Total:		**1**	**0**

BOYLE, Steven — Midfield

b.Edinburgh 11-12-80

Source: Rotho Colts.

1998–99	Dunfermline Ath	1	1
Total:		**1**	**1**

BOYLE, Wesley — Forward

H: 5 10 W: 11 01 b.Portadown 30-3-79

Source: Trainee. *Honours:* Northern Ireland Under-21.

1995–96	Leeds U	0	0
1996–97	Leeds U	1	0
1997–98	Leeds U	0	0
1998–99	Leeds U	0	0
Total:		**1**	**0**

BRABIN, Gary — Midfield

H: 5 11 W: 14 08 b.Liverpool 9-12-70

Source: Trainee.

1989–90	Stockport Co	1	0
1990–91	Stockport Co	1	0
From Runcorn			
1994–95	Doncaster R	28	8
1995–96	Doncaster R	31	3
1995–96	Bury	5	0
1996–97	Blackpool	32	2
1997–98	Blackpool	24	3
1998–99	Blackpool	7	0
1998–99	Lincoln C (loan)	4	0
1998–99	Hull C	21	4
Total:		**154**	**20**

BRACE, Deryn — Defender

H: 5 7 W: 10 12 b.Haverfordwest 15-3-75

Source: Trainee. *Honours:* Wales Under-21.

1993–94	Norwich C	0	0
1993–94	Wrexham	1	0
1994–95	Wrexham	14	0
1995–96	Wrexham	16	1
1996–97	Wrexham	26	1
1997–98	Wrexham	8	0
1998–99	Wrexham	17	0
Total:		**82**	**2**

BRACEWELL, Paul — Midfield

H: 5 9 W: 12 03 b.Heswall 19-7-62

Source: Apprentice. *Honours:* England Under-21, 3 full caps.

1979–80	Stoke C	6	0
1980–81	Stoke C	40	2
1981–82	Stoke C	42	1
1982–83	Stoke C	41	2
1983–84	Sunderland	38	4
1984–85	Everton	37	2
1985–86	Everton	38	3
1986–87	Everton	0	0
1987–88	Everton	0	0
1988–89	Everton	20	2
1989–90	Everton	0	0
1989–90	Sunderland	37	2
1990–91	Sunderland	37	0
1991–92	Sunderland	39	0
1992–93	Newcastle U	25	2
1993–94	Newcastle U	32	1
1994–95	Newcastle U	16	0
1995–96	Sunderland	38	0
1996–97	Sunderland	38	0
1997–98	Sunderland	1	0
1997–98	Fulham	36	0
1998–99	Fulham	26	1
Total:		**587**	**22**

BRACEY, Lee — Goalkeeper

H: 6 2 W: 13 02 b.Barking 11-9-68

Source: Trainee.

1987–88	West Ham U	0	0
1988–89	Swansea C	30	0
1989–90	Swansea C	31	0
1990–91	Swansea C	35	0
1991–92	Swansea C	3	0
1991–92	Halifax T	32	0
1992–93	Halifax T	41	0
1993–94	Bury	40	0
1994–95	Bury	6	0
1995–96	Bury	21	0
1996–97	Bury	0	0
1996–97	Ipswich T (loan)	0	0
1997–98	Ipswich T	0	0
1998–99	Ipswich T	0	0
Total:		**239**	**0**

BRADBURY, Lee — Forward

H: 6 2 W: 13 10 b.Isle of Wight 3-7-75

Source: Cowes. *Honours:* England Under-21.

1995–96	Portsmouth	12	0
1995–96	Exeter C (loan)	14	5
1996–97	Portsmouth	42	15
1997–98	Manchester C	27	7
1998–99	Manchester C	13	3
1998–99	Crystal Palace	22	4
1998–99	Birmingham C (loan)	7	0
Total:		**137**	**34**

BRADLEY, Russell — Defender

H: 6 2 W: 13 02 b.Birmingham 28-3-66

Source: Dudley T.

1987–88	Nottingham F	0	0
1988–89	Nottingham F	0	0
1988–89	Hereford U (loan)	12	1
1989–90	Hereford U	33	1
1990–91	Hereford U	41	2
1991–92	Hereford U	3	0
1991–92	Halifax T	26	2
1992–93	Halifax T	30	1
1993–94	Scunthorpe U	34	1
1994–95	Scunthorpe U	25	2
1995–96	Scunthorpe U	38	1
1996–97	Scunthorpe U	22	1
1996–97	Hartlepool U (loan)	12	1
1997–98	Hartlepool U	43	1
1998–99	Hartlepool U	0	0
Total:		**319**	**14**

BRADLEY, Shayne — Forward

H: 6 0 W: 13 06 b.Gloucester 8-12-79

Source: Trainee. *Honours:* England Schools.

1997–98	Southampton	0	0
1998–99	Southampton	3	0
1998–99	Swindon T (loan)	7	0
Total:		**10**	**0**

BRADSHAW, Carl — Defender

H: 5 10 W: 11 08 b.Sheffield 2-10-68

Source: Apprentice. *Honours:* England Youth.

1986–87	Sheffield W	9	2
1986–87	Barnsley (loan)	6	1
1987–88	Sheffield W	20	2
1988–89	Sheffield W	3	0
1988–89	Manchester C	5	0
1989–90	Manchester C	0	0
1989–90	Sheffield U	30	3
1990–91	Sheffield U	27	1
1991–92	Sheffield U	18	2
1992–93	Sheffield U	32	1
1993–94	Sheffield U	40	1
1994–95	Norwich C	26	1
1995–96	Norwich C	21	1
1996–97	Norwich C	17	0
1997–98	Norwich C	1	0
1997–98	Wigan Ath	28	1
1998–99	Wigan Ath	39	6
Total:		**322**	**22**

BRADSHAW, Mark — Defender

H: 5 10 W: 11 00 b.Ashton-under-Lyne 7-9-69

Source: Trainee.

1986–87	Blackpool	4	0
1987–88	Blackpool	16	0
1988–89	Blackpool	0	0
1989–90	Blackpool	21	1
1990–91	Blackpool	1	0
1990–91	York C (loan)	1	0
From Macclesfield T			
1998–99	Halifax T	41	4
Total:		**84**	**5**

BRADY, Garry — Midfield

H: 5 10 W: 10 09 b.Glasgow 7-9-76

Source: Trainee.

1993–94	Tottenham H	0	0
1994–95	Tottenham H	0	0
1995–96	Tottenham H	0	0
1996–97	Tottenham H	0	0
1997–98	Tottenham H	9	0
1998–99	Newcastle U	9	0
Total:		**18**	**0**

BRADY, Matthew — Forward

H: 6 0 W: 10 04 b.Barnet 27-10-77

Source: Trainee.

1994–95	Barnet	1	0
1995–96	Barnet	2	0
1996–97	Barnet	7	0
1997–98	Barnet	0	0
1998–99	Barnet	0	0
Total:		**10**	**0**

BRAMBLE, Titus — Defender

H: 6 1 W: 13 10 b.Ipswich 21-7-81

Source: Trainee.

1998–99	Ipswich T	4	0
Total:		**4**	**0**

BRAMMER, Dave — Midfield

H: 5 10 W: 12 00 b.Bromborough 28-2-75

Source: Trainee.

1992–93	Wrexham	2	0
1993–94	Wrexham	22	2
1994–95	Wrexham	14	1
1995–96	Wrexham	11	2
1996–97	Wrexham	21	1
1997–98	Wrexham	33	4
1998–99	Wrexham	34	2
1998–99	Port Vale	9	0
Total:		**146**	**12**

BRANAGAN, Keith — Goalkeeper

H: 6 0 W: 13 02 b.Fulham 10-7-66

Honours: Eire B. 1 full cap.

1983–84	Cambridge U	1	0
1984–85	Cambridge U	19	0
1985–86	Cambridge U	9	0
1986–87	Cambridge U	46	0
1987–88	Cambridge U	35	0
1987–88	Millwall	0	0
1988–89	Millwall	0	0
1989–90	Millwall	16	0
1989–90	Brentford (loan)	2	0
1990–91	Millwall	18	0
1991–92	Millwall	12	0
1991–92	Gillingham (loan)	1	0
1991–92	Fulham (loan)	0	0
1992–93	Bolton W	46	0
1993–94	Bolton W	10	0
1994–95	Bolton W	43	0
1995–96	Bolton W	31	0
1996–97	Bolton W	36	0
1997–98	Bolton W	34	0
1998–99	Bolton W	3	0
Total:		**362**	**0**

BRANCA, Marco — Forward

H: 6 0 W: 12 09 b.Grosseto 6-1-65

1981–82	Grosseto	0	0
1982–83	Cagliari	0	0
1983–84	Cagliari	0	0
1984–85	Cagliari	25	2
1985–86	Cagliari	27	2
1986–87	Udinese	18	2
1987–88	Sampdoria	9	1
1988–89	Udinese	28	4
1989–90	Udinese	27	9
1990–91	Sampdoria	20	5
1991–92	Fiorentina	23	5
1992–93	Udinese	29	8
1993–94	Udinese	29	14
1994–95	Parma	25	7
1995–96	Roma	7	2
1995–96	Internazionale	24	17
1996–97	Internazionale	21	5
1997–98	Internazionale	7	1
1997–98	Middlesbrough	11	9
1998–99	Middlesbrough	1	0
Total:		**331**	**93**

BRANCH, Graham — Midfield

H: 6 2 W: 12 02 b.Liverpool 12-2-72

Source: Heswall.

1991–92	Tranmere R	4	0
1992–93	Tranmere R	3	0
1992–93	Bury (loan)	4	1
1993–94	Tranmere R	13	0
1994–95	Tranmere R	1	0
1995–96	Tranmere R	21	2
1996–97	Tranmere R	35	5
1997–98	Tranmere R	25	3
1997–98	Wigan Ath (loan)	3	0
1998–99	Stockport Co	14	3
1998–99	Burnley	20	1
Total:		**143**	**15**

BRANCH, Michael — Forward

H: 5 10 W: 11 07 b.Liverpool 18-10-78

Source: Trainee. *Honours:* England Schools, Youth, Under-21.

1995–96	Everton	3	0
1996–97	Everton	25	3
1997–98	Everton	6	0
1998–99	Everton	7	0
1998–99	Manchester C (loan)	4	0
Total:		**45**	**3**

BRANNAN, Ged — Defender

H: 6 0 W: 12 05 b.Liverpool 15-1-72

Source: Trainee.

1990–91	Tranmere R	18	1
1991–92	Tranmere R	18	1
1992–93	Tranmere R	38	1
1993–94	Tranmere R	45	9
1994–95	Tranmere R	41	2
1995–96	Tranmere R	44	0
1996–97	Tranmere R	34	6
1996–97	Manchester C	11	1
1997–98	Manchester C	32	3
1998–99	Manchester C	0	0
1998–99	Norwich C (loan)	11	1
1998–99	Motherwell	25	5
Total:		**317**	**30**

BRANSTON, Guy — Defender

H: 6 1 W: 13 11 b.Leicester 9-1-79

Source: Trainee.

1997–98	Leicester C	0	0
1997–98	Colchester U (loan)	12	1
1998–99	Leicester C	0	0
1998–99	Colchester U (loan)	1	0
1998–99	Plymouth Arg (loan)	7	1
Total:		**20**	**2**

BRASS, Chris — Defender

H: 5 9 W: 12 06 b.Easington 24-7-75

Source: Trainee.

1993–94	Burnley	0	0
1994–95	Burnley	5	0
1994–95	Torquay U (loan)	7	0
1995–96	Burnley	9	0
1996–97	Burnley	39	0
1997–98	Burnley	40	1
1998–99	Burnley	34	0
Total:		**134**	**1**

BRATTBAKK, Harald — Forward

H: 5 9 W: 11 00 b.Norway 1-2-71

Honours: Norway 9 full caps, 3 goals.

1990	Rosenborg	3	0
1991	Rosenborg	11	1
1992	Bodo Glimt*	0	0
1993	Bodo Glimt	22	10
1994	Rosenborg	22	17
1995	Rosenborg	26	26
1996	Rosenborg	26	28
1997	Rosenborg	26	23
1997–98	Celtic	18	7
1998–99	Celtic	24	5
Total:		**178**	**117**

BRAY, Justin — Goalkeeper

H: 5 11 W: 11 00 b.Great Yarmouth 1-11-79

Source: Trainee.

1997–98	Wolverhampton W	0	0
1998–99	Wolverhampton W	0	0

BRAYSON, Paul — Forward

H: 5 6 W: 10 10 b.Newcastle 16-9-77

Source: Trainee. *Honours:* England Youth.

1995–96	Newcastle U	0	0
1996–97	Newcastle U	0	0
1996–97	Swansea C (loan)	11	5
1997–98	Newcastle U	0	0
1997–98	Reading	6	1
1998–99	Reading	28	0
Total:		**45**	**6**

BRAZIER, Matthew — Midfield

H: 5 8 W: 11 08 b.Whipps Cross 2-7-76

Source: Trainee.

1994–95	QPR	0	0
1995–96	QPR	11	0
1996–97	QPR	27	2
1997–98	QPR	11	0
1997–98	Fulham	7	1
1998–99	Fulham	2	0
1998–99	Cardiff C (loan)	11	2
Total:		**69**	**5**

BREACKER, Tim — Defender

H: 5 11 W: 13 00 b.Bicester 2-7-65

Source: Apprentice. *Honours:* England Under-21.

1983–84	Luton T	2	0
1984–85	Luton T	35	0
1985–86	Luton T	36	0
1986–87	Luton T	29	1
1987–88	Luton T	40	1
1988–89	Luton T	22	0
1989–90	Luton T	38	1
1990–91	Luton T	8	0
1990–91	West Ham U	24	1
1991–92	West Ham U	34	2
1992–93	West Ham U	39	2
1993–94	West Ham U	40	3
1994–95	West Ham U	33	0
1995–96	West Ham U	22	0
1996–97	West Ham U	26	0
1997–98	West Ham U	19	0
1998–99	West Ham U	3	0
1998–99	QPR	18	1
Total:		**468**	**12**

BREBNER, Grant — Midfield

H: 5 10 W: 11 11 b.Edinburgh 6-12-77

Source: Trainee. *Honours:* Scotland Under-21.

1994–95	Manchester U	0	0
1995–96	Manchester U	0	0
1996–97	Manchester U	0	0
1997–98	Manchester U	0	0
1997–98	Cambridge U (loan)	6	1
1997–98	Hibernian (loan)	9	1
1998–99	Reading	39	9
Total:		**54**	**11**

BRECKIN, Ian — Defender

H: 5 11 W: 11 07 b.Rotherham 24-2-75

Source: Trainee.

1993–94	Rotherham U	10	0
1994–95	Rotherham U	41	2
1995–96	Rotherham U	39	1
1996–97	Rotherham U	42	3
1997–98	Chesterfield	43	1
1998–99	Chesterfield	44	2
Total:		**219**	**9**

BREEN, Gary — Defender

H: 6 1 W: 11 12 b.London 12-12-73

Source: Charlton Ath. *Honours:* Eire Under-21, 20 full caps, 3 goals.

1991–92	Maidstone U	19	0
1992–93	Gillingham	29	0
1993–94	Gillingham	22	0
1994–95	Peterborough U	44	1
1995–96	Peterborough U	25	0
1995–96	Birmingham C	18	1
1996–97	Birmingham C	22	1
1996–97	Coventry C	9	0
1997–98	Coventry C	30	1
1998–99	Coventry C	25	0
Total:		**243**	**4**

BRENNAN, Damien — Defender

b.Dublin 30-8-80

Source: Belvedere.

1997–98	Huddersfield T	0	0
1998–99	Huddersfield T	0	0

BRENNAN, Dean — Midfield

H: 5 9 W: 11 04 b.Dublin 17-6-80

1997–98	Sheffield W	0	0
1998–99	Sheffield W	0	0

BRENNAN, Jim — Defender

H: 5 9 W: 11 06 b.Toronto 8-5-77

Source: Sora Lazio. *Honours:* Canada full caps.

1994–95	Bristol C	0	0
1995–96	Bristol C	0	0
1996–97	Bristol C	8	0
1997–98	Bristol C	6	0
1998–99	Bristol C	29	1
Total:		**43**	**1**

BRENNAN, Karl — Midfield

H: 5 6 W: 11 00 b.Leicester 19-3-81

Source: Trainee.

1997–98	Leicester C	0	0
1998–99	Leicester C	0	0

BRESLAN, Geoff — Midfield

H: 5 9 W: 10 02 b.Torbay 4-6-80

Source: Trainee.

1997–98	Exeter C	1	0
1998–99	Exeter C	34	4
Total:		**35**	**4**

BREVETT, Rufus — Defender

H: 5 8 W: 11 08 b.Derby 24-9-69

Source: Trainee.

1987–88	Doncaster R	17	0
1988–89	Doncaster R	23	0
1989–90	Doncaster R	42	0
1990–91	Doncaster R	27	3
1990–91	QPR	10	0
1991–92	QPR	7	0
1992–93	QPR	15	0
1993–94	QPR	7	0
1994–95	QPR	19	0
1995–96	QPR	27	1
1996–97	QPR	44	0
1997–98	QPR	23	0
1997–98	Fulham	11	0
1998–99	Fulham	45	1
Total:		**317**	**5**

BRIDGE-WILKINSON, Marc — Midfield

H: 5 6 W: 10 08 b.Nuneaton 16-3-79

Source: Trainee.

1996–97	Derby Co	0	0
1997–98	Derby Co	0	0
1998–99	Derby Co	1	0
1998–99	Carlisle U (loan)	7	0
Total:		**8**	**0**

BRIDGE, Wayne — Forward

H: 5 10 W: 12 04 b.Southampton 5-8-80

Source: Trainee. *Honours:* England Youth, Under-21.

1997–98	Southampton	0	0
1998–99	Southampton	23	0
Total:		**23**	**0**

BRIDGES, Michael — Forward

H: 6 1 W: 11 00 b.North Shields 5-8-78

Source: Trainee. *Honours:* England Schools, Youth, Under-21.

1995–96	Sunderland	15	4
1996–97	Sunderland	25	3
1997–98	Sunderland	9	1
1998–99	Sunderland	30	8
Total:		**79**	**16**

BRIGGS, John — Midfield

H: 5 11 W: 10 10 b.Stockton 9-11-79

Source: Trainee.

1998–99	Hartlepool U	0	0

BRIGHT, Mark — Forward

H: 6 2 W: 13 00 b.Stoke 6-6-62

Source: Leek T.

1981–82	Port Vale	2	0
1982–83	Port Vale	1	1
1983–84	Port Vale	26	9
1984–85	Leicester C	16	0
1985–86	Leicester C	24	6
1986–87	Leicester C	2	0
1986–87	Crystal Palace	28	8
1987–88	Crystal Palace	38	25
1988–89	Crystal Palace	46	20
1989–90	Crystal Palace	36	12
1990–91	Crystal Palace	32	9
1991–92	Crystal Palace	42	17
1992–93	Crystal Palace	5	1
1992–93	Sheffield W	30	11
1993–94	Sheffield W	40	19
1994–95	Sheffield W	37	11
1995–96	Sheffield W	25	7
1996–97	Sheffield W	1	0
1996–97	Millwall (loan)	3	1
1996–97	Sion	0	0
1996–97	Charlton Ath	6	2
From Sion			
1997–98	Charlton Ath	16	7
1998–99	Charlton Ath	6	1
Total:		**462**	**167**

BRIGHTWELL, David — Defender

H: 6 2 W: 12 09 b.Lutterworth 7-1-71

Source: Trainee.

1987–88	Manchester C	0	0
1988–89	Manchester C	0	0
1989–90	Manchester C	0	0
1990–91	Manchester C	0	0
1990–91	Chester C (loan)	6	0
1991–92	Manchester C	4	0
1992–93	Manchester C	8	0
1993–94	Manchester C	22	1
1994–95	Manchester C	9	0
1995–96	Manchester C	0	0
1995–96	Lincoln C (loan)	5	0
1995–96	Stoke C (loan)	1	0
1995–96	Bradford C	22	0
1996–97	Bradford C	2	0
1996–97	Blackpool (loan)	2	0
1997–98	Northampton T	35	1
1998–99	Carlisle U	41	4
Total:		**157**	**6**

BRIGHTWELL, Ian — Midfield

H: 5 9 W: 12 05 b.Lutterworth 9-4-68

Source: Congleton T. *Honours:* England Schools, Youth, Under-21.

1986–87	Manchester C	16	1
1987–88	Manchester C	33	5
1988–89	Manchester C	26	6
1989–90	Manchester C	28	2
1990–91	Manchester C	33	0
1991–92	Manchester C	40	1
1992–93	Manchester C	21	1
1993–94	Manchester C	7	0
1994–95	Manchester C	30	0
1995–96	Manchester C	29	0
1996–97	Manchester C	37	2
1997–98	Manchester C	21	0
1998–99	Coventry C	0	0
Total:		**321**	**18**

BRIGHTWELL, Stuart — Midfield

H: 5 5 W: 11 01 b.Easington 31-1-79

Source: Trainee. *Honours:* England Schools, Youth.

1995–96	Manchester U	0	0
1996–97	Manchester U	0	0
1997–98	Manchester U	0	0
1998–99	Hartlepool U	17	1
Total:		**17**	**1**

BRISCO, Neil — Midfield

H: 6 0 W: 11 05 b.Billinge 26-1-78

Source: Trainee.

1996–97	Manchester C	0	0
1997–98	Manchester C	0	0
1998–99	Port Vale	1	0
Total:		**1**	**0**

BRISCOE, Anthony — Forward

H: 6 0 W: 11 01 b.Birmingham 16-8-78

Source: Trainee.

1996–97	Shrewsbury T	1	0
1997–98	Shrewsbury T	0	0
1998–99	Shrewsbury T	0	0
Total:		**1**	**0**

BRISCOE, Lee — Forward

H: 5 11 W: 11 13 b.Pontefract 30-9-75

Source: Trainee. *Honours:* England Under-21.

1993–94	Sheffield W	1	0
1994–95	Sheffield W	6	0
1995–96	Sheffield W	26	0
1996–97	Sheffield W	6	0
1997–98	Sheffield W	7	0
1997–98	Manchester C (loan)	5	1
1998–99	Sheffield W	16	1
Total:		**67**	**2**

BRISSETT, Jason — Forward

H: 5 10 W: 12 05 b.Redbridge 7-9-74

Source: Arsenal Trainee.

1993–94	Peterborough U	30	0
1994–95	Peterborough U	5	0
1994–95	Bournemouth	25	0
1995–96	Bournemouth	43	3
1996–97	Bournemouth	25	4
1997–98	Bournemouth	31	1
1998–99	Walsall	35	2
Total:		**194**	**10**

BRISTOW, Jason — Defender

H: 6 2 W: 11 00 b.Basingstoke 23-4-80

Source: Trainee.

1998–99	Reading	0	0

BRITTON, Gerard — Forward

H: 6 0 W: 11 00 b.Glasgow 20-10-70

Source: Celtic BC.

1987–88	Celtic	0	0
1988–89	Celtic	0	0

1989–90	Celtic	0	0
1990–91	Celtic	2	0
1991–92	Celtic	0	0
1991–92	Reading (loan)	2	0
1992–93	Partick Th	40	12
1993–94	Partick Th	22	3
1993–94	Dundee	17	1
1994–95	Dundee	26	12
1995–96	Dundee	25	2
1996–97	Dunfermline Ath	33	13
1997–98	Dunfermline Ath	16	3
1998–99	Dunfermline Ath	21	2
1998–99	Raith R	5	1
Total:		**209**	**49**

BROAD, Stephen — Defender

H: 6 2 W: 12 00 b.Epsom 10-6-80

Source: Trainee.

1997–98	Chelsea	0	0
1998–99	Chelsea	0	0

BROADBENT, David — Forward

H: 5 9 W: 10 06 b.Pembury 26-9-79

Source: Trainee.

1997–98	Newcastle U	0	0
1998–99	Newcastle U	0	0

BROADHURST, Karl — Defender

H: 6 1 W: 11 07 b.Portsmouth 18-3-80

Source: Trainee.

1998–99	Bournemouth	0	0

BROCK, Stuart — Goalkeeper

H: 6 1 W: 13 03 b.Sandwell 26-9-76

Source: Trainee.

1994–95	Aston Villa	0	0
1995–96	Aston Villa	0	0
1996–97	Aston Villa	0	0
1996–97	Northampton T	0	0
1997–98	Northampton T	0	0
1998–99	Northampton T	0	0

BRODIE, Steve — Forward

H: 5 7 W: 10 08 b.Sunderland 14-1-73

Source: Trainee.

1991–92	Sunderland	0	0
1992–93	Sunderland	0	0
1993–94	Sunderland	4	0
1994–95	Sunderland	8	0
1995–96	Sunderland	0	0
1995–96	Doncaster R (loan)	5	1
1996–97	Sunderland	0	0
1996–97	Scarborough	24	5
1997–98	Scarborough	44	10
1998–99	Scarborough	43	12
Total:		**128**	**28**

BROMBY, Leigh — Defender

H: 6 0 W: 11 05 b.Dewsbury 2-6-80

Honours: England Schools.

1998–99	Sheffield W	0	0

BROOKER, Paul — Forward

H: 5 8 W: 10 01 b.Hammersmith 25-11-76

Source: Trainee.

1995–96	Fulham	20	2
1996–97	Fulham	26	2
1997–98	Fulham	9	0
1998–99	Fulham	1	0
Total:		**56**	**4**

BROOMES, Marlon — Defender

H: 6 1 W: 12 12 b.Meriden 28-11-77

Source: Trainee. *Honours:* England Schools, Youth, Under-21.

1994–95	Blackburn R	0	0
1995–96	Blackburn R	0	0
1996–97	Blackburn R	0	0
1996–97	Swindon T (loan)	12	1
1997–98	Blackburn R	4	0
1998–99	Blackburn R	13	0
Total:		**29**	**1**

BROUGHTON, Drewe — Forward

H: 6 3 W: 12 01 b.Hitchin 25-10-78

Source: Trainee.

1996–97	Norwich C	8	1
1997–98	Norwich C	1	0
1997–98	Wigan Ath (loan)	4	0
1998–99	Norwich C	0	0
1998–99	Brentford	1	0
1998–99	Peterborough U	25	7
Total:		**39**	**8**

BROWN, Aaron — Midfield

H: 5 10 W: 11 12 b.Bristol 14-3-80

Source: Trainee. *Honours:* England Schools.

1997–98	Bristol C	0	0
1998–99	Bristol C	14	0
Total:		**14**	**0**

BROWN, Carlos — Midfield

H: 5 11 W: 10 06 b.Edmonton 22-4-81

Source: Trainee.

1998–99	QPR	0	0

BROWN, Daniel — Midfield

H: 6 0 W: 12 06 b.Bethnal Green 12-9-80

Source: Trainee.

1997–98	Leyton Orient	0	0
1998–99	Leyton Orient	0	0

BROWN, David — Forward

H: 5 10 W: 12 08 b.Bolton 2-10-78

Source: Trainee.

1995–96	Manchester U	0	0
1996–97	Manchester U	0	0
1997–98	Manchester U	0	0
1997–98	Hull C (loan)	7	2
1998–99	Hull C	42	11
Total:		**49**	**13**

BROWN, Grant — Defender

H: 6 0 W: 11 12 b.Sunderland 19-11-69

Source: Trainee.

1987–88	Leicester C	2	0
1988–89	Leicester C	12	0
1989–90	Lincoln C	34	2
1990–91	Lincoln C	32	1
1991–92	Lincoln C	37	1
1992–93	Lincoln C	40	1
1993–94	Lincoln C	38	3
1994–95	Lincoln C	39	3
1995–96	Lincoln C	34	0
1996–97	Lincoln C	34	1
1997–98	Lincoln C	15	0
1998–99	Lincoln C	22	1
Total:		**339**	**13**

BROWN, Greg — Defender

H: 5 10 W: 12 04 b.Wythenshawe 31-7-78

Source: Trainee.

1995–96	Chester C	3	0
1996–97	Chester C	1	0
1997–98	Chester C	0	0
1997–98	Macclesfield T	2	0
1998–99	Macclesfield T	5	0
Total:		**11**	**0**

BROWN, Jon — Midfield

H: 5 11 W: 11 03 b.Barnsley 8-9-66

Source: Denaby U.

1990–91	Exeter C	29	0
1991–92	Exeter C	35	0
1992–93	Exeter C	40	1
1993–94	Exeter C	23	0
1994–95	Exeter C	37	2
1998–99	Halifax T	40	0
Total:		**204**	**3**

BROWN, Keith — Defender

H: 6 0 W: 11 00 b.Edinburgh 24-12-79

1996–97	Blackburn R	0	0
1997–98	Blackburn R	0	0
1998–99	Blackburn R	0	0

BROWN, Kenny — Defender

H: 5 9 W: 11 06 b.Upminster 11-7-67

Source: Apprentice.

1984–85	Norwich C	0	0
1985–86	Norwich C	0	0
1986–87	Norwich C	18	0
1987–88	Norwich C	7	0
1988–89	Plymouth Arg	39	1
1989–90	Plymouth Arg	44	0
1990–91	Plymouth Arg	43	3
1991–92	West Ham U	27	3
1992–93	West Ham U	15	2
1993–94	West Ham U	9	0
1994–95	West Ham U	9	0
1995–96	West Ham U	3	0
1995–96	Huddersfield T (loan)	5	0
1995–96	Reading (loan)	12	1
1995–96	Southend U (loan)	6	0
1995–96	Crystal Palace (loan)	6	2
1996–97	West Ham U	0	0
1996–97	Reading (loan)	5	0
1996–97	Birmingham C	11	0
1997–98	Millwall	45	0
1998–99	Millwall	0	0
1998–99	Gillingham	4	0
Total:		**308**	**12**

BROWN, Michael — Goalkeeper

H: 5 9 W: 10 07 b.Stranraer 6-11-79

Source: Trainee.

1996–97	Manchester C	0	0
1997–98	Manchester C	0	0
1998–99	Manchester C	0	0

BROWN, Michael R
Midfield

H: 5 9 W: 10 07 b.Hartlepool 25-1-77

Source: Trainee. *Honours:* England Under-21.

1994–95	Manchester C	0	0
1995–96	Manchester C	21	0
1996–97	Manchester C	11	0
1996–97	Hartlepool U (loan)	6	1
1997–98	Manchester C	26	0
1998–99	Manchester C	31	2
Total:		**95**	**3**

BROWN, Mickey
Forward

H: 5 9 W: 10 12 b.Birmingham 8-2-68

Source: Apprentice.

1985–86	Shrewsbury T	0	0
1986–87	Shrewsbury T	22	2
1987–88	Shrewsbury T	41	5
1988–89	Shrewsbury T	41	0
1989–90	Shrewsbury T	43	1
1990–91	Shrewsbury T	43	1
1991–92	Bolton W	27	3
1992–93	Bolton W	6	0
1992–93	Shrewsbury T	17	1
1993–94	Shrewsbury T	41	7
1994–95	Shrewsbury T	9	3
1994–95	Preston NE	0	0
1995–96	Preston NE	10	1
1996–97	Preston NE	6	0
1996–97	Rochdale (loan)	5	0
1996–97	Shrewsbury T	19	1
1997–98	Shrewsbury T	30	2
1998–99	Shrewsbury T	34	2
Total:		**394**	**29**

BROWN, Simon
Goalkeeper

H: 6 2 W: 15 01 b.Chelmsford 3-12-76

Source: Trainee.

1995–96	Tottenham H	0	0
1996–97	Tottenham H	0	0
1997–98	Tottenham H	0	0
1997–98	Lincoln C (loan)	1	0
1998–99	Tottenham H	0	0
1998–99	Fulham (loan)	0	0
Total:		**1**	**0**

BROWN, Steve
Defender

H: 6 1 W: 13 10 b.Brighton 13-5-72

Source: Trainee.

1990–91	Charlton Ath	0	0
1991–92	Charlton Ath	1	0
1992–93	Charlton Ath	0	0
1993–94	Charlton Ath	19	0
1994–95	Charlton Ath	42	3
1995–96	Charlton Ath	19	0
1996–97	Charlton Ath	27	0
1997–98	Charlton Ath	34	2
1998–99	Charlton Ath	18	0
Total:		**160**	**5**

BROWN, Steve
Forward

H: 6 0 W: 13 10 b.Rochford 6-12-73

Source: Trainee.

1992–93	Southend U	10	2
1993–94	Scunthorpe U	0	0
1993–94	Colchester U	34	11
1994–95	Colchester U	28	6
1994–95	Gillingham	8	2
1995–96	Gillingham	1	0
1995–96	Lincoln C	26	3
1996–97	Lincoln C	15	2
1997–98	Lincoln C	31	3
1998–99	Macclesfield T	2	0
Total:		**155**	**29**

BROWN, Steve
Midfield

H: 5 11 W: 11 12 b.Northampton 6-7-66

1985–86	Northampton T	0	0
From Irthlingborough D			
1989–90	Northampton T	21	1
1990–91	Northampton T	40	2
1991–92	Northampton T	35	3
1992–93	Northampton T	38	9
1993–94	Northampton T	24	4
1993–94	Wycombe W	9	2
1994–95	Wycombe W	40	1
1995–96	Wycombe W	38	0
1996–97	Wycombe W	34	5
1997–98	Wycombe W	40	3
1998–99	Wycombe W	38	3
Total:		**357**	**33**

BROWN, Wayne
Goalkeeper

H: 6 1 W: 11 06 b.Southampton 14-1-77

Source: Trainee.

1993–94	Bristol C	1	0
1994–95	Bristol C	0	0
1995–96	Bristol C	0	0
From Weston-S-Mare			
1996–97	Chester C	2	0
1997–98	Chester C	13	0
1998–99	Chester C	23	0
Total:		**39**	**0**

BROWN, Wayne
Defender

H: 6 0 W: 12 00 b.Barking 20-8-77

Source: Trainee.

1995–96	Ipswich T	0	0

1996–97	Ipswich T	0	0
1997–98	Ipswich T	1	0
1997–98	Colchester U (loan)	2	0
1998–99	Ipswich T	1	0
Total:		**4**	**0**

BROWN, Wes — Defender

H: 6 1 W: 11 11 b.Manchester 13-10-79

Source: Trainee. *Honours:* England Schools, Youth, Under-21, 1 full cap.

1996–97	Manchester U	0	0
1997–98	Manchester U	2	0
1998–99	Manchester U	14	0
Total:		**16**	**0**

BROWNE, Bevan — Midfield

b.Wellingborough 29-3-80

Source: Nottingham F Trainee.

1998–99	Leicester C	0	0

BROWNE, Stafford

b.Cuckfield 4-1-72

Source: Hastings T.

1998–99	Brighton & HA	3	0
Total:		**3**	**0**

BROWNE, Tony — Defender

b.Isle of Sheppey 12-2-77

Source: West Ham U.

1998–99	Brighton & HA	13	0
Total:		**13**	**0**

BROWNING, Marcus — Midfield

H: 6 0 W: 12 10 b.Bristol 22-4-71

Source: Trainee. *Honours:* Wales 5 full caps.

1989–90	Bristol R	1	0
1990–91	Bristol R	0	0
1991–92	Bristol R	11	0
1992–93	Bristol R	19	1
1992–93	Hereford U (loan)	7	5
1993–94	Bristol R	31	4
1994–95	Bristol R	41	2
1995–96	Bristol R	45	4
1996–97	Bristol R	26	2
1996–97	Huddersfield T	13	0
1997–98	Huddersfield T	14	0
1998–99	Huddersfield T	6	0
1998–99	Gillingham	4	0
Total:		**218**	**18**

BRUCE, Paul — Forward

H: 5 10 W: 12 01 b.London 18-2-78

Source: Trainee.

1996–97	QPR	0	0
1997–98	QPR	5	1
1998–99	QPR	0	0
1998–99	Cambridge U (loan)	4	0
Total:		**9**	**1**

BRUCE, Steve — Defender

H: 6 0 W: 13 00 b.Corbridge 31-12-60

Source: Apprentice. *Honours:* England Youth.

1978–79	Gillingham	0	0
1979–80	Gillingham	40	6
1980–81	Gillingham	41	4
1981–82	Gillingham	45	6
1982–83	Gillingham	39	7
1983–84	Gillingham	40	6
1984–85	Norwich C	39	1
1985–86	Norwich C	42	8
1986–87	Norwich C	41	3
1987–88	Norwich C	19	2
1987–88	Manchester U	21	2
1988–89	Manchester U	38	2
1989–90	Manchester U	34	3
1990–91	Manchester U	31	13
1991–92	Manchester U	37	5
1992–93	Manchester U	42	5
1993–94	Manchester U	41	3
1994–95	Manchester U	35	2
1995–96	Manchester U	30	1
1996–97	Birmingham C	32	0
1997–98	Birmingham C	40	2
1998–99	Sheffield U	10	0
Total:		**737**	**81**

BRUMWELL, Phil — Midfield

H: 5 8 W: 11 00 b.Darlington 8-8-75

Source: Trainee.

1994–95	Sunderland	0	0
1995–96	Darlington	28	0
1996–97	Darlington	38	1
1997–98	Darlington	35	0
1998–99	Darlington	37	0
Total:		**138**	**1**

BRYAN, Derek — Forward

H: 5 10 W: 11 05 b.London 11-11-74

Source: Hampton.

1997–98	Brentford	11	2
1998–99	Brentford	20	4
Total:		**31**	**6**

BRYAN, Marvin — Defender

H: 6 0 W: 12 02 b.Paddington 2-8-75

Source: Trainee.

1992–93	QPR	0	0
1993–94	QPR	0	0
1994–95	QPR	0	0
1994–95	Doncaster R (loan)	5	1
1995–96	Blackpool	46	1
1996–97	Blackpool	34	1
1997–98	Blackpool	43	1
1998–99	Blackpool	41	1
Total:		**169**	**5**

BRYANT, Matthew — Defender

H: 6 1 W: 13 01 b.Bristol 21-9-70

Source: Trainee.

1989–90	Bristol C	0	0
1990–91	Bristol C	22	1
1990–91	Walsall (loan)	13	0
1991–92	Bristol C	43	2
1992–93	Bristol C	41	1
1993–94	Bristol C	28	0
1994–95	Bristol C	37	3
1995–96	Bristol C	32	0
1996–97	Gillingham	39	0
1997–98	Gillingham	35	0
1998–99	Gillingham	23	0
Total:		**313**	**7**

BRYSON, Ian — Midfield

H: 5 11 W: 12 07 b.Kilmarnock 26-11-62

1981–82	Kilmarnock	14	3
1982–83	Kilmarnock	28	1
1983–84	Kilmarnock	25	4
1984–85	Kilmarnock	36	3
1985–86	Kilmarnock	38	14
1986–87	Kilmarnock	32	10
1987–88	Kilmarnock	42	5
1988–89	Sheffield U	37	8
1989–90	Sheffield U	39	9
1990–91	Sheffield U	29	7
1991–92	Sheffield U	34	9
1992–93	Sheffield U	16	3
1993–94	Barnsley	16	3
1993–94	Preston NE	25	2
1994–95	Preston NE	41	5
1995–96	Preston NE	44	9
1996–97	Preston NE	41	3
1997–98	Rochdale	15	1
1998–99	Rochdale	39	0
Total:		**591**	**99**

BUBB, Alvin — Midfield

H: 5 5 W: 10 00 b.Paddington 11-10-80

Source: Trainee.

1998–99	QPR	0	0

BUBB, Byron — Midfield

b.Harrow 17-12-81

Source: Scholarship.

1998–99	Millwall	3	0
Total:		**3**	**0**

BUCHAN, James — Midfield

H: 5 10 W: 10 10 b.Manchester 3-4-77

Source: Stonehaven. *Honours:* Scotland Under-21.

1995–96	Aberdeen	4	1
1996–97	Aberdeen	14	0
1997–98	Aberdeen	10	0
1998–99	Aberdeen	23	2
Total:		**51**	**3**

BUCKLE, Paul — Midfield

H: 5 8 W: 11 10 b.Welwyn 16-12-70

Source: Trainee.

1987–88	Brentford	1	0
1988–89	Brentford	0	0
1989–90	Brentford	10	0
1990–91	Brentford	26	0
1991–92	Brentford	15	1
1992–93	Brentford	5	0
1993–94	Brentford	0	0
1993–94	Torquay U	16	2
1994–95	Torquay U	32	3
1995–96	Torquay U	11	4
1995–96	Exeter C	22	2
1996–97	Northampton T	0	0
1996–97	Wycombe W	0	0
1996–97	Colchester U	24	0
1997–98	Colchester U	38	5
1998–99	Colchester U	43	2
Total:		**243**	**19**

BUCKLEY, Adam — Midfield

H: 5 9 W: 11 00 b.Nottingham 2-8-79

1997–98	Grimsby T	0	0
1998–99	Grimsby T	2	0
Total:		**2**	**0**

BUGGIE, Lee — Forward

b.Bury 11-2-81

Source: Trainee.

1998–99	Bolton W	0	0
1998–99	Bury	0	0

BULL, Gary — Forward

H: 5 10 W: 12 02 b.Tipton 12-6-66

Source: Swindon T Apprentice.

1986–87	Southampton	0	0
1987–88	Southampton	0	0
1987–88	Cambridge U	9	3
1988–89	Cambridge U	10	1
From Barnet			
1991–92	Barnet	42	20
1992–93	Barnet	41	17
1993–94	Nottingham F	11	0
1994–95	Nottingham F	1	1
1994–95	Birmingham C (loan)	10	6
1995–96	Nottingham F	0	0
1995–96	Brighton & HA (loan)	10	2
1995–96	Birmingham C (loan)	6	0
1995–96	York C	15	8
1996–97	York C	41	2
1997–98	York C	27	1
1998–99	Scunthorpe U	24	0
Total:		**247**	**61**

BULL, Ronnie — Defender

b.Hackney 26-12-80

1998–99	Millwall	1	0
Total:		**1**	**0**

BULL, Steve — Forward

H: 5 11 W: 11 04 b.Tipton 28-3-65

Source: Apprentice. *Honours:* England Under-21, B, 13 full caps, 4 goals.

1985–86	WBA	1	0
1986–87	WBA	3	2
1986–87	Wolverhampton W	30	15
1987–88	Wolverhampton W	44	34
1988–89	Wolverhampton W	45	37
1989–90	Wolverhampton W	42	24
1990–91	Wolverhampton W	43	26
1991–92	Wolverhampton W	43	20
1992–93	Wolverhampton W	36	16
1993–94	Wolverhampton W	27	14
1994–95	Wolverhampton W	31	16
1995–96	Wolverhampton W	44	15
1996–97	Wolverhampton W	43	23
1997–98	Wolverhampton W	31	7
1998–99	Wolverhampton W	15	3
Total:		**478**	**252**

BULLARD, Jimmy — Midfield

H: 5 10 W: 11 07 b.Newham 23-10-78

Source: Gravesend & N.

1998–99	West Ham U	0	0

BULLIMORE, Wayne — Midfield

H: 5 10 W: 12 00 b.Mansfield 12-9-70

Source: Trainee. *Honours:* FA Schools.

1988–89	Manchester U	0	0
1989–90	Manchester U	0	0
1990–91	Manchester U	0	0
1990–91	Barnsley	0	0
1991–92	Barnsley	18	1
1992–93	Barnsley	17	0
1993–94	Barnsley	0	0
1993–94	Stockport Co	0	0
1993–94	Scunthorpe U	18	3
1994–95	Scunthorpe U	35	6
1995–96	Scunthorpe U	14	2
1995–96	Bradford C	2	0
1996–97	Bradford C	0	0
1996–97	Doncaster R (loan)	4	0
1996–97	Peterborough U	6	0
1997–98	Peterborough U	15	1
1998–99	Scarborough	35	1
Total:		**164**	**14**

BULLOCK, Darren — Midfield

H: 5 9 W: 12 10 b.Worcester 12-2-69

Source: Nuneaton Bor.

1993–94	Huddersfield T	20	3
1994–95	Huddersfield T	39	6
1995–96	Huddersfield T	42	6
1996–97	Huddersfield T	27	1
1996–97	Swindon T	13	1
1997–98	Swindon T	31	0
1998–99	Swindon T	22	1
1998–99	Bury	12	1
Total:		**206**	**19**

BULLOCK, Martin — Midfield

H: 5 6 W: 9 04 b.Derby 5-3-75

Source: Eastwood T. *Honours:* England Under-21.

1993–94	Barnsley	0	0
1994–95	Barnsley	29	0
1995–96	Barnsley	41	1
1996–97	Barnsley	28	0

1997–98	Barnsley	33	0
1998–99	Barnsley	32	2
Total:		**163**	**3**

BULLOCK, Matthew — Midfield

H: 5 8 W: 11 00 b.Stoke 1-11-80

Source: Trainee.

1997–98	Stoke C	0	0
1998–99	Stoke C	0	0

BULLOCK, Tony — Goalkeeper

H: 6 1 W: 14 01 b.Warrington 18-2-72

Source: Northwich V, Leek T.

1996–97	Barnsley	0	0
1997–98	Barnsley	0	0
1998–99	Barnsley	32	0
Total:		**32**	**0**

BULMAN, Dannie — Midfield

H: 5 9 W: 11 12 b.Ashford 24-1-79

Source: Ashford T.

1998–99	Wycombe W	11	1
Total:		**11**	**1**

BUNDY, Scott — Forward

H: 6 3 W: 12 00 b.Southampton 20-10-77

Source: Trainee.

1996–97	Portsmouth	0	0
1997–98	Portsmouth	0	0
1998–99	Portsmouth	0	0

BUNN, James — Forward

b.Tottenham 12-1-78

Source: Trainee. *Honours:* England Schools.

1996–97	Tottenham H	0	0
1997–98	Tottenham H	0	0
1998–99	Tottenham H	0	0

BURCHILL, Mark — Forward

H: 5 8 W: 9 9 b.Broxburn 18-8-80

Source: Celtic BC. *Honours:* Scotland Under-21.

1997–98	Celtic	0	0
1998–99	Celtic	21	9
Total:		**21**	**9**

BURDOCK, Gary — Forward

b.Dublin 9-3-80

Source: Trainee.

1997–98	Middlesbrough	0	0
1998–99	Middlesbrough	0	0

BURGESS, Ben — Forward

H: 6 3 W: 14 04 b.Buxton 9-11-81

Source: Trainee.

1998–99	Blackburn R	0	0

BURGESS, Daryl — Defender

H: 5 11 W: 11 04 b.Birmingham 24-1-71

Source: Trainee.

1989–90	WBA	34	0
1990–91	WBA	25	0
1991–92	WBA	36	2
1992–93	WBA	18	1
1993–94	WBA	43	2
1994–95	WBA	22	0
1995–96	WBA	45	2
1996–97	WBA	33	1
1997–98	WBA	27	1
1998–99	WBA	20	0
Total:		**303**	**9**

BURGESS, Mark — Defender

H: 5 11 W: 11 09 b.Ipswich 3-2-79

Source: Trainee.

1997–98	Ipswich T	0	0
1998–99	Ipswich T	0	0

BURGESS, Richard — Forward

H: 5 8 W: 11 00 b.Bromsgrove 18-8-78

Source: Trainee.

1996–97	Aston Villa	0	0
1997–98	Stoke C	0	0
1998–99	Stoke C	0	0

BURGHALL, Terry — Forward

H: 6 0 W: 11 06 b.Liverpool 25-9-78

Source: Liverpool Trainee.

1996–97	Newcastle U	0	0
1997–98	Newcastle U	0	0
1998–99	Newcastle U	0	0

BURKE, Alexander — Midfield

H: 5 7 W: 9 11 b.Glasgow 11-11-77

Source: Kilmarnock BC. *Honours:* Scotland Under-21.

1995–96	Kilmarnock	0	0
1996–97	Kilmarnock	17	3
1997–98	Kilmarnock	19	3
1998–99	Kilmarnock	19	0
Total:		**55**	**6**

BURLEY, Craig — Midfield

H: 6 1 W: 12 13 b.Ayr 24-9-71

Source: Trainee. *Honours:* Scotland Schools, Youth, Under-21, 30 full caps, 3 goals.

1989–90	Chelsea	0	0
1990–91	Chelsea	1	0
1991–92	Chelsea	8	0
1992–93	Chelsea	3	0
1993–94	Chelsea	23	3
1994–95	Chelsea	25	2
1995–96	Chelsea	22	0
1996–97	Chelsea	31	2
1997–98	Celtic	35	10
1998–99	Celtic	21	9
Total:		**169**	**26**

BURNETT, Wayne — Midfield

H: 5 10 W: 12 00 b.Lambeth 4-9-71

Source: Trainee.

1989–90	Leyton Orient	3	0
1990–91	Leyton Orient	1	0
1991–92	Leyton Orient	36	0
1992–93	Blackburn R	0	0
1993–94	Plymouth Arg	32	2
1994–95	Plymouth Arg	32	1
1995–96	Plymouth Arg	6	0
1995–96	Bolton W	1	0
1996–97	Bolton W	1	0
1996–97	Huddersfield T	35	0
1997–98	Huddersfield T	15	0
1997–98	Grimsby T	21	1
1998–99	Grimsby T	20	2
Total:		**203**	**6**

BURNS, Alex — Forward

H: 5 9 W: 12 09 b.Bellshill 4-8-73

Source: Shotts Bon-Accord.

1992–93	Motherwell	0	0
1993–94	Motherwell	4	1
1994–95	Motherwell	14	3
1995–96	Motherwell	28	3
1996–97	Motherwell	30	1
1997–98	Motherwell	0	0
From Heracles.			
1998–99	Southend U	31	5
Total:		**107**	**13**

BURNS, John — Midfield

H: 5 10 W: 11 02 b.Dublin 4-12-77

Source: Belvedere, Trainee.

1994–95	Nottingham F	0	0
1995–96	Nottingham F	0	0
1996–97	Nottingham F	0	0
1997–98	Nottingham F	0	0
1998–99	Nottingham F	0	0

BURNS, Liam — Defender

H: 6 0 W: 13 03 b.Belfast 30-10-78

Source: Trainee. *Honours:* Northern Ireland Under-21.

1997–98	Port Vale	1	0
1998–99	Port Vale	4	0
Total:		**5**	**0**

BURROWS, David — Defender

H: 5 8 W: 11 08 b.Dudley 25-10-68

Source: Apprentice. *Honours:* England Under-21, B.

1985–86	WBA	1	0
1986–87	WBA	15	1
1987–88	WBA	21	0
1988–89	WBA	9	0
1988–89	Liverpool	21	0
1989–90	Liverpool	26	0
1990–91	Liverpool	35	0
1991–92	Liverpool	30	1
1992–93	Liverpool	30	2
1993–94	Liverpool	4	0
1993–94	West Ham U	25	1
1994–95	West Ham U	4	0
1994–95	Everton	19	0
1994–95	Coventry C	11	0
1995–96	Coventry C	11	0
1996–97	Coventry C	18	0
1997–98	Coventry C	33	0
1998–99	Coventry C	23	0
Total:		**336**	**5**

BURROWS, Mark — Defender

H: 6 3 W: 12 08 b.Kettering 14-8-80

Source: Trainee.

1997–98	Coventry C	0	0
1998–99	Coventry C	0	0

BURT, David — Midfield

H: 5 9 W: 10 11 b.Newcastle 5-2-78

Source: Trainee.

1997–98	Newcastle U	0	0
1998–99	Newcastle U	0	0

BURTON, Deon — Forward

H: 5 9 W: 11 10 b.Reading 25-10-76

Source: Trainee. *Honours:* Jamaica 19 full caps, 4 goals.

1993–94	Portsmouth	2	0
1994–95	Portsmouth	7	2
1995–96	Portsmouth	32	7
1996–97	Portsmouth	21	1
1996–97	Cardiff C (loan)	5	2
1997–98	Derby Co	29	3
1998–99	Derby Co	21	9
1998–99	Barnsley (loan)	3	0
Total:		**120**	**24**

BURTON, Sagi — Defender

H: 6 2 W: 13 06 b.Birmingham 25-11-77

Source: Trainee.

1995–96	Crystal Palace	0	0
1996–97	Crystal Palace	0	0
1997–98	Crystal Palace	2	0
1998–99	Crystal Palace	23	1
Total:		**25**	**1**

BUSHELL, Steve — Midfield

H: 5 9 W: 11 06 b.Manchester 28-12-72

Source: Trainee.

1990–91	York C	15	0
1991–92	York C	16	0
1992–93	York C	8	0
1993–94	York C	31	4
1994–95	York C	10	1
1995–96	York C	23	0
1996–97	York C	31	3
1997–98	York C	40	2
1998–99	Blackpool	31	3
Total:		**205**	**13**

BUTLER, Ian — Defender

H: 5 8 W: 11 05 b.Barnsley 9-11-79

Source: Trainee.

1997–98	Barnsley	0	0
1998–99	Barnsley	0	0

BUTLER, Lee — Goalkeeper

H: 6 2 W: 13 00 b.Sheffield 30-5-66

Source: Haworth Colliery. *Honours:*

1986–87	Lincoln C	30	0
1987–88	Aston Villa	0	0
1988–89	Aston Villa	4	0
1989–90	Aston Villa	0	0
1990–91	Aston Villa	4	0
1990–91	Hull C (loan)	4	0
1991–92	Barnsley	43	0
1992–93	Barnsley	28	0
1993–94	Barnsley	37	0
1994–95	Barnsley	9	0
1995–96	Barnsley	3	0
1995–96	Scunthorpe U (loan)	2	0
1996–97	Wigan Ath	46	0
1997–98	Wigan Ath	17	0
1998–99	Dunfermline Ath	35	0
Total:		**262**	**0**

BUTLER, Martin — Forward

H: 5 11 W: 11 12 b.Wordsley 15-9-74

Source: Trainee.

1993–94	Walsall	15	3
1994–95	Walsall	8	0
1995–96	Walsall	28	4
1996–97	Walsall	23	1
1997–98	Cambridge U	31	10
1998–99	Cambridge U	46	17
Total:		**151**	**35**

BUTLER, Paul — Defender

H: 6 0 W: 13 05 b.Manchester 2-11-72

Source: Trainee.

1990–91	Rochdale	2	0
1991–92	Rochdale	25	0
1992–93	Rochdale	16	2
1993–94	Rochdale	38	2
1994–95	Rochdale	39	3
1995–96	Rochdale	38	3
1996–97	Bury	41	2
1997–98	Bury	43	2
1998–99	Sunderland	44	2
Total:		**286**	**16**

BUTLER, Peter — Midfield

H: 5 9 W: 11 01 b.Halifax 27-8-66

Source: Apprentice.

1984–85	Huddersfield T	4	0
1985–86	Huddersfield T	1	0
1985–86	Cambridge U (loan)	14	1
1986–87	Bury	11	0
1986–87	Cambridge U	29	4

Butler, Steve

1987–88	Cambridge U	26	5
1987–88	Southend U	15	3
1988–89	Southend U	35	2
1989–90	Southend U	41	2
1990–91	Southend U	42	2
1991–92	Southend U	9	0
1991–92	Huddersfield T (loan)	7	0
1992–93	West Ham U	39	2
1993–94	West Ham U	26	1
1994–95	West Ham U	5	0
1994–95	Notts Co	20	0
1995–96	Notts Co	0	0
1995–96	Grimsby T (loan)	3	0
1995–96	WBA (loan)	9	0
1996–97	WBA	17	0
1997–98	WBA	34	0
1998–99	Halifax T	33	1
Total:		**420**	**23**

BUTLER, Steve — Forward

H: 6 1 W: 12 02 b.Birmingham 21-1-62

Source: Windsor & Eton, Wokingham T.

1984–85	Brentford	3	1
1985–86	Brentford	18	2
To Maidstone U (1986)			
1989–90	Maidstone U	44	21
1990–91	Maidstone U	32	20
1990–91	Watford	10	1
1991–92	Watford	43	8
1992–93	Watford	9	0
1992–93	Bournemouth (loan)	1	0
1992–93	Cambridge U	23	6
1993–94	Cambridge U	33	21
1994–95	Cambridge U	37	14
1995–96	Cambridge U	16	10
1995–96	Gillingham	20	5
1996–97	Gillingham	38	9
1997–98	Gillingham	43	6
1998–99	Gillingham	7	0
1998–99	Peterborough U	14	2
Total:		**391**	**126**

BUTLER, Thomas — Midfield

H: 5 8 W: 10 07 b.Ballymun 25-4-81

Source: Trainee.

1998–99	Sunderland	0	0

BUTLER, Tony — Defender

H: 6 2 W: 12 03 b.Stockport 28-9-72

Source: Trainee.

1990–91	Gillingham	6	0
1991–92	Gillingham	5	0
1992–93	Gillingham	41	0
1993–94	Gillingham	27	1
1994–95	Gillingham	33	2
1995–96	Gillingham	36	2
1996–97	Blackpool	42	0
1997–98	Blackpool	37	0
1998–99	Blackpool	20	0
1998–99	Port Vale	4	0
Total:		**251**	**5**

BUTT, Nicky — Midfield

H: 5 10 W: 11 05 b.Manchester 21-1-75

Source: Trainee. *Honours:* England Schools, Youth, Under-21, 8 full caps.

1992–93	Manchester U	1	0
1993–94	Manchester U	1	0
1994–95	Manchester U	22	1
1995–96	Manchester U	32	2
1996–97	Manchester U	26	5
1997–98	Manchester U	33	3
1998–99	Manchester U	31	2
Total:		**146**	**13**

BUTTERFIELD, Danny — Defender

H: 5 9 W: 11 00 b.Boston 21-11-79

Source: Trainee. *Honours:* England Youth.

1997–98	Grimsby T	7	0
1998–99	Grimsby T	12	0
Total:		**19**	**0**

BUTTERS, Guy — Defender

H: 6 3 W: 13 12 b.Hillingdon 30-10-69

Source: Trainee. *Honours:* England Under-21.

1988–89	Tottenham H	28	1
1989–90	Tottenham H	7	0
1989–90	Southend U (loan)	16	3
1990–91	Portsmouth	23	0
1991–92	Portsmouth	33	2
1992–93	Portsmouth	15	1
1993–94	Portsmouth	15	1
1994–95	Portsmouth	24	0
1994–95	Oxford U (loan)	3	1
1995–96	Portsmouth	37	2
1996–97	Portsmouth	7	0
1996–97	Gillingham	30	0
1997–98	Gillingham	31	7
1998–99	Gillingham	23	3
Total:		**292**	**21**

BUXTON, Nick — Goalkeeper

H: 6 0 W: 13 00 b.Doncaster 6-9-76

1996–97	Bury	0	0
From Goole T.			
1997–98	Scarborough	3	0

1998–99	Scarborough	0	0
Total:		**3**	**0**

BYFIELD, Darren — Forward

H: 5 11 W: 11 11 b.Sutton Coldfield 29-9-76

Source: Trainee.

1993–94	Aston Villa	0	0
1994–95	Aston Villa	0	0
1995–96	Aston Villa	0	0
1996–97	Aston Villa	0	0
1997–98	Aston Villa	7	0
1998–99	Aston Villa	0	0
1998–99	Preston NE (loan)	5	1
Total:		**12**	**1**

BYRNE, Chris — Midfield

H: 5 9 W: 10 02 b.Hulme 9-2-75

Source: Crewe Alex, Macclesfield T.

1997–98	Sunderland	8	0
1997–98	Stockport Co	26	7
1998–99	Stockport Co	11	2
Total:		**45**	**9**

BYRNE, Des — Defender

b.Dublin 10-4-81

Source: Trainee.

1998–99	Stockport Co	2	0
Total:		**2**	**0**

BYRNE, Niall — Forward

H: 5 8 W: 11 00 b.Dublin 3-9-79

Source: Trainee.

1996–97	Liverpool	0	0
1997–98	Liverpool	0	0
1998–99	Liverpool	0	0

BYRNE, Paul — Midfield

H: 5 11 W: 13 00 b.Dublin 30-6-72

Source: Trainee. *Honours:* Eire Youth.

1989–90	Oxford U	3	0
1990–91	Oxford U	2	0
1991–92	Oxford U	1	0
From Bangor			
1993–94	Celtic	22	2
1994–95	Celtic	6	2
1994–95	Brighton & HA (loan)	8	1
1995–96	Southend U	41	5
1996–97	Southend U	32	1
1997–98	Southend U	10	0
1998–99	Southend U	0	0
Total:		**125**	**11**

BYWATER, Steve — Goalkeeper

b.Manchester 7-6-81

Source: Trainee. *Honours:* England Youth.

1997–98	Rochdale	0	0
1998–99	West Ham U	0	0

CABALLERO, Fabian — Forward

b.Argentina 31-1-78

Source: Cerro Porteno.

1998–99	Arsenal	1	0
Total:		**1**	**0**

CADAMARTERI, Danny — Forward

H: 5 8 W: 12 11 b.Bradford 12-10-79

Source: Trainee. *Honours:* England Youth, Under-21.

1996–97	Everton	1	0
1997–98	Everton	26	4
1998–99	Everton	30	4
Total:		**57**	**8**

CADETTE, Nathan — Midfield

H: 5 8 W: 11 11 b.Cardiff 6-1-80

Source: Trainee.

1997–98	Cardiff C	4	0
1998–99	Cardiff C	0	0
Total:		**4**	**0**

CAHILL, Tim — Midfield

H: 5 10 W: 10 11 b.Sydney 6-12-79

Source: Sydney U.

1997–98	Millwall	1	0
1998–99	Millwall	36	6
Total:		**37**	**6**

CAIG, Tony — Goalkeeper

H: 6 1 W: 12 00 b.Whitehaven 11-4-74

Source: Trainee.

1992–93	Carlisle U	1	0
1993–94	Carlisle U	20	0
1994–95	Carlisle U	40	0
1995–96	Carlisle U	33	0
1996–97	Carlisle U	46	0
1997–98	Carlisle U	46	0
1998–99	Carlisle U	37	0
1998–99	Blackpool	10	0
Total:		**233**	**0**

CALDERWOOD, Colin — Defender

H: 6 0 W: 13 00 b.Glasgow 20-1-65

Source: Amateur. *Honours:* Scotland 34 full caps, 1 goal. Football League.

1981–82	Mansfield T	1	0
1982–83	Mansfield T	28	0
1983–84	Mansfield T	30	1
1984–85	Mansfield T	41	0
1985–86	Swindon T	46	2
1986–87	Swindon T	46	1
1987–88	Swindon T	34	1
1988–89	Swindon T	43	4
1989–90	Swindon T	46	3
1990–91	Swindon T	23	2
1991–92	Swindon T	46	5
1992–93	Swindon T	46	2
1993–94	Tottenham H	26	0
1994–95	Tottenham H	36	2
1995–96	Tottenham H	29	0
1996–97	Tottenham H	34	0
1997–98	Tottenham H	26	4
1998–99	Tottenham H	12	0
1998–99	Aston Villa	8	0
Total:		**601**	**27**

CALDWELL, Gary — Defender

H: 5 11 W: 11 10 b.Stirling 12-4-82

Source: Trainee.

1998–99	Newcastle U	0	0

CALDWELL, Stephen — Defender

H: 6 0 W: 11 05 b.Stirling 12-9-80

Source: Trainee.

1997–98	Newcastle U	0	0
1998–99	Newcastle U	0	0

CALLAGHAN, Stuart — Midfield

H: 5 8 W: 10 03 b.Calderbank 20-7-76

Source: Blantyre BC.

1994–95	Hearts	0	0
1995–96	Hearts	1	0
1996–97	Hearts	4	0
1997–98	Hearts	1	0
1998–99	Hearts	2	0
Total:		**8**	**0**

CALVO-GARCIA, Alexander — Midfield

H: 5 11 W: 11 10 b.Ordizia 1-1-72

Source: Eibar.

1996–97	Scunthorpe U	13	1
1997–98	Scunthorpe U	44	6
1998–99	Scunthorpe U	43	9
Total:		**100**	**16**

CAMERON, Colin — Forward

H: 5 6 W: 9 06 b.Kirkcaldy 23-10-72

Source: Lochore Welfare. *Honours:* Scotland B, 2 full caps.

1990–91	Raith R	0	0
1991–92	Sligo R (loan)	0	0
1992–93	Raith R	16	1
1993–94	Raith R	41	6
1994–95	Raith R	35	7
1995–96	Raith R	30	9
1995–96	Hearts	4	2
1996–97	Hearts	36	7
1997–98	Hearts	31	8
1998–99	Hearts	11	6
Total:		**204**	**46**

CAMPAGNA, Sam — Midfield

b.Worcester 19-11-80

Source: Trainee.

1998–99	Swindon T	2	0
Total:		**2**	**0**

CAMPBELL, Andy — Forward

H: 6 0 W: 11 13 b.Middlesbrough 18-4-79

Source: Trainee. *Honours:* England Youth.

1995–96	Middlesbrough	2	0
1996–97	Middlesbrough	3	0
1997–98	Middlesbrough	7	0
1998–99	Middlesbrough	8	0
1998–99	Sheffield U (loan)	11	3
Total:		**31**	**3**

CAMPBELL, James — Defender

H: 6 2 W: 11 12 b.Kent 16-11-79

Source: Trainee.

1998–99	Peterborough U	0	0

CAMPBELL, Jamie — Defender

H: 6 1 W: 12 07 b.Birmingham 21-10-72

Source: Trainee.

1991–92	Luton T	11	0
1992–93	Luton T	9	1
1993–94	Luton T	16	0

1994–95	Luton T	0	0
1994–95	Mansfield T (loan)	3	1
1994–95	Cambridge U (loan)	12	0
1995–96	Barnet	24	1
1996–97	Barnet	43	4
1997–98	Cambridge U	46	2
1998–99	Cambridge U	45	4
Total:		**209**	**13**

CAMPBELL, Jamie — Midfield

b.Glasgow 2-12-80

Source: Trainee.

1998–99	Oldham Ath	0	0

CAMPBELL, Kevin — Forward

H: 6 1 W: 13 08 b.Lambeth 4-2-70

Source: Trainee. *Honours:* England Under-21, B.

1987–88	Arsenal	1	0
1988–89	Arsenal	0	0
1988–89	Leyton Orient (loan)	16	9
1989–90	Arsenal	15	2
1989–90	Leicester C (loan)	11	5
1990–91	Arsenal	22	9
1991–92	Arsenal	31	13
1992–93	Arsenal	37	4
1993–94	Arsenal	37	14
1994–95	Arsenal	23	4
1995–96	Nottingham F	21	3
1996–97	Nottingham F	17	6
1997–98	Nottingham F	42	23
1998–99	Trabzonspor	17	5
1998–99	Everton	8	9
Total:		**298**	**106**

CAMPBELL, Neil — Forward

H: 6 2 W: 13 10 b.Middlesbrough 26-1-77

Source: Trainee.

1995–96	York C	0	0
1996–97	York C	11	1
1997–98	York C	1	0
1997–98	Scarborough	34	7
1998–99	Scarborough	11	0
1998–99	Southend U	12	2
Total:		**69**	**10**

CAMPBELL, Paul — Midfield

H: 6 1 W: 11 00 b.Middlesbrough 29-1-80

Source: Trainee.

1997–98	Darlington	6	1
1998–99	Darlington	9	1
Total:		**15**	**2**

CAMPBELL, Sean — Midfield

b.Bristol 31-12-74

1997–98	Peterborough U	0	0
1998–99	Peterborough U	0	0

CAMPBELL, Sol — Defender

H: 6 2 1 W: 14 04 b.Newham 18-9-74

Source: Trainee. *Honours:* England Youth, Under-21, 27 full caps.

1992–93	Tottenham H	1	1
1993–94	Tottenham H	34	0
1994–95	Tottenham H	30	0
1995–96	Tottenham H	31	1
1996–97	Tottenham H	38	0
1997–98	Tottenham H	34	0
1998–99	Tottenham H	37	6
Total:		**205**	**8**

CAMPBELL, Stuart — Midfield

H: 5 10 W: 10 08 b.Corby 9-12-77

Source: Trainee. *Honours:* Scotland Under-21.

1996–97	Leicester C	10	0
1997–98	Leicester C	11	0
1998–99	Leicester C	12	0
Total:		**33**	**0**

CANAVAN, Michael — Forward

H: 6 1 W: 12 02 b.South Shields 17 9 80

Source: Trainee.

1998–99	Middlesbrough	0	0

CANHAM, Scott — Midfield

H: 5 10 W: 11 08 b.London 5-11-74

Source: Trainee.

1993–94	West Ham U	0	0
1994–95	West Ham U	0	0
1995–96	West Ham U	0	0
1995–96	Torquay U (loan)	3	0
1995–96	Brentford (loan)	14	0
1996–97	Brentford	13	1
1997–98	Brentford	22	0
1998–99	Leyton Orient	8	0
Total:		**60**	**1**

CANOVILLE, Dean — Midfield

H: 6 0 W: 11 10 b.Perivale 30-11-78

Source: Trainee.

1995–96	Millwall	0	0
1996–97	Millwall	2	0

1997–98	Millwall	0	0
1998–99	Millwall	0	0
Total:		**2**	**0**

CANOVILLE, Lee — Defender

b.Ealing 14-3-81

Source: Trainee. *Honours:* FA Schools, England Youth.

1998–99	Arsenal	0	0

CAPLETON, Mel — Goalkeeper

H: 6 0 W: 13 03 b.London 24-10-73

Source: Trainee.

1992–93	Southend U	0	0
1993–94	Blackpool	0	0
1994–95	Blackpool	10	0
1995–96	Blackpool	1	0
1996–97	Leyton Orient	0	0
1997–98	Leyton Orient	0	0
1998–99	Leyton Orient	0	0
From Grays Ath.			
1998–99	Southend U	14	0
Total:		**25**	**0**

CAPPER, David — Defender

H: 6 1 W: 12 02 b.Stoke 8-9-78

Source: Trainee.

1997–98	Sheffield U	0	0
1998–99	Sheffield U	0	0

CARBON, Matt — Defender

H: 6 2 W: 12 05 b.Nottingham 8-6-75

Source: Trainee. *Honours:* England Under-21.

1992–93	Lincoln C	1	0
1993–94	Lincoln C	9	0
1994–95	Lincoln C	33	7
1995–96	Lincoln C	26	3
1995–96	Derby Co	6	0
1996–97	Derby Co	10	0
1997–98	Derby Co	4	0
1997–98	WBA	16	1
1998–99	WBA	39	2
Total:		**144**	**13**

CARBONARI, Horace Angel — Defender

H: 6 3 W: 13 02 b.Rosario 2-5-73

Source: Rosario Central.

1998–99	Derby Co	29	5
Total:		**29**	**5**

CARBONE, Benito — Forward

H: 5 6 W: 10 09 b.Begnara 14-8-71

1988–89	Torino	3	0
1989–90	Torino	5	0
1990–91	Reggina	31	5
1991–92	Casert	31	4
1992–93	Ascoli	28	6
1993–94	Torino	28	3
1994–95	Napoli	29	5
1995–96	Internazionale	31	2
1996–97	Internazionale	1	0
1996–97	Sheffield W	25	6
1997–98	Sheffield W	33	9
1998–99	Sheffield W	31	8
Total:		**276**	**48**

CARDEN, Paul — Midfield

H: 5 9 W: 11 10 b.Liverpool 29-3-79

Source: Trainee.

1996–97	Blackpool	1	0
1997–98	Blackpool	0	0
1997–98	Rochdale	7	0
1998–99	Rochdale	25	0
Total:		**33**	**0**

CAREY, Brian — Defender

H: 6 3 W: 13 02 b.Cork 31-5-68

Source: Cork C. *Honours:* Eire 3 full caps.

1989–90	Manchester U	0	0
1990–91	Manchester U	0	0
1990–91	Wrexham (loan)	3	0
1991–92	Manchester U	0	0
1991–92	Wrexham (loan)	13	1
1992–93	Manchester U	0	0
1993–94	Leicester C	27	0
1994–95	Leicester C	12	0
1995–96	Leicester C	19	1
1996–97	Wrexham	38	0
1997–98	Wrexham	43	1
1998–99	Wrexham	36	2
Total:		**191**	**5**

CAREY, Louis — Defender

H: 5 10 W: 12 05 b.Bristol 20-1-77

Source: Trainee. *Honours:* Scotland Under-21.

1995–96	Bristol C	23	0
1996–97	Bristol C	42	0
1997–98	Bristol C	38	0
1998–99	Bristol C	41	0
Total:		**144**	**0**

CAREY, Shaun — Midfield

H: 5 10 W: 11 03 b.Kettering 13-5-76

Source: Trainee.

1994–95	Norwich C	0	0
1995–96	Norwich C	9	0
1996–97	Norwich C	14	0
1997–98	Norwich C	14	0
1998–99	Norwich C	10	0
Total:		**47**	**0**

CARLISLE, Clarke — Defender

H: 6 1 W: 12 07 b.Preston 14-10-79

Source: Trainee.

1997–98	Blackpool	11	2
1998–99	Blackpool	39	1
Total:		**50**	**3**

CARLISLE, Wayne — Midfield

H: 6 0 W: 11 06 b.Lisburn 9-9-79

Source: Trainee.

1996–97	Crystal Palace	0	0
1997–98	Crystal Palace	0	0
1998–99	Crystal Palace	6	0
Total:		**6**	**0**

CARPENTER, Richard — Midfield

H: 6 0 W: 13 01 b.Sheppey 30-9-72

Source: Trainee.

1990–91	Gillingham	9	1
1991–92	Gillingham	3	0
1992–93	Gillingham	28	0
1993–94	Gillingham	40	3
1994–95	Gillingham	29	0
1995–96	Gillingham	12	0
1996–97	Gillingham	1	0
1996–97	Fulham	34	5
1997–98	Fulham	24	2
1998–99	Cardiff C	42	1
Total:		**222**	**12**

CARR-LAWTON, Colin — Forward

H: 5 10 W: 11 06 b.South Shields 5-9-78

Source: Trainee.

1996–97	Burnley	0	0
1997–98	Burnley	1	0
1998–99	Burnley	4	0
Total:		**5**	**0**

CARR, Darren — Defender

H: 6 2 W: 13 07 b.Bristol 4-9-68

Source: Trainee.

1985–86	Bristol R	1	0
1986–87	Bristol R	20	0
1987–88	Bristol R	9	0
1987–88	Newport Co	9	0
1987–88	Sheffield U	3	0
1988–89	Sheffield U	10	1
1989–90	Sheffield U	0	0
1990–91	Sheffield U	0	0
1990–91	Crewe Alex	36	0
1991–92	Crewe Alex	36	3
1992–93	Crewe Alex	32	2
1993–94	Chesterfield	28	1
1994–95	Chesterfield	35	2
1995–96	Chesterfield	1	0
1996–97	Chesterfield	12	0
1997–98	Chesterfield	10	1
1998–99	Gillingham	30	2
Total:		**272**	**12**

CARR, Graeme — Midfield

H: 5 10 W: 11 00 b.Chester-le-Street 28-10-78

Source: Trainee.

1997–98	Scarborough	0	0
1998–99	Scarborough	10	0
Total:		**10**	**0**

CARR, Stephen — Defender

H: 5 9 W: 12 04 b.Dublin 29-8-76

Source: Trainee. *Honours:* Eire Under-21, 3 full caps.

1993–94	Tottenham H	1	0
1994–95	Tottenham H	0	0
1995–96	Tottenham H	0	0
1996–97	Tottenham H	26	0
1997–98	Tottenham H	38	0
1998–99	Tottenham H	37	0
Total:		**102**	**0**

CARRAGHER, James — Midfield

H: 6 1 W: 13 00 b.Liverpool 28-1-78

Source: Trainee. *Honours:* England Youth, Under-21, B, 1 full cap.

1995–96	Liverpool	0	0
1996–97	Liverpool	2	1
1997–98	Liverpool	20	0
1998–99	Liverpool	34	1
Total:		**56**	**2**

CARRAGHER, Matthew — Defender

H: 5 9 W: 11 06 b.Liverpool 14-1-76

Source: Trainee.

1993–94	Wigan Ath	32	0
1994–95	Wigan Ath	41	0
1995–96	Wigan Ath	28	0
1996–97	Wigan Ath	18	0
1997–98	Port Vale	26	0
1998–99	Port Vale	10	0
Total:		**155**	**0**

CARRICK, Michael — Forward

b.Wallsend 28-7-81

Source: Trainee.

1998–99	West Ham U	0	0

CARROLL, Dave — Midfield

H: 6 0 W: 11 12 b.Paisley 20-9-66

Source: Ruislip Manor. *Honours:* England Schools.

1993–94	Wycombe W	41	6
1994–95	Wycombe W	41	6
1995–96	Wycombe W	46	8
1996–97	Wycombe W	43	9
1997–98	Wycombe W	39	1
1998–99	Wycombe W	32	6
Total:		**242**	**36**

CARROLL, Roy — Goalkeeper

H: 6 2 W: 13 05 b.Enniskillen 30-9-77

Source: Trainee. *Honours:* Northern Ireland Under-21, 2 full caps.

1995–96	Hull C	23	0
1996–97	Hull C	23	0
1996–97	Wigan Ath	0	0
1997–98	Wigan Ath	29	0
1998–99	Wigan Ath	43	0
Total:		**118**	**0**

CARRUTHERS, Martin — Forward

H: 5 11 W: 11 07 b.Nottingham 7-8-72

Source: Trainee.

1990–91	Aston Villa	0	0
1991–92	Aston Villa	3	0
1992–93	Aston Villa	1	0
1992–93	Hull C (loan)	13	6
1993–94	Stoke C	34	5
1994–95	Stoke C	32	5
1995–96	Stoke C	24	3
1996–97	Stoke C	1	0
1996–97	Peterborough U	14	4
1997–98	Peterborough U	39	15
1998–99	Peterborough U	14	2
1998–99	York C (loan)	6	0
1998–99	Darlington	11	2
Total:		**192**	**42**

CARRUTHERS, Matt — Forward

b.Dover 22-7-76

Source: Dover Ath.

1998–99	Mansfield T	5	0
Total:		**5**	**0**

CARSLEY, Lee — Midfield

H: 5 9 W: 12 00 b.Birmingham 28-2-74

Source: Trainee. *Honours:* Eire 11 full caps.

1992–93	Derby Co	0	0
1993–94	Derby Co	0	0
1994–95	Derby Co	23	2
1995–96	Derby Co	35	1
1996–97	Derby Co	24	0
1997–98	Derby Co	34	1
1998–99	Derby Co	22	1
1998–99	Blackburn R	8	0
Total:		**146**	**5**

CARSON, Danny — Midfield

H: 5 6 W: 10 07 b.Huyton 2-2-81

Source: Trainee.

1998–99	Chester C	2	0
Total:		**2**	**0**

CARSS, Tony — Midfield

H: 5 10 W: 11 08 b.Alnwick 31-3-76

Source: Bradford C Trainee.

1994–95	Blackburn R	0	0
1995–96	Darlington	28	2
1996–97	Darlington	29	0
1997–98	Cardiff C	42	1
1998–99	Chesterfield	4	0
Total:		**103**	**3**

CARTER, Alfonso — Midfield

b.Birmingham 23-8-80

Source: Trainee.

1998–99	Walsall	1	0
Total:		**1**	**0**

CARTER, Jimmy — Midfield

H: 5 10 W: 11 02 b.Hammersmith 9-11-65

Source: Apprentice.

1983–84	Crystal Palace	0	0

1984–85	Crystal Palace	0	0
1985–86	QPR	0	0
1986–87	Millwall	12	1
1987–88	Millwall	26	0
1988–89	Millwall	20	5
1989–90	Millwall	28	2
1990–91	Millwall	24	2
1990–91	Liverpool	5	0
1991–92	Liverpool	0	0
1991–92	Arsenal	6	0
1992–93	Arsenal	16	2
1993–94	Arsenal	0	0
1993–94	Oxford U (loan)	5	0
1994–95	Arsenal	3	0
1994–95	Oxford U (loan)	4	0
1995–96	Portsmouth	35	4
1996–97	Portsmouth	27	1
1997–98	Portsmouth	10	0
1998–99	Millwall	16	0
Total:		**237**	**17**

CARTER, Michael — Forward

b.Darlington 13-11-80

Source: Trainee.

1998–99	Darlington	1	1
Total:		**1**	**1**

CARTER, Nicky — Forward

H: 5 11 W: 11 07 b.Stoke 29-11-81

Source: Trainee.

1998–99	Nottingham F	0	0

CARTER, Tim — Goalkeeper

H: 6 2 W: 12 08 b.Bristol 5-10-67

Source: Apprentice. *Honours:* England Youth.

1985–86	Bristol R	2	0
1986–87	Bristol R	38	0
1987–88	Bristol R	7	0
1987–88	Newport Co (loan)	1	0
1987–88	Carlisle U (loan)	4	0
1987–88	Sunderland	1	0
1988–89	Sunderland	2	0
1988–89	Bristol C (loan)	3	0
1989–90	Sunderland	18	0
1990–91	Sunderland	1	0
1991–92	Sunderland	2	0
1991–92	Birmingham C (loan)	2	0
1992–93	Sunderland	13	0
1993–94	Hartlepool U	18	0
1993–94	Millwall	2	0
1994–95	Millwall	2	0
1995–96	Oxford U	12	0
1995–96	Millwall	4	0
1996–97	Millwall	46	0
1997–98	Millwall	12	0
1998–99	Halifax T	10	0
Total:		**200**	**0**

CARTWRIGHT, Jamie — Midfield

H: 5 7 W: 9 06 b.Lichfield 11-10-79

Source: Trainee.

1996–97	Stoke C	0	0
1997–98	Stoke C	0	0
1998–99	Stoke C	0	0

CARTWRIGHT, Lee — Forward

H: 5 8 W: 10 06 b.Rossendale 19-9-72

Source: Trainee.

1990–91	Preston NE	14	1
1991–92	Preston NE	33	4
1992–93	Preston NE	34	3
1993–94	Preston NE	39	1
1994–95	Preston NE	36	1
1995–96	Preston NE	26	3
1996–97	Preston NE	14	1
1997–98	Preston NE	36	2
1998–99	Preston NE	27	4
Total:		**259**	**20**

CARTWRIGHT, Mark — Goalkeeper

H: 6 2 W: 13 06 b.Chester 13-1-73

Source: York C.

1994–95	Wrexham	0	0
1995–96	Wrexham	0	0
1996–97	Wrexham	3	0
1997–98	Wrexham	4	0
1998–99	Wrexham	30	0
Total:		**37**	**0**

CASEY, Ryan — Midfield

H: 6 0 W: 10 12 b.Coventry 3-1-79

Source: Trainee.

1996–97	Swansea C	10	0
1997–98	Swansea C	6	0
1998–99	Swansea C	10	1
Total:		**26**	**1**

CASIRAGHI, Pierluigi — Forward

H: 5 11 W: 12 02 b.Milan 4-3-69

Honours: Italy 44 full caps, 13 goals.

1985–86	Monza	12	1
1986–87	Monza	25	6
1987–88	Monza	30	12
1988–89	Monza	27	9
1989–90	Juventus	23	4

1990–91	Juventus	24	8
1991–92	Juventus	33	7
1992–93	Juventus	18	1
1993–94	Lazio	26	4
1994–95	Lazio	34	12
1995–96	Lazio	28	14
1996–97	Lazio	24	8
1997–98	Lazio	28	3
1998–99	Chelsea	10	1
Total:		**342**	**90**

CASKEY, Darren — Midfield

H: 5 8 W: 11 09 b.Basildon 21-8-74

Source: Trainee. *Honours:* England Schools, Youth.

1991–92	Tottenham H	0	0
1992–93	Tottenham H	0	0
1993–94	Tottenham H	25	4
1994–95	Tottenham H	4	0
1995–96	Tottenham H	3	0
1995–96	Watford (loan)	6	1
1995–96	Reading	15	2
1996–97	Reading	35	0
1997–98	Reading	23	0
1998–99	Reading	42	7
Total:		**153**	**14**

CASPER, Chris — Defender

H: 6 0 W: 12 02 b.Burnley 28-4-75

Source: Trainee. *Honours:* England Youth, Under-21.

1992–93	Manchester U	0	0
1993–94	Manchester U	0	0
1994–95	Manchester U	0	0
1995–96	Manchester U	0	0
1995–96	Bournemouth (loan)	16	1
1996–97	Manchester U	2	0
1997–98	Manchester U	0	0
1997–98	Swindon T (loan)	9	1
1998–99	Manchester U	0	0
1998–99	Reading	32	0
Total:		**59**	**2**

CASS, Matthew — Defender

H: 5 7 W: 10 05 b.Liverpool 16-12-79

Source: Trainee.

1998–99	QPR	0	0

CASSIDY, Jamie — Midfield

H: 5 9 W: 10 08 b.Liverpool 21-11-77

Source: Trainee. *Honours:* England Schools, Youth.

1994–95	Liverpool	0	0
1995–96	Liverpool	0	0
1996–97	Liverpool	0	0
1997–98	Liverpool	0	0
1998–99	Liverpool	0	0

CASTLE, Steve — Midfield

H: 5 11 W: 11 07 b.Ilford 17-5-66

Source: Apprentice.

1984–85	Orient	21	1
1985–86	Orient	23	4
1986–87	Orient	24	5
1987–88	Orient	42	10
1988–89	Orient	24	6
1989–90	Orient	27	7
1990–91	Orient	45	12
1991–92	Orient	37	10
1992–93	Plymouth Arg	31	11
1993–94	Plymouth Arg	44	21
1994–95	Plymouth Arg	26	3
1995–96	Birmingham C	15	1
1995–96	Gillingham (loan)	6	1
1996–97	Birmingham C	8	0
1996–97	Leyton Orient (loan)	4	1
1996–97	Peterborough U	0	0
1997–98	Peterborough U	37	3
1998–99	Peterborough U	26	4
Total:		**440**	**100**

CASTLEDINE, Stewart — Midfield

H: 6 1 W: 12 00 b.Wandsworth 22-1-73

Source: Trainee.

1991–92	Wimbledon	2	0
1992–93	Wimbledon	0	0
1993–94	Wimbledon	3	1
1994–95	Wimbledon	6	1
1995–96	Wimbledon	4	1
1995–96	Wycombe W (loan)	7	3
1996–97	Wimbledon	6	1
1997–98	Wimbledon	6	0
1998–99	Wimbledon	1	0
Total:		**35**	**7**

CATAROCHE, David — Midfield

H: 5 7 W: 11 07 b.Leeds 13-12-80

Source: Trainee.

1997–98	Barnsley	0	0
1998–99	Barnsley	0	0

CAVE, Vincent — Midfield

b.Harrow 16-5-79

Source: Trainee.

1997–98	Watford	0	0
1998–99	Watford	0	0

CAWLEY, Alan — Midfield

H: 6 2 W: 10 01 b.Sligo 3-1-82

Source: Belvedere.

1998–99	Leeds U	0	0

CHADWICK, Gareth — Midfield

b.Warrington 23-9-79

Source: Trainee.

1998–99	Crewe Alex	0	0

CHADWICK, Luke — Forward

H: 5 11 W: 10 09 b.Cambridge 18-11-80

Source: Trainee. *Honours:* England Youth.

1998–99	Manchester U	0	0

CHALK, Martyn — Forward

H: 5 6 W: 11 03 b.Swindon 30-8-69

Source: Louth U.

1990–91	Derby Co	0	0
1991–92	Derby Co	7	1
1992–93	Derby Co	0	0
1993–94	Derby Co	0	0
1994–95	Stockport Co	33	6
1995–96	Stockport Co	10	0
1995–96	Wrexham	19	4
1996–97	Wrexham	43	1
1997–98	Wrexham	26	1
1998–99	Wrexham	28	0
Total:		**166**	**13**

CHALLINOR, Dave — Defender

H: 6 1 W: 12 00 b.Chester 2-10-75

Source: Brombrough Pool. *Honours:* England Schools.

1994–95	Tranmere R	0	0
1995–96	Tranmere R	0	0
1996–97	Tranmere R	5	0
1997–98	Tranmere R	32	1
1998–99	Tranmere R	34	2
Total:		**71**	**3**

CHALLIS, Trevor — Defender

H: 5 8 W: 11 06 b.Paddington 23-10-75

Source: Trainee. *Honours:* England Youth, Under-21.

1994–95	QPR	0	0
1995–96	QPR	11	0
1996–97	QPR	2	0
1997–98	QPR	0	0
1998–99	Bristol R	38	0
Total:		**51**	**0**

CHAMBERLAIN, Alec — Goalkeeper

H: 6 2 W: 13 10 b.March 20-6-64

Source: Ramsey T.

1981–82	Ipswich T	0	0
1982–83	Colchester U	0	0
1983–84	Colchester U	46	0
1984–85	Colchester U	46	0
1985–86	Colchester U	46	0
1986–87	Colchester U	46	0
1987–88	Everton	0	0
1987–88	Tranmere R (loan)	15	0
1988–89	Luton T	6	0
1989–90	Luton T	38	0
1990–91	Luton T	38	0
1991–92	Luton T	24	0
1992–93	Luton T	32	0
1992–93	Chelsea (loan)	0	0
1993–94	Sunderland	43	0
1994–95	Sunderland	18	0
1994–95	Liverpool (loan)	0	0
1995–96	Sunderland	29	0
1996–97	Watford	4	0
1997–98	Watford	46	0
1998–99	Watford	46	0
Total:		**523**	**0**

CHAMBERS, Adam — Defender

H: 5 10 W: 11 08 b.Sandwell 20-11-80

Source: Trainee. *Honours:* England Youth.

1998–99	WBA	0	0

CHAMBERS, James — Defender

H: 5 10 W: 11 08 b.Sandwell 20-11-80

Source: Trainee. *Honours:* England Youth.

1998–99	WBA	0	0

CHAMBERS, Leroy — Forward

H: 5 11 W: 11 08 b.Sheffield 25-10-72

Source: Trainee.

1991–92	Sheffield W	0	0
1992–93	Sheffield W	0	0
1993–94	Sheffield W	0	0
1994–95	Chester C	13	0
1995–96	Chester C	8	1
1996–97	Chesterfield	0	0
From Boston U.			
1997–98	Macclesfield T	21	4
1998–99	Macclesfield T	0	0
Total:		**42**	**5**

CHANNING, Justin — Defender

H: 5 11 W: 11 07 b.Reading 19-11-68

Source: Apprentice. *Honours:* England Youth.

1986–87	QPR	2	0
1987–88	QPR	14	1
1988–89	QPR	9	1
1989–90	QPR	23	2
1990–91	QPR	5	0
1991–92	QPR	0	0
1992–93	QPR	2	1
1992–93	Bristol R	25	3
1993–94	Bristol R	29	5
1994–95	Bristol R	40	2
1995–96	Bristol R	36	0
1996–97	Leyton Orient	40	5
1997–98	Leyton Orient	34	0
1998–99	Leyton Orient	0	0
Total:		**259**	**20**

CHAPMAN, Ben — Defender

H: 5 6 W: 11 00 b.Scunthorpe 2-3-79

Source: Trainee.

1997–98	Grimsby T	0	0
1998–99	Grimsby T	1	0
Total:		**1**	**0**

CHAPPLE, Phil — Defender

H: 6 2 W: 13 01 b.Norwich 21-11-66

Source: Apprentice.

1984–85	Norwich C	0	0
1985–86	Norwich C	0	0
1986–87	Norwich C	0	0
1987–88	Norwich C	0	0
1987–88	Cambridge U	6	1
1988–89	Cambridge U	46	3
1989–90	Cambridge U	45	5
1990–91	Cambridge U	43	5
1991–92	Cambridge U	29	3
1992–93	Cambridge U	18	2
1993–94	Charlton Ath	44	5
1994–95	Charlton Ath	21	2
1995–96	Charlton Ath	16	2
1996–97	Charlton Ath	26	2
1997–98	Charlton Ath	35	4
1998–99	Peterborough U	1	0
Total:		**330**	**34**

CHARBONNIER, Lionel — Goalkeeper

H: 6 1 W: 11 07 b.Poitiers 25-10-66

Source: Poitiers. *Honours:* France 1 full cap.

1988–89	Auxerre	1	0
1989–90	Auxerre	0	0
1990–91	Auxerre	0	0
1991–92	Auxerre	7	0
1992–93	Auxerre	9	0
1993–94	Auxerre	7	0
1994–95	Auxerre	24	0
1995–96	Auxerre	23	0
1996–97	Auxerre	31	0
1997–98	Auxerre	24	0
1998–99	Rangers	11	0
Total:		**137**	**0**

CHARLERY, Ken — Forward

H: 6 1 W: 13 12 b.Stepney 28-11-64

Source: Fisher Ath, Basildon U, Beckton U.

1989–90	Maidstone U	30	2
1990–91	Maidstone U	29	9
1990–91	Peterborough U	4	0
1991–92	Peterborough U	37	16
1992–93	Peterborough U	10	3
1992–93	Watford	32	11
1993–94	Watford	16	2
1993–94	Peterborough U	26	8
1994–95	Peterborough U	44	16
1995–96	Birmingham C	17	4
1995–96	Southend U (loan)	3	0
1995–96	Peterborough U	19	7
1996–97	Peterborough U	37	5
1996–97	Stockport Co	10	0
1997–98	Barnet	32	5
1998–99	Barnet	42	16
Total:		**388**	**104**

CHARLES, Gary — Defender

H: 5 9 W: 11 06 b.London 13-4-70

Source: Trainee. *Honours:* England Under-21, 2 full caps.

1987–88	Nottingham F	0	0
1988–89	Nottingham F	1	0
1988–89	Leicester C (loan)	8	0
1989–90	Nottingham F	1	0
1990–91	Nottingham F	10	0
1991–92	Nottingham F	30	1
1992–93	Nottingham F	14	0
1993–94	Derby Co	43	1
1994–95	Derby Co	18	2
1994–95	Aston Villa	16	0
1995–96	Aston Villa	34	1
1996–97	Aston Villa	0	0
1997–98	Aston Villa	18	1
1998–99	Aston Villa	11	1
Total:		**204**	**7**

CHARLTON, Simon — Defender

H: 5 8 W: 11 10 b.Huddersfield 25-10-71

Source: Trainee. *Honours:* FA Schools.

1989–90	Huddersfield T	3	0
1990–91	Huddersfield T	30	0

1991–92	Huddersfield T	45	0
1992–93	Huddersfield T	46	1
1993–94	Southampton	33	1
1994–95	Southampton	25	1
1995–96	Southampton	26	0
1996–97	Southampton	27	0
1997–98	Southampton	3	0
1998–99	Birmingham C	28	0
1997–98	Birmingham C	24	0
Total:		**290**	**3**

CHARNOCK, Phil — Midfield

H: 5 10 W: 11 03 b.Southport 14-2-75

Source: Trainee.

1992–93	Liverpool	0	0
1993–94	Liverpool	0	0
1994–95	Liverpool	0	0
1995–96	Liverpool	0	0
1995–96	Blackpool (loan)	4	0
1996–97	Liverpool	0	0
1996–97	Crewe Alex	32	1
1997–98	Crewe Alex	33	3
1998–99	Crewe Alex	44	2
Total:		**113**	**6**

CHARVET, Laurent — Defender

H: 5 11 W: 12 10 b.Beziers 8-5-73

1994–95	Cannes	19	4
1995–96	Cannes	31	8
1996–97	Cannes	38	6
1997–98	Cannes	11	1
1997–98	Chelsea	11	2
1998–99	Newcastle U	31	1
Total:		**141**	**22**

CHENERY, Ben — Defender

H: 6 1 W: 11 11 b.Ipswich 28-1-77

Source: Trainee.

1994–95	Luton T	0	0
1995–96	Luton T	2	0
1996–97	Luton T	0	0
1997–98	Cambridge U	36	2
1998–99	Cambridge U	44	0
Total:		**82**	**2**

CHERRY, Steve — Goalkeeper

H: 6 1 W: 13 00 b.Nottingham 5-8-60

Source: Apprentice. *Honours:* England Youth.

1977–78	Derby Co	0	0
1978–79	Derby Co	0	0
1979–80	Derby Co	4	0
1980–81	Port Vale (loan)	4	0
1981–82	Derby Co	4	0
1982–83	Derby Co	31	0
1983–84	Derby Co	38	0
1984–85	Walsall	41	0
1985–86	Walsall	30	0
1986–87	Walsall	0	0
1986–87	Plymouth Arg	21	0
1987–88	Plymouth Arg	37	0
1988–89	Plymouth Arg	15	0
1988–89	Chesterfield (loan)	10	0
1988–89	Notts Co	18	0
1989–90	Notts Co	46	0
1990–91	Notts Co	46	0
1991–92	Notts Co	42	0
1992–93	Notts Co	44	0
1993–94	Notts Co	45	0
1994–95	Notts Co	25	0
1995–96	Watford	4	0
1995–96	Plymouth Arg (loan)	16	0
1996–97	Rotherham U	20	0
1997–98	Notts Co	0	0
1998–99	Mansfield T	1	0
1998–99	Oldham Ath	0	0
Total:		**542**	**0**

CHESTERFIELD, Gavin — Defender

H: 5 10 W: 11 12 b.Neath 18-8-79

Source: Trainee.

1998–99	Exeter C	0	0

CHETTLE, Steve — Defender

H: 6 1 W: 13 04 b.Nottingham 27-9-68

Source: Apprentice. *Honours:* England Under-21.

1986–87	Nottingham F	0	0
1987–88	Nottingham F	30	0
1988–89	Nottingham F	28	2
1989–90	Nottingham F	22	1
1990–91	Nottingham F	37	2
1991–92	Nottingham F	22	1
1992–93	Nottingham F	30	0
1993–94	Nottingham F	46	1
1994–95	Nottingham F	41	0
1995–96	Nottingham F	37	0
1996–97	Nottingham F	32	0
1997–98	Nottingham F	45	1
1998–99	Nottingham F	34	2
Total:		**404**	**10**

CHRISTIE, Iyseden — Forward

H: 5 10 W: 12 02 b.Coventry 14-11-76

Source: Trainee.

1994–95	Coventry C	0	0
1995–96	Coventry C	1	0
1996–97	Coventry C	0	0
1996–97	Bournemouth (loan)	4	0

1996–97	Mansfield T (loan)	8	0
1997–98	Mansfield T	39	10
1998–99	Mansfield T	42	8
Total:		**94**	**18**

CHRISTIE, Kevin — Midfield

H: 6 1 W: 12 03 b.Aberdeen 1-4-76

Source: Lewis Utd.

1994–95	Aberdeen	0	0
1995–96	Aberdeen	2	0
1996–97	East Fife	9	1
1996–97	Motherwell	4	0
1997–98	Motherwell	21	0
1998–99	Motherwell	5	0
Total:		**41**	**1**

CHRISTIE, Malcolm — Forward

H: 6 0 W: 11 00 b.Peterborough 11-4-79

Source: Nuneaton B.

1998–99	Derby Co	2	0
Total:		**2**	**0**

CLAPHAM, Jamie — Defender

H: 5 9 W: 11 08 b.Lincoln 7-12-75

Source: Trainee.

1994–95	Tottenham H	0	0
1995–96	Tottenham H	0	0
1996–97	Tottenham H	1	0
1996–97	Leyton Orient (loan)	6	0
1996–97	Bristol R (loan)	5	0
1997–98	Tottenham H	0	0
1997–98	Ipswich T	22	0
1998–99	Ipswich T	46	3
Total:		**80**	**3**

CLARE, Daryl — Forward

H: 5 9 W: 12 00 b.Jersey 1-8-78

Source: Trainee. *Honours:* Eire Under-21.

1995–96	Grimsby T	1	0
1996–97	Grimsby T	0	0
1997–98	Grimsby T	22	3
1998–99	Grimsby T	22	3
Total:		**45**	**6**

CLARIDGE, Rob — Forward

H: 6 0 W: 11 10 b.Bristol 13-3-80

Source: Trainee.

1998–99	Bristol R	0	0

CLARIDGE, Steve — Forward

H: 5 9 W: 13 00 b.Portsmouth 10-4-66

Source: Portsmouth, Fareham T.

1984–85	Bournemouth	6	1
1985–86	Bournemouth	1	0
From Weymouth			
1988–89	Crystal Palace	0	0
1988–89	Aldershot	37	9
1989–90	Aldershot	25	10
1989–90	Cambridge U	20	4
1990–91	Cambridge U	30	12
1991–92	Cambridge U	29	12
1992–93	Luton T	16	2
1992–93	Cambridge U	29	7
1993–94	Cambridge U	24	11
1993–94	Birmingham C	18	7
1994–95	Birmingham C	42	20
1995–96	Birmingham C	28	8
1995–96	Leicester C	14	5
1996–97	Leicester C	32	11
1997–98	Leicester C	17	0
1997–98	Portsmouth (loan)	10	2
1997–98	Wolverhampton W	5	0
1998–99	Portsmouth	39	9
Total:		**422**	**130**

CLARK, Billy — Midfield

H: 6 0 W: 12 03 b.Christchurch 19-5-67

Source: Trainee.

1984–85	Bournemouth	1	0
1985–86	Bournemouth	1	0
1986–87	Bournemouth	0	0
1987–88	Bournemouth	2	0
1987–88	Bristol R	31	1
1988–89	Bristol R	11	0
1989–90	Bristol R	0	0
1990–91	Bristol R	14	1
1991–92	Bristol R	24	1
1992–93	Bristol R	24	1
1993–94	Bristol R	36	1
1994–95	Bristol R	42	6
1995–96	Bristol R	39	2
1996–97	Bristol R	27	1
1997–98	Bristol R	0	0
1997–98	Exeter C	31	3
1998–99	Exeter C	10	0
Total:		**293**	**17**

CLARK, Dean — Midfield

H: 5 10 W: 12 06 b.Hillingdon 31-3-80

Source: Trainee.

1997–98	Brentford	4	0
1998–99	Brentford	0	0
Total:		**4**	**0**

CLARK, Ian — Midfield

H: 5 10 W: 11 02 b.Stockton 23-10-74

Source: Stockton.

1995–96	Doncaster R	23	1
1996–97	Doncaster R	20	2
1997–98	Doncaster R	2	0
1997–98	Hartlepool U	24	7
1998–99	Hartlepool U	39	2
Total:		**108**	**12**

CLARK, Lee — Midfield

H: 5 8 W: 11 07 b.Wallsend 27-10-72

Source: Trainee. *Honours:* England Schools, Youth, Under-21.

1989–90	Newcastle U	0	0
1990–91	Newcastle U	19	2
1991–92	Newcastle U	29	5
1992–93	Newcastle U	46	9
1993–94	Newcastle U	29	2
1994–95	Newcastle U	19	1
1995–96	Newcastle U	28	2
1996–97	Newcastle U	25	2
1997–98	Sunderland	46	13
1998–99	Sunderland	27	3
Total:		**268**	**39**

CLARK, Martin — Defender

H: 5 9 W: 10 12 b.Accrington 12-9-70

Source: Accrington S.

1992–93	Crewe Alex	0	0
1993–94	Crewe Alex	0	0
From Southport			
1997–98	Rotherham U	28	0
1998–99	Rotherham U	1	0
Total:		**29**	**0**

CLARK, Paul — Midfield

H: 5 9 W: 13 13 b.Benfleet 14-9-58

Source: Apprentice. *Honours:* England Schools, Youth.

1976–77	Southend U	25	0
1977–78	Southend U	8	1
1977–78	Brighton & HA	26	3
1978–79	Brighton & HA	33	4
1979–80	Brighton & HA	11	2
1980–81	Brighton & HA	9	0
1981–82	Reading (loan)	2	0
1982–83	Southend U	31	1
1983–84	Southend U	20	0
1984–85	Southend U	29	1
1985–86	Southend U	39	1
1986–87	Southend U	46	0
1987–88	Southend U	30	0
1988–89	Southend U	16	0
1989–90	Southend U	25	0
1990–91	Southend U	40	0
1991–92	Gillingham	42	0
1992–93	Gillingham	35	1
1993–94	Gillingham	13	0
1994–95	Cambridge U	0	0
1995–96	Cambridge U	2	0
1996–97	Cambridge U	0	0
1996–97	Leyton Orient	0	0
1997–98	Leyton Orient	0	0
1998–99	Leyton Orient	0	0
Total:		**482**	**14**

CLARK, Peter — Defender

H: 6 1 W: 12 04 b.Romford 10-12-79

Source: Arsenal Trainee.

1998–99	Carlisle U	36	0
Total:		**36**	**0**

CLARK, Simon — Defender

H: 6 0 W: 12 10 b.Boston 12-3-67

Source: Boston U, Holbeach, Kings Lynn, Hendon, Stevenage Borough.

1993–94	Peterborough U	1	0
1994–95	Peterborough U	32	0
1995–96	Peterborough U	40	1
1996–97	Peterborough U	34	3
1997–98	Leyton Orient	39	4
1998–99	Leyton Orient	40	4
Total:		**186**	**12**

CLARKE, Adrian — Midfield

H: 5 9 W: 11 00 b.Cambridge 28-9-74

Source: Trainee. *Honours:* England Schools.

1993–94	Arsenal	0	0
1994–95	Arsenal	1	0
1995–96	Arsenal	6	0
1996–97	Arsenal	0	0
1996–97	Rotherham U (loan)	2	0
1996–97	Southend U (loan)	7	0
1997–98	Southend U	45	5
1998–99	Southend U	24	3
Total:		**85**	**8**

CLARKE, Andy — Forward

H: 5 10 W: 11 07 b.Islington 22-7-67

Source: Barnet.

1990–91	Wimbledon	12	3
1991–92	Wimbledon	34	3
1992–93	Wimbledon	33	5
1993–94	Wimbledon	23	2
1994–95	Wimbledon	25	1
1995–96	Wimbledon	18	2
1996–97	Wimbledon	11	1

1997–98	Wimbledon	14	0
1998–99	Wimbledon	0	0
1998–99	Port Vale (loan)	6	0
1998–99	Northampton T (loan)	4	0
1998–99	Peterborough U	0	0
Total:		**180**	**17**

CLARKE, Clive — Defender

H: 6 1 W: 12 05 b.Dublin 14-1-80

Source: Trainee.

1996–97	Stoke C	0	0
1997–98	Stoke C	0	0
1998–99	Stoke C	2	0
Total:		**2**	**0**

CLARKE, Darrell — Midfield

H: 5 10 W: 10 11 b.Mansfield 16-12-77

Source: Trainee.

1995–96	Mansfield T	3	0
1996–97	Mansfield T	19	2
1997–98	Mansfield T	35	4
1998–99	Mansfield T	33	5
Total:		**90**	**11**

CLARKE, Matthew — Goalkeeper

H: 6 4 W: 13 10 b.Sheffield 3-11-73

Source: Trainee.

1992–93	Rotherham U	9	0
1993–94	Rotherham U	30	0
1994–95	Rotherham U	45	0
1995–96	Rotherham U	40	0
1996–97	Sheffield W	1	0
1997–98	Sheffield W	3	0
1998–99	Sheffield W	0	0
Total:		**128**	**0**

CLARKE, Peter — Defender

H: 6 0 W: 12 00 b.Southport 3-1-82

Source: Trainee. *Honours:* England Youth.

1998–99	Everton	0	0

CLARKE, Richard — Defender

H: 5 11 W: 10 10 b.Enfield 15-2-80

Source: Trainee.

1998–99	Luton T	0	0

CLARKE, Steve — Defender

H: 5 10 W: 12 07 b.Saltcoats 29-8-63

Source: Beith Jun. *Honours:* Scotland Youth, Under-21, B, 6 full caps. Football League.

1981–82	St Mirren	0	0
1982–83	St Mirren	31	0
1983–84	St Mirren	33	2
1984–85	St Mirren	33	0
1985–86	St Mirren	31	3
1986–87	St Mirren	23	1
1986–87	Chelsea	16	0
1987–88	Chelsea	38	1
1988–89	Chelsea	36	0
1989–90	Chelsea	24	3
1990–91	Chelsea	18	1
1991–92	Chelsea	31	1
1992–93	Chelsea	20	0
1993–94	Chelsea	39	0
1994–95	Chelsea	29	0
1995–96	Chelsea	22	0
1996–97	Chelsea	31	0
1997–98	Chelsea	26	1
1998–99	Newcastle U	0	0
Total:		**481**	**13**

CLARKE, Tim — Goalkeeper

H: 6 3 W: 15 12 b.Stourbridge 19-9-68

Source: Halesowen T.

1990–91	Coventry C	0	0
1991–92	Huddersfield T	39	0
1992–93	Huddersfield T	31	0
1992–93	Rochdale (loan)	2	0
1993–94	Shrewsbury T	0	0
1994–95	Shrewsbury T	16	0
1995–96	Shrewsbury T	15	0
From Witton Alb.			
1996–97	York C	17	0
1996–97	Scunthorpe U	15	0
1997–98	Scunthorpe U	41	0
1998–99	Scunthorpe U	22	0
Total:		**198**	**0**

CLARKSON, Ian — Defender

H: 5 11 W: 12 00 b.Solihull 4-12-70

Source: Trainee.

1988–89	Birmingham C	9	0
1989–90	Birmingham C	20	0
1990–91	Birmingham C	37	0
1991–92	Birmingham C	42	0
1992–93	Birmingham C	28	0
1993–94	Birmingham C	0	0
1993–94	Stoke C	14	0
1994–95	Stoke C	18	0
1995–96	Stoke C	43	0
1996–97	Northampton T	45	0

1997–98	Northampton T	42	1
1998–99	Northampton T	5	0
Total:		**303**	**1**

CLARKSON, Phil — Midfield

H: 5 10 W: 12 08 b.Garstang 13-11-68

Source: Fleetwood T.

1991–92	Crewe Alex	28	6
1992–93	Crewe Alex	35	13
1993–94	Crewe Alex	7	2
1994–95	Crewe Alex	23	6
1995–96	Crewe Alex	5	0
1995–96	Scunthorpe U	24	6
1996–97	Scunthorpe U	28	13
1996–97	Blackpool	17	5
1997–98	Blackpool	45	13
1998–99	Blackpool	44	9
Total:		**256**	**73**

CLAYTON, Gary — Midfield

H: 5 10 W: 12 08 b.Sheffield 2-2-63

Source: Rotherham U Apprentice, Burton Alb.

1986–87	Doncaster R	35	5
1987–88	Cambridge U	45	5
1988–89	Cambridge U	46	1
1989–90	Cambridge U	10	1
1990–91	Cambridge U	6	0
1990–91	Peterborough U (loan)	4	0
1991–92	Cambridge U	11	3
1992–93	Cambridge U	36	3
1993–94	Cambridge U	25	4
1993–94	Huddersfield T	17	1
1994–95	Huddersfield T	2	0
1995–96	Plymouth Arg	36	2
1996–97	Plymouth Arg	1	0
1997–98	Plymouth Arg	1	0
1997–98	Torquay U	41	2
1998–99	Torquay U	15	0
Total:		**331**	**27**

CLEAVER, Chris — Forward

H: 5 10 W: 11 07 b.Hitchin 24-3-79

Source: Trainee.

1996–97	Peterborough U	13	1
1997–98	Peterborough U	14	2
1998–99	Peterborough U	2	0
Total:		**29**	**3**

CLEGG, Michael — Defender

H: 5 8 W: 11 10 b.Ashton-under-Lyne 3-7-77

Source: Trainee. *Honours:* England Under-21.

1995–96	Manchester U	0	0
1996–97	Manchester U	4	0
1997–98	Manchester U	3	0
1998–99	Manchester U	0	0
Total:		**7**	**0**

CLELAND, Alec — Defender

H: 5 9 W: 11 10 b.Glasgow 10-12-70

Source: 'S' Form. *Honours:* Scotland Under-21, B.

1987–88	Dundee U	1	0
1988–89	Dundee U	9	0
1989–90	Dundee U	15	0
1990–91	Dundee U	20	2
1991–92	Dundee U	31	4
1992–93	Dundee U	24	0
1993–94	Dundee U	33	1
1994–95	Dundee U	18	1
1994–95	Rangers	10	0
1995–96	Rangers	25	1
1996–97	Rangers	32	0
1997–98	Rangers	29	3
1998–99	Everton	18	0
Total:		**265**	**12**

CLEMENCE, Stephen — Midfield

H: 5 11 W: 11 07 b.Liverpool 31-3-78

Source: Trainee. *Honours:* England Schools, Youth, Under-21.

1994–95	Tottenham H	0	0
1995–96	Tottenham H	0	0
1996–97	Tottenham H	0	0
1997–98	Tottenham H	17	0
1998–99	Tottenham H	18	0
Total:		**35**	**0**

CLEMENT, Neil — Defender

H: 6 0 W: 12 03 b.Reading 3-10-78

Source: Trainee. *Honours:* England Schools, Youth.

1995–96	Chelsea	0	0
1996–97	Chelsea	1	0
1997–98	Chelsea	0	0
1998–99	Chelsea	0	0
1998–99	Reading (loan)	11	1
1998–99	Preston NE (loan)	4	0
Total:		**16**	**1**

CLEMENT, Philippe — Midfield

H: 6 2 W: 13 00 b.Antwerp 22-3-74

1996–97	Genk	23	0
1997–98	Genk	30	2
1998–99	Coventry C	12	0
Total:		**65**	**2**

CLENCH, Philip — Midfield

b.Chester 23-3-79

Source: Trainee.

1997–98	Chester C	0	0
1998–99	Chester C	0	0

CLITHEROE, Lee — Forward

H: 5 10 W: 10 07 b.Chorley 18-11-78

Source: Trainee.

1997–98	Oldham Ath	3	0
1998–99	Oldham Ath	2	0
Total:		**5**	**0**

CLODE, Mark — Defender

H: 5 10 W: 10 10 b.Plymouth 24-2-73

Source: Trainee.

1991–92	Plymouth Arg	0	0
1992–93	Plymouth Arg	0	0
1993–94	Swansea C	28	1
1994–95	Swansea C	33	1
1995–96	Swansea C	30	0
1996–97	Swansea C	18	1
1997–98	Swansea C	8	0
1998–99	Swansea C	2	0
Total:		**119**	**3**

CLOUGH, Nigel — Midfield

H: 5 10 W: 12 03 b.Sunderland 19-3-66

Source: AC Hunters. *Honours:* England Under-21, B, 14 full caps.

1984–85	Nottingham F	9	1
1985–86	Nottingham F	39	15
1986–87	Nottingham F	42	14
1987–88	Nottingham F	34	19
1988–89	Nottingham F	36	14
1989–90	Nottingham F	38	9
1990–91	Nottingham F	37	14
1991–92	Nottingham F	34	5
1992–93	Nottingham F	42	10
1993–94	Liverpool	27	7
1994–95	Liverpool	10	0
1995–96	Liverpool	2	0
1995–96	Manchester C	15	2
1996–97	Manchester C	23	2
1996–97	Nottingham F (loan)	13	1
1997–98	Manchester C	0	0
1997–98	Sheffield W (loan)	1	0
1998–99	Manchester C	0	0
Total:		**402**	**113**

CLYDE, Glynn — Goalkeeper

H: 6 2 W: 11 07 b.Derry 16-1-79

Source: Barnsley Trainee. *Honours:*

1997–98	Macclesfield T	0	0
1998–99	Macclesfield T	0	0

COATES, Jonathan — Midfield

H: 5 8 W: 10 04 b.Swansea 27-5-75

Source: Trainee. *Honours:* Wales Under-21.

1993–94	Swansea C	4	1
1994–95	Swansea C	5	0
1995–96	Swansea C	18	0
1996–97	Swansea C	40	3
1997–98	Swansea C	44	7
1998–99	Swansea C	33	0
Total:		**144**	**11**

COBIAN, Juan — Defender

H: 5 6 W: 10 10 b.Buenos Aires 11-9-75

Source: Boca Juniors.

1998–99	Sheffield W	9	0
Total:		**9**	**0**

COCKRILL, Darren — Forward

H: 6 1 W: 13 00 b.Great Yarmouth 28-2-80

Source: Trainee.

1998–99	Cambridge U	0	0

COID, Daniel — Midfield

H: 5 11 W: 11 07 b.Liverpool 3-10-81

Source: Trainee.

1998–99	Blackpool	1	0
Total:		**1**	**0**

COLDICOTT, Stacy — Midfield

H: 5 8 W: 12 00 b.Redditch 29-4-74

Source: Trainee.

1991–92	WBA	0	0
1992–93	WBA	14	0
1993–94	WBA	5	0
1994–95	WBA	11	0
1995–96	WBA	33	0
1996–97	WBA	19	3
1996–97	Cardiff C (loan)	6	0
1997–98	WBA	22	0
1998–99	Grimsby T	37	0
Total:		**147**	**3**

COLE, Andy — Forward

H: 5 10 W: 12 04 b.Nottingham 15-10-71

Source: Trainee. *Honours:* England Schools, Youth, Under-21, B, 5 full caps. Football League.

1989–90	Arsenal	0	0
1990–91	Arsenal	1	0
1991–92	Arsenal	0	0
1991–92	Fulham (loan)	13	3
1991–92	Bristol C (loan)	12	8
1992–93	Bristol C	29	12
1992–93	Newcastle U	12	12
1993–94	Newcastle U	40	34
1994–95	Newcastle U	18	9
1994–95	Manchester U	18	12
1995–96	Manchester U	34	11
1996–97	Manchester U	20	6
1997–98	Manchester U	33	15
1998–99	Manchester U	32	17
Total:		**262**	**139**

COLE, Ashley — Defender

b.Stepney 20-12-80

Source: Trainee. *Honours:* England Youth.

1998–99	Arsenal	0	0

COLE, Joe — Midfield

H: 5 9 W: 11 00 b.North London 8-11-81

Source: Trainee. *Honours:* England Schools, Youth.

1998–99	West Ham U	8	0
Total:		**8**	**0**

COLEMAN, Chris — Defender

H: 6 2 W: 14 04 b.Swansea 10-6-70

Source: Apprentice. *Honours:* Wales Under-21, 24 full caps, 4 goals.

1987–88	Swansea C	30	0
1988–89	Swansea C	43	0
1989–90	Swansea C	46	2
1990–91	Swansea C	41	0
1991–92	Crystal Palace	18	4
1992–93	Crystal Palace	38	5
1993–94	Crystal Palace	46	3
1994–95	Crystal Palace	35	1
1995–96	Crystal Palace	17	0
1995–96	Blackburn R	20	0
1996–97	Blackburn R	8	0
1997–98	Blackburn R	0	0
1997–98	Fulham	26	1
1998–99	Fulham	45	4
Total:		**413**	**20**

COLEMAN, Simon — Defender

H: 6 0 W: 12 03 b.Worksop 13-6-68

Source: Apprentice.

1985–86	Mansfield T	0	0
1986–87	Mansfield T	2	0
1987–88	Mansfield T	44	2
1988–89	Mansfield T	45	5
1989–90	Mansfield T	5	0
1989–90	Middlesbrough	36	1
1990–91	Middlesbrough	19	1
1991–92	Derby Co	43	2
1992–93	Derby Co	25	0
1993–94	Derby Co	2	0
1993–94	Sheffield W	15	1
1994–95	Sheffield W	1	0
1994–95	Bolton W	22	4
1995–96	Bolton W	12	1
1996–97	Bolton W	0	0
1997–98	Bolton W	0	0
1997–98	Wolverhampton W (loan)	4	0
1997–98	Southend U	14	0
1998–99	Southend U	42	4
Total:		**331**	**21**

COLGAN, Nick — Goalkeeper

H: 6 1 W: 13 06 b.Drogheda 19-9-73

Source: Drogheda. *Honours:* Eire Under-21.

1992–93	Chelsea	0	0
1993–94	Chelsea	0	0
1993–94	Crewe Alex (loan)	0	0
1994–95	Chelsea	0	0
1994–95	Grimsby T (loan)	0	0
1995–96	Chelsea	0	0
1995–96	Millwall (loan)	0	0
1996–97	Chelsea	1	0
1997–98	Chelsea	0	0
1997–98	Brentford (loan)	5	0
1997–98	Reading (loan)	5	0
1998–99	Bournemouth	0	0
Total:		**11**	**0**

COLLETER, Patrick — Defender

H: 5 8 W: 11 04 b.Brest 6-11-65

1986–87	Brest	23	2
1987–88	Brest	37	2
1988–89	Brest	32	2
1989–90	Brest	35	2
1990–91	Montpellier	31	0
1991–92	Paris St Germain	28	0
1992–93	Paris St Germain	36	0
1993–94	Paris St Germain	32	0
1994–95	Paris St Germain	28	1
1995–96	Paris St Germain	33	0
1996–97	Bordeaux	30	1

1997–98	Marseille	31	0
1998–99	Marseille	10	0
1998–99	Southampton	16	1
Total:		**402**	**11**

COLLETT, Andy — Goalkeeper

H: 5 11 W: 12 10 b.Middlesbrough 28-10-73

Source: Trainee.

1991–92	Middlesbrough	0	0
1992–93	Middlesbrough	2	0
1993–94	Middlesbrough	0	0
1994–95	Middlesbrough	0	0
1994–95	Bristol R	4	0
1995–96	Bristol R	26	0
1996–97	Bristol R	44	0
1997–98	Bristol R	30	0
1998–99	Bristol R	3	0
Total:		**109**	**0**

COLLINS, Chris — Defender

H: 6 0 W: 13 01 b.Chatham 26-9-79

Source: Trainee.

1997–98	Southampton	0	0
1998–99	Southampton	0	0

COLLINS, Derek — Defender

H: 5 8 W: 10 07 b.Glasgow 15-4-69

Source: Renfrew Waverley. *Honours:*

1987–88	Morton	28	1
1988–89	Morton	35	1
1989–90	Morton	38	0
1990–91	Morton	37	2
1991–92	Morton	44	1
1992–93	Morton	41	0
1993–94	Morton	37	1
1994–95	Morton	33	1
1995–96	Morton	36	1
1996–97	Morton	35	0
1997–98	Morton	34	3
1998–99	Hibernian	16	0
Total:		**414**	**11**

COLLINS, James — Midfield

H: 5 8 W: 10 00 b.Liverpool 28-5-78

Source: Trainee.

1996–97	Crewe Alex	0	0
1997–98	Crewe Alex	1	0
1998–99	Crewe Alex	6	1
Total:		**7**	**1**

COLLINS, John — Midfield

H: 5 8 W: 10 06 b.Galashiels 30-1-68

Source: Hutchison Vale BC. *Honours:* Scotland Youth, Under-21, 53 full caps, 11 goals.

1984–85	Hibernian	0	0
1985–86	Hibernian	19	1
1986–87	Hibernian	30	1
1987–88	Hibernian	44	6
1988–89	Hibernian	35	2
1989–90	Hibernian	35	6
1990–91	Celtic	35	1
1991–92	Celtic	38	11
1992–93	Celtic	43	8
1993–94	Celtic	38	8
1994–95	Celtic	34	8
1995–96	Celtic	29	11
1996–97	Monaco	28	6
1997–98	Monaco	25	1
1998–99	Everton	20	1
Total:		**453**	**71**

COLLINS, Lee — Midfield

H: 5 9 W: 11 02 b.Bellshill 3-2-74

Source: Possil U.

1993–94	Albion R	20	0
1994–95	Albion R	17	0
1995–96	Albion R	8	1
1995–96	Swindon T	5	0
1996–97	Swindon T	4	0
1997–98	Swindon T	26	1
1998–99	Swindon T	4	0
Total:		**84**	**2**

COLLINS, Lee — Defender

H: 6 2 W: 13 05 b.Bellshill 10-9-77

Source: Trainee.

1996–97	Aston Villa	0	0
1997–98	Aston Villa	0	0
1998–99	Aston Villa	0	0
1998–99	Stoke C	4	0
Total:		**4**	**0**

COLLINS, Sam — Defender

H: 6 2 W: 14 04 b.Pontefract 5-6-77

Source: Trainee.

1994–95	Huddersfield T	0	0
1995–96	Huddersfield T	0	0
1996–97	Huddersfield T	4	0
1997–98	Huddersfield T	10	0
1998–99	Huddersfield T	23	0
Total:		**37**	**0**

COLLINS, Simon — Midfield

H: 6 0 W: 12 05 b.Pontefract 16-12-73

Source: Trainee.

1992–93	Huddersfield T	1	0
1993–94	Huddersfield T	1	0
1994–95	Huddersfield T	4	0
1995–96	Huddersfield T	30	3
1996–97	Huddersfield T	16	0
1996–97	Plymouth Arg	12	1
1997–98	Plymouth Arg	32	2
1998–99	Plymouth Arg	40	2
Total:		**136**	**8**

COLLINS, Wayne — Midfield

H: 6 0 W: 11 07 b.Manchester 4-3-69

Source: Winsford U.

1993–94	Crewe Alex	35	2
1994–95	Crewe Alex	40	11
1995–96	Crewe Alex	42	1
1996–97	Sheffield W	12	1
1997–98	Sheffield W	19	5
1997–98	Fulham	13	1
1998–99	Fulham	21	2
Total:		**182**	**23**

COLLYMORE, Stan — Forward

H: 6 2 W: 14 04 b.Stone 22-1-71

Source: Stafford R. *Honours:* England 3 full caps.

1990–91	Crystal Palace	6	0
1991–92	Crystal Palace	12	1
1992–93	Crystal Palace	2	0
1992–93	Southend U	30	15
1993–94	Nottingham F	28	19
1994–95	Nottingham F	37	22
1995–96	Liverpool	31	14
1996–97	Liverpool	30	12
1996–97	Aston Villa	0	0
1997–98	Aston Villa	25	6
1998–99	Aston Villa	20	1
Total:		**221**	**90**

COLWELL, Richard — Defender

H: 5 9 W: 11 02 b.Wordsley 2-9-79

Source: Trainee.

1997–98	Coventry C	0	0
1998–99	Coventry C	0	0

COMBE, Alan — Goalkeeper

H: 6 1 W: 12 02 b.Edinburgh 3-4-74

Source: Kelty Hearts.

1992–93	Cowdenbeath	18	0
1993–94	St Mirren	16	0
1994–95	St Mirren	21	0
1995–96	St Mirren	21	0
1996–97	St Mirren	36	0
1997–98	St Mirren	30	0
1998–99	Dundee U	10	0
Total:		**152**	**0**

CONLON, Barry — Forward

H: 6 2 W: 13 07 b.Drogheda 1-10-78

Source: QPR Trainee. *Honours:* Eire Under-21.

1997–98	Manchester C	7	0
1997–98	Plymouth Arg (loan)	13	2
1998–99	Manchester C	0	0
1998–99	Southend U	34	7
Total:		**54**	**9**

CONNELLY, Gordon — Midfield

H: 6 0 W: 11 07 b.Glasgow 1-11-76

1998–99	York C	28	4
Total:		**28**	**4**

CONNELLY, Sean — Defender

H: 5 10 W: 11 10 b.Sheffield 26-6-70

Source: Hallam.

1991–92	Stockport Co	0	0
1992–93	Stockport Co	7	0
1993–94	Stockport Co	32	0
1994–95	Stockport Co	39	0
1995–96	Stockport Co	43	0
1996–97	Stockport Co	45	0
1997–98	Stockport Co	45	2
1998–99	Stockport Co	35	1
Total:		**246**	**3**

CONNOLLY, David — Forward

H: 5 8 W: 12 00 b.Willesden 6-6-77

Source: Trainee. *Honours:* Eire 18 full caps, 7 goals.

1994–95	Watford	2	0
1995–96	Watford	11	8
1996–97	Watford	13	2
1997–98	Watford	0	0
1998–99	Wolverhampton W	32	6
Total:		**58**	**16**

CONNOLLY, Karl — Forward

H: 5 10 W: 11 01 b.Prescot 9-2-70

Source: Napoli (Liverpool Sunday League).

1990–91	Wrexham	0	0
1991–92	Wrexham	36	8
1992–93	Wrexham	42	9

1993–94	Wrexham	39	2
1994–95	Wrexham	45	10
1995–96	Wrexham	46	18
1996–97	Wrexham	30	14
1997–98	Wrexham	35	7
1998–99	Wrexham	44	11
Total:		**317**	**79**

CONNOLLY, Patrick — Forward

H: 5 9 W: 11 00 b.Glasgow 25-6-70

Honours: 'S' Form. Scotland Under-21.

1986–87	Dundee U	0	0
1987–88	Dundee U	0	0
1988–89	Dundee U	2	0
1989–90	Dundee U	15	5
1990–91	Dundee U	10	2
1991–92	Dundee U	5	0
1992–93	Dundee U	42	16
1993–94	Dundee U	28	5
1994–95	Dundee U	6	0
1995–96	Dundee U	6	1
1995–96	Airdrieonians	6	3
1996–97	Airdrieonians	35	8
1997–98	Airdrieonians	23	8
1997–98	St Johnstone	4	0
1998–99	St Johnstone	9	1
Total:		**191**	**49**

CONNOLLY, Patrick — Midfield

b.Preston 3-3-80

Source: Trainee.

1998–99	Blackburn R	0	0

CONNOR, Dan — Goalkeeper

H: 6 2 W: 12 09 b.Dublin 31-1-81

Source: Trainee.

1997–98	Peterborough U	0	0
1998–99	Peterborough U	2	0
Total:		**2**	**0**

CONNOR, Paul — Forward

H: 6 2 W: 11 05 b.Bishop Auckland 12-1-79

Source: Trainee.

1996–97	Middlesbrough	0	0
1997–98	Middlesbrough	0	0
1997–98	Hartlepool U (loan)	5	0
1998–99	Middlesbrough	0	0
1998–99	Stoke C (loan)	3	2
Total:		**8**	**2**

CONROY, Mike — Forward

H: 6 0 W: 13 03 b.Glasgow 31-12-65

Source: Apprentice.

1983–84	Coventry C	0	0
1983–84	Clydebank	2	0
1984–85	Clydebank	26	11
1985–86	Clydebank	28	7
1986–87	Clydebank	36	9
1987–88	Clydebank	22	11
1987–88	St Mirren	10	1
1988–89	Reading	13	4
1989–90	Reading	34	2
1990–91	Reading	33	1
1991–92	Burnley	38	24
1992–93	Burnley	39	6
1993–94	Preston NE	32	12
1994–95	Preston NE	25	10
1995–96	Fulham	40	9
1996–97	Fulham	43	21
1997–98	Fulham	11	2
1997–98	Blackpool	6	0
1998–99	Blackpool	8	0
1998–99	Chester C (loan)	15	3
Total:		**461**	**133**

CONVERY, Mark — Forward

H: 5 6 W: 10 05 b.Newcastle 29-5-81

Source: Trainee.

1998–99	Sunderland	0	0

COOK, Aaron — Defender

H: 6 0 W: 11 10 b.Caerphilly 6-12-79

Source: Trainee.

1997–98	Portsmouth	1	0
1998–99	Portsmouth	0	0
1998–99	Crystal Palace	0	0
Total:		**1**	**0**

COOK, Andy — Midfield

H: 5 9 W: 12 00 b.Romsey 10-8-69

Source: Apprentice.

1987–88	Southampton	2	0
1988–89	Southampton	3	0
1989–90	Southampton	4	1
1990–91	Southampton	7	0
1991–92	Southampton	0	0
1991–92	Exeter C	38	0
1992–93	Exeter C	32	1
1993–94	Swansea C	28	0
1994–95	Swansea C	1	0
1995–96	Swansea C	33	0
1996–97	Swansea C	0	0
1996–97	Portsmouth	8	0

1997–98	Portsmouth	1	0
1997–98	Millwall	3	0
1998–99	Millwall	2	0
Total:		**162**	**2**

COOK, Jamie — Forward

H: 5 10 W: 10 10 b.Oxford 2-8-79

Source: Trainee.

1997–98	Oxford U	20	2
1998–99	Oxford U	19	1
Total:		**39**	**3**

COOK, Paul — Midfield

H: 5 11 W: 11 00 b.Liverpool 22-6-67

Source: Marine.

1984–85	Wigan Ath	2	0
1985–86	Wigan Ath	13	2
1986–87	Wigan Ath	27	4
1987–88	Wigan Ath	41	8
1988–89	Norwich C	4	0
1989–90	Norwich C	2	0
1989–90	Wolverhampton W	28	2
1990–91	Wolverhampton W	42	6
1991–92	Wolverhampton W	43	8
1992–93	Wolverhampton W	44	1
1993–94	Wolverhampton W	36	2
1994–95	Coventry C	34	3
1995–96	Coventry C	3	0
1995–96	Tranmere R	15	1
1996–97	Tranmere R	36	3
1997–98	Tranmere R	9	0
1997–98	Stockport Co	25	3
1998–99	Stockport Co	24	0
1998–99	Burnley (loan)	12	1
Total:		**440**	**44**

COOKE, Andy — Forward

H: 5 11 W: 12 08 b.Stoke 20-1-74

Source: Newtown.

1994–95	Burnley	0	0
1995–96	Burnley	23	5
1996–97	Burnley	31	13
1997–98	Burnley	34	16
1998–99	Burnley	36	9
Total:		**124**	**43**

COOKE, Terry — Forward

H: 5 8 W: 10 03 b.Marston Green 5-8-76

Source: Trainee. *Honours:* England Youth, Under-21.

1994–95	Manchester U	0	0
1995–96	Manchester U	4	0
1995–96	Sunderland (loan)	6	0
1996–97	Manchester U	0	0
1996–97	Birmingham C (loan)	4	0
1997–98	Manchester U	0	0
1998–99	Manchester U	0	0
1998–99	Wrexham (loan)	10	0
1998–99	Manchester C	21	7
Total:		**45**	**7**

COOKSEY, Scott — Goalkeeper

H: 6 3 W: 13 10 b.Birmingham 24-6-72

Source: Derby Co, Shrewsbury T, Bromsgrove R.

1993–94	Peterborough U	3	0
1994–95	Peterborough U	12	0
1995–96	Peterborough U	0	0
1996–97	Peterborough U	0	0
1997–98	Peterborough U	0	0
From Hednesford T.			
1998–99	Shrewsbury T	2	0
Total:		**17**	**0**

COOPER, Colin — Defender

H: 5 11 W: 11 11 b.Sedgefield 28-2-67

Honours: England Under-21, 2 full caps.

1984–85	Middlesbrough	0	0
1985–86	Middlesbrough	11	0
1986–87	Middlesbrough	46	0
1987–88	Middlesbrough	43	2
1988–89	Middlesbrough	35	2
1989–90	Middlesbrough	21	2
1990–91	Middlesbrough	32	0
1991–92	Millwall	36	2
1992–93	Millwall	41	4
1993–94	Nottingham F	37	7
1994–95	Nottingham F	35	1
1995–96	Nottingham F	37	5
1996–97	Nottingham F	36	2
1997–98	Nottingham F	35	5
1998–99	Nottingham F	0	0
1998–99	Middlesbrough	32	1
Total:		**477**	**33**

COOPER, James — Midfield

b.Wordsley 6-2-80

Source: Trainee.

1998–99	WBA	0	0

COOPER, Kevin — Forward

H: 5 8 W: 10 07 b.Derby 8-2-75

Source: Trainee.

1993–94	Derby Co	0	0
1994–95	Derby Co	1	0
1995–96	Derby Co	1	0
1996–97	Derby Co	0	0
1996–97	Stockport Co (loan)	12	3

Cooper, Mark

1997–98	Stockport Co	38	8
1998–99	Stockport Co	38	1
Total:		**90**	**12**

COOPER, Mark — Midfield

H: 5 10 W: 12 10 b.Wakefield 18-12-68

Source: Trainee.

1987–88	Bristol C	0	0
1988–89	Bristol C	0	0
1989–90	Exeter C	5	0
1989–90	Southend U (loan)	5	0
1990–91	Exeter C	42	11
1991–92	Exeter C	3	1
1991–92	Birmingham C	33	4
1992–93	Birmingham C	6	0
1992–93	Fulham	9	0
1992–93	Huddersfield T (loan)	10	4
1993–94	Fulham	5	0
1993–94	Wycombe W	2	1
1993–94	Exeter C	21	8
1994–95	Exeter C	40	6
1995–96	Exeter C	27	6
1996–97	Hartlepool U	33	9
1997–98	Hartlepool U	0	0
1997–98	Macclesfield T (loan)	8	2
1997–98	Leyton Orient	1	0
1998–99	Leyton Orient	0	0
Total:		**250**	**52**

COOPER, Richard — Defender

H: 5 9 W: 10 07 b.Nottingham 27-9-79

Source: Trainee. *Honours:* England Schools, Youth.

1996–97	Nottingham F	0	0
1997–98	Nottingham F	0	0
1998–99	Nottingham F	0	0

COOPER, Steve — Defender

H: 5 9 W: 11 03 b.Pontypridd 10-12-79

1998–99	Wrexham	0	0

COOTE, Adrian — Forward

H: 6 1 W: 12 00 b.Gt Yarmouth 30-9-78

Source: Trainee. *Honours:* Northern Ireland Under-21, 2 full caps.

1997–98	Norwich C	23	2
1998–99	Norwich C	6	0
Total:		**29**	**2**

COPPINGER, James — Midfield

H: 5 7 W: 10 03 b.Middlesbrough 10-1-81

Source: Darlington Trainee. *Honours:* England Youth.

1997–98	Newcastle U	0	0
1998–99	Newcastle U	0	0

CORAZZIN, Carlo — Forward

H: 5 10 W: 12 07 b.Canada 25-12-71

Source: Vancouver 86ers. *Honours:* Canada full caps.

1993–94	Cambridge U	28	10
1994–95	Cambridge U	46	19
1995–96	Cambridge U	31	10
1995–96	Plymouth Arg	6	1
1996–97	Plymouth Arg	30	5
1997–98	Plymouth Arg	38	16
1998–99	Northampton T	39	16
Total:		**218**	**77**

CORBETT, James — Midfield

H: 5 10 W: 10 12 b.Hackney 6-7-80

Source: Trainee.

1997–98	Gillingham	16	2
1998–99	Blackburn R	0	0
Total:		**16**	**2**

CORDEN, Wayne — Midfield

H: 5 10 W: 11 05 b.Leek 1-11-75

Source: Trainee.

1994–95	Port Vale	1	0
1995–96	Port Vale	2	0
1996–97	Port Vale	12	0
1997–98	Port Vale	33	1
1998–99	Port Vale	16	0
Total:		**64**	**1**

CORICA, Steve — Midfield

H: 5 8 W: 10 10 b.Cairns 24-3-73

Source: Marconi. *Honours:* Australia full caps.

1995–96	Leicester C	16	2
1995–96	Wolverhampton W	17	0
1996–97	Wolverhampton W	36	2
1997–98	Wolverhampton W	1	0
1998–99	Wolverhampton W	31	2
Total:		**101**	**6**

CORNFORTH, John — Midfield

H: 5 11 W: 14 06 b.Whitley Bay 7-10-67

Source: Apprentice. *Honours:* Wales 2 full caps.

1984–85	Sunderland	1	0
1985–86	Sunderland	0	0

1986–87 Sunderland 0 0
1986–87 Doncaster R (loan) 7 3
1987–88 Sunderland 12 2
1988–89 Sunderland 15 0
1989–90 Sunderland 2 0
1989–90 Shrewsbury T (loan) 3 0
1989–90 Lincoln C (loan) 9 1
1990–91 Sunderland 2 0
1991–92 Swansea C 17 0
1992–93 Swansea C 44 5
1993–94 Swansea C 38 6
1994–95 Swansea C 33 3
1995–96 Swansea C 17 2
1995–96 Birmingham C 8 0
1996–97 Birmingham C 0 0
1996–97 Wycombe W 10 0
1997–98 Wycombe W 24 5
1997–98 Peterborough U (loan) 4 0
1998–99 Wycombe W 13 1
Total: 259 28

CORNOCK, Grant — Midfield

H: 6 3 W: 12 06 b.Watford 2-2-80

Source: Trainee.

1998–99 Watford 0 0

CORNS, Stuart — Forward

H: 5 11 W: 12 00 b.Shrewsbury 1-7-79

Source: Trainee.

1997–98 Shrewsbury T 0 0
1998–99 Shrewsbury T 0 0

CORNWALL, Luke — Forward

H: 5 11 W: 11 00 b.Lambeth 23-7-80

Source: Trainee.

1998–99 Fulham 4 1
Total: 4 1

CORR, Barry — Goalkeeper

H: 6 1 W: 12 13 b.Glasgow 13-1-81

Source: Celtic BC.

1997–98 Celtic 0 0
1998–99 Celtic 1 0
Total: 1 0

CORRIGAN, Noel — Midfield

H: 5 10 W: 11 00 b.Belfast 29-12-79

Source: Trainee.

1998–99 Bolton W 0 0

CORT, Carl — Forward

H: 6 4 W: 12 07 b.Southwark 1-11-77

Source: Trainee. *Honours:* England Under-21.

1996–97 Wimbledon 1 0
1996–97 Lincoln C (loan) 6 1
1997–98 Wimbledon 22 4
1998–99 Wimbledon 16 3
Total: 45 8

CORT, Leon — Defender

b.Southwark 11-7-79

Source: Dulwich H.

1997–98 Millwall 0 0
1998–99 Millwall 0 0

COSGROVE, Stephen — Midfield

H: 5 9 W: 10 05 b.Glasgow 29-12-80

Source: Trainee.

1998–99 Manchester U 0 0

COSTA, Riccardo — Forward

H: 5 7 W: 10 08 b.Lisbon 10-1-73

1998–99 Darlington 3 1
Total: 3 1

COTON, Tony — Goalkeeper

H: 6 2 W: 13 07 b.Tamworth 19-5-61

Source: Mile Oak R. *Honours:* England B.

1978–79 Birmingham C 0 0
1979–80 Birmingham C 0 0
1979–80 Hereford U (loan) 0 0
1980–81 Birmingham C 3 0
1981–82 Birmingham C 15 0
1982–83 Birmingham C 28 0
1983–84 Birmingham C 41 0
1984–85 Birmingham C 7 0
1984–85 Watford 33 0
1985–86 Watford 40 0
1986–87 Watford 31 0
1987–88 Watford 37 0
1988–89 Watford 46 0
1989–90 Watford 46 0
1990–91 Manchester C 33 0
1991–92 Manchester C 37 0
1992–93 Manchester C 40 0
1993–94 Manchester C 31 0
1994–95 Manchester C 23 0
1995–96 Manchester C 0 0
1995–96 Manchester U 0 0
1996–97 Sunderland 10 0

1997–98	Sunderland	0	0
1998–99	Sunderland	0	0
Total:		**501**	**0**

COTTEE, Tony — Forward

H: 5 8 W: 11 05 b.West Ham 11-7-65

Source: Apprentice. *Honours:* England Youth, Under-21, 7 full caps.

1982–83	West Ham U	8	5
1983–84	West Ham U	39	15
1984–85	West Ham U	41	17
1985–86	West Ham U	42	20
1986–87	West Ham U	42	22
1987–88	West Ham U	40	13
1988–89	Everton	36	13
1989–90	Everton	27	13
1990–91	Everton	29	10
1991–92	Everton	24	8
1992–93	Everton	26	12
1993–94	Everton	39	16
1994–95	Everton	3	0
1994–95	West Ham U	31	13
1995–96	West Ham U	33	10
1996–97	West Ham U	3	0
From Selangor			
1997–98	Leicester C	19	4
1997–98	Birmingham C (loan)	5	1
1998–99	Leicester C	31	10
Total:		**518**	**202**

COUBROUGH, James — Midfield

b.Bradford 4-10-80

Source: Trainee.

1998–99	Sheffield W	0	0

COUGHLAN, Graham — Defender

H: 6 3 W: 14 00 b.Dublin 18-11-74

Source: Bray Wanderers.

1995–96	Blackburn R	0	0
1996–97	Blackburn R	0	0
1996–97	Swindon T (loan)	3	0
1997–98	Blackburn R	0	0
1998–99	Blackburn R	0	0
Total:		**3**	**0**

COUSINS, Jason — Defender

H: 5 10 W: 12 07 b.Hayes 4-10-70

Source: Trainee.

1989–90	Brentford	13	0
1990–91	Brentford	8	0
From Wycombe W			
1993–94	Wycombe W	37	1
1994–95	Wycombe W	41	2
1995–96	Wycombe W	30	0
1996–97	Wycombe W	37	0
1997–98	Wycombe W	29	0
1998–99	Wycombe W	34	2
Total:		**229**	**5**

COUZENS, Andy — Midfield

H: 5 10 W: 11 11 b.Shipley 4-6-75

Source: Trainee. *Honours:* England Under-21.

1992–93	Leeds U	0	0
1993–94	Leeds U	0	0
1994–95	Leeds U	4	0
1995–96	Leeds U	14	0
1996–97	Leeds U	10	1
1997–98	Carlisle U	27	2
1998–99	Carlisle U	15	0
1998–99	Blackpool	6	0
Total:		**76**	**3**

COWAN, Tom — Defender

H: 5 8 W: 11 10 b.Bellshill 28-8-69

Source: Netherdale BC.

1988–89	Clyde	16	2
1988–89	Rangers	4	0
1989–90	Rangers	3	0
1990–91	Rangers	5	0
1991–92	Sheffield U	20	0
1992–93	Sheffield U	21	0
1993–94	Sheffield U	4	0
1993–94	Stoke C (loan)	14	0
1993–94	Huddersfield T (loan)	10	0
1994–95	Huddersfield T	37	2
1995–96	Huddersfield T	43	2
1996–97	Huddersfield T	42	4
1997–98	Huddersfield T	0	0
1998–99	Huddersfield T	5	0
1998–99	Burnley	12	0
Total:		**236**	**10**

COWANS, Gordon — Midfield

H: 5 7 W: 9 07 b.Durham 27-10-58

Source: Apprentice. *Honours:* England Youth, Under-21, B, 10 full caps, 2 goals.

1975–76	Aston Villa	1	0
1976–77	Aston Villa	18	3
1977–78	Aston Villa	35	7
1978–79	Aston Villa	34	4
1979–80	Aston Villa	42	6
1980–81	Aston Villa	42	5
1981–82	Aston Villa	42	6
1982–83	Aston Villa	42	10
1983–84	Aston Villa	0	0
1984–85	Aston Villa	30	1
1985–86	Bari	20	0
1986–87	Bari	38	3

1987–88	Bari	36	0
1988–89	Aston Villa	33	2
1989–90	Aston Villa	34	4
1990–91	Aston Villa	38	1
1991–92	Aston Villa	12	0
1991–92	Blackburn R	26	1
1992–93	Blackburn R	24	1
1993–94	Aston Villa	11	0
1993–94	Derby Co	19	0
1994–95	Derby Co	17	0
1994–95	Wolverhampton W	21	0
1995–96	Wolverhampton W	16	0
1995–96	Sheffield U	20	0
1996–97	Bradford C	24	0
1996–97	Stockport Co	7	0
1997–98	Burnley	6	0
1998–99	Burnley	0	0
Total:		**688**	**54**

COWE, Steve — Forward

H: 5 7 W: 10 02 b.Gloucester 29-9-74

Source: Trainee.

1993–94	Aston Villa	0	0
1994–95	Aston Villa	0	0
1995–96	Aston Villa	0	0
1995–96	Swindon T	11	1
1996–97	Swindon T	38	6
1997–98	Swindon T	17	2
1998–99	Swindon T	5	0
Total:		**71**	**9**

COWELL, Claydon — Midfield

b.Colchester 3-9-80

Source: Arsenal Trainee.

1998–99	Ipswich T	0	0

COWLING, Lee — Defender

H: 5 9 W: 11 00 b.Doncaster 22-9-77

Source: Trainee.

1994–95	Nottingham F	0	0
1995–96	Nottingham F	0	0
1996–97	Nottingham F	0	0
1997–98	Nottingham F	0	0
1998–99	Nottingham F	0	0

COX, Ian — Defender

H: 6 0 W: 12 00 b.Croydon 25-3-71

Source: Carshalton Ath.

1993–94	Crystal Palace	0	0
1994–95	Crystal Palace	11	0
1995–96	Crystal Palace	4	0
1995–96	Bournemouth	8	0
1996–97	Bournemouth	44	8
1997–98	Bournemouth	46	3
1998–99	Bournemouth	46	5
Total:		**159**	**16**

COX, Jimmy — Forward

H: 5 6 W: 10 07 b.Gloucester 11-4-80

Source: Trainee.

1998–99	Luton T	8	0
Total:		**8**	**0**

COX, Neil — Defender

H: 6 0 W: 13 02 b.Scunthorpe 8-10-71

Source: Trainee. *Honours:* England Under-21.

1989–90	Scunthorpe U	0	0
1990–91	Scunthorpe U	17	1
1990–91	Aston Villa	0	0
1991–92	Aston Villa	7	0
1992–93	Aston Villa	15	1
1993–94	Aston Villa	20	2
1994–95	Middlesbrough	40	1
1995–96	Middlesbrough	35	2
1996–97	Middlesbrough	31	0
1997–98	Bolton W	21	1
1998–99	Bolton W	44	4
Total:		**230**	**12**

COYLE, Owen — Forward

H: 5 9 W: 9 12 b.Paisley 14-7-66

Source: Renfrew YM. *Honours:* Eire Under-21, B, 1 full cap.

1984–85	Dumbarton	0	0
1985–86	Dumbarton	16	5
1986–87	Dumbarton	43	17
1987–88	Dumbarton	41	14
1988–89	Dumbarton	3	0
1988–89	Clydebank	36	16
1989–90	Clydebank	27	17
1989–90	Airdrieonians	10	10
1990–91	Airdrieonians	28	20
1991–92	Airdrieonians	43	11
1992–93	Airdrieonians	42	9
1993–94	Bolton W	30	7
1994–95	Bolton W	19	5
1995–96	Bolton W	5	0
1995–96	Dundee U	28	5
1996–97	Dundee U	10	0
1996–97	Motherwell	15	7
1997–98	Motherwell	36	10
1998–99	Motherwell	26	7
1998–99	Dunfermline Ath	11	1
Total:		**469**	**161**

COYNE, Chris — Defender

H: 6 1 W: 13 10 b.Brisbane 20-12-78

Source: Perth SC.

1995–96	West Ham U	0	0
1996–97	West Ham U	0	0
1997–98	West Ham U	0	0
1998–99	West Ham U	1	0
1998–99	Brentford (loan)	7	0
1998–99	Southend U (loan)	1	0
Total:		**9**	**0**

COYNE, Danny — Goalkeeper

H: 5 11 W: 12 05 b.Prestatyn 27-8-73

Source: Trainee. *Honours:* Wales Under-21, 1 full cap.

1991–92	Tranmere R	0	0
1992–93	Tranmere R	1	0
1993–94	Tranmere R	5	0
1994–95	Tranmere R	5	0
1995–96	Tranmere R	46	0
1996–97	Tranmere R	21	0
1997–98	Tranmere R	16	0
1998–99	Tranmere R	17	0
Total:		**111**	**0**

COYNE, Tommy — Forward

H: 5 11 W: 12 00 b.Glasgow 14-11-62

Source: Hillwood BC. *Honours:* Eire B, 22 full caps, 6 goals.

1981–82	Clydebank	31	9
1982–83	Clydebank	38	18
1983–84	Clydebank	11	10
1983–84	Dundee U	18	3
1984–85	Dundee U	21	3
1985–86	Dundee U	13	2
1986–87	Dundee	20	9
1987–88	Dundee	43	33
1988–89	Dundee	26	9
1988–89	Celtic	7	0
1989–90	Celtic	23	7
1990–91	Celtic	26	18
1991–92	Celtic	39	15
1992–93	Celtic	10	3
1992–93	Tranmere R	12	1
1993–94	Motherwell	26	12
1994–95	Motherwell	31	16
1995–96	Motherwell	14	4
1996–97	Motherwell	27	11
1997–98	Motherwell	34	15
1998–99	Dundee	16	0
Total:		**486**	**198**

CRADDOCK, Jody — Defender

H: 6 0 W: 11 01 b.Bromsgrove 25-7-75

Source: Christchurch.

1993–94	Cambridge U	20	0
1994–95	Cambridge U	38	0
1995–96	Cambridge U	46	3
1996–97	Cambridge U	41	1
1997–98	Sunderland	32	0
1998–99	Sunderland	6	0
Total:		**183**	**4**

CRAIGAN, Stephen — Defender

H: 5 10 W: 10 09 b.Newtonards 29-10-76

Source: Blantyre Vics.

1995–96	Motherwell	0	0
1996–97	Motherwell	0	0
1997–98	Motherwell	14	0
1998–99	Motherwell	10	0
Total:		**24**	**0**

CRAMB, Colin — Forward

H: 6 0 W: 12 09 b.Lanark 23-6-74

Source: Hamilton A BC.

1990–91	Hamilton A	3	2
1991–92	Hamilton A	12	1
1992–93	Hamilton A	33	7
1993–94	Southampton	1	0
1994–95	Falkirk	8	1
1994–95	Hearts	6	1
1995–96	Doncaster R	21	7
1996–97	Doncaster R	41	18
1997–98	Bristol C	40	9
1998–99	Bristol C	13	0
1998–99	Walsall (loan)	4	4
Total:		**182**	**50**

CRAVEN, Dean — Midfield

H: 5 6 W: 10 10 b.Shrewsbury 17-2-79

Source: WBA Trainee.

1997–98	Shrewsbury T	1	0
1998–99	Shrewsbury T	10	0
Total:		**11**	**0**

CRAWFORD, Dale — Forward

H: 5 9 W: 11 01 b.Sunderland 14-9-81

Source: Trainee.

1998–99	Leeds U	0	0

CRAWFORD, Jimmy — Midfield

H: 5 11 W: 11 06 b.Chicago 1-5-74

Source: Bohemians.

1994–95	Newcastle U	0	0
1995–96	Newcastle U	0	0
1996–97	Newcastle U	2	0
1996–97	Rotherham U (loan)	11	0
1997–98	Newcastle U	0	0
1997–98	Dundee U (loan)	2	0
1997–98	Reading	6	0
1998–99	Reading	11	0
Total:		**32**	**0**

CRAWFORD, Steve — Forward

H: 5 10 W: 10 07 b.Dunfermline 9-1-74

Source: Rosyth Recreation. *Honours:* Scotland Under-21, B, 1 full cap.

1992–93	Raith R	20	3
1993–94	Raith R	36	5
1994–95	Raith R	31	11
1995–96	Raith R	28	3
1996–97	Millwall	42	11
1997–98	Hibernian	35	9
1998–99	Hibernian	35	14
Total:		**227**	**56**

CREANEY, Gerry — Forward

H: 5 11 W: 13 07 b.Coatbridge 13-4-70

Source: Celtic BC. *Honours:* Scotland Under-21.

1987–88	Celtic	0	0
1988–89	Celtic	0	0
1989–90	Celtic	6	1
1990–91	Celtic	31	7
1991–92	Celtic	32	14
1992–93	Celtic	26	9
1993–94	Celtic	18	5
1993–94	Portsmouth	18	11
1994–95	Portsmouth	39	18
1995–96	Portsmouth	3	3
1995–96	Manchester C	15	3
1995–96	Oldham Ath (loan)	9	2
1996–97	Manchester C	5	1
1996–97	Ipswich T (loan)	6	1
1997–98	Manchester C	1	0
1997–98	Burnley (loan)	10	8
1997–98	Chesterfield (loan)	4	0
1998–99	Manchester C	0	0
1998–99	Notts Co	16	3
Total:		**239**	**86**

CRESSWELL, Richard — Forward

H: 6 1 W: 11 07 b.Bridlington 20-9-77

Source: Trainee. *Honours:* England Under-21.

1995–96	York C	16	1
1996–97	York C	17	0
1996–97	Mansfield T (loan)	5	1
1997–98	York C	26	4
1998–99	York C	36	16
1998–99	Sheffield W	7	1
Total:		**107**	**23**

CRICHTON, Paul — Goalkeeper

H: 6 1 W: 13 08 b.Pontefract 3-10-68

Source: Apprentice.

1986–87	Nottingham F	0	0
1986–87	Notts Co (loan)	5	0
1986–87	Darlington (loan)	5	0
1986–87	Peterborough U (loan)	4	0
1987–88	Nottingham F	0	0
1987–88	Darlington (loan)	3	0
1987–88	Swindon T (loan)	4	0
1987–88	Rotherham U (loan)	6	0
1988–89	Nottingham F	0	0
1988–89	Torquay U (loan)	13	0
1988–89	Peterborough U	31	0
1989–90	Peterborough U	16	0
1990–91	Doncaster R	20	0
1991–92	Doncaster R	16	0
1992–93	Doncaster R	41	0
1993–94	Grimsby T	46	0
1994–95	Grimsby T	43	0
1995–96	Grimsby T	44	0
1996–97	Grimsby T	0	0
1996–97	WBA	30	0
1997–98	WBA	2	0
1997–98	Aston Villa (loan)	0	0
1998–99	WBA	0	0
1998–99	Burnley	29	0
Total:		**358**	**0**

CRITCHLEY, Neil — Midfield

b.Crewe 18-10-78

Source: Trainee.

1997–98	Crewe Alex	0	0
1998–99	Crewe Alex	0	0

CRITTENDEN, Nick — Defender

H: 5 10 W: 11 00 b.Ascot 11-11-78

Source: Trainee.

1997–98	Chelsea	2	0
1998–99	Chelsea	0	0
1998–99	Plymouth Arg (loan)	2	0
Total:		**4**	**0**

CROFT, Gary — Defender

H: 5 8 W: 10 08 b.Stafford 17-2-74

Source: Trainee. *Honours:* England Under-21.

1990–91	Grimsby T	1	0
1991–92	Grimsby T	0	0
1992–93	Grimsby T	32	0
1993–94	Grimsby T	36	1
1994–95	Grimsby T	44	1
1995–96	Grimsby T	36	1
1995–96	Blackburn R	0	0
1996–97	Blackburn R	5	0
1997–98	Blackburn R	23	1
1998–99	Blackburn R	12	0
Total:		**189**	**4**

CRONIN, Gary — Midfield

H: 5 10 W: 10 00 b.Dublin 16-3-79

Source: Stella Maris.

1997–98	Middlesbrough	0	0
1998–99	Middlesbrough	0	0

CROOKES, Dale — Midfield

H: 5 9 W: 12 03 b.Sheffield 10-3-80

Source: Trainee.

1997–98	Barnsley	0	0
1998–99	Barnsley	0	0

CROOKS, Lee — Defender

H: 6 1 W: 12 09 b.Wakefield 14-1-78

Source: Trainee. *Honours:* England Youth.

1994–95	Manchester C	0	0
1995–96	Manchester C	0	0
1996–97	Manchester C	15	0
1997–98	Manchester C	5	0
1998–99	Manchester C	34	1
Total:		**54**	**1**

CROSBY, Andy — Defender

H: 6 2 W: 13 07 b.Rotherham 3-3-73

Source: Leeds U Trainee.

1991–92	Doncaster R	22	0
1992–93	Doncaster R	29	0
1993–94	Doncaster R	0	0
1993–94	Darlington	25	0
1994–95	Darlington	35	0
1995–96	Darlington	45	1
1996–97	Darlington	42	1
1997–98	Darlington	34	1
1998–99	Chester C	41	4
Total:		**273**	**7**

CROSS, Jonathan — Midfield

H: 5 10 W: 11 07 b.Wallasey 2-3-75

Source: Trainee.

1991–92	Wrexham	6	0
1992–93	Wrexham	37	7
1993–94	Wrexham	25	2
1994–95	Wrexham	24	1
1995–96	Wrexham	7	0
1996–97	Wrexham	18	2
1996–97	Hereford U (loan)	5	1
1997–98	Wrexham	2	0
1997–98	Tranmere R (loan)	0	0
1998–99	Chester C	35	1
Total:		**159**	**14**

CROSS, Matthew — Defender

H: 5 6 W: 12 03 b.Bury 25-3-80

Source: Trainee.

1997–98	Barnsley	0	0
1998–99	Barnsley	0	0

CROSSLAND, Mark — Midfield

H: 5 11 W: 12 02 b.Ashton-under-Lyne 14-12-78

Source: Lincoln C Trainee.

1996–97	Bury	0	0
1997–98	Bury	0	0
1998–99	Bury	0	0

CROSSLEY, Mark — Goalkeeper

H: 6 0 W: 15 09 b.Barnsley 16-6-69

Source: Trainee. *Honours:* England Under-21, Wales B, 2 full caps.

1987–88	Nottingham F	0	0
1988–89	Nottingham F	2	0
1989–90	Nottingham F	8	0
1989–90	Manchester U (loan)	0	0
1990–91	Nottingham F	38	0
1991–92	Nottingham F	36	0
1992–93	Nottingham F	37	0
1993–94	Nottingham F	37	0
1994–95	Nottingham F	42	0
1995–96	Nottingham F	38	0
1996–97	Nottingham F	33	0
1997–98	Nottingham F	0	0
1997–98	Millwall (loan)	13	0
1998–99	Nottingham F	12	0
Total:		**296**	**0**

CROSSLEY, Ryan — Defender

H: 6 0 W: 12 00 b.Halifax 23-7-80

Source: Trainee.

1998–99	Huddersfield T	0	0

CROUCH, Peter — Forward

H: 6 2 W: 11 12 b.Macclesfield 30-1-81

Source: Trainee. *Honours:* England Youth.

1998–99	Tottenham H	0	0

CROUDSON, Steve — Goalkeeper

H: 6 0 W: 12 00 b.Grimsby 14-9-79

Source: Trainee.

1998–99	Grimsby T	2	0
Total:		**2**	**0**

CROWE, Barry — Defender

H: 5 4 W: 10 05 b.Liverpool 15-6-80

Source: Trainee.

1998–99	Tranmere R	0	0

CROWE, Dean — Forward

H: 5 5 W: 11 02 b.Stockport 6-6-79

Source: Trainee.

1996–97	Stoke C	0	0
1997–98	Stoke C	16	4
1998–99	Stoke C	38	8
Total:		**54**	**12**

CROWE, Glen — Forward

H: 5 10 W: 13 01 b.Dublin 25-12-77

Source: Trainee.

1995–96	Wolverhampton W	2	1
1996–97	Exeter C (loan)	10	5
1996–97	Wolverhampton W	6	0
1997–98	Wolverhampton W	2	0
1997–98	Cardiff C (loan)	8	1
1998–99	Wolverhampton W	0	0
1998–99	Exeter C (loan)	9	0
1998–99	Plymouth Arg	11	1
Total:		**48**	**8**

CROWE, Jason — Defender

H: 5 9 W: 10 09 b.Sidcup 30-9-78

Source: Trainee. *Honours:* England Schools, Youth.

1995–96	Arsenal	0	0
1996–97	Arsenal	0	0
1997–98	Arsenal	0	0
1998–99	Arsenal	0	0
1998–99	Crystal Palace (loan)	8	0
Total:		**8**	**0**

CROWE, Seamie — Midfield

H: 5 7 W: 11 07 b.Galway 18-11-80

Source: Trainee.

1997–98	Wolverhampton W	0	0
1998–99	Wolverhampton W	0	0

CRUYFF, Jordi — Forward

H: 6 1 W: 10 12 b.Amsterdam 9-2-74

Source: Ajax. *Honours:* Holland 9 full caps, 1 goal.

1992–93	Barcelona	0	0
1993–94	Barcelona	0	0
1994–95	Barcelona	28	9
1995–96	Barcelona	13	2
1996–97	Manchester U	16	2
1997–98	Manchester U	5	0
1998–99	Manchester U	5	2
Total:		**67**	**15**

CUERVO, Philippe — Midfield

H: 5 11 W: 11 03 b.Ris-oranges 13-8-69

1996–97	St Etienne	21	0
1997–98	Swindon T	23	0
1998–99	Swindon T	6	0
Total:		**50**	**0**

CULKIN, Nick — Goalkeeper

H: 6 2 W: 13 05 b.York 6-7-78

Source: York C.

1995–96	Manchester U	0	0
1996–97	Manchester U	0	0
1997–98	Manchester U	0	0
1998–99	Manchester U	0	0

CULLEN, Jon — Midfield

H: 6 0 W: 11 10 b.Durham 10-1-73

Source: Trainee.

1990–91	Doncaster R	1	0
1991–92	Doncaster R	8	0
1992–93	Doncaster R	0	0
1993–94	Doncaster R	0	0
From Morpeth T			
1996–97	Hartlepool U	6	0
1997–98	Hartlepool U	28	12
1997–98	Sheffield U	2	0
1998–99	Sheffield U	2	0
Total:		**47**	**12**

CULLIP, Danny — Defender

H: 6 1 W: 12 07 b.Bracknell 17-9-76

Source: Trainee.

1995–96	Oxford U	0	0
1996–97	Fulham	29	1
1997–98	Fulham	21	1
1997–98	Brentford	13	0
1998–99	Brentford	2	0
Total:		**65**	**2**

CULSHAW, Thomas — Defender

H: 5 10 W: 12 02 b.Liverpool 10-10-78

Source: Trainee. *Honours:* England Schools.

1995–96	Liverpool	0	0
1996–97	Liverpool	0	0
1997–98	Liverpool	0	0
1998–99	Liverpool	0	0

CULVERHOUSE, Ian — Defender

H: 5 10 W: 11 02 b.Bishop's Stortford 22-9-64

Source: Apprentice. *Honours:* England Youth.

1982–83	Tottenham H	0	0
1983–84	Tottenham H	2	0
1984–85	Tottenham H	0	0
1985–86	Tottenham H	0	0
1985–86	Norwich C	30	0
1986–87	Norwich C	25	0
1987–88	Norwich C	33	0
1988–89	Norwich C	38	0
1989–90	Norwich C	32	0
1990–91	Norwich C	34	0
1991–92	Norwich C	21	0
1992–93	Norwich C	41	0
1993–94	Norwich C	42	0
1994–95	Norwich C	0	0
1994–95	Swindon T	9	0
1995–96	Swindon T	46	0
1996–97	Swindon T	31	0
1997–98	Swindon T	11	0
From Kingstonian.			
1998–99	Brighton & HA	35	0
Total:		**430**	**0**

CUMMINS, Michael — Midfield

H: 6 0 W: 12 08 b.Dublin 1-6-78

Source: Trainee. *Honours:* Eire Youth, Under-21.

1995–96	Middlesbrough	0	0
1996–97	Middlesbrough	0	0
1997–98	Middlesbrough	0	0
1998–99	Middlesbrough	1	0
Total:		**1**	**0**

CUNDY, Jason — Defender

H: 6 0 W: 13 10 b.Wimbledon 12-11-69

Source: Trainee. *Honours:* England Under-21.

1988–89	Chelsea	0	0
1989–90	Chelsea	0	0
1990–91	Chelsea	29	0
1991–92	Chelsea	12	1
1991–92	Tottenham H (loan)	10	0
1992–93	Tottenham H	15	1
1993–94	Tottenham H	0	0
1994–95	Tottenham H	0	0
1995–96	Tottenham H	1	0
1995–96	Crystal Palace (loan)	4	0
1996–97	Tottenham H	0	0
1996–97	Bristol C (loan)	6	1
1996–97	Ipswich T	13	2
1997–98	Ipswich T	41	3
1998–99	Ipswich T	4	0
Total:		**135**	**8**

CUNNINGHAM, Darren — Midfield

b.Telford 23-8-79

1998–99	WBA	0	0

CUNNINGHAM, Kenny — Defender

H: 5 11 W: 11 02 b.Dublin 28-6-71

Source: Tolka R. *Honours:* Eire Under-21, B, 23 full caps.

1989–90	Millwall	5	0
1990–91	Millwall	23	0
1991–92	Millwall	17	0
1992–93	Millwall	37	0
1993–94	Millwall	39	1
1994–95	Millwall	15	0
1994–95	Wimbledon	28	0
1995–96	Wimbledon	33	0
1996–97	Wimbledon	36	0
1997–98	Wimbledon	32	0
1998–99	Wimbledon	35	0
Total:		**300**	**1**

CURBISHLEY, Alan — Midfield

H: 5 10 W: 11 07 b.Forest Gate 8-11-57

Source: Apprentice. *Honours:* England Schools, Youth, Under-21.

1974–75	West Ham U	2	0
1975–76	West Ham U	14	2
1976–77	West Ham U	10	1
1977–78	West Ham U	32	1
1978–79	West Ham U	27	1
1979–80	Birmingham C	42	3
1980–81	Birmingham C	29	6
1981–82	Birmingham C	29	1

1982–83	Birmingham C	30	1
1982–83	Aston Villa	7	0
1983–84	Aston Villa	26	1
1984–85	Aston Villa	3	0
1984–85	Charlton Ath	23	2
1985–86	Charlton Ath	30	4
1986–87	Charlton Ath	10	0
1987–88	Brighton & HA	34	6
1988–89	Brighton & HA	37	6
1989–90	Brighton & HA	45	1
1990–91	Charlton Ath	25	0
1991–92	Charlton Ath	1	0
1992–93	Charlton Ath	1	0
1993–94	Charlton Ath	1	0
1994–95	Charlton Ath	0	0
1995–96	Charlton Ath	0	0
1996–97	Charlton Ath	0	0
1997–98	Charlton Ath	0	0
1998–99	Charlton Ath	0	0
Total:		**458**	**36**

CURCIC, Sasa — Midfield

H: 5 9 W: 11 00 b.Belgrade 14-2-72

Honours: Yugoslavia 13 full caps, 1 goal.

1991–92	OFK Belgrade	17	2
1992–93	OFK Belgrade	32	3
1993–94	Partizan Belgrade	33	8
1994–95	Partizan Belgrade	31	6
1995–96	Partizan Belgrade	10	2
1995–96	Bolton W	28	4
1996–97	Aston Villa	22	0
1997–98	Aston Villa	7	0
1997–98	Crystal Palace	8	1
1998–99	Crystal Palace	15	4
Total:		**203**	**30**

CURETON, Jamie — Forward

H: 5 7 W: 11 00 b.Bristol 28-8-75

Source: Trainee. *Honours:* England Youth.

1992–93	Norwich C	0	0
1993–94	Norwich C	0	0
1994–95	Norwich C	17	4
1995–96	Norwich C	12	2
1995–96	Bournemouth (loan)	5	0
1996–97	Norwich C	0	0
1996–97	Bristol R	38	11
1997–98	Bristol R	43	13
1998–99	Bristol R	46	25
Total:		**161**	**55**

CURLE, Keith — Defender

H: 6 0 W: 12 07 b.Bristol 14-11-63

Source: Apprentice. *Honours:* England B, 3 full caps.

1981–82	Bristol R	20	2
1982–83	Bristol R	12	2
1983–84	Bristol R	0	0
1983–84	Torquay U	16	5
1983–84	Bristol C	6	0
1984–85	Bristol C	40	0
1985–86	Bristol C	44	1
1986–87	Bristol C	28	0
1987–88	Bristol C	3	0
1987–88	Reading	30	0
1988–89	Reading	10	0
1988–89	Wimbledon	18	0
1989–90	Wimbledon	38	2
1990–91	Wimbledon	37	1
1991–92	Manchester C	40	5
1992–93	Manchester C	39	3
1993–94	Manchester C	29	1
1994–95	Manchester C	31	2
1995–96	Manchester C	32	0
1996–97	Wolverhampton W	21	2
1997–98	Wolverhampton W	40	1
1998–99	Wolverhampton W	44	4
Total:		**578**	**31**

CURRAN, Chris — Defender

H: 5 11 W: 11 09 b.Birmingham 17-9-71

Source: Trainee.

1989–90	Torquay U	1	0
1990–91	Torquay U	13	0
1991–92	Torquay U	17	0
1992–93	Torquay U	34	0
1993–94	Torquay U	41	1
1994–95	Torquay U	27	2
1995–96	Torquay U	19	1
1995–96	Plymouth Arg	8	0
1996–97	Plymouth Arg	22	0
1997–98	Exeter C	9	0
1998–99	Exeter C	34	4
Total:		**225**	**8**

CURRAN, Danny — Midfield

b.Essex 13-6-81

Source: Trainee.

1998–99	Leyton Orient	1	0
Total:		**1**	**0**

CURRIE, Darren — Midfield

H: 5 10 W: 12 07 b.Hampstead 29-11-74

Source: Trainee.

1993–94	West Ham U	0	0
1994–95	West Ham U	0	0
1994–95	Shrewsbury T (loan)	17	2
1995–96	West Ham U	0	0
1995–96	Leyton Orient (loan)	10	0
1995–96	Shrewsbury T	13	2
1996–97	Shrewsbury T	37	2
1997–98	Shrewsbury T	16	4

1997–98	Plymouth Arg	7	0
1998–99	Barnet	38	4
Total:		**138**	**14**

CURRIE, Michael — Forward

H: 5 10 W: 11 00 b.Westminster 19-10-79

Source: Trainee.

1997–98	QPR	0	0
1998–99	QPR	0	0

CURTIS, John — Defender

H: 5 10 W: 11 07 b.Nuneaton 3-9-78

Source: Trainee. *Honours:* England Schools, Youth, Under-21, B.

1995–96	Manchester U	0	0
1996–97	Manchester U	0	0
1997–98	Manchester U	8	0
1998–99	Manchester U	4	0
Total:		**12**	**0**

CURTIS, Tom — Midfield

H: 5 8 W: 10 08 b.Exeter 1-3-73

Source: School.

1991–92	Derby Co	0	0
1992–93	Derby Co	0	0
1993–94	Chesterfield	36	3
1994–95	Chesterfield	40	2
1995–96	Chesterfield	46	0
1996–97	Chesterfield	40	3
1997–98	Chesterfield	36	1
1998–99	Chesterfield	24	3
Total:		**222**	**12**

CURTOLO, David — Midfield

H: 5 9 W: 11 00 b.Stockholm 30-9-80

1997–98	Aston Villa	0	0
1998–99	Aston Villa	0	0

CUSACK, Nick — Midfield

H: 6 0 W: 12 05 b.Rotherham 24-12-65

Source: Alvechurch.

1987–88	Leicester C	16	1
1988–89	Peterborough U	44	10
1989–90	Motherwell	31	11
1990–91	Motherwell	29	4
1991–92	Motherwell	17	2
1991–92	Darlington	21	6
1992–93	Oxford U	39	4
1993–94	Oxford U	20	6
1993–94	Wycombe W (loan)	4	0
1994–95	Oxford U	2	0
1994–95	Fulham	27	7
1995–96	Fulham	42	5
1996–97	Fulham	45	2
1997–98	Fulham	2	0
1997–98	Swansea C	32	0
1998–99	Swansea C	43	1
Total:		**414**	**59**

CUSS, Paul — Goalkeeper

H: 6 1 W: 13 07 b.Minden 19-4-79

Source: Trainee.

1997–98	Huddersfield T	0	0
1998–99	Huddersfield T	0	0

CUTLER, Neil — Goalkeeper

H: 6 1 W: 12 00 b.Birmingham 3-9-76

Source: Trainee. *Honours:* England Schools, Youth.

1993–94	WBA	0	0
1994–95	WBA	0	0
1995–96	WBA	0	0
1995–96	Coventry C (loan)	0	0
1995–96	Chester C (loan)	1	0
1996–97	Crewe Alex	0	0
1996–97	Chester C (loan)	5	0
1997–98	Crewe Alex	0	0
1998–99	Chester C	23	0
Total:		**29**	**0**

D'AURIA, David — Midfield

H: 5 8 W: 12 00 b.Swansea 26-3-70

Source: Trainee.

1987–88	Swansea C	4	0
1988–89	Swansea C	14	2
1989–90	Swansea C	7	0
1990–91	Swansea C	20	4
From Barry T			
1994–95	Scarborough	34	7
1995–96	Scarborough	18	1
1995–96	Scunthorpe U	27	5
1996–97	Scunthorpe U	39	3
1997–98	Scunthorpe U	41	10
1998–99	Hull C	42	4
Total:		**246**	**36**

D'JAFFO, Laurent — Forward

H: 6 0 W: 13 05 b.France 5-11-70

1997–98	Ayr U	24	10
1998–99	Bury	37	8
Total:		**61**	**18**

DA COSTA, Nelson — Defender

H: 5 10 W: 12 03 b.Angola 8-12-78

Source: Belenenses.

1996–97	Stockport Co	0	0
1997–98	Macclesfield T	0	0
1998–99	Macclesfield T	0	0

DABELSTEEN, Thomas — Midfield

b.Copenhagen 6-3-73

1998–99	Scarborough	5	1
Total:		**5**	**1**

DABIZAS, Nikos — Defender

H: 6 0 W: 11 11 b.Amypeo 3-8-73

Honours: Greece 28 full caps.

1994–95	Olympiakos	26	2
1995–96	Olympiakos	27	1
1996–97	Olympiakos	31	0
1997–98	Olympiakos	20	5
1997–98	Newcastle U	11	1
1998–99	Newcastle U	30	3
Total:		**145**	**12**

DACOURT, Olivier — Midfield

H: 5 9 W: 11 00 b.Montreuil 25-9-74

1992–93	Strasbourg	6	0
1993–94	Strasbourg	8	0
1994–95	Strasbourg	18	0
1995–96	Strasbourg	34	0
1996–97	Strasbourg	31	1
1997–98	Strasbourg	30	3
1998–99	Everton	30	2
Total:		**157**	**6**

DAHLIN, Martin — Forward

H: 6 1 W: 13 03 b.Lund 16-4-68

Source: Lund BK. *Honours:* Sweden 58 full caps, 28 goals.

1988	Malmo	21	17
1989	Malmo	17	4
1990	Malmo	19	7
1991	Malmo	22	11
1991–92	Moenchengladbach	12	2
1992–93	Moenchengladbach	20	10
1993–94	Moenchengladbach	27	12
1994–95	Moenchengladbach	24	11
1995–96	Moenchengladbach	23	15
1996–97	Roma	3	0
1997–98	Blackburn R	21	4
1998–99	Blackburn R	5	0
Total:		**214**	**93**

DAILLY, Christian — Defender

H: 6 0 W: 12 05 b.Dundee 23-10-73

Source: 'S' Form. *Honours:* Scotland B, Under-21, 14 full caps, 1 goal.

1990–91	Dundee U	18	5
1991–92	Dundee U	8	0
1992–93	Dundee U	14	4
1993–94	Dundee U	38	4
1994–95	Dundee U	33	4
1995–96	Dundee U	30	1
1996–97	Derby Co	36	3
1997–98	Derby Co	30	1
1998–99	Derby Co	1	0
1998–99	Blackburn R	17	0
Total:		**225**	**22**

DAIR, Jason — Midfield

H: 5 11 W: 10 08 b.Dunfermline 15-6-74

Source: Castlebridge. *Honours:* Scotland Under 21.

1991–92	Raith R	4	0
1992–93	Raith R	15	1
1993–94	Raith R	38	6
1994–95	Raith R	18	1
1995–96	Raith R	19	3
1996–97	Millwall	24	1
1997–98	Raith R	25	0
1998–99	Dunfermline Ath	10	0
Total:		**153**	**12**

DAISH, Liam — Defender

H: 6 2 W: 13 05 b.Portsmouth 23-9-68

Source: Apprentice. *Honours:* Eire Under-21, B, 5 full caps.

1986–87	Portsmouth	1	0
1987–88	Portsmouth	0	0
1988–89	Cambridge U	28	0
1989–90	Cambridge U	42	1
1990–91	Cambridge U	13	1
1991–92	Cambridge U	22	0
1992–93	Cambridge U	16	0
1993–94	Cambridge U	18	2
1993–94	Birmingham C	19	0
1994–95	Birmingham C	37	3
1995–96	Birmingham C	17	0
1995–96	Coventry C	11	1
1996–97	Coventry C	20	1
1997–98	Coventry C	0	0
1998–99	Coventry C	0	0
Total:		**244**	**9**

DALEY, Tony — Midfield

H: 5 9 W: 11 00 b.Birmingham 18-11-67

Source: Apprentice. *Honours:* England Youth, 7 full caps.

1984–85	Aston Villa	5	0
1985–86	Aston Villa	23	2
1986–87	Aston Villa	33	3
1987–88	Aston Villa	14	3
1988–89	Aston Villa	29	5
1989–90	Aston Villa	32	6
1990–91	Aston Villa	23	2
1991–92	Aston Villa	34	7
1992–93	Aston Villa	13	2
1993–94	Aston Villa	27	1
1994–95	Wolverhampton W	1	0
1995–96	Wolverhampton W	18	3
1996–97	Wolverhampton W	0	0
1997–98	Wolverhampton W	2	0
1998–99	Watford	12	1
Total:		**266**	**35**

DALGLISH, Paul — Forward

H: 5 9 W: 10 10 b.Glasgow 18-2-77

Honours: Scotland Under-21.

1995–96	Celtic	0	0
1996–97	Liverpool	0	0
1997–98	Liverpool	0	0
1997–98	Newcastle U	0	0
1997–98	Bury (loan)	12	0
1998–99	Newcastle U	11	1
1998–99	Norwich C (loan)	5	0
Total:		**28**	**1**

DALLA BONA, Samuele — Defender

H: 6 1 W: 12 00 b.S. Dona di Piave 6-2-81

1997–98	Atalanta	0	0
1998–99	Chelsea	0	0

DALTON, Paul — Forward

H: 6 0 W: 13 00 b.Middlesbrough 25-4-67

Source: Brandon U.

1987–88	Manchester U	0	0
1988–89	Manchester U	0	0
1988–89	Hartlepool U	17	2
1989–90	Hartlepool U	45	11
1990–91	Hartlepool U	46	11
1991–92	Hartlepool U	43	13
1992–93	Plymouth Arg	32	9
1993–94	Plymouth Arg	40	12
1994–95	Plymouth Arg	26	4
1995–96	Huddersfield T	29	5
1996–97	Huddersfield T	29	4
1997–98	Huddersfield T	31	13
1998–99	Huddersfield T	9	3
Total:		**347**	**87**

DANIELSSON, Helgi — Midfield

H: 5 11 W: 10 10 b.Reykjavik 13-7-81

Source: Fylkir.

1998–99	Peterborough U	0	0

DARBY, Duane — Forward

H: 5 11 W: 12 06 b.Birmingham 17-10-73

Source: Trainee.

1991–92	Torquay U	14	2
1992–93	Torquay U	34	12
1993–94	Torquay U	36	8
1994–95	Torquay U	24	4
1995–96	Doncaster R	17	4
1995–96	Hull C	8	1
1996–97	Hull C	41	13
1997–98	Hull C	29	13
1998–99	Notts Co	0	0
1998–99	Hull C (loan)	8	0
Total:		**211**	**57**

DARBY, Julian — Midfield

H: 6 0 W: 11 04 b.Bolton 3-10-67

Source: Trainee. *Honours:* England Schools.

1984–85	Bolton W	0	0
1985–86	Bolton W	2	0
1986–87	Bolton W	28	0
1987–88	Bolton W	35	2
1988–89	Bolton W	44	5
1989–90	Bolton W	46	10
1990–91	Bolton W	45	9
1991–92	Bolton W	44	6
1992–93	Bolton W	21	4
1993–94	Bolton W	5	0
1993–94	Coventry C	26	5
1994–95	Coventry C	29	0
1995–96	Coventry C	0	0
1995–96	WBA	22	1
1996–97	WBA	17	0
1997–98	Preston NE	12	0
1997–98	Rotherham U (loan)	3	0
1998–99	Preston NE	20	1
Total:		**399**	**43**

DARCHEVILLE, Jean-Claude — Forward

H: 5 8 W: 13 09 b.French Guyana 25-7-75

1995–96	Rennes	10	1
1996–97	Rennes	9	1

1997–98	Rennes	24	3
1998–99	Nottingham F	16	2
Total:		**59**	**7**

DARCY, Ross — Defender

H: 6 0 W: 12 02 b.Balbriggan 21-3-78

Source: Trainee. *Honours:* Eire Under-21.

1995–96	Tottenham H	0	0
1996–97	Tottenham H	0	0
1997–98	Tottenham H	0	0
1998–99	Tottenham H	0	0

DARLINGTON, Jermaine — Defender

H: 5 10 W: 12 05 b.London 11-4-74

Source: Aylesbury U.

1998–99	QPR	4	0
Total:		**4**	**0**

DARNBROUGH, Lee — Goalkeeper

H: 6 1 W: 12 12 b.Ashton 15-9-77

Source: Trainee. *Honours:* England Youth.

1994–95	Oldham Ath	0	0
1995–96	Oldham Ath	0	0
1996–97	Oldham Ath	0	0
1997–98	Oldham Ath	0	0
1998–99	Oldham Ath	0	0

DASOVIC, Nick — Midfield

H: 6 1 W: 12 04 b.Vancouver 5-12-68

Source: Trelleborg.

1996–97	St Johnstone	14	0
1997–98	St Johnstone	19	0
1998–99	St Johnstone	31	1
Total:		**64**	**1**

DAVENPORT, Peter — Midfield

H: 5 11 W: 12 10 b.Birkenhead 24-3-61

Source: Everton, Cammell Laird. *Honours:* England B, 1 full cap.

1981–82	Nottingham F	5	4
1982–83	Nottingham F	18	6
1983–84	Nottingham F	33	15
1984–85	Nottingham F	35	16
1985–86	Nottingham F	27	13
1985–86	Manchester U	11	1
1986–87	Manchester U	39	14
1987–88	Manchester U	34	5
1988–89	Manchester U	8	2
1988–89	Middlesbrough	24	4
1989–90	Middlesbrough	35	3
1990–91	Sunderland	29	7
1991–92	Sunderland	36	4
1992–93	Sunderland	34	4
1993–94	Airdrie	38	9
1994–95	St Johnstone	22	4
1994–95	Stockport Co	6	1
From Southport.			
1997–98	Macclesfield T	4	1
1998–99	Macclesfield T	1	0
Total:		**439**	**113**

DAVEY, Simon — Midfield

H: 5 10 W: 11 02 b.Swansea 1-10-70

Source: Trainee.

1986–87	Swansea C	1	0
1987–88	Swansea C	4	0
1988–89	Swansea C	3	0
1989–90	Swansea C	18	2
1990–91	Swansea C	18	2
1991–92	Swansea C	5	0
1992–93	Carlisle U	38	5
1993–94	Carlisle U	42	9
1994–95	Carlisle U	25	4
1994–95	Preston NE	13	3
1995–96	Preston NE	38	10
1996–97	Preston NE	37	6
1997–98	Preston NE	18	2
1997–98	Darlington (loan)	11	0
1998–99	Preston NE	0	0
Total:		**271**	**43**

DAVIDSON, Callum — Defender

H: 5 10 W: 11 00 b.Stirling 26-6-76

Source: 'S' Form. *Honours:* Scotland Under-21, 7 full caps.

1994–95	St Johnstone	7	1
1995–96	St Johnstone	2	0
1996–97	St Johnstone	20	2
1997–98	St Johnstone	15	1
1997–98	Blackburn R	1	0
1998–99	Blackburn R	34	1
Total:		**79**	**5**

DAVIDSON, Ross — Defender

H: 5 9 W: 12 04 b.Chertsey 13-11-73

Source: Walton & Hersham. *Honours:*

1993–94	Sheffield U	0	0
1994–95	Sheffield U	1	0
1995–96	Sheffield U	1	0
1995–96	Chester C	19	1
1996–97	Chester C	40	2
1997–98	Chester C	24	1
1998–99	Chester C	40	1
Total:		**125**	**5**

DAVIES, Gareth — Defender

H: 6 1 W: 11 03 b.Hereford 11-12-73

Source: Trainee. *Honours:* Wales Under-21.

1991–92	Hereford U	4	0
1992–93	Hereford U	32	1
1993–94	Hereford U	31	0
1994–95	Hereford U	28	0
1995–96	Crystal Palace	20	2
1996–97	Crystal Palace	6	0
1996–97	Cardiff C (loan)	6	2
1997–98	Crystal Palace	1	0
1997–98	Reading	18	0
1998–99	Reading	1	0
1998–99	Swindon T	6	0
Total:		**153**	**5**

DAVIES, Jamie — Forward

H: 6 0 W: 11 09 b.Swansea 12-2-80

Source: Trainee.

1998–99	Swansea C	1	0
Total:		**1**	**0**

DAVIES, Kevin — Forward

H: 6 0 W: 13 11 b.Sheffield 26-3-77

Source: Trainee. *Honours:* England Youth, Under-21.

1993–94	Chesterfield	24	4
1994–95	Chesterfield	41	11
1995–96	Chesterfield	30	4
1996–97	Chesterfield	34	3
1996–97	Southampton	0	0
1997–98	Southampton	25	9
1998–99	Blackburn R	21	1
Total:		**175**	**32**

DAVIES, Kevin — Midfield

H: 6 0 W: 12 00 b.Sheffield 15-11-78

Source: Trainee.

1997–98	Sheffield U	0	0
1998–99	Sheffield U	0	0

DAVIES, Lawrence — Forward

H: 6 1 W: 11 11 b.Abergavenny 3-9-77

Source: Trainee.

1996–97	Leeds U	0	0
1997–98	Bradford C	4	0
1997–98	Darlington (loan)	2	0
1998–99	Bradford C	0	0
1998–99	Hartlepool U (loan)	3	0
1998–99	Brighton & HA	8	0
Total:		**17**	**0**

DAVIES, Simon — Midfield

H: 5 11 W: 12 04 b.Davenham 23-4-74

Source: Trainee. *Honours:* Wales 1 full cap.

1992–93	Manchester U	0	0
1993–94	Manchester U	0	0
1993–94	Exeter C (loan)	6	1
1994–95	Manchester U	5	0
1995–96	Manchester U	6	0
1996–97	Manchester U	0	0
1996–97	Huddersfield T (loan)	3	0
1997–98	Luton T	20	1
1998–99	Luton T	2	0
1998–99	Macclesfield T	12	2
Total:		**54**	**4**

DAVIES, Simon — Midfield

H: 5 10 W: 12 03 b.Haverfordwest 23-10-79

Source: Trainee. *Honours:* Wales Under-21.

1997–98	Peterborough U	6	0
1998–99	Peterborough U	43	4
Total:		**49**	**4**

DAVIS, Danny — Midfield

H: 5 10 W: 11 04 b.Brighton 3-10-80

Source: Trainee.

1998–99	Brighton & HA	1	0
Total:		**1**	**0**

DAVIS, Kelvin — Goalkeeper

H: 6 1 W: 13 11 b.Bedford 29-9-76

Source: Trainee. *Honours:* England Youth, Under-21.

1993–94	Luton T	1	0
1994–95	Luton T	9	0
1994–95	Torquay U (loan)	2	0
1995–96	Luton T	6	0
1996–97	Luton T	0	0
1997–98	Luton T	32	0
1997–98	Hartlepool U (loan)	2	0
1998–99	Luton T	44	0
Total:		**96**	**0**

DAVIS, Neil — Forward

H: 5 10 W: 11 07 b.Bloxwich 15-8-73

Source: Redditch U.

1991–92	Aston Villa	0	0
1992–93	Aston Villa	0	0
1993–94	Aston Villa	0	0
1994–95	Aston Villa	0	0
1995–96	Aston Villa	2	0
1996–97	Aston Villa	0	0
1996–97	Wycombe W (loan)	13	0

1997–98	Aston Villa	0	0
1998–99	Walsall	1	0
Total:		**16**	**0**

DAVIS, Ryan — Defender

H: 5 7 W: 10 02 b.Stoke 16-11-79

Source: Trainee.

1998–99	Sheffield W	0	0

DAVIS, Sean — Midfield

H: 5 11 W: 12 09 b.Clapham 20-9-79

Source: Trainee.

1996–97	Fulham	1	0
1997–98	Fulham	0	0
1998–99	Fulham	6	0
Total:		**7**	**0**

DAVIS, Sol — Defender

H: 5 7 W: 11 00 b.Cheltenham 4-9-79

Source: Trainee.

1997–98	Swindon T	6	0
1998–99	Swindon T	25	0
Total:		**31**	**0**

DAVIS, Steve — Defender

H: 6 1 W: 13 05 b.Birmingham 26-7-65

Source: Stoke C Apprentice. *Honours:* England Youth.

1983–84	Crewe Alex	24	0
1984–85	Crewe Alex	40	0
1985–86	Crewe Alex	45	1
1986–87	Crewe Alex	33	0
1987–88	Crewe Alex	3	0
1987–88	Burnley	33	5
1988–89	Burnley	37	0
1989–90	Burnley	31	1
1990–91	Burnley	46	5
1991–92	Barnsley	9	0
1992–93	Barnsley	11	0
1993–94	Barnsley	0	0
1994–95	Barnsley	36	2
1995–96	Barnsley	27	5
1996–97	Barnsley	24	3
1997–98	Barnsley	0	0
1997–98	York C (loan)	2	1
1997–98	Oxford U	15	2
1998–99	Oxford U	3	0
Total:		**419**	**25**

DAVIS, Steve — Defender

H: 6 2 W: 14 07 b.Hexham 30-10-68

Source: Trainee.

1987–88	Southampton	0	0
1988–89	Southampton	0	0
1989–90	Southampton	4	0
1989–90	Burnley (loan)	9	0
1990–91	Southampton	3	0
1990–91	Notts Co (loan)	2	0
1991–92	Burnley	40	6
1992–93	Burnley	37	2
1993–94	Burnley	42	7
1994–95	Burnley	43	7
1995–96	Luton T	36	2
1996–97	Luton T	44	8
1997–98	Luton T	38	5
1998–99	Luton T	20	6
1998–99	Burnley	19	4
Total:		**337**	**47**

DAVISON, Aidan — Goalkeeper

H: 6 2 W: 14 00 b.Sedgefield 11-5-68

Source: Billingham Synthonia. *Honours:* Northern Ireland 3 full caps.

1987–88	Notts Co	0	0
1988–89	Notts Co	1	0
1989–90	Notts Co	0	0
1989–90	Leyton Orient (loan)	0	0
1989–90	Bury	0	0
1989–90	Chester C (loan)	0	0
1990–91	Bury	0	0
1990–91	Blackpool (loan)	0	0
1991–92	Millwall	33	0
1992–93	Millwall	1	0
1993–94	Bolton W	31	0
1994–95	Bolton W	4	0
1995–96	Bolton W	2	0
1996–97	Bolton W	0	0
1996–97	Ipswich T (loan)	0	0
1996–97	Hull C (loan)	9	0
1996–97	Bradford C	10	0
1997–98	Grimsby T	42	0
1998–99	Grimsby T	35	0
Total:		**168**	**0**

DAWS, Nick — Midfield

H: 5 11 W: 12 13 b.Salford 15-3-70

Source: Altrincham.

1992–93	Bury	36	1
1993–94	Bury	37	1
1994–95	Bury	34	2
1995–96	Bury	37	1
1996–97	Bury	46	2
1997–98	Bury	46	2
1998–99	Bury	46	2
Total:		**282**	**11**

DAWSON, Andrew — Defender

H: 5 10 W: 11 02 b.Northallerton 20-10-78

Source: Trainee.

1995–96	Nottingham F	0	0
1996–97	Nottingham F	0	0
1997–98	Nottingham F	0	0
1998–99	Nottingham F	0	0
1998–99	Scunthorpe U	24	0
Total:		**24**	**0**

DAWSON, Andrew — Defender

H: 6 0 W: 12 00 b.York 8-12-79

Source: Trainee.

1998–99	York C	11	1
Total:		**11**	**1**

DAWSON, Chris — Defender

H: 5 10 W: 10 02 b.Coventry 22-8-79

Source: Trainee.

1998–99	Bolton W	0	0

DAWSON, Kevin — Defender

H: 6 0 W: 10 07 b.Northallerton 18-6-81

Source: Trainee.

1998–99	Nottingham F	0	0

DAY, Chris — Goalkeeper

H: 6 3 W: 13 06 b.Walthamstow 28-7-75

Source: Trainee. *Honours:* England Under-21.

1992–93	Tottenham H	0	0
1993–94	Tottenham H	0	0
1994–95	Tottenham H	0	0
1995–96	Tottenham H	0	0
1996–97	Crystal Palace	24	0
1997–98	Watford	0	0
1998–99	Watford	0	0
Total:		**24**	**0**

DAY, Jamie — Midfield

H: 5 10 W: 11 04 b.Sidcup 13-9-79

Source: Trainee. *Honours:* England Schools.

1997–98	Arsenal	0	0
1998–99	Arsenal	0	0
1998–99	Bournemouth	2	0
Total:		**2**	**0**

DE FREITAS, Fabian — Forward

H: 6 0 W: 12 00 b.Paramaribo 28-7-72

Source: Volendam.

1994–95	Bolton W	13	2
1995–96	Bolton W	27	5
1996–97	Bolton W	0	0
1997–98	Osasuna	25	4
1998–99	WBA	37	7
Total:		**102**	**18**

DE GOEY, Ed — Goalkeeper

H: 6 6 W: 15 04 b.Gouda 20-12-66

Honours: Holland 31 full caps.

1985–86	Sparta	12	0
1986–87	Sparta	34	0
1987–88	Sparta	34	0
1988–89	Sparta	31	0
1989–90	Sparta	34	0
1990–91	Feyenoord	34	0
1991–92	Feyenoord	34	0
1992–93	Feyenoord	33	0
1993–94	Feyenoord	34	0
1994–95	Feyenoord	32	0
1995–96	Feyenoord	34	0
1997–98	Chelsea	28	0
1998–99	Chelsea	35	0
Total:		**409**	**0**

DE SOUZA, Miguel — Forward

H: 5 11 W: 13 08 b.Newham 11-2-70

Source: Dagenham & Redbridge.

1993–94	Birmingham C	7	0
1994–95	Birmingham C	8	0
1994–95	Bury (loan)	3	0
1994–95	Wycombe W	7	6
1995–96	Wycombe W	43	18
1996–97	Wycombe W	33	5
1996–97	Peterborough U	8	2
1997–98	Peterborough U	24	3
1998–99	Peterborough U	3	0
1998–99	Southend U (loan)	2	0
1998–99	Rochdale (loan)	5	0
Total:		**143**	**34**

DE ZEEUW, Arjan — Defender

H: 6 3 W: 13 03 b.Castricum 16-4-70

Source: Vitesse 22.

1992–93	Telstar	30	1
1993–94	Telstar	31	2
1994–95	Telstar	29	1
1995–96	Telstar	12	1
1995–96	Barnsley	31	1
1996–97	Barnsley	43	2

1997–98	Barnsley	26	0
1998–99	Barnsley	38	4
Total:		**240**	**12**

DEAN, Michael — Midfield

H: 5 9 W: 11 10 b.Weymouth 9-3-78

Source: Trainee.

1995–96	Bournemouth	5	0
1996–97	Bournemouth	12	0
1997–98	Bournemouth	8	0
1998–99	Bournemouth	9	0
Total:		**34**	**0**

DEANE, Brian — Forward

H: 6 3 W: 14 00 b.Leeds 7-2-68

Source: Apprentice. *Honours:* England B, 3 full caps.

1985–86	Doncaster R	3	0
1986–87	Doncaster R	20	2
1987–88	Doncaster R	43	10
1988–89	Sheffield U	43	22
1989–90	Sheffield U	45	21
1990–91	Sheffield U	38	13
1991–92	Sheffield U	30	12
1992–93	Sheffield U	41	14
1993–94	Leeds U	41	11
1994–95	Leeds U	35	9
1995–96	Leeds U	34	7
1996–97	Leeds U	28	5
1997–98	Sheffield U	24	11
From Benfica.			
1998–99	Middlesbrough	26	6
Total:		**451**	**143**

DEARDEN, Kevin — Goalkeeper

H: 5 11 W: 13 12 b.Luton 8-3-70

Source: Trainee.

1988–89	Tottenham H	0	0
1988–89	Cambridge U (loan)	15	0
1989–90	Tottenham H	0	0
1989–90	Hartlepool U (loan)	10	0
1989–90	Oxford U (loan)	0	0
1989–90	Swindon T (loan)	1	0
1990–91	Tottenham H	0	0
1990–91	Peterborough U (loan)	7	0
1990–91	Hull C (loan)	3	0
1991–92	Tottenham H	0	0
1991–92	Rochdale (loan)	2	0
1991–92	Birmingham C (loan)	12	0
1992–93	Tottenham H	1	0
1992–93	Portsmouth (loan)	0	0
1993–94	Tottenham H	0	0
1993–94	Brentford	35	0
1994–95	Brentford	43	0
1995–96	Brentford	41	0
1996–97	Brentford	44	0
1997–98	Brentford	35	0
1998–99	Brentford	7	0
1998–99	Barnet (loan)	1	0
Total:		**257**	**0**

DEBENHAM, Rob — Defender

H: 5 8 W: 10 07 b.Doncaster 28-11-79

Source: Trainee.

1997–98	Doncaster R	6	0
1998–99	Bury	0	0
Total:		**6**	**0**

DEGN, Peter — Midfield

H: 5 10 W: 13 04 b.Denmark 6-4-77

1995–96	Aarhus	9	0
1996–97	Aarhus	31	2
1997–98	Aarhus	23	0
1998–99	Aarhus	13	3
1998–99	Everton	4	0
Total:		**80**	**5**

DEL RIO, Walter — Defender

H: 6 0 W: 12 06 b.Buenos Aires 16-6-76

Source: Boca Juniors.

1998–99	Crystal Palace	2	0
Total:		**2**	**0**

DELANEY, Mark — Midfield

H: 6 1 W: 11 07 b.Haverfordwest 13-5-76

Source: Carmarthen T.

1998–99	Cardiff C	28	0
1998–99	Aston Villa	2	0
Total:		**30**	**0**

DELANY, Dean — Goalkeeper

b.Dublin 15-9-80

1997–98	Everton	0	0
1998–99	Everton	0	0

DELANY, Derek — Midfield

b.Drogheda 23-9-80

1998–99	Ipswich T	0	0

DELAP, Rory — Defender

H: 6 0 W: 13 00 b.Sutton Coldfield 6-7-76

Source: Trainee. *Honours:* Eire 3 full caps.

1992–93	Carlisle U	1	0
1993–94	Carlisle U	1	0
1994–95	Carlisle U	3	0

1995–96	Carlisle U	19	3
1996–97	Carlisle U	32	4
1997–98	Carlisle U	9	0
1997–98	Derby Co	13	0
1998–99	Derby Co	23	0
Total:		**101**	**7**

DELLAS, Traianos — Defender

H: 6 4 W: 15 00 b.Salonika 31-1-76

Source: Aris Salonika.

1997–98	Sheffield U	9	0
1998–99	Sheffield U	17	3
Total:		**26**	**3**

DELORGE, Laurent — Midfield

H: 5 10 W: 11 12 b.Leuven 21-7-79

Source: Gent.

1998–99	Coventry C	0	0

DEMPSEY, Gary — Midfield

b.Wexford 15-1-81

Source: Trainee.

1997–98	Everton	0	0
1998–99	Everton	0	0

DEMPSIE, Mark — Midfield

H: 5 9 W: 10 06 b.Bellshill 19-10-80

Source: Hibernian BC.

1996–97	Hibernian	0	0
1997–98	Hibernian	0	0
1998–99	Hibernian	8	0
Total:		**8**	**0**

DEN BIEMAN, Ivo — Midfield

H: 6 2 W: 12 10 b.Wamel 4-2-67

Source: SV Leones.

1990–91	Montrose	36	5
1991–92	Montrose	42	6
1992–93	Dundee	24	3
1993–94	Dunfermline Ath	41	3
1994–95	Dunfermline Ath	31	5
1995–96	Dunfermline Ath	26	1
1996–97	Dunfermline Ath	28	1
1997–98	Dunfermline Ath	25	0
1998–99	Dunfermline Ath	2	0
Total:		**255**	**24**

DENHAM, Greig — Defender

H: 6 0 W: 12 02 b.Glasgow 5-10-76

Source: Cumbernauld Utd.

1994–95	Motherwell	0	0
1995–96	Motherwell	13	0
1996–97	Motherwell	9	0
1997–98	Motherwell	18	0
1998–99	Motherwell	1	0
Total:		**41**	**0**

DENNEY, Phil — Forward

H: 6 1 W: 13 04 b.Bury 6-1-79

Source: Trainee.

1998–99	Bury	0	0

DENNIS, Kevin — Forward

H: 5 10 W: 12 00 b.Islington 14-12-76

Source: Arsenal Trainee.

1996–97	Brentford	12	0
1997–98	Brentford	5	0
1998–99	Brentford	0	0
Total:		**17**	**0**

DENNIS, Shaun — Defender

H: 6 1 W: 13 07 b.Kirkcaldy 20-12-69

Source: Lochgelly Albert. *Honours:* Scotland Under-21.

1988–89	Raith R	10	0
1989–90	Raith R	18	0
1990–91	Raith R	35	1
1991–92	Raith R	42	0
1992–93	Raith R	31	1
1993–94	Raith R	43	3
1994–95	Raith R	26	1
1995–96	Raith R	25	0
1996–97	Raith R	16	0
1996–97	Hibernian	4	1
1997–98	Hibernian	5	0
1998–99	Hibernian	31	3
Total:		**286**	**10**

DENYS, Ryan — Forward

H: 5 6 W: 11 02 b.Brentford 16-8-78

Source: Trainee.

1997–98	Brentford	19	1
1998–99	Brentford	0	0
Total:		**19**	**1**

DERRY, Shaun — Midfield

H: 5 10 W: 10 13 b.Nottingham 6-12-77

Source: Trainee.

1995–96	Notts Co	12	0
1996–97	Notts Co	39	2
1997–98	Notts Co	28	2
1997–98	Sheffield U	12	0
1998–99	Sheffield U	26	0
Total:		**117**	**4**

DESAILLY, Marcel — Defender

H: 6 2 W: 12 06 b.Accra 17-9-68

Honours: France 56 full caps, 2 goals.

1986–87	Nantes	15	0
1987–88	Nantes	11	0
1988–89	Nantes	36	1
1989–90	Nantes	36	1
1990–91	Nantes	34	1
1991–92	Nantes	32	2
1992–93	Marseille	31	1
1993–94	Marseille	15	0
1993–94	AC Milan	21	1
1994–95	AC Milan	22	1
1995–96	AC Milan	32	2
1996–97	AC Milan	29	1
1997–98	AC Milan	33	0
1998–99	Chelsea	31	0
Total:		**378**	**11**

DEVANEY, Martin — Midfield

H: 5 10 W: 11 12 b.Cheltenham 1-6-80

Source: Trainee.

1997–98	Coventry C	0	0
1998–99	Coventry C	0	0

DEVENNEY, Michael — Defender

H: 5 8 W: 10 05 b.Bolton 8-2-80

Source: Trainee.

1998–99	Burnley	0	0

DEVINE, Sean — Forward

H: 5 11 W: 13 00 b.Lewisham 6-9-72

Source: Omonia.

1995–96	Barnet	35	19
1996–97	Barnet	31	11
1997–98	Barnet	40	16
1998–99	Barnet	20	1
1998–99	Wycombe W	12	8
Total:		**138**	**55**

DEVITO, Claudio — Midfield

H: 5 9 W: 11 02 b.Peterborough 21-7-78

Source: Trainee.

1996–97	Northampton T	0	0
1997–98	Northampton T	0	0
1997–98	Barnet	1	0
1998–99	Barnet	0	0
Total:		**1**	**0**

DEVLIN, Mark — Midfield

H: 5 10 W: 11 13 b.Irvine 8-1-73

Source: Trainee.

1990–91	Stoke C	21	2
1991–92	Stoke C	0	0
1992–93	Stoke C	3	0
1993–94	Stoke C	0	0
1994–95	Stoke C	0	0
1995–96	Stoke C	10	0
1996–97	Stoke C	21	0
1997–98	Stoke C	0	0
1997–98	Exeter C (loan)	33	2
1998–99	Stoke C	0	0
Total:		**88**	**4**

DEVLIN, Paul — Forward

H: 5 8 W: 11 05 b.Birmingham 14-4-72

Source: Stafford R.

1991–92	Notts Co	2	0
1992–93	Notts Co	32	3
1993–94	Notts Co	41	7
1994–95	Notts Co	40	9
1995–96	Notts Co	26	6
1995–96	Birmingham C	16	7
1996–97	Birmingham C	38	16
1997–98	Birmingham C	22	5
1997–98	Sheffield U	10	1
1998–99	Sheffield U	33	5
1998–99	Notts Co (loan)	5	0
Total:		**265**	**59**

DEVOS, Jason — Defender

H: 6 4 W: 13 07 b.Ontario 2-1-74

Source: Montreal Impact. *Honours:* Canada 30 full caps.

1996–97	Darlington	8	0
1997–98	Darlington	24	3
1998–99	Darlington	12	2
1998–99	Dundee U	25	0
Total:		**69**	**5**

DEWHURST, Rob — Defender

H: 6 3 W: 14 00 b.Keighley 10-9-71

Source: Trainee.

1990–91	Blackburn R	13	0
1991–92	Blackburn R	0	0
1991–92	Darlington (loan)	11	1
1992–93	Blackburn R	0	0
1992–93	Huddersfield T (loan)	7	0
1993–94	Blackburn R	0	0
1993–94	Hull C	27	2
1994–95	Hull C	41	8
1995–96	Hull C	16	0
1996–97	Hull C	22	0
1997–98	Hull C	24	3
1998–99	Hull C	8	0
Total:		**169**	**14**

DI CANIO, Paolo — Forward

H: 5 9 W: 11 07 b.Rome 9-7-68

Source: Milan AC.

1985–86	Lazio	0	0
1986–87	Ternana	27	2
1987–88	Lazio	0	0
1988–89	Lazio	30	1
1989–90	Lazio	24	3
1990–91	Juventus	23	3
1991–92	Juventus	24	0
1992–93	Juventus	31	3
1993–94	Napoli	26	5
1994–95	Juventus	0	0
1994–95	AC Milan	15	1
1995–96	AC Milan	22	5
1996–97	Celtic	26	12
1997–98	Sheffield W	35	12
1998–99	Sheffield W	6	3
1998–99	West Ham U	13	4
Total:		**302**	**54**

DI LELLA, Gus — Midfield

H: 5 9 W: 11 09 b.Buenos Aires 6-10-73

1997–98	Darlington	5	0
From Blyth S			
1997–98	Hartlepool U	5	2
1998–99	Hartlepool U	23	2
Total:		**33**	**4**

DI MATTEO, Roberto — Midfield

H: 5 10 W: 12 00 b.Schaffhausen 29-5-70

Honours: Italy 33 full caps, 1 goal.

1988–89	Schaffhausen	18	0
1989–90	Schaffhausen	31	2
1990–91	Schaffhausen	1	0
1991–92	Zurich	34	6
1992–93	Aarau	32	1
1993–94	Lazio	29	4
1994–95	Lazio	28	1
1995–96	Lazio	31	2
1996–97	Chelsea	34	7
1997–98	Chelsea	30	4
1998–99	Chelsea	30	2
Total:		**298**	**29**

DIAWARA, Kaba — Forward

b.Toulon 16-12-75

Source: Toulon.

1994–95	Bordeaux	0	0
1995–96	Bordeaux	1	1
1996–97	Bordeaux	29	7
1997–98	Bordeaux	13	1
1997–98	Rennes	12	3
1998–99	Bordeaux	17	5
1998–99	Arsenal	12	0
Total:		**84**	**17**

DIAZ, Isidro — Midfield

H: 5 7 W: 9 03 b.Valencia 15-5-72

Source: Balaguer.

1995–96	Wigan Ath	37	10
1996–97	Wigan Ath	39	6
1997–98	Wolverhampton W	1	0
1997–98	Wigan Ath	2	0
1998–99	Rochdale	14	2
Total:		**93**	**18**

DIBBLE, Andy — Goalkeeper

H: 6 3 W: 16 10 b.Cwmbran 8-5-65

Source: Apprentice. *Honours:* Wales Schools, Youth, Under-21, 3 full caps.

1981–82	Cardiff C	1	0
1982–83	Cardiff C	20	0
1983–84	Cardiff C	41	0
1984–85	Luton T	13	0
1985–86	Luton T	7	0
1985–86	Sunderland (loan)	12	0
1986–87	Luton T	1	0
1986–87	Huddersfield T (loan)	5	0
1987–88	Luton T	9	0
1988–89	Manchester C	38	0
1989–90	Manchester C	31	0
1990–91	Manchester C	3	0
1990–91	Aberdeen (loan)	5	0
1990–91	Middlesbrough (loan)	19	0
1991–92	Manchester C	2	0
1991–92	Bolton W (loan)	13	0
1991–92	WBA (loan)	9	0
1992–93	Manchester C	2	0
1992–93	Oldham Ath (loan)	0	0

1993–94	Manchester C	11	0
1994–95	Manchester C	15	0
1995–96	Manchester C	0	0
1996–97	Manchester C	13	0
1996–97	Rangers	7	0
1997–98	Luton T	1	0
1997–98	Middlesbrough	2	0
1998–99	Middlesbrough	0	0
From Altrincham			
1998–99	Hartlepool U	0	0
Total:		**280**	**0**

DICHIO, Daniele — Forward

H: 6 3 W: 12 08 b.Hammersmith 19-10-74

Source: Trainee. *Honours:* England Schools, Under-21.

1993–94	QPR	0	0
1993–94	Barnet (loan)	9	2
1994–95	QPR	9	3
1995–96	QPR	29	10
1996–97	QPR	37	7
1997–98	Sampdoria	0	0
1997–98	Lecce	4	1
1997–98	Sunderland	13	0
1998–99	Sunderland	36	10
Total:		**137**	**33**

DICKMAN, Elliot — Defender

H: 5 8 W: 9 08 b.Hexham 11-10-78

Source: Trainee. *Honours:* England Schools, Youth.

1996–97	Sunderland	0	0
1997–98	Sunderland	0	0
1998–99	Sunderland	0	0

DICKMAN, Jonjo — Defender

H: 5 8 W: 10 05 b.Hexham 22-9-81

1998–99	Sunderland	0	0

DICKOV, Paul — Forward

H: 5 5 W: 11 09 b.Glasgow 1-11-72

Source: Trainee. *Honours:* Scotland Under-21.

1992–93	Arsenal	3	2
1993–94	Arsenal	1	0
1993–94	Luton T (loan)	15	1
1993–94	Brighton & HA (loan)	8	5
1994–95	Arsenal	9	0
1995–96	Arsenal	7	1
1996–97	Arsenal	1	0
1996–97	Manchester C	29	5
1997–98	Manchester C	30	9
1998–99	Manchester C	35	10
Total:		**138**	**33**

DICKS, Julian — Defender

H: 5 10 W: 13 00 b.Bristol 8-8-68

Source: Apprentice. *Honours:* England Under-21, B.

1985–86	Birmingham C	23	0
1986–87	Birmingham C	34	0
1987–88	Birmingham C	32	1
1987–88	West Ham U	8	0
1988–89	West Ham U	34	2
1989–90	West Ham U	40	9
1990–91	West Ham U	13	4
1991–92	West Ham U	23	3
1992–93	West Ham U	34	11
1993–94	West Ham U	7	0
1993–94	Liverpool	24	3
1994–95	Liverpool	0	0
1994–95	West Ham U	29	5
1995–96	West Ham U	34	10
1996–97	West Ham U	31	6
1997–98	West Ham U	0	0
1998–99	West Ham U	9	0
Total:		**375**	**54**

DIETRICH, Klaus — Defender

H: 6 0 W: 11 10 b.Vienna 26-6-74

1996–97	Graz	6	2
1997–98	Graz	7	0
1998–99	Hibernian	1	0
Total:		**14**	**2**

DIGBY, Fraser — Goalkeeper

H: 6 1 W: 12 12 b.Sheffield 23-4-67

Source: Apprentice. *Honours:* England Schools, Youth, Under-21.

1984–85	Manchester U	0	0
1985–86	Manchester U	0	0
1985–86	Oldham Ath (loan)	0	0
1985–86	Swindon T (loan)	0	0
1986–87	Manchester U	0	0
1986–87	Swindon T	39	0
1987–88	Swindon T	31	0
1988–89	Swindon T	46	0
1989–90	Swindon T	45	0
1990–91	Swindon T	41	0
1991–92	Swindon T	21	0
1992–93	Swindon T	33	0
1992–93	Manchester U (loan)	0	0
1993–94	Swindon T	28	0
1994–95	Swindon T	39	0
1995–96	Swindon T	25	0
1996–97	Swindon T	31	0
1997–98	Swindon T	38	0
1998–99	Crystal Palace	18	0
Total:		**435**	**0**

DIGNAM, Michael — Midfield

b.Havering 10-8-78

Source: Trainee.

1997–98	Shrewsbury T	0	0
1998–99	Shrewsbury T	0	0

DIJKSTRA, Sieb — Goalkeeper

H: 6 5 W: 14 10 b.Kerkrade 20-10-66

Source: Roda JC.

1991–92	Motherwell	1	0
1992–93	Motherwell	35	0
1993–94	Motherwell	44	0
1994–95	QPR	11	0
1995–96	QPR	0	0
1995–96	Bristol C (loan)	8	0
1995–96	Wycombe W (loan)	13	0
1996–97	Dundee U	22	0
1997–98	Dundee U	36	0
1998–99	Dundee U	27	0
Total:		**197**	**0**

DILLON, Paul — Defender

H: 5 9 W: 10 11 b.Limerick 22-10-78

Source: Trainee.

1996–97	Rotherham U	13	1
1997–98	Rotherham U	16	0
1998–99	Rotherham U	26	1
Total:		**55**	**2**

DINNING, Tony — Defender

H: 6 0 W: 12 00 b.Wallsend 12-4-75

Source: Trainee.

1993–94	Newcastle U	0	0
1994–95	Stockport Co	40	1
1995–96	Stockport Co	10	1
1996–97	Stockport Co	20	2
1997–98	Stockport Co	30	4
1998–99	Stockport Co	41	5
Total:		**141**	**13**

DIUK, Wayne — Midfield

H: 5 9 W: 11 00 b.Nottingham 26-5-80

Source: Trainee.

1996–97	Notts Co	1	0
1997–98	Notts Co	1	0
1998–99	Notts Co	0	0
Total:		**2**	**0**

DIXON, Alan — Midfield

H: 5 8 W: 11 02 b.Dublin 9-10-79

Source: Trainee.

1996–97	Wolverhampton W	0	0
1997–98	Wolverhampton W	0	0
1998–99	Wolverhampton W	0	0

DIXON, Calvin — Midfield

b.Walsall 20-10-80

Source: Trainee.

1998–99	Stoke C	0	0

DIXON, George — Goalkeeper

H: 6 0 W: 14 02 b.Whitehaven 24-10-78

Source: Trainee.

1996–97	Carlisle U	0	0
1997–98	Carlisle U	0	0
1998–99	Carlisle U	0	0

DIXON, Kevin — Midfield

H: 5 9 W: 12 03 b.Easington 27-6-80

Source: Trainee. *Honours:* England Youth.

1997–98	Leeds U	0	0
1998–99	Leeds U	0	0

DIXON, Lee — Defender

H: 5 8 W: 11 08 b.Manchester 17-3-64

Source: Local. *Honours:* England B, 22 full caps, 1 goal.

1982–83	Burnley	3	0
1983–84	Burnley	1	0
1983–84	Chester C	16	1
1984–85	Chester	41	0
1985–86	Bury	45	5
1986–87	Stoke C	42	3
1987–88	Stoke C	29	2
1987–88	Arsenal	6	0
1988–89	Arsenal	33	1
1989–90	Arsenal	38	5
1990–91	Arsenal	38	5
1991–92	Arsenal	38	4
1992–93	Arsenal	29	0
1993–94	Arsenal	33	0
1994–95	Arsenal	39	1
1995–96	Arsenal	38	2
1996–97	Arsenal	32	2
1997–98	Arsenal	28	0
1998–99	Arsenal	36	0
Total:		**565**	**31**

DJORDJIC, Bojan — Midfield

b.Belgrade 6-2-82

Source: On loan to Brommapojkarna.

1998–99	Manchester U	0	0

DOANE, Ben — Defender

H: 5 10 W: 12 00 b.Sheffield 22-12-79

Source: Trainee.

1998–99	Sheffield U	0	0

DOBBIN, Jim — Midfield

H: 5 9 W: 11 07 b.Dunfermline 17-9-63

Source: Whitburn BC. *Honours:* Scotland Youth.

1980–81	Celtic	0	0
1981–82	Celtic	0	0
1982–83	Celtic	0	0
1983–84	Celtic	2	0
1983–84	Motherwell (loan)	2	0
1983–84	Doncaster R	11	2
1984–85	Doncaster R	17	1
1985–86	Doncaster R	31	6
1986–87	Doncaster R	5	4
1986–87	Barnsley	30	4
1987–88	Barnsley	16	2
1988–89	Barnsley	41	5
1989–90	Barnsley	28	1
1990–91	Barnsley	14	0
1991–92	Grimsby T	32	6
1992–93	Grimsby T	39	6
1993–94	Grimsby T	29	4
1994–95	Grimsby T	38	2
1995–96	Grimsby T	26	3
1996–97	Rotherham U	19	0
1997–98	Doncaster R	31	0
1997–98	Scarborough	1	0
1997–98	Grimsby T	2	0
1998–99	Grimsby T	4	0
Total:		**418**	**46**

DOBIE, Scott — Forward

H: 6 2 W: 12 09 b.Workington 10-10-78

Source: Trainee.

1996–97	Carlisle U	2	1
1997–98	Carlisle U	23	0
1998–99	Carlisle U	33	6
1998–99	Clydebank (loan)	6	0
Total:		**64**	**7**

DOBSON, Tony — Defender

H: 6 1 W: 12 06 b.Coventry 5-2-69

Source: Apprentice. *Honours:* England Under-21.

1986–87	Coventry C	1	0
1987–88	Coventry C	1	0
1988–89	Coventry C	16	0
1989–90	Coventry C	30	0
1990–91	Coventry C	6	1
1990–91	Blackburn R	17	0
1991–92	Blackburn R	5	0
1992–93	Blackburn R	19	0
1993–94	Blackburn R	0	0
1993–94	Portsmouth	24	2
1994–95	Portsmouth	14	0
1994–95	Oxford U (loan)	5	0
1995–96	Portsmouth	9	0
1995–96	Peterborough U (loan)	4	0
1996–97	Portsmouth	6	0
1997–98	WBA	11	0
1998–99	WBA	0	0
1998–99	Gillingham (loan)	2	0
1998–99	Northampton T	11	0
Total:		**181**	**3**

DOBSON, Warren — Goalkeeper

H: 6 1 W: 13 08 b.North Shields 5-11-78

Source: QPR Trainee.

1997–98	Hartlepool U	1	0
1998–99	Plymouth Arg	0	0
Total:		**1**	**0**

DODD, Jason — Defender

H: 5 9 W: 12 08 b.Bath 2-11-70

Source: Bath C. *Honours:* England Under-21.

1988–89	Southampton	0	0
1989–90	Southampton	22	0
1990–91	Southampton	19	0
1991–92	Southampton	28	0
1992–93	Southampton	30	1
1993–94	Southampton	10	0
1994–95	Southampton	26	2
1995–96	Southampton	37	2
1996–97	Southampton	23	1
1997–98	Southampton	36	1
1998–99	Southampton	28	1
Total:		**259**	**8**

DODDS, Billy — Forward

H: 5 8 W: 10 10 b.New Cumnock 5-2-69

Source: Apprentice. *Honours:* Scotland B, 9 full caps, 3 goals.

1986–87	Chelsea	1	0
1987–88	Chelsea	0	0
1987–88	Partick T (loan)	30	9

1988–89	Chelsea	2	0
1989–90	Dundee	30	13
1990–91	Dundee	37	15
1991–92	Dundee	42	19
1992–93	Dundee	41	16
1993–94	Dundee	24	5
1993–94	St Johnstone	20	6
1994–95	Aberdeen	35	15
1995–96	Aberdeen	31	7
1996–97	Aberdeen	31	15
1997–98	Aberdeen	34	10
1998–99	Aberdeen	6	0
1998–99	Dundee U	30	17
Total:		**394**	**147**

DODS, Darren — Defender

H: 6 1 W: 12 13 b.Edinburgh 7-6-75

Source: Hutchison Vale BC. *Honours:* Scotland Under-21.

1994–95	Hibernian	1	0
1995–96	Hibernian	15	0
1996–97	Hibernian	20	0
1997–98	Hibernian	28	1
1998–99	St Johnstone	34	2
Total:		**98**	**3**

DOESBURG, Michel — Defender

H: 5 10 W: 12 01 b.Beverwijk 10-8-68

1986–87	Haarlem	18	0
1987–88	Haarlem	8	0
1988–89	Haarlem	25	0
1989–90	Haarlem	23	0
1990–91	Wageningen	32	2
1991–92	Wageningen	33	1
1992–93	Heerenveen	31	2
1993–94	Heerenveen	29	0
1994–95	Heerenveen	30	0
1995–96	Heerenveen	21	0
1995–96	AZ	9	0
1996–97	AZ	24	0
1997–98	AZ*	0	0
1998–99	Motherwell	30	0
Total:		**313**	**5**

DOHERTY, Gary — Defender

H: 6 1 W: 13 00 b.Donegal 31-1-80

Source: Trainee.

1997–98	Luton T	10	0
1998–99	Luton T	20	6
Total:		**30**	**6**

DOHERTY, Gerard — Midfield

b.Derry 24-8-81

Source: Derry C.

1998–99	Derby Co	0	0

DOHERTY, Kevin — Midfield

b.Dublin 18-4-80

1998–99	Liverpool	0	0

DOHERTY, Lee — Defender

b.Camden Town 6-2-80

Source: Arsenal Trainee.

1998–99	Charlton Ath	0	0
1998–99	Brighton & HA	3	0
Total:		**3**	**0**

DOHERTY, Martin — Midfield

H: 6 1 W: 12 02 b.Urmston 17-10-78

Source: Trainee.

1997–98	Bolton W	0	0
1998–99	Bolton W	0	0

DOHERTY, Tom — Midfield

H: 5 8 W: 11 07 b.Bristol 17-3-79

Source: Trainee.

1997–98	Bristol C	30	2
1998–99	Bristol C	23	1
Total:		**53**	**3**

DOIG, Chris — Defender

H: 6 2 W: 12 06 b.Dumfries 13-2-81

Source: Trainee.

1997–98	Nottingham F	0	0
1998–99	Nottingham F	2	0
Total:		**2**	**0**

DOLAN, Jim — Forward

H: 5 10 W: 10 07 b.Salsburgh 22-2-69

Source: Motherwell BC.

1987–88	Motherwell	0	0
1988–89	Motherwell	5	0
1989–90	Motherwell	12	0
1990–91	Motherwell	8	1
1991–92	Motherwell	32	2
1992–93	Motherwell	25	2
1993–94	Motherwell	36	0
1994–95	Motherwell	31	0

1995–96	Motherwell	27	0
1996–97	Motherwell	18	0
1996–97	Dundee U	13	0
1997–98	Dundee U	26	0
1998–99	Dundee U	5	0
1998–99	Dunfermline Ath	10	0
Total:		**248**	**5**

DOLAN, Joe — Defender

H: 6 3 W: 12 12 b.Harrow 27-5-80

Source: Chelsea Trainee.

1998–99	Millwall	9	1
Total:		**9**	**1**

DOMI, Didier — Defender

H: 5 10 W: 11 04 b.Sarcelles 2-5-79

1995–96	Paris St Germain	1	0
1996–97	Paris St Germain	12	0
1997–98	Paris St Germain	27	0
1998–99	Paris St Germain	8	0
1998–99	Newcastle U	14	0
Total:		**62**	**0**

DOMINGUEZ, Jose — Forward

H: 5 3 W: 10 00 b.Lisbon 16-2-74

Source: Benfica. *Honours:* Portugal 3 full caps.

1993–94	Birmingham C	5	0
1994–95	Birmingham C	30	3
1995–96	Sporting Lisbon	30	1
1996–97	Sporting Lisbon	32	3
1997–98	Tottenham H	18	2
1998–99	Tottenham H	13	2
Total:		**128**	**11**

DONALDSON, David — Midfield

H: 5 7 W: 9 08 b.Gravesend 17-12-78

Source: Arsenal Trainee.

1997–98	Bradford C	0	0
1998–99	Bradford C	0	0

DONALDSON, O'Neill — Forward

H: 6 0 W: 12 04 b.Birmingham 24-11-69

Source: Hinckley.

1991–92	Shrewsbury T	19	2
1992–93	Shrewsbury T	0	0
1993–94	Shrewsbury T	9	2
1994–95	Doncaster R	9	2
1994–95	Mansfield T (loan)	4	6
1994–95	Sheffield W	1	0
1995–96	Sheffield W	3	1
1996–97	Sheffield W	5	2
1997–98	Sheffield W	5	0
1997–98	Oxford U (loan)	6	2
1997–98	Stoke C	2	0
1998–99	Torquay U	12	1
Total:		**75**	**18**

DONIS, George — Midfield

H: 6 0 W: 12 00 b.Greece 29-10-69

Source: Panaryiakos. *Honours:* Greece 22 full caps, 4 goals.

1990–91	Yannina	22	3
1991–92	Panathinaikos	30	4
1992–93	Panathinaikos	25	7
1993–94	Panathinaikos	24	7
1994–95	Panathinaikos	28	9
1995–96	Panathinaikos	29	7
1996–97	Blackburn R	22	2
1997–98	Blackburn R	0	0
From AEK Athens.			
1998–99	Sheffield U	7	1
Total:		**187**	**40**

DONLEVY, Andrew — Defender

H: 5 11 W: 10 12 b.Hong Kong 13-4-81

Source: Trainee.

1997–98	Coventry C	0	0
1998–99	Coventry C	0	0

DONNELLY, Mark — Defender

H: 6 1 W: 12 07 b.Leeds 22-12-79

Source: Trainee.

1996–97	Doncaster R	2	0
1997–98	Doncaster R	9	1
1998–99	Bury	0	0
Total:		**11**	**1**

DONNELLY, Paul — Defender

H: 5 10 W: 11 07 b.Dublin 31-8-79

Source: Trainee.

1996–97	Leeds U	0	0
1997–98	Leeds U	0	0
1998–99	Leeds U	0	0

DONNELLY, Simon — Forward

H: 5 9 W: 10 12 b.Glasgow 1-12-74

Source: Celtic BC. *Honours:* Scotland Under-21, 10 full caps.

1993–94	Celtic	12	5
1994–95	Celtic	17	0
1995–96	Celtic	35	6
1996–97	Celtic	29	4
1997–98	Celtic	30	10
1998–99	Celtic	23	5
Total:		**146**	**30**

DONOVAN, Kevin — Forward

H: 5 8 W: 12 12 b.Halifax 17-12-71

Source: Trainee.

1989–90	Huddersfield T	1	0
1990–91	Huddersfield T	6	1
1991–92	Huddersfield T	10	0
1991–92	Halifax T (loan)	6	0
1992–93	Huddersfield T	3	0
1992–93	WBA	32	6
1993–94	WBA	37	8
1994–95	WBA	33	5
1995–96	WBA	34	0
1996–97	WBA	32	0
1997–98	Grimsby T	46	16
1998–99	Grimsby T	28	0
Total:		**268**	**36**

DOOLAN, John — Midfield

H: 6 1 W: 13 00 b.Liverpool 7-5-74

Source: Trainee.

1992–93	Everton	0	0
1993–94	Everton	0	0
1994–95	Mansfield T	24	1
1995–96	Mansfield T	42	2
1996–97	Mansfield T	41	6
1997–98	Mansfield T	24	1
1997–98	Barnet	17	0
1998–99	Barnet	42	2
Total:		**190**	**12**

DORIGO, Tony — Defender

H: 5 9 W: 11 03 b.Adelaide 31-12-65

Source: Apprentice. *Honours:* England Under-21, B, 15 full caps.

1983–84	Aston Villa	1	0
1984–85	Aston Villa	31	0
1985–86	Aston Villa	38	1
1986–87	Aston Villa	41	0
1987–88	Chelsea	40	0
1988–89	Chelsea	40	6
1989–90	Chelsea	35	3
1990–91	Chelsea	31	2
1991–92	Leeds U	38	3
1992–93	Leeds U	33	1
1993–94	Leeds U	37	0
1994–95	Leeds U	28	0
1995–96	Leeds U	17	1
1996–97	Leeds U	18	0
1997–98	Torino	30	2
1998–99	Derby Co	18	1
Total:		**476**	**20**

DORNER, Mario — Forward

H: 5 10 W: 13 02 b.Baden 21-3-70

Source: Susome Dorner, Wustef, Modling. *Honours:* Austria Under-21.

1997–98	Motherwell	2	0
1997–98	Darlington	27	10
1998–99	Darlington	22	3
Total:		**51**	**13**

DOUGLAS, Andrew — Forward

H: 5 9 W: 10 05 b.Penrith 27-5-80

Source: Trainee.

1998–99	Carlisle U	1	0
Total:		**1**	**0**

DOUGLAS, Andrew — Forward

H: 5 7 W: 10 09 b.Edmonton 7-2-80

Source: Arsenal Trainee.

1998–99	Sheffield W	0	0

DOUGLAS, Robert — Goalkeeper

H: 6 3 W: 14 12 b.Lanark 24-4-72

Source: Forth Wanderers. *Honours:* Scotland B.

1992–93	Meadowbank T	0	0
1993–94	Meadowbank T	4	0
1994–95	Meadowbank T	8	0
1995–96	Livingston	24	0
1996–97	Livingston	36	0
1997–98	Dundee	36	0
1998–99	Dundee	35	0
Total:		**143**	**0**

DOUGLAS, Stuart — Forward

H: 5 8 W: 11 05 b.London 9-4-78

Source: Trainee.

1995–96	Luton T	8	1
1996–97	Luton T	9	0
1997–98	Luton T	17	1
1998–99	Luton T	42	9
Total:		**76**	**11**

DOW, Andrew — Midfield

H: 5 9 W: 11 00 b.Dundee 7-2-73

Source: Sporting Club 85. *Honours:* Scotland Under-21.

1990–91	Dundee	0	0
1991–92	Dundee	4	0
1992–93	Dundee	14	1
1993–94	Chelsea	14	0
1994–95	Chelsea	0	0
1994–95	Bradford C (loan)	5	0
1995–96	Chelsea	1	0
1995–96	Hibernian	8	1
1996–97	Hibernian	22	2
1997–98	Hibernian	32	0
1998–99	Aberdeen	25	0
Total:		**125**	**4**

DOWIE, Iain — Forward

H: 6 1 W: 13 07 b.Hatfield 9-1-65

Source: Hendon. *Honours:* Northern Ireland Under-21, 56 full caps, 12 goals.

1988–89	Luton T	8	0
1989–90	Luton T	29	9
1989–90	Fulham (loan)	5	1
1990–91	Luton T	29	7
1990–91	West Ham U	12	4
1991–92	West Ham U	0	0
1991–92	Southampton	30	9
1992–93	Southampton	36	11
1993–94	Southampton	39	5
1994–95	Southampton	17	5
1994–95	Crystal Palace	15	4
1995–96	Crystal Palace	4	2
1995–96	West Ham U	33	8
1996–97	West Ham U	23	0
1997–98	West Ham U	12	0
1997–98	QPR	11	1
1998–99	QPR	19	1
Total:		**322**	**67**

DOWNER, Simon — Midfield

b.Romford 19-10-81

Source: Trainee.

1998–99	Leyton Orient	1	0
Total:		**1**	**0**

DOWNEY, Glen — Defender

H: 6 1 W: 12 07 b.Newcastle 20-9-78

1997–98	Hartlepool U	0	0
1998–99	Hartlepool U	0	0

DOYLE, Daire — Midfield

H: 5 10 W: 11 06 b.Dublin 18-10-80

Source: Cherry Orchard.

1998–99	Coventry C	0	0

DOYLE, Kevin — Midfield

H: 5 11 W: 12 02 b.Wexford 13-10-80

Source: Trainee.

1997–98	Leeds U	0	0
1998–99	Leeds U	0	0

DOYLE, Maurice — Midfield

H: 5 8 W: 10 07 b.Ellesmere Port 17-10-69

Source: Trainee.

1987–88	Crewe Alex	4	0
1988–89	Crewe Alex	4	2
1989–90	QPR	0	0
1990–91	Crewe Alex (loan)	7	2
1990–91	Wolverhampton W (loan)	0	0
1991–92	QPR	0	0
1992–93	QPR	5	0
1993–94	QPR	1	0
1994–95	QPR	0	0
1994–95	Millwall	0	0
1995–96	Millwall	18	0
1996–97	Millwall	28	1
1997–98	Millwall	20	0
1998–99	Shrewsbury T	0	0
Total:		**87**	**5**

DOYLE, Robert — Midfield

b.Dublin 15-4-82

Source: Trainee.

1998–99	Blackburn R	0	0

DOZZELL, Jason — Midfield

H: 6 2 W: 13 07 b.Ipswich 9-12-67

Source: School. *Honours:* England Youth, Under-21.

1983–84	Ipswich T	5	1
1984–85	Ipswich T	14	2
1985–86	Ipswich T	41	3
1986–87	Ipswich T	42	2
1987–88	Ipswich T	39	1
1988–89	Ipswich T	29	11
1989–90	Ipswich T	46	8
1990–91	Ipswich T	30	6
1991–92	Ipswich T	45	11
1992–93	Ipswich T	41	7
1993–94	Tottenham H	32	8
1994–95	Tottenham H	7	0
1995–96	Tottenham H	28	3

1996–97	Tottenham H	17	2
1997–98	Ipswich T	8	1
1997–98	Northampton T	21	4
1998–99	Colchester U	29	4
Total:		**474**	**74**

DRAPER, Mark — Forward

H: 5 10 W: 12 04 b.Long Eaton 11-11-70

Source: Trainee. *Honours:* England Under-21.

1988–89	Notts Co	20	3
1989–90	Notts Co	34	3
1990–91	Notts Co	45	9
1991–92	Notts Co	35	1
1992–93	Notts Co	44	11
1993–94	Notts Co	44	13
1994–95	Leicester C	39	5
1995–96	Aston Villa	36	2
1996–97	Aston Villa	29	0
1997–98	Aston Villa	31	3
1998–99	Aston Villa	23	2
Total:		**380**	**52**

DREYER, John — Defender

H: 6 1 W: 13 02 b.Alnwick 11-6-63

Source: Wallingford T.

1984–85	Oxford U	0	0
1985–86	Oxford U	0	0
1985–86	Torquay U (loan)	5	0
1985–86	Fulham (loan)	12	2
1986–87	Oxford U	25	2
1987–88	Oxford U	35	0
1988–89	Luton T	18	1
1989–90	Luton T	38	2
1990–91	Luton T	38	3
1991–92	Luton T	42	2
1992–93	Luton T	38	2
1993–94	Luton T	40	3
1994–95	Stoke C	18	2
1994–95	Bolton W (loan)	2	0
1995–96	Stoke C	19	0
1996–97	Stoke C	12	1
1996–97	Bradford C	28	1
1997–98	Bradford C	17	0
1998–99	Bradford C	21	0
Total:		**408**	**21**

DRURY, Adam — Defender

H: 5 10 W: 11 06 b.Cottenham 29-8-78

Source: Trainee.

1995–96	Peterborough U	1	0
1996–97	Peterborough U	5	1
1997–98	Peterborough U	31	0
1998–99	Peterborough U	40	0
Total:		**77**	**1**

DRYDEN, Richard — Defender

H: 6 0 W: 14 09 b.Stroud 14-6-69

Source: Trainee.

1986–87	Bristol R	6	0
1987–88	Bristol R	6	0
1988–89	Bristol R	1	0
1988–89	Exeter C	21	0
1989–90	Exeter C	30	7
1990–91	Manchester C (loan)	0	0
1991–92	Notts Co	29	1
1992–93	Notts Co	2	0
1992–93	Plymouth Arg (loan)	5	0
1992–93	Birmingham C	11	0
1993–94	Birmingham C	34	0
1994–95	Birmingham C	3	0
1994–95	Bristol C	19	1
1995–96	Bristol C	18	1
1996–97	Southampton	29	1
1997–98	Southampton	13	0
1998–99	Southampton	4	0
Total:		**231**	**11**

DRYSDALE, Leon — Defender

H: 5 9 W: 10 12 b.Walsall 3-2-81

Source: Trainee.

1998–99	Shrewsbury T	2	0
Total:		**2**	**0**

DUBERRY, Michael — Defender

H: 6 1 W: 14 00 b.Enfield 14-10-75

Source: Trainee. *Honours:* England Under-21.

1993–94	Chelsea	1	0
1994–95	Chelsea	0	0
1995–96	Chelsea	22	0
1995–96	Bournemouth (loan)	7	0
1996–97	Chelsea	15	1
1997–98	Chelsea	23	0
1998–99	Chelsea	25	0
Total:		**93**	**1**

DUBLIN, Dion — Forward

H: 6 2 W: 12 04 b.Leicester 22-4-69

Honours: England 4 full caps.

1987–88	Norwich C	0	0
1988–89	Cambridge U	21	6
1989–90	Cambridge U	46	15
1990–91	Cambridge U	46	16
1991–92	Cambridge U	43	15
1992–93	Manchester U	7	1
1993–94	Manchester U	5	1
1994–95	Coventry C	31	13
1995–96	Coventry C	34	14
1996–97	Coventry C	34	13

1997–98	Coventry C	36	18
1998–99	Coventry C	10	3
1998–99	Aston Villa	24	11
Total:		**337**	**126**

DUBLIN, Keith — Defender

H: 6 0 W: 12 10 b.Brent 29-1-66

Source: Apprentice. *Honours:* England Youth.

1983–84	Chelsea	1	0
1984–85	Chelsea	11	0
1985–86	Chelsea	11	0
1986–87	Chelsea	28	0
1987–88	Brighton & HA	46	5
1988–89	Brighton & HA	43	0
1989–90	Brighton & HA	43	0
1990–91	Watford	43	0
1991–92	Watford	46	0
1992–93	Watford	46	1
1993–94	Watford	33	1
1994–95	Southend U	40	2
1995–96	Southend U	43	3
1996–97	Southend U	46	0
1997–98	Southend U	41	4
1998–99	Southend U	9	0
1998–99	Colchester U (loan)	2	0
Total:		**532**	**16**

DUCROS, Andrew — Forward

H: 5 6 W: 9 08 b.Evesham 16-9-77

Source: Trainee. *Honours:* England Schools, Youth.

1994–95	Coventry C	0	0
1995–96	Coventry C	0	0
1996–97	Coventry C	5	0
1997–98	Coventry C	3	0
1998–99	Coventry C	0	0
Total:		**8**	**0**

DUDFIELD, Lawrie — Forward

H: 6 0 W: 11 05 b.London 7-5-80

Source: Kettering T.

1997–98	Leicester C	0	0
1998–99	Leicester C	0	0

DUDLEY, Craig — Forward

H: 5 11 W: 11 02 b.Ollerton 12-9-79

Source: Trainee. *Honours:* England Youth.

1996–97	Notts Co	10	2
1997–98	Notts Co	17	1
1997–98	Shrewsbury T (loan)	4	0
1998–99	Notts Co	4	0
1998–99	Hull C (loan)	7	2
Total:		**42**	**5**

DUERDEN, Ian — Forward

H: 5 10 W: 12 07 b.Burnley 27-3-78

Source: Trainee.

1996–97	Burnley	0	0
1997–98	Burnley	1	0
1998–99	Halifax T	2	0
Total:		**3**	**0**

DUFF, Damien — Forward

H: 5 8 W: 9 07 b.Ballyboden 2-3-79

Honours: Eire Youth, 9 full caps.

1995–96	Blackburn R	0	0
1996–97	Blackburn R	1	0
1997–98	Blackburn R	26	4
1998–99	Blackburn R	28	1
Total:		**55**	**5**

DUFFIELD, Peter — Forward

H: 5 6 W: 10 04 b.Middlesbrough 4 2 69

1986–87	Middlesbrough	0	0
1987–88	Sheffield U	11	1
1987–88	Halifax T (loan)	12	6
1988–89	Sheffield U	38	11
1989–90	Sheffield U	5	2
1990–91	Sheffield U	2	0
1990–91	Rotherham U (loan)	17	4
1991–92	Sheffield U	2	0
1992–93	Sheffield U	0	0
1992–93	Blackpool (loan)	5	1
1992–93	Bournemouth (loan)	0	0
1992–93	Stockport Co (loan)	7	4
1992–93	Crewe Alex (loan)	2	0
1993–94	Sheffield U	0	0
1993–94	Hamilton A	36	19
1994–95	Hamilton A	36	20
1995–96	Airdrieonians	24	6
1995–96	Raith R	9	5
1996–97	Raith R	33	5
1997–98	Raith R	0	0
1998–99	Raith R	0	0
1998–99	Darlington	14	2
Total:		**253**	**86**

DUFFY, Neil Cornelius — Midfield

H: 6 1 W: 11 13 b.Glasgow 5-6-67

Source: Shamrock SA.

1989–90	Dundee U	0	0
1990–91	Falkirk	25	2
1991–92	Falkirk	39	2
1992–93	Falkirk	34	5
1993–94	Falkirk	23	9
1993–94	Dundee	9	2

1994–95	Dundee	24	3
1995–96	Dundee	31	3
1996–97	Dundee U	13	1
1997–98	Dundee U	7	0
1998–99	Dundee U	15	0
Total:		**220**	**27**

DUGUID, Karl — Forward

H: 5 11 W: 11 00 b.Letchworth 21-3-78

Source: Trainee.

1995–96	Colchester U	16	1
1996–97	Colchester U	20	3
1997–98	Colchester U	21	3
1998–99	Colchester U	33	4
Total:		**90**	**11**

DUKE, David — Midfield

H: 5 10 W: 11 00 b.Inverness 7-11-78

Source: Redby CA.

1997–98	Sunderland	0	0
1998–99	Sunderland	0	0

DUNBAVIN, Ian — Goalkeeper

b.Knowsley 27-5-80

Source: Trainee.

1998–99	Liverpool	0	0

DUNCAN, Andy — Defender

H: 5 11 W: 13 04 b.Hexham 20-10-77

Source: Trainee. *Honours:* England Schools.

1996–97	Manchester U	0	0
1997–98	Manchester U	0	0
1997–98	Cambridge U	19	0
1998–99	Cambridge U	45	1
Total:		**64**	**1**

DUNDEE, Sean — Forward

H: 6 1 W: 13 00 b.Durban 7-12-72

Source: Bayview, D'Alberton Carries.

1992–93	Stuttgart Kickers	6	0
1993–94	Stuttgart Kickers	1	0
From Ditzingen			
1995–96	Karlsruhe	32	16
1996–97	Karlsruhe	29	17
1997–98	Karlsruhe	24	3
1998–99	Liverpool	3	0
Total:		**95**	**36**

DUNFIELD, Terry — Midfield

H: 5 7 W: 10 03 b.Canada 20-2-82

Source: Trainee.

1998–99	Manchester C	0	0

DUNGEY, James — Goalkeeper

H: 5 8 W: 12 00 b.Plymouth 7-2-78

Source: Trainee. *Honours:* England Schools, Youth.

1994–95	Plymouth Arg	4	0
1995–96	Plymouth Arg	0	0
1996–97	Plymouth Arg	6	0
1997–98	Plymouth Arg	0	0
1997–98	Exeter C	1	0
From Bodmin T.			
1998–99	Plymouth Arg	7	0
Total:		**18**	**0**

DUNN, David — Midfield

H: 5 10 W: 12 00 b.Blackburn 27-12-79

Source: Trainee. *Honours:* England Youth, Under-21.

1997–98	Blackburn R	0	0
1998–99	Blackburn R	15	1
Total:		**15**	**1**

DUNN, Iain — Midfield

H: 5 10 W: 10 07 b.Derwent 1-4-70

Source: School. *Honours:* England Schools, Youth.

1988–89	York C	26	6
1989–90	York C	18	2
1990–91	York C	33	3
1991–92	Chesterfield	13	1
From Goole T			
1992–93	Huddersfield T	28	3
1993–94	Huddersfield T	34	6
1994–95	Huddersfield T	39	5
1995–96	Huddersfield T	14	0
1996–97	Huddersfield T	5	0
1996–97	Scunthorpe U (loan)	3	0
1996–97	Chesterfield	11	0
1997–98	Chesterfield	7	0
1998–99	Chesterfield	0	0
Total:		**231**	**26**

DUNN, Thomas — Defender

H: 5 10 W: 12 00 b.Hartlepool 21-12-79

Source: Trainee.

1998–99	Middlesbrough	0	0

DUNNE, Joe — Defender

H: 5 9 W: 11 08 b.Dublin 25-5-73

Source: Trainee. *Honours:* Eire Youth, Under-21.

1990–91	Gillingham	26	0
1991–92	Gillingham	11	0
1992–93	Gillingham	4	0
1993–94	Gillingham	37	0
1994–95	Gillingham	35	1
1995–96	Gillingham	2	0
1995–96	Colchester U	5	1
1996–97	Colchester U	35	0
1997–98	Colchester U	25	2
1998–99	Colchester U	36	0
Total:		**216**	**4**

DUNNE, Richard — Defender

H: 6 2 W: 15 10 b.Dublin 21-9-79

Source: Trainee. *Honours:* Eire Under-21.

1996–97	Everton	7	0
1997–98	Everton	3	0
1998–99	Everton	16	0
Total:		**26**	**0**

DUNNING, Darren — Midfield

H: 5 6 W: 11 12 b.Scarborough 8-1-81

Source: Trainee.

1998–99	Blackburn R	0	0

DUNNING, Richard — Defender

H: 5 7 W: 11 10 b.Scarborough 8-1-81

Source: Trainee.

1998–99	Blackburn R	0	0

DUNWELL, Michael — Forward

H: 5 11 W: 12 02 b.Stockton 6-1-80

Source: Trainee.

1998–99	Hartlepool U	1	0
Total:		**1**	**0**

DURIE, Gordon — Forward

H: 6 0 W: 12 00 b.Paisley 6-12-65

Source: Hill of Beath Hawthorn. *Honours:* Scotland B, Under-21, 43 full caps, 7 goals.

1981–82	East Fife	13	1
1982–83	East Fife	25	2
1983–84	East Fife	34	16
1984–85	East Fife	9	7
1984–85	Hibernian	22	8
1985–86	Hibernian	25	6
1985–86	Chelsea	1	0
1986–87	Chelsea	25	5
1987–88	Chelsea	26	12
1988–89	Chelsea	32	17
1989–90	Chelsea	15	5
1990–91	Chelsea	24	12
1991–92	Tottenham H	31	7
1992–93	Tottenham H	17	3
1993–94	Tottenham H	10	1
1993–94	Rangers	24	12
1994–95	Rangers	21	6
1995–96	Rangers	27	17
1996–97	Rangers	16	5
1997–98	Rangers	26	4
1998–99	Rangers	5	0
Total:		**428**	**146**

DURKAN, Kieron — Midfield

H: 5 10 W: 12 09 b.Chester 1-12-73

Source: Trainee. *Honours:* Eire Under-21.

1991–92	Wrexham	1	0
1992–93	Wrexham	1	0
1993–94	Wrexham	10	1
1994–95	Wrexham	30	2
1995–96	Wrexham	8	0
1995–96	Stockport Co	16	0
1996–97	Stockport Co	41	3
1997–98	Stockport Co	7	1
1997–98	Macclesfield T	4	0
1998–99	Macclesfield T	26	3
Total:		**144**	**10**

DURNIN, John — Midfield

H: 5 10 W: 11 10 b.Liverpool 18-8-65

Source: Waterloo Dock.

1985–86	Liverpool	0	0
1986–87	Liverpool	0	0
1987–88	Liverpool	0	0
1988–89	Liverpool	0	0
1988–89	WBA (loan)	5	2
1988–89	Oxford U	19	3
1989–90	Oxford U	42	13
1990–91	Oxford U	26	9
1991–92	Oxford U	37	8
1992–93	Oxford U	37	11
1993–94	Portsmouth	28	6
1994–95	Portsmouth	16	2
1995–96	Portsmouth	41	3
1996–97	Portsmouth	34	3
1997–98	Portsmouth	34	10
1998–99	Portsmouth	26	7
Total:		**345**	**77**

DURRANT, Iain

Midfield

H: 5 8 W: 9 07 b.Glasgow 29-10-66

Source: Glasgow United. *Honours:* Scotland Youth, Under-21, 16 full caps.

1984–85	Rangers	5	0
1985–86	Rangers	30	2
1986–87	Rangers	39	4
1987–88	Rangers	40	10
1988–89	Rangers	8	2
1989–90	Rangers	0	0
1990–91	Rangers	4	1
1991–92	Rangers	13	0
1992–93	Rangers	30	3
1993–94	Rangers	23	0
1994–95	Rangers	25	4
1994–95	Everton (loan)	5	0
1995–96	Rangers	15	0
1996–97	Rangers	8	0
1997–98	Rangers	8	0
1998–99	Kilmarnock	36	4
Total:		**289**	**30**

DUXBURY, Lee

Midfield

H: 5 10 W: 10 07 b.Keighley 7-10-69

Source: Trainee.

1988–89	Bradford C	1	0
1989–90	Bradford C	12	1
1989–90	Rochdale (loan)	10	0
1990–91	Bradford C	45	5
1991–92	Bradford C	46	5
1992–93	Bradford C	42	5
1993–94	Bradford C	43	9
1994–95	Bradford C	20	0
1994–95	Huddersfield T	26	2
1995–96	Huddersfield T	3	0
1995–96	Bradford C	30	4
1996–97	Bradford C	33	3
1996–97	Oldham Ath	12	1
1997–98	Oldham Ath	38	5
1998–99	Oldham Ath	41	6
Total:		**402**	**46**

DYCHE, Sean

Defender

H: 6 0 W: 13 05 b.Kettering 28-6-71

Source: Trainee.

1988–89	Nottingham F	0	0
1989–90	Nottingham F	0	0
1989–90	Chesterfield	22	2
1990–91	Chesterfield	28	2
1991–92	Chesterfield	42	3
1992–93	Chesterfield	20	1
1993–94	Chesterfield	20	0
1994–95	Chesterfield	22	0
1995–96	Chesterfield	41	0
1996–97	Chesterfield	36	0
1997–98	Bristol C	11	0
1998–99	Bristol C	6	0
1998–99	Luton T (loan)	14	1
Total:		**262**	**9**

DYER, Alex

Midfield

H: 5 11 W: 12 00 b.Forest Gate 14-11-65

Source: Watford Apprentice.

1983–84	Blackpool	9	0
1984–85	Blackpool	36	8
1985–86	Blackpool	39	8
1986–87	Blackpool	24	3
1986–87	Hull C	17	4
1987–88	Hull C	28	8
1988–89	Hull C	15	2
1988–89	Crystal Palace	7	2
1989–90	Crystal Palace	10	0
1990–91	Charlton Ath	35	7
1991–92	Charlton Ath	13	0
1992–93	Charlton Ath	30	6
1993–94	Oxford U	38	5
1994–95	Oxford U	38	1
1995–96	Oxford U	0	0
1995–96	Lincoln C	1	0
1995–96	Barnet	35	2
1996–97	Barnet	0	0
1997–98	Huddersfield T	12	1
1997–98	Notts Co	10	0
1998–99	Notts Co	29	0
Total:		**426**	**57**

DYER, Bruce

Forward

H: 5 11 W: 12 06 b.Ilford 13-4-75

Source: Trainee. *Honours:* England Under-21.

1992–93	Watford	2	0
1993–94	Watford	29	6
1993–94	Crystal Palace	11	0
1994–95	Crystal Palace	16	1
1995–96	Crystal Palace	35	13
1996–97	Crystal Palace	43	17
1997–98	Crystal Palace	24	4
1998–99	Crystal Palace	6	2
1998–99	Barnsley	28	7
Total:		**194**	**50**

DYER, Kieron

Midfield

H: 5 8 W: 10 01 b.Ipswich 29-12-78

Source: Trainee. *Honours:* England Youth, Under-21, B.

1996–97	Ipswich T	13	0
1997–98	Ipswich T	41	4
1998–99	Ipswich T	37	5
Total:		**91**	**9**

DYER, Wayne — Midfield

H: 6 1 W: 11 07 b.Birmingham 24-11-77

Source: Trainee.

1996–97	Birmingham C	0	0
1997–98	Oxford U	0	0
From Barry T.			
1998–99	Walsall	1	0
Total:		**1**	**0**

DYSON, James — Defender

H: 6 2 W: 12 00 b.Wordsley 20-4-79

Source: Trainee.

1997–98	Birmingham C	0	0
1998–99	Birmingham C	0	0

DYSON, Jon — Defender

H: 6 0 W: 12 12 b.Mirfield 18-12-71

Source: School.

1991–92	Huddersfield T	0	0
1992–93	Huddersfield T	15	0
1993–94	Huddersfield T	22	0
1994–95	Huddersfield T	28	2
1995–96	Huddersfield T	17	0
1996–97	Huddersfield T	23	0
1997–98	Huddersfield T	36	1
1998–99	Huddersfield T	14	1
Total:		**155**	**4**

EADEN, Nicky — Defender

H: 5 9 W: 12 02 b.Sheffield 12-12-72

Source: Trainee.

1991–92	Barnsley	0	0
1992–93	Barnsley	2	0
1993–94	Barnsley	37	2
1994–95	Barnsley	45	1
1995–96	Barnsley	46	2
1996–97	Barnsley	46	3
1997–98	Barnsley	35	0
1998–99	Barnsley	40	1
Total:		**251**	**9**

EADIE, Darren — Forward

H: 5 9 W: 11 03 b.Chippenham 10-6-75

Source: Trainee. *Honours:* England Youth, Under-21.

1992–93	Norwich C	0	0
1993–94	Norwich C	15	3
1994–95	Norwich C	26	2
1995–96	Norwich C	31	6
1996–97	Norwich C	42	17
1997–98	Norwich C	19	3
1998–99	Norwich C	22	3
Total:		**155**	**34**

EARLE, Robbie — Midfield

H: 5 9 W: 10 10 b.Newcastle-Under-Lyme 27-1-65

Source: Stoke C. *Honours:* Jamaica 10 full caps, 1 goal.

1981–82	Port Vale	0	0
1982–83	Port Vale	8	1
1983–84	Port Vale	12	0
1984–85	Port Vale	46	15
1985–86	Port Vale	46	15
1986–87	Port Vale	35	6
1987–88	Port Vale	25	4
1988–89	Port Vale	44	13
1989–90	Port Vale	43	12
1990–91	Port Vale	35	11
1991–92	Wimbledon	40	14
1992–93	Wimbledon	42	7
1993–94	Wimbledon	42	9
1994–95	Wimbledon	9	0
1995–96	Wimbledon	37	11
1996–97	Wimbledon	32	7
1997–98	Wimbledon	22	3
1998–99	Wimbledon	35	5
Total:		**553**	**133**

EARNSHAW, Mark — Midfield

H: 5 9 W: 11 02 b.Leeds 11-11-78

Source: Trainee.

1997–98	Oldham Ath	0	0
1998–99	Oldham Ath	0	0

EARNSHAW, Robert — Forward

H: 5 6 W: 9 09 b.Zambia 6-4-81

Source: Trainee. *Honours:* Wales Under-21.

1997–98	Cardiff C	5	0
1998–99	Cardiff C	5	1
1998–99	Middlesbrough (loan)	0	0
Total:		**10**	**1**

EASTON, Clint — Midfield

H: 5 11 W: 10 04 b.Barking 1-10-77

Source: Trainee. *Honours:* England Youth.

1996–97	Watford	17	1
1997–98	Watford	12	0
1998–99	Watford	7	0
Total:		**36**	**1**

EASTON, Craig — Midfield

H: 5 9 W: 9 08 b.Bellshill 26-2-79

Source: Dundee U BC. *Honours:* Scotland Under-21, Under-18.

1995–96	Dundee U	0	0
1996–97	Dundee U	2	0
1997–98	Dundee U	29	1
1998–99	Dundee U	30	1
Total:		**61**	**2**

EASTWOOD, Philip — Forward

H: 5 10 W: 12 02 b.Blackburn 6-4-78

Source: Trainee.

1996–97	Burnley	0	0
1997–98	Burnley	3	0
1998–99	Burnley	13	1
Total:		**16**	**1**

EATON, Adam — Defender

b.Wigan 2-5-80

Source: Trainee.

1997–98	Everton	0	0
1998–99	Everton	0	0

EBBRELL, John — Midfield

H: 5 10 W: 11 11 b.Bromborough 1-10-69

Honours: FA Schools, England Schools, Youth, Under-21, B.

1986–87	Everton	0	0
1987–88	Everton	0	0
1988–89	Everton	4	0
1989–90	Everton	17	0
1990–91	Everton	36	3
1991–92	Everton	39	1
1992–93	Everton	24	1
1993–94	Everton	39	4
1994–95	Everton	26	0
1995–96	Everton	25	4
1996–97	Everton	7	0
1996–97	Sheffield U	1	0
1997–98	Sheffield U	0	0
1998–99	Sheffield U	0	0
Total:		**218**	**13**

EBDON, Marcus — Midfield

H: 5 10 W: 11 02 b.Pontypool 17-10-70

Source: Trainee. *Honours:* Wales Under-21.

1988–89	Everton	0	0
1989–90	Everton	0	0
1990–91	Everton	0	0
1991–92	Peterborough U	15	2
1992–93	Peterborough U	28	4
1993–94	Peterborough U	10	0
1994–95	Peterborough U	35	6
1995–96	Peterborough U	39	2
1996–97	Peterborough U	20	1
1996–97	Chesterfield	12	1
1997–98	Chesterfield	33	2
1998–99	Chesterfield	40	1
Total:		**232**	**19**

ECKHARDT, Jeff — Defender

H: 6 0 W: 12 01 b.Sheffield 7-10-65

1984–85	Sheffield U	7	0
1985–86	Sheffield U	33	2
1986–87	Sheffield U	22	0
1987–88	Sheffield U	12	0
1987–88	Fulham	29	1
1988–89	Fulham	43	2
1989–90	Fulham	40	2
1990–91	Fulham	29	2
1991–92	Fulham	43	7
1992–93	Fulham	30	6
1993–94	Fulham	35	5
1994–95	Stockport Co	27	1
1995–96	Stockport Co	35	6
1996–97	Cardiff C	35	5
1997–98	Cardiff C	21	3
1998–99	Cardiff C	35	5
Total:		**476**	**47**

EDDS, Gareth — Midfield

H: 5 11 W: 10 12 b.Sydney 3-2-81

Source: Trainee.

1997–98	Nottingham F	0	0
1998–99	Nottingham F	0	0

EDGE, Roland — Defender

H: 5 10 W: 11 10 b.Gillingham 25-11-78

Source: Trainee.

1997–98	Gillingham	0	0
1998–99	Gillingham	8	0
Total:		**8**	**0**

EDGHILL, Phil — Midfield

H: 6 0 W: 9 08 b.Oldham 13-9-79

Source: Trainee.

1998–99	Rochdale	0	0

EDGHILL, Richard — Defender

H: 5 9 W: 11 00 b.Oldham 23-9-74

Source: Trainee. *Honours:* England Under-21.

1992–93	Manchester C	0	0
1993–94	Manchester C	22	0
1994–95	Manchester C	14	0
1995–96	Manchester C	13	0
1996–97	Manchester C	0	0
1997–98	Manchester C	36	0
1998–99	Manchester C	38	0
Total:		**123**	**0**

EDINBURGH, Justin — Defender

H: 5 10 W: 12 01 b.Basildon 18-12-69

Source: Trainee.

1988–89	Southend U	15	0
1989–90	Southend U	22	0
1989–90	Tottenham H (loan)	0	0
1990–91	Tottenham H	16	1
1991–92	Tottenham H	23	0
1992–93	Tottenham H	32	0
1993–94	Tottenham H	25	0
1994–95	Tottenham H	31	0
1995–96	Tottenham H	22	0
1996–97	Tottenham H	24	0
1997–98	Tottenham H	16	0
1998–99	Tottenham H	16	0
Total:		**242**	**1**

EDINHO — Forward

H: 5 8 W: 12 12 b.Brazil 21-2-67

1994–95	Chaves	32	14
1995–96	Guimaraes	32	15
1996–97	Bradford C	15	5
1997–98	Bradford C	41	10
1998–99	Bradford C	3	0
1998–99	Dunfermline Ath	9	1
Total:		**132**	**45**

EDMONDSON, Darren — Defender

H: 6 0 W: 12 10 b.Ulverston 4-11-71

Source: Trainee.

1990–91	Carlisle U	31	0
1991–92	Carlisle U	27	2
1992–93	Carlisle U	34	0
1993–94	Carlisle U	22	3
1994–95	Carlisle U	38	2
1995–96	Carlisle U	42	1
1996–97	Carlisle U	20	1
1996–97	Huddersfield T	10	0
1997–98	Huddersfield T	19	0
1998–99	Huddersfield T	3	0
1998–99	Plymouth Arg (loan)	4	0
Total:		**250**	**9**

EDWARDS, Andy — Defender

H: 6 2 W: 12 00 b.Epping 17-9-71

Source: Trainee.

1988–89	Southend U	1	0
1989–90	Southend U	8	0
1990–91	Southend U	2	1
1991–92	Southend U	9	0
1992–93	Southend U	41	0
1993–94	Southend U	42	1
1994–95	Southend U	44	3
1995–96	Birmingham C	37	1
1996–97	Birmingham C	3	0
1996–97	Peterborough U	25	0
1997–98	Peterborough U	46	2
1998–99	Peterborough U	41	2
Total:		**299**	**10**

EDWARDS, Christian — Defender

H: 6 2 W: 12 03 b.Caerphilly 23-11-75

Source: Trainee. *Honours:* Wales Under-21, B, 1 full cap.

1994–95	Swansea C	9	0
1995–96	Swansea C	38	2
1996–97	Swansea C	36	0
1997–98	Swansea C	32	2
1997–98	Nottingham F	0	0
1998–99	Nottingham F	12	0
1998–99	Bristol C (loan)	3	0
Total:		**130**	**4**

EDWARDS, Jake — Forward

H: 6 1 W: 12 08 b.Manchester 11-5-76

Source: USA (College).

1998–99	Wrexham	9	1
Total:		**9**	**1**

EDWARDS, Michael — Defender

H: 6 0 W: 12 10 b.North Ferriby 25-4-80

Source: Trainee.

1997–98	Hull C	21	0
1998–99	Hull C	30	0
Total:		**51**	**0**

EDWARDS, Neil — Goalkeeper

H: 5 8 W: 11 02 b.Aberdare 5-12-70

Source: Trainee.

1988–89	Leeds U	0	0
1989–90	Leeds U	0	0
1990–91	Leeds U	0	0
1990–91	Huddersfield T (loan)	0	0
1991–92	Stockport Co	39	0
1992–93	Stockport Co	35	0
1993–94	Stockport Co	26	0
1994–95	Stockport Co	19	0
1995–96	Stockport Co	45	0
1996–97	Stockport Co	0	0
1997–98	Stockport Co	0	0
1997–98	Rochdale	27	0
1998–99	Rochdale	45	0
Total:		**236**	**0**

EDWARDS, Paul — Goalkeeper

H: 6 0 W: 11 05 b.Liverpool 22-2-65

Source: St Helens T.

Season	Club	Apps	Goals
1988–89	Crewe Alex	10	0
1989–90	Crewe Alex	8	0
1990–91	Crewe Alex	9	0
1991–92	Crewe Alex	2	0
1992–93	Shrewsbury T	42	0
1993–94	Shrewsbury T	42	0
1994–95	Shrewsbury T	31	0
1995–96	Shrewsbury T	31	0
1996–97	Shrewsbury T	23	0
1997–98	Shrewsbury T	34	0
1998–99	Shrewsbury T	43	0
Total:		**275**	**0**

EDWARDS, Rob — Midfield

H: 5 8 W: 12 04 b.Manchester 23-2-70

Source: Trainee.

Season	Club	Apps	Goals
1987–88	Crewe Alex	6	1
1988–89	Crewe Alex	4	0
1989–90	Crewe Alex	4	0
1990–91	Crewe Alex	29	11
1991–92	Crewe Alex	28	6
1992–93	Crewe Alex	23	7
1993–94	Crewe Alex	12	2
1994–95	Crewe Alex	17	2
1995–96	Crewe Alex	32	15
1995–96	Huddersfield T	13	7
1996–97	Huddersfield T	33	3
1997–98	Huddersfield T	38	1
1998–99	Huddersfield T	45	2
Total:		**284**	**57**

EDWARDS, Robert — Defender

H: 6 0 W: 12 07 b.Kendal 1-7-73

Source: Trainee. *Honours:* Wales Youth, Under-21, 4 full caps.

Season	Club	Apps	Goals
1989–90	Carlisle U	12	0
1990–91	Carlisle U	36	5
1990–91	Bristol C	0	0
1991–92	Bristol C	20	1
1992–93	Bristol C	18	0
1993–94	Bristol C	38	2
1994–95	Bristol C	30	0
1995–96	Bristol C	19	0
1996–97	Bristol C	31	0
1997–98	Bristol C	37	2
1998–99	Bristol C	23	0
Total:		**264**	**10**

EDWORTHY, Marc — Defender

H: 5 11 W: 10 03 b.Barnstaple 24-12-72

Source: Trainee.

Season	Club	Apps	Goals
1990–91	Plymouth Arg	0	0
1991–92	Plymouth Arg	15	0
1992–93	Plymouth Arg	15	0
1993–94	Plymouth Arg	12	0
1994–95	Plymouth Arg	27	1
1995–96	Crystal Palace	44	0
1996–97	Crystal Palace	45	0
1997–98	Crystal Palace	34	0
1998–99	Crystal Palace	3	0
1998–99	Coventry C	22	0
Total:		**217**	**1**

EHIOGU, Ugo — Defender

H: 6 2 W: 14 10 b.Hackney 3-11-72

Source: Trainee. *Honours:* England Under-21, B, 1 full cap.

Season	Club	Apps	Goals
1990–91	WBA	2	0
1991–92	Aston Villa	8	0
1992–93	Aston Villa	4	0
1993–94	Aston Villa	17	0
1994–95	Aston Villa	39	3
1995–96	Aston Villa	36	1
1996–97	Aston Villa	38	3
1997–98	Aston Villa	37	2
1998–99	Aston Villa	25	2
Total:		**206**	**11**

EKOKU, Efan — Forward

H: 6 2 W: 12 00 b.Manchester 8-6-67

Source: Sutton U. *Honours:* Nigeria 4 full caps.

Season	Club	Apps	Goals
1990–91	Bournemouth	20	3
1991–92	Bournemouth	28	11
1992–93	Bournemouth	14	7
1992–93	Norwich C	4	3
1993–94	Norwich C	27	12
1994–95	Norwich C	6	0
1994–95	Wimbledon	24	9
1995–96	Wimbledon	31	7
1996–97	Wimbledon	30	11
1997–98	Wimbledon	16	4
1998–99	Wimbledon	22	6
Total:		**222**	**73**

ELKINS, Gary — Defender

H: 5 9 W: 13 04 b.Wallingford 4-5-66

Source: Apprentice. *Honours:* England Youth.

Season	Club	Apps	Goals
1983–84	Fulham	0	0
1984–85	Fulham	21	0
1985–86	Fulham	13	0
1986–87	Fulham	9	0
1987–88	Fulham	29	0

1988–89	Fulham	22	1
1989–90	Fulham	10	1
1989–90	Exeter C (loan)	5	0
1990–91	Wimbledon	10	0
1991–92	Wimbledon	18	1
1992–93	Wimbledon	18	0
1993–94	Wimbledon	18	1
1994–95	Wimbledon	36	1
1995–96	Wimbledon	10	0
1996–97	Wimbledon	0	0
1996–97	Swindon T	23	1
1997–98	Swindon T	0	0
1998–99	Swindon T	0	0
Total:		**242**	**6**

ELLINGTON, Lee — Forward

H: 5 10 W: 11 07 b.Bradford 3-7-80

Source: Trainee.

1996–97	Hull C	2	0
1997–98	Hull C	7	2
1998–99	Hull C	6	0
Total:		**15**	**2**

ELLINGTON, Nathan — Forward

H: 5 10 W: 12 10 b.Bradford 2-7-81

Source: Walton & Hersham.

1998–99	Bristol R	10	1
Total:		**10**	**1**

ELLIOT, David — Forward

H: 5 9 W: 11 00 b.Glasgow 13-11-69

Source: Celtic BC.

1987–88	Celtic	0	0
1988–89	Celtic	4	0
1989–90	Celtic	2	0
1990–91	Partick T	37	13
1991–92	St Mirren	28	1
1992–93	St Mirren	40	5
1993–94	St Mirren	36	8
1994–95	St Mirren	28	3
1995–96	Falkirk	32	0
1996–97	Falkirk	17	1
1996–97	Hibernian	7	0
1997–98	Hibernian	4	0
1998–99	Hibernian	8	0
1998–99	Wigan Ath (loan)	0	0
Total:		**243**	**31**

ELLIOTT, Matt — Defender

H: 6 3 W: 14 05 b.Wandsworth 1-11-68

Source: Epsom & Ewell. *Honours:* Scotland 7 full caps.

1988–89	Charlton Ath	0	0
1988–89	Torquay U	13	2
1989–90	Torquay U	33	2
1990–91	Torquay U	45	6
1991–92	Torquay U	33	5
1991–92	Scunthorpe U (loan)	8	1
1992–93	Scunthorpe U	39	6
1993–94	Scunthorpe U	14	1
1993–94	Oxford U	32	5
1994–95	Oxford U	45	4
1995–96	Oxford U	45	8
1996–97	Oxford U	26	4
1996–97	Leicester C	16	4
1997–98	Leicester C	37	7
1998–99	Leicester C	37	3
Total:		**423**	**58**

ELLIOTT, Robbie — Defender

H: 5 10 W: 10 13 b.Gosforth 25-12-73

Source: Trainee. *Honours:* England Under-21.

1990–91	Newcastle U	6	0
1991–92	Newcastle U	9	0
1992–93	Newcastle U	0	0
1993–94	Newcastle U	15	0
1994–95	Newcastle U	14	2
1995–96	Newcastle U	6	0
1996–97	Newcastle U	29	7
1997–98	Bolton W	4	0
1998–99	Bolton W	22	0
Total:		**105**	**9**

ELLIOTT, Steve — Defender

H: 6 1 W: 13 12 b.Derby 29-10-78

Source: Trainee.

1996–97	Derby Co	0	0
1997–98	Derby Co	3	0
1998–99	Derby Co	11	0
Total:		**14**	**0**

ELLIOTT, Stuart — Defender

H: 5 8 W: 11 05 b.London 27-8-77

Source: Trainee.

1995–96	Newcastle U	0	0
1996–97	Newcastle U	0	0
1996–97	Hull C (loan)	3	0
1997–98	Newcastle U	0	0
1997–98	Swindon T (loan)	2	0
1998–99	Newcastle U	0	0
1998–99	Gillingham (loan)	5	0
1998–99	Hartlepool U (loan)	5	0
1998–99	Wrexham (loan)	9	0
Total:		**24**	**0**

ELLIOTT, Tony — Goalkeeper

H: 6 0 W: 13 06 b.Nuneaton 30-11-69

Honours: England Schools, Youth.

1986–87	Birmingham C	0	0
1987–88	Birmingham C	0	0
1988–89	Birmingham C	0	0
1988–89	Hereford U	23	0
1989–90	Hereford U	29	0
1990–91	Hereford U	5	0
1991–92	Hereford U	18	0
1992–93	Huddersfield T	15	0
1993–94	Carlisle U	6	0
1994–95	Carlisle U	3	0
1995–96	Carlisle U	13	0
1996–97	Cardiff C	36	0
1997–98	Cardiff C	3	0
1997–98	Scarborough	15	0
1998–99	Scarborough	20	0
Total:		**186**	**0**

ELLIS, Tony — Forward

H: 5 11 W: 11 00 b.Salford 20-10-64

Source: Horwich RMI, Northwich Vic.

1986–87	Oldham Ath	5	0
1987–88	Oldham Ath	3	0
1987–88	Preston NE	24	4
1988–89	Preston NE	45	19
1989–90	Preston NE	17	3
1989–90	Stoke C	24	6
1990–91	Stoke C	38	9
1991–92	Stoke C	15	4
1992–93	Preston NE	35	22
1993–94	Preston NE	37	26
1994–95	Blackpool	40	17
1995–96	Blackpool	43	14
1996–97	Blackpool	45	15
1997–98	Blackpool	18	8
1997–98	Bury	22	6
1998–99	Bury	16	2
1998–99	Stockport Co	16	6
Total:		**443**	**161**

ELLISON, Lee — Forward

H: 5 11 W: 12 06 b.Darlington 13-1-73

Source: Trainee.

1990–91	Darlington	13	3
1991–92	Darlington	27	10
1992–93	Darlington	3	0
1992–93	Hartlepool U (loan)	4	1
1993–94	Darlington	29	4
1994–95	Leicester C	0	0
1995–96	Crewe Alex	1	0
1996–97	Crewe Alex	3	2
1996–97	Hereford U	1	0
1996–97	Mansfield T	0	0

From Bishop Auckland

1997–98	Darlington	8	3
1998–99	Darlington	20	0
Total:		**109**	**23**

EMBERSON, Carl — Goalkeeper

H: 6 2 W: 14 10 b.Epsom 13-7-73

Source: Trainee.

1991–92	Millwall	0	0
1992–93	Millwall	0	0
1992–93	Colchester U (loan)	13	0
1993–94	Millwall	0	0
1994–95	Colchester U	20	0
1995–96	Colchester U	41	0
1996–97	Colchester U	35	0
1997–98	Colchester U	46	0
1998–99	Colchester U	37	0
Total:		**192**	**0**

EMBLEN, Neil — Midfield

H: 6 1 W: 13 03 b.Bromley 19-6-71

Source: Tonbridge, Sittingbourne.

1993–94	Millwall	12	0
1994–95	Wolverhampton W	27	7
1995–96	Wolverhampton W	33	2
1996–97	Wolverhampton W	28	0
1997–98	Wolverhampton W	7	0
1997–98	Crystal Palace	13	0
1998–99	Wolverhampton W	33	2
Total:		**153**	**11**

EMBLEN, Paul — Forward

H: 5 11 W: 12 12 b.Bromley 3-4-76

Source: Tonbridge A.

1996–97	Charlton Ath	0	0
1997–98	Charlton Ath	4	0
1997–98	Brighton & HA (loan)	15	4
1998–99	Charlton Ath	0	0
1998–99	Wycombe W	35	2
Total:		**54**	**6**

EMERSON — Defender

H: 6 1 W: 14 07 b.Porto Alegre 30-3-72

Source: Benfica.

1997–98	Sheffield W	6	0
1998–99	Sheffield W	38	1
Total:		**44**	**1**

EMERSON, Paul — Defender

H: 6 1 W: 11 06 b.Newtonards 29-8-78

Source: Trainee.

1997–98	Leicester C	0	0
1998–99	Leicester C	0	0

ENCKELMAN, Peter — Goalkeeper

H: 6 2 W: 12 05 b.Turku 10-3-77

Source: TPS Turku.

1998–99	Aston Villa	0	0

ERANIO, Stefano — Midfield

H: 5 10 W: 12 00 b.Genoa 29-12-68

Honours: Italy 20 full caps, 3 goals.

1984–85	Genoa	9	0
1985–86	Genoa	13	0
1986–87	Genoa	36	3
1987–88	Genoa	34	0
1988–89	Genoa	35	4
1989–90	Genoa	25	0
1990–91	Genoa	32	4
1991–92	Genoa	29	2
1992–93	AC Milan	21	2
1993–94	AC Milan	21	1
1994–95	AC Milan	11	0
1995–96	AC Milan	24	1
1996–97	AC Milan	21	2
1997–98	Derby Co	23	5
1998–99	Derby Co	25	0
Total:		**359**	**24**

ERIBENNE, Chukkie — Forward

H: 5 10 W: 11 12 b.London 2-11-80

Source: Trainee.

1997–98	Coventry C	0	0
1998–99	Coventry C	0	0

ETHERINGTON, Craig — Midfield

b.Basildon 16-9-79

Source: Trainee.

1997–98	West Ham U	0	0
1998–99	West Ham U	0	0
1998–99	Halifax T (loan)	4	0
Total:		**4**	**0**

ETHERINGTON, Matthew — Forward

H: 5 10 W: 10 07 b.Truro 14-8-81

Source: School. *Honours:* England Youth.

1996–97	Peterborough U	1	0
1997–98	Peterborough U	2	0
1998–99	Peterborough U	29	3
Total:		**32**	**3**

EUELL, Jason — Forward

H: 5 11 W: 11 02 b.Lambeth 6-2-77

Source: Trainee. *Honours:* England Youth, Under-21.

1995–96	Wimbledon	9	2
1996–97	Wimbledon	7	2
1997–98	Wimbledon	19	4
1998–99	Wimbledon	33	10
Total:		**68**	**18**

EUSTACE, John — Midfield

H: 5 11 W: 11 12 b.Solihull 3-11-79

Source: Trainee.

1996–97	Coventry C	0	0
1997–98	Coventry C	0	0
1998–99	Coventry C	0	0
1998–99	Dundee U	11	1
Total:		**11**	**1**

EUSTACE, Scott — Defender

H: 6 1 W: 13 06 b.Leicester 13-6-75

Source: Trainee.

1993–94	Leicester C	1	0
1994–95	Leicester C	0	0
1995–96	Mansfield T	27	1
1996–97	Mansfield T	42	4
1997–98	Mansfield T	29	1
1998–99	Mansfield T	0	0
1998–99	Cambridge U	16	0
Total:		**115**	**6**

EVANS, Gareth — Defender

H: 6 0 W: 11 11 b.Leeds 15-2-81

Source: Trainee. *Honours:* England Youth.

1997–98	Leeds U	0	0
1998–99	Leeds U	0	0

EVANS, Graham — Forward

b.Wrexham 16-6-80

Source: Caersws.

1998–99	Aston Villa	0	0

EVANS, James — Midfield

b.Epsom 3-10-78

Source: Trainee.

1997–98	Tottenham H	0	0
1998–99	Bristol C	0	0

EVANS, James — Midfield

b.Glasgow 27-1-82

Source: Fortuna Dusseldorf.

1998–99	Bolton W	0	0

EVANS, Kevin — Defender

H: 6 2 W: 12 10 b.Carmarthen 16-12-80

Source: Trainee. *Honours:* Wales Under-21.

1997–98	Leeds U	0	0
1998–99	Leeds U	0	0

EVANS, Micky — Forward

H: 6 0 W: 12 03 b.Plymouth 1-1-73

Source: Trainee. *Honours:* Eire 1 full cap.

1990–91	Plymouth Arg	4	0
1991–92	Plymouth Arg	13	0
1992–93	Plymouth Arg	23	1
1992–93	Blackburn R (loan)	0	0
1993–94	Plymouth Arg	22	9
1994–95	Plymouth Arg	23	4
1995–96	Plymouth Arg	45	12
1996–97	Plymouth Arg	33	12
1996–97	Southampton	12	4
1997–98	Southampton	10	0
1997–98	WBA	10	1
1998–99	WBA	20	2
Total:		**215**	**45**

EVANS, Nicky — Midfield

H: 5 8 W: 12 05 b.Carmarthen 12-5-80

Source: Trainee.

1998–99	Hartlepool U	1	0
Total:		**1**	**0**

EVANS, Paul — Midfield

H: 5 7 W: 12 00 b.Oswestry 1-9-74

Source: Trainee. *Honours:* Wales Under-21.

1991–92	Shrewsbury T	2	0
1992–93	Shrewsbury T	4	0
1993–94	Shrewsbury T	13	0
1994–95	Shrewsbury T	32	5
1995–96	Shrewsbury T	34	3
1996–97	Shrewsbury T	42	6
1997–98	Shrewsbury T	39	6
1998–99	Shrewsbury T	32	6
1998–99	Brentford	14	3
Total:		**212**	**29**

EVANS, Rhys — Goalkeeper

H: 6 1 W: 12 01 b.Swindon 27-1-82

Source: Trainee. *Honours:* England Schools, Youth.

1998–99	Chelsea	0	0

EVANS, Stephen — Midfield

H: 5 11 W: 11 02 b.Caerphilly 25-9-80

Source: Trainee.

1998–99	Crystal Palace	4	0
Total:		**4**	**0**

EVANS, Tom — Goalkeeper

H: 6 1 W: 13 02 b.Doncaster 31-12-76

Source: Trainee.

1995–96	Sheffield U	0	0
1996–97	Crystal Palace	0	0
1996–97	Coventry C (loan)	0	0
1997–98	Scunthorpe U	5	0
1998–99	Scunthorpe U	24	0
Total:		**29**	**0**

EVANS, Wayne — Defender

H: 5 10 W: 12 03 b.Welshpool 25-8-71

Source: Welshpool.

1993–94	Walsall	41	0
1994–95	Walsall	36	0
1995–96	Walsall	24	0
1996–97	Walsall	28	0
1997–98	Walsall	43	1
1998–99	Walsall	11	0
Total:		**183**	**1**

EVANS, Wayne — Midfield

H: 5 9 W: 9 12 b.Carmarthen 23-10-80

Source: Trainee.

1997–98	Manchester U	0	0
1998–99	Manchester U	0	0

EVATT, Ian — Defender

b.Coventry 19-11-81

Source: Trainee.

1998–99	Derby Co	0	0

EVERS, Sean — Midfield

H: 5 9 W: 9 11 b.Hitchin 10-10-77

Source: Trainee.

1995–96	Luton T	1	0
1996–97	Luton T	1	0

1997–98	Luton T	23	3
1998–99	Luton T	27	3
1998–99	Reading	1	0
Total:		**53**	**6**

EYDELIE, Jean-Jacques — Midfield

b.Angouleme 3-2-66

Source: Angouleme, Laval, Tours, Nantes, Marseille, Benfica, Bastia, Sion.

1997–98	Walsall	11	0
1998–99	Walsall	0	0
Total:		**11**	**0**

EYJOLFSSON, Siggi — Forward

H: 6 2 W: 12 09 b.Reykjavik 1-12-73

Source: IA Akranes

1998–99	Walsall	10	1
Total:		**10**	**1**

EYRE, John — Forward

H: 5 11 W: 13 00 b.Hull 9-10-74

Source: Trainee.

1993–94	Oldham Ath	2	0
1994–95	Oldham Ath	8	1
1994–95	Scunthorpe U (loan)	9	8
1995–96	Scunthorpe U	39	10
1996–97	Scunthorpe U	42	8
1997–98	Scunthorpe U	42	10
1998–99	Scunthorpe U	41	15
Total:		**183**	**52**

EYRE, Richard — Midfield

H: 5 8 W: 11 08 b.Poynton 15-9-76

Source: Trainee.

1995–96	Port Vale	0	0
1996–97	Port Vale	0	0
1997–98	Port Vale	1	0
1998–99	Port Vale	11	0
Total:		**12**	**0**

EYRES, David — Forward

H: 5 11 W: 11 05 b.Liverpool 26-2-64

Source: Rhyl.

1989–90	Blackpool	35	7
1990–91	Blackpool	36	6
1991–92	Blackpool	41	9
1992–93	Blackpool	46	16
1993–94	Burnley	45	19
1994–95	Burnley	39	8
1995–96	Burnley	42	6
1996–97	Burnley	36	3
1997–98	Burnley	13	1
1997–98	Preston NE	28	4
1998–99	Preston NE	34	8
Total:		**395**	**87**

FACEY, Delroy — Forward

H: 5 10 W: 14 10 b.Huddersfield 22-4-80

Source: Trainee.

1996–97	Huddersfield T	3	0
1997–98	Huddersfield T	3	0
1998–99	Huddersfield T	20	3
Total:		**26**	**3**

FAIRCLOUGH, Chris — Defender

H: 5 11 W: 11 07 b.Nottingham 12-4-64

Source: Apprentice. *Honours:* England Under-21, B.

1981–82	Nottingham F	0	0
1982–83	Nottingham F	15	0
1983–84	Nottingham F	31	0
1984–85	Nottingham F	35	0
1985–86	Nottingham F	0	0
1986–87	Nottingham F	26	1
1987–88	Tottenham H	40	4
1988–89	Tottenham H	20	1
1988–89	Leeds U	11	0
1989–90	Leeds U	42	8
1990–91	Leeds U	34	4
1991–92	Leeds U	31	2
1992–93	Leeds U	30	3
1993–94	Leeds U	40	4
1994–95	Leeds U	5	0
1995–96	Bolton W	33	0
1996–97	Bolton W	46	8
1997–98	Bolton W	11	0
1998–99	Notts Co	16	1
1998–99	York C (loan)	11	0
Total:		**477**	**36**

FAIRCLOUGH, David — Defender

H: 6 1 W: 11 08 b.Drogheda 26-4-78

1998–99	Tranmere R	0	0

FAIRHURST, Scott — Defender

H: 5 11 W: 10 12 b.Manchester 29-11-78

Source: Trainee.

1998–99	Oldham Ath	0	0

FALCONER, Willie — Midfield

H: 6 1 W: 11 09 b.Aberdeen 5-4-66

Source: Lewis United. *Honours:* Scotland Schools, Youth.

1982–83	Aberdeen	1	0
1983–84	Aberdeen	8	1

1984–85	Aberdeen	16	4
1985–86	Aberdeen	8	0
1986–87	Aberdeen	8	0
1987–88	Aberdeen	36	8
1988–89	Watford	33	5
1989–90	Watford	30	3
1990–91	Watford	35	4
1991–92	Middlesbrough	25	5
1992–93	Middlesbrough	28	5
1993–94	Sheffield U	23	3
1993–94	Celtic	14	1
1994–95	Celtic	26	4
1995–96	Celtic	2	0
1995–96	Motherwell	15	5
1996–97	Motherwell	21	2
1997–98	Motherwell	22	3
1998–99	Dundee	33	4
Total:		**384**	**57**

FALLON, Rory — Forward

H: 6 2 W: 11 09 b.Gisbourne 20-3-82

Source: North Shore U.

1998–99	Barnsley	0	0

FARLEY, Adam — Defender

b.Liverpool 12-1-80

Source: Trainee.

1997–98	Everton	0	0
1998–99	Everton	1	0
Total:		**1**	**0**

FARRELL, Andy — Midfield

H: 5 11 W: 12 00 b.Colchester 7-10-65

Source: School.

1983–84	Colchester U	15	0
1984–85	Colchester U	38	0
1985–86	Colchester U	24	1
1986–87	Colchester U	28	4
1987–88	Burnley	45	3
1988–89	Burnley	36	4
1989–90	Burnley	36	2
1990–91	Burnley	37	2
1991–92	Burnley	39	3
1992–93	Burnley	42	3
1993–94	Burnley	22	2
1994–95	Burnley	0	0
1994–95	Wigan Ath	31	0
1995–96	Wigan Ath	23	1
1996–97	Rochdale	40	2
1997–98	Rochdale	40	4
1998–99	Rochdale	38	0
Total:		**534**	**31**

FARRELL, Dave — Forward

H: 5 9 W: 11 07 b.Birmingham 11-11-71

Source: Redditch U.

1992–93	Aston Villa	2	0
1992–93	Scunthorpe U (loan)	5	1
1993–94	Aston Villa	4	0
1994–95	Aston Villa	0	0
1995–96	Aston Villa	0	0
1995–96	Wycombe W	33	7
1996–97	Wycombe W	27	1
1997–98	Peterborough U	42	6
1998–99	Peterborough U	37	4
Total:		**150**	**19**

FARRELL, Sean — Forward

H: 6 1 W: 13 07 b.Watford 28-2-69

Source: Apprentice.

1986–87	Luton T	0	0
1987–88	Luton T	0	0
1987–88	Colchester U (loan)	9	1
1988–89	Luton T	0	0
1989–90	Luton T	1	0
1990–91	Luton T	20	1
1991–92	Luton T	4	0
1991–92	Northampton T (loan)	4	1
1991–92	Fulham	25	10
1992–93	Fulham	35	12
1993–94	Fulham	34	9
1994–95	Peterborough U	33	8
1995–96	Peterborough U	26	9
1996–97	Peterborough U	7	3
1996–97	Notts Co	14	1
1997–98	Notts Co	35	15
1998–99	Notts Co	11	3
Total:		**258**	**73**

FARRELLY, Gareth — Midfield

H: 6 1 W: 13 07 b.Dublin 28-8-75

Source: Home Farm. *Honours:* Eire Under-21, 5 full caps.

1992–93	Aston Villa	0	0
1993–94	Aston Villa	0	0
1994–95	Aston Villa	0	0
1994–95	Rotherham U (loan)	10	2
1995–96	Aston Villa	5	0
1996–97	Aston Villa	3	0
1997–98	Everton	26	1
1998–99	Everton	1	0
Total:		**45**	**3**

FAULCONBRIDGE, Craig — Forward

H: 6 1 W: 13 00 b.Nuneaton 20-4-78

Source: Trainee.

1996–97	Coventry C	0	0

1997–98	Coventry C	0	0
1997–98	Dunfermline Ath	7	1
1998–99	Dunfermline Ath	6	0
1998–99	Coventry C	0	0
1998–99	Hull C (loan)	10	0
Total:		**23**	**1**

FAVATA, Sebastian — Defender

H: 5 10 W: 11 07 b.Carshalton 18-10-80

Source: Trainee.

1998–99	Wimbledon	0	0

FEAR, Peter — Midfield

H: 5 10 W: 11 07 b.Sutton 10-9-73

Source: Trainee. *Honours:* England Under-21.

1992–93	Wimbledon	4	0
1993–94	Wimbledon	23	1
1994–95	Wimbledon	14	1
1995–96	Wimbledon	4	0
1996–97	Wimbledon	18	0
1997–98	Wimbledon	8	2
1998–99	Wimbledon	2	0
Total:		**73**	**4**

FEATHERSTONE, James — Forward

H: 6 0 W: 12 12 b.Wharfedale 12-11-79

Source: Blackburn R Trainee.

1997–98	Scunthorpe U	1	0
1998–99	Scunthorpe U	0	0
Total:		**1**	**0**

FEENEY, Lee — Forward

b.Newry 21-3-78

Honours: Northern Ireland Under-21.

1997–98	Linfield	18	3
1998–99	Rangers	1	0
Total:		**19**	**3**

FEENEY, Warren — Forward

H: 5 10 W: 11 00 b.Belfast 17-1-81

Source: Trainee.

1997–98	Leeds U	0	0
1998–99	Leeds U	0	0

FENN, Neale — Forward

H: 5 10 W: 12 08 b.Edmonton 18-1-77

Source: Trainee. *Honours:* Eire Youth, Under-21.

1995–96	Tottenham H	0	0
1996–97	Tottenham H	4	0
1997–98	Tottenham H	4	0
1997–98	Leyton Orient (loan)	3	0
1997–98	Norwich C (loan)	7	1
1998–99	Tottenham H	0	0
1998–99	Swindon T (loan)	4	0
1998–99	Lincoln C (loan)	4	0
Total:		**26**	**1**

FENTON, Anthony — Defender

H: 5 10 W: 10 02 b.Preston 23-11-79

Source: Trainee.

1996–97	Manchester C	0	0
1997–98	Manchester C	0	0
1998–99	Manchester C	0	0
1998–99	Portsmouth	0	0

FENTON, Graham — Forward

H: 5 10 W: 11 09 b.Wallsend 22-5-74

Source: Trainee. *Honours:* England Under-21.

1991–92	Aston Villa	0	0
1992–93	Aston Villa	0	0
1993–94	Aston Villa	12	1
1993–94	WBA (loan)	7	3
1994–95	Aston Villa	17	2
1995–96	Aston Villa	3	0
1995–96	Blackburn R	14	6
1996–97	Blackburn R	13	1
1997–98	Leicester C	23	3
1998–99	Leicester C	9	0
Total:		**98**	**16**

FENTON, Nick — Defender

H: 6 1 W: 11 08 b.Preston 23-11-79

Source: Trainee. *Honours:* England Youth.

1996–97	Manchester C	0	0
1997–98	Manchester C	0	0
1998–99	Manchester C	15	0
Total:		**15**	**0**

FERDINAND, Les — Forward

H: 5 11 W: 13 05 b.Acton 18-12-66

Source: Hayes. *Honours:* England B, 17 full caps, 5 goals.

1986–87	QPR	2	0
1987–88	QPR	1	0
1987–88	Brentford (loan)	3	0
1988–89	QPR	0	0
1988–89	Besiktas (loan)	24	14
1989–90	QPR	9	2
1990–91	QPR	18	8
1991–92	QPR	23	10
1992–93	QPR	37	20
1993–94	QPR	36	16
1994–95	QPR	37	24
1995–96	Newcastle U	37	25

1996–97	Newcastle U	31	16
1997–98	Tottenham H	21	5
1998–99	Tottenham H	24	5
Total:		**303**	**145**

FERDINAND, Rio — Defender

H: 6 2 W: 12 00 b.Peckham 8-11-78

Source: Trainee. *Honours:* England Youth, Under-21, 8 full caps.

1995–96	West Ham U	1	0
1996–97	West Ham U	15	2
1996–97	Bournemouth (loan)	10	0
1997–98	West Ham U	35	0
1998–99	West Ham U	31	0
Total:		**92**	**2**

FERGUSON, Allan — Goalkeeper

H: 5 10 W: 12 07 b.Lanark 21-3-69

Source: Netherdale Com.

1987–88	Hamilton A	6	0
1988–89	Hamilton A	31	0
1989–90	Hamilton A	34	0
1990–91	Hamilton A	37	0
1991–92	Hamilton A	16	0
1992–93	Hamilton A	37	0
1993–94	Hamilton A	40	0
1994–95	Hamilton A	24	0
1995–96	Hamilton A	26	0
1996–97	Hamilton A	27	0
1997–98	Hamilton A	25	0
1998–99	St Johnstone	3	0
Total:		**306**	**0**

FERGUSON, Barry — Midfield

H: 5 11 W: 11 01 b.Glasgow 2-2-78

Source: Rangers SABC. *Honours:* Scotland Under-21, 1 full cap.

1994–95	Rangers	0	0
1995–96	Rangers	0	0
1996–97	Rangers	1	0
1997–98	Rangers	7	0
1998–99	Rangers	23	1
Total:		**31**	**1**

FERGUSON, Barry — Defender

H: 6 3 W: 13 00 b.Dublin 7-9-79

Source: Home Farm. *Honours:* Eire Under-21.

1998–99	Coventry C	0	0

FERGUSON, Darren — Midfield

H: 5 10 W: 10 04 b.Glasgow 9-2-72

Source: Trainee. *Honours:* Scotland Under-21.

1990–91	Manchester U	5	0
1991–92	Manchester U	4	0
1992–93	Manchester U	15	0
1993–94	Manchester U	3	0
1993–94	Wolverhampton W	14	0
1994–95	Wolverhampton W	24	0
1995–96	Wolverhampton W	33	1
1996–97	Wolverhampton W	16	3
1997–98	Wolverhampton W	26	0
1998–99	Wolverhampton W	4	0
Total:		**144**	**4**

FERGUSON, Derek — Midfield

H: 5 8 W: 11 12 b.Glasgow 31-7-67

Source: Gartcosh United. *Honours:* Scotland Schools, Youth, Under-21, 2 full caps.

1983–84	Rangers	1	0
1984–85	Rangers	8	0
1985–86	Rangers	19	0
1986–87	Rangers	30	1
1987–88	Rangers	32	4
1988–89	Rangers	16	2
1989–90	Rangers	5	0
1989–90	Dundee (loan)	4	0
1990–91	Hearts	28	2
1991–92	Hearts	38	1
1992–93	Hearts	37	1
1993–94	Sunderland	41	0
1994–95	Sunderland	23	0
1995–96	Falkirk	26	0
1996–97	Falkirk	14	3
1997–98	Falkirk	4	0
1998–99	Dunfermline Ath	21	0
Total:		**347**	**14**

FERGUSON, Duncan — Forward

H: 6 4 W: 14 06 b.Stirling 27-12-71

Source: Carse T. *Honours:* Scotland Under-21, 7 full caps.

1990–91	Dundee U	9	1
1991–92	Dundee U	38	15
1992–93	Dundee U	30	12
1993–94	Rangers	10	1
1994–95	Rangers	4	1
1994–95	Everton	23	7
1995–96	Everton	18	5
1996–97	Everton	33	10
1997–98	Everton	29	11
1998–99	Everton	13	4
1998–99	Newcastle U	7	2
Total:		**214**	**69**

FERGUSON, Ian — Midfield

H: 5 10 W: 10 11 b.Glasgow 15-3-67

Source: Clyde BC. *Honours:* Scotland B, Under-21, 9 full caps.

1984–85	Clyde	2	0
1985–86	Clyde	19	4
1986–87	Clyde	5	0
1986–87	St Mirren	35	4
1987–88	St Mirren	22	6
1987–88	Rangers	8	1
1988–89	Rangers	30	6
1989–90	Rangers	24	0
1990–91	Rangers	11	1
1991–92	Rangers	16	1
1992–93	Rangers	30	4
1993–94	Rangers	35	5
1994–95	Rangers	16	1
1995–96	Rangers	18	2
1996–97	Rangers	24	1
1997–98	Rangers	11	0
1998–99	Rangers	13	0
Total:		**319**	**36**

FERNANDES, Tamer — Goalkeeper

H: 6 3 W: 14 05 b.Paddington 7-12-74

Source: Trainee.

1993–94	Brentford	1	0
1994–95	Brentford	4	0
1995–96	Brentford	5	0
1996–97	Brentford	2	0
1997–98	Brentford	0	0
1997–98	Peterborough U (loan)	0	0
1997–98	Colchester U	0	0
1998–99	Colchester U	8	0
Total:		**20**	**0**

FERNANDO — Midfield

H: 5 10 W: 13 00 b.Valencia 11-9-65

Source: Valencia.

1998–99	Wolverhampton W	19	2
Total:		**19**	**2**

FERRANTE, Michael — Midfield

b.Melbourne 28-4-81

Source: Australia IOS.

1998–99	West Ham U	0	0

FERRARESI, Fabio — Midfield

H: 5 9 W: 11 02 b.Fano 24-5-79

Source: Cesena.

1998–99	Aston Villa	0	0

FERRER, Albert — Defender

H: 5 9 W: 11 00 b.Barcelona 6-6-70

Honours: Spain 35 full caps.

1989–90	Tenerife	17	0
1990–91	Barcelona	26	0
1991–92	Barcelona	12	1
1992–93	Barcelona	32	0
1993–94	Barcelona	34	0
1994–95	Barcelona	31	0
1995–96	Barcelona	28	0
1996–97	Barcelona	18	0
1997–98	Barcelona	24	0
1998–99	Chelsea	30	0
Total:		**252**	**1**

FERRI, Jean-Michel — Midfield

H: 6 0 W: 12 00 b.Lyon 7-2-69

1987–88	Nantes	5	0
1988–89	Nantes	2	0
1989–90	Nantes	30	2
1990–91	Nantes	37	3
1991–92	Nantes	24	4
1992–93	Nantes	34	4
1993–94	Nantes	36	4
1994–95	Nantes	33	1
1995–96	Nantes	26	0
1996–97	Nantes	33	2
1997–98	Nantes	30	1
From Istanbul.			
1998–99	Liverpool	2	0
Total:		**292**	**21**

FESTA, Gianluca — Defender

H: 5 11 W: 13 00 b.Cagliari 15-3-69

1986–87	Cagliari	3	0
1987–88	Fersuicis (loan)	26	2
1988–89	Cagliari	27	0
1989–90	Cagliari	36	0
1990–91	Cagliari	28	0
1991–92	Cagliari	31	0
1992–93	Cagliari	31	0
1993–94	Internazionale	4	0
1993–94	Roma (loan)	21	1
1994–95	Internazionale	26	2
1995–96	Internazionale	31	1
1996–97	Internazionale	5	0
1996–97	Middlesbrough	13	1
1997–98	Middlesbrough	38	2
1998–99	Middlesbrough	25	2
Total:		**345**	**11**

FETTIS, Alan — Goalkeeper

H: 6 2 W: 13 00 b.Newtownards 1-2-71

Source: Ards. *Honours:* Northern Ireland 25 full caps.

1991–92	Hull C	43	0
1992–93	Hull C	20	0
1993–94	Hull C	37	0
1994–95	Hull C	28	2
1995–96	Hull C	7	0
1995–96	WBA (loan)	3	0
1996–97	Nottingham F	4	0
1997–98	Nottingham F	0	0
1997–98	Blackburn R	8	0
1998–99	Blackburn R	2	0
Total:		**152**	**2**

FICKLING, Ashley — Defender

H: 5 10 W: 11 08 b.Sheffield 15-11-72

Source: Trainee. *Honours:* England Schools.

1991–92	Sheffield U	0	0
1992–93	Sheffield U	0	0
1992–93	Darlington (loan)	14	0
1993–94	Darlington (loan)	1	0
1994–95	Sheffield U	0	0
1994–95	Grimsby T	1	0
1995–96	Grimsby T	11	0
1996–97	Grimsby T	27	2
1997–98	Grimsby T	0	0
1997–98	Darlington (loan)	8	0
1998–99	Scunthorpe U	29	0
Total:		**91**	**2**

FILAN, John — Goalkeeper

H: 6 2 W: 14 04 b.Sydney 8-2-70

Source: Budapest St George.

1992–93	Cambridge U	6	0
1993–94	Cambridge U	46	0
1994–95	Cambridge U	16	0
1994–95	Nottingham F (loan)	0	0
1994–95	Coventry C	2	0
1995–96	Coventry C	13	0
1996–97	Coventry C	1	0
1997–98	Blackburn R	7	0
1998–99	Blackburn R	26	0
Total:		**117**	**0**

FINNAN, Steve — Midfield

H: 5 10 W: 12 00 b.Limerick 20-4-76

Source: Welling U.

1995–96	Birmingham C	12	1
1995–96	Notts Co (loan)	17	2
1996–97	Birmingham C	3	0
1996–97	Notts Co	23	0
1997–98	Notts Co	44	5
1998–99	Notts Co	13	0
1998–99	Fulham	22	2
Total:		**134**	**10**

FINNEY, Steve — Forward

H: 5 11 W: 12 08 b.Hexham 31-10-73

Source: Trainee.

1991–92	Preston NE	2	1
1992–93	Preston NE	4	0
1993–94	Manchester C	0	0
1994–95	Manchester C	0	0
1995–96	Swindon T	30	12
1996–97	Swindon T	20	2
1997–98	Swindon T	23	4
1997–98	Cambridge U (loan)	7	2
1998–99	Carlisle U	33	6
1998–99	Leyton Orient	5	0
Total:		**124**	**27**

FINNIGAN, John — Midfield

H: 5 8 W: 10 11 b.Wakefield 29-3-76

Source: Trainee.

1992–93	Nottingham F	0	0
1993–94	Nottingham F	0	0
1994–95	Nottingham F	0	0
1995–96	Nottingham F	0	0
1996–97	Nottingham F	0	0
1997–98	Nottingham F	0	0
1997–98	Lincoln C (loan)	6	0
1998–99	Lincoln C	37	1
Total:		**43**	**1**

FISH, David — Goalkeeper

H: 6 1 W: 11 07 b.Ashton-under-Lyne 4-8-80

Source: Trainee.

1998–99	Stockport Co	0	0

FISH, Mark — Defender

H: 6 4 W: 12 11 b.Cape Town 14-3-74

Source: Arcadia Shepherds. *Honours:* South Africa 46 full caps, 2 goals.

1992	Jomo Cosmos	14	1
1993	Jomo Cosmos	41	1
1994	Orlando Pirates	37	5
1995	Orlando Pirates	38	1
1996–97	Lazio	15	1
1997–98	Bolton W	22	2
1998–99	Bolton W	36	1
Total:		**203**	**12**

FISHER, Neil — Midfield

H: 5 10 W: 11 00 b.St Helens 7-11-70

Source: Trainee.

1990–91	Bolton W	0	0
1991–92	Bolton W	7	1
1992–93	Bolton W	4	0
1993–94	Bolton W	2	0
1994–95	Bolton W	11	0
1995–96	Chester C	44	2
1996–97	Chester C	29	1
1997–98	Chester C	35	1
From Connahs Quay			
1998–99	Chester C	8	0
Total:		**140**	**5**

FITCHETT, Scott — Midfield

H: 5 8 W: 9 06 b.Manchester 20-1-79

Source: Trainee.

1995–96	Nottingham F	0	0
1996–97	Nottingham F	0	0
1997–98	Nottingham F	0	0
1998–99	Nottingham F	0	0

FITZGERALD, Scott — Defender

H: 6 0 W: 12 12 b.Westminster 13-8-69

Source: Trainee. *Honours:* Eire Under-21, B.

1988–89	Wimbledon	0	0
1989–90	Wimbledon	1	0
1990–91	Wimbledon	0	0
1991–92	Wimbledon	36	1
1992–93	Wimbledon	20	0
1993–94	Wimbledon	28	0
1994–95	Wimbledon	17	0
1995–96	Wimbledon	4	0
1995–96	Sheffield U (loan)	6	0
1996–97	Wimbledon	0	0
1996–97	Millwall (loan)	7	0
1997–98	Millwall	18	0
1998–99	Millwall	32	1
Total:		**169**	**2**

FITZHENRY, Neil — Defender

H: 6 0 W: 12 02 b.Billinge 24-9-78

Source: Trainee.

1997–98	Wigan Ath	3	0
1998–99	Wigan Ath	1	0
Total:		**4**	**0**

FITZPATRICK, Ian — Forward

H: 5 9 W: 10 00 b.Manchester 22-9-80

Source: Trainee. *Honours:* England Schools.

1998–99	Manchester U	0	0

FITZPATRICK, Lee — Midfield

H: 5 10 W: 11 07 b.Manchester 31-10-78

Source: Trainee.

1996–97	Blackburn R	0	0
1997–98	Blackburn R	0	0
1998–99	Blackburn R	0	0

FITZPATRICK, Trevor — Forward

H: 6 1 W: 12 10 b.Surrey 19-2-80

Source: Trainee.

1997–98	Southend U	3	0
1998–99	Southend U	23	5
Total:		**26**	**5**

FJORTOFT, Jan Aage — Forward

H: 6 4 W: 13 12 b.Aalesund 10-1-67

Honours: Norway 71 full caps, 20 goals.

1987	Hamar	22	10
1988	Lillestrom	24	14
1989	Lillestrom	11	6
1989–90	Rapid Vienna	33	17
1990–91	Rapid Vienna	33	16
1991–92	Rapid Vienna	34	16
1992–93	Rapid Vienna	28	13
1993–94	Swindon T	36	12
1994–95	Swindon T	36	16
1994–95	Middlesbrough	8	3
1995–96	Middlesbrough	28	6
1996–97	Middlesbrough	5	0
1996–97	Sheffield U	17	10
1997–98	Sheffield U	17	9
1997–98	Barnsley	15	6
1998–99	Barnsley	19	3
Total:		**366**	**157**

FLACK, Steve — Forward

H: 6 1 W: 11 04 b.Cambridge 29-5-71

Source: Cambridge C.

1995–96	Cardiff C	10	1
1996–97	Cardiff C	1	0
1996–97	Exeter C	27	4
1997–98	Exeter C	41	14
1998–99	Exeter C	44	11
Total:		**123**	**30**

FLAHAVAN, Aaron — Goalkeeper

H: 6 1 W: 11 12 b.Southampton 15-12-75

Source: Trainee.

1993–94	Portsmouth	0	0
1994–95	Portsmouth	0	0
1995–96	Portsmouth	0	0
1996–97	Portsmouth	24	0
1997–98	Portsmouth	26	0
1998–99	Portsmouth	13	0
Total:		**63**	**0**

FLASH, Richard — Defender

H: 5 11 W: 12 00 b.Birmingham 8-4-76

Source: Trainee.

1994–95	Manchester U	0	0
1995–96	Manchester U	0	0
1995–96	Wolverhampton W	0	0
1996–97	Watford	1	0
1997–98	Watford	0	0
1997–98	Lincoln C (loan)	5	0
1998–99	Plymouth Arg	5	0
Total:		**11**	**0**

FLECK, Robert — Forward

H: 5 7 W: 11 09 b.Glasgow 11-8-65

Source: Possil YM. *Honours:* Scotland Youth, Under-21, 4 full caps.

1983–84	Partick T	2	1
1983–84	Rangers	1	0
1984–85	Rangers	8	0
1985–86	Rangers	15	3
1986–87	Rangers	40	19
1987–88	Rangers	21	7
1987–88	Norwich C	18	7
1988–89	Norwich C	33	10
1989–90	Norwich C	27	7
1990–91	Norwich C	29	5
1991–92	Norwich C	36	11
1992–93	Chelsea	31	2
1993–94	Chelsea	9	1
1993–94	Bolton W (loan)	7	1
1994–95	Chelsea	0	0
1994–95	Bristol C (loan)	10	1
1995–96	Chelsea	0	0
1995–96	Norwich C	41	10
1996–97	Norwich C	36	4
1997–98	Norwich C	27	2
1997–98	Reading	5	0
1998–99	Reading	4	1
Total:		**400**	**92**

FLEMING, Craig — Defender

H: 5 11 W: 13 00 b.Halifax 6-10-71

Source: Trainee.

1988–89	Halifax T	1	0
1989–90	Halifax T	10	0
1990–91	Halifax T	46	0
1991–92	Oldham Ath	32	1
1992–93	Oldham Ath	24	0
1993–94	Oldham Ath	37	0
1994–95	Oldham Ath	5	0
1995–96	Oldham Ath	22	0
1996–97	Oldham Ath	44	0
1997–98	Norwich C	22	1
1998–99	Norwich C	37	3
Total:		**280**	**5**

FLEMING, Curtis — Defender

H: 5 10 W: 12 05 b.Manchester 8-10-68

Source: St Patrick's Ath. *Honours:* Eire Youth, Under-21, B, 10 full caps.

1991–92	Middlesbrough	28	0
1992–93	Middlesbrough	24	0
1993–94	Middlesbrough	40	0
1994–95	Middlesbrough	21	0
1995–96	Middlesbrough	13	1
1996–97	Middlesbrough	30	0
1997–98	Middlesbrough	31	1
1998–99	Middlesbrough	14	1
Total:		**201**	**3**

FLEMING, Derek — Defender

H: 5 7 W: 10 02 b.Falkirk 5-12-73

Source: Broxburn Ath.

1992–93	Meadowbank T	4	0
1993–94	Meadowbank T	38	2
1994–95	Meadowbank T	7	1
1994–95	Dunfermline Ath	29	1
1995–96	Dunfermline Ath	33	3
1996–97	Dunfermline Ath	26	2
1997–98	Dunfermline Ath	2	0
1997–98	Dundee	17	0
1998–99	Dundee	1	0
Total:		**157**	**9**

FLEMING, Terry — Midfield

H: 5 9 W: 10 01 b.Marston Green 5-1-73

Source: Trainee.

1990–91	Coventry C	2	0
1991–92	Coventry C	0	0
1992–93	Coventry C	11	0
1993–94	Northampton T	31	1
1994–95	Preston NE	27	2
1995–96	Preston NE	5	0

1995–96	Lincoln C	22	0
1996–97	Lincoln C	37	0
1997–98	Lincoln C	40	3
1998–99	Lincoln C	43	0
Total:		**218**	**6**

FLETCHER, Carl — Midfield

H: 5 10 W: 11 07 b.Camberley 7-4-80

Source: Trainee.

1997–98	Bournemouth	1	0
1998–99	Bournemouth	1	0
Total:		**2**	**0**

FLETCHER, Steve — Forward

H: 6 2 W: 14 09 b.Hartlepool 26-6-72

Source: Trainee.

1990–91	Hartlepool U	14	2
1991–92	Hartlepool U	18	2
1992–93	Bournemouth	31	4
1993–94	Bournemouth	36	6
1994–95	Bournemouth	40	6
1995–96	Bournemouth	7	1
1996–97	Bournemouth	35	7
1997–98	Bournemouth	42	12
1998–99	Bournemouth	39	8
Total:		**262**	**48**

FLITCROFT, David — Midfield

H: 5 11 W: 13 05 b.Bolton 14-1-74

Source: Trainee.

1991–92	Preston NE	0	0
1992–93	Preston NE	8	2
1993–94	Preston NE	0	0
1993–94	Lincoln C (loan)	2	0
1993–94	Chester C	8	1
1994–95	Chester C	32	0
1995–96	Chester C	9	1
1996–97	Chester C	32	6
1997–98	Chester C	44	4
1998–99	Chester C	42	6
Total:		**177**	**20**

FLITCROFT, Garry — Midfield

H: 6 0 W: 11 08 b.Bolton 6-11-72

Source: Trainee. *Honours:* England Schools, Under-21.

1991–92	Manchester C	0	0
1991–92	Bury (loan)	12	0
1992–93	Manchester C	32	5
1993–94	Manchester C	21	3
1994–95	Manchester C	37	5
1995–96	Manchester C	25	0
1995–96	Blackburn R	3	0
1996–97	Blackburn R	28	3
1997–98	Blackburn R	33	0
1998–99	Blackburn R	8	2
Total:		**199**	**18**

FLITCROFT, Steven — Midfield

H: 5 10 W: 11 01 b.Bolton 17-10-81

Source: Trainee. *Honours:* England Schools.

1998–99	Blackburn R	0	0

FLO, Havard — Forward

H: 6 2 W: 13 08 b.Volda 4-4-70

Source: Stryn, Sogndal. *Honours:* Norway 16 full caps, 3 goals.

1994–95	Aarhus	19	5
1995–96	Aarhus	23	10
1996–97	Aarhus	11	12
1996–97	Werder Bremen	14	0
1997–98	Werder Bremen	25	5
1998–99	Werder Bremen	16	0
1998–99	Wolverhampton W	19	5
Total:		**127**	**37**

FLO, Tore Andre — Forward

H: 6 4 W: 13 08 b.Strin 15-6-73

Honours: Norway 37 full caps, 20 goals.

1994	Sogndal	22	5
1995	Tromso	26	18
1996	Brann	24	19
1997	Brann	16	9
1997–98	Chelsea	34	11
1998–99	Chelsea	30	10
Total:		**152**	**72**

FLOGEL, Thomas — Midfield

H: 5 9 W: 11 02 b.Vienna 7-6-71

Source: FK Austria. *Honours:* Austria 9 full caps.

1989–90	FK Austria	16	1
1990–91	FK Austria	28	5
1991–92	FK Austria	35	6
1992–93	FK Austria	35	10
1993–94	FK Austria	35	5
1994–95	FK Austria	36	7
1995–96	FK Austria	29	4
1996–97	FK Austria	34	4
1997–98	Hearts	29	5
1998–99	Hearts	20	2
Total:		**297**	**49**

FLOOD, James — Forward

H: 5 9 W: 11 02 b.Stockport 21-9-79

Source: Trainee.

1998–99	Stockport Co	0	0

FLOWERS, Tim — Goalkeeper

H: 6 3 W: 14 04 b.Kenilworth 3-2-67

Source: Apprentice. *Honours:* England Youth, Under-21, 11 full caps.

1984–85	Wolverhampton W	38	0
1985–86	Wolverhampton W	25	0
1985–86	Southampton (loan)	0	0
1986–87	Southampton	9	0
1986–87	Swindon T (loan)	2	0
1987–88	Southampton	9	0
1987–88	Swindon T (loan)	5	0
1988–89	Southampton	7	0
1989–90	Southampton	35	0
1990–91	Southampton	37	0
1991–92	Southampton	41	0
1992–93	Southampton	42	0
1993–94	Southampton	12	0
1993–94	Blackburn R	29	0
1994–95	Blackburn R	39	0
1995–96	Blackburn R	37	0
1996–97	Blackburn R	36	0
1997–98	Blackburn R	25	0
1998–99	Blackburn R	11	0
Total:		**439**	**0**

FLYNN, Mike — Defender

H: 6 0 W: 11 02 b.Oldham 23-2-69

Source: Trainee.

1986–87	Oldham Ath	0	0
1987–88	Oldham Ath	31	1
1988–89	Oldham Ath	9	0
1988–89	Norwich C	0	0
1989–90	Norwich C	0	0
1989–90	Preston NE	23	1
1990–91	Preston NE	35	1
1991–92	Preston NE	43	3
1992–93	Preston NE	35	2
1992–93	Stockport Co	10	0
1993–94	Stockport Co	46	1
1994–95	Stockport Co	43	2
1995–96	Stockport Co	46	6
1996–97	Stockport Co	46	2
1997–98	Stockport Co	34	1
1998–99	Stockport Co	46	1
Total:		**447**	**21**

FLYNN, Sean — Midfield

H: 5 8 W: 11 09 b.Birmingham 13-3-68

Source: Halesowen T.

1991–92	Coventry C	22	2
1992–93	Coventry C	7	0
1993–94	Coventry C	36	3
1994–95	Coventry C	32	4
1995–96	Derby Co	42	2
1996–97	Derby Co	17	1
1996–97	Stoke C (loan)	5	0
1997–98	WBA	35	2
1998–99	WBA	38	2
Total:		**234**	**16**

FOE, Marc Vivien — Midfield

H: 6 2 W: 13 06 b.Yaounde 1-5-75

Source: Canon Yaounde. *Honours:* Cameroon 30 full caps.

1994–95	Lens	15	3
1995–96	Lens	19	2
1996–97	Lens	28	2
1997–98	Lens	18	2
1998–99	Lens	5	2
1998–99	West Ham U	13	0
Total:		**98**	**11**

FOLAN, Tony — Forward

H: 6 0 W: 11 00 b.Lewisham 18-9-78

Source: Trainee. *Honours:* Eire Under-21.

1995–96	Crystal Palace	0	0
1996–97	Crystal Palace	0	0
1997–98	Crystal Palace	1	0
1998–99	Crystal Palace	0	0
1998–99	Brentford	29	4
Total:		**30**	**4**

FOLEY, Dominic — Forward

H: 6 1 W: 12 08 b.Cork 7-7-76

Source: St James Gate.

1995–96	Wolverhampton W	5	0
1996–97	Wolverhampton W	5	1
1997–98	Wolverhampton W	5	0
1997–98	Watford (loan)	8	1
1998–99	Wolverhampton W	5	2
1998–99	Notts Co (loan)	2	0
Total:		**30**	**4**

FOLLAND, Robbie — Forward

H: 5 9 W: 10 07 b.Swansea 16-9-79

Source: Trainee.

1997–98	Oxford U	2	0
1998–99	Oxford U	0	0
Total:		**2**	**0**

FOLLETT, Richard — Defender

H: 5 9 W: 10 02 b.Leamington Spa 29-8-79

Source: Trainee.

1996–97	Nottingham F	0	0
1997–98	Nottingham F	0	0
1998–99	Nottingham F	0	0
1998–99	Scunthorpe U (loan)	0	0

FORAN, Mark — Defender

H: 6 3 W: 13 04 b.Aldershot 30-10-73

Source: Trainee.

1991–92	Millwall	0	0
1992–93	Millwall	0	0
1993–94	Millwall	0	0
1993–94	Sheffield U	0	0
1994–95	Sheffield U	4	1
1994–95	Rotherham U (loan)	3	0
1995–96	Sheffield U	7	0
1995–96	Wycombe W (loan)	5	0
1995–96	Peterborough U	17	1
1996–97	Peterborough U	4	0
1996–97	Lincoln C (loan)	2	0
1996–97	Oldham Ath (loan)	1	0
1997–98	Peterborough U	4	0
1997–98	Crewe Alex	12	1
1998–99	Crewe Alex	6	0
Total:		**65**	**3**

FORBES, Adrian — Forward

H: 5 7 W: 11 02 b.Greenford 23-1-79

Source: Trainee. *Honours:* England Youth.

1996–97	Norwich C	10	0
1997–98	Norwich C	33	4
1998–99	Norwich C	15	0
Total:		**58**	**4**

FORBES, Steve — Midfield

H: 6 1 W: 13 03 b.Hackney 24-12-75

Source: Sittingbourne.

1994–95	Millwall	1	0
1995–96	Millwall	4	0
1996–97	Millwall	0	0
1996–97	Colchester U	1	1
1997–98	Colchester U	35	1
1998–99	Colchester U	15	2
1998–99	Peterborough U (loan)	3	0
Total:		**59**	**4**

FORD, Bobby — Midfield

H: 5 8 W: 11 00 b.Bristol 22-9-74

Source: Trainee.

1992–93	Oxford U	0	0
1993–94	Oxford U	14	0
1994–95	Oxford U	23	2
1995–96	Oxford U	28	3
1996–97	Oxford U	33	0
1997–98	Oxford U	18	2
1997–98	Sheffield U	23	1
1998–99	Sheffield U	30	0
Total:		**169**	**8**

FORD, John — Defender

H: 6 1 W: 13 04 b.Birmingham 12-4-68

Source: Cradley T.

1991–92	Swansea C	44	0
1992–93	Swansea C	43	3
1993–94	Swansea C	27	1
1994–95	Swansea C	46	3
1995–96	Bradford C	19	0
1996–97	Gillingham	4	0
1996–97	Barnet	13	1
1997–98	Barnet	19	0
1998–99	Barnet	15	1
Total:		**230**	**9**

FORD, Liam — Forward

H: 5 7 W: 10 03 b.Bradford 8-9-79

Source: Trainee.

1998–99	Plymouth Arg	1	0
Total:		**1**	**0**

FORD, Mark — Midfield

H: 5 7 W: 10 08 b.Pontefract 10-10-75

Source: Trainee. *Honours:* England Youth, Under-21.

1992–93	Leeds U	0	0
1993–94	Leeds U	1	0
1994–95	Leeds U	0	0
1995–96	Leeds U	12	0
1996–97	Leeds U	16	1
1997–98	Burnley	36	1
1998–99	Burnley	12	0
Total:		**77**	**2**

FORD, Mike — Defender

H: 6 0 W: 12 12 b.Bristol 9-2-66

Source: Apprentice.

1983–84	Leicester C	0	0
From Devizes T			
1984–85	Cardiff C	20	1
1985–86	Cardiff C	44	4
1986–87	Cardiff C	36	1
1987–88	Cardiff C	45	7
1988–89	Oxford U	10	1
1989–90	Oxford U	31	2
1990–91	Oxford U	28	1
1991–92	Oxford U	9	1
1992–93	Oxford U	44	4
1993–94	Oxford U	41	1
1994–95	Oxford U	18	0
1995–96	Oxford U	44	2
1996–97	Oxford U	42	4
1997–98	Oxford U	22	2
1998–99	Cardiff C	25	0
Total:		**459**	**31**

FORD, Ryan — Midfield

H: 5 9 W: 10 04 b.Worksop 3-9-80

Source: Trainee.

1997–98	Manchester U	0	0
1998–99	Manchester U	0	0

FORD, Tony — Midfield

H: 5 9 W: 13 00 b.Grimsby 14-5-59

Source: Apprentice. *Honours:* England B.

1975–76	Grimsby T	15	0
1976–77	Grimsby T	6	0
1977–78	Grimsby T	34	2
1978–79	Grimsby T	45	16
1979–80	Grimsby T	37	5
1980–81	Grimsby T	28	4
1981–82	Grimsby T	35	7
1982–83	Grimsby T	37	4
1983–84	Grimsby T	42	8
1984–85	Grimsby T	42	6
1985–86	Grimsby T	34	3
1985–86	Sunderland (loan)	9	1
1986–87	Stoke C	41	6
1987–88	Stoke C	44	7
1988–89	Stoke C	27	0
1988–89	WBA	11	1
1989–90	WBA	42	8
1990–91	WBA	46	5
1991–92	WBA	15	0
1991–92	Grimsby T	22	1
1992–93	Grimsby T	17	2
1993–94	Grimsby T	29	0
1993–94	Bradford C (loan)	5	0
1994–95	Scunthorpe U	38	2
1995–96	Scunthorpe U	38	7
From Barrow			
1996–97	Mansfield T	27	2
1997–98	Mansfield T	34	3
1998–99	Mansfield T	42	2
Total:		**842**	**102**

FORINTON, Howard — Forward

H: 5 11 W: 11 00 b.Boston 18-9-75

Source: Yeovil T.

1997–98	Birmingham C	1	0
1998–99	Birmingham C	3	1
1998–99	Plymouth Arg (loan)	9	3
Total:		**13**	**4**

FORREST, Craig — Goalkeeper

H: 6 4 W: 14 04 b.Vancouver 20-9-67

Source: Apprentice. *Honours:* Canada 37 full caps.

1985–86	Ipswich T	0	0
1986–87	Ipswich T	0	0
1987–88	Ipswich T	0	0
1987–88	Colchester U (loan)	11	0
1988–89	Ipswich T	28	0
1989–90	Ipswich T	45	0
1990–91	Ipswich T	43	0
1991–92	Ipswich T	46	0
1992–93	Ipswich T	11	0
1993–94	Ipswich T	27	0
1994–95	Ipswich T	36	0
1995–96	Ipswich T	21	0
1996–97	Ipswich T	6	0
1996–97	Chelsea (loan)	3	0
1997–98	West Ham U	13	0
1998–99	West Ham U	2	0
Total:		**292**	**0**

FORREST, Martyn — Midfield

H: 5 10 W: 12 02 b.Bury 2-1-79

1997–98	Bury	0	0
1998–99	Bury	1	0
Total:		**1**	**0**

FORRESTER, Jamie — Forward

H: 5 6 W: 10 12 b.Bradford 1-11-74

Source: Auxerre. *Honours:* England Schools, Youth.

1992–93	Leeds U	6	0
1993–94	Leeds U	3	0
1994–95	Leeds U	0	0
1994–95	Southend U (loan)	5	0
1994–95	Grimsby T (loan)	9	1
1995–96	Leeds U	0	0
1995–96	Grimsby T	28	5
1996–97	Grimsby T	13	1
1996–97	Scunthorpe U	10	6
1997–98	Scunthorpe U	45	11
1998–99	Scunthorpe U	46	20
Total:		**165**	**44**

FORRESTER, Mark — Forward

H: 5 8 W: 10 02 b.Stockton 15-4-81

Source: Trainee.

1998–99	Torquay U	5	0
Total:		**5**	**0**

FORSSELL, Mikael — Forward

H: 5 10 W: 10 10 b.Steinfurt 15-3-81

1997	HJK Helsinki	1	0
1998	HJK Helsinki	16	1
1998–99	Chelsea	10	1
Total:		**27**	**2**

FORSTER, Nicky — Forward

H: 5 9 W: 11 05 b.Caterham 8-9-73

Source: Horley T. *Honours:* England Under-21.

1992–93	Gillingham	26	6
1993–94	Gillingham	41	18
1994–95	Brentford	46	24
1995–96	Brentford	38	5
1996–97	Brentford	25	10
1996–97	Birmingham C	7	3
1997–98	Birmingham C	28	3
1998–99	Birmingham C	33	5
Total:		**244**	**74**

FORSYTH, Mike — Defender

H: 5 11 W: 12 07 b.Liverpool 20-3-66

Source: Apprentice. *Honours:* England Youth, Under-21, B.

1983–84	WBA	8	0
1984–85	WBA	10	0
1985–86	WBA	11	0
1985–86	Northampton T (loan)	0	0
1985–86	Derby Co	0	0
1986–87	Derby Co	41	1
1987–88	Derby Co	39	3
1988–89	Derby Co	38	0
1989–90	Derby Co	38	0
1990–91	Derby Co	35	0
1991–92	Derby Co	43	1
1992–93	Derby Co	41	1
1993–94	Derby Co	28	2
1994–95	Derby Co	27	0
1994–95	Notts Co	7	0
1995–96	Notts Co	0	0
1996–97	Notts Co	0	0
1996–97	Hereford U (loan)	12	0
1996–97	Wycombe W	23	2
1997–98	Wycombe W	25	0
1998–99	Wycombe W	4	0
Total:		**425**	**10**

FORSYTH, Paul — Forward

H: 5 8 W: 10 05 b.Dublin 11-4-81

Source: Trainee.

1998–99	Blackburn R	0	0

FORSYTH, Richard — Midfield

H: 5 10 W: 13 01 b.Dudley 3-10-70

Source: Kidderminster H.

1995–96	Birmingham C	26	2
1996–97	Stoke C	40	8
1997–98	Stoke C	37	7
1998–99	Stoke C	18	2
Total:		**121**	**19**

FORTUNE-WEST, Leo — Forward

H: 6 4 W: 13 01 b.Stratford 9-4-71

Source: Tiptree, Dagenham, Dartford, Bishops Stortford, Stevenage Bor.

1995–96	Gillingham	40	12
1996–97	Gillingham	7	2
1996–97	Leyton Orient (loan)	5	0
1997–98	Gillingham	20	4
1998–99	Lincoln C	9	1
1998–99	Brentford	11	0
1998–99	Rotherham U	20	12
Total:		**112**	**31**

FORTUNE, Jonathan — Defender

H: 6 2 W: 11 00 b.Islington 23-8-80

Source: Trainee.

1998–99	Charlton Ath	0	0

FOSTER, Craig — Midfield

H: 5 11 W: 12 00 b.Melbourne 15-4-69

Source: Marconi.

1997–98	Portsmouth	16	2
1998–99	Portsmouth	0	0
1998–99	Crystal Palace	32	2
Total:		**48**	**4**

FOSTER, John — Defender

H: 5 11 W: 12 13 b.Blackley 19-9-73

Source: Trainee. *Honours:* England Schools.

1992–93	Manchester C	0	0
1993–94	Manchester C	1	0
1994–95	Manchester C	11	0
1995–96	Manchester C	4	0
1996–97	Manchester C	3	0
1997–98	Manchester C	0	0
1997–98	Carlisle U	7	0
1998–99	Bury	7	0
Total:		**33**	**0**

FOSTER, Stephen — Defender

H: 6 1 W: 13 00 b.Mansfield 3-12-74

Source: Trainee.

1993–94	Mansfield T	5	0
From Woking			
1997–98	Bristol R	34	0
1998–99	Bristol R	43	1
Total:		**82**	**1**

FOSTER, Stephen — Defender

H: 5 11 W: 11 00 b.Warrington 10-9-80

Source: Trainee. *Honours:* England Schools.

1998–99	Crewe Alex	1	0
Total:		**1**	**0**

FOSTER, Steve — Forward

H: 5 9 W: 13 01 b.Manchester 30-12-81

Source: Trainee.

1998–99	Blackburn R	0	0

FOTIADIS, Andrew — Forward

H: 5 11 W: 11 07 b.Hitchin 6-9-77

Source: School. *Honours:* England Schools.

1996–97	Luton T	17	3
1997–98	Luton T	15	1
1998–99	Luton T	21	2
Total:		**53**	**6**

FOWLER, Jason — Midfield

H: 6 3 W: 12 04 b.Bristol 20-8-74

Source: Trainee.

1992–93	Bristol C	1	0
1993–94	Bristol C	1	0
1994–95	Bristol C	13	0
1995–96	Bristol C	10	0
1996–97	Cardiff C	37	5
1997–98	Cardiff C	38	5
1998–99	Cardiff C	37	3
Total:		**137**	**13**

FOWLER, Robbie — Forward

H: 5 11 W: 11 10 b.Liverpool 9-4-75

Source: Trainee. *Honours:* England Youth, B, Under-21, 9 full caps, 2 goals.

1991–92	Liverpool	0	0
1992–93	Liverpool	0	0
1993–94	Liverpool	28	12
1994–95	Liverpool	42	25
1995–96	Liverpool	38	28
1996–97	Liverpool	32	18
1997–98	Liverpool	20	9
1998–99	Liverpool	25	14
Total:		**185**	**106**

FOX, Martin — Defender

H: 5 8 W: 11 02 b.Sutton-in-Ashfield 21-4-79

Source: Trainee.

1997–98	Leicester C	0	0
1998–99	Leicester C	0	0

FOX, Peter — Goalkeeper

H: 5 11 W: 13 10 b.Scunthorpe 5-7-57

Source: Apprentice.

1972–73	Sheffield W	1	0
1973–74	Sheffield W	0	0
1974–75	Sheffield W	20	0
1975–76	Sheffield W	27	0
1976–77	Sheffield W	1	0
1976–77	West Ham U (loan)	0	0
1977–78	Sheffield W	0	0
1977–78	Barnsley (loan)	1	0
1977–78	Stoke C	0	0
1978–79	Stoke C	1	0
1979–80	Stoke C	23	0
1980–81	Stoke C	42	0
1981–82	Stoke C	38	0
1982–83	Stoke C	35	0
1983–84	Stoke C	42	0
1984–85	Stoke C	14	0
1985–86	Stoke C	37	0
1986–87	Stoke C	39	0
1987–88	Stoke C	17	0
1988–89	Stoke C	29	0
1989–90	Stoke C	38	0
1990–91	Stoke C	44	0
1991–92	Stoke C	0	0
1992–93	Stoke C	10	0
1992–93	Wrexham (loan)	0	0
1993–94	Exeter C	26	0
1994–95	Exeter C	31	0
1995–96	Exeter C	46	0
1996–97	Exeter C	5	0
1997–98	Exeter C	0	0
1998–99	Exeter C	0	0
Total:		**567**	**0**

FOX, Ruel — Forward

H: 5 6 W: 10 05 b.Ipswich 14-1-68

Source: Apprentice. *Honours:* England B.

1985–86	Norwich C	0	0
1986–87	Norwich C	3	0
1987–88	Norwich C	34	2
1988–89	Norwich C	4	0
1989–90	Norwich C	7	3
1990–91	Norwich C	28	4
1991–92	Norwich C	37	2
1992–93	Norwich C	34	4
1993–94	Norwich C	25	7
1993–94	Newcastle U	14	2
1994–95	Newcastle U	40	10
1995–96	Newcastle U	4	0
1995–96	Tottenham H	26	6
1996–97	Tottenham H	25	1
1997–98	Tottenham H	32	3
1998–99	Tottenham H	20	3
Total:		**333**	**47**

FOY, Keith — Midfield

H: 5 11 W: 12 03 b.Crumlin 30-12-81

Source: Trainee.

1998–99	Nottingham F	0	0

FOYLE, Martin — Forward

H: 5 10 W: 12 00 b.Salisbury 2-5-63

Source: Amateur.

1980–81	Southampton	0	0
1981–82	Southampton	0	0
1982–83	Southampton	7	1
1983–84	Southampton	5	0
1983–84	Blackburn R (loan)	0	0
1984–85	Aldershot	44	15
1985–86	Aldershot	20	9
1986–87	Aldershot	34	11
1986–87	Oxford U	4	0
1987–88	Oxford U	33	10
1988–89	Oxford U	40	14
1989–90	Oxford U	13	2
1990–91	Oxford U	36	10
1991–92	Port Vale	43	11
1992–93	Port Vale	16	4
1993–94	Port Vale	37	18
1994–95	Port Vale	42	16
1995–96	Port Vale	25	8
1996–97	Port Vale	37	3
1997–98	Port Vale	39	8
1998–99	Port Vale	35	9
Total:		**510**	**149**

FRAIL, Stephen — Defender

H: 5 11 W: 12 03 b.Glasgow 10-8-69

Source: Possilpark YM.

1985–86	Dundee	0	0
1986–87	Dundee	0	0
1987–88	Dundee	4	0
1988–89	Dundee	23	1
1989–90	Dundee	6	0
1990–91	Dundee	26	0
1991–92	Dundee	3	0
1992–93	Dundee	7	0
1993–94	Dundee	32	0
1993–94	Hearts	9	2
1994–95	Hearts	25	2
1995–96	Hearts	0	0
1996–97	Hearts	9	0
1997–98	Hearts	11	0
1997–98	Tranmere R	6	0
1998–99	Tranmere R	5	0
Total:		**166**	**5**

FRAIN, John — Defender

H: 5 9 W: 11 09 b.Birmingham 8-10-68

Source: Apprentice.

1985–86	Birmingham C	3	0
1986–87	Birmingham C	3	1
1987–88	Birmingham C	14	2
1988–89	Birmingham C	28	3
1989–90	Birmingham C	38	1
1990–91	Birmingham C	42	3
1991–92	Birmingham C	44	5
1992–93	Birmingham C	45	6
1993–94	Birmingham C	26	2
1994–95	Birmingham C	7	0
1995–96	Birmingham C	23	0
1996–97	Birmingham C	1	0
1996–97	Northampton T	13	0
1997–98	Northampton T	45	1
1998–99	Northampton T	41	0
Total:		**373**	**24**

FRAMPTON, Andrew — Defender

H: 5 11 W: 10 10 b.Wimbledon 3-9-79

Source: Trainee.

1998–99	Crystal Palace	6	0
Total:		**6**	**0**

FRAMPTON, Kevin — Midfield

H: 5 11 W: 11 00 b.Carlisle 18-3-80

Source: Trainee.

1998–99	Sunderland	0	0

FRANCIS, Damien — Midfield

H: 6 0 W: 10 10 b.Wandsworth 27-2-79

Source: Trainee.

1996–97	Wimbledon	0	0
1997–98	Wimbledon	2	0
1998–99	Wimbledon	0	0
Total:		**2**	**0**

FRANCIS, Kevin — Forward

H: 6 7 W: 16 12 b.Moseley 6-12-67

Source: Mile Oak R.

1988–89	Derby Co	0	0
1989–90	Derby Co	8	0
1990–91	Derby Co	2	0
1990–91	Stockport Co	13	5
1991–92	Stockport Co	35	15
1992–93	Stockport Co	42	28
1993–94	Stockport Co	45	28
1994–95	Stockport Co	17	12
1994–95	Birmingham C	15	8

1995–96	Birmingham C	19	3
1996–97	Birmingham C	19	1
1997–98	Birmingham C	20	1
1997–98	Oxford U	15	7
1998–99	Oxford U	18	1
Total:		**268**	**109**

FRANCIS, Steve — Goalkeeper

H: 6 0 W: 14 00 b.Billericay 29-5-64

Source: Apprentice. *Honours:* England Youth.

1981–82	Chelsea	29	0
1982–83	Chelsea	37	0
1983–84	Chelsea	0	0
1984–85	Chelsea	2	0
1985–86	Chelsea	3	0
1986–87	Chelsea	0	0
1986–87	Reading	14	0
1987–88	Reading	34	0
1988–89	Reading	22	0
1989–90	Reading	46	0
1990–91	Reading	34	0
1991–92	Reading	32	0
1992–93	Reading	34	0
1993–94	Huddersfield T	46	0
1994–95	Huddersfield T	43	0
1995–96	Huddersfield T	43	0
1996–97	Huddersfield T	42	0
1997–98	Huddersfield T	9	0
1998–99	Huddersfield T	3	0
1998–99	Northampton T	3	0
Total:		**476**	**0**

FRANDSEN, Per — Midfield

H: 6 1 W: 12 06 b.Copenhagen 6-2-70

Honours: Denmark 18 full caps.

1990	B 1903	25	15
1990–91	Lille	19	4
1991–92	Lille	27	8
1992–93	Lille	32	3
1993–94	Lille	31	4
1994–95	FC Copenhagen	29	12
1995–96	FC Copenhagen	26	7
1996–97	Bolton W	41	5
1997–98	Bolton W	38	2
1998–99	Bolton W	44	8
Total:		**312**	**68**

FRASER, John — Midfield

H: 5 10 W: 11 01 b.Dunfermline 17-1-78

Source: Oakley Utd.

1995–96	Dunfermline Ath	0	0
1996–97	Dunfermline Ath	2	0
1997–98	Dunfermline Ath	7	0
1998–99	Dunfermline Ath	6	0
Total:		**15**	**0**

FRASER, Stuart — Goalkeeper

H: 6 0 W: 12 00 b.Cheltenham 1-8-78

1996–97	Stoke C	0	0
1997–98	Stoke C	0	0
1998–99	Stoke C	1	0
Total:		**1**	**0**

FRASER, Stuart — Defender

H: 5 9 W: 10 06 b.Edinburgh 9-1-80

Source: Trainee.

1997–98	Luton T	1	0
1998–99	Luton T	8	0
Total:		**9**	**0**

FREEDMAN, Dougie — Forward

H: 5 9 W: 12 05 b.Glasgow 21-1-74

Source: Trainee. *Honours:* Scotland Under-21, B.

1991–92	QPR	0	0
1992–93	QPR	0	0
1993–94	QPR	0	0
1994–95	Barnet	42	24
1995–96	Barnet	5	3
1995–96	Crystal Palace	39	20
1996–97	Crystal Palace	44	11
1997–98	Crystal Palace	7	0
1997–98	Wolverhampton W	29	10
1998–99	Nottingham F	31	9
Total:		**197**	**77**

FREEMAN, Darren — Forward

H: 5 11 W: 13 00 b.Brighton 22-8-73

Source: Horsham T.

1994–95	Gillingham	2	0
1995–96	Gillingham	10	0
1996–97	Fulham	39	9
1997–98	Fulham	7	0
1998–99	Brentford	22	6
Total:		**80**	**15**

FREEMAN, David — Forward

H: 5 10 W: 11 07 b.Dublin 25-11-79

Source: Cherry Orchard.

1996–97	Nottingham F	0	0
1997–98	Nottingham F	0	0
1998–99	Nottingham F	0	0

FREESTONE, Chris — Forward

H: 5 10 W: 12 00 b.Nottingham 4-9-71

Source: Arnold T.

1994–95	Middlesbrough	1	0
1995–96	Middlesbrough	3	1
1996–97	Middlesbrough	3	0
1996–97	Carlisle U (loan)	5	2
1997–98	Middlesbrough	2	0
1997–98	Northampton T	25	11
1998–99	Northampton T	32	2
1998–99	Hartlepool U	10	3
Total:		**81**	**19**

FREESTONE, Roger — Goalkeeper

H: 6 3 W: 14 06 b.Newport 19-8-68

Source: Trainee. *Honours:* Wales Under-21.

1986–87	Newport Co	13	0
1986–87	Chelsea	6	0
1987–88	Chelsea	15	0
1988–89	Chelsea	21	0
1989–90	Chelsea	0	0
1989–90	Swansea C (loan)	14	0
1989–90	Hereford U (loan)	8	0
1990–91	Chelsea	0	0
1991–92	Swansea C	42	0
1992–93	Swansea C	46	0
1993–94	Swansea C	46	0
1994–95	Swansea C	45	1
1995–96	Swansea C	45	2
1996–97	Swansea C	45	0
1997–98	Swansea C	43	0
1998–99	Swansea C	38	0
Total:		**427**	**3**

FRENCH, Daniel — Midfield

H: 5 11 W: 11 01 b.Peterborough 25-11-79

Source: Trainee.

1998–99	Peterborough U	0	0

FRENCH, Hamish — Midfield

H: 5 10 W: 11 07 b.Aberdeen 7-2-64

Source: Keith.

1987–88	Dundee U	20	2
1988–89	Dundee U	18	3
1989–90	Dundee U	12	2
1990–91	Dundee U	19	3
1991–92	Dundee U	6	1
1991–92	Dunfermline Ath	31	2
1992–93	Dunfermline Ath	38	12
1993–94	Dunfermline Ath	36	15
1994–95	Dunfermline Ath	25	12
1995–96	Dunfermline Ath	23	4
1996–97	Dunfermline Ath	35	3
1997–98	Dunfermline Ath	34	2
1998–99	Dunfermline Ath	21	2
Total:		**318**	**63**

FRENCH, James — Forward

H: 6 1 W: 12 02 b.Germany 24-10-79

Source: Trainee.

1998–99	Bristol R	0	0

FRENCH, Jon — Midfield

H: 5 10 W: 10 10 b.Bristol 25-9-76

Source: Trainee.

1995–96	Bristol R	10	1
1996–97	Bristol R	4	0
1997–98	Bristol R	3	0
1998–99	Hull C	15	0
Total:		**32**	**1**

FREUND, Steffen — Midfield

H: 5 11 W: 12 06 b.Brandenburg 19-1-70

Source: Motor Sud, Stahl Brandenburg. *Honours:* Germany 21 full caps.

1989–90	Brandenburg	9	0
1990–91	Brandenburg	22	0
1991–92	Schalke	33	1
1992–93	Schalke	20	2
1993–94	Borussia Dortmund	19	0
1994–95	Borussia Dortmund	28	2
1995–96	Borussia Dortmund	30	2
1996–97	Borussia Dortmund	2	0
1997–98	Borussia Dortmund	25	2
1998–99	Borussia Dortmund	13	0
1998–99	Tottenham H	17	0
Total:		**218**	**9**

FRIARS, Sean — Forward

H: 5 8 W: 10 07 b.Derry 15-5-79

Source: Trainee. *Honours:* Northern Ireland Under-21.

1995–96	Liverpool	0	0
1996–97	Liverpool	0	0
1997–98	Liverpool	0	0
1998–99	Ipswich T	0	0

FRIEDEL, Brad — Goalkeeper

H: 6 3 W: 14 00 b.Lakewood 18-5-71

Honours: USA 59 full caps.

1997–98	Liverpool	11	0
1998–99	Liverpool	12	0
Total:		**23**	**0**

FROGGATT, Steve — Forward

H: 5 11 W: 11 00 b.Lincoln 9-3-73

Source: Trainee. *Honours:* England Under-21.

1990–91	Aston Villa	0	0
1991–92	Aston Villa	9	0
1992–93	Aston Villa	17	1
1993–94	Aston Villa	9	1
1994–95	Wolverhampton W	20	2
1995–96	Wolverhampton W	18	1
1996–97	Wolverhampton W	27	2
1997–98	Wolverhampton W	33	2
1998–99	Wolverhampton W	8	0
1998–99	Coventry C	23	1
Total:		**164**	**10**

FRY, Chris — Midfield

H: 5 10 W: 10 07 b.Cardiff 23-10-69

Source: Trainee.

1988–89	Cardiff C	9	0
1989–90	Cardiff C	23	1
1990–91	Cardiff C	23	0
1991–92	Hereford U	37	3
1992–93	Hereford U	37	4
1993–94	Hereford U	16	3
1993–94	Colchester U	17	0
1994–95	Colchester U	33	8
1995–96	Colchester U	38	2
1996–97	Colchester U	42	6
1997–98	Exeter C	28	1
1998–99	Exeter C	32	2
Total:		**335**	**30**

FUGLESTAD, Erik — Defender

H: 5 9 W: 11 02 b.Randaberg 13-8-74

Source: Trainee.

1994	Viking	1	0
1995	Viking	25	2
1996	Viking	23	1
1997	Viking	25	1
1997–98	Norwich C	24	2
1998–99	Norwich C	24	0
Total:		**122**	**6**

FULLARTON, Jamie — Midfield

H: 5 9 W: 10 09 b.Bellshill 20-7-74

1991–92	St Mirren	1	0
1992–93	St Mirren	25	0
1993–94	St Mirren	37	0
1994–95	St Mirren	17	1
1995–96	St Mirren	22	2
1996–97	Bastia	17	0
1997–98	Crystal Palace	25	1
1998–99	Crystal Palace	7	0
1998–99	Bolton W (loan)	1	0
Total:		**152**	**4**

FULTON, Stephen — Midfield

H: 5 10 W: 11 00 b.Greenock 10-8-70

Source: Celtic BC. *Honours:* Scotland Under-21, B.

1986–87	Celtic	0	0
1987–88	Celtic	0	0
1988–89	Celtic	3	0
1989–90	Celtic	16	0
1990–91	Celtic	21	0
1991–92	Celtic	30	2
1992–93	Celtic	6	0
1993–94	Bolton W	4	0
1993–94	Peterborough U (loan)	3	0
1994–95	Falkirk	28	3
1995–96	Falkirk	5	0
1995–96	Hearts	26	2
1996–97	Hearts	29	1
1997–98	Hearts	36	5
1998–99	Hearts	27	2
Total:		**234**	**15**

FUMACA, Jose Antunes — Midfield

H: 6 0 W: 11 08 b.Belem 15-7-76

Source: Catunese.

1998–99	Birmingham C	0	0
1998–99	Colchester U	1	0
1998–99	Barnsley	0	0
Total:		**1**	**0**

FURLONG, Lee — Midfield

b.Liverpool 9-8-79

1998–99	Wigan Ath	0	0

FURLONG, Paul — Forward

H: 6 0 W: 11 00 b.London 1-10-68

Source: Enfield.

1991–92	Coventry C	37	4
1992–93	Watford	41	19
1993–94	Watford	38	18
1994–95	Chelsea	36	10
1995–96	Chelsea	28	3
1996–97	Birmingham C	43	10
1997–98	Birmingham C	25	15
1998–99	Birmingham C	29	13
Total:		**277**	**92**

FUTCHER, Andy — Defender

H: 5 7 W: 10 07 b.Enfield 10-2-78

Source: Trainee. *Honours:* England Schools, Youth.

1994–95	Wimbledon	0	0
1995–96	Wimbledon	0	0
1996–97	Wimbledon	0	0
1997–98	Wimbledon	0	0
1998–99	Wimbledon	0	0

GABBIADINI, Marco — Forward

H: 5 10 W: 13 04 b.Nottingham 21-1-68

Source: Apprentice. *Honours:* England Under-21, B.

1984–85	York C	1	0
1985–86	York C	22	4
1986–87	York C	29	9
1987–88	York C	8	1
1987–88	Sunderland	35	21
1988–89	Sunderland	36	18
1989–90	Sunderland	46	21
1990–91	Sunderland	31	9
1991–92	Sunderland	9	5
1991–92	Crystal Palace	15	5
1991–92	Derby Co	20	6
1992–93	Derby Co	44	9
1993–94	Derby Co	39	13
1994–95	Derby Co	32	11
1995–96	Derby Co	39	11
1996–97	Derby Co	14	0
1996–97	Birmingham C (loan)	2	0
1996–97	Oxford U (loan)	5	1
1997–98	Stoke C	8	0
1997–98	York C	7	1
1998–99	Darlington	40	23
Total:		**482**	**168**

GABBIDON, Daniel — Defender

H: 5 10 W: 11 02 b.Cwmbran 8-8-79

Source: Trainee. *Honours:* Wales Under-21.

1998–99	WBA	2	0
Total:		**2**	**0**

GADSBY, Matthew — Defender

H: 6 1 W: 11 12 b.Sutton Coldfield 6-9-79

Source: Trainee.

1997–98	Walsall	1	0
1998–99	Walsall	6	0
Total:		**7**	**0**

GAGE, Kevin — Defender

H: 5 9 W: 12 11 b.Chiswick 21-4-64

Source: Apprentice. *Honours:* England Youth.

1980–81	Wimbledon	1	0
1981–82	Wimbledon	21	1
1982–83	Wimbledon	26	4
1983–84	Wimbledon	24	4
1984–85	Wimbledon	37	2
1985–86	Wimbledon	29	1
1986–87	Wimbledon	30	3
1987–88	Aston Villa	44	2
1988–89	Aston Villa	28	3
1989–90	Aston Villa	22	3
1990–91	Aston Villa	21	0
1991–92	Aston Villa	0	0
1991–92	Sheffield U	22	2
1992–93	Sheffield U	27	0
1993–94	Sheffield U	21	0
1994–95	Sheffield U	40	5
1995–96	Sheffield U	2	0
1995–96	Preston NE	7	0
1996–97	Preston NE	16	0
1997–98	Preston NE	0	0
1997–98	Hull C	10	0
1998–99	Hull C	3	0
Total:		**431**	**30**

GAIN, Peter — Midfield

H: 6 1 W: 11 00 b.Hammersmith 2-11-76

Source: Trainee.

1995–96	Tottenham H	0	0
1996–97	Tottenham H	0	0
1997–98	Tottenham H	0	0
1998–99	Tottenham H	0	0
1998–99	Lincoln C (loan)	4	0
Total:		**4**	**0**

GALE, Shaun — Defender

H: 6 1 W: 12 02 b.Reading 8-10-69

Source: Trainee.

1989–90	Portsmouth	0	0
1990–91	Portsmouth	3	0
1991–92	Portsmouth	0	0
1992–93	Portsmouth	0	0
1993–94	Portsmouth	0	0
1994–95	Barnet	27	2
1995–96	Barnet	44	1
1996–97	Barnet	43	2
1997–98	Exeter C	43	4
1998–99	Exeter C	27	0
Total:		**187**	**9**

GALL, Kevin — Forward

H: 5 9 W: 11 01 b.Merthyr 4-2-82

Source: Trainee.

1998–99	Newcastle U	0	0

GALLACHER, Kevin — Forward

H: 5 8 W: 11 03 b.Clydebank 23-11-66

Source: Duntocher BC. *Honours:* Scotland Youth, Under-21, B, 43 full caps, 8 goals.

1983–84	Dundee U	0	0
1984–85	Dundee U	0	0
1985–86	Dundee U	20	3
1986–87	Dundee U	37	10
1987–88	Dundee U	26	4
1988–89	Dundee U	31	9
1989–90	Dundee U	17	1
1989–90	Coventry C	15	3
1990–91	Coventry C	32	11
1991–92	Coventry C	33	8
1992–93	Coventry C	20	6
1992–93	Blackburn R	9	5
1993–94	Blackburn R	30	7
1994–95	Blackburn R	1	1
1995–96	Blackburn R	16	2
1996–97	Blackburn R	34	10
1997–98	Blackburn R	33	16
1998–99	Blackburn R	16	5
Total:		**370**	**101**

GALLEN, Kevin — Forward

H: 5 11 W: 12 10 b.Hammersmith 21-9-75

Source: Trainee. *Honours:* England Schools, Youth, Under-21.

1992–93	QPR	0	0
1993–94	QPR	0	0
1994–95	QPR	37	10
1995–96	QPR	30	8
1996–97	QPR	2	3
1997–98	QPR	27	3
1998–99	QPR	44	8
Total:		**140**	**32**

GALLIMORE, Tony — Defender

H: 5 11 W: 13 00 b.Crewe 21-2-72

Source: Trainee.

1989–90	Stoke C	1	0
1990–91	Stoke C	7	0
1991–92	Stoke C	3	0
1991–92	Carlisle U (loan)	16	0
1992–93	Stoke C	0	0
1992–93	Carlisle U (loan)	8	1
1993–94	Carlisle U	40	1
1994–95	Carlisle U	40	5
1995–96	Carlisle U	36	2
1995–96	Grimsby T	10	1
1996–97	Grimsby T	42	1
1997–98	Grimsby T	35	2
1998–99	Grimsby T	43	0
Total:		**281**	**13**

GALLOWAY, Mick — Midfield

H: 5 11 W: 12 05 b.Nottingham 13-10-74

Source: Trainee.

1993–94	Notts Co	0	0
1994–95	Notts Co	7	0
1995–96	Notts Co	9	0
1996–97	Notts Co	5	0
1996–97	Gillingham (loan)	9	1
1997–98	Gillingham	39	1
1998–99	Gillingham	25	3
Total:		**94**	**5**

GANNON, Jim — Defender

H: 6 2 W: 13 00 b.Southwark 7-9-68

Source: Dundalk.

1988–89	Sheffield U	0	0
1989–90	Sheffield U	0	0
1989–90	Halifax T (loan)	2	0
1989–90	Stockport Co	7	1
1990–91	Stockport Co	41	6
1991–92	Stockport Co	43	16
1992–93	Stockport Co	46	12
1993–94	Stockport Co	35	4
1993–94	Notts Co (loan)	2	0
1994–95	Stockport Co	45	7
1995–96	Stockport Co	23	1
1996–97	Stockport Co	40	4
1997–98	Stockport Co	36	1
1998–99	Stockport Co	38	0
Total:		**358**	**52**

GARCIA, Richard — Forward

b.Perth 4-9-81

Source: Trainee.

1998–99	West Ham U	0	0

GARCIA, Tony — Forward

H: 6 0 W: 12 00 b.Pierre Patte 18-3-72

1998–99	Notts Co	19	2
Total:		**19**	**2**

GARCIN, Eric — Midfield

H: 6 0 W: 12 05 b.Lille 6-12-65

Source: Toulouse.

1997–98	Motherwell	11	1
1998–99	Dundee	3	0
Total:		**14**	**1**

GARDE, Remi — Midfield

H: 5 9 W: 11 07 b.L'Arbresle 3-4-66

Honours: France 6 full caps.

1987–88	Lyon	1	0
1988–89	Lyon	32	5
1989–90	Lyon	31	4
1990–91	Lyon	24	3
1991–92	Lyon	24	1
1992–93	Lyon	33	9
1993–94	Strasbourg	21	1
1994–95	Strasbourg	31	2
1995–96	Strasbourg	16	0
1996–97	Arsenal	11	0
1997–98	Arsenal	10	0
1998–99	Arsenal	10	0
Total:		**244**	**25**

GARDNER, Anthony — Defender

H: 6 5 W: 13 00 b.Staffordshire 19-9-80

Source: Trainee.

1998–99	Port Vale	15	1
Total:		**15**	**1**

GARDNER, Jimmy — Midfield

H: 5 11 W: 11 08 b.Dunfermline 27-9-67

Source: Ayresome North.

1986–87	Queen's Park	1	0
1987–88	Queen's Park	1	0
1988–89	Motherwell	0	0
1989–90	Motherwell	1	0
1990–91	Motherwell	0	0
1991–92	Motherwell	12	0
1992–93	Motherwell	3	0
1993–94	St Mirren	21	1
1994–95	St Mirren	20	0
1995–96	Scarborough	6	1
1995–96	Cardiff C	35	4
1996–97	Cardiff C	28	1
1997–98	Exeter C	23	1
1998–99	Exeter C	27	0
Total:		**178**	**8**

GARDNER, Lee — Defender

b.Doncaster 18-5-78

1997–98	Birmingham C	0	0
1998–99	Birmingham C	0	0

GARDNER, Ricardo — Midfield

H: 5 9 W: 11 00 b.St Andrews 25-9-78

Source: Harbour View. *Honours:* Jamaica 21 full caps.

1998–99	Bolton W	30	2
Total:		**30**	**2**

GARNER, Darren — Midfield

H: 5 9 W: 12 07 b.Plymouth 10-12-71

Source: Trainee.

1988–89	Plymouth Arg	1	0
1989–90	Plymouth Arg	1	0
1990–91	Plymouth Arg	5	1
1991–92	Plymouth Arg	10	0
1992–93	Plymouth Arg	10	0
1993–94	Plymouth Arg	0	0
From Dorchester T.			
1995–96	Rotherham U	31	1
1996–97	Rotherham U	30	2
1997–98	Rotherham U	40	3
1998–99	Rotherham U	40	4
Total:		**168**	**11**

GARNETT, Shaun — Defender

H: 6 2 W: 13 01 b.Wallasey 22-11-69

Source: Trainee.

1987–88	Tranmere R	1	0
1988–89	Tranmere R	0	0
1989–90	Tranmere R	4	0
1990–91	Tranmere R	16	1
1991–92	Tranmere R	8	0
1992–93	Tranmere R	5	1
1992–93	Chester C (loan)	9	0
1992–93	Preston NE (loan)	10	2
1992–93	Wigan Ath (loan)	13	1
1993–94	Tranmere R	26	2
1994–95	Tranmere R	34	1
1995–96	Tranmere R	18	0
1995–96	Swansea C	9	0
1996–97	Swansea C	6	0
1996–97	Oldham Ath	23	1
1997–98	Oldham Ath	34	3
1998–99	Oldham Ath	37	2
Total:		**253**	**14**

GARRATT, Martin — Midfield

H: 5 10 W: 11 00 b.York 22-2-80

1998–99	York C	38	1
Total:		**38**	**1**

GARRITY, Michael — Midfield

b.Liverpool 6-5-80

Source: Trainee.

1998–99	WBA	0	0

GARVEY, Steve — Midfield

H: 5 9 W: 11 01 b.Stalybridge 22-11-73

Source: Trainee.

1990–91	Crewe Alex	1	0
1991–92	Crewe Alex	11	0
1992–93	Crewe Alex	10	1
1993–94	Crewe Alex	0	0
1994–95	Crewe Alex	28	3
1995–96	Crewe Alex	29	2
1996–97	Crewe Alex	16	0
1997–98	Crewe Alex	13	2
1997–98	Chesterfield (loan)	3	0
1998–99	Blackpool	15	1
Total:		**126**	**9**

GASCOIGNE, Paul — Midfield

H: 5 10 W: 12 09 b.Gateshead 27-5-67

Source: Apprentice. *Honours:* England, Under-21 B, 57 full caps, 10 goals.

1984–85	Newcastle U	2	0
1985–86	Newcastle U	31	9
1986–87	Newcastle U	24	5
1987–88	Newcastle U	35	7
1988–89	Tottenham H	32	6
1989–90	Tottenham H	34	6
1990–91	Tottenham H	26	7
1991–92	Tottenham H	0	0
1992–93	Lazio	22	4
1993–94	Lazio	17	2
1994–95	Lazio	2	0
1995–96	Rangers	28	14
1996–97	Rangers	26	13
1997–98	Rangers	20	3
1997–98	Middlesbrough	7	0
1998–99	Middlesbrough	26	3
Total:		**332**	**79**

GATTUSO, Gennaro — Forward

H: 5 9 W: 12 01 b.Corigliano Calabro 9-1-78

1995–96	Perugia	2	0
1996–97	Perugia	8	0
1997–98	Rangers	29	3
1998–99	Rangers	5	0
Total:		**44**	**3**

GAUGHAN, Steve — Midfield

H: 5 11 W: 11 04 b.Doncaster 14-4-70

Source: Hatfield Main.

1987–88	Doncaster R	4	0
1988–89	Doncaster R	34	2
1989–90	Doncaster R	29	1
1990–91	Sunderland	0	0
1991–92	Sunderland	0	0
1991–92	Darlington	20	0
1992–93	Darlington	37	1
1993–94	Darlington	32	3
1994–95	Darlington	41	8
1995–96	Darlington	41	3
1996–97	Chesterfield	18	0
1997–98	Chesterfield	2	0
1997–98	Darlington	24	1
1998–99	Darlington	23	2
Total:		**305**	**21**

GAVIN, Jason — Defender

H: 6 0 W: 11 12 b.Dublin 14-3-80

Source: Trainee.

1996–97	Middlesbrough	0	0
1997–98	Middlesbrough	0	0
1998–99	Middlesbrough	2	0
Total:		**2**	**0**

GAYLE, Brian — Defender

H: 6 2 W: 13 12 b.Kingston 6-3-65

1984–85	Wimbledon	12	1
1985–86	Wimbledon	13	0
1986–87	Wimbledon	32	1
1987–88	Wimbledon	26	1
1988–89	Manchester C	41	3
1989–90	Manchester C	14	0
1989–90	Ipswich T	20	0
1990–91	Ipswich T	33	4
1991–92	Ipswich T	5	0
1991–92	Sheffield U	33	3
1992–93	Sheffield U	31	2
1993–94	Sheffield U	13	3
1994–95	Sheffield U	35	1
1995–96	Sheffield U	5	0
1996–97	Exeter C	10	0
1996–97	Rotherham U	20	0
1996–97	Bristol R (loan)	7	0
1997–98	Bristol R	16	0
1997–98	Shrewsbury T	23	0
1998–99	Shrewsbury T	43	1
Total:		**432**	**20**

GAYLE, John — Forward

H: 6 3 W: 15 00 b.Bromsgrove 30-7-64

Source: Burton Alb.

1988–89	Wimbledon	2	0
1989–90	Wimbledon	11	1
1990–91	Wimbledon	7	1
1990–91	Birmingham C	22	6
1991–92	Birmingham C	3	1
1992–93	Birmingham C	19	3
1993–94	Birmingham C	0	0
1993–94	Walsall (loan)	4	1
1993–94	Coventry C	3	0
1994–95	Coventry C	0	0
1994–95	Burnley	14	3
1994–95	Stoke C	4	0
1995–96	Stoke C	10	3
1995–96	Gillingham (loan)	9	3
1996–97	Stoke C	12	1
1996–97	Northampton T	13	1
1997–98	Northampton T	35	6
1998–99	Scunthorpe U	37	4
Total:		**205**	**34**

GAYLE, Marcus — Forward

H: 6 1 W: 12 09 b.Hammersmith 27-9-70

Source: Trainee. *Honours:* England Youth. Jamaica 9 full caps, 2 goals.

1988–89	Brentford	3	0
1989–90	Brentford	9	0
1990–91	Brentford	33	6
1991–92	Brentford	38	6
1992–93	Brentford	38	4
1993–94	Brentford	35	6
1993–94	Wimbledon	10	0
1994–95	Wimbledon	23	2
1995–96	Wimbledon	34	5
1996–97	Wimbledon	36	8
1997–98	Wimbledon	30	2
1998–99	Wimbledon	35	10
Total:		**324**	**49**

GEARY, Derek — Defender

H: 5 6 W: 10 08 b.Dublin 19-6-80

1997–98	Sheffield W	0	0
1998–99	Sheffield W	0	0

GEMMILL, Scot — Midfield

H: 5 11 W: 11 06 b.Paisley 2-1-71

Source: School. *Honours:* Scotland Under-21, 15 full caps.

1989–90	Nottingham F	0	0
1990–91	Nottingham F	4	0
1991–92	Nottingham F	39	8
1992–93	Nottingham F	33	1
1993–94	Nottingham F	31	8
1994–95	Nottingham F	19	1
1995–96	Nottingham F	31	1
1996–97	Nottingham F	24	0
1997–98	Nottingham F	44	2
1998–99	Nottingham F	20	0
1998–99	Everton	7	1
Total:		**252**	**22**

GEORGE, Liam — Forward

H: 5 9 W: 11 04 b.Luton 2-2-79

Source: Trainee.

1996–97	Luton T	0	0
1997–98	Luton T	1	0
1998–99	Luton T	12	0
Total:		**13**	**0**

GEORGIADIS, George — Midfield

H: 5 8 W: 10 11 b.Kavala 8-3-72

1990–91	Doxa	10	0
1991–92	Doxa	32	6
1992–93	Doxa	13	4
1992–93	Panathinaikos	21	4
1993–94	Panathinaikos	31	6
1994–95	Panathinaikos	30	9
1995–96	Panathinaikos	31	10
1996–97	Panathinaikos	31	9
1997–98	Panathinaikos	32	21
1998–99	Newcastle U	10	0
Total:		**241**	**69**

GERMAIN, Steve — Forward

b.Cannes 22-6-81

1998–99	Colchester U	6	0
Total:		**6**	**0**

GERRARD, Paul — Goalkeeper

H: 6 2 W: 14 04 b.Heywood 22-1-73

Source: Trainee. *Honours:* England Under-21.

1991–92	Oldham Ath	0	0
1992–93	Oldham Ath	25	0
1993–94	Oldham Ath	16	0
1994–95	Oldham Ath	42	0
1995–96	Oldham Ath	36	1
1996–97	Everton	5	0
1997–98	Everton	4	0
1998–99	Everton	0	0
1998–99	Oxford U (loan)	16	0
Total:		**144**	**1**

GERRARD, Steven — Midfield

H: 6 1 W: 13 00 b.Whiston 30-5-80

Source: Trainee. *Honours:* England Youth.

1997–98	Liverpool	0	0
1998–99	Liverpool	12	0
Total:		**12**	**0**

GHENT, Matthew — Goalkeeper

H: 6 3 W: 14 01 b.Burton 5-10-80

Source: Trainee. *Honours:* England Schools, Youth.

1997–98	Aston Villa	0	0
1998–99	Aston Villa	0	0

GIALLANZA, Gaetano — Forward

H: 6 0 W: 11 03 b.Dornach 6-6-74

1996–97	Basle	32	19
1997–98	Nantes	12	2
1997–98	Bolton W	3	0
1998–99	Bolton W	0	0
Total:		**47**	**21**

GIBB, Ali — Forward

H: 5 9 W: 11 07 b.Salisbury 17-2-76

Source: Trainee.

1994–95	Norwich C	0	0
1995–96	Norwich C	0	0
1995–96	Northampton T	23	2
1996–97	Northampton T	18	1
1997–98	Northampton T	35	1
1998–99	Northampton T	41	0
Total:		**117**	**4**

GIBBENS, Kevin — Midfield

H: 5 10 W: 13 02 b.Southampton 4-11-79

Source: Trainee.

1997–98	Southampton	2	0
1998–99	Southampton	4	0
Total:		**6**	**0**

GIBBS, Nigel — Defender

H: 5 7 W: 11 06 b.St Albans 20-11-65

Source: Apprentice. *Honours:* England Youth, Under-21.

1983–84	Watford	3	0
1984–85	Watford	12	0
1985–86	Watford	40	1
1986–87	Watford	15	0
1987–88	Watford	30	0
1988–89	Watford	46	1
1989–90	Watford	41	0
1990–91	Watford	34	0
1991–92	Watford	43	1
1992–93	Watford	7	0
1993–94	Watford	0	0
1994–95	Watford	11	0
1995–96	Watford	9	0
1996–97	Watford	45	1
1997–98	Watford	38	1
1998–99	Watford	10	0
Total:		**384**	**5**

GIBBS, Paul — Defender

H: 5 10 W: 11 09 b.Gorleston 26-10-72

Source: Diss T.

1994–95	Colchester U	9	0
1995–96	Colchester U	24	3
1996–97	Colchester U	20	0
1997–98	Torquay U	41	7
1998–99	Plymouth Arg	27	3
Total:		**121**	**13**

GIBSON, Mark — Midfield

b.Hitchin 24-8-81

Source: Trainee.

1997–98	Cambridge U	0	0
1998–99	Cambridge U	0	0

GIBSON, Neil — Midfield

H: 5 11 W: 11 08 b.St Asaph 10-10-79

Source: Trainee. *Honours:* Wales Under-21.

1997–98	Tranmere R	0	0
1998–99	Tranmere R	1	0
Total:		**1**	**0**

GIBSON, Paul — Goalkeeper

H: 6 2 W: 13 06 b.Sheffield 1-11-76

Source: Trainee.

1995–96	Manchester U	0	0
1996–97	Manchester U	0	0
1997–98	Manchester U	0	0
1997–98	Mansfield T (loan)	13	0
1998–99	Manchester U	0	0
1998–99	Hull C (loan)	4	0
1998–99	Notts Co	1	0
Total:		**18**	**0**

GIBSON, Robin — Forward

H: 5 7 W: 10 07 b.Crewe 15-11-79

Source: Trainee.

1998–99	Wrexham	7	1
Total:		**7**	**1**

GIER, Robert — Midfield

H: 5 9 W: 11 07 b.Bracknell 6-1-81

Source: Trainee.

1998–99	Wimbledon	0	0

GIGGS, Ryan — Forward

H: 5 11 W: 10 10 b.Cardiff 29-11-73

Source: School. *Honours:* England Schools, Wales Youth, Under-21, 24 full caps, 5 goals.

1990–91	Manchester U	2	1
1991–92	Manchester U	38	4
1992–93	Manchester U	41	9
1993–94	Manchester U	38	13
1994–95	Manchester U	29	1
1995–96	Manchester U	33	11
1996–97	Manchester U	26	3
1997–98	Manchester U	29	8
1998–99	Manchester U	24	3
Total:		**260**	**53**

GILCHRIST, Phil — Defender

H: 6 0 W: 13 04 b.Stockton 25-8-73

Source: Trainee.

1990–91	Nottingham F	0	0
1991–92	Middlesbrough	0	0
1992–93	Hartlepool U	24	0
1993–94	Hartlepool U	35	0
1994–95	Hartlepool U	23	0
1994–95	Oxford U	18	1
1995–96	Oxford U	42	3
1996–97	Oxford U	38	2
1997–98	Oxford U	39	2
1998–99	Oxford U	39	2
Total:		**258**	**10**

GILKES, Michael — Midfield

H: 5 8 W: 10 10 b.Hackney 20-7-65

Source: Leicester C.

1984–85	Reading	16	2
1985–86	Reading	9	2
1986–87	Reading	7	0
1987–88	Reading	39	4
1988–89	Reading	46	9
1989–90	Reading	42	2
1990–91	Reading	21	1
1991–92	Reading	20	0
1991–92	Chelsea (loan)	1	0
1991–92	Southampton (loan)	6	0
1992–93	Reading	38	12
1993–94	Reading	39	2
1994–95	Reading	40	8
1995–96	Reading	44	0
1996–97	Reading	32	1
1996–97	Wolverhampton W	5	1
1997–98	Wolverhampton W	3	0
1998–99	Wolverhampton W	30	0
Total:		**438**	**44**

GILL, Jeremy — Defender

H: 5 11 W: 11 00 b.Clevedon 8-9-70

Source: Yeovil T.

1997–98	Birmingham C	3	0
1998–99	Birmingham C	3	0
Total:		**6**	**0**

GILL, Matthew — Midfield

H: 5 11 W: 11 10 b.Cambridge 8-11-80

Source: Trainee.

1997–98	Peterborough U	2	0
1998–99	Peterborough U	26	0
Total:		**28**	**0**

GILL, Wayne — Midfield

H: 5 9 W: 11 00 b.Chorley 28-11-75

Source: Trainee.

1994–95	Blackburn R	0	0
1995–96	Blackburn R	0	0
1996–97	Blackburn R	0	0
1997–98	Blackburn R	0	0
1997–98	Dundee U	2	0
1998–99	Blackburn R	0	0
Total:		**2**	**0**

GILLESPIE, Keith — Midfield

H: 5 9 W: 11 05 b.Larne 18-2-75

Source: Trainee. *Honours:* Northern Ireland Youth, Under-21, 26 full caps, 1 goal.

1992–93	Manchester U	0	0
1993–94	Manchester U	0	0
1993–94	Wigan Ath (loan)	8	4
1994–95	Manchester U	9	1
1994–95	Newcastle U	17	2
1995–96	Newcastle U	28	4
1996–97	Newcastle U	32	1
1997–98	Newcastle U	29	4
1998–99	Newcastle U	7	0
1998–99	Blackburn R	16	1
Total:		**146**	**17**

GILLIES, Richard — Forward

H: 5 10 W: 11 00 b.Glasgow 24-8-76

Source: St Mirren BC.

1992–93	St Mirren	8	1
1993–94	St Mirren	22	2
1994–95	St Mirren	24	3
1995–96	St Mirren	33	3

1996–97	St Mirren	29	6
1997–98	Aberdeen	21	0
1998–99	Aberdeen	11	0
Total:		**148**	**15**

GINOLA, David — Forward

H: 5 11 W: 11 10 b.Gassin 25-1-67

Honours: France 17 full caps, 3 goals.

1985–86	Toulon	14	0
1986–87	Toulon	34	0
1987–88	Toulon	33	4
1988–89	Racing Paris	29	7
1989–90	Racing Paris	32	1
1990–91	Brest	33	1
1991–92	Brest	17	9
1991–92	Paris St Germain	15	2
1992–93	Paris St Germain	34	6
1993–94	Paris St Germain	38	13
1994–95	Paris St Germain	28	11
1995–96	Newcastle U	34	5
1996–97	Newcastle U	24	1
1997–98	Tottenham H	34	6
1998–99	Tottenham H	30	3
Total:		**429**	**69**

GIOACCHINI, Stefano — Forward

b.Rome 25-11-76

1994–95	Perugia	5	0
1995–96	Cosenza	17	0
1996–97	Cosenza	26	3
1997–98	Venezia	18	1
1998–99	Venezia	3	0
1998–99	Coventry C	3	0
Total:		**72**	**4**

GITTENS, Jon — Defender

H: 5 11 W: 12 10 b.Moseley 22-1-64

Source: Paget R.

1985–86	Southampton	4	0
1986–87	Southampton	14	0
1987–88	Swindon T	29	0
1988–89	Swindon T	29	1
1989–90	Swindon T	40	4
1990–91	Swindon T	28	1
1990–91	Southampton	8	0
1991–92	Southampton	11	0
1991–92	Middlesbrough (loan)	12	1
1992–93	Middlesbrough	13	0
1993–94	Portsmouth	30	1
1994–95	Portsmouth	38	0
1995–96	Portsmouth	15	1
1996–97	Torquay U	33	3
1997–98	Torquay U	45	6
1998–99	Exeter C	44	2
Total:		**393**	**20**

GIVEN, Shay — Goalkeeper

H: 6 0 W: 11 08 b.Lifford 24-4-76

Source: Celtic. *Honours:* Eire Under-21, 23 full caps.

1994–95	Blackburn R	0	0
1994–95	Swindon T (loan)	0	0
1995–96	Blackburn R	0	0
1995–96	Swindon T (loan)	5	0
1995–96	Sunderland (loan)	17	0
1996–97	Blackburn R	2	0
1997–98	Newcastle U	24	0
1998–99	Newcastle U	31	0
Total:		**79**	**0**

GLASGOW, Byron — Midfield

H: 5 6 W: 10 11 b.Tooting 18-2-79

Source: Bognor Regis T.

1996–97	Reading	4	0
1997–98	Reading	3	0
1998–99	Reading	32	1
Total:		**39**	**1**

GLASS, Jimmy — Goalkeeper

H: 6 1 W: 13 04 b.Swindon 1-8-73

Source: Trainee.

1991–92	Crystal Palace	0	0
1992–93	Crystal Palace	0	0
1993–94	Crystal Palace	0	0
1994–95	Crystal Palace	0	0
1994–95	Portsmouth (loan)	3	0
1995–96	Crystal Palace	0	0
1995–96	Bournemouth	13	0
1996–97	Bournemouth	35	0
1997–98	Bournemouth	46	0
1998–99	Swindon T	3	0
1998–99	Carlisle U (loan)	3	1
Total:		**103**	**1**

GLASS, Stephen — Midfield

H: 5 8 W: 10 11 b.Dundee 23-5-76

Source: Crombie Sports. *Honours:* Scotland Under-21, B, 1 full cap.

1994–95	Aberdeen	19	1
1995–96	Aberdeen	32	3
1996–97	Aberdeen	24	1
1997–98	Aberdeen	31	2
1998–99	Newcastle U	22	3
Total:		**128**	**10**

GLEDHILL, Lee — Defender

H: 5 10 W: 11 02 b.Bury 7-11-80

Source: Trainee.

1998–99	Barnet	1	0
Total:		**1**	**0**

GLENNON, Matthew — Goalkeeper

H: 6 2 W: 13 11 b.Stockport 8-10-78

Source: Trainee.

1997–98	Bolton W	0	0
1998–99	Bolton W	0	0

GLOVER, Lee — Forward

H: 5 11 W: 11 09 b.Kettering 24-4-70

Source: Trainee. *Honours:* Scotland Under-21.

1986–87	Nottingham F	0	0
1987–88	Nottingham F	20	3
1988–89	Nottingham F	0	0
1989–90	Nottingham F	0	0
1989–90	Leicester C (loan)	5	1
1989–90	Barnsley (loan)	8	0
1990–91	Nottingham F	8	1
1991–92	Nottingham F	16	0
1991–92	Luton T (loan)	1	0
1992–93	Nottingham F	14	0
1993–94	Nottingham F	18	5
1994–95	Port Vale	28	4
1995–96	Port Vale	24	3
1996–97	Rotherham U	22	1
1996–97	Huddersfield T (loan)	11	0
1997–98	Rotherham U	37	17
1998–99	Rotherham U	19	10
Total:		**231**	**45**

GOATER, Shaun — Forward

H: 6 0 W: 12 10 b.Bermuda 25-2-70

Honours: Bermuda full caps.

1988–89	Manchester U	0	0
1989–90	Manchester U	0	0
1989–90	Rotherham U	12	2
1990–91	Rotherham U	22	2
1991–92	Rotherham U	24	9
1992–93	Rotherham U	23	7
1993–94	Rotherham U	39	13
1993–94	Notts Co (loan)	1	0
1994–95	Rotherham U	45	19
1995–96	Rotherham U	44	18
1996–97	Bristol C	42	23
1997–98	Bristol C	33	17
1997–98	Manchester C	7	3
1998–99	Manchester C	43	17
Total:		**335**	**130**

GODBOLD, Jamie — Midfield

H: 5 4 W: 9 0 b.Great Yarmouth 10-1-80

Source: Trainee.

1996–97	Stoke C	0	0
1997–98	Stoke C	0	0
1998–99	Stoke C	0	0

GOLDBAEK, Bjarne — Midfield

H: 5 10 W: 11 06 b.Denmark 6-10-68

Honours: Denmark 15 full caps.

1991–92	Kaiserslautern	24	2
1992–93	Kaiserslautern	28	5
1993–94	Kaiserslautern	3	0
1993–94	Tennis Borussia	24	5
1994–95	Cologne	14	0
1995–96	Cologne	16	2
1996–97	FC Copenhagen	32	7
1997–98	FC Copenhagen	30	6
1998–99	FC Copenhagen	12	3
1998–99	Chelsea	23	5
Total:		**206**	**35**

GOOD, Iain — Defender

H: 6 0 W: 11 07 b.Glasgow 9-8-77

Source: Queens Park.

1995–96	Aberdeen	0	0
1996–97	Aberdeen	0	0
1997–98	Aberdeen	0	0
1998–99	Aberdeen	1	0
Total:		**1**	**0**

GOODEN, Ty — Midfield

H: 5 8 W: 12 06 b.Canvey Island 23-10-72

Source: Arsenal, Wycombe W.

1993–94	Swindon T	4	0
1994–95	Swindon T	16	2
1995–96	Swindon T	26	3
1996–97	Swindon T	13	1
1997–98	Swindon T	39	2
1998–99	Swindon T	38	1
Total:		**136**	**9**

GOODFELLOW, Marc — Midfield

b.Burton 20-9-81

1998–99	Stoke C	0	0

GOODHIND, Warren — Defender

H: 5 11 W: 11 02 b.Johannesburg 16-8-77

Source: Trainee.

1996–97	Barnet	3	0
1997–98	Barnet	35	1
1998–99	Barnet	15	1
Total:		**53**	**2**

GOODING, Mick — Midfield

H: 5 8 W: 10 10 b.Newcastle 12-4-59

Source: Bishop Auckland.

1979–80	Rotherham U	34	3
1980–81	Rotherham U	37	4
1981–82	Rotherham U	22	2
1982–83	Rotherham U	9	1
1982–83	Chesterfield	12	0
1983–84	Chesterfield	0	0
1983–84	Rotherham U	26	7
1984–85	Rotherham U	44	10
1985–86	Rotherham U	40	8
1986–87	Rotherham U	46	8
1987–88	Peterborough U	44	18
1988–89	Peterborough U	3	3
1988–89	Wolverhampton W	31	4
1989–90	Wolverhampton W	13	0
1989–90	Reading	27	3
1990–91	Reading	44	7
1991–92	Reading	40	3
1992–93	Reading	40	3
1993–94	Reading	41	7
1994–95	Reading	39	0
1995–96	Reading	40	3
1996–97	Reading	43	0
1997–98	Reading	0	0
1998–99	Southend U	23	0
Total:		**698**	**94**

GOODLAD, Mark — Goalkeeper

H: 6 0 W: 13 02 b.Barnsley 9-9-80

Source: Trainee.

1996–97	Nottingham F	0	0
1997–98	Nottingham F	0	0
1998–99	Nottingham F	0	0
1998–99	Scarborough (loan)	3	0
Total:		**3**	**0**

GOODMAN, Don — Forward

H: 5 10 W: 12 12 b.Leeds 9-5-66

Source: School.

1983–84	Bradford C	2	0
1984–85	Bradford C	25	5
1985–86	Bradford C	20	4
1986–87	Bradford C	23	5
1986–87	WBA	10	2
1987–88	WBA	40	7
1988–89	WBA	36	15
1989–90	WBA	39	21
1990–91	WBA	22	8
1991–92	WBA	11	7
1991–92	Sunderland	22	11
1992–93	Sunderland	41	16
1993–94	Sunderland	35	10
1994–95	Sunderland	18	3
1994–95	Wolverhampton W	24	3
1995–96	Wolverhampton W	44	16
1996–97	Wolverhampton W	27	6
1997–98	Wolverhampton W	30	8
From Hiroshima			
1998–99	Barnsley (loan)	8	0
1998–99	Motherwell	8	1
Total:		**485**	**148**

GOODMAN, Jon — Forward

H: 6 0 W: 12 03 b.Walthamstow 2-6-71

Source: Bromley. *Honours:* Eire 4 full caps. Football League.

1990–91	Millwall	23	5
1991–92	Millwall	17	3
1992–93	Millwall	35	12
1993–94	Millwall	19	7
1994–95	Millwall	15	8
1994–95	Wimbledon	19	4
1995–96	Wimbledon	27	6
1996–97	Wimbledon	13	1
1997–98	Wimbledon	0	0
1998–99	Wimbledon	1	0
Total:		**169**	**46**

GOODRIDGE, Greg — Forward

H: 5 6 W: 11 02 b.Barbados 10-7-71

Source: Lambada. *Honours:* Barbados full caps.

1993–94	Torquay U	8	1
1994–95	Torquay U	30	3
1995–96	QPR	7	1
1996–97	Bristol C	28	6
1997–98	Bristol C	31	6
1998–99	Bristol C	30	2
Total:		**134**	**19**

GOODWIN, Tommy — Defender

H: 6 0 W: 12 02 b.Leicester 8-11-79

Source: Trainee.

1998–99	Leicester C	0	0

GOODYEAR, Craig — Midfield

H: 5 7 W: 12 01 b.Barnsley 7-11-80

Source: Trainee.

1997–98	Barnsley	0	0
1998–99	Barnsley	0	0

GORAM, Andy — Goalkeeper

H: 5 11 W: 11 06 b.Bury 13-4-64

Source: West Bromwich Apprentice, Scotland Under-21, 43 full caps.

1981–82	Oldham Ath	3	0
1982–83	Oldham Ath	38	0
1983–84	Oldham Ath	22	0
1984–85	Oldham Ath	41	0
1985–86	Oldham Ath	41	0
1986–87	Oldham Ath	41	0
1987–88	Oldham Ath	9	0
1987–88	Hibernian	33	1
1988–89	Hibernian	36	0
1989–90	Hibernian	34	0
1990–91	Hibernian	35	0
1991–92	Rangers	44	0
1992–93	Rangers	34	0
1993–94	Rangers	8	0
1994–95	Rangers	19	0
1995–96	Rangers	30	0
1996–97	Rangers	25	0
1997–98	Rangers	24	0
1998–99	Notts Co	1	0
1998–99	Sheffield U	7	0
1998–99	Motherwell	13	0
Total:		**538**	**1**

GORDON, Dean — Defender

H: 6 0 W: 13 08 b.Thornton Heath 10-2-73

Source: Trainee. *Honours:* England Under-21.

1991–92	Crystal Palace	4	0
1992–93	Crystal Palace	10	0
1993–94	Crystal Palace	45	5
1994–95	Crystal Palace	41	2
1995–96	Crystal Palace	34	8
1996–97	Crystal Palace	30	3
1997–98	Crystal Palace	37	2
1998–99	Middlesbrough	38	3
Total:		**239**	**23**

GORDON, Gavin — Forward

H: 6 1 W: 12 00 b.Manchester 24-6-79

Source: Trainee.

1995–96	Hull C	13	3
1996–97	Hull C	20	4
1997–98	Hull C	5	2
1997–98	Lincoln C	13	3
1998–99	Lincoln C	27	5
Total:		**78**	**17**

GOSS, Jeremy — Midfield

H: 5 9 W: 11 08 b.Oekolia 11-5-65

Source: Amateur. *Honours:* England Youth, Wales 9 full caps.

1982–83	Norwich C	0	0
1983–84	Norwich C	1	0
1984–85	Norwich C	5	0
1985–86	Norwich C	0	0
1986–87	Norwich C	1	0
1987–88	Norwich C	22	2
1988–89	Norwich C	0	0
1989–90	Norwich C	7	0
1990–91	Norwich C	19	1
1991–92	Norwich C	33	1
1992–93	Norwich C	25	1
1993–94	Norwich C	34	6
1994–95	Norwich C	25	2
1995–96	Norwich C	16	1
1996–97	Hearts	10	0
1997–98	Colchester U	0	0
1998–99	Colchester U	0	0
Total:		**198**	**14**

GOTTSKALKSSON, Olafur — Goalkeeper

H: 6 3 W: 13 12 b.Keflavik 12-3-68

Honours: Iceland 7 full caps.

1988	IA Akranes	18	0
1989	IA Akranes	15	0
1990	KR	18	0
1991	KR	18	0
1992	KR	18	0
1993	KR	17	0
1994	Keflavik	18	0
1995	Keflavik	17	0
1996	Keflavik	18	0
1997	Keflavik	10	0
1997–98	Hibernian	16	0
1998–99	Hibernian	36	0
Total:		**219**	**0**

GOUGH, Richard — Defender

H: 6 2 W: 11 09 b.Stockholm 5-4-62

Source: Wits University. *Honours:* Scotland Under-21, 61 full caps, 6 goals.

1980–81	Dundee U	4	0
1981–82	Dundee U	30	1
1982–83	Dundee U	34	8
1983–84	Dundee U	33	3
1984–85	Dundee U	33	6
1985–86	Dundee U	31	5
1986–87	Tottenham H	40	2
1987–88	Tottenham H	9	0

1987–88	Rangers	31	5
1988–89	Rangers	35	4
1989–90	Rangers	26	0
1990–91	Rangers	26	0
1991–92	Rangers	33	2
1992–93	Rangers	25	2
1993–94	Rangers	37	3
1994–95	Rangers	25	1
1995–96	Rangers	29	3
1996–97	Rangers	27	5
From Kansas City W			
1997–98	Rangers	24	1
From San Jose Clash			
1998–99	Nottingham F	7	0
Total:		**539**	**51**

GOUGH, Steven — Midfield

H: 5 11 W: 11 10 b.Burton 16-9-80

Source: Trainee.

1997–98	Nottingham F	0	0
1998–99	Nottingham F	0	0

GOULD, Jonathan — Goalkeeper

H: 6 1 W: 12 07 b.Paddington 18-7-68

Source: Clevedon T. *Honours:* Scotland B.

1990–91	Halifax T	23	0
1991–92	Halifax T	9	0
1991–92	WBA	0	0
1992–93	Coventry C	9	0
1993–94	Coventry C	9	0
1994–95	Coventry C	7	0
1995–96	Coventry C	0	0
1995–96	Bradford C (loan)	9	0
1996–97	Bradford C	9	0
1996–97	Gillingham (loan)	3	0
1997–98	Celtic	35	0
1998–99	Celtic	28	0
Total:		**141**	**0**

GOWER, Mark — Midfield

b.Edmonton 5-10-78

Source: Trainee. *Honours:* England Schools, Youth.

1996–97	Tottenham H	0	0
1997–98	Tottenham H	0	0
1998–99	Tottenham H	0	0
1998–99	Motherwell	9	1
Total:		**9**	**1**

GRADY, James — Forward

H: 5 7 W: 10 00 b.Paisley 14-3-71

Source: Arthurlie J.

1994–95	Clydebank	36	7
1995–96	Clydebank	36	10
1996–97	Clydebank	36	8
1997–98	Dundee	36	15
1998–99	Dundee	26	3
Total:		**170**	**43**

GRAHAM, David — Forward

H: 5 10 W: 11 02 b.Edinburgh 6-10-78

Source: Rangers SABC. *Honours:* Scotland Under-21.

1995–96	Rangers	0	0
1996–97	Rangers	0	0
1997–98	Rangers	0	0
1998–99	Rangers	3	0
1998–99	Dunfermline Ath	21	2
Total:		**24**	**2**

GRAHAM, Gareth — Midfield

H: 5 7 W: 10 02 b.Belfast 6-12-78

Source: Trainee. *Honours:* Northern Ireland Under-21.

1996–97	Crystal Palace	0	0
1997–98	Crystal Palace	0	0
1998–99	Crystal Palace	1	0
Total:		**1**	**0**

GRAHAM, Mark — Midfield

H: 5 7 W: 10 08 b.Newry 24-10-74

Source: Trainee.

1993–94	QPR	0	0
1994–95	QPR	0	0
1995–96	QPR	0	0
1996–97	QPR	18	0
1997–98	QPR	0	0
1998–99	QPR	0	0
Total:		**18**	**0**

GRAHAM, Paul — Midfield

H: 5 9 W: 10 09 b.Sefton North 28-7-80

Source: Trainee.

1998–99	Burnley	0	0

GRAHAM, Richard — Defender

H: 6 2 W: 12 09 b.Dewsbury 28-11-74

Source: Trainee.

1993–94	Oldham Ath	5	0
1994–95	Oldham Ath	32	3
1995–96	Oldham Ath	32	1
1996–97	Oldham Ath	19	1
1997–98	Oldham Ath	34	4
1998–99	Oldham Ath	11	3
Total:		**133**	**12**

GRAHAM, Richard — Midfield

H: 5 8 W: 10 06 b.Newry 5-8-79

Source: Trainee. *Honours:* Northern Ireland Youth, Under-21.

1996–97	QPR	0	0
1997–98	QPR	0	0
1998–99	QPR	2	0
Total:		**2**	**0**

GRAINGER, Martin — Defender

H: 5 10 W: 11 07 b.Enfield 23-8-72

Source: Trainee.

1989–90	Colchester U	7	2
1990–91	Colchester U	0	0
1991–92	Colchester U	0	0
1992–93	Colchester U	31	3
1993–94	Colchester U	8	2
1993–94	Brentford	31	2
1994–95	Brentford	37	7
1995–96	Brentford	33	3
1995–96	Birmingham C	8	0
1996–97	Birmingham C	23	3
1997–98	Birmingham C	33	2
1998–99	Birmingham C	40	4
Total:		**251**	**28**

GRANT, Brian — Midfield

H: 5 9 W: 10 07 b.Bannockburn 19-6-64

Source: Fallin Violet.

1981–82	Stirling Albion	1	0
1982–83	Stirling Alb	1	0
1983–84	Stirling Alb	24	3
1984–85	Aberdeen	0	0
1985–86	Aberdeen	0	0
1986–87	Aberdeen	15	4
1987–88	Aberdeen	7	1
1988–89	Aberdeen	26	1
1989–90	Aberdeen	31	6
1990–91	Aberdeen	32	2
1991–92	Aberdeen	33	6
1992–93	Aberdeen	29	3
1993–94	Aberdeen	30	2
1994–95	Aberdeen	32	2
1995–96	Aberdeen	25	0
1996–97	Aberdeen	2	0
1996–97	Hibernian	12	0
1997–98	Hibernian	5	0
1997–98	Dundee	8	0
1998–99	Dundee	4	0
Total:		**317**	**30**

GRANT, Gareth — Forward

H: 5 10 W: 10 04 b.Leeds 6-9-80

Source: Trainee.

1997–98	Bradford C	3	0
1998–99	Bradford C	5	0
1998–99	Halifax T (loan)	3	0
Total:		**11**	**0**

GRANT, Kim — Forward

H: 5 10 W: 11 05 b.Ghana 25-9-72

Source: Trainee. *Honours:* Ghana full caps.

1990–91	Charlton Ath	12	2
1991–92	Charlton Ath	4	0
1992–93	Charlton Ath	21	2
1993–94	Charlton Ath	30	1
1994–95	Charlton Ath	26	6
1995–96	Charlton Ath	30	7
1995–96	Luton T	10	3
1996–97	Luton T	25	2
1997–98	Luton T	0	0
1997–98	Millwall	39	8
1998–99	Millwall	16	3
1998–99	Notts Co (loan)	6	1
Total:		**219**	**35**

GRANT, Martin — Midfield

b.Kirkcaldy 16-1-82

Source: Trainee.

1998–99	Coventry C	0	0

GRANT, Peter — Midfield

H: 5 10 W: 11 08 b.Bellshill 30-8-65

Source: Celtic BC. *Honours:* Scotland Schools, Youth B, Under-21, 2 full caps.

1982–83	Celtic	0	0
1983–84	Celtic	3	0
1984–85	Celtic	20	4
1985–86	Celtic	30	1
1986–87	Celtic	37	1
1987–88	Celtic	37	2
1988–89	Celtic	21	0
1989–90	Celtic	26	0
1990–91	Celtic	27	0
1991–92	Celtic	22	0
1992–93	Celtic	31	2
1993–94	Celtic	28	0
1994–95	Celtic	28	2
1995–96	Celtic	30	3
1996–97	Celtic	23	0
1997–98	Norwich C	35	3
1998–99	Norwich C	33	0
Total:		**431**	**18**

GRANT, Roderick — Forward

H: 5 11 W: 11 00 b.Gloucester 16-9-66

Source: Strathbrock Juniors.

1986–87	Cowdenbeath	24	14
1987–88	Cowdenbeath	32	11
1988–89	Cowdenbeath	8	2
1988–89	St Johnstone	28	5
1989–90	St Johnstone	37	19
1990–91	St Johnstone	30	7
1991–92	St Johnstone	25	2
1992–93	Dunfermline Ath	32	4
1993–94	Partick Th	37	13
1994–95	Partick Th	23	5
1995–96	St Johnstone	27	5
1996–97	St Johnstone	33	19
1997–98	St Johnstone	34	6
1998–99	St Johnstone	25	0
Total:		**395**	**112**

GRANT, Stephen — Forward

H: 6 1 W: 12 00 b.Birr 14-4-77

Source: Athlone T. *Honours:* Eire Schools, Under-21.

1995–96	Sunderland	0	0
1996–97	Sunderland	0	0
From Shamrock R.			
1997–98	Stockport Co	16	3
1998–99	Stockport Co	13	1
Total:		**29**	**4**

GRANT, Tony — Midfield

H: 5 10 W: 10 10 b.Liverpool 14-11-74

Source: Trainee. *Honours:* England Under-21.

1993–94	Everton	0	0
1994–95	Everton	5	0
1995–96	Everton	13	1
1995–96	Swindon T (loan)	3	1
1996–97	Everton	18	0
1997–98	Everton	7	1
1998–99	Everton	16	0
Total:		**62**	**3**

GRANVILLE, Danny — Defender

H: 6 1 W: 12 11 b.Islington 19-1-75

Source: Trainee. *Honours:* England Under-21.

1993–94	Cambridge U	11	5
1994–95	Cambridge U	16	2
1995–96	Cambridge U	35	0
1996–97	Cambridge U	37	0
1996–97	Chelsea	5	0
1997–98	Chelsea	13	0
1998–99	Leeds U	9	0
Total:		**126**	**7**

GRAVES, Wayne — Midfield

H: 5 8 W: 10 07 b.Scunthorpe 18-9-80

Source: Trainee.

1997–98	Scunthorpe U	3	0
1998–99	Scunthorpe U	0	0
Total:		**3**	**0**

GRAY, Andy — Midfield

H: 5 11 W: 14 04 b.Lambeth 22-2-64

Source: Corinthian C, Dulwich H. *Honours:* England Under-21, 1 full cap.

1984–85	Crystal Palace	21	5
1985–86	Crystal Palace	30	10
1986–87	Crystal Palace	30	6
1987–88	Crystal Palace	17	6
1987–88	Aston Villa	19	1
1988–89	Aston Villa	18	3
1988–89	QPR	11	2
1989–90	Crystal Palace	35	6
1990–91	Crystal Palace	30	4
1991–92	Crystal Palace	25	2
1991–92	Tottenham H (loan)	14	1
1992–93	Tottenham H	17	1
1992–93	Swindon T (loan)	3	0
1993–94	Tottenham H	2	1
From Marbella			
1995–96	Falkirk	16	0
1996–97	Falkirk	0	0
1997–98	Bury	21	1
1997–98	Millwall	12	1
1998–99	Millwall	0	0
Total:		**321**	**50**

GRAY, Andy — Midfield

H: 6 0 W: 13 00 b.Harrogate 15-11-77

Source: Trainee.

1995–96	Leeds U	15	0
1996–97	Leeds U	7	0
1997–98	Leeds U	0	0
1997–98	Bury (loan)	6	1
1998–99	Leeds U	0	0
1998–99	Nottingham F	8	0
1998–99	Preston NE (loan)	5	0
1998–99	Oldham Ath (loan)	4	0
Total:		**45**	**1**

GRAY, David — Forward

H: 6 2 W: 13 07 b.Rossendale 19-1-80

1998–99	Rochdale	3	0
Total:		**3**	**0**

GRAY, Ian — Goalkeeper

H: 6 2 W: 13 00 b.Manchester 25-2-75

Source: Trainee.

1993–94	Oldham Ath	0	0
1994–95	Oldham Ath	0	0
1994–95	Rochdale (loan)	12	0
1995–96	Rochdale	20	0
1996–97	Rochdale	46	0
1997–98	Stockport Co	3	0
1998–99	Stockport Co	3	0
Total:		**84**	**0**

GRAY, Julian — Midfield

b.Lewisham 21-9-79

Source: Trainee.

1998–99	Arsenal	0	0

GRAY, Kevin — Defender

H: 5 11 W: 14 02 b.Sheffield 7-1-72

Source: Trainee.

1988–89	Mansfield T	1	0
1989–90	Mansfield T	16	0
1990–91	Mansfield T	31	1
1991–92	Mansfield T	18	0
1992–93	Mansfield T	33	0
1993–94	Mansfield T	42	2
1994–95	Huddersfield T	5	0
1995–96	Huddersfield T	38	0
1996–97	Huddersfield T	39	1
1997–98	Huddersfield T	35	1
1998–99	Huddersfield T	34	1
Total:		**292**	**6**

GRAY, Martin — Midfield

H: 5 9 W: 11 04 b.Stockton 17-8-71

Source: Trainee.

1989–90	Sunderland	0	0
1990–91	Sunderland	0	0
1990–91	Aldershot (loan)	5	0
1991–92	Sunderland	1	0
1992–93	Sunderland	12	1
1993–94	Sunderland	22	0
1994–95	Sunderland	22	0
1995–96	Sunderland	7	0
1995–96	Fulham (loan)	6	0
1995–96	Oxford U	7	0
1996–97	Oxford U	43	2
1997–98	Oxford U	31	2
1998–99	Oxford U	40	0
Total:		**196**	**5**

GRAY, Michael — Defender

H: 5 7 W: 10 08 b.Sunderland 3-8-74

Source: Trainee. *Honours:* England 3 full caps.

1992–93	Sunderland	27	2
1993–94	Sunderland	22	1
1994–95	Sunderland	16	0
1995–96	Sunderland	46	4
1996–97	Sunderland	34	3
1997–98	Sunderland	44	2
1998–99	Sunderland	37	2
Total:		**226**	**14**

GRAY, Phil — Forward

H: 5 9 W: 12 07 b.Belfast 2-10-68

Source: Apprentice. *Honours:* Northern Ireland Schools, Youth, Under-23, 21 full caps, 5 goals.

1986–87	Tottenham H	1	0
1987–88	Tottenham H	1	0
1988–89	Tottenham H	1	0
1989–90	Tottenham H	0	0
1989–90	Barnsley (loan)	3	0
1990–91	Tottenham H	6	0
1990–91	Fulham (loan)	3	0
1991–92	Luton T	14	3
1992–93	Luton T	45	19
1993–94	Sunderland	41	14
1994–95	Sunderland	42	12
1995–96	Sunderland	32	8
1996–97	Sunderland	0	0
1997–98	Luton T	17	2
1998–99	Luton T	35	8
Total:		**241**	**66**

GRAY, Stuart — Defender

H: 5 11 W: 11 02 b.Harrogate 18-12-73

Source: Giffnock N. *Honours:* Scotland Under-21.

1992–93	Celtic	1	0
1993–94	Celtic	0	0
1994–95	Celtic	11	0
1995–96	Celtic	5	1
1996–97	Celtic	11	0
1997–98	Celtic	0	0
1997–98	Reading	7	0
1998–99	Reading	27	2
Total:		**62**	**3**

GRAY, Wayne — Forward

H: 5 10 W: 12 07 b.London 7-11-80

Source: Trainee.

1998–99	Wimbledon	0	0

GRAYSON, Simon — Defender

H: 6 0 W: 13 04 b.Ripon 16-12-69

Source: Trainee.

1987–88	Leeds U	2	0
1988–89	Leeds U	0	0
1989–90	Leeds U	0	0
1990–91	Leeds U	0	0
1991–92	Leeds U	0	0
1991–92	Leicester C	13	0
1992–93	Leicester C	24	1
1993–94	Leicester C	40	1
1994–95	Leicester C	34	0
1995–96	Leicester C	41	2
1996–97	Leicester C	36	0
1997–98	Aston Villa	33	0
1998–99	Aston Villa	15	0
Total:		**238**	**4**

GRAZIOLI, Guiliano — Forward

H: 5 11 W: 12 00 b.London 23-3-75

Source: Wembley.

1995–96	Peterborough U	3	1
1996–97	Peterborough U	4	0
1997–98	Peterborough U	0	0
1998–99	Peterborough U	34	15
Total:		**41**	**16**

GREAVES, Mark — Defender

H: 6 1 W: 13 00 b.Hull 22-1-75

Source: Brigg Town.

1996–97	Hull C	30	2
1997–98	Hull C	25	2
1998–99	Hull C	25	0
Total:		**80**	**4**

GREEN, Alex — Midfield

H: 6 0 W: 12 05 b.Bolton 4-1-80

Source: Trainee.

1998–99	Bury	0	0

GREEN, Francis — Forward

H: 5 9 W: 11 04 b.Derby 23-4-80

Source: Ilkeston T.

1997–98	Peterborough U	4	1
1998–99	Peterborough U	7	1
Total:		**11**	**2**

GREEN, Richard — Defender

H: 6 1 W: 14 00 b.Wolverhampton 22-11-67

Source: Apprentice.

1986–87	Shrewsbury T	15	0
1987–88	Shrewsbury T	31	2
1988–89	Shrewsbury T	39	3
1989–90	Shrewsbury T	40	0
1990–91	Shrewsbury T	0	0
1990–91	Swindon T	0	0
1991–92	Swindon T	0	0
1991–92	Gillingham	12	4
1992–93	Gillingham	39	3
1993–94	Gillingham	39	4
1994–95	Gillingham	37	1
1995–96	Gillingham	35	2
1996–97	Gillingham	29	2
1997–98	Gillingham	25	0
1998–99	Gillingham	0	0
1998–99	Walsall	30	1
Total:		**371**	**22**

GREEN, Robert — Goalkeeper

H: 6 3 W: 12 12 b.Chertsey 18-1-80

Source: Trainee. *Honours:* England Youth.

1997–98	Norwich C	0	0
1998–99	Norwich C	2	0
Total:		**2**	**0**

GREEN, Ryan — Defender

H: 5 8 W: 10 10 b.Cardiff 20-10-80

Source: Danes Court. *Honours:* Wales Under-21, 2 full caps.

1997–98	Wolverhampton W	0	0
1998–99	Wolverhampton W	1	0
Total:		**1**	**0**

GREEN, Scott — Defender

H: 5 10 W: 13 04 b.Walsall 15-1-70

Source: Trainee.

1988–89	Derby Co	0	0
1989–90	Derby Co	0	0
1989–90	Bolton W	5	2
1990–91	Bolton W	41	6
1991–92	Bolton W	37	2
1992–93	Bolton W	41	6
1993–94	Bolton W	22	4
1994–95	Bolton W	31	1
1995–96	Bolton W	31	3
1996–97	Bolton W	12	1
1997–98	Wigan Ath	38	1
1998–99	Wigan Ath	37	0
Total:		**295**	**26**

GREENACRE, Chris — Forward

H: 5 11 W: 10 06 b.Halifax 23-12-77

Source: Trainee.

1995–96	Manchester C	0	0
1996–97	Manchester C	4	0
1997–98	Manchester C	3	1
1997–98	Cardiff C (loan)	11	2
1997–98	Blackpool (loan)	4	0
1998–99	Manchester C	1	0
1998–99	Scarborough (loan)	12	2
Total:		**35**	**5**

GREENALL, Colin — Defender

H: 5 11 W: 12 12 b.Billinge 30-12-63

Source: Apprentice.

1980–81	Blackpool	12	0
1981–82	Blackpool	18	0
1982–83	Blackpool	24	1
1983–84	Blackpool	39	4
1984–85	Blackpool	44	3
1985–86	Blackpool	43	1
1986–87	Blackpool	3	0
1986–87	Gillingham	37	2
1987–88	Gillingham	25	2
1987–88	Oxford U	12	0
1988–89	Oxford U	40	2
1989–90	Oxford U	15	0
1989–90	Bury (loan)	3	0
1990–91	Bury	31	0
1991–92	Bury	37	5
1991–92	Preston NE	9	1
1992–93	Preston NE	20	0
1993–94	Chester C	42	1
1994–95	Lincoln C	39	3
1995–96	Lincoln C	4	0
1995–96	Wigan Ath	37	2
1996–97	Wigan Ath	46	2
1997–98	Wigan Ath	39	4
1998–99	Wigan Ath	40	6
Total:		**659**	**39**

GREENE, David — Defender

H: 6 3 W: 14 03 b.Luton 26-10-73

Source: Trainee. *Honours:* Eire Under-21.

1991–92	Luton T	0	0
1992–93	Luton T	1	0
1993–94	Luton T	10	0
1994–95	Luton T	8	0
1995–96	Luton T	0	0
1995–96	Colchester U (loan)	14	1
1995–96	Brentford (loan)	11	0
1996–97	Colchester U	44	2
1997–98	Colchester U	38	4
1998–99	Colchester U	42	8
Total:		**168**	**15**

GREENING, Jonathan — Forward

H: 6 0 W: 11 03 b.Scarborough 2-1-79

Source: Trainee. *Honours:* England Youth, Under-21.

1996–97	York C	5	0
1997–98	York C	20	2
1997–98	Manchester U	0	0
1998–99	Manchester U	3	0
Total:		**28**	**2**

GREGAN, Sean — Midfield

H: 6 2 W: 12 03 b.Stockton 29-3-74

Source: Trainee.

1991–92	Darlington	17	0
1992–93	Darlington	17	1
1993–94	Darlington	23	1
1994–95	Darlington	25	2
1995–96	Darlington	38	0
1996–97	Darlington	16	0
1996–97	Preston NE	21	1
1997–98	Preston NE	35	2
1998–99	Preston NE	41	3
Total:		**233**	**10**

GREGG, Matt — Goalkeeper

H: 5 11 W: 12 00 b.Cheltenham 30-11-78

Source: Trainee.

1995–96	Torquay U	1	0
1996–97	Torquay U	1	0
1997–98	Torquay U	19	0
1998–99	Torquay U	11	0
1998–99	Crystal Palace	0	0
1998–99	Swansea C (loan)	5	0
Total:		**37**	**0**

GREGORY, Andrew — Midfield

H: 5 10 W: 11 04 b.Barnsley 8-10-76

Source: Trainee.

1995–96	Barnsley	0	0
1996–97	Barnsley	0	0
1997–98	Barnsley	0	0
1998–99	Barnsley	0	0

GREGORY, David — Midfield

H: 5 10 W: 12 03 b.Polstead 23-1-70

Source: Trainee.

1987–88	Ipswich T	0	0
1988–89	Ipswich T	2	0
1989–90	Ipswich T	4	0
1990–91	Ipswich T	21	1
1991–92	Ipswich T	1	0
1992–93	Ipswich T	3	1

1993–94	Ipswich T	0	0
1994–95	Ipswich T	1	0
1994–95	Hereford U (loan)	2	0
1995–96	Peterborough U	3	0
1995–96	Colchester U	10	0
1996–97	Colchester U	38	1
1997–98	Colchester U	44	5
1998–99	Colchester U	44	11
Total:		**173**	**19**

GREGORY, Neil — Forward

H: 6 0 W: 12 10 b.Ndola 7-10-72

Source: Trainee.

1992–93	Ipswich T	0	0
1993–94	Ipswich T	0	0
1993–94	Chesterfield (loan)	3	1
1994–95	Ipswich T	3	0
1994–95	Scunthorpe U (loan)	10	7
1995–96	Ipswich T	17	2
1996–97	Ipswich T	17	6
1996–97	Torquay U (loan)	5	0
1997–98	Ipswich T	8	1
1997–98	Peterborough U (loan)	3	1
1997–98	Colchester U	15	7
1998–99	Colchester U	38	4
Total:		**119**	**29**

GRIDELET, Phil — Midfield

H: 5 11 W: 13 00 b.Edgware 30-4-67

Source: Watford, Hendon, Barnet.

1990–91	Barnsley	4	0
1991–92	Barnsley	0	0
1992–93	Barnsley	2	0
1992–93	Rotherham U (loan)	9	0
1993–94	Barnsley	0	0
1993–94	Southend U	29	0
1994–95	Southend U	29	5
1995–96	Southend U	40	2
1996–97	Southend U	41	1
1997–98	Southend U	37	2
1998–99	Southend U	0	0
Total:		**191**	**10**

GRIEMINK, Bart — Goalkeeper

H: 6 3 W: 15 04 b.Holland 29-3-72

Source: WKE.

1995–96	Birmingham C	20	0
1996–97	Birmingham C	0	0
1996–97	Barnsley (loan)	0	0
1996–97	Peterborough U	27	0
1997–98	Peterborough U	0	0
1998–99	Peterborough U	17	0
Total:		**64**	**0**

GRIEVES, Danny — Midfield

H: 5 11 W: 11 06 b.Watford 21-9-78

Source: Trainee.

1996–97	Watford	0	0
1997–98	Watford	0	0
1998–99	Watford	0	0

GRIFFIN, Andy — Defender

H: 5 8 W: 10 10 b.Wigan 17-3-79

Source: Trainee. *Honours:* England Youth, Under-21.

1996–97	Stoke C	34	1
1997–98	Stoke C	23	1
1997–98	Newcastle U	4	0
1998–99	Newcastle U	14	0
Total:		**75**	**2**

GRIFFIN, Anthony — Defender

H: 5 11 W: 11 02 b.Bournemouth 22-3-79

Source: Trainee.

1997–98	Bournemouth	0	0
1998–99	Bournemouth	6	0
Total:		**6**	**0**

GRIFFIN, Charlie — Forward

b.Bath 25-6-79

Source: Bristol R Schoolboy.

1998–99	Swindon T	5	1
Total:		**5**	**1**

GRIFFIN, Daniel — Defender

H: 5 10 W: 10 05 b.Belfast 10-8-77

Source: St Andrews, Belfast. *Honours:* Northern Ireland Under-21, 9 full caps, 1 goal.

1993–94	St Johnstone	0	0
1994–95	St Johnstone	3	0
1995–96	St Johnstone	31	1
1996–97	St Johnstone	29	1
1997–98	St Johnstone	13	0
1998–99	St Johnstone	19	1
Total:		**95**	**3**

GRIFFITHS, Andy — Midfield

H: 5 10 W: 11 04 b.Wirral 21-11-78

Source: Trainee.

1997–98	Wrexham	0	0
1998–99	Wrexham	0	0

GRIFFITHS, Carl — Forward

H: 5 10 W: 11 05 b.Oswestry 15-7-71

Source: Trainee. *Honours:* Wales Youth, Under-21.

1988–89	Shrewsbury T	28	6
1989–90	Shrewsbury T	18	4
1990–91	Shrewsbury T	19	4
1991–92	Shrewsbury T	27	8
1992–93	Shrewsbury T	42	27
1993–94	Shrewsbury T	9	5
1993–94	Manchester C	16	4
1994–95	Manchester C	2	0
1995–96	Manchester C	0	0
1995–96	Portsmouth	14	2
1995–96	Peterborough U	4	1
1996–97	Peterborough U	12	1
1996–97	Leyton Orient	13	6
1997–98	Leyton Orient	33	18
1998–99	Leyton Orient	24	8
1998–99	Wrexham (loan)	4	3
1998–99	Port Vale	3	1
Total:		**268**	**98**

GRIFFITHS, Gareth — Defender

H: 6 4 W: 14 01 b.Winsford 10-4-70

Source: Rhyl.

1992–93	Port Vale	0	0
1993–94	Port Vale	4	2
1994–95	Port Vale	20	0
1995–96	Port Vale	41	2
1996–97	Port Vale	26	0
1997–98	Port Vale	3	0
1997–98	Shrewsbury T (loan)	6	0
1998–99	Wigan Ath	20	0
Total:		**120**	**4**

GRIFFITHS, Peter — Midfield

H: 5 9 W: 11 06 b.St Helier 13-3-80

Source: Trainee.

1998–99	Macclesfield T	4	1
Total:		**4**	**1**

GRIM, Robert — Midfield

H: 5 11 W: 11 08 b.London 10-9-78

Source: Trainee.

1995–96	Nottingham F	0	0
1996–97	Nottingham F	0	0
1997–98	Nottingham F	0	0
1998–99	Nottingham F	0	0

GRIMANDI, Gilles — Defender

H: 6 0 W: 12 07 b.Gap 11-11-70

Source: FC Gap.

1991–92	Monaco	5	0
1992–93	Monaco	8	0
1993–94	Monaco	19	1
1994–95	Monaco	9	0
1995–96	Monaco	25	1
1996–97	Monaco	24	1
1997–98	Arsenal	22	1
1998–99	Arsenal	8	0
Total:		**120**	**4**

GRITTON, Martin — Forward

H: 6 1 W: 12 02 b.Glasgow 1-6-78

Source: Porthleven.

1998–99	Plymouth Arg	2	0
Total:		**2**	**0**

GROBBELAAR, Bruce — Goalkeeper

H: 6 1 W: 12 08 b.Durban 6-10-57

Source: Vancouver Whitecaps. *Honours:* Zimbabwe full caps.

1979–80	Crewe Alex	24	1
1980–81	Liverpool	0	0
1981–82	Liverpool	42	0
1982–83	Liverpool	42	0
1983–84	Liverpool	42	0
1984–85	Liverpool	42	0
1985–86	Liverpool	42	0
1986–87	Liverpool	31	0
1987–88	Liverpool	38	0
1988–89	Liverpool	21	0
1989–90	Liverpool	38	0
1990–91	Liverpool	31	0
1991–92	Liverpool	37	0
1992–93	Liverpool	5	0
1992–93	Stoke C (loan)	4	0
1993–94	Liverpool	29	0
1994–95	Southampton	30	0
1995–96	Southampton	2	0
1996–97	Plymouth Arg	36	0
1997–98	Oxford U	0	0
1997–98	Oldham Ath	4	0
From Chesham U.			
1998–99	Bury	1	0
1998–99	Lincoln C	2	0
Total:		**543**	**1**

GRODAS, Frode — Goalkeeper

H: 6 2 W: 14 07 b.Volda 24-10-64

Honours: Norway 43 full caps.

1988	Lillestrom	22	0
1989	Lillestrom	22	0

1990	Lillestrom	7	0
1991	Lillestrom	22	1
1992	Lillestrom	22	0
1993	Lillestrom	19	0
1994	Lillestrom	22	0
1995	Lillestrom	25	0
1996	Lillestrom	21	0
1996–97	Chelsea	21	0
1997–98	Chelsea	0	0
1997–98	Tottenham H	0	0
1998–99	Tottenham H	0	0
Total:		**203**	**1**

GRONDIN, David — Defender

b.Paris 8-5-80

Source: St Etienne, France Youth.

1998–99	Arsenal	1	0
Total:		**1**	**0**

GROVES, Paul — Midfield

H: 5 11 W: 13 00 b.Derby 28-2-66

Source: Burton Alb.

1987–88	Leicester C	1	1
1988–89	Leicester C	15	0
1989–90	Leicester C	0	0
1989–90	Lincoln C (loan)	8	1
1989–90	Blackpool	19	1
1990–91	Blackpool	46	11
1991–92	Blackpool	42	9
1992–93	Grimsby T	46	12
1993–94	Grimsby T	46	11
1994–95	Grimsby T	46	5
1995–96	Grimsby T	46	10
1996–97	WBA	29	4
1997–98	Grimsby T	46	7
1998–99	Grimsby T	46	14
Total:		**436**	**86**

GUDJOHNSEN, Eidur — Forward

H: 6 0 W: 13 00 b.Reykjavik 15-9-78

Honours: Iceland Youth, 1 full cap.

1994–95	Valur	17	7
1995–96	PSV Eindhoven	13	3
1996–97	PSV Eindhoven	0	0
1998	KR	0	0
1998–99	Bolton W	14	5
Total:		**44**	**15**

GUDJONSSON, Bjarni — Forward

H: 5 8 W: 10 10 b.Akranes 26-2-79

Honours: Iceland Under-21, 1 full cap.

1995	IA Akranes	2	0
1996	IA Akranes	17	13
1997	IA Akranes	6	2
1997–98	Newcastle U	0	0
1998–99	Newcastle U	0	0
Total:		**25**	**15**

GUDMUNDSSON, Johann — Midfield

H: 6 0 W: 12 00 b.Reykjavik 5-12-77

1994	Keflavik	1	0
1995	Keflavik	14	4
1996	Keflavik	17	4
1997	Keflavik	17	5
1997–98	Watford	0	0
1998–99	Watford	13	2
Total:		**62**	**15**

GUDNASON, Haukar — Forward

H: 5 10 W: 12 00 b.Keflavik 8-9-78

1995	Keflavik	3	1
1996	Keflavik	15	4
1997	Keflavik	16	6
1997–98	Liverpool	0	0
1998–99	Liverpool	0	0
Total:		**34**	**11**

GUERIN, Vincent — Midfield

H: 5 8 W: 11 06 b.Bologne 22-11-65

Source: Joinville le Pont, Brest, Matra Racing, Montpellier.
Honours: France 19 full caps, 2 goals.

1992–93	Paris St Germain	31	4
1993–94	Paris St Germain	35	7
1994–95	Paris St Germain	30	2
1995–96	Paris St Germain	31	1
1996–97	Paris St Germain	34	2
1997–98	Paris St Germain	21	0
1998–99	Hearts	19	1
Total:		**201**	**17**

GUGGI, Peter — Midfield

H: 5 10 W: 11 12 b.Graz 25-9-67

1990–91	Alpine	21	3
1991–92	Linz ASK	14	0
1992–93	Wiener SC	13	2
1993–94	Wiener SC	28	2
1994–95	Modling	14	1
1994–95	Rapid	16	2
1995–96	Rapid	29	3
1996–97	Rapid	26	0
1997–98	Admira Wacker	30	2
1998–99	Hibernian	8	2
Total:		**199**	**17**

GUINAN, Stephen — Forward

H: 6 1 W: 13 06 b.Birmingham 24-12-75

Source: Trainee.

1992–93	Nottingham F	0	0
1993–94	Nottingham F	0	0
1994–95	Nottingham F	0	0
1995–96	Nottingham F	2	0
1995–96	Darlington (loan)	3	1
1996–97	Nottingham F	2	0
1996–97	Burnley (loan)	6	0
1997–98	Nottingham F	2	0
1997–98	Crewe Alex (loan)	3	0
1998–99	Nottingham F	0	0
1998–99	Halifax T (loan)	12	2
1998–99	Plymouth Arg (loan)	11	7
Total:		**41**	**10**

GUIVARC'H, Stephane — Forward

H: 6 0 W: 13 00 b.Concarneau 6-9-70

Source: Brest, Guincamp. *Honours:* France 13 full caps, 1 goal.

1995–96	Auxerre	23	3
1996–97	Rennes	36	22
1997–98	Auxerre	32	21
1998–99	Newcastle U	4	1
1998–99	Rangers	14	5
Total:		**109**	**52**

GUNNLAUGSSON, Arnar — Forward

H: 5 10 W: 11 06 b.Akranes 6-3-73

Honours: Iceland 30 full caps, 2 goals.

1990	IA Akranes	12	3
1991	IA Akranes*	0	0
1992	IA Akranes	18	15
1992–93	Feyenoord	4	0
1993–94	Feyenoord	5	0
1994–95	Nuremberg	28	8
1995	IA Akranes	7	15
From Sochaux.			
1997	IA Akranes	2	1
1997–98	Bolton W	15	0
1998–99	Bolton W	27	13
1998–99	Leicester C	9	0
Total:		**127**	**55**

GUPPY, Steve — Midfield

H: 5 11 W: 12 00 b.Winchester 29-3-69

Source: Southampton. *Honours:* England Under-21, B.

1993–94	Wycombe W	41	8
1994–95	Newcastle U	0	0
1994–95	Port Vale	27	2
1995–96	Port Vale	44	4
1996–97	Port Vale	34	6
1996–97	Leicester C	13	0
1997–98	Leicester C	37	2
1998–99	Leicester C	38	4
Total:		**234**	**26**

GURNEY, Andy — Defender

H: 5 11 W: 12 02 b.Bristol 25-1-74

Source: Trainee.

1992–93	Bristol R	0	0
1993–94	Bristol R	3	0
1994–95	Bristol R	38	1
1995–96	Bristol R	43	6
1996–97	Bristol R	24	2
1997–98	Torquay U	44	9
1998–99	Torquay U	20	1
1998–99	Reading	8	0
Total:		**180**	**19**

HAALAND, Alf-Inge — Midfield

H: 6 1 W: 12 06 b.Stavanger 23-11-72

Source: Bryne. *Honours:* Norway 33 full caps.

1993–94	Nottingham F	3	0
1994–95	Nottingham F	20	1
1995–96	Nottingham F	17	0
1996–97	Nottingham F	35	6
1997–98	Leeds U	32	7
1998–99	Leeds U	29	1
Total:		**136**	**15**

HAARHOFF, James — Midfield

b.Lusaka 27-5-81

Source: Trainee.

1998–99	Birmingham C	0	0

HACKETT, Stephen — Defender

b.Dublin 17-9-80

Source: Trainee.

1997–98	Wolverhampton W	0	0
1998–99	Wolverhampton W	0	0

HACKETT, Warren — Defender

H: 6 0 W: 12 05 b.Plaistow 16-12-71

Source: Tottenham H Trainee.

1990–91	Leyton Orient	0	0
1991–92	Leyton Orient	22	0
1992–93	Leyton Orient	17	0
1993–94	Leyton Orient	33	3
1994–95	Doncaster R	39	2
1995–96	Doncaster R	7	0
1995–96	Mansfield T	32	3
1996–97	Mansfield T	36	1
1997–98	Mansfield T	23	1

1998–99	Mansfield T	26	0
1998–99	Barnet	7	0
Total:		**242**	**10**

HACKWORTH, Tony — Forward

H: 6 1 W: 13 07 b.Durham 19-5-80

Source: Trainee. *Honours:* England Youth.

1997–98	Leeds U	0	0
1998–99	Leeds U	0	0

HADLEY, Shaun — Midfield

H: 5 8 W: 10 05 b.Birmingham 6-2-80

Source: Trainee.

1998–99	Torquay U	2	0
Total:		**2**	**0**

HAILS, Julian — Midfield

H: 5 10 W: 11 02 b.Lincoln 20-11-67

Source: Hemel Hempstead.

1989–90	Fulham	0	0
1990–91	Fulham	0	0
1991–92	Fulham	18	1
1992–93	Fulham	46	6
1993–94	Fulham	37	4
1994–95	Fulham	8	1
1994–95	Southend U	26	2
1995–96	Southend U	42	4
1996–97	Southend U	37	0
1997–98	Southend U	44	0
1998–99	Southend U	11	1
Total:		**269**	**19**

HALE, Matt — Defender

H: 5 6 W: 10 01 b.Bristol 2-2-79

Source: Trainee.

1997–98	Bristol C	0	0
1998–99	Bristol C	0	0

HALES, Lee — Forward

H: 5 10 W: 11 00 b.Gillingham 1-5-81

Source: Trainee.

1998–99	Charlton Ath	0	0

HALEY, Grant — Defender

H: 5 8 W: 10 02 b.Bristol 20-9-79

Source: Trainee.

1998–99	Peterborough U	0	0

HALL, Daniel — Midfield

b.Rugby 29-12-81

Source: Trainee. *Honours:* England Youth.

1998–99	Coventry C	0	0

HALL, Gareth — Defender

H: 5 8 W: 12 00 b.Croydon 12-3-69

Source: Apprentice. *Honours:* England Schools, Wales Under-21, 9 full caps.

1986–87	Chelsea	1	0
1987–88	Chelsea	13	0
1988–89	Chelsea	22	0
1989–90	Chelsea	13	1
1990–91	Chelsea	24	0
1991–92	Chelsea	10	0
1992–93	Chelsea	37	2
1993–94	Chelsea	7	0
1994–95	Chelsea	6	0
1995–96	Chelsea	5	1
1995–96	Sunderland	14	0
1996–97	Sunderland	32	0
1997–98	Sunderland	2	0
1997–98	Brentford (loan)	6	0
1998–99	Swindon T	41	1
Total:		**233**	**5**

HALL, Marcus — Defender

H: 6 1 W: 12 02 b.Coventry 24-3-76

Source: Trainee. *Honours:* England Under-21, B.

1994–95	Coventry C	5	0
1995–96	Coventry C	25	0
1996–97	Coventry C	13	0
1997–98	Coventry C	25	1
1998–99	Coventry C	5	0
Total:		**73**	**1**

HALL, Paul — Forward

H: 5 8 W: 10 02 b.Manchester 3-7-72

Source: Trainee. *Honours:* Jamaica 29 full caps, 9 goals.

1989–90	Torquay U	10	0
1990–91	Torquay U	17	0
1991–92	Torquay U	38	1
1992–93	Torquay U	28	0
1992–93	Portsmouth	0	0
1993–94	Portsmouth	28	4
1994–95	Portsmouth	43	5
1995–96	Portsmouth	46	10
1996–97	Portsmouth	42	13
1997–98	Portsmouth	29	5
1998–99	Coventry C	9	0
1998–99	Bury (loan)	7	0
Total:		**297**	**38**

HALL, Richard — Defender

H: 6 2 W: 13 11 b.Ipswich 14-3-72

Source: Trainee. *Honours:* England Under-21.

1989–90	Scunthorpe U	1	0
1990–91	Scunthorpe U	21	3
1990–91	Southampton	1	0
1991–92	Southampton	26	3
1992–93	Southampton	28	4
1993–94	Southampton	4	0
1994–95	Southampton	37	4
1995–96	Southampton	30	1
1996–97	West Ham U	7	0
1997–98	West Ham U	0	0
1998–99	West Ham U	0	0
Total:		**155**	**15**

HALL, Wayne — Defender

H: 5 9 W: 10 06 b.Rotherham 25-10-68

Source: Darlington.

1988–89	York C	2	0
1989–90	York C	27	3
1990–91	York C	46	1
1991–92	York C	37	3
1992–93	York C	42	1
1993–94	York C	45	0
1994–95	York C	37	0
1995–96	York C	23	0
1996–97	York C	13	0
1997–98	York C	32	0
1998–99	York C	27	1
Total:		**331**	**9**

HALLE, Gunnar — Defender

H: 6 0 W: 12 07 b.Larvik 11-8-65

Source: Lillestrom. *Honours:* Norway 62 full caps, 5 goals.

1990–91	Oldham Ath	17	0
1991–92	Oldham Ath	10	0
1992–93	Oldham Ath	41	5
1993–94	Oldham Ath	23	1
1994–95	Oldham Ath	40	5
1995–96	Oldham Ath	37	3
1996–97	Oldham Ath	20	3
1996–97	Leeds U	20	0
1997–98	Leeds U	33	2
1998–99	Leeds U	17	2
Total:		**258**	**21**

HALLIDAY, Stephen — Forward

H: 5 10 W: 12 07 b.Sunderland 3-5-76

Source: Charlton Ath.

1993–94	Hartlepool U	11	0
1994–95	Hartlepool U	28	5
1995–96	Hartlepool U	39	7
1996–97	Hartlepool U	31	8
1997–98	Hartlepool U	31	5
1998–99	Motherwell	4	0
Total:		**144**	**25**

HALLIWELL, Bryn — Goalkeeper

H: 5 11 W: 12 00 b.Epsom 1-10-80

Source: Trainee.

1998–99	Wimbledon	0	0

HALLWORTH, Jon — Goalkeeper

H: 6 3 W: 14 08 b.Stockport 26-10-65

Source: School.

1983–84	Ipswich T	0	0
1984–85	Ipswich T	0	0
1984–85	Swindon T (loan)	0	0
1984–85	Fulham (loan)	0	0
1984–85	Bristol R (loan)	2	0
1985–86	Ipswich T	6	0
1986–87	Ipswich T	6	0
1987–88	Ipswich T	33	0
1988–89	Ipswich T	0	0
1988–89	Oldham Ath	16	0
1989–90	Oldham Ath	15	0
1990–91	Oldham Ath	46	0
1991–92	Oldham Ath	41	0
1992–93	Oldham Ath	16	0
1993–94	Oldham Ath	19	0
1994–95	Oldham Ath	6	0
1995–96	Oldham Ath	11	0
1996–97	Oldham Ath	4	0
1997–98	Cardiff C	43	0
1998–99	Cardiff C	41	0
Total:		**305**	**0**

HAMANN, Dietmar — Midfield

H: 6 3 W: 12 06 b.Waldsasson 27-8-73

Source: Wacker Munich. *Honours:* Germany 17 full caps, 1 goal.

1993–94	Bayern Munich	5	1
1994–95	Bayern Munich	30	0
1995–96	Bayern Munich	20	2
1996–97	Bayern Munich	22	1
1997–98	Bayern Munich	28	2
1998–99	Newcastle U	23	4
Total:		**128**	**10**

HAMILTON, Des — Defender

H: 5 11 W: 12 13 b.Bradford 15-8-76

Source: Trainee. *Honours:* England Under-21.

1993–94	Bradford C	2	1
1994–95	Bradford C	30	1
1995–96	Bradford C	24	3

1996–97	Bradford C	32	0
1996–97	Newcastle U	0	0
1997–98	Newcastle U	12	0
1998–99	Newcastle U	0	0
1998–99	Sheffield U (loan)	6	0
1998–99	Huddersfield T (loan)	10	1
Total:		**116**	**6**

HAMILTON, Gary — Forward

b.Bambridge 6-10-80

Source: Trainee.

1997–98	Blackburn R	0	0
1998–99	Blackburn R	0	0

HAMILTON, Ian — Midfield

H: 5 10 W: 12 03 b.Stevenage 14-12-67

Source: Apprentice.

1985–86	Southampton	0	0
1986–87	Southampton	0	0
1987–88	Southampton	0	0
1987–88	Cambridge U	9	1
1988–89	Cambridge U	15	0
1988–89	Scunthorpe U	27	1
1989–90	Scunthorpe U	43	6
1990–91	Scunthorpe U	34	2
1991–92	Scunthorpe U	41	9
1992–93	WBA	46	7
1993–94	WBA	42	3
1994–95	WBA	35	4
1995–96	WBA	41	3
1996–97	WBA	39	5
1997–98	WBA	37	1
1997–98	Sheffield U	8	1
1998–99	Sheffield U	30	2
Total:		**447**	**45**

HAMILTON, James — Midfield

H: 6 0 W: 10 10 b.Aberdeen 9-2-76

Source: Keith. *Honours:* Scotland Under-21.

1993–94	Dundee	1	0
1994–95	Dundee	28	12
1995–96	Dundee	33	14
1996–97	Dundee	12	1
1996–97	Hearts	18	4
1997–98	Hearts	32	14
1998–99	Hearts	25	6
1998–99	Aberdeen	7	1
Total:		**156**	**52**

HAMILTON, Steven — Defender

H: 5 9 W: 12 10 b.Baillieston 19-3-75

Source: Troon Juniors.

1994–95	Kilmarnock	0	0
1995–96	Kilmarnock	0	0
1996–97	Kilmarnock	6	0
1997–98	Kilmarnock	6	0
1998–99	Kilmarnock	5	0
Total:		**17**	**0**

HAMLET, Gareth — Forward

H: 6 0 W: 13 06 b.Huddersfield 10-1-80

Source: Trainee.

1998–99	Halifax T	0	0

HAMMOND, Nicky — Goalkeeper

H: 6 0 W: 11 13 b.Hornchurch 7-9-67

Source: Apprentice.

1985–86	Arsenal	0	0
1986–87	Arsenal	0	0
1986–87	Bristol R (loan)	3	0
1986–87	Peterborough U (loan)	0	0
1986–87	Aberdeen (loan)	0	0
1987–88	Swindon T	4	0
1988–89	Swindon T	0	0
1989–90	Swindon T	0	0
1990–91	Swindon T	5	0
1991–92	Swindon T	25	0
1992–93	Swindon T	13	0
1993–94	Swindon T	13	0
1994–95	Swindon T	7	0
1995–96	Plymouth Arg	4	0
1995–96	Reading	5	0
1996–97	Reading	1	0
1997–98	Reading	18	0
1998–99	Reading	1	0
Total:		**99**	**0**

HAMPSHIRE, Steve — Forward

H: 5 10 W: 10 10 b.Edinburgh 17-10-79

Source: Trainee.

1997–98	Chelsea	0	0
1998–99	Chelsea	0	0

HAMSHAW, Matthew — Midfield

b.Rotherham 1-1-82

Source: Trainee.

1998–99	Sheffield W	0	0

HANDYSIDE, Peter — Defender

H: 6 1 W: 13 03 b.Dumfries 31-7-74

Source: Trainee. *Honours:* Scotland Under-21.

1992–93	Grimsby T	11	0
1993–94	Grimsby T	13	0
1994–95	Grimsby T	35	0
1995–96	Grimsby T	30	0

1996–97	Grimsby T	9	1
1997–98	Grimsby T	42	0
1998–99	Grimsby T	31	2
Total:		**171**	**3**

HANLON, Ritchie — Midfield

H: 5 10 W: 11 12 b.Kenton 25-5-78

Source: Chelsea Trainee.

1996–97	Southend U	2	0
1997–98	Southend U	0	0
From Rushden & D.			
1998–99	Peterborough U	4	1
Total:		**6**	**1**

HANMER, Gary — Defender

H: 5 6 W: 10 02 b.Shrewsbury 12-10-73

Source: Newtown.

1996–97	WBA	0	0
1997–98	Shrewsbury T	39	1
1998–99	Shrewsbury T	46	0
Total:		**85**	**1**

HANN, Matthew — Midfield

H: 5 9 W: 10 04 b.Saffron Walden 6-9-80

Source: Trainee.

1998–99	Peterborough U	4	0
Total:		**4**	**0**

HANNAH, David — Midfield

H: 5 11 W: 11 01 b.Coatbridge 4-8-74

Source: Hamilton Th. *Honours:* Scotland Under-21.

1991–92	Dundee U	0	0
1992–93	Dundee U	5	0
1993–94	Dundee U	10	2
1994–95	Dundee U	32	2
1995–96	Dundee U	7	1
1996–97	Dundee U	12	1
1996–97	Celtic	18	0
1997–98	Celtic	15	0
1998–99	Celtic	9	0
1998–99	Dundee U	13	1
Total:		**121**	**7**

HANSEN, Bo — Forward

H: 5 10 W: 11 00 b.Jutland 16-6-72

1994–95	Brondby	31	11
1995–96	Brondby	14	4
1996–97	Brondby	20	2
1997–98	Brondby	21	14
1998–99	Brondby	16	12
1998–99	Bolton W	8	0
Total:		**110**	**43**

HANSON, Christian — Defender

H: 6 1 W: 11 05 b.Middlesbrough 3-8-81

Source: Trainee. *Honours:* England Schools, Youth.

1998–99	Middlesbrough	0	0

HANSON, Dave — Forward

H: 6 0 W: 13 07 b.Huddersfield 19-11-68

Source: Manchester U, Farsley Celtic.

1993–94	Bury	1	0
From Halifax T, Hednesford T			
1995–96	Leyton Orient	11	1
1996–97	Leyton Orient	25	3
1996–97	Chesterfield (loan)	3	1
1997–98	Leyton Orient	12	1
1998–99	Halifax T	31	2
Total:		**83**	**8**

HAPGOOD, Leon — Forward

H: 5 6 W: 10 00 b.Torbay 7-8-79

Source: Trainee.

1996–97	Torquay U	1	0
1997–98	Torquay U	22	3
1998–99	Torquay U	17	0
Total:		**40**	**3**

HARDY, Phil — Defender

H: 5 7 W: 11 08 b.Chester 9-4-73

Source: Trainee. *Honours:* Eire Under-21.

1989–90	Wrexham	1	0
1990–91	Wrexham	32	0
1991–92	Wrexham	42	0
1992–93	Wrexham	32	0
1993–94	Wrexham	25	0
1994–95	Wrexham	44	0
1995–96	Wrexham	42	0
1996–97	Wrexham	13	0
1997–98	Wrexham	34	0
1998–99	Wrexham	33	0
Total:		**298**	**0**

HAREWOOD, Marlon — Forward

H: 6 1 W: 13 03 b.Hampstead 25-8-79

Source: Trainee.

1996–97	Nottingham F	0	0
1997–98	Nottingham F	1	0
1998–99	Nottingham F	23	1
1998–99	Ipswich T (loan)	6	1
Total:		**30**	**2**

HARGREAVES, Chris — Midfield

H: 5 11 W: 12 02 b.Cleethorpes 12-5-72

Source: Trainee.

1989–90	Grimsby T	19	2
1990–91	Grimsby T	18	3
1991–92	Grimsby T	10	0
1992–93	Grimsby T	4	0
1992–93	Scarborough (loan)	3	0
1993–94	Grimsby T	0	0
1993–94	Hull C	28	0
1994–95	Hull C	21	0
1995–96	WBA	1	0
1995–96	Hereford U (loan)	17	2
1996–97	Hereford U	44	4
1997–98	Hereford U	0	0
From Hereford U.			
1998–99	Plymouth Arg	32	2
Total:		**197**	**13**

HARKES, John — Midfield

H: 5 10 W: 12 03 b.New Jersey 8-3-67

Source: USSF. *Honours:* USA full caps.

1990–91	Sheffield W	23	2
1991–92	Sheffield W	29	3
1992–93	Sheffield W	29	2
1993–94	Derby Co	33	2
1994–95	Derby Co	33	0
1995–96	Derby Co	8	0
1995–96	West Ham U	11	0
1996–97	West Ham U	0	0
1997–98	West Ham U	0	0
From DC United.			
1998–99	Nottingham F	3	0
Total:		**169**	**9**

HARKIN, Maurice — Forward

H: 5 9 W: 11 05 b.Derry 16-8-79

Source: Trainee.

1996–97	Wycombe W	4	0
1997–98	Wycombe W	35	2
1998–99	Wycombe W	2	0
Total:		**41**	**2**

HARKNESS, Steve — Defender

H: 5 10 W: 11 02 b.Carlisle 27-8-71

Source: Trainee. *Honours:* England Youth.

1988–89	Carlisle U	13	0
1989–90	Liverpool	0	0
1990–91	Liverpool	0	0
1991–92	Liverpool	11	0
1992–93	Liverpool	10	0
1993–94	Liverpool	11	0
1993–94	Huddersfield T (loan)	5	0
1994–95	Liverpool	8	1
1994–95	Southend U (loan)	6	0
1995–96	Liverpool	24	1
1996–97	Liverpool	7	0
1997–98	Liverpool	25	0
1998–99	Liverpool	6	0
Total:		**126**	**2**

HARLE, Mike — Defender

H: 6 0 W: 12 06 b.Lewisham 31-10-72

Source: Sittingbourne.

1993–94	Millwall	0	0
1994–95	Millwall	0	0
1995–96	Millwall	0	0
1995–96	Bury (loan)	1	0
1996–97	Millwall	21	1
1997–98	Barnet	43	2
1998–99	Barnet	11	0
Total:		**76**	**3**

HARLEY, Jon — Midfield

H: 5 10 W: 11 10 b.Maidstone 26-9-79

Source: Trainee.

1996–97	Chelsea	0	0
1997–98	Chelsea	3	0
1998–99	Chelsea	0	0
Total:		**3**	**0**

HARPER, Kevin — Forward

H: 5 7 W: 12 00 b.Oldham 15-1-76

Source: Hutcheson Vale BC. *Honours:* Scotland Under-21.

1993–94	Hibernian	2	0
1994–95	Hibernian	23	5
1995–96	Hibernian	16	3
1996–97	Hibernian	26	5
1997–98	Hibernian	27	1
1998–99	Hibernian	2	1
1998–99	Derby Co	27	1
Total:		**123**	**16**

HARPER, Lee — Goalkeeper

H: 6 1 W: 13 11 b.Chelsea 30-10-71

Source: Sittingbourne.

1994–95	Arsenal	0	0
1995–96	Arsenal	0	0
1996–97	Arsenal	1	0
1997–98	QPR	36	0
1998–99	QPR	15	0
Total:		**52**	**0**

HARPER, Steve — Midfield

H: 5 10 W: 11 12 b.Newcastle-under-Lyme 3-2-69

Source: Trainee.

1987–88	Port Vale	21	2
1988–89	Port Vale	7	0
1988–89	Preston NE	5	0
1989–90	Preston NE	36	10
1990–91	Preston NE	36	0
1991–92	Burnley	35	3
1992–93	Burnley	34	5
1993–94	Burnley	0	0
1993–94	Doncaster R	31	2
1994–95	Doncaster R	33	9
1995–96	Doncaster R	1	0
1995–96	Mansfield T	29	5
1996–97	Mansfield T	40	2
1997–98	Mansfield T	46	5
1998–99	Mansfield T	45	6
Total:		**399**	**49**

HARPER, Steve — Goalkeeper

H: 6 1 W: 13 09 b.Easington 3-2-74

Source: Seaham Red Star.

1993–94	Newcastle U	0	0
1994–95	Newcastle U	0	0
1995–96	Newcastle U	0	0
1995–96	Bradford C (loan)	1	0
1996–97	Newcastle U	0	0
1996–97	Stockport Co (loan)	0	0
1997–98	Newcastle U	0	0
1997–98	Hartlepool U (loan)	15	0
1997–98	Huddersfield T (loan)	24	0
1998–99	Newcastle U	8	0
Total:		**48**	**0**

HARRIES, Paul — Forward

H: 6 1 W: 13 00 b.Sydney 19-11-77

Source: NSWSF.

1997–98	Portsmouth	1	0
1998–99	Crystal Palace	0	0
1998–99	Torquay U (loan)	5	0
Total:		**6**	**0**

HARRIS, Andrew — Defender

H: 5 10 W: 12 02 b.Springs 26-2-77

Source: Trainee.

1993–94	Liverpool	0	0
1994–95	Liverpool	0	0
1995–96	Liverpool	0	0
1996–97	Southend U	44	0
1997–98	Southend U	27	0
1998–99	Southend U	1	0
Total:		**72**	**0**

HARRIS, Danny — Defender

H: 5 11 W: 11 07 b.Exeter 18-12-79

Source: Trainee.

1998–99	Exeter C	0	0

HARRIS, Jamie — Forward

H: 6 3 W: 13 06 b.Swansea 28-6-79

Source: Mumbles R.

1997–98	Swansea C	6	0
1998–99	Swansea C	0	0
Total:		**6**	**0**

HARRIS, Jason — Forward

H: 6 1 W: 11 10 b.Sutton 24-11-76

Source: Trainee.

1995–96	Crystal Palace	0	0
1996–97	Crystal Palace	2	0
1996–97	Bristol R (loan)	6	2
1997–98	Crystal Palace	0	0
1997–98	Lincoln C (loan)	1	0
1997–98	Leyton Orient	35	6
1998–99	Leyton Orient	2	1
1998–99	Preston NE	34	6
Total:		**80**	**15**

HARRIS, Michael — Defender

b.Liverpool 6-12-80

Source: Trainee.

1998–99	Newcastle U	0	0

HARRIS, Neil — Forward

H: 5 11 W: 12 08 b.Orsett 12-7-77

Source: Cambridge C.

1997–98	Millwall	3	0
1998–99	Millwall	39	15
Total:		**42**	**15**

HARRIS, Richard — Defender

H: 5 11 W: 10 09 b.Croydon 23-10-80

Source: Trainee.

1997–98	Crystal Palace	0	0
1998–99	Crystal Palace	1	0
Total:		**1**	**0**

HARRISON, Craig — Defender

H: 6 0 W: 11 08 b.Gateshead 10-11-77

Source: Trainee.

1996–97	Middlesbrough	0	0

1997–98	Middlesbrough	20	0
1998–99	Middlesbrough	4	0
1998–99	Preston NE (loan)	6	0
Total:		**30**	**0**

HARRISON, Edward — Midfield

b.Carlisle 14-2-80

Source: Trainee.

1997–98	Carlisle U	10	0
1998–99	Carlisle U	0	0
Total:		**10**	**0**

HARRISON, Gerry — Defender

H: 5 8 W: 12 05 b.Lambeth 15-4-72

Source: Trainee. *Honours:* England Schools.

1989–90	Watford	3	0
1990–91	Watford	6	0
1991–92	Bristol C	4	0
1991–92	Cardiff C (loan)	10	1
1992–93	Bristol C	33	1
1993–94	Bristol C	1	0
1993–94	Hereford U (loan)	6	0
1993–94	Huddersfield T	0	0
1994–95	Burnley	19	2
1995–96	Burnley	35	1
1996–97	Burnley	35	0
1997–98	Burnley	35	0
1998–99	Sunderland	0	0
1998–99	Luton T (loan)	14	0
1998–99	Hull C (loan)	8	0
Total:		**209**	**5**

HARRISON, Lee — Goalkeeper

H: 6 2 W: 12 07 b.Billericay 12-9-71

Source: Trainee.

1990–91	Charlton Ath	0	0
1991–92	Charlton Ath	0	0
1991–92	Fulham (loan)	0	0
1991–92	Gillingham (loan)	2	0
1992–93	Charlton Ath	0	0
1992–93	Fulham (loan)	0	0
1993–94	Fulham	0	0
1994–95	Fulham	7	0
1995–96	Fulham	5	0
1996–97	Barnet	21	0
1997–98	Barnet	46	0
1998–99	Barnet	43	0
Total:		**124**	**0**

HARRISON, Ross — Forward

H: 5 9 W: 10 04 b.Leamington Spa 28-12-79

Source: Trainee.

1998–99	Reading	0	0

HARRISON, Thomas — Midfield

H: 5 9 W: 12 06 b.Edinburgh 22-1-74

1997–98	Carlisle U	0	0
1998–99	Carlisle U	0	0

HARSLEY, Paul — Midfield

H: 5 10 W: 11 03 b.Scunthorpe 29-5-78

Source: Trainee.

1996–97	Grimsby T	0	0
1997–98	Scunthorpe U	15	1
1998–99	Scunthorpe U	34	0
Total:		**49**	**1**

HART, Gary — Forward

H: 5 9 W: 12 08 b.Harlow 6-11-75

Source: Stansted.

1998–99	Brighton & HA	44	12
Total:		**44**	**12**

HART, Michael — Forward

H: 5 10 W: 11 06 b.Bellshill 10-2-80

Source: Stoneywood.

1997–98	Aberdeen	0	0
1998–99	Aberdeen	14	0
Total:		**14**	**0**

HARTE, Ian — Defender

H: 6 0 W: 12 04 b.Drogheda 31-8-77

Source: Trainee. *Honours:* Eire 19 full caps, 2 goals.

1995–96	Leeds U	4	0
1996–97	Leeds U	14	2
1997–98	Leeds U	12	0
1998–99	Leeds U	35	4
Total:		**65**	**6**

HARTFIELD, Charlie — Midfield

H: 6 0 W: 13 08 b.London 4-9-71

Source: Trainee.

1989–90	Arsenal	0	0
1990–91	Arsenal	0	0
1991–92	Sheffield U	7	0
1992–93	Sheffield U	17	0
1993–94	Sheffield U	5	0
1994–95	Sheffield U	25	1
1995–96	Sheffield U	0	0
1996–97	Sheffield U	2	0
1996–97	Fulham (loan)	2	0
1997–98	Sheffield U	0	0
1997–98	Swansea C	22	2

1998–99	Swansea C	0	0
1998–99	Lincoln C (loan)	3	1
Total:		**83**	**4**

HARTLEY, Paul — Midfield

H: 5 9 W: 10 04 b.Baillieston 19-10-76

Source: Mill United BC. *Honours:* Scotland Under-21.

1994–95	Hamilton A	16	0
1995–96	Hamilton A	31	11
1996–97	Millwall	44	4
1997–98	Raith R	30	10
1998–99	Hibernian	12	5
Total:		**133**	**30**

HARTSON, John — Forward

H: 6 0 W: 13 00 b.Swansea 5-4-75

Source: Trainee. *Honours:* Wales Under-21, 17 full caps, 2 goals.

1992–93	Luton T	0	0
1993–94	Luton T	34	6
1994–95	Luton T	20	5
1994–95	Arsenal	15	7
1995–96	Arsenal	19	4
1996–97	Arsenal	19	3
1996–97	West Ham U	11	5
1997–98	West Ham U	32	15
1998–99	West Ham U	17	4
1998–99	Wimbledon	14	2
Total:		**181**	**51**

HASLAM, Nathan — Midfield

b.Middlesbrough 13-1-81

Source: Trainee. *Honours:* England Youth.

1998–99	Sheffield W	0	0

HASLAM, Steven — Midfield

H: 5 11 W: 11 00 b.Sheffield 6-9-79

Source: Trainee. *Honours:* England Schools, Youth.

1996–97	Sheffield W	0	0
1997–98	Sheffield W	0	0
1998–99	Sheffield W	2	0
Total:		**2**	**0**

HASSELBAINK, Jimmy Floyd — Forward

H: 6 0 W: 13 08 b.Paramaribo 27-3-72

Honours: Holland 5 full caps, 2 goals.

1995–96	Campomairorense	31	12
1996–97	Boavista	29	20
1997–98	Leeds U	33	16
1998–99	Leeds U	36	18
Total:		**129**	**66**

HASSELL, Bobby — Defender

H: 5 10 W: 11 13 b.Derby 4-6-80

Source: Trainee.

1997–98	Mansfield T	9	0
1998–99	Mansfield T	3	0
Total:		**12**	**0**

HATELEY, Mark — Forward

H: 6 2 W: 13 00 b.Liverpool 7-11-61

Source: Apprentice. *Honours:* England Youth, Under-21, 32 full caps, 9 goals.

1978–79	Coventry C	1	0
1979–80	Coventry C	4	0
1980–81	Coventry C	19	3
1981–82	Coventry C	34	13
1982–83	Coventry C	35	9
1983–84	Portsmouth	38	22
1984–85	AC Milan	21	7
1985–86	AC Milan	22	8
1986–87	AC Milan	23	2
1987–88	Monaco	28	14
1988–89	Monaco	18	6
1989–90	Monaco	13	2
1990–91	Rangers	33	10
1991–92	Rangers	30	21
1992–93	Rangers	37	19
1993–94	Rangers	42	22
1994–95	Rangers	23	13
1995–96	QPR	14	2
1996–97	QPR	13	1
1996–97	Leeds U (loan)	6	0
1996–97	Rangers	4	1
1997–98	Hull C	9	0
1998–99	Hull C	12	3
Total:		**479**	**178**

HATHAWAY, Ian — Midfield

H: 5 6 W: 10 12 b.Wordsley 22-8-68

Source: WBA Apprentice, Bedworth U.

1988–89	Mansfield T	12	1
1989–90	Mansfield T	22	1
1990–91	Mansfield T	10	0
1990–91	Rotherham U	5	1
1991–92	Rotherham U	8	0
1992–93	Rotherham U	0	0
1993–94	Torquay U	41	7
1994–95	Torquay U	38	5
1995–96	Torquay U	26	1
1996–97	Torquay U	35	1
1997–98	Colchester U	12	0
1998–99	Colchester U	0	0
Total:		**209**	**17**

HAWE, Steven — Forward

b.Machbrafelt 23-12-80

Source: Trainee.

1997–98	Blackburn R	0	0
1998–99	Blackburn R	0	0

HAWES, Steve — Midfield

H: 5 8 W: 12 04 b.High Wycombe 17-7-78

Source: Trainee.

1995–96	Sheffield U	2	0
1996–97	Sheffield U	2	0
1997–98	Sheffield U	0	0
1997–98	Doncaster R (loan)	11	0
1998–99	Hull C	19	0
Total:		**34**	**0**

HAWKINS, Peter — Defender

H: 6 0 W: 11 04 b.Maidstone 19-9-78

Source: Trainee.

1996–97	Wimbledon	0	0
1997–98	Wimbledon	0	0
1998–99	Wimbledon	0	0

HAWLEY, Jon — Defender

H: 6 1 W: 12 08 b.Lincoln 25-1-78

Source: Trainee.

1996–97	Portsmouth	0	0
1997–98	Portsmouth	0	0
1998–99	Portsmouth	0	0

HAWORTH, Simon — Forward

H: 6 1 W: 13 01 b.Cardiff 30-3-77

Source: Trainee. *Honours:* Wales Under-21, 5 full caps.

1995–96	Cardiff C	13	0
1996–97	Cardiff C	24	9
1997–98	Coventry C	10	0
1998–99	Coventry C	1	0
1998–99	Wigan Ath	20	10
Total:		**68**	**19**

HAXTHAUSEN, Michael — Goalkeeper

H: 5 10 W: 11 00 b.Helsingor 23-10-79

Source: Trainee.

1998–99	Peterborough U	0	0

HAY, Chris — Forward

H: 6 0 W: 12 05 b.Glasgow 28-8-74

Source: Giffnock N.

1993–94	Celtic	2	0
1994–95	Celtic	5	0
1995–96	Celtic	4	0
1996–97	Celtic	14	4
1997–98	Swindon T	36	14
1998–99	Swindon T	27	6
Total:		**88**	**24**

HAYDON, Nicky — Midfield

H: 5 9 W: 11 07 b.Barking 10-8-78

Source: Trainee.

1995–96	Colchester U	0	0
1996–97	Colchester U	1	1
1997–98	Colchester U	17	0
1998–99	Colchester U	13	1
Total:		**31**	**2**

HAYFIELD, Matt — Midfield

H: 5 10 W: 11 07 b.Bristol 8-8-75

Source: Trainee.

1995–96	Bristol R	6	0
1996–97	Bristol R	17	0
1997–98	Bristol R	18	0
1998–99	Shrewsbury T	2	0
Total:		**43**	**0**

HAYLES, Barry — Forward

H: 5 9 W: 13 00 b.London 17-4-72

Source: Stevenage Bor.

1997–98	Bristol R	45	23
1998–99	Bristol R	17	9
1998–99	Fulham	30	8
Total:		**92**	**40**

HAYTER, James — Forward

H: 5 9 W: 10 13 b.Newport (IW) 9-4-79

Source: Trainee.

1996–97	Bournemouth	2	0
1997–98	Bournemouth	5	0
1998–99	Bournemouth	20	2
Total:		**27**	**2**

HAYWARD, Steve — Midfield

H: 5 11 W: 12 07 b.Walsall 8-9-71

Source: Trainee. *Honours:* England Youth.

1988–89	Derby Co	0	0
1989–90	Derby Co	3	0

1990–91	Derby Co	1	0
1991–92	Derby Co	7	0
1992–93	Derby Co	7	1
1993–94	Derby Co	5	0
1994–95	Derby Co	3	0
1994–95	Carlisle U	9	2
1995–96	Carlisle U	38	4
1996–97	Carlisle U	43	7
1997–98	Fulham	35	4
1998–99	Fulham	42	3
Total:		**193**	**21**

HAZAN, Alon — Midfield

H: 6 1 W: 13 08 b.Ashdod 14-9-67

Source: Ironi Ashdod. *Honours:* Israel 63 full caps, 4 goals.

1997–98	Watford	10	0
1998–99	Watford	23	2
Total:		**33**	**2**

HAZELL, Reuben — Defender

H: 5 11 W: 11 11 b.Birmingham 24-4-79

Source: Trainee.

1996–97	Aston Villa	0	0
1997–98	Aston Villa	0	0
1998–99	Aston Villa	0	0

HEALD, Greg — Defender

H: 6 1 W: 13 01 b.Enfield 26-9-71

Source: Enfield. *Honours:* England Schools.

1994–95	Peterborough U	29	0
1995–96	Peterborough U	40	4
1996–97	Peterborough U	36	2
1997–98	Barnet	43	3
1998–99	Barnet	19	2
Total:		**167**	**11**

HEALD, Paul — Goalkeeper

H: 6 2 W: 12 05 b.Wath-on-Dearne 20-9-68

Source: Trainee.

1987–88	Sheffield U	0	0
1988–89	Sheffield U	0	0
1988–89	Leyton Orient	28	0
1989–90	Leyton Orient	37	0
1990–91	Leyton Orient	38	0
1991–92	Leyton Orient	2	0
1991–92	Coventry C (loan)	2	0
1992–93	Leyton Orient	26	0
1992–93	Crystal Palace (loan)	0	0
1993–94	Leyton Orient	0	0
1993–94	Swindon T (loan)	2	0
1994–95	Leyton Orient	45	0
1995–96	Wimbledon	18	0
1996–97	Wimbledon	2	0
1997–98	Wimbledon	0	0
1998–99	Wimbledon	0	0
Total:		**200**	**0**

HEALY, Brian — Midfield

H: 6 1 W: 13 02 b.Glasgow 27-12-68

Source: West Auckland, Billingham T, Bishop Auckland, Gateshead, Spennymoor U, Morecambe.

1998–99	Torquay U	19	2
Total:		**19**	**2**

HEALY, Colin — Midfield

H: 5 11 W: 11 00 b.Cork 14-3-80

Source: Wilton U.

1998–99	Celtic	3	0
Total:		**3**	**0**

HEALY, David — Forward

H: 5 8 W: 10 09 b.Downpatrick 5-8-79

Source: Trainee. *Honours:* Northern Ireland Under-21.

1997–98	Manchester U	0	0
1998–99	Manchester U	0	0

HEANEY, Neil — Forward

H: 5 9 W: 11 07 b.Middlesbrough 3-11-71

Source: Trainee. *Honours:* England Youth, Under-21.

1989–90	Arsenal	0	0
1990–91	Arsenal	0	0
1990–91	Hartlepool U (loan)	3	0
1991–92	Arsenal	1	0
1991–92	Cambridge U (loan)	13	4
1992–93	Arsenal	5	0
1993–94	Arsenal	1	0
1993–94	Southampton	2	0
1994–95	Southampton	34	2
1995–96	Southampton	17	2
1996–97	Southampton	8	1
1996–97	Manchester C	15	1
1997–98	Manchester C	3	0
1997–98	Charlton Ath (loan)	6	0
1998–99	Manchester C	0	0
1998–99	Bristol C (loan)	3	0
Total:		**111**	**10**

HEARY, Thomas — Midfield

H: 5 10 W: 10 06 b.Dublin 14-2-78

Source: Trainee.

1995–96	Huddersfield T	0	0
1996–97	Huddersfield T	5	0
1997–98	Huddersfield T	3	0
1998–99	Huddersfield T	3	0
Total:		**11**	**0**

HEATH, Robert — Midfield

H: 5 9 W: 10 07 b.Newcastle-Under-Lyme 31-8-78

1996–97	Stoke C	0	0
1997–98	Stoke C	6	0
1998–99	Stoke C	10	0
Total:		**16**	**0**

HEATHCOTE, Mike — Defender

H: 6 2 W: 12 08 b.Durham 10-9-65

Source: Middlesbrough, Spennymoor U.

1987–88	Sunderland	1	0
1987–88	Halifax T (loan)	7	1
1988–89	Sunderland	0	0
1989–90	Sunderland	8	0
1989–90	York C (loan)	3	0
1990–91	Shrewsbury T	39	6
1991–92	Shrewsbury T	5	0
1991–92	Cambridge U	22	5
1992–93	Cambridge U	42	2
1993–94	Cambridge U	40	5
1994–95	Cambridge U	24	1
1995–96	Plymouth Arg	44	4
1996–97	Plymouth Arg	42	1
1997–98	Plymouth Arg	36	4
1998–99	Plymouth Arg	43	3
Total:		**356**	**32**

HEBEL, Dirk — Midfield

H: 5 10 W: 12 01 b.Cologne 24-11-72

Source: Cologne.

1997–98	Tranmere R	0	0
1998–99	Brentford	15	0
Total:		**15**	**0**

HECKINGBOTTOM, Marc — Midfield

H: 5 7 W: 12 01 b.Barnsley 21-2-80

Source: Trainee.

1998–99	Barnsley	0	0

HECKINGBOTTOM, Paul — Defender

H: 6 0 W: 12 03 b.Barnsley 17-7-77

Source: Manchester U Trainee.

1995–96	Sunderland	0	0
1996–97	Sunderland	0	0
1997–98	Sunderland	0	0
1997–98	Scarborough (loan)	29	0
1998–99	Sunderland	0	0
1998–99	Hartlepool U (loan)	5	1
1998–99	Darlington (loan)	10	0
Total:		**44**	**1**

HEDMAN, Magnus — Goalkeeper

H: 6 3 W: 14 00 b.Stockholm 19-3-73

Honours: Sweden 16 full caps.

1990	AIK Stockholm	2	0
1991	AIK Stockholm	2	0
1992	AIK Stockholm	7	0
1993	AIK Stockholm	26	0
1994	AIK Stockholm	26	0
1995	AIK Stockholm	25	0
1996	AIK Stockholm	26	0
1997	AIK Stockholm	13	0
1997–98	Coventry C	14	0
1998–99	Coventry C	36	0
Total:		**177**	**0**

HEGGEM, Vegard — Defender

H: 5 11 W: 12 00 b.Trondheim 13-7-75

Honours: Norway 9 full caps, 1 goal.

1995	Rosenborg	15	1
1996	Rosenborg	14	1
1997	Rosenborg	23	3
1998–99	Liverpool	29	2
Total:		**81**	**7**

HEGGS, Carl — Forward

H: 6 1 W: 12 10 b.Leicester 11-10-70

Source: Doncaster R Trainee, Paget R.

1991–92	WBA	3	0
1992–93	WBA	17	2
1993–94	WBA	6	0
1994–95	WBA	14	1
1994–95	Bristol R (loan)	5	1
1995–96	Swansea C	32	5
1996–97	Swansea C	14	2
1997–98	Northampton T	33	4
1998–99	Northampton T	13	1
Total:		**137**	**16**

HEINOLA, Antti — Defender

H: 5 7 W: 10 05 b.Helsinki 20-3-73

Honours: Finland 5 full caps.

1991–92	HJK Helsinki	18	0
1992–93	HJK Helsinki	20	0
1993–94	HJK Helsinki	19	2
1994–95	HJK Helsinki	23	3
1995–96	Emmen	10	0
1996–97	Emmen	9	0
1996–97	Heracles	13	0
1997–98	Heracles	18	3
1997–98	QPR	10	0
1998–99	QPR	23	0
Total:		**163**	**8**

HENCHOZ, Stephane — Defender

H: 6 2 W: 12 08 b.Billens 7-9-74

Source: Bulle. *Honours:* Switzerland 37 full caps.

1992–93	Neuchatel Xamax	35	0
1993–94	Neuchatel Xamax	21	1
1994–95	Neuchatel Xamax	35	0
1995–96	Hamburg	31	2
1996–97	Hamburg	18	0
1997–98	Blackburn R	36	0
1998–99	Blackburn R	34	0
Total:		**210**	**3**

HENDERSON, Kevin — Forward

H: 5 10 W: 12 04 b.Ashington 8-6-74

Source: Morpeth Town.

1997–98	Burnley	7	0
1998–99	Burnley	7	1
Total:		**14**	**1**

HENDERSON, Tommy — Midfield

H: 5 6 W: 10 10 b.Bury St Edmunds 9-10-79

Source: Trainee.

1998–99	Norwich C	0	0

HENDON, Ian — Defender

H: 6 0 W: 12 10 b.Ilford 5-12-71

Source: Trainee. *Honours:* England Youth, Under-21.

1989–90	Tottenham H	0	0
1990–91	Tottenham H	2	0
1991–92	Tottenham H	2	0
1991–92	Portsmouth (loan)	4	0
1991–92	Leyton Orient (loan)	6	0
1992–93	Tottenham H	0	0
1992–93	Barnsley (loan)	6	0
1993–94	Leyton Orient	36	2
1994–95	Leyton Orient	29	0
1994–95	Birmingham C (loan)	4	0
1995–96	Leyton Orient	38	2
1996–97	Leyton Orient	28	1
1996–97	Notts Co	12	0
1997–98	Notts Co	38	0
1998–99	Notts Co	32	6
1998–99	Northampton T	7	0
Total:		**244**	**11**

HENDRIE, John — Forward

H: 5 7 W: 12 02 b.Lennoxtown 24-10-63

Source: Apprentice. *Honours:* Scotland Youth.

1981–82	Coventry C	6	0
1982–83	Coventry C	12	2
1983–84	Coventry C	3	0
1983–84	Hereford U (loan)	6	0
1984–85	Bradford C	46	9
1985–86	Bradford C	42	10
1986–87	Bradford C	42	14
1987–88	Bradford C	43	13
1988–89	Newcastle U	34	4
1989–90	Leeds U	27	5
1990–91	Middlesbrough	41	3
1991–92	Middlesbrough	38	3
1992–93	Middlesbrough	32	9
1993–94	Middlesbrough	29	13
1994–95	Middlesbrough	39	15
1995–96	Middlesbrough	13	1
1996–97	Middlesbrough	0	0
1996–97	Barnsley	36	15
1997–98	Barnsley	20	1
1998–99	Barnsley	9	1
Total:		**518**	**118**

HENDRIE, Lee — Forward

H: 5 10 W: 11 00 b.Birmingham 18-5-77

Source: Trainee. *Honours:* England Youth, Under-21, B, 1 full cap.

1993–94	Aston Villa	0	0
1994–95	Aston Villa	0	0
1995–96	Aston Villa	3	0
1996–97	Aston Villa	4	0
1997–98	Aston Villa	17	3
1998–99	Aston Villa	32	3
Total:		**56**	**6**

HENDRY, Colin — Defender

H: 6 1 W: 12 07 b.Keith 7-12-65

Source: Islavale. *Honours:* Scotland B, 39 full caps, 1 goal.

1983–84	Dundee	4	0
1984–85	Dundee	4	0
1985–86	Dundee	20	0
1986–87	Dundee	13	2
1986–87	Blackburn R	13	3
1987–88	Blackburn R	44	12
1988–89	Blackburn R	38	7
1989–90	Blackburn R	7	0
1989–90	Manchester C	25	3
1990–91	Manchester C	32	1
1991–92	Manchester C	6	1
1991–92	Blackburn R	30	4
1992–93	Blackburn R	41	1
1993–94	Blackburn R	23	0
1994–95	Blackburn R	38	4
1995–96	Blackburn R	33	1
1996–97	Blackburn R	35	1
1997–98	Blackburn R	34	1
1998–99	Rangers	19	0
Total:		**459**	**41**

HENRIKSEN, Tony — Goalkeeper

H: 6 3 W: 13 09 b.Hammel 25-4-73

Source: Randers Freja.

1996–97	Southend U	0	0
1997–98	Southend U	0	0
1998–99	Southend U	0	0

HENRY, Anthony — Defender

b.London 13-9-79

Source: Trainee.

1997–98	West Ham U	0	0
1998–99	West Ham U	0	0

HENRY, John — Forward

H: 5 9 W: 10 00 b.Vale of Leven 31-12-71

Source: Clydebank BC.

1990–91	Clydebank	3	1
1991–92	Clydebank	35	8
1992–93	Clydebank	32	12
1993–94	Clydebank	44	7
1994–95	Kilmarnock	30	4
1995–96	Kilmarnock	28	3
1996–97	Kilmarnock	22	2
1997–98	Kilmarnock	26	1
1998–99	Kilmarnock	11	3
Total:		**231**	**41**

HENRY, Nick — Midfield

H: 5 6 W: 10 12 b.Liverpool 21-2-69

Source: Trainee.

1987–88	Oldham Ath	5	0
1988–89	Oldham Ath	18	0
1989–90	Oldham Ath	41	0
1990–91	Oldham Ath	43	4
1991–92	Oldham Ath	42	6
1992–93	Oldham Ath	32	6
1993–94	Oldham Ath	22	0
1994–95	Oldham Ath	34	2
1995–96	Oldham Ath	14	0
1996–97	Oldham Ath	22	1
1996–97	Sheffield U	9	0
1997–98	Sheffield U	1	0
1998–99	Sheffield U	6	0
1998–99	Walsall	8	0
Total:		**297**	**19**

HENSHAW, Terrence — Defender

H: 5 10 W: 10 10 b.Nottingham 29-2-80

Source: Trainee.

1998–99	Notts Co	0	0

HERBERT, Craig — Defender

H: 5 10 W: 11 00 b.Coventry 9-11-75

Source: Torquay U.

1993–94	WBA	0	0
1994–95	WBA	8	0
1995–96	WBA	0	0
1996–97	WBA	0	0
1997–98	Shrewsbury T	24	0
1998–99	Shrewsbury T	8	0
Total:		**40**	**0**

HERITAGE, Paul — Goalkeeper

H: 6 1 W: 13 06 b.Sheffield 17-4-79

Source: Trainee.

1996–97	Sheffield U	0	0
1997–98	Sheffield U	0	0
1997–98	Barnsley	0	0
1998–99	Carlisle U	0	0

HERRERA, Robbie — Defender

H: 5 7 W: 10 06 b.Torbay 12-6-70

Source: Trainee.

1987–88	QPR	0	0
1988–89	QPR	2	0
1989–90	QPR	1	0
1990–91	QPR	3	0
1991–92	QPR	0	0
1991–92	Torquay U (loan)	11	0
1992–93	QPR	0	0
1992–93	Torquay U (loan)	5	0
1993–94	QPR	0	0
1993–94	Fulham	23	1
1994–95	Fulham	27	0
1995–96	Fulham	43	0
1996–97	Fulham	26	0
1997–98	Fulham	26	0
1998–99	Torquay U	40	0
Total:		**207**	**1**

HESKEY, Emile — Forward

H: 6 2 W: 13 12 b.Leicester 11-1-78

Source: Trainee. *Honours:* England Youth, Under-21, B, 2 full caps.

1994–95	Leicester C	1	0
1995–96	Leicester C	30	7
1996–97	Leicester C	35	10
1997–98	Leicester C	35	10
1998–99	Leicester C	30	6
Total:		**131**	**33**

HESSENTHALER, Andy — Midfield

H: 5 7 W: 11 05 b.Gravesend 17-6-65

Source: Dartford, Redbridge Forest.

1991–92	Watford	35	1
1992–93	Watford	45	3
1993–94	Watford	42	5
1994–95	Watford	43	2
1995–96	Watford	30	0
1996–97	Gillingham	38	2
1997–98	Gillingham	42	0
1998–99	Gillingham	39	7
Total:		**314**	**20**

HESSEY, Sean — Defender

H: 6 0 W: 12 03 b.Liverpool 19-9-78

Source: Liverpool Trainee.

1997–98	Wigan Ath	0	0
1997–98	Leeds U	0	0
1997–98	Huddersfield T	1	0
1998–99	Huddersfield T	10	0
Total:		**11**	**0**

HEUVEL, Arafath — Midfield

H: 6 0 W: 12 00 b.Amsterdam 13-10-75

1998–99	Colchester U	0	0

HEWITT, Jamie — Midfield

H: 5 10 W: 10 08 b.Chesterfield 17-5-68

Source: School.

1984–85	Chesterfield	0	0
1985–86	Chesterfield	17	0
1986–87	Chesterfield	42	2
1987–88	Chesterfield	28	2
1988–89	Chesterfield	40	1
1989–90	Chesterfield	42	6
1990–91	Chesterfield	43	0
1991–92	Chesterfield	37	3
1992–93	Doncaster R	27	0
1993–94	Doncaster R	6	0
1993–94	Chesterfield	29	3
1994–95	Chesterfield	38	3
1995–96	Chesterfield	28	2
1996–97	Chesterfield	37	1
1997–98	Chesterfield	44	1
1998–99	Chesterfield	40	2
Total:		**498**	**26**

HEWLETT, Matthew — Midfield

H: 6 2 W: 12 12 b.Bristol 25-2-76

Source: Trainee. *Honours:* England Youth.

1993–94	Bristol C	12	0
1994–95	Bristol C	1	0
1995–96	Bristol C	27	2
1996–97	Bristol C	36	2
1997–98	Bristol C	34	4
1998–99	Bristol C	10	1
1998–99	Burnley (loan)	2	0
Total:		**122**	**9**

HEY, Tony — Midfield

H: 5 9 W: 11 07 b.Berlin 19-9-70

1996–97	Fortuna Cologne	32	9
1997–98	Birmingham C	9	0
1998–99	Birmingham C	0	0
Total:		**41**	**9**

HEYWOOD, Matthew — Defender

H: 6 3 W: 14 00 b.Chatham 26-8-79

Source: Trainee.

1998–99	Burnley	13	0
Total:		**13**	**0**

HIBBERT, Anthony — Midfield

H: 5 8 W: 11 01 b.Liverpool 20-2-81

Source: Trainee.

1998–99	Everton	0	0

HIBBINS, John — Midfield

H: 6 2 W: 12 09 b.Sheffield 17-11-79

Source: Trainee.

1998–99	Sheffield W	0	0

HIBBURT, James — Defender

H: 6 0 W: 12 08 b.Ashford 30-10-79

Source: Trainee. *Honours:* England Schools.

1996–97	Crystal Palace	0	0
1997–98	Crystal Palace	0	0
1998–99	Crystal Palace	2	0
Total:		**2**	**0**

HICKS, Graham — Defender

b.Oldham 17-2-81

Source: Trainee.

1998–99	Rochdale	1	0
Total:		**1**	**0**

HICKS, Mark — Forward

b.Belfast 24-7-81

1998–99	Millwall	1	0
Total:		**1**	**0**

HICKS, Stuart — Defender

H: 6 1 W: 13 03 b.Peterborough 30-5-67

Source: Peterborough U Apprentice, Wisbech T.

1987–88	Colchester U	7	0
1988–89	Colchester U	37	0
1989–90	Colchester U	20	0
1990–91	Scunthorpe U	46	1
1991–92	Scunthorpe U	21	0
1992–93	Doncaster R	36	0
1993–94	Doncaster R	0	0
1993–94	Huddersfield T	22	1
1993–94	Preston NE	4	0
1994–95	Preston NE	8	0
1994–95	Scarborough	6	0
1995–96	Scarborough	41	1
1996–97	Scarborough	38	1
1997–98	Leyton Orient	35	1
1998–99	Leyton Orient	29	0
Total:		**350**	**5**

HIDEN, Martin — Defender

H: 6 1 W: 12 00 b.Stainz 11-3-73

Honours: Austria 6 full caps, 1 goal.

1992–93	Sturm Graz	20	1
1993–94	Sturm Graz	33	4
1994–95	Salzburg	27	1
1995–96	Salzburg	31	1
1996–97	Sturm Graz	28	3
1997–98	Rapid Vienna	20	0
1997–98	Leeds U	11	0
1998–99	Leeds U	14	0
Total:		**184**	**10**

HIGGINBOTHAM, Danny — Defender

H: 6 1 W: 12 03 b.Manchester 29-12-78

Source: Trainee.

1997–98	Manchester U	1	0
1998–99	Manchester U	0	0
Total:		**1**	**0**

HIGGINS, Alex — Midfield

H: 5 9 W: 10 12 b.Sheffield 22-7-81

Source: Trainee. *Honours:* England Schools.

1998–99	Sheffield W	0	0

HIGGINS, Paul — Defender

H: 5 7 W: 10 02 b.Ilkeston 6-1-81

Source: Trainee.

1997–98	Nottingham F	0	0
1998–99	Nottingham F	0	0

HIGNETT, Craig — Forward

H: 5 9 W: 11 03 b.Whiston 12-1-70

Source: Liverpool Trainee.

1987–88	Crewe Alex	0	0
1988–89	Crewe Alex	1	0
1989–90	Crewe Alex	35	8
1990–91	Crewe Alex	38	13
1991–92	Crewe Alex	33	13
1992–93	Crewe Alex	14	8
1992–93	Middlesbrough	21	4
1993–94	Middlesbrough	29	5
1994–95	Middlesbrough	26	8
1995–96	Middlesbrough	22	5
1996–97	Middlesbrough	22	4
1997–98	Middlesbrough	36	7
1998–99	Aberdeen	13	2
1998–99	Barnsley	24	9
Total:		**314**	**86**

HILEY, Scott — Defender

H: 5 9 W: 11 12 b.Plymouth 27-9-68

Source: Trainee.

1986–87	Exeter C	0	0
1987–88	Exeter C	15	1
1988–89	Exeter C	37	5
1989–90	Exeter C	46	0
1990–91	Exeter C	46	2
1991–92	Exeter C	33	1
1992–93	Exeter C	33	3
1992–93	Birmingham C	7	0
1993–94	Birmingham C	28	0
1994–95	Birmingham C	9	0
1995–96	Birmingham C	5	0
1995–96	Manchester C	6	0
1996–97	Manchester C	3	0
1997–98	Manchester C	0	0
1998–99	Southampton	29	0
Total:		**297**	**12**

HILL, Clint — Defender

H: 6 0 W: 11 06 b.Liverpool 19-10-78

Source: Trainee.

1997–98	Tranmere R	14	0
1998–99	Tranmere R	33	4
Total:		**47**	**4**

HILL, Colin — Defender

H: 6 0 W: 12 11 b.Uxbridge 12-11-63

Source: Apprentice. *Honours:* Northern Ireland 27 full caps, 1 goal.

1981–82	Arsenal	0	0
1982–83	Arsenal	7	0
1983–84	Arsenal	37	1
1984–85	Arsenal	2	0
1985–86	Arsenal	0	0
1985–86	Brighton & HA (loan)	0	0
From Maritimo			
1987–88	Colchester U	25	0
1988–89	Colchester U	44	0
1989–90	Sheffield U	43	0
1990–91	Sheffield U	24	0
1991–92	Sheffield U	15	1
1991–92	Leicester C (loan)	10	0
1992–93	Leicester C	46	0
1993–94	Leicester C	31	0
1994–95	Leicester C	24	0
1995–96	Leicester C	27	0
1996–97	Leicester C	7	0
1997	Trelleborg	11	0
1997–98	Northampton T	27	0
1998–99	Northampton T	27	0
Total:		**407**	**2**

HILL, Danny — Midfield

H: 5 8 W: 11 08 b.Edmonton 1-10-74

Source: Trainee. *Honours:* England Under-21.

1992–93	Tottenham H	4	0
1993–94	Tottenham H	3	0
1994–95	Tottenham H	3	0
1995–96	Tottenham H	0	0
1995–96	Birmingham C (loan)	5	0
1995–96	Watford (loan)	1	0
1996–97	Tottenham H	0	0
1997–98	Tottenham H	0	0
1997–98	Cardiff C (loan)	7	0
1998–99	Oxford U	9	0
1998–99	Cardiff C	26	2
Total:		**58**	**2**

HILL, Keith — Defender

H: 6 1 W: 12 07 b.Bolton 17-5-69

Source: Apprentice.

1986–87	Blackburn R	0	0
1987–88	Blackburn R	1	0
1988–89	Blackburn R	15	1
1989–90	Blackburn R	25	0
1990–91	Blackburn R	22	2
1991–92	Blackburn R	32	0
1992–93	Blackburn R	1	0
1992–93	Plymouth Arg	36	0
1993–94	Plymouth Arg	29	1
1994–95	Plymouth Arg	34	1
1995–96	Plymouth Arg	24	0
1996–97	Rochdale	43	3
1997–98	Rochdale	37	2
1998–99	Rochdale	33	1
Total:		**332**	**11**

HILL, Kevin — Midfield

H: 5 8 W: 10 03 b.Exeter 6-3-76

Source: Torrington.

1997–98	Torquay U	37	7
1998–99	Torquay U	35	5
Total:		**72**	**12**

HILL, Matthew — Defender

b.Bristol 26-3-81

Source: Trainee.

1998–99	Bristol C	3	0
Total:		**3**	**0**

HILLIER, David — Midfield

H: 5 10 W: 12 07 b.Blackheath 19-12-69

Source: Trainee. *Honours:* England Under-21.

1987–88	Arsenal	0	0
1988–89	Arsenal	0	0
1989–90	Arsenal	0	0
1990–91	Arsenal	16	0
1991–92	Arsenal	27	1
1992–93	Arsenal	30	1
1993–94	Arsenal	15	0
1994–95	Arsenal	9	0
1995–96	Arsenal	5	0
1996–97	Arsenal	2	0
1996–97	Portsmouth	21	2
1997–98	Portsmouth	30	2
1998–99	Portsmouth	16	0
1998–99	Bristol R	13	0
Total:		**184**	**6**

HILLIER, Ian — Defender

H: 5 11 W: 11 05 b.Neath 26-12-79

Source: Trainee. *Honours:* Wales Schools, Youth.

1998–99	Tottenham H	0	0

HILLS, John — Defender

H: 5 8 W: 10 08 b.St Annes-on-Sea 21-4-78

Source: Trainee.

1995–96	Blackpool	0	0
1995–96	Everton	0	0
1996–97	Everton	3	0
1996–97	Swansea C (loan)	11	0
1997–98	Everton	0	0

1997–98	Swansea C (loan)	7	1
1997–98	Blackpool	19	1
1998–99	Blackpool	28	1
Total:		**68**	**3**

HIMSWORTH, Gary — Midfield

H: 5 8 W: 11 00 b.York 19-12-69

Source: Trainee.

1987–88	York C	31	2
1988–89	York C	32	2
1989–90	York C	23	4
1990–91	York C	2	0
1990–91	Scarborough	23	1
1991–92	Scarborough	36	4
1992–93	Scarborough	33	1
1993–94	Darlington	28	3
1994–95	Darlington	38	2
1995–96	Darlington	28	3
1995–96	York C	8	1
1996–97	York C	33	2
1997–98	York C	15	0
1998–99	York C	13	0
1998–99	Darlington	14	1
Total:		**357**	**26**

HINCHCLIFFE, Andy — Defender

H: 5 10 W: 12 10 b.Manchester 5-2-69

Source: Apprentice. *Honours:* England Youth, Under-21, 7 full caps.

1986–87	Manchester C	0	0
1987–88	Manchester C	42	1
1988–89	Manchester C	39	5
1989–90	Manchester C	31	2
1990–91	Everton	21	1
1991–92	Everton	18	0
1992–93	Everton	25	1
1993–94	Everton	26	0
1994–95	Everton	29	2
1995–96	Everton	28	2
1996–97	Everton	18	1
1997–98	Everton	17	0
1997–98	Sheffield W	15	1
1998–99	Sheffield W	32	3
Total:		**341**	**19**

HINDS, Leigh — Forward

H: 5 8 W: 10 10 b.Beckenham 17-8-78

Source: Trainee.

1996–97	Wimbledon	0	0
1997–98	Wimbledon	0	0
1998–99	Wimbledon	0	0

HINDS, Richard — Defender

H: 6 2 W: 12 00 b.Sheffield 22-8-80

Source: Schoolboy.

1998–99	Tranmere R	2	0
Total:		**2**	**0**

HINER, Daniel — Midfield

b.Sheffield 4-10-78

Source: Trainee.

1997–98	Sheffield W	0	0
1998–99	Sheffield W	0	0

HINSHELWOOD, Danny — Defender

H: 5 9 W: 11 00 b.Bromley 12-2-75

Source: Trainee. *Honours:* England Youth.

1992–93	Nottingham F	0	0
1993–94	Nottingham F	0	0
1994–95	Nottingham F	0	0
1995–96	Nottingham F	0	0
1995–96	Portsmouth	5	0
1996–97	Portsmouth	0	0
1996–97	Torquay U (loan)	9	0
1997–98	Portsmouth	0	0
1998–99	Portsmouth	0	0
1998–99	Brighton & HA	4	0
Total:		**18**	**0**

HIRST, David — Forward

H: 5 11 W: 14 10 b.Cudworth 7-12-67

Source: Apprentice. *Honours:* England Youth, Under-21, B, 3 full caps, 1 goal.

1985–86	Barnsley	28	9
1986–87	Sheffield W	21	6
1987–88	Sheffield W	24	3
1988–89	Sheffield W	32	7
1989–90	Sheffield W	38	14
1990–91	Sheffield W	41	24
1991–92	Sheffield W	33	18
1992–93	Sheffield W	22	11
1993–94	Sheffield W	7	1
1994–95	Sheffield W	15	3
1995–96	Sheffield W	30	13
1996–97	Sheffield W	25	6
1997–98	Sheffield W	6	0
1997–98	Southampton	28	9
1998–99	Southampton	2	0
Total:		**352**	**124**

HISLOP, Shaka — Goalkeeper

H: 6 4 W: 14 04 b.Hackney 22-2-69

Source: Howard Univ, USA. *Honours:* England Under-21.

1992–93	Reading	12	0
1993–94	Reading	46	0
1994–95	Reading	46	0
1995–96	Newcastle U	24	0
1996–97	Newcastle U	16	0
1997–98	Newcastle U	13	0
1998–99	West Ham U	37	0
Total:		**194**	**0**

HITCHCOCK, Kevin — Goalkeeper

H: 6 1 W: 13 00 b.Custom House 5-10-62

Source: Barking.

1983–84	Nottingham F	0	0
1983–84	Mansfield T (loan)	14	0
1984–85	Mansfield T	43	0
1985–86	Mansfield T	46	0
1986–87	Mansfield T	46	0
1987–88	Mansfield T	33	0
1987–88	Chelsea	8	0
1988–89	Chelsea	3	0
1989–90	Chelsea	0	0
1990–91	Chelsea	3	0
1990–91	Northampton T (loan)	17	0
1991–92	Chelsea	21	0
1992–93	Chelsea	20	0
1992–93	West Ham U (loan)	0	0
1993–94	Chelsea	2	0
1994–95	Chelsea	12	0
1995–96	Chelsea	12	0
1996–97	Chelsea	12	0
1997–98	Chelsea	0	0
1998–99	Chelsea	3	0
Total:		**295**	**0**

HITCHEN, Steve — Defender

H: 5 8 W: 11 07 b.Salford 28-11-76

Source: Trainee.

1995–96	Blackburn R	0	0
1996–97	Blackburn R	0	0
1997–98	Macclesfield T	2	0
1998–99	Macclesfield T	35	0
Total:		**37**	**0**

HJELDE, Jon Olav — Defender

H: 6 2 W: 13 05 b.Levanger 30-7-72

1994	Rosenborg	1	0
1995	Rosenborg	7	0
1996	Rosenborg	16	1
1997	Rosenborg	3	0
1997–98	Nottingham F	28	1
1998–99	Nottingham F	17	1
Total:		**72**	**3**

HOBSON, Gary — Defender

H: 6 2 W: 13 02 b.North Ferriby 12-11-72

Source: Trainee.

1990–91	Hull C	4	0
1991–92	Hull C	16	0
1992–93	Hull C	21	0
1993–94	Hull C	36	0
1994–95	Hull C	36	0
1995–96	Hull C	29	0
1995–96	Brighton & HA	9	0
1996–97	Brighton & HA	37	1
1997–98	Brighton & HA	33	0
1998–99	Brighton & HA	13	0
Total:		**234**	**1**

HOCKING, Matthew — Defender

H: 5 11 W: 12 00 b.Boston 30-1-78

Source: Trainee.

1995–96	Sheffield U	0	0
1996–97	Sheffield U	0	0
1997–98	Sheffield U	0	0
1997–98	Hull C	31	1
1998–99	Hull C	26	1
1998–99	York C (loan)	6	0
Total:		**63**	**2**

HOCKLEY, David — Midfield

H: 5 11 W: 11 05 b.Gillingham 23-2-81

Source: Trainee.

1998–99	Charlton Ath	0	0

HOCKTON, Danny — Forward

H: 6 0 W: 11 11 b.Barking 7-2-79

Source: Trainee.

1996–97	Millwall	2	0
1997–98	Millwall	26	3
1998–99	Millwall	8	1
Total:		**36**	**4**

HODGE, John — Forward

H: 5 7 W: 11 06 b.Skelmersdale 1-4-69

Source: Exmouth.

1991–92	Exeter C	23	1
1992–93	Exeter C	42	9
1993–94	Swansea C	27	2
1994–95	Swansea C	44	7
1995–96	Swansea C	41	1
1996–97	Swansea C	0	0

1996–97	Walsall	37	4
1997–98	Walsall	39	8
1998–99	Gillingham	34	1
Total:		**287**	**33**

HODGES, Danny — Defender

H: 6 0 W: 12 07 b.Greenwich 14-9-76

Source: Trainee. *Honours:* England Youth.

1995–96	Wimbledon	0	0
1996–97	Wimbledon	0	0
1997–98	Wimbledon	0	0
1998–99	Wimbledon	0	0

HODGES, Glyn — Midfield

H: 6 0 W: 12 10 b.Streatham 30-4-63

Source: Apprentice. *Honours:* Wales Youth, Under-21, B, 18 full caps.

1980–81	Wimbledon	30	5
1981–82	Wimbledon	34	2
1982–83	Wimbledon	37	9
1983–84	Wimbledon	42	15
1984–85	Wimbledon	22	3
1985–86	Wimbledon	30	6
1986–87	Wimbledon	37	9
1987–88	Newcastle U	7	0
1987–88	Watford	24	3
1988–89	Watford	27	5
1989–90	Watford	35	7
1990–91	Crystal Palace	7	0
1990–91	Sheffield U	12	4
1991–92	Sheffield U	26	2
1992–93	Sheffield U	31	4
1993–94	Sheffield U	31	2
1994–95	Sheffield U	25	4
1995–96	Sheffield U	22	3
1995–96	Derby Co	9	0
From Sin Tao			
1996–97	Derby Co	0	0
From Sin Tao			
1997–98	Hull C	18	4
1997–98	Nottingham F	0	0
1998–99	Nottingham F	5	0
1998–99	Scarborough	1	0
Total:		**512**	**87**

HODGES, John — Goalkeeper

H: 6 0 W: 11 05 b.Leicester 22-1-80

Source: Trainee.

1998–99	Leicester C	0	0

HODGES, Kevin — Midfield

H: 5 8 W: 11 02 b.Bridport 12-6-60

Source: Apprentice.

1977–78	Plymouth Arg	0	0
1978–79	Plymouth Arg	12	0
1979–80	Plymouth Arg	44	5
1980–81	Plymouth Arg	41	5
1981–82	Plymouth Arg	46	11
1982–83	Plymouth Arg	46	11
1983–84	Plymouth Arg	43	4
1984–85	Plymouth Arg	45	10
1985–86	Plymouth Arg	46	16
1986–87	Plymouth Arg	35	5
1987–88	Plymouth Arg	37	6
1988–89	Plymouth Arg	31	1
1989–90	Plymouth Arg	44	4
1990–91	Plymouth Arg	42	3
1991–92	Plymouth Arg	14	0
1991–92	Torquay U (loan)	3	0
1992–93	Plymouth Arg	4	0
1992–93	Torquay U	8	1
1993–94	Torquay U	29	2
1994–95	Torquay U	28	1
1995–96	Torquay U	2	0
1996–97	Torquay U	1	0
1997–98	Torquay U	0	0
1998–99	Torquay U	0	0
Total:		**601**	**85**

HODGES, Lee — Forward

H: 6 0 W: 12 00 b.Epping 4-9-73

Source: Trainee.

1991–92	Tottenham H	0	0
1992–93	Tottenham H	4	0
1992–93	Plymouth Arg (loan)	7	2
1993–94	Tottenham H	0	0
1993–94	Wycombe W (loan)	4	0
1994–95	Barnet	34	4
1995–96	Barnet	40	17
1996–97	Barnet	31	5
1997–98	Reading	24	6
1998–99	Reading	1	0
Total:		**145**	**34**

HODGES, Lee — Midfield

H: 5 5 W: 10 02 b.Newham 2-3-78

Source: Trainee. *Honours:* England Schools.

1994–95	West Ham U	0	0
1995–96	West Ham U	0	0
1996–97	West Ham U	0	0
1996–97	Exeter C (loan)	17	0
1996–97	Leyton Orient (loan)	3	0
1997–98	West Ham U	2	0
1997–98	Plymouth Arg (loan)	9	0
1998–99	West Ham U	1	0

1998–99	Ipswich T (loan)	4	0
1998–99	Southend U (loan)	10	1
Total:		**46**	**1**

HODGSON, Ben — Forward

H: 6 2 W: 13 08 b.Nottingham 25-1-76

Source: Yeading.

1997–98	Wycombe W	0	0
1998–99	Wycombe W	0	0

HODGSON, Dougie — Defender

H: 6 2 W: 13 10 b.Frankston 27-2-69

Source: Heidelberg.

1994–95	Sheffield U	1	0
1995–96	Sheffield U	16	0
1995–96	Plymouth Arg (loan)	5	0
1996–97	Sheffield U	13	0
1996–97	Burnley (loan)	1	0
1996–97	Oldham Ath	12	0
1997–98	Oldham Ath	28	4
1998–99	Oldham Ath	1	0
1998–99	Northampton T (loan)	8	1
Total:		**85**	**5**

HODGSON, Richard — Forward

H: 5 10 W: 11 06 b.Sunderland 1-10-79

Source: Trainee.

1996–97	Nottingham F	0	0
1997–98	Nottingham F	0	0
1998–99	Nottingham F	0	0

HODGSON, Steven — Goalkeeper

H: 5 11 W: 11 00 b.Macclesfield 23-12-81

Source: Scholarship. *Honours:* England Youth.

1998–99	Manchester C	0	0

HODSON, Matthew — Midfield

b.Derby 20-9-79

Source: Trainee.

1997–98	Wycombe W	0	0
1998–99	Colchester U	0	0

HOGGETH, Gary — Goalkeeper

H: 6 0 W: 11 07 b.South Shields 7-10-79

Source: Trainee.

1997–98	Doncaster R	8	0
1998–99	Bury	0	0
Total:		**8**	**0**

HOLBROOK, Adam — Midfield

H: 5 9 W: 11 04 b.Newport (IW) 17-10-80

Source: Trainee.

1998–99	Portsmouth	0	0

HOLCROFT, Peter — Midfield

H: 5 9 W: 11 07 b.Liverpool 3-1-76

Source: Trainee.

1994–95	Everton	0	0
1995–96	Everton	0	0
1996–97	Everton	0	0
1996–97	Swindon T	3	0
1997–98	Swindon T	0	0
1997–98	Exeter C (loan)	6	0
1998–99	Swindon T	0	0
Total:		**9**	**0**

HOLDEN, Dean — Defender

H: 6 0 W: 11 00 b.Salford 15-9-79

Source: Trainee. *Honours:* England Youth.

1997–98	Bolton W	0	0
1998–99	Bolton W	0	0

HOLDSWORTH, David — Defender

H: 6 1 W: 12 10 b.Walthamstow 8-11-68

Source: Trainee. *Honours:* England Youth, Under-21.

1986–87	Watford	0	0
1987–88	Watford	0	0
1988–89	Watford	33	1
1989–90	Watford	44	3
1990–91	Watford	15	2
1991–92	Watford	33	2
1992–93	Watford	39	0
1993–94	Watford	28	0
1994–95	Watford	39	1
1995–96	Watford	27	1
1996–97	Watford	0	0
1996–97	Sheffield U	37	1
1997–98	Sheffield U	40	2
1998–99	Sheffield U	16	1
1998–99	Birmingham C	8	1
Total:		**359**	**15**

HOLDSWORTH, Dean — Forward

H: 5 11 W: 11 13 b.Walthamstow 8-11-68

Source: Trainee.

1986–87	Watford	2	0
1987–88	Carlisle U (loan)	4	1
1987–88	Port Vale (loan)	6	2
1988–89	Watford	10	2
1988–89	Swansea C (loan)	5	1

1988–89	Brentford (loan)	7	1
1989–90	Watford	4	1
1989–90	Brentford	39	24
1990–91	Brentford	30	5
1991–92	Brentford	41	24
1992–93	Wimbledon	36	19
1993–94	Wimbledon	42	17
1994–95	Wimbledon	28	7
1995–96	Wimbledon	33	10
1996–97	Wimbledon	25	5
1997–98	Wimbledon	5	0
1997–98	Bolton W	20	3
1998–99	Bolton W	32	12
Total:		**369**	**134**

HOLLAND, Chris — Midfield

H: 5 9 W: 11 05 b.Whalley 11-9-76

Source: Trainee. *Honours:* England Youth, Under-21.

1993–94	Preston NE	1	0
1993–94	Newcastle U	3	0
1994–95	Newcastle U	0	0
1995–96	Newcastle U	0	0
1996–97	Newcastle U	0	0
1996–97	Birmingham C	32	0
1997–98	Birmingham C	10	0
1998–99	Birmingham C	14	0
Total:		**60**	**0**

HOLLAND, Matt — Midfield

H: 5 10 W: 11 10 b.Bury 11-4-74

Source: Trainee.

1992–93	West Ham U	0	0
1993–94	West Ham U	0	0
1994–95	West Ham U	0	0
1994–95	Bournemouth	16	1
1995–96	Bournemouth	43	10
1996–97	Bournemouth	45	7
1997–98	Ipswich T	46	10
1998–99	Ipswich T	46	5
Total:		**196**	**33**

HOLLAND, Paul — Midfield

H: 5 11 W: 12 10 b.Lincoln 8-7-73

Source: School. *Honours:* England Schools, Under-21.

1990–91	Mansfield T	1	0
1991–92	Mansfield T	38	6
1992–93	Mansfield T	39	3
1993–94	Mansfield T	38	7
1994–95	Mansfield T	33	9
1995–96	Sheffield U	18	1
1995–96	Chesterfield	17	2
1996–97	Chesterfield	25	3
1997–98	Chesterfield	35	3
1998–99	Chesterfield	33	3
Total:		**277**	**37**

HOLLIGAN, Gavin — Forward

H: 6 0 W: 13 00 b.Lambeth 13-6-80

Source: Kingstonian.

1998–99	West Ham U	1	0
Total:		**1**	**0**

HOLLOWAY, Chris — Midfield

H: 5 10 W: 11 10 b.Swansea 5-2-80

Source: Trainee. *Honours:* Wales Under-21.

1997–98	Exeter C	6	0
1998–99	Exeter C	34	1
Total:		**40**	**1**

HOLLOWAY, Darren — Defender

H: 6 0 W: 12 04 b.Bishop Auckland 3-10-77

Source: Trainee. *Honours:* England Under-21.

1995–96	Sunderland	0	0
1996–97	Sunderland	0	0
1997–98	Sunderland	32	0
1997–98	Carlisle U (loan)	5	0
1998–99	Sunderland	6	0
Total:		**43**	**0**

HOLLOWAY, Ian — Midfield

H: 5 7 W: 10 10 b.Kingswood 12-3-63

Source: Apprentice.

1980–81	Bristol R	1	0
1981–82	Bristol R	1	0
1982–83	Bristol R	31	7
1983–84	Bristol R	36	1
1984–85	Bristol R	42	6
1985–86	Wimbledon	19	2
1985–86	Brentford (loan)	13	2
1986–87	Brentford	16	0
1986–87	Torquay U (loan)	5	0
1987–88	Brentford	1	0
1987–88	Bristol R	43	5
1988–89	Bristol R	44	6
1989–90	Bristol R	46	8
1990–91	Bristol R	46	7
1991–92	QPR	40	0
1992–93	QPR	24	2
1993–94	QPR	25	0
1994–95	QPR	31	1
1995–96	QPR	27	1
1996–97	Bristol R	31	1
1997–98	Bristol R	39	0
1998–99	Bristol R	37	0
Total:		**598**	**49**

HOLLUND, Martin — Goalkeeper

H: 6 0 W: 12 05 b.Stord 11-8-74

1994	Brann	3	0
1995	Brann	15	0
1996	Brann	0	0
1997	Brann	6	0
1997–98	Hartlepool U	28	0
1998–99	Hartlepool U	41	0
Total:		**93**	**0**

HOLMES, Derek — Midfield

H: 6 0 W: 12 02 b.Lanark 18-10-78

Source: Royal Albert.

1995–96	Hearts	0	0
1996–97	Hearts	1	0
1997–98	Hearts	1	1
1997–98	Cowdenbeath	13	5
1998–99	Hearts	6	0
Total:		**21**	**6**

HOLMES, Matty — Midfield

H: 5 7 W: 11 00 b.Luton 1-8-69

Source: Trainee.

1988–89	Bournemouth	4	1
1988–89	Cardiff C (loan)	1	0
1989–90	Bournemouth	22	2
1990–91	Bournemouth	42	2
1991–92	Bournemouth	46	3
1992–93	West Ham U	18	0
1993–94	West Ham U	34	3
1994–95	West Ham U	24	1
1995–96	Blackburn R	9	1
1996–97	Blackburn R	0	0
1997–98	Charlton Ath	16	1
1998–99	Charlton Ath	0	0
Total:		**216**	**14**

HOLMES, Paul — Defender

H: 5 10 W: 11 00 b.Stocksbridge 18-2-68

Source: Apprentice.

1985–86	Doncaster R	5	1
1986–87	Doncaster R	16	0
1987–88	Doncaster R	26	0
1988–89	Torquay U	25	0
1989–90	Torquay U	44	2
1990–91	Torquay U	33	1
1991–92	Torquay U	36	1
1992–93	Birmingham C	12	0
1992–93	Everton	4	0
1993–94	Everton	15	0
1994–95	Everton	1	0
1995–96	Everton	1	0
1995–96	WBA	18	0
1996–97	WBA	38	1
1997–98	WBA	30	0
1998–99	WBA	17	0
Total:		**321**	**6**

HOLMES, Peter — Midfield

H: 5 11 W: 10 05 b.Bishop Auckland 18-11-80

Source: Trainee. *Honours:* England Schools.

1997–98	Sheffield W	0	0
1998–99	Sheffield W	0	0

HOLMES, Richard — Defender

b.Grantham 7-11-80

Source: Trainee.

1998–99	Notts Co	8	0
Total:		**8**	**0**

HOLMES, Shaun — Defender

H: 5 9 W: 10 07 b.Derry 27-12-80

Source: Trainee.

1997–98	Manchester C	0	0
1998–99	Manchester C	0	0

HOLMES, Steve — Defender

H: 6 2 W: 13 00 b.Middlesbrough 13-1-71

Source: Guisborough T.

1993–94	Preston NE	0	0
1994–95	Preston NE	5	1
1994–95	Hartlepool U (loan)	5	2
From Guisborough T			
1995–96	Preston NE	8	0
1995–96	Lincoln C	23	2
1996–97	Lincoln C	28	4
1997–98	Lincoln C	46	4
1998–99	Lincoln C	37	6
Total:		**152**	**19**

HOLMES, Tommy — Defender

H: 6 0 W: 12 06 b.Bevington 1-9-79

Source: Trainee.

1997–98	Tranmere R	0	0
1998–99	Tranmere R	0	0

HOLSGROVE, Lee — Defender

H: 6 1 W: 12 06 b.Wendover 13-12-79

Source: Trainee.

1996–97	Millwall	0	0
1997–98	Millwall	0	0
1997–98	Wycombe W	0	0
1998–99	Wycombe W	1	0
Total:		**1**	**0**

HOLSGROVE, Paul
Midfield

H: 6 2 W: 13 03 b.Wellington 26-8-69

Source: Trainee.

1986–87	Aldershot	0	0
1987–88	Aldershot	2	0
1988–89	Aldershot	1	0
1988–89	Wimbledon (loan)	0	0
1989–90	Aldershot	0	0
1989–90	WBA (loan)	0	0
From Wokingham T			
1990–91	Luton T	1	0
1991–92	Luton T	1	0
From Heracles			
1992–93	Millwall	11	0
1993–94	Millwall	0	0
1994–95	Reading	24	3
1995–96	Reading	30	1
1996–97	Reading	14	2
1997–98	Reading	2	0
1997–98	Grimsby T (loan)	10	0
1997–98	Crewe Alex	8	1
1997–98	Stoke C	12	1
1998–99	Stoke C	0	0
1998–99	Brighton & HA	0	0
1998–99	Hibernian	17	1
Total:		**133**	**9**

HOLSTER, Marco
Midfield

H: 5 6 W: 10 11 b.Weesp 4-12-71

Source: BFC, Huizen.

1993–94	AZ	33	9
1994–95	AZ	32	5
1995–96	AZ	25	3
1996–97	Heracles	28	6
1997–98	Heracles*	0	0
1998–99	Ipswich T	10	0
Total:		**128**	**23**

HOLT, Andy
Defender

H: 6 1 W: 11 02 b.Manchester 21-5-78

Source: Trainee.

1996–97	Oldham Ath	1	0
1997–98	Oldham Ath	14	1
1998–99	Oldham Ath	43	5
Total:		**58**	**6**

HOLT, Gary
Midfield

H: 6 1 W: 11 11 b.Irvine 9-3-73

Source: Celtic.

1994–95	Stoke C	0	0
1995–96	Kilmarnock	26	0
1996–97	Kilmarnock	12	1
1997–98	Kilmarnock	27	2
1998–99	Kilmarnock	33	3
Total:		**98**	**6**

HOLT, Michael
Forward

H: 5 10 W: 11 03 b.Barnoldswick 28-7-77

Source: Trainee.

1995–96	Blackburn R	0	0
1996–97	Preston NE	19	3
1997–98	Preston NE	14	2
1998–99	Preston NE	3	0
1998–99	Macclesfield T (loan)	4	1
1998–99	Rochdale	24	7
Total:		**64**	**13**

HOOPER, Dean
Defender

H: 5 10 W: 12 12 b.Harefield 13-4-71

Source: Hayes.

1994–95	Swindon T	4	0
From Hayes			
1995–96	Swindon T	0	0
1995–96	Peterborough U (loan)	4	0
1996–97	Swindon T	0	0
1997–98	Swindon T	0	0
From Kingstonian.			
1998–99	Peterborough U	38	2
Total:		**46**	**2**

HOPE, Chris
Defender

H: 6 1 W: 12 08 b.Sheffield 14-11-73

Source: Darlington.

1991–92	Nottingham F	0	0
1992–93	Nottingham F	0	0
1993–94	Scunthorpe U	41	0
1994–95	Scunthorpe U	24	0
1995–96	Scunthorpe U	40	3
1996–97	Scunthorpe U	46	3
1997–98	Scunthorpe U	46	5
1998–99	Scunthorpe U	46	5
Total:		**243**	**16**

HOPE, Richard
Defender

H: 6 2 W: 12 06 b.Stockton 22-6-78

Source: Trainee.

1995–96	Blackburn R	0	0
1996–97	Blackburn R	0	0
1996–97	Darlington	20	0
1997–98	Darlington	35	1
1998–99	Darlington	8	0
1998–99	Northampton T	19	0
Total:		**82**	**1**

HOPKIN, David — Midfield

H: 6 1 W: 13 13 b.Greenock 21-8-70

Source: Pt Glasgow R BC. *Honours:* Scotland B, 5 full caps, 2 goals.

1989–90	Morton	8	0
1990–91	Morton	10	0
1991–92	Morton	0	0
1992–93	Chelsea	4	0
1993–94	Chelsea	21	0
1994–95	Chelsea	15	1
1995–96	Crystal Palace	42	8
1996–97	Crystal Palace	41	13
1997–98	Leeds U	25	1
1998–99	Leeds U	34	4
Total:		**200**	**27**

HOPKINS, Steve — Defender

H: 5 10 W: 11 04 b.St Asaph 12-4-80

Honours: Wales Under-21.

1998–99	Wrexham	0	0

HOPPER, Tony — Midfield

H: 5 11 W: 12 08 b.Carlisle 31-5-76

Source: Trainee.

1992–93	Carlisle U	1	0
1993–94	Carlisle U	0	0
1994–95	Carlisle U	5	0
1995–96	Carlisle U	5	0
1996–97	Carlisle U	20	1
1997–98	Carlisle U	19	0
1998–99	Carlisle U	23	0
Total:		**73**	**1**

HORLAVILLE, Christopher — Forward

b.Rouen 1-3-69

1991–92	Rouen	32	15
1992–93	Rouen	29	13
1993–94	Rouen	41	14
1994–95	Cannes	36	11
1995–96	Cannes	35	12
1996–97	Guincamp	13	0
1997–98	Le Havre	26	3
1998–99	Port Vale	2	0
Total:		**214**	**68**

HORLOCK, Kevin — Midfield

H: 6 0 W: 12 00 b.Erith 1-11-72

Source: Trainee. *Honours:* Northern Ireland 17 full caps.

1991–92	West Ham U	0	0
1992–93	West Ham U	0	0
1992–93	Swindon T	14	1
1993–94	Swindon T	38	0
1994–95	Swindon T	38	1
1995–96	Swindon T	45	12
1996–97	Swindon T	28	8
1996–97	Manchester C	18	4
1997–98	Manchester C	25	5
1998–99	Manchester C	37	9
Total:		**243**	**40**

HORNE, Barry — Midfield

H: 5 9 W: 12 07 b.St Asaph 18-5-62

Source: Rhyl. *Honours:* Wales 59 full caps, 2 goals.

1984–85	Wrexham	44	6
1985–86	Wrexham	46	3
1986–87	Wrexham	46	8
1987–88	Portsmouth	39	3
1988–89	Portsmouth	31	4
1988–89	Southampton	11	0
1989–90	Southampton	29	4
1990–91	Southampton	38	1
1991–92	Southampton	34	1
1992–93	Everton	34	1
1993–94	Everton	32	1
1994–95	Everton	31	0
1995–96	Everton	26	1
1996–97	Birmingham C	33	0
1997–98	Birmingham C	0	0
1997–98	Huddersfield T	30	0
1998–99	Huddersfield T	20	1
Total:		**524**	**34**

HORSFIELD, Geoff — Forward

H: 6 0 W: 11 07 b.Barnsley 1-11-73

1992–93	Scarborough	6	1
1993–94	Scarborough	6	0
From Witton Alb			
1998–99	Halifax T	10	7
1998–99	Fulham	28	15
Total:		**50**	**23**

HOTTE, Mark — Midfield

H: 5 11 W: 11 00 b.Bradford 27-9-78

Source: Trainee.

1997–98	Oldham Ath	1	0
1998–99	Oldham Ath	1	0
Total:		**2**	**0**

HOUGHTON, Ray — Midfield

H: 5 7 W: 10 10 b.Glasgow 9-1-62

Source: Amateur. *Honours:* Eire 73 full caps, 6 goals.

1979–80	West Ham U	0	0

1980–81	West Ham U	0	0
1981–82	West Ham U	1	0
1982–83	Fulham	42	5
1983–84	Fulham	40	3
1984–85	Fulham	42	8
1985–86	Fulham	5	0
1985–86	Oxford U	35	4
1986–87	Oxford U	37	5
1987–88	Oxford U	11	1
1987–88	Liverpool	28	5
1988–89	Liverpool	38	7
1989–90	Liverpool	19	1
1990–91	Liverpool	32	7
1991–92	Liverpool	36	8
1992–93	Aston Villa	39	3
1993–94	Aston Villa	30	2
1994–95	Aston Villa	26	1
1994–95	Crystal Palace	10	2
1995–96	Crystal Palace	41	4
1996–97	Crystal Palace	21	1
1997–98	Reading	25	1
1998–99	Reading	18	0
Total:		**576**	**68**

HOUGHTON, Scott — Midfield

H: 5 7 W: 12 03 b.Hitchin 22-10-71

Source: Trainee. *Honours:* England Schools, Youth.

1990–91	Tottenham H	0	0
1990–91	Ipswich T (loan)	8	1
1991–92	Tottenham H	10	2
1992–93	Tottenham H	0	0
1992–93	Cambridge U (loan)	0	0
1992–93	Gillingham (loan)	3	0
1992–93	Charlton Ath (loan)	6	0
1993–94	Luton T	15	1
1994–95	Luton T	1	0
1994–95	Walsall	38	8
1995–96	Walsall	40	6
1996–97	Peterborough U	32	8
1997–98	Peterborough U	30	4
1998–99	Peterborough U	8	1
1998–99	Southend U	27	3
Total:		**218**	**34**

HOULT, Russell — Goalkeeper

H: 6 4 W: 14 07 b.Ashby 22-11-72

Source: Trainee.

1990–91	Leicester C	0	0
1991–92	Leicester C	0	0
1991–92	Lincoln C (loan)	2	0
1991–92	Blackpool (loan)	0	0
1992–93	Leicester C	10	0
1993–94	Leicester C	0	0
1993–94	Bolton W (loan)	4	0
1994–95	Leicester C	0	0
1994–95	Lincoln C (loan)	15	0
1994–95	Derby Co (loan)	15	0
1995–96	Derby Co	41	0
1996–97	Derby Co	32	0
1997–98	Derby Co	2	0
1998–99	Derby Co	23	0
Total:		**144**	**0**

HOUSHAM, Steven — Midfield

H: 5 10 W: 12 03 b.Gainsborough T 24-2-76

Source: Trainee.

1993–94	Scunthorpe U	0	0
1994–95	Scunthorpe U	4	0
1995–96	Scunthorpe U	28	0
1996–97	Scunthorpe U	34	3
1997–98	Scunthorpe U	24	1
1998–99	Scunthorpe U	16	0
Total:		**106**	**4**

HOWARD, Jonathan — Forward

H: 5 11 W: 11 07 b.Sheffield 7-10-71

Source: Trainee.

1990–91	Rotherham U	1	0
1991–92	Rotherham U	10	3
1992–93	Rotherham U	17	2
1993–94	Rotherham U	8	0
1994–95	Rotherham U	0	0
1994–95	Chesterfield	12	1
1995–96	Chesterfield	30	2
1996–97	Chesterfield	35	9
1997–98	Chesterfield	35	6
1998–99	Chesterfield	37	9
Total:		**185**	**32**

HOWARD, Mike — Defender

H: 5 9 W: 11 13 b.Birkenhead 2-12-78

Source: Tranmere R Trainee.

1997–98	Swansea C	3	0
1998–99	Swansea C	39	1
Total:		**42**	**1**

HOWARD, Steve — Forward

H: 6 2 W: 14 06 b.Durham 10-5-76

Source: Tow Law T.

1995–96	Hartlepool U	39	7
1996–97	Hartlepool U	32	8
1997–98	Hartlepool U	43	7
1998–99	Hartlepool U	28	5
1998–99	Northampton T	12	0
Total:		**154**	**27**

HOWARTH, Lee — Defender

H: 6 3 W: 13 09 b.Bolton 3-1-68

Source: Chorley.

1991–92	Peterborough U	7	0
1992–93	Peterborough U	30	0
1993–94	Peterborough U	25	0
1994–95	Mansfield T	40	2
1995–96	Mansfield T	17	0
1995–96	Barnet	19	0
1996–97	Barnet	38	1
1997–98	Barnet	45	4
1998–99	Barnet	0	0
Total:		**221**	**7**

HOWARTH, Neil — Defender

H: 6 3 W: 13 07 b.Bolton 15-11-71

Source: Trainee.

1989–90 Burnley 1 0

From Macclesfield T.

1997–98	Macclesfield T	41	3
1998–99	Macclesfield T	19	0
Total:		**61**	**3**

HOWARTH, Paul — Defender

H: 5 6 W: 10 01 b.Nottingham 21-11-80

Source: Trainee.

1997–98	Nottingham F	0	0
1998–99	Nottingham F	0	0

HOWE, Bobby — Midfield

H: 5 7 W: 10 06 b.Annitsford 6-11-73

Source: Trainee.

1991–92	Nottingham F	0	0
1992–93	Nottingham F	0	0
1993–94	Nottingham F	4	0
1994–95	Nottingham F	0	0
1995–96	Nottingham F	9	2
1996–97	Nottingham F	1	0
1996–97	Ipswich T (loan)	3	0
1997–98	Nottingham F	0	0
1997–98	Swindon T	10	0
1998–99	Swindon T	23	3
Total:		**50**	**5**

HOWE, Eddie — Defender

H: 5 9 W: 11 02 b.Amersham 29-11-77

Source: Trainee.

1995–96	Bournemouth	5	0
1996–97	Bournemouth	13	0
1997–98	Bournemouth	40	1
1998–99	Bournemouth	45	2
Total:		**103**	**3**

HOWELLS, David — Midfield

H: 6 0 W: 12 03 b.Guildford 15-12-67

Source: Trainee. *Honours:* England Youth.

1984–85	Tottenham H	0	0
1985–86	Tottenham H	1	1
1986–87	Tottenham H	1	0
1987–88	Tottenham H	11	0
1988–89	Tottenham H	27	3
1989–90	Tottenham H	34	5
1990–91	Tottenham H	29	4
1991–92	Tottenham H	31	1
1992–93	Tottenham H	18	1
1993–94	Tottenham H	18	1
1994–95	Tottenham H	26	1
1995–96	Tottenham H	29	3
1996–97	Tottenham H	32	2
1997–98	Tottenham H	20	0
1998–99	Southampton	9	1
1998–99	Bristol C (loan)	8	1
Total:		**294**	**24**

HOWEY, Lee — Defender

H: 6 2 W: 13 09 b.Sunderland 1-1-69

Source: AC Hemptinne Eghezee.

1992–93	Sunderland	1	0
1993–94	Sunderland	14	3
1994–95	Sunderland	15	2
1995–96	Sunderland	27	3
1996–97	Sunderland	12	0
1997–98	Burnley	23	0
1998–99	Burnley	3	0
1998–99	Northampton T	25	6
Total:		**120**	**14**

HOWEY, Steve — Defender

H: 6 1 W: 11 12 b.Sunderland 26-10-71

Source: Trainee. *Honours:* England 4 full caps.

1988–89	Newcastle U	1	0
1989–90	Newcastle U	0	0
1990–91	Newcastle U	11	0
1991–92	Newcastle U	21	1
1992–93	Newcastle U	41	2
1993–94	Newcastle U	14	0
1994–95	Newcastle U	30	1
1995–96	Newcastle U	28	1
1996–97	Newcastle U	8	1
1997–98	Newcastle U	14	0
1998–99	Newcastle U	14	0
Total:		**182**	**6**

HOWIE, Scott — Goalkeeper

H: 6 3 W: 13 07 b.Motherwell 4-1-72

Source: Ferguslie U. *Honours:* Scotland Under-21.

1991–92	Clyde	15	0
1992–93	Clyde	39	0
1993–94	Clyde	1	0
1993–94	Norwich C	2	0
1994–95	Motherwell	3	0
1995–96	Motherwell	36	0
1996–97	Motherwell	30	0
1997–98	Motherwell	0	0
1997–98	Reading	7	0
1998–99	Reading	42	0
Total:		**175**	**0**

HOYLAND, Jamie — Midfield

H: 6 0 W: 14 07 b.Sheffield 23-1-66

Source: Apprentice. *Honours:* England Youth.

1983–84	Manchester C	1	0
1984–85	Manchester C	1	0
1985–86	Manchester C	0	0
1986–87	Bury	36	2
1987–88	Bury	44	8
1988–89	Bury	46	9
1989–90	Bury	46	16
1990–91	Sheffield U	21	0
1991–92	Sheffield U	26	4
1992–93	Sheffield U	22	2
1993–94	Sheffield U	18	0
1993–94	Bristol C (loan)	6	0
1994–95	Sheffield U	2	0
1994–95	Burnley	30	2
1995–96	Burnley	23	0
1996–97	Burnley	25	1
1997–98	Burnley	9	0
1997–98	Carlisle U (loan)	5	0
1998–99	Scarborough	44	3
Total:		**405**	**47**

HREIDARSSON, Hermann — Defender

H: 6 0 W: 13 01 b.Iceland 11-7-74

Honours: Iceland 20 full caps.

1993	IBV	2	0
1994	IBV	18	2
1995	IBV	18	1
1996	IBV	17	2
1997	IBV	11	0
1997–98	Crystal Palace	30	2
1998–99	Crystal Palace	7	0
1998–99	Brentford	33	4
Total:		**136**	**11**

HRISTOV, Georgi — Forward

H: 6 0 W: 12 09 b.Bitola 30-1-76

Honours: Macedonia 24 full caps, 9 goals.

1994–95	Partizan Belgrade	12	3
1995–96	Partizan Belgrade	25	9
1997–98	Barnsley	23	4
1998–99	Barnsley	3	0
Total:		**63**	**16**

HUCK, Willie — Midfield

H: 5 10 W: 11 09 b.Paris 17-3-79

Source: Monaco.

1998–99	Arsenal	0	0
1998–99	Bournemouth	8	0
Total:		**8**	**0**

HUCKERBY, Darren — Forward

H: 5 11 W: 11 04 b.Nottingham 23-4-76

Source: Trainee. *Honours:* England Under-21, B.

1993–94	Lincoln C	6	1
1994–95	Lincoln C	6	2
1995–96	Lincoln C	16	2
1995–96	Newcastle U	1	0
1996–97	Newcastle U	0	0
1996–97	Millwall (loan)	6	3
1996–97	Coventry C	25	5
1997–98	Coventry C	34	14
1998–99	Coventry C	34	9
Total:		**128**	**36**

HUDSON, Danny — Midfield

H: 5 8 W: 10 03 b.Mexborough 25-6-79

Source: Trainee.

1997–98	Rotherham U	10	0
1998–99	Rotherham U	26	4
Total:		**36**	**4**

HUDSON, Mark — Midfield

b.Guilford 30-3-82

Source: Trainee.

1998–99	Fulham	0	0

HUDSON, Niall — Midfield

H: 5 10 W: 10 02 b.Ilkeston 7-1-82

Source: Trainee.

1998–99	Nottingham F	0	0

HUGHES, Aaron — Defender

H: 6 0 W: 11 02 b.Magherafelt 8-11-79

Source: Trainee. *Honours:* Northern Ireland 8 full caps.

1996–97	Newcastle U	0	0
1997–98	Newcastle U	4	0
1998–99	Newcastle U	14	0
Total:		**18**	**0**

HUGHES, Andy — Midfield

H: 6 0 W: 11 00 b.Manchester 2-1-78

Source: Trainee.

1995–96	Oldham Ath	15	1
1996–97	Oldham Ath	8	0
1997–98	Oldham Ath	10	0
1997–98	Notts Co	15	2
1998–99	Notts Co	30	3
Total:		**78**	**6**

HUGHES, Bryan — Midfield

H: 5 9 W: 10 00 b.Liverpool 19-6-76

Source: Trainee.

1993–94	Wrexham	11	0
1994–95	Wrexham	38	9
1995–96	Wrexham	22	0
1996–97	Wrexham	23	3
1996–97	Birmingham C	11	0
1997–98	Birmingham C	40	5
1998–99	Birmingham C	28	3
Total:		**173**	**20**

HUGHES, Ceri — Midfield

H: 5 10 W: 12 07 b.Pontypridd 26-2-71

Source: Trainee. *Honours:* Wales Youth, Under-21, 8 full caps.

1989–90	Luton T	1	0
1990–91	Luton T	17	1
1991–92	Luton T	18	0
1992–93	Luton T	29	2
1993–94	Luton T	42	7
1994–95	Luton T	9	2
1995–96	Luton T	23	1
1996–97	Luton T	36	4
1997–98	Wimbledon	17	1
1998–99	Wimbledon	14	0
Total:		**206**	**18**

HUGHES, Danny — Midfield

H: 5 10 W: 13 00 b.Bangor 13-2-80

Source: Trainee.

1998–99	Wolverhampton W	0	0
1998–99	Hartlepool U	8	0
Total:		**8**	**0**

HUGHES, David — Midfield

H: 5 11 W: 11 07 b.St Albans 30-12-72

Source: Trainee. *Honours:* England Schools.

1991–92	Southampton	0	0
1992–93	Southampton	0	0
1993–94	Southampton	2	0
1994–95	Southampton	12	2
1995–96	Southampton	11	1
1996–97	Southampton	6	0
1997–98	Southampton	14	0
1998–99	Southampton	9	0
Total:		**54**	**3**

HUGHES, David — Defender

H: 6 4 W: 14 02 b.Wrexham 1-2-78

Source: Trainee. *Honours:* Wales Under-21, B.

1996–97	Aston Villa	7	0
1997–98	Aston Villa	0	0
1997–98	Carlisle U (loan)	1	0
1998–99	Aston Villa	0	0
Total:		**8**	**0**

HUGHES, Garry — Defender

H: 6 1 W: 11 09 b.Birmingham 19-11-79

Source: Trainee.

1998–99	Northampton T	0	0

HUGHES, Ian — Midfield

H: 5 10 W: 12 08 b.Bangor 2-8-74

Source: Trainee. *Honours:* Wales Under-21.

1991–92	Bury	17	0
1992–93	Bury	15	0
1992–93	Bury	15	0
1993–94	Bury	38	0
1994–95	Bury	23	1
1995–96	Bury	32	0
1996–97	Bury	22	0
1997–98	Bury	13	0
1997–98	Blackpool	21	0
1998–99	Blackpool	33	1
Total:		**229**	**2**

HUGHES, John — Defender

H: 6 0 W: 13 07 b.Edinburgh 9-9-64

Source: Newtongrange Star.

1988–89	Berwick R	27	10
1989–90	Berwick R	14	4
1989–90	Swansea C	24	4
1990–91	Falkirk	32	2
1991–92	Falkirk	38	2
1992–93	Falkirk	15	0
1993–94	Falkirk	29	3
1994–95	Falkirk	20	0
1995–96	Celtic	26	2
1996–97	Celtic	6	0
1996–97	Hibernian	4	0
1997–98	Hibernian	25	1
1998–99	Hibernian	23	3
Total:		**283**	**31**

HUGHES, Lee — Forward

H: 5 10 W: 11 06 b.Birmingham 22-5-76

Source: Kidderminster H.

1997–98	WBA	37	14
1998–99	WBA	42	31
Total:		**79**	**45**

HUGHES, Mark — Forward

H: 5 9 W: 13 04 b.Wrexham 1-11-63

Source: Apprentice. *Honours:* Wales Youth, Under-21, 72 full caps, 16 goals.

1980–81	Manchester U	0	0
1981–82	Manchester U	0	0
1982–83	Manchester U	0	0
1983–84	Manchester U	11	4
1984–85	Manchester U	38	16
1985–86	Manchester U	40	17
1986–87	Barcelona	28	4
1987–88	Bayern Munich (loan)	18	6
1988–89	Manchester U	38	14
1989–90	Manchester U	37	13
1990–91	Manchester U	31	10
1991–92	Manchester U	39	11
1992–93	Manchester U	41	15
1993–94	Manchester U	36	11
1994–95	Manchester U	34	8
1995–96	Chelsea	31	8
1996–97	Chelsea	35	8
1997–98	Chelsea	29	9
1998–99	Southampton	32	1
Total:		**518**	**155**

HUGHES, Michael — Midfield

H: 5 6 W: 10 08 b.Larne 2-8-71

Source: Carrick R. *Honours:* Northern Ireland Under-21, 47 full caps, 3 goals.

1988–89	Manchester C	1	0
1989–90	Manchester C	0	0
1990–91	Manchester C	1	0
1991–92	Manchester C	24	1
1992–93	Strasbourg	36	2
1993–94	Strasbourg	34	7
1994–95	Strasbourg	13	0
1994–95	West Ham U (loan)	17	2
1995–96	West Ham U (loan)	28	0
1996–97	West Ham U	33	3
1997–98	West Ham U	5	0
1997–98	Wimbledon	29	4
1998–99	Wimbledon	30	2
Total:		**251**	**21**

HUGHES, Paul — Midfield

H: 5 11 W: 12 06 b.Hammersmith 19-4-76

Source: Trainee. *Honours:* England Schools.

1994–95	Chelsea	0	0
1995–96	Chelsea	0	0
1996–97	Chelsea	12	2
1997–98	Chelsea	9	0
1998–99	Chelsea	0	0
1998–99	Stockport Co (loan)	7	0
1998–99	Norwich C (loan)	4	1
Total:		**32**	**3**

HUGHES, Richard — Defender

H: 5 9 W: 9 12 b.Glasgow 25-6-79

Source: Atalanta. *Honours:* Scotland Youth, Under-21.

1997–98	Arsenal	0	0
1998–99	Bournemouth	44	2
Total:		**44**	**2**

HUGHES, Stephen — Midfield

H: 6 0 W: 12 05 b.Wokingham 18-9-76

Source: Trainee. *Honours:* England Schools, Youth, Under-21.

1994–95	Arsenal	1	0
1995–96	Arsenal	1	0
1996–97	Arsenal	14	1
1997–98	Arsenal	17	2
1998–99	Arsenal	14	1
Total:		**47**	**4**

HULBERT, Robin — Midfield

b.Plymouth 14-3-80

Source: Trainee. *Honours:* England Youth.

1997–98	Swindon T	1	0
1997–98	Newcastle U (loan)	0	0
1998–99	Swindon T	16	0
Total:		**17**	**0**

HULME, Kevin — Midfield

H: 5 10 W: 13 07 b.Farnworth 7-12-67

Source: Radcliffe Borough.

1988–89	Bury	5	0
1989–90	Bury	19	1
1989–90	Chester C (loan)	4	0
1990–91	Bury	24	7
1991–92	Bury	30	4
1992–93	Bury	32	9
1993–94	Doncaster R	34	8
1994–95	Bury	28	0
1995–96	Bury	1	0
1995–96	Lincoln C	5	0
From Macclesfield T			
1998–99	Halifax T	30	4
Total:		**212**	**33**

HULSE, Robert — Midfield

b.Crewe 25-10-79

Source: Trainee.

1998–99	Crewe Alex	0	0

HUMES, Tony — Defender

H: 6 0 W: 12 00 b.Blyth 19-3-66

Source: Apprentice.

1983–84	Ipswich T	0	0
1984–85	Ipswich T	0	0
1985–86	Ipswich T	0	0
1986–87	Ipswich T	22	2
1987–88	Ipswich T	27	0
1988–89	Ipswich T	26	3
1989–90	Ipswich T	24	3
1990–91	Ipswich T	16	2
1991–92	Ipswich T	5	0
1991–92	Wrexham	8	0
1992–93	Wrexham	38	0
1993–94	Wrexham	27	1
1994–95	Wrexham	29	0
1995–96	Wrexham	27	3
1996–97	Wrexham	34	4
1997–98	Wrexham	24	0
1998–99	Wrexham	12	0
Total:		**319**	**18**

HUMPHREYS, Richie — Forward

H: 5 11 W: 14 07 b.Sheffield 30-11-77

Source: Trainee. *Honours:* England Youth, Under-21.

1995–96	Sheffield W	5	0
1996–97	Sheffield W	29	3
1997–98	Sheffield W	7	0
1998–99	Sheffield W	19	1
Total:		**60**	**4**

HUNT, Andy — Forward

H: 6 0 W: 11 12 b.Thurrock 9-6-70

Source: Kettering T.

1990–91	Newcastle U	16	2
1991–92	Newcastle U	27	9
1992–93	Newcastle U	0	0
1992–93	WBA (loan)	10	9
1993–94	WBA	35	12
1994–95	WBA	39	13
1995–96	WBA	45	14
1996–97	WBA	45	15
1997–98	WBA	38	13
1998–99	Charlton Ath	34	7
Total:		**289**	**94**

HUNT, David — Defender

H: 5 10 W: 12 00 b.Durham 5-3-80

Source: Trainee.

1996–97	Darlington	1	0
1997–98	Darlington	0	0
1998–99	Darlington	0	0
Total:		**1**	**0**

HUNT, James — Midfield

H: 5 8 W: 10 03 b.Derby 17-12-76

Source: Trainee.

1994–95	Notts Co	0	0
1995–96	Notts Co	10	1
1996–97	Notts Co	9	0
1997–98	Northampton T	21	0
1998–99	Northampton T	35	2
Total:		**75**	**3**

HUNT, Jonathan — Midfield

H: 5 10 W: 11 13 b.London 2-11-71

Source: Barnet, Slough T. *Honours:*

1991–92	Barnet	14	0
1992–93	Barnet	19	0
1993–94	Southend U	42	6
1994–95	Southend U	7	0
1994–95	Birmingham C	20	5
1995–96	Birmingham C	45	11

1996–97	Birmingham C	12	2
1997–98	Derby Co	19	1
1998–99	Derby Co	6	1
1998–99	Sheffield U	13	2
1998–99	Ipswich T (loan)	6	0
Total:		**203**	**28**

HUNTER, Barry — Defender

H: 6 3 W: 13 02 b.Coleraine 18-11-68

Source: Crusaders. *Honours:* Northern Ireland 13 full caps, 1 goal.

1993–94	Wrexham	23	1
1994–95	Wrexham	37	0
1995–96	Wrexham	31	3
1996–97	Reading	27	2
1997–98	Reading	0	0
1998–99	Reading	3	0
1998–99	Southend U (loan)	5	2
Total:		**126**	**8**

HUNTER, Gordon — Defender

H: 5 10 W: 10 05 b.Wallyford 3-5-67

Source: Musselburgh Windsor. *Honours:* Scotland Youth, Under-21.

1983–84	Hibernian	1	0
1984–85	Hibernian	6	0
1985–86	Hibernian	25	0
1986–87	Hibernian	29	0
1987–88	Hibernian	35	0
1988–89	Hibernian	33	1
1989–90	Hibernian	34	0
1990–91	Hibernian	20	1
1991–92	Hibernian	37	2
1992–93	Hibernian	23	0
1993–94	Hibernian	29	1
1994–95	Hibernian	29	2
1995–96	Hibernian	22	0
1996–97	Hibernian	17	0
From Canberra Cosmos			
1998–99	Dundee	3	0
Total:		**343**	**7**

HUNTER, Roy — Midfield

H: 5 10 W: 12 08 b.Saltburn 29-10-73

Source: Trainee.

1991–92	WBA	6	1
1992–93	WBA	1	0
1993–94	WBA	2	0
1994–95	WBA	0	0
1995–96	Northampton T	34	0
1996–97	Northampton T	36	6
1997–98	Northampton T	28	3
1998–99	Northampton T	18	1
Total:		**125**	**11**

HURST, Chris — Midfield

H: 5 11 W: 11 06 b.Barnsley 3-10-73

Source: Emley.

1997–98	Huddersfield T	3	0
1998–99	Huddersfield T	0	0
Total:		**3**	**0**

HURST, Paul — Defender

H: 5 4 W: 9 0 b.Sheffield 25-9-74

Source: Trainee.

1993–94	Rotherham U	4	0
1994–95	Rotherham U	13	0
1995–96	Rotherham U	40	1
1996–97	Rotherham U	30	3
1997–98	Rotherham U	30	0
1998–99	Rotherham U	32	2
Total:		**149**	**6**

HURST, Richard — Goalkeeper

H: 6 0 W: 13 01 b.Hammersmith 23-12-76

Source: Trainee.

1994–95	QPR	0	0
1995–96	QPR	0	0
1996–97	QPR	0	0
1997–98	QPR	0	0
1998–99	QPR	0	0

HUSSEY, Stuart — Midfield

b.Southampton 4-12-80

Source: Portsmouth Trainee.

1998–99	Bristol C	0	0

HUTCHINGS, Carl — Midfield

H: 6 1 W: 12 00 b.Hammersmith 24-9-74

Source: Trainee.

1993–94	Brentford	29	0
1994–95	Brentford	39	0
1995–96	Brentford	23	0
1996–97	Brentford	28	2
1997–98	Brentford	43	5
1998–99	Bristol C	21	2
Total:		**183**	**9**

HUTCHINSON, James — Midfield

b.Nottingham 24-3-80

1998–99	Derby Co	0	0

HUTCHINSON, Thomas — Midfield

b.Kingston 23-2-82

1998–99	Fulham	0	0

HUTCHISON, Don — Midfield

H: 6 2 W: 12 04 b.Gateshead 9-5-71

Source: Trainee. *Honours:* Scotland 2 full caps, 1 goal.

1989–90	Hartlepool U	13	2
1990–91	Hartlepool U	11	0
1990–91	Liverpool	0	0
1991–92	Liverpool	3	0
1992–93	Liverpool	31	7
1993–94	Liverpool	11	0
1994–95	West Ham U	23	9
1995–96	West Ham U	12	2
1995–96	Sheffield U	19	2
1996–97	Sheffield U	41	3
1997–98	Sheffield U	18	0
1997–98	Everton	11	1
1998–99	Everton	33	3
Total:		**226**	**29**

HUTT, Stephen — Midfield

H: 6 2 W: 12 00 b.Middlesbrough 19-2-79

Source: Trainee.

1995–96	Hartlepool U	1	0
1996–97	Hartlepool U	0	0
1997–98	Hartlepool U	4	0
1998–99	Hartlepool U	4	0
Total:		**9**	**0**

HUTTON, John — Forward

H: 5 10 W: 11 12 b.Easington 23-9-80

Source: Trainee.

1998–99	Sheffield W	0	0

HUXFORD, Richard — Defender

H: 5 10 W: 11 06 b.Scunthorpe 25-7-69

Source: Kettering T.

1992–93	Barnet	33	1
1993–94	Millwall	31	0
1993–94	Birmingham C (loan)	5	0
1994–95	Millwall	1	0
1994–95	Bradford C	33	1
1995–96	Bradford C	26	1
1996–97	Bradford C	2	0
1996–97	Peterborough U (loan)	7	0
1996–97	Burnley	9	0
1997–98	Burnley	4	0
1997–98	Dunfermline Ath (loan)	10	0
1998–99	Dunfermline Ath	25	0
Total:		**186**	**3**

HYDE, Graham — Midfield

H: 5 8 W: 12 04 b.Doncaster 10-11-70

Source: Trainee.

1988–89	Sheffield W	0	0
1989–90	Sheffield W	0	0
1990–91	Sheffield W	0	0
1991–92	Sheffield W	13	0
1992–93	Sheffield W	20	1
1993–94	Sheffield W	36	1
1994–95	Sheffield W	35	5
1995–96	Sheffield W	26	1
1996–97	Sheffield W	19	2
1997–98	Sheffield W	22	1
1998–99	Sheffield W	1	0
1998–99	Birmingham C	13	0
Total:		**185**	**11**

HYDE, Micah — Midfield

H: 5 10 W: 11 12 b.Newham 10-11-74

Source: Trainee.

1993–94	Cambridge U	18	2
1994–95	Cambridge U	27	0
1995–96	Cambridge U	24	4
1996–97	Cambridge U	38	7
1997–98	Watford	40	4
1998–99	Watford	44	2
Total:		**191**	**19**

HYDE, Paul — Goalkeeper

H: 6 1 W: 14 09 b.Hayes 7-4-63

Source: Hayes.

1993–94	Wycombe W	42	0
1994–95	Wycombe W	46	0
1995–96	Wycombe W	17	0
1995–96	Leicester C	0	0
1996–97	Leicester C	0	0
1996–97	Leyton Orient	13	0
1997–98	Leyton Orient	28	0
1998–99	Leyton Orient	0	0
Total:		**146**	**0**

IFEJIAGWA, Emeka — Defender

H: 6 3 W: 14 00 b.Nigeria 30-10-77

Source: Udoji U.

1998–99	Charlton Ath	0	0
1998–99	Brighton & HA (loan)	2	1
Total:		**2**	**1**

IFILL, Paul — Forward

b.Brighton 20-10-79

Source: Trainee.

1998–99	Millwall	15	1
Total:		**15**	**1**

IGOE, Sammy — Midfield

H: 5 6 W: 9 07 b.Spelthorne 30-9-75

Source: Trainee.

1993–94	Portsmouth	0	0
1994–95	Portsmouth	1	0
1995–96	Portsmouth	22	0
1996–97	Portsmouth	40	2
1997–98	Portsmouth	31	3
1998–99	Portsmouth	40	5
Total:		**134**	**10**

ILIC, Sasa — Goalkeeper

H: 6 4 W: 14 00 b.Melbourne 18-7-72

Source: Daewoo Royals, St Leonards Stamcroft. *Honours:* Yugoslavia 1 full cap.

1997–98	Charlton Ath	14	0
1998–99	Charlton Ath	23	0
Total:		**37**	**0**

IMPEY, Andrew — Midfield

H: 5 8 W: 11 06 b.Hammersmith 13-9-71

Source: Yeading. *Honours:* England Under-21.

1990–91	QPR	0	0
1991–92	QPR	13	0
1992–93	QPR	40	2
1993–94	QPR	33	3
1994–95	QPR	40	3
1995–96	QPR	29	3
1996–97	QPR	32	2
1997–98	West Ham U	19	0
1998–99	West Ham U	8	0
1998–99	Leicester C	18	0
Total:		**232**	**13**

INCE, James — Midfield

b.Chelmsford 27-3-80

Source: Trainee.

1998–99	WBA	0	0

INCE, Paul — Midfield

H: 5 10 W: 12 02 b.Ilford 21-10-67

Source: Trainee. *Honours:* England Youth, Under-21, B, 45 full caps, 2 goals.

1985–86	West Ham U	0	0
1986–87	West Ham U	10	1
1987–88	West Ham U	28	3
1988–89	West Ham U	33	3
1989–90	West Ham U	1	0
1989–90	Manchester U	26	0
1990–91	Manchester U	31	3
1991–92	Manchester U	33	3
1992–93	Manchester U	41	5
1993–94	Manchester U	39	8
1994–95	Manchester U	36	5
1995–96	Internazionale	30	3
1996–97	Internazionale	24	6
1997–98	Liverpool	31	8
1998–99	Liverpool	34	6
Total:		**397**	**54**

INGHAM, Andrew — Midfield

b.Leeds 21-8-81

Source: Trainee.

1997–98	Cambridge U	0	0
1998–99	Cambridge U	0	0

INGLEDOW, Jamie — Midfield

H: 5 7 W: 11 01 b.Barnsley 23-8-80

Source: Trainee.

1998–99	Rotherham U	21	2
Total:		**21**	**2**

INGLETHORPE, Alex — Midfield

H: 5 11 W: 11 04 b.Epsom 14-11-71

Source: School.

1990–91	Watford	1	0
1991–92	Watford	2	0
1992–93	Watford	0	0
1993–94	Watford	9	2
1994–95	Watford	0	0
1994–95	Barnet (loan)	6	3
1994–95	Leyton Orient	0	0
1995–96	Leyton Orient	30	9
1996–97	Leyton Orient	16	8
1997–98	Leyton Orient	38	9
1998–99	Leyton Orient	23	4
Total:		**125**	**35**

INGLIS, John — Defender

H: 6 0 W: 13 00 b.Edinburgh 16-10-66

Source: Hutchison Vale.

1983–84	East Fife	4	1

1984–85	East Fife	9	0
1985–86	East Fife	30	0
1986–87	East Fife	13	0
1986–87	Brechin C	15	0
1987–88	Brechin C	26	3
1988–89	Brechin C	12	1
1988–89	Meadowbank T	12	1
1989–90	Meadowbank T	38	3
1990–91	St Johnstone	31	1
1991–92	St Johnstone	40	0
1992–93	St Johnstone	39	0
1993–94	St Johnstone	25	1
1994–95	St Johnstone	5	0
1994–95	Aberdeen	17	1
1995–96	Aberdeen	24	1
1996–97	Aberdeen	15	0
1997–98	Aberdeen	25	1
1998–99	Aberdeen	17	1
Total:		**397**	**15**

INGLIS, Kevin — Midfield

b.Glasgow 26-8-80

Source: Trainee.

1998–99	Ipswich T	0	0

INGRAM, Denny — Defender

H: 5 11 W: 12 02 b.Sunderland 27-6-76

Source: Trainee.

1993–94	Hartlepool U	13	0
1994–95	Hartlepool U	35	0
1995–96	Hartlepool U	33	2
1996–97	Hartlepool U	37	1
1997–98	Hartlepool U	36	3
1998–99	Hartlepool U	38	4
Total:		**192**	**10**

INGRAM, Rae — Defender

H: 5 11 W: 12 02 b.Manchester 6-12-74

Source: Trainee.

1993–94	Manchester C	0	0
1994–95	Manchester C	0	0
1995–96	Manchester C	5	0
1996–97	Manchester C	18	0
1997–98	Manchester C	0	0
1997–98	Macclesfield T (loan)	5	0
1998–99	Macclesfield T	29	0
Total:		**57**	**0**

INGRAM, Stuart — Forward

H: 6 1 W: 11 07 b.Stockton 7-11-79

Source: Trainee.

1998–99	Sunderland	0	0

INMAN, Niall — Midfield

H: 5 9 W: 11 06 b.Wakefield 6-2-78

Source: Trainee. *Honours:* Eire Youth, Under-21.

1995–96	Peterborough U	1	0
1996–97	Peterborough U	3	0
1997–98	Peterborough U	4	1
1998–99	Peterborough U	3	1
Total:		**11**	**2**

INNES, Christopher — Defender

H: 6 0 W: 12 02 b.Broxburn 13-7-76

Source: Blackburn Juniors.

1996–97	Stenhousemuir	24	1
1997–98	Stenhousemuir	30	2
1998–99	Kilmarnock	4	1
Total:		**58**	**4**

INNES, Mark — Defender

H: 5 10 W: 12 04 b.Bellshill 27-9-78

Source: Trainee.

1995–96	Oldham Ath	0	0
1996–97	Oldham Ath	0	0
1997–98	Oldham Ath	4	0
1998–99	Oldham Ath	13	1
Total:		**17**	**1**

IORFA, Dominic — Forward

H: 6 0 W: 12 12 b.Lagos 1-10-68

Source: Antwerp. *Honours:* Nigeria full caps.

1989–90	QPR	1	0
1990–91	QPR	6	0
1991–92	QPR	1	0
1992–93	QPR	0	0
1992–93	Peterborough U	26	1
1993–94	Peterborough U	34	8
1994–95	Southend U	8	1
1995–96	Southend U	2	0
1995–96	Falkirk	4	1
1996–97	Falkirk	0	0
1997–98	Falkirk	0	0
From Billericay T.			
1998–99	Southend U	2	0
Total:		**84**	**11**

IPOUA, Guy — Forward

H: 6 1 W: 13 10 b.Douala 14-1-76

Source: Atletico Madrid, Novelda.

1998–99	Bristol R	24	3
Total:		**24**	**3**

IRELAND, Craig — Defender

H: 6 3 W: 13 09 b.Dundee 29-11-75

Source: Aberdeen Lads.

1994–95	Aberdeen	0	0
1995–96	Aberdeen	0	0
1995–96	Dunfermline Ath	10	0
1996–97	Dunfermline Ath	9	1
1997–98	Dunfermline Ath	12	1
1998–99	Dunfermline Ath	23	0
Total:		**54**	**2**

IRIEKPEN, Ezomo — Defender

b.Nigeria 14-5-82

Source: Trainee.

1998–99	West Ham U	0	0

IROHA, Ben — Midfield

H: 5 8 W: 11 06 b.Calabar 29-11-69

Source: Elche. *Honours:* Nigeria 31 full caps, 1 goal.

1998–99	Bristol R	0	0
1998–99	Watford	10	0
Total:		**10**	**0**

IRONS, Kenny — Midfield

H: 5 10 W: 11 02 b.Liverpool 4-11-70

Source: Trainee.

1989–90	Tranmere R	3	0
1990–91	Tranmere R	32	6
1991–92	Tranmere R	43	7
1992–93	Tranmere R	42	7
1993–94	Tranmere R	34	3
1994–95	Tranmere R	38	4
1995–96	Tranmere R	32	3
1996–97	Tranmere R	41	5
1997–98	Tranmere R	43	4
1998–99	Tranmere R	43	15
Total:		**351**	**54**

IRVINE, Brian — Defender

H: 6 2 W: 13 00 b.Bellshill 24-5-65

Source: Victoria Park. *Honours:* Scotland 9 full caps.

1983–84	Falkirk	3	0
1984–85	Falkirk	35	0
1985–86	Aberdeen	1	0
1986–87	Aberdeen	20	1
1987–88	Aberdeen	16	1
1988–89	Aberdeen	27	2
1989–90	Aberdeen	31	1
1990–91	Aberdeen	29	2
1991–92	Aberdeen	41	4
1992–93	Aberdeen	39	5
1993–94	Aberdeen	42	7
1994–95	Aberdeen	17	1
1995–96	Aberdeen	18	3
1996–97	Aberdeen	25	1
1997–98	Dundee	36	1
1998–99	Dundee	33	3
Total:		**413**	**32**

IRVINE, Stuart — Forward

H: 5 9 W: 11 07 b.Hartlepool 1-3-79

Source: Trainee.

1996–97	Hartlepool U	4	1
1997–98	Hartlepool U	9	0
1998–99	Hartlepool U	18	1
Total:		**31**	**2**

IRWIN, Denis — Defender

H: 5 8 W: 10 10 b.Cork 31-10-65

Source: Apprentice. *Honours:* Eire Schools, Youth, Under-21, B, 52 full caps, 4 goals.

1983–84	Leeds U	12	0
1984–85	Leeds U	41	1
1985–86	Leeds U	19	0
1986–87	Oldham Ath	41	1
1987–88	Oldham Ath	43	0
1988–89	Oldham Ath	41	2
1989–90	Oldham Ath	42	1
1990–91	Manchester U	34	0
1991–92	Manchester U	38	4
1992–93	Manchester U	40	5
1993–94	Manchester U	42	2
1994–95	Manchester U	40	2
1995–96	Manchester U	31	1
1996–97	Manchester U	31	1
1997–98	Manchester U	25	2
1998–99	Manchester U	29	2
Total:		**549**	**24**

ISMAEL, Valerien — Defender

H: 6 2 W: 13 01 b.Strasbourg 28-9-75

1993–94	Strasbourg	4	0
1994–95	Strasbourg	13	0
1995–96	Strasbourg	19	0
1996–97	Strasbourg	31	1
1997–98	Strasbourg	18	0
1997–98	Crystal Palace	13	0
1998–99	Crystal Palace	0	0
Total:		**98**	**1**

IVERSEN, Steffen — Forward

H: 6 1 W: 11 08 b.Oslo 10-11-76

Honours: Norway 7 full caps, 4 goals.

1996	Rosenborg	25	10
1996–97	Tottenham H	16	6
1997–98	Tottenham H	13	0
1998–99	Tottenham H	27	9
Total:		**81**	**25**

IZZET, Kemal — Midfield

H: 5 8 W: 10 05 b.Whitechapel 29-9-80

Source: Trainee.

1998–99	Charlton Ath	0	0

IZZET, Muzzy — Midfield

H: 5 10 W: 11 02 b.Mile End 31-10-74

Source: Trainee.

1993–94	Chelsea	0	0
1994–95	Chelsea	0	0
1995–96	Chelsea	0	0
1995–96	Leicester C (loan)	9	1
1996–97	Leicester C	35	3
1997–98	Leicester C	36	4
1998–99	Leicester C	31	5
Total:		**111**	**13**

JAASKELAINEN, Jussi — Goalkeeper

H: 6 3 W: 12 10 b.Mikkeli 19-4-75

Honours: Finland 4 full caps.

1992	MP	6	0
1993	MP	6	0
1994	MP	26	0
1995	MP	26	0
1996	VPS	27	0
1997	VPS	27	0
1997–98	Bolton W	0	0
1998–99	Bolton W	34	0
Total:		**152**	**0**

JACK, Rodney — Forward

H: 5 7 W: 10 07 b.Kingston, Jamaica 28-9-72

Source: Lambada. *Honours:* St Vincent full caps.

1995–96	Torquay U	14	2
1996–97	Torquay U	33	10
1997–98	Torquay U	40	12
1998–99	Crewe Alex	39	9
Total:		**126**	**33**

JACKSON, Darren — Forward

H: 5 10 W: 10 10 b.Edinburgh 25-7-66

Source: Broxburn Am. *Honours:* Scotland 28 full caps, 4 goals.

1985–86	Meadowbank T	39	17
1986–87	Meadowbank T	9	5
1986–87	Newcastle U	23	3
1987–88	Newcastle U	31	2
1988–89	Newcastle U	15	2
1988–89	Dundee U	1	0
1989–90	Dundee U	25	7
1990–91	Dundee U	33	12
1991–92	Dundee U	28	11
1992–93	Hibernian	36	13
1993–94	Hibernian	40	7
1994–95	Hibernian	31	10
1995–96	Hibernian	36	9
1996–97	Hibernian	30	11
1997–98	Celtic	23	3
1998–99	Celtic	6	0
1998–99	Coventry C (loan)	3	0
1998–99	Hearts	9	1
Total:		**418**	**113**

JACKSON, Elliott — Goalkeeper

H: 6 3 W: 14 06 b.Swindon 27-8-77

Source: Trainee.

1996–97	Oxford U	3	0
1997–98	Oxford U	3	0
1998–99	Oxford U	1	0
Total:		**7**	**0**

JACKSON, John — Goalkeeper

H: 6 1 W: 11 10 b.Stockton 30-6-80

Source: Trainee.

1998–99	Middlesbrough	0	0

JACKSON, Justin — Forward

H: 5 11 W: 11 06 b.Nottingham 10-12-74

Source: Woking.

1997–98	Notts Co	15	1
1998–99	Notts Co	10	0
1998–99	Rotherham U (loan)	2	1
1998–99	Halifax T	16	4
Total:		**43**	**6**

JACKSON, Mark — Defender

H: 6 0 W: 12 10 b.Barnsley 30-9-77

Source: Trainee. *Honours:* England Youth.

1995–96	Leeds U	1	0
1996–97	Leeds U	17	0
1997–98	Leeds U	1	0

1998–99	Leeds U	0	0
1998–99	Huddersfield T (loan)	5	0
Total:		**24**	**0**

JACKSON, Matt — Defender

H: 6 0 W: 13 00 b.Leeds 19-10-71

Source: School. *Honours:* England Schools, Under-21.

1990–91	Luton T	0	0
1990–91	Preston NE (loan)	4	0
1991–92	Luton T	9	0
1991–92	Everton	30	1
1992–93	Everton	27	3
1993–94	Everton	38	0
1994–95	Everton	29	0
1995–96	Everton	14	0
1995–96	Charlton Ath (loan)	8	0
1996–97	Everton	0	0
1996–97	QPR (loan)	7	0
1996–97	Birmingham C (loan)	10	0
1996–97	Norwich C	19	2
1997–98	Norwich C	41	3
1998–99	Norwich C	37	1
Total:		**273**	**10**

JACKSON, Michael — Defender

H: 5 11 W: 11 09 b.Chester 4-12-73

Source: Trainee.

1991–92	Crewe Alex	1	0
1992–93	Crewe Alex	4	0
1993–94	Bury	39	0
1994–95	Bury	24	2
1995–96	Bury	31	4
1996–97	Bury	31	3
1996–97	Preston NE	7	0
1997–98	Preston NE	40	2
1998–99	Preston NE	44	8
Total:		**221**	**19**

JACKSON, Richard — Defender

H: 5 9 W: 9 07 b.Whitby 18-4-80

Source: Trainee.

1997–98	Scarborough	2	0
1998–99	Scarborough	20	0
1998–99	Derby Co	0	0
Total:		**22**	**0**

JACOBS, Wayne — Defender

H: 5 8 W: 11 02 b.Sheffield 3-2-69

Source: Apprentice.

1986–87	Sheffield W	0	0
1987–88	Sheffield W	6	0
1987–88	Hull C	6	0
1988–89	Hull C	33	0
1989–90	Hull C	46	3
1990–91	Hull C	19	1
1991–92	Hull C	25	0
1992–93	Hull C	0	0
1993–94	Rotherham U	42	2
1994–95	Bradford C	38	1
1995–96	Bradford C	28	0
1996–97	Bradford C	39	3
1997–98	Bradford C	36	2
1998–99	Bradford C	44	3
Total:		**362**	**15**

JACOBSEN, Anders — Defender

H: 6 3 W: 13 07 b.Oslo 18-4-68

Source: Start.

1998–99	Sheffield U	12	0
Total:		**12**	**0**

JAFFA, Graeme — Forward

H: 5 6 W: 9 08 b.Falkirk 8-5-79

Source: Trainee.

1997–98	Leicester C	0	0
1998–99	Leicester C	0	0

JAGIELKA, Steve — Forward

H: 5 8 W: 11 03 b.Manchester 10-3-78

Source: Trainee.

1996–97	Stoke C	0	0
1997–98	Shrewsbury T	16	1
1998–99	Shrewsbury T	31	1
Total:		**47**	**2**

JAMES, David — Goalkeeper

H: 6 5 W: 14 02 b.Welwyn 1-8-70

Source: Trainee. *Honours:* England Youth, Under-21, B, 1 full cap.

1988–89	Watford	0	0
1989–90	Watford	0	0
1990–91	Watford	46	0
1991–92	Watford	43	0
1992–93	Liverpool	29	0
1993–94	Liverpool	14	0
1994–95	Liverpool	42	0
1995–96	Liverpool	38	0
1996–97	Liverpool	38	0
1997–98	Liverpool	27	0
1998–99	Liverpool	26	0
Total:		**303**	**0**

JAMES, Julian — Defender

H: 5 10 W: 12 06 b.Tring 22-3-70

Source: Trainee. *Honours:* England Under-21.

1987–88	Luton T	3	0
1988–89	Luton T	1	0
1989–90	Luton T	20	1
1990–91	Luton T	17	1
1991–92	Luton T	28	2
1991–92	Preston NE (loan)	6	0
1992–93	Luton T	43	2
1993–94	Luton T	33	3
1994–95	Luton T	42	3
1995–96	Luton T	27	0
1996–97	Luton T	44	1
1997–98	Luton T	24	0
1998–99	Luton T	0	0
Total:		**288**	**13**

JAMES, Kevin — Defender

H: 6 0 W: 12 00 b.Edinburgh 3-12-75

Source: Musselburgh Ath.

1994–95	Falkirk	1	0
1995–96	Falkirk	14	2
1996–97	Falkirk	18	3
1997–98	Falkirk	17	4
1998–99	Falkirk	13	0
1998–99	Hearts	4	0
Total:		**67**	**9**

JAMES, Kevin — Forward

H: 5 8 W: 10 05 b.Merthyr 26-3-80

Source: Trainee.

1997–98	Southampton	0	0
1998–99	Southampton	0	0

JAMES, Kevin — Forward

H: 5 9 W: 10 07 b.Southwark 3-1-80

Source: Trainee.

1998–99	Charlton Ath	0	0

JAMES, Lutel — Forward

H: 5 8 W: 11 00 b.Manchester 2-6-72

1992–93	Scarborough	6	0
From Hyde U.			
1998–99	Bury	17	2
Total:		**23**	**2**

JAMES, Owen — Defender

H: 5 11 W: 12 00 b.Derby 1-9-78

Source: Trainee.

1997–98	Sheffield U	0	0
1998–99	Sheffield U	0	0

JAMES, Tony — Defender

H: 6 3 W: 13 08 b.Sheffield 27-6-67

Source: Gainsborough T.

1988–89	Lincoln C	28	0
1989–90	Lincoln C	1	0
1989–90	Leicester C	31	2
1990–91	Leicester C	38	8
1991–92	Leicester C	13	0
1992–93	Leicester C	16	0
1993–94	Leicester C	9	1
1994–95	Hereford U	18	2
1995–96	Hereford U	17	2
1996–97	Plymouth Arg	34	1
1997–98	Plymouth Arg	0	0
1998–99	Plymouth Arg	0	0
Total:		**205**	**16**

JANSEN, Matt — Forward

H: 5 11 W: 11 03 b.Carlisle 20-10-77

Source: Trainee. *Honours:* England Under-21.

1995–96	Carlisle U	0	0
1996–97	Carlisle U	19	1
1997–98	Carlisle U	23	9
1997–98	Crystal Palace	8	3
1998–99	Crystal Palace	18	7
1998–99	Blackburn R	11	3
Total:		**79**	**23**

JANSSON, Jan — Midfield

H: 5 11 W: 13 00 b.Kalmar 26-1-68

Honours: Sweden Under-21, 7 full caps.

1993	Norrkoping	23	8
1994	Norrkoping	19	0
1995	Norrkoping	25	0
1996	Norrkoping	6	1
1996–97	Port Vale	11	1
1997–98	Port Vale	33	5
1998–99	Port Vale	7	0
Total:		**124**	**15**

JARMAN, Lee — Defender

H: 6 3 W: 14 01 b.Cardiff 16-12-77

Source: Trainee. *Honours:* Wales Under-21.

1995–96	Cardiff C	32	0
1996–97	Cardiff C	32	0

1997–98	Cardiff C	23	0
1998–99	Cardiff C	6	1
Total:		**93**	**1**

JARRETT, Jason — Midfield

H: 6 0 W: 12 04 b.Bury 14-9-79

Source: Trainee.

1998–99	Blackpool	2	0
Total:		**2**	**0**

JASZCZUN, Tommy — Defender

H: 5 11 W: 11 02 b.Kettering 16-9-77

Source: Trainee.

1996–97	Aston Villa	0	0
1997–98	Aston Villa	0	0
1998–99	Aston Villa	0	0

JEAN, Earl — Forward

H: 5 7 W: 11 00 b.St Lucia 9-10-71

Source: Oliveirense, Union Coimbra, Leca, Felgueiras. *Honours:* St Lucia full caps.

1996–97	Ipswich T	1	0
1996–97	Rotherham U	18	6
1997–98	Plymouth Arg	36	4
1998–99	Plymouth Arg	29	3
Total:		**84**	**13**

JEANNE, Leon — Midfield

H: 5 6 W: 10 00 b.Cardiff 17-11-80

Source: Trainee. *Honours:* Wales Under-21.

1997–98	QPR	0	0
1998–99	QPR	10	0
Total:		**10**	**0**

JEFFERS, Francis — Forward

H: 5 10 W: 10 02 b.Liverpool 25-1-81

Source: Trainee. *Honours:* England Schools, Youth.

1997–98	Everton	1	0
1998–99	Everton	15	6
Total:		**16**	**6**

JELLEYMAN, Gareth — Defender

H: 5 10 W: 10 02 b.Holywell 14-11-80

Source: Trainee. *Honours:* Wales Under-21.

1998–99	Peterborough U	0	0

JEMSON, Nigel — Forward

H: 5 11 W: 13 00 b.Preston 10-8-69

Source: Trainee. *Honours:* England Under-21.

1985–86	Preston NE	1	0
1986–87	Preston NE	4	3
1987–88	Preston NE	27	5
1987–88	Nottingham F	0	0
1988–89	Nottingham F	0	0
1988–89	Bolton W (loan)	5	0
1988–89	Preston NE (loan)	9	2
1989–90	Nottingham F	18	4
1990–91	Nottingham F	23	8
1991–92	Nottingham F	6	1
1991–92	Sheffield W	20	4
1992–93	Sheffield W	13	0
1993–94	Sheffield W	18	5
1993–94	Grimsby T (loan)	6	2
1994–95	Notts Co	11	1
1994–95	Watford (loan)	4	0
1994–95	Coventry C (loan)	0	0
1995–96	Notts Co	3	0
1995–96	Rotherham U (loan)	16	5
1996–97	Oxford U	44	18
1997–98	Oxford U	24	9
1997–98	Bury	15	1
1998–99	Bury	14	0
Total:		**281**	**68**

JENKINS, Iain — Defender

H: 5 9 W: 11 10 b.Whiston 24-12-72

Source: Trainee. *Honours:* Northern Ireland 5 full caps.

1990–91	Everton	1	0
1991–92	Everton	3	0
1992–93	Everton	1	0
1992–93	Bradford C (loan)	6	0
1993–94	Chester C	34	0
1994–95	Chester C	40	0
1995–96	Chester C	13	0
1996–97	Chester C	39	0
1997–98	Chester C	34	1
1997–98	Dundee U	7	0
1998–99	Dundee U	6	0
Total:		**184**	**1**

JENKINS, Jamie — Defender

H: 5 8 W: 10 07 b.Pontypool 1-1-79

Source: Trainee.

1997–98	Bournemouth	0	0
1998–99	Bournemouth	1	0
Total:		**1**	**0**

JENKINS, Lee — Midfield

H: 5 9 W: 10 00 b.Pontypool 28-6-79

Source: Trainee.

1996–97	Swansea C	23	2
1997–98	Swansea C	21	0
1998–99	Swansea C	12	0
Total:		**56**	**2**

JENKINS, Steve — Defender

H: 6 0 W: 12 08 b.Merthyr 16-7-72

Source: Trainee. *Honours:* Wales Under-21, 12 full caps.

1990–91	Swansea C	1	0
1991–92	Swansea C	34	0
1992–93	Swansea C	33	0
1993–94	Swansea C	40	1
1994–95	Swansea C	42	0
1995–96	Swansea C	15	0
1995–96	Huddersfield T	31	1
1996–97	Huddersfield T	33	0
1997–98	Huddersfield T	29	1
1998–99	Huddersfield T	36	1
Total:		**294**	**4**

JENKINS, Steve — Defender

H: 6 2 W: 13 10 b.Bristol 2-1-80

Source: Trainee.

1997–98	Southampton	0	0
1998–99	Southampton	0	0
1998–99	Brentford (loan)	1	0
Total:		**1**	**0**

JENKINSON, Leigh — Midfield

H: 6 0 W: 14 01 b.Thorne 9-7-69

Source: Trainee. *Honours:* Wales B.

1987–88	Hull C	3	1
1988–89	Hull C	11	0
1989–90	Hull C	22	0
1990–91	Hull C	26	0
1990–91	Rotherham U (loan)	7	0
1991–92	Hull C	42	8
1992–93	Hull C	26	4
1992–93	Coventry C	5	0
1993–94	Coventry C	16	0
1993–94	Birmingham C (loan)	3	0
1994–95	Coventry C	11	1
1995–96	St Johnstone	18	2
1996–97	St Johnstone	25	5
1997–98	St Johnstone	24	3
1998–99	Wigan Ath	7	0
1998–99	Hearts	5	0
Total:		**251**	**24**

JENSEN, Claus — Midfield

H: 5 11 W: 12 00 b.Nykobing 29-4-77

Source: Stubbekobing, Nykobing. *Honours:* Denmark Under-21.

1995–96	Naestved	4	0
1996–97	Lyngby	31	3
1997–98	Lyngby	31	11
1998–99	Bolton W	44	2
Total:		**110**	**16**

JEPSON, Ronnie — Forward

H: 6 0 W: 14 00 b.Stoke 12-5-63

Source: Nantwich T.

1988–89	Port Vale	2	0
1989–90	Port Vale	5	0
1989–90	Peterborough U (loan)	18	5
1990–91	Port Vale	15	0
1990–91	Preston NE	14	3
1991–92	Preston NE	24	5
1992–93	Exeter C	38	8
1993–94	Exeter C	16	13
1993–94	Huddersfield T	23	5
1994–95	Huddersfield T	41	19
1995–96	Huddersfield T	43	12
1996–97	Bury	31	9
1997–98	Bury	16	0
1997–98	Oldham Ath	9	4
1998–99	Burnley	15	1
Total:		**310**	**84**

JERKAN, Nikola — Defender

H: 6 2 W: 12 07 b.Sinj 8-12-64

Source: Zagreb, Cibalia Vinkovci, Hajduk Split. *Honours:* Croatia 30 full caps, 1 goal.

1990–91	Oviedo	34	0
1991–92	Oviedo	33	0
1992–93	Oviedo	38	0
1993–94	Oviedo	32	0
1994–95	Oviedo	31	0
1995–96	Oviedo	35	1
1996–97	Nottingham F	14	0
1997–98	Nottingham F	0	0
1998–99	Nottingham F	0	0
Total:		**217**	**1**

JERMYN, Mark — Defender

H: 5 11 W: 12 00 b.West Germany 16-4-81

Source: Trainee.

1998–99	Torquay U	1	0
Total:		**1**	**0**

JESS, Eoin — Forward

H: 5 10 W: 11 07 b.Aberdeen 13-12-70

Source: Rangers 'S' Form. *Honours:* Scotland Under-21, 18 full caps, 2 goals.

1987–88	Aberdeen	0	0
1988–89	Aberdeen	2	0
1989–90	Aberdeen	11	3
1990–91	Aberdeen	27	13
1991–92	Aberdeen	39	12
1992–93	Aberdeen	31	12
1993–94	Aberdeen	41	6
1994–95	Aberdeen	25	1
1995–96	Aberdeen	25	3
1995–96	Coventry C	12	1
1996–97	Coventry C	27	0
1997–98	Aberdeen	34	9
1998–99	Aberdeen	36	14
Total:		**310**	**74**

JEVONS, Phillip — Midfield

H: 5 11 W: 11 07 b.Liverpool 1-8-79

Source: Trainee.

1996–97	Everton	0	0
1997–98	Everton	0	0
1998–99	Everton	1	0
Total:		**1**	**0**

JEWELL, Paul — Forward

H: 5 8 W: 12 01 b.Liverpool 28-9-64

Source: Apprentice.

1982–83	Liverpool	0	0
1983–84	Liverpool	0	0
1984–85	Wigan Ath	26	9
1985–86	Wigan Ath	29	6
1986–87	Wigan Ath	39	9
1987–88	Wigan Ath	43	11
1988–89	Bradford C	39	4
1989–90	Bradford C	30	4
1990–91	Bradford C	38	4
1991–92	Bradford C	30	6
1992–93	Bradford C	46	16
1993–94	Bradford C	30	5
1994–95	Bradford C	38	14
1995–96	Bradford C	18	3
1995–96	Grimsby T (loan)	5	1
1996–97	Bradford C	0	0
1997–98	Bradford C	0	0
1998–99	Bradford C	0	0
Total:		**411**	**92**

JIHAI, Sun — Defender

H: 5 10 W: 10 07 b.Dalian 30-9-77

Source: Dalian Wanda. *Honours:* China full caps.

1998–99	Crystal Palace	23	0
Total:		**23**	**0**

JOACHIM, Julian — Midfield

H: 5 6 W: 12 00 b.Boston 20-9-74

Source: Trainee. *Honours:* England Youth, Under-21.

1992–93	Leicester C	26	10
1993–94	Leicester C	36	11
1994–95	Leicester C	15	3
1995–96	Leicester C	22	1
1995–96	Aston Villa	11	1
1996–97	Aston Villa	15	3
1997–98	Aston Villa	26	8
1998–99	Aston Villa	36	14
Total:		**187**	**51**

JOBLING, Kevin — Midfield

H: 5 8 W: 12 00 b.Sunderland 1-1-68

Source: Apprentice.

1985–86	Leicester C	0	0
1986–87	Leicester C	3	0
1987–88	Leicester C	6	0
1987–88	Grimsby T	15	1
1988–89	Grimsby T	32	4
1989–90	Grimsby T	33	1
1990–91	Grimsby T	45	0
1991–92	Grimsby T	36	2
1992–93	Grimsby T	14	0
1993–94	Grimsby T	11	0
1993–94	Scunthorpe U (loan)	0	0
1994–95	Grimsby T	38	1
1995–96	Grimsby T	3	0
1996–97	Grimsby T	28	0
1997–98	Grimsby T	30	1
1998–99	Shrewsbury T	41	1
Total:		**335**	**11**

JOBSON, Richard — Defender

H: 6 2 W: 12 12 b.Holderness 9-5-63

Source: Burton Alb. *Honours:* England B.

1982–83	Watford	13	1
1983–84	Watford	13	2
1984–85	Watford	2	1
1984–85	Hull C	8	0
1985–86	Hull C	36	7
1986–87	Hull C	40	5
1987–88	Hull C	44	2
1988–89	Hull C	46	1
1989–90	Hull C	45	2
1990–91	Hull C	2	0

1990–91	Oldham Ath	44	1
1991–92	Oldham Ath	36	2
1992–93	Oldham Ath	40	2
1993–94	Oldham Ath	37	5
1994–95	Oldham Ath	20	0
1995–96	Oldham Ath	12	0
1995–96	Leeds U	12	1
1996–97	Leeds U	10	0
1997–98	Leeds U	0	0
1997–98	Southend U (loan)	8	1
1997–98	Manchester C	6	1
1998–99	Manchester C	0	0
Total:		**474**	**34**

JOHANSEN, Martin — Midfield

H: 5 8 W: 11 01 b.Glostrup 22-7-72

1990	KB Copenhagen	20	4
1991	KB Copenhagen	0	0
1991–92	B1903	25	8
1992–93	FC Copenhagen	21	12
1993–94	FC Copenhagen	22	11
1994–95	FC Copenhagen	25	4
1995–96	FC Copenhagen	24	2
1996–97	FC Copenhagen	24	2
1997–98	Coventry C	2	0
1998–99	Coventry C	0	0
Total:		**163**	**43**

JOHANSEN, Michael — Midfield

H: 5 6 W: 10 05 b.Glostrup 22-7-72

1990	KB Copenhagen	15	1
1991–92	B 1903	26	1
1992–93	FC Copenhagen	28	1
1993–94	FC Copenhagen	28	4
1994–95	FC Copenhagen	27	4
1995–96	FC Copenhagen	31	8
1996–97	Bolton W	33	5
1997–98	Bolton W	16	1
1998–99	Bolton W	43	7
Total:		**247**	**32**

JOHANSEN, Stig — Forward

H: 5 9 W: 12 05 b.Norway 13-6-72

Honours: Norway 3 full caps.

1995	Bodo Glimt	26	19
1996	Bodo Glimt	26	14
1997	Bodo Glimt	18	12
1997–98	Southampton	6	0
1997–98	Bristol C (loan)	3	0
1998–99	Southampton	0	0
Total:		**79**	**45**

JOHANSSON, Jonatan — Midfield

H: 6 1 W: 12 08 b.Stockholm 16-8-75

Source: Flora Tallinn. *Honours:* Finland 8 full caps, 2 goals.

1997–98	Rangers	6	0
1998–99	Rangers	25	8
Total:		**31**	**8**

JOHNROSE, Lenny — Midfield

H: 5 11 W: 12 06 b.Preston 27-11-69

Source: Trainee.

1987–88	Blackburn R	1	0
1988–89	Blackburn R	0	0
1989–90	Blackburn R	8	3
1990–91	Blackburn R	26	7
1991–92	Blackburn R	7	1
1991–92	Preston NE (loan)	3	1
1991–92	Hartlepool U	15	2
1992–93	Hartlepool U	38	6
1993–94	Hartlepool U	13	3
1993–94	Bury	14	0
1994–95	Bury	26	4
1995–96	Bury	34	6
1996–97	Bury	43	4
1997–98	Bury	44	3
1998–99	Bury	27	1
1998–99	Burnley	12	1
Total:		**311**	**42**

JOHNSEN, Ronny — Defender

H: 6 3 W: 13 02 b.Sandefjord 10-6-69

Honours: Norway 45 full caps, 2 goals.

1992	Lyn	12	1
1993	Lyn	19	6
1994	Lillestrom	10	3
1995	Lillestrom	13	1
1995–96	Besiktas	22	1
1996–97	Manchester U	31	0
1997–98	Manchester U	22	2
1998–99	Manchester U	22	3
Total:		**151**	**17**

JOHNSON, Alan — Defender

H: 6 0 W: 14 02 b.Wigan 19-2-71

Source: Trainee.

1988–89	Wigan Ath	8	1
1989–90	Wigan Ath	33	1
1990–91	Wigan Ath	43	5
1991–92	Wigan Ath	44	4
1992–93	Wigan Ath	36	1
1993–94	Wigan Ath	16	1
1993–94	Lincoln C	16	0
1994–95	Lincoln C	25	0
1995–96	Lincoln C	22	0

1995–96	Preston NE (loan)	2	0
1996–97	Rochdale	46	4
1997–98	Rochdale	0	0
1998–99	Rochdale	16	0
Total:		**307**	**17**

JOHNSON, Andrew — Forward

H: 5 6 W: 10 00 b.Bedford 10-2-81

Source: Trainee. *Honours:* England Youth.

1997–98	Birmingham C	0	0
1998–99	Birmingham C	4	0
Total:		**4**	**0**

JOHNSON, Andy — Midfield

H: 6 1 W: 13 03 b.Bristol 2-5-74

Source: Trainee. *Honours:* Wales 4 full caps.

1991–92	Norwich C	2	0
1992–93	Norwich C	2	1
1993–94	Norwich C	2	0
1994–95	Norwich C	7	0
1995–96	Norwich C	26	7
1996–97	Norwich C	27	5
1997–98	Nottingham F	34	4
1998–99	Nottingham F	28	0
Total:		**128**	**17**

JOHNSON, Damien — Midfield

H: 5 10 W: 11 02 b.Lisburn 18-11-78

Source: Trainee. *Honours:* Northern Ireland Under-21, 1 full cap.

1995–96	Blackburn R	0	0
1996–97	Blackburn R	0	0
1997–98	Blackburn R	0	0
1997–98	Nottingham F (loan)	6	0
1998–99	Blackburn R	21	1
Total:		**27**	**1**

JOHNSON, David — Forward

H: 5 6 W: 12 00 b.Kingston, Jam 15-8-76

Source: Trainee. *Honours:* England Schools, B.

1994–95	Manchester U	0	0
1995–96	Bury	36	5
1996–97	Bury	44	8
1997–98	Bury	17	5
1997–98	Ipswich T	31	20
1998–99	Ipswich T	42	13
Total:		**170**	**51**

JOHNSON, David — Goalkeeper

b.Bolton 18-3-80

Source: Trainee.

1998–99	Sheffield U	0	0

JOHNSON, Gavin — Defender

H: 5 11 W: 11 07 b.Eye 10-10-70

Source: Trainee.

1988–89	Ipswich T	4	0
1989–90	Ipswich T	6	0
1990–91	Ipswich T	7	0
1991–92	Ipswich T	42	5
1992–93	Ipswich T	40	5
1993–94	Ipswich T	16	1
1994–95	Ipswich T	17	0
1995–96	Luton T	5	0
1995–96	Wigan Ath	27	3
1996–97	Wigan Ath	37	3
1997–98	Wigan Ath	20	2
1998–99	Dunfermline Ath	18	0
Total:		**239**	**19**

JOHNSON, Grant — Midfield

H: 5 11 W: 11 03 b.Dundee 24-3-72

Source: Broughty Ferry. *Honours:* Scotland Under-21.

1990–91	Dundee U	0	0
1991–92	Dundee U	10	1
1992–93	Dundee U	17	1
1993–94	Dundee U	10	0
1994–95	Dundee U	13	1
1995–96	Dundee U	28	4
1996–97	Dundee U	7	0
1997–98	Dundee U	0	0
1997–98	Huddersfield T	29	1
1998–99	Huddersfield T	36	4
Total:		**150**	**12**

JOHNSON, Lee — Midfield

b.Newmarket 7-6-81

Source: Trainee.

1998–99	Watford	0	0

JOHNSON, Marvin — Defender

H: 6 1 W: 13 00 b.Wembley 29-10-68

Source: Apprentice.

1986–87	Luton T	0	0
1987–88	Luton T	9	0
1988–89	Luton T	16	0
1989–90	Luton T	12	0
1990–91	Luton T	26	0
1991–92	Luton T	0	0
1992–93	Luton T	40	3
1993–94	Luton T	17	0
1994–95	Luton T	46	1
1995–96	Luton T	36	0
1996–97	Luton T	44	0
1997–98	Luton T	14	2
1998–99	Luton T	42	0
Total:		**302**	**6**

JOHNSON, Michael — Defender

H: 5 11 W: 11 00 b.Nottingham 4-7-73

Source: Trainee.

Season	Club	Apps	Goals
1991–92	Notts Co	5	0
1992–93	Notts Co	37	0
1993–94	Notts Co	34	0
1994–95	Notts Co	31	0
1995–96	Notts Co	0	0
1995–96	Birmingham C	33	0
1996–97	Birmingham C	35	0
1997–98	Birmingham C	38	3
1998–99	Birmingham C	45	5
Total:		**258**	**8**

JOHNSON, Richard — Midfield

H: 5 10 W: 12 07 b.Kurri Kurri 27-4-74

Source: Trainee.

Season	Club	Apps	Goals
1991–92	Watford	2	0
1992–93	Watford	1	0
1993–94	Watford	27	0
1994–95	Watford	35	3
1995–96	Watford	20	1
1996–97	Watford	37	2
1997–98	Watford	42	7
1998–99	Watford	40	4
Total:		**204**	**17**

JOHNSON, Ross — Defender

H: 6 0 W: 13 00 b.Brighton 2-1-76

Source: Trainee.

Season	Club	Apps	Goals
1993–94	Brighton & HA	2	0
1994–95	Brighton & HA	0	0
1995–96	Brighton & HA	20	0
1996–97	Brighton & HA	29	0
1997–98	Brighton & HA	38	0
1998–99	Brighton & HA	34	2
Total:		**123**	**2**

JOHNSON, Seth — Midfield

H: 5 10 W: 11 00 b.Birmingham 12-3-79

Source: Trainee. *Honours:* England Youth, Under-21.

Season	Club	Apps	Goals
1996–97	Crewe Alex	11	1
1997–98	Crewe Alex	40	1
1998–99	Crewe Alex	42	4
Total:		**93**	**6**

JOHNSON, Tommy — Forward

H: 5 11 W: 12 07 b.Newcastle 15-1-71

Source: Trainee. *Honours:* England Under-21.

Season	Club	Apps	Goals
1988–89	Notts Co	10	4
1989–90	Notts Co	40	18
1990–91	Notts Co	37	16
1991–92	Notts Co	31	9
1991–92	Derby Co	12	2
1992–93	Derby Co	35	8
1993–94	Derby Co	37	13
1994–95	Derby Co	14	7
1994–95	Aston Villa	14	4
1995–96	Aston Villa	23	5
1996–97	Aston Villa	20	4
1996–97	Celtic	4	1
1997–98	Celtic	2	0
1998–99	Celtic	3	3
Total:		**282**	**94**

JOHNSTON, Allan — Forward

H: 5 7 W: 9 07 b.Glasgow 14-12-73

Source: Tynecastle BC. *Honours:* Scotland Under-21, B, 6 full caps, 2 goals.

Season	Club	Apps	Goals
1991–92	Hearts	0	0
1992–93	Hearts	2	1
1993–94	Hearts	28	1
1994–95	Hearts	21	1
1995–96	Hearts	33	9
1996–97	Rennes	23	2
1996–97	Sunderland	6	1
1997–98	Sunderland	40	11
1998–99	Sunderland	40	7
Total:		**193**	**33**

JOHNSTON, Ray — Goalkeeper

H: 6 1 W: 13 13 b.Bristol 5-5-81

Source: Trainee. *Honours:* England Schools.

Season	Club	Apps	Goals
1998–99	Bristol R	1	0
Total:		**1**	**0**

JONES, Barry — Defender

H: 5 10 W: 11 07 b.Prescot 20-6-70

Source: Prescot T.

Season	Club	Apps	Goals
1988–89	Liverpool	0	0
1989–90	Liverpool	0	0
1990–91	Liverpool	0	0
1991–92	Liverpool	0	0
1992–93	Wrexham	42	2
1993–94	Wrexham	33	2
1994–95	Wrexham	44	0
1995–96	Wrexham	40	0
1996–97	Wrexham	22	0
1997–98	Wrexham	14	1
1997–98	York C	23	2
1998–99	York C	45	2
Total:		**263**	**9**

JONES, Bradley — Goalkeeper

H: 6 3 W: 12 01 b.Armadale 19-3-82

Source: Trainee.

1998–99	Middlesbrough	0	0

JONES, David — Midfield

H: 5 7 W: 9 10 b.Goole 17-11-78

Source: Goole T.

1997–98	Blackpool	0	0
1998–99	Blackpool	0	0

JONES, Eifion — Defender

H: 6 3 W: 13 00 b.Llanrug 28-9-80

Source: Trainee.

1997–98	Liverpool	0	0
1998–99	Liverpool	0	0

JONES, Gary — Forward

H: 6 1 W: 13 00 b.Huddersfield 6-4-69

Source: Rossington Main.

1988–89	Doncaster R	17	2
1989–90	Doncaster R	3	0
From Boston U			
1993–94	Southend U	22	3
1993–94	Lincoln C (loan)	4	2
1994–95	Southend U	25	11
1995–96	Southend U	23	2
1995–96	Notts Co	18	5
1996–97	Notts Co	27	3
1996–97	Scunthorpe U (loan)	11	5
1997–98	Notts Co	44	28
1998–99	Notts Co	28	2
1998–99	Hartlepool U	12	1
Total:		**234**	**64**

JONES, Gary — Forward

H: 6 3 W: 13 05 b.Chester 10-5-75

Source: Trainee.

1993–94	Tranmere R	6	2
1994–95	Tranmere R	19	3
1995–96	Tranmere R	23	1
1996–97	Tranmere R	30	6
1997–98	Tranmere R	43	8
1998–99	Tranmere R	26	5
Total:		**147**	**25**

JONES, Gary — Midfield

H: 5 11 W: 11 07 b.Birkenhead 3-6-77

1997–98	Swansea C	8	0
1997–98	Rochdale	17	2
1998–99	Rochdale	20	0
Total:		**45**	**2**

JONES, Graeme — Forward

H: 6 0 W: 14 04 b.Gateshead 13-3-70

Source: Bridlington T.

1993–94	Doncaster R	28	4
1994–95	Doncaster R	32	12
1995–96	Doncaster R	32	10
1996–97	Wigan Ath	40	31
1997–98	Wigan Ath	33	9
1998–99	Wigan Ath	20	3
Total:		**185**	**69**

JONES, Jason — Goalkeeper

H: 6 2 W: 12 10 b.Wrexham 10-5-79

Source: Liverpool Trainee.

1997–98	Swansea C	1	0
1998–99	Swansea C	3	0
Total:		**4**	**0**

JONES, Jon — Forward

H: 5 11 W: 11 05 b.Wrexham 27-10-78

Source: Trainee.

1996–97	Chester C	17	1
1997–98	Chester C	7	1
1998–99	Chester C	8	0
Total:		**32**	**2**

JONES, Keith — Midfield

H: 5 9 W: 10 11 b.Dulwich 14-10-65

Source: Apprentice. *Honours:* England Schools, Youth.

1982–83	Chelsea	2	0
1983–84	Chelsea	0	0
1984–85	Chelsea	19	2
1985–86	Chelsea	14	2
1986–87	Chelsea	17	3
1987–88	Chelsea	0	0
1987–88	Brentford	36	1
1988–89	Brentford	40	3
1989–90	Brentford	42	2
1990–91	Brentford	45	6
1991–92	Brentford	6	1
1991–92	Southend U	34	5
1992–93	Southend U	29	1
1993–94	Southend U	20	5
1994–95	Southend U	7	0
1994–95	Charlton Ath	31	1
1995–96	Charlton Ath	25	0
1996–97	Charlton Ath	19	0
1997–98	Charlton Ath	44	3
1998–99	Charlton Ath	22	1
Total:		**452**	**36**

JONES, Lee — Forward

H: 5 8 W: 10 06 b.Wrexham 29-5-73

Source: Trainee. *Honours:* Wales Under-21, 2 full caps.

1990–91	Wrexham	18	5
1991–92	Wrexham	21	5
1991–92	Liverpool	0	0
1992–93	Liverpool	0	0
1993–94	Liverpool	0	0
1993–94	Crewe Alex (loan)	8	1
1994–95	Liverpool	1	0
1995–96	Liverpool	0	0
1995–96	Wrexham (loan)	20	9
1996–97	Liverpool	2	0
1996–97	Wrexham (loan)	6	0
1996–97	Tranmere R (loan)	8	5
1997–98	Tranmere R	34	9
1998–99	Tranmere R	30	2
Total:		**148**	**36**

JONES, Lee — Goalkeeper

H: 6 3 W: 15 10 b.Pontypridd 9-8-70

Source: Porth.

1993–94	Swansea C	0	0
1994–95	Swansea C	2	0
1995–96	Swansea C	1	0
1995–96	Crewe Alex (loan)	0	0
1996–97	Swansea C	1	0
1997–98	Swansea C	2	0
1997–98	Bristol R	8	0
1998–99	Bristol R	32	0
Total:		**46**	**0**

JONES, Mark — Forward

H: 5 9 W: 12 06 b.Walsall 7-9-79

Source: Trainee. *Honours:* England Schools.

1996–97	Wolverhampton W	0	0
1997–98	Wolverhampton W	0	0
1998–99	Wolverhampton W	2	0
Total:		**2**	**0**

JONES, Mark — Midfield

b.Havering 4-8-79

Source: Trainee.

1996–97	Southend U	1	0
1997–98	Southend U	0	0
1998–99	Southend U	0	0
Total:		**1**	**0**

JONES, Matthew — Midfield

H: 5 11 W: 11 09 b.Llanelli 1-9-80

Source: Trainee. *Honours:* Wales Youth, Under-21, B.

1997–98	Leeds U	0	0
1998–99	Leeds U	8	0
Total:		**8**	**0**

JONES, Matthew — Forward

H: 6 0 W: 11 03 b.Shrewsbury 11-10-80

Source: Trainee.

1998–99	Shrewsbury T	1	0
Total:		**1**	**0**

JONES, Nathan — Defender

H: 5 7 W: 10 12 b.Rhondda 28-5-73

Source: Cardiff C Trainee, Maesteg Park, Ton Pentre, Merthyr T.

1995–96	Luton T	0	0
Badajoz, Numancia			
1997–98	Southend U	39	0
1998–99	Southend U	17	0
1998–99	Scarborough (loan)	9	0
Total:		**65**	**0**

JONES, Paul — Goalkeeper

H: 6 2 W: 15 03 b.Chirk 18-4-67

Source: Bridgnorth, Kidderminster H. *Honours:* Wales 11 full caps.

1991–92	Wolverhampton W	0	0
1992–93	Wolverhampton W	16	0
1993–94	Wolverhampton W	0	0
1994–95	Wolverhampton W	9	0
1995–96	Wolverhampton W	8	0
1996–97	Stockport Co	46	0
1997–98	Southampton	38	0
1998–99	Southampton	31	0
Total:		**148**	**0**

JONES, Rob — Defender

H: 5 8 W: 11 00 b.Wrexham 5-11-71

Source: Trainee. *Honours:* England Under-21, 8 full caps.

1987–88	Crewe Alex	5	0
1988–89	Crewe Alex	19	1
1989–90	Crewe Alex	11	0
1990–91	Crewe Alex	32	1
1991–92	Crewe Alex	8	0
1991–92	Liverpool	28	0
1992–93	Liverpool	30	0
1993–94	Liverpool	38	0
1994–95	Liverpool	31	0
1995–96	Liverpool	33	0

1996–97	Liverpool	2	0
1997–98	Liverpool	21	0
1998–99	Liverpool	0	0
Total:		**258**	**2**

JONES, Scott — Defender

H: 5 10 W: 12 01 b.Sheffield 1-5-75

Source: Trainee.

1993–94	Barnsley	0	0
1994–95	Barnsley	0	0
1995–96	Barnsley	4	0
1996–97	Barnsley	18	0
1997–98	Barnsley	12	1
1997–98	Mansfield T (loan)	6	0
1997–98	Notts Co (loan)	0	0
1998–99	Barnsley	29	3
Total:		**69**	**4**

JONES, Steve — Forward

H: 5 11 W: 12 00 b.Cambridge 17-3-70

Source: Billericay T.

1992–93	West Ham U	6	2
1993–94	West Ham U	8	2
1994–95	West Ham U	2	0
1994–95	Bournemouth	30	9
1995–96	Bournemouth	44	17
1995–96	West Ham U	0	0
1996–97	West Ham U	8	0
1996–97	Charlton Ath	2	0
1997–98	Charlton Ath	23	7
1997–98	Bournemouth (loan)	5	4
1998–99	Charlton Ath	25	1
Total:		**153**	**42**

JONES, Steve — Defender

H: 5 10 W: 12 02 b.Bristol 25-12-70

Source: Cheltenham T.

1995–96	Swansea C	17	0
1996–97	Swansea C	46	1
1997–98	Swansea C	0	0
1998–99	Swansea C	32	2
Total:		**95**	**3**

JONES, Stuart — Goalkeeper

H: 6 1 W: 13 11 b.Bristol 24-10-77

Source: Weston-Super-Mare.

1997–98	Sheffield W	0	0
1998–99	Sheffield W	0	0
1998–99	Crewe Alex (loan)	0	0

JONES, Thomas — Forward

H: 5 10 W: 11 02 b.Middlesbrough 26-3-80

Source: Trainee.

1998–99	Middlesbrough	0	0

JONES, Vinnie — Midfield

H: 6 0 W: 11 12 b.Watford 5-1-65

Source: Wealdstone. *Honours:* Wales 9 full caps.

1986–87	Wimbledon	22	4
1987–88	Wimbledon	24	2
1988–89	Wimbledon	31	3
1989–90	Leeds U	45	5
1990–91	Leeds U	1	0
1990–91	Sheffield U	31	2
1991–92	Sheffield U	4	0
1991–92	Chelsea	35	3
1992–93	Chelsea	7	1
1992–93	Wimbledon	27	1
1993–94	Wimbledon	33	2
1994–95	Wimbledon	33	3
1995–96	Wimbledon	31	3
1996–97	Wimbledon	29	3
1997–98	Wimbledon	24	0
1997–98	QPR	7	1
1998–99	QPR	2	0
Total:		**386**	**33**

JONK, Wim — Midfield

H: 6 1 W: 12 02 b.Volendam 12-10-66

Honours: Holland 48 full caps, 11 goals.

1986–87	Volendam	36	23
1987–88	Volendam	23	5
1988–89	Ajax	17	6
1989–90	Ajax	13	3
1990–91	Ajax	17	1
1991–92	Ajax	26	5
1992–93	Ajax	23	3
1993–94	Internazionale	25	6
1994–95	Internazionale	29	2
1995–96	PSV Eindhoven	29	6
1996–97	PSV Eindhoven	32	9
1997–98	PSV Eindhoven	28	5
1998–99	Sheffield W	38	2
Total:		**336**	**76**

JONSSON, Siggi — Defender

H: 5 11 W: 12 06 b.Akranes 26-9-66

Source: IA Akranes. *Honours:* Iceland 54 full caps, 2 goals.

1984–85	Sheffield W	3	0
1985–86	Sheffield W	10	2
1985–86	Barnsley (loan)	5	0
1986–87	Sheffield W	13	0
1987–88	Sheffield W	13	1

1988–89	Sheffield W	28	1
1989–90	Arsenal	6	1
1990–91	Arsenal	2	0
1991–92	Arsenal	0	0
1992	IA Akranes	11	0
1993	IA Akranes	16	1
1994	IA Akranes	13	3
1995	IA Akranes	16	2
1996	Orebro	20	0
1997	Orebro	22	2
1997–98	Dundee U	15	0
1998–99	Dundee U	14	1
Total:		**207**	**14**

JORDAN, Andrew — Defender

H: 6 0 W: 13 01 b.Manchester 14-12-79

Source: Trainee.

1997–98	Bristol C	0	0
1998–99	Bristol C	1	0
Total:		**1**	**0**

JORDAN, Scott — Midfield

H: 5 9 W: 11 02 b.Newcastle 19-7-75

Source: Trainee.

1992–93	York C	1	0
1993–94	York C	0	0
1994–95	York C	37	3
1995–96	York C	26	1
1996–97	York C	15	1
1997–98	York C	16	0
1998–99	York C	32	5
Total:		**127**	**10**

JORDAN, Stephen — Midfield

b.Warrington 6-3-82

Source: Scholarship.

1998–99	Manchester C	0	0

JOSEPH, Marc — Defender

H: 6 1 W: 12 12 b.Leicester 10-11-76

Source: Trainee.

1995–96	Cambridge U	12	0
1996–97	Cambridge U	8	0
1997–98	Cambridge U	41	0
1998–99	Cambridge U	29	0
Total:		**90**	**0**

JOSEPH, Matt — Defender

H: 5 7 W: 10 02 b.Bethnal Green 30-9-72

Source: Trainee.

1991–92	Arsenal	0	0
1992–93	Gillingham	0	0
1993–94	Cambridge U	27	2
1994–95	Cambridge U	39	2
1995–96	Cambridge U	42	2
1996–97	Cambridge U	44	0
1997–98	Cambridge U	7	0
1997–98	Leyton Orient	14	1
1998–99	Leyton Orient	34	0
Total:		**207**	**7**

JOSEPH, Roger — Defender

H: 5 11 W: 11 10 b.Paddington 24-12-65

Source: Juniors. *Honours:* England B.

1984–85	Brentford	1	0
1985–86	Brentford	28	1
1986–87	Brentford	32	1
1987–88	Brentford	43	0
1988–89	Wimbledon	31	0
1989–90	Wimbledon	19	0
1990–91	Wimbledon	38	0
1991–92	Wimbledon	26	0
1992–93	Wimbledon	32	0
1993–94	Wimbledon	13	0
1994–95	Wimbledon	3	0
1994–95	Millwall (loan)	5	0
1995–96	Wimbledon	0	0
1996–97	Leyton Orient	15	0
1996–97	WBA	2	0
1997–98	Leyton Orient	25	0
1998–99	Leyton Orient	24	0
Total:		**337**	**2**

JOY, Ian — Midfield

H: 5 10 W: 11 00 b.San Diego 14-7-81

Source: Trainee.

1998–99	Tranmere R	0	0

JOYCE, Warren — Midfield

H: 5 9 W: 12 01 b.Oldham 20-1-65

Source: School.

1982–83	Bolton W	8	0
1983–84	Bolton W	45	3
1984–85	Bolton W	45	5
1985–86	Bolton W	31	4
1986–87	Bolton W	44	5
1987–88	Bolton W	11	0
1987–88	Preston NE	22	0
1988–89	Preston NE	40	9
1989–90	Preston NE	44	11
1990–91	Preston NE	42	9
1991–92	Preston NE	29	5
1992–93	Plymouth Arg	30	3
1993–94	Burnley	22	4
1994–95	Burnley	5	0
1994–95	Hull C (loan)	9	3
1995–96	Burnley	43	5

1996–97	Hull C	45	5
1997–98	Hull C	45	4
1998–99	Hull C	29	2
Total:		**589**	**77**

JUANJO — Midfield

H: 5 8 W: 10 00 b.Barcelona 4-5-77

1997–98	Barcelona B	36	4
1998–99	Hearts	11	0
Total:		**47**	**4**

JUKES, Nathan — Midfield

H: 5 11 W: 11 13 b.Worcester 10-4-79

Source: Trainee.

1997–98	Portsmouth	0	0
1998–99	Portsmouth	0	0

JULES, Mark — Defender

H: 5 7 W: 10 09 b.Bradford 5-9-71

Source: Trainee.

1990–91	Bradford C	0	0
1991–92	Scarborough	41	8
1992–93	Scarborough	36	8
1993–94	Chesterfield	33	1
1994–95	Chesterfield	23	0
1995–96	Chesterfield	32	2
1996–97	Chesterfield	42	0
1997–98	Chesterfield	33	1
1998–99	Chesterfield	23	0
Total:		**263**	**20**

JUPP, Duncan — Defender

H: 6 0 W: 12 11 b.Guildford 25-1-75

Source: Trainee. *Honours:* Scotland Under-21.

1992–93	Fulham	3	0
1993–94	Fulham	30	0
1994–95	Fulham	36	2
1995–96	Fulham	36	0
1996–97	Wimbledon	6	0
1997–98	Wimbledon	3	0
1998–99	Wimbledon	6	0
Total:		**120**	**2**

KACHLOUL, Hassan — Midfield

H: 6 1 W: 12 09 b.Agadir 19-2-73

Honours: Morocco 12 full caps.

1992–93	Nimes	17	1
1993–94	Nimes	37	17
1994–95	Nimes	32	8
1995–96	Dunkerque	28	6
1996–97	Metz	7	0
1997–98	St Etienne	16	0
1998–99	Southampton	22	5
Total:		**159**	**37**

KAMARK, Pontus — Defender

H: 5 11 W: 12 02 b.Vasteras 5-4-69

Honours: Sweden 45 full caps.

1985	Vasteras	1	0
1986	Vasteras	10	0
1987	Vasteras	18	1
1988	Vasteras	26	5
1989	IFK Gothenburg	18	3
1990	IFK Gothenburg	8	0
1991	IFK Gothenburg	26	0
1992	IFK Gothenburg	24	0
1993	IFK Gothenburg	26	0
1994	IFK Gothenburg	22	0
1995	IFK Gothenburg	20	1
1995–96	Leicester C	1	0
1996–97	Leicester C	10	0
1997–98	Leicester C	35	0
1998–99	Leicester C	19	0
Total:		**264**	**10**

KANCHELSKIS, Andrei — Forward

H: 5 10 W: 12 12 b.Kirovograd 23-1-69

Honours: USSR/CIS 23 full caps, 3 goals; Russia 36 full caps, 5 goals.

1988	Dynamo Kiev	7	1
1989	Dynamo Kiev	15	0
1990	Donetsk	16	2
1991	Donetsk	5	1
1990–91	Manchester U	1	0
1991–92	Manchester U	34	5
1992–93	Manchester U	27	3
1993–94	Manchester U	31	6
1994–95	Manchester U	30	14
1995–96	Everton	32	16
1996–97	Everton	20	4
1997–98	Fiorentina	17	2
1998–99	Rangers	30	8
Total:		**265**	**62**

KANDOL, Tresor — Forward

H: 6 1 W: 11 07 b.Banga 30-8-81

Source: Trainee.

1998–99	Luton T	4	0
Total:		**4**	**0**

KANE, Paul — Midfield

H: 5 8 W: 9 09 b.Edinburgh 20-6-65

Source: Salvesen BC. *Honours:* Scotland Youth.

1982–83	Hibernian	0	0
1983–84	Hibernian	13	1
1984–85	Hibernian	34	8
1985–86	Hibernian	32	5
1986–87	Hibernian	37	1
1987–88	Hibernian	44	10

1988–89	Hibernian	35	5
1989–90	Hibernian	31	3
1990–91	Hibernian	21	0
1990–91	Oldham Ath	17	0
1991–92	Oldham Ath	4	0
1991–92	Aberdeen	25	2
1992–93	Aberdeen	27	4
1993–94	Aberdeen	39	3
1994–95	Aberdeen	27	2
1995–96	Barnsley (loan)	4	0
1996	Viking	15	3
1997–98	St Johnstone	27	1
1998–99	St Johnstone	34	3
Total:		**466**	**51**

KANU, Nwankwo — Forward

b.Owerri 1-8-76

Honours: Nigeria 11 full caps, 2 goals.

1991–92	Federation Works	30	9
1992–93	Iwanyanwu	30	6
1993–94	Ajax	6	2
1994–95	Ajax	18	10
1995–96	Ajax	30	13
1996–97	Internazionale	0	0
1997–98	Internazionale	11	1
1998–99	Internazionale	1	0
1998–99	Arsenal	12	6
Total:		**138**	**47**

KATCHURO, Petr — Forward

H: 6 0 W: 12 06 b.Minsk 2-8-72

Honours: Russia Youth, Belarus 23 full caps, 4 goals.

1993–94	Dynamo 93	15	7
1993–94	Dynamo Minsk	13	14
1994–95	Dynamo Minsk	22	14
1995	Dynamo Minsk	15	15
1996	Dynamo Minsk	10	9
1996–97	Sheffield U	40	12
1997–98	Sheffield U	16	0
1998–99	Sheffield U	16	6
Total:		**147**	**77**

KAVANAGH, Graham — Midfield

H: 5 10 W: 12 06 b.Dublin 2-12-73

Source: Home Farm. *Honours:* Eire Under-21, 3 full caps.

1991–92	Middlesbrough	0	0
1992–93	Middlesbrough	10	0
1993–94	Middlesbrough	11	2
1993–94	Darlington (loan)	5	0
1994–95	Middlesbrough	7	0
1995–96	Middlesbrough	7	1
1996–97	Middlesbrough	0	0
1996–97	Stoke C	38	4
1997–98	Stoke C	44	5
1998–99	Stoke C	36	11
Total:		**158**	**23**

KAVANAGH, Jason — Defender

H: 5 8 W: 12 09 b.Meriden 23-11-71

Source: Birmingham C Schoolboy. *Honours:* England Schools, FA Schools, Youth.

1988–89	Derby Co	0	0
1989–90	Derby Co	0	0
1990–91	Derby Co	11	0
1991–92	Derby Co	25	0
1992–93	Derby Co	10	0
1993–94	Derby Co	19	0
1994–95	Derby Co	25	1
1995–96	Derby Co	9	0
1996–97	Derby Co	0	0
1996–97	Wycombe W	27	0
1997–98	Wycombe W	45	1
1998–99	Wycombe W	18	0
1998–99	Stoke C	8	0
Total:		**197**	**2**

KAVELASHVILI, Mikhail — Midfield

H: 5 11 W: 12 01 b.Tbilisi 22-7-71

Source: Spartak Vladikavkaz. *Honours:* Georgia 20 full caps, 3 goals.

1995–96	Manchester C	4	1
1996–97	Manchester C	24	2
1997–98	Manchester C	0	0
1998–99	Manchester C	0	0
Total:		**28**	**3**

KAVEN, Mikko — Goalkeeper

H: 6 1 W: 11 11 b.Lahti 19-2-75

1994	Kuusysi	18	0
1995	Kuusysi	18	0
1996	Kuusysi	26	0
1997	HJK Helsinki	5	0
1998–99	Motherwell	16	0
Total:		**83**	**0**

KAY, John — Defender

H: 5 10 W: 11 08 b.Sunderland 29-1-64

Source: Apprentice.

1981–82	Arsenal	0	0
1982–83	Arsenal	7	0
1983–84	Arsenal	7	0
1984–85	Wimbledon	21	1
1984–85	Middlesbrough (loan)	8	0
1985–86	Wimbledon	26	1
1986–87	Wimbledon	16	0
1987–88	Sunderland	46	0
1988–89	Sunderland	11	0
1989–90	Sunderland	32	0
1990–91	Sunderland	30	0

1991–92	Sunderland	41	0
1992–93	Sunderland	36	0
1993–94	Sunderland	3	0
1994–95	Sunderland	0	0
1995–96	Sunderland	0	0
1995–96	Shrewsbury T (loan)	7	0
1996–97	Preston NE	7	0
1996–97	Scarborough	34	0
1997–98	Scarborough	40	0
1998–99	Scarborough	24	0
Total:		**396**	**2**

KEANE, Robbie — Forward

H: 5 9 W: 11 07 b.Dublin 8-7-80

Source: Trainee. *Honours:* Eire 9 full caps, 2 goals.

1997–98	Wolverhampton W	38	11
1998–99	Wolverhampton W	33	11
Total:		**71**	**22**

KEANE, Roy — Midfield

H: 5 11 W: 12 01 b.Cork 10-8-71

Source: Cobh Ramb. *Honours:* Eire Youth, Under-21, 42 full caps, 5 goals.

1990–91	Nottingham F	35	8
1991–92	Nottingham F	39	8
1992–93	Nottingham F	40	6
1993–94	Manchester U	37	5
1994–95	Manchester U	25	2
1995–96	Manchester U	29	6
1996–97	Manchester U	21	2
1997–98	Manchester U	9	2
1998–99	Manchester U	35	2
Total:		**270**	**41**

KEARTON, Jason — Goalkeeper

H: 6 1 W: 12 03 b.Ipswich (Aus) 9-7-69

Source: Brisbane Lions.

1988–89	Everton	0	0
1989–90	Everton	0	0
1990–91	Everton	0	0
1991–92	Everton	0	0
1991–92	Stoke C (loan)	16	0
1991–92	Blackpool (loan)	14	0
1992–93	Everton	5	0
1993–94	Everton	0	0
1994–95	Everton	1	0
1994–95	Notts Co (loan)	10	0
1995–96	Everton	0	0
1995–96	Preston NE (loan)	0	0
1996–97	Everton	0	0
1996–97	Crewe Alex	30	0
1997–98	Crewe Alex	43	0
1998–99	Crewe Alex	46	0
Total:		**165**	**0**

KEATES, Dean — Midfield

H: 5 5 W: 10 07 b.Walsall 30-6-78

Source: Trainee.

1996–97	Walsall	2	0
1997–98	Walsall	33	1
1998–99	Walsall	43	2
Total:		**78**	**3**

KEEBLE, Chris — Midfield

H: 5 9 W: 11 00 b.Colchester 17-9-78

Source: Trainee.

1997–98	Ipswich T	1	0
1998–99	Ipswich T	0	0
Total:		**1**	**0**

KEEN, Kevin — Midfield

H: 5 7 W: 10 10 b.Amersham 25-2-67

Source: Wycombe W and Apprentice. *Honours:* England Schools, Youth.

1983–84	West Ham U	0	0
1984–85	West Ham U	0	0
1985–86	West Ham U	0	0
1986–87	West Ham U	13	0
1987–88	West Ham U	23	1
1988–89	West Ham U	24	3
1989–90	West Ham U	44	10
1990–91	West Ham U	40	0
1991–92	West Ham U	29	0
1992–93	West Ham U	46	7
1993–94	Wolverhampton W	41	7
1994–95	Wolverhampton W	1	0
1994–95	Stoke C	21	2
1995–96	Stoke C	33	3
1996–97	Stoke C	16	1
1997–98	Stoke C	40	1
1998–99	Stoke C	44	2
Total:		**415**	**37**

KEEN, Peter — Goalkeeper

H: 6 0 W: 11 10 b.Middlesbrough 16-11-76

Source: Trainee.

1995–96	Newcastle U	0	0
1996–97	Newcastle U	0	0
1997–98	Newcastle U	0	0
1998–99	Newcastle U	0	0

KEIDAL, Ralf — Midfield

H: 5 8 W: 10 12 b.Wurzburg 6-3-77

Source: Schweinfurt.

1997–98	Newcastle U	0	0
1998–99	Newcastle U	0	0

KEISTER, John — Midfield

H: 5 7 W: 10 10 b.Manchester 11-11-70

Source: Faweh FC.

1993–94	Walsall	22	1
1994–95	Walsall	11	0
1995–96	Walsall	21	0
1996–97	Walsall	36	1
1997–98	Walsall	13	0
1998–99	Walsall	2	0
Total:		**105**	**2**

KEITH, Joseph — Defender

b.London 1-10-78

Source: Trainee.

1997–98	West Ham U	0	0
1998–99	West Ham U	0	0

KELL, Richard — Midfield

b.Bishop Auckland 15-9-79

Source: Trainee.

1998–99	Middlesbrough	0	0

KELLER, Francois — Midfield

H: 6 0 W: 12 00 b.Colmar 27-10-73

1996–97	Strasbourg	17	1
1997–98	Strasbourg	18	0
1998–99	Fulham	1	0
Total:		**36**	**1**

KELLER, Kasey — Goalkeeper

H: 6 2 W: 13 12 b.Washington 27-11-69

Source: Portland Univ. *Honours:* USA 35 full caps.

1991–92	Millwall	1	0
1992–93	Millwall	45	0
1993–94	Millwall	44	0
1994–95	Millwall	44	0
1995–96	Millwall	42	0
1996–97	Leicester C	31	0
1997–98	Leicester C	32	0
1998–99	Leicester C	36	0
Total:		**275**	**0**

KELLER, Marc — Midfield

H: 5 9 W: 12 03 b.Colmar 14-1-68

Honours: France 6 full caps, 1 goal.

1987–88	Mulhouse	27	1
1988–89	Mulhouse	25	8
1989–90	Mulhouse	36	2
1990–91	Strasbourg*	0	0
1991–92	Strasbourg*	0	0
1992–93	Strasbourg	34	8
1993–94	Strasbourg	27	6
1994–95	Strasbourg	21	2
1995–96	Strasbourg	33	8
1996–97	Karlsruhe	33	9
1997–98	Karlsruhe	28	4
1998–99	West Ham U	21	5
Total:		**285**	**53**

KELLY, Alan — Goalkeeper

H: 6 3 W: 14 02 b.Preston 11-8-68

Source: Trainee. *Honours:* Eire Youth, Under-21, Under-23, 22 full caps.

1985–86	Preston NE	13	0
1986–87	Preston NE	22	0
1987–88	Preston NE	19	0
1988–89	Preston NE	0	0
1989–90	Preston NE	42	0
1990–91	Preston NE	23	0
1991–92	Preston NE	23	0
1992–93	Sheffield U	33	0
1993–94	Sheffield U	30	0
1994–95	Sheffield U	38	0
1995–96	Sheffield U	35	0
1996–97	Sheffield U	39	0
1997–98	Sheffield U	19	0
1998–99	Sheffield U	22	0
Total:		**358**	**0**

KELLY, Brian — Midfield

b.Dublin 6-2-81

Source: Trainee.

1998–99	Middlesbrough	0	0

KELLY, David — Forward

H: 5 11 W: 11 10 b.Birmingham 25-11-65

Source: Alvechurch. *Honours:* Eire Under-21, Under-23, B, 26 full caps, 9 goals.

1983–84	Walsall	6	3
1984–85	Walsall	32	7
1985–86	Walsall	28	10
1986–87	Walsall	42	23
1987–88	Walsall	39	20
1988–89	West Ham U	25	6
1989–90	West Ham U	16	1
1989–90	Leicester C	10	7
1990–91	Leicester C	44	14
1991–92	Leicester C	12	1
1991–92	Newcastle U	25	11
1992–93	Newcastle U	45	24
1993–94	Wolverhampton W	36	11
1994–95	Wolverhampton W	42	15
1995–96	Wolverhampton W	5	0
1995–96	Sunderland	10	2

1996–97	Sunderland	24	0
1997–98	Tranmere R	29	11
1998–99	Tranmere R	27	4
Total:		**497**	**170**

KELLY, Gary — Goalkeeper

H: 5 11 W: 12 08 b.Fulwood 3-8-66

Source: Apprentice. *Honours:* Eire Under-21, B.

1984–85	Newcastle U	0	0
1985–86	Newcastle U	0	0
1986–87	Newcastle U	3	0
1987–88	Newcastle U	37	0
1988–89	Newcastle U	9	0
1988–89	Blackpool (loan)	5	0
1989–90	Newcastle U	4	0
1989–90	Bury	38	0
1990–91	Bury	46	0
1991–92	Bury	46	0
1992–93	Bury	42	0
1993–94	Bury	1	0
1993–94	West Ham U (loan)	0	0
1994–95	Bury	38	0
1995–96	Bury	25	0
1996–97	Oldham Ath	42	0
1997–98	Oldham Ath	26	0
1998–99	Oldham Ath	45	0
Total:		**407**	**0**

KELLY, Gary — Defender

H: 5 8 W: 11 00 b.Drogheda 9-7-74

Source: Home Farm. *Honours:* Eire Youth, 28 full caps, 1 goal.

1991–92	Leeds U	2	0
1992–93	Leeds U	0	0
1993–94	Leeds U	42	0
1994–95	Leeds U	42	0
1995–96	Leeds U	34	0
1996–97	Leeds U	36	2
1997–98	Leeds U	34	0
1998–99	Leeds U	0	0
Total:		**190**	**2**

KELLY, Paddy — Defender

H: 6 0 W: 11 07 b.Kirkcaldy 26-4-78

Source: Celtic BC. *Honours:* Scotland Under-18.

1995–96	Celtic	0	0
1996–97	Celtic	1	0
1997–98	Newcastle U	0	0
1997–98	Reading (loan)	3	0
1998–99	Newcastle U	0	0
Total:		**4**	**0**

KELLY, Ray — Forward

H: 5 11 W: 12 00 b.Ballinasloe 29-12-76

Source: Athlone T.

1994–95	Manchester C	0	0
1995–96	Manchester C	0	0
1996–97	Manchester C	0	0
1997–98	Manchester C	1	0
1997–98	Wrexham (loan)	10	1
1998–99	Manchester C	0	0
Total:		**11**	**1**

KELLY, Seamus — Goalkeeper

H: 6 1 W: 13 13 b.Tullamore 6-5-74

Source: UCD.

1998–99	Cardiff C	5	0
Total:		**5**	**0**

KENDALL, Lee — Goalkeeper

H: 5 10 W: 10 05 b.Newport 8-1-81

Source: Trainee.

1997–98	Crystal Palace	0	0
1998–99	Crystal Palace	0	0

KENNA, Jeff — Defender

H: 5 11 W: 12 03 b.Dublin 27-8-70

Source: Trainee. *Honours:* Eire Youth, Under-21, B, 26 full caps.

1988–89	Southampton	0	0
1989–90	Southampton	0	0
1990–91	Southampton	2	0
1991–92	Southampton	14	0
1992–93	Southampton	29	2
1993–94	Southampton	41	2
1994–95	Southampton	28	0
1994–95	Blackburn R	9	1
1995–96	Blackburn R	32	0
1996–97	Blackburn R	37	0
1997–98	Blackburn R	37	0
1998–99	Blackburn R	23	0
Total:		**252**	**5**

KENNA, Warren — Defender

H: 6 1 W: 13 06 b.Southampton 18-5-80

Source: Trainee.

1998–99	Peterborough U	0	0

KENNEDY, Alan — Forward

H: 5 8 W: 11 00 b.Dublin 17-10-81

Source: Trainee.

1998–99	Leeds U	0	0

KENNEDY, John — Defender

H: 5 8 W: 10 07 b.Cambridge 19-8-78

Source: Trainee.

1997–98	Ipswich T	1	0
1998–99	Ipswich T	7	0
Total:		**8**	**0**

KENNEDY, Mark — Forward

H: 5 11 W: 11 00 b.Dublin 15-5-76

Source: Belvedere, Trainee. *Honours:* Eire Under-21, 22 full caps, 1 goal.

1992–93	Millwall	1	0
1993–94	Millwall	12	4
1994–95	Millwall	30	5
1994–95	Liverpool	6	0
1995–96	Liverpool	4	0
1996–97	Liverpool	5	0
1997–98	Liverpool	1	0
1997–98	QPR (loan)	8	2
1997–98	Wimbledon	4	0
1998–99	Wimbledon	17	0
Total:		**88**	**11**

KENNEDY, Paul — Defender

H: 5 9 W: 12 02 b.Stockport 8-10-79

Source: Trainee.

1998–99	Barnsley	0	0

KENNEDY, Peter — Defender

H: 5 10 W: 11 05 b.Lisburn 10-9-73

Source: Portadown. *Honours:* Northern Ireland 2 full caps.

1996–97	Notts Co	22	0
1997–98	Watford	34	11
1998–99	Watford	46	6
Total:		**102**	**17**

KENNEDY, Richard — Midfield

H: 5 10 W: 10 05 b.Waterford 28-8-78

Source: Trainee.

1996–97	Crystal Palace	0	0
1997–98	Crystal Palace	0	0
1998–99	Wycombe W	0	0

KENNY, Patrick — Goalkeeper

H: 6 1 W: 14 06 b.Halifax 17-5-78

Source: Bradford PA.

1998–99	Bury	0	0

KENTON, Darren — Defender

H: 5 11 W: 11 10 b.Wandsworth 13-9-78

Source: Trainee.

1997–98	Norwich C	11	0
1998–99	Norwich C	22	1
Total:		**33**	**1**

KEOWN, Martin — Defender

H: 6 1 W: 12 04 b.Oxford 24-7-66

Source: Apprentice. *Honours:* England Youth, Under-21, B, 23 full caps, 3 goals.

1983–84	Arsenal	0	0
1984–85	Arsenal	0	0
1984–85	Brighton & HA (loan)	16	0
1985–86	Arsenal	22	0
1985–86	Brighton & HA (loan)	7	1
1986–87	Aston Villa	36	0
1987–88	Aston Villa	42	3
1988–89	Aston Villa	34	0
1989–90	Everton	20	0
1990–91	Everton	24	0
1991–92	Everton	39	0
1992–93	Everton	13	0
1992–93	Arsenal	16	0
1993–94	Arsenal	33	0
1994–95	Arsenal	31	1
1995–96	Arsenal	34	0
1996–97	Arsenal	33	1
1997–98	Arsenal	18	0
1998–99	Arsenal	34	1
Total:		**452**	**7**

KERNAGHAN, Alan — Defender

H: 6 2 W: 14 01 b.Otley 25-4-67

Source: Apprentice. *Honours:* Eire 22 full caps, 1 goal.

1984–85	Middlesbrough	8	1
1985–86	Middlesbrough	6	0
1986–87	Middlesbrough	13	0
1987–88	Middlesbrough	35	6
1988–89	Middlesbrough	23	0
1989–90	Middlesbrough	37	4
1990–91	Middlesbrough	24	0
1990–91	Charlton Ath (loan)	13	0
1991–92	Middlesbrough	38	2
1992–93	Middlesbrough	22	2
1993–94	Middlesbrough	6	1
1993–94	Manchester C	24	0
1994–95	Manchester C	22	1
1994–95	Bolton W (loan)	11	0
1995–96	Manchester C	6	0
1995–96	Bradford C (loan)	5	0
1996–97	Manchester C	10	0
1997–98	Manchester C	1	0
1997–98	St Johnstone (loan)	28	2
1998–99	St Johnstone	26	3
Total:		**358**	**22**

KERR, Brian — Midfield

H: 5 8 W: 11 00 b.Motherwell 12-10-81

Source: Trainee.

1998–99	Newcastle U	0	0

KERR, David — Midfield

H: 5 11 W: 12 01 b.Dumfries 6-9-74

Source: Trainee.

1991–92	Manchester C	0	0
1992–93	Manchester C	1	0
1993–94	Manchester C	2	0
1994–95	Manchester C	2	0
1995–96	Manchester C	1	0
1995–96	Mansfield T (loan)	5	0
1996–97	Mansfield T	9	0
1997–98	Mansfield T	18	2
1998–99	Mansfield T	35	2
Total:		**73**	**4**

KERR, Dylan — Defender

H: 5 9 W: 11 04 b.Valletta 14-1-67

Source: Arcadia Shepherds.

1988–89	Leeds U	3	0
1989–90	Leeds U	5	0
1990–91	Leeds U	0	0
1991–92	Leeds U	0	0
1991–92	Doncaster R (loan)	7	1
1991–92	Blackpool (loan)	12	1
1992–93	Leeds U	5	0
1993–94	Reading	45	2
1994–95	Reading	36	1
1995–96	Reading	8	2
1996–97	Reading	0	0
1996–97	Carlisle U	1	0
1996–97	Kilmarnock	27	0
1997–98	Kilmarnock	14	0
1998–99	Kilmarnock	16	0
Total:		**179**	**7**

KERR, Stewart — Goalkeeper

H: 6 2 W: 13 00 b.Bellshill 13-11-74

Source: Celtic BC. *Honours:* Scotland Under-21.

1993–94	Celtic	0	0
1994–95	Celtic	0	0
1994–95	Brighton & HA (loan)	2	0
1995–96	Celtic	0	0
1996–97	Celtic	26	0
1997–98	Celtic	0	0
1998–99	Celtic	4	0
Total:		**32**	**0**

KERRIGAN, Steve — Forward

H: 6 1 W: 12 04 b.Baillieston 9-10-72

Source: Newmains J.

1992–93	Albion R	29	8
1993–94	Albion R	24	6
1993–94	Clydebank	15	0
1994–95	Clydebank	14	0
1995–96	Clydebank	1	0
1995–96	Stranraer	21	5
1996–97	Ayr U	27	14
1997–98	Ayr U	6	3
1997–98	Shrewsbury T	14	2
1998–99	Shrewsbury T	37	10
Total:		**188**	**48**

KERSEY, Lee — Defender

H: 5 11 W: 13 02 b.Harlow 12-8-79

Source: Trainee.

1997–98	Tottenham H	0	0
1998–99	Tottenham H	0	0

KERSLAKE, David — Defender

H: 5 9 W: 12 04 b.Stepney 19-6-66

Source: Apprentice. *Honours:* England Schools, Youth, Under-21. Football League.

1983–84	QPR	0	0
1984–85	QPR	1	0
1985–86	QPR	14	1
1986–87	QPR	3	0
1987–88	QPR	18	5
1988–89	QPR	21	0
1989–90	QPR	1	0
1989–90	Swindon T	28	0
1990–91	Swindon T	37	0
1991–92	Swindon T	39	1
1992–93	Swindon T	31	0
1992–93	Leeds U	8	0
1993–94	Tottenham H	17	0
1994–95	Tottenham H	18	0
1995–96	Tottenham H	2	0
1996–97	Tottenham H	0	0
1996–97	Swindon T (loan)	8	0
1997–98	Ipswich T	7	0
1997–98	Wycombe W (loan)	10	0
1997–98	Swindon T	10	0
1998–99	Swindon T	14	0
Total:		**287**	**7**

KETSBAIA, Temuri — Forward

H: 5 8 W: 10 12 b.Gale 18-3-68

Source: Dynamo Sukhumi. *Honours:* Georgia 35 full caps, 11 goals.

1987	Dynamo Tbilisi	14	4

1988	Dynamo Tbilisi	13	0
1989	Dynamo Tbilisi	27	4
1990	Dynamo Tbilisi	0	0
1991–92	Anorthosis	26	13
1992–93	Anorthosis	24	4
1993–94	Anorthosis	26	19
1994–95	AEK Athens	22	5
1995–96	AEK Athens	32	14
1996–97	AEK Athens	30	5
1997–98	Newcastle U	31	3
1998–99	Newcastle U	26	5
Total:		**271**	**76**

KEWELL, Harry — Forward

H: 6 0 W: 12 10 b.Sydney 22-9-78

Source: NSW Soccer Academy. *Honours:* Australia full caps.

1995–96	Leeds U	2	0
1996–97	Leeds U	1	0
1997–98	Leeds U	29	5
1998–99	Leeds U	38	6
Total:		**70**	**11**

KEY, Lance — Goalkeeper

H: 6 3 W: 15 00 b.Kettering 13-5-68

Source: Histon.

1991–92	Sheffield W	0	0
1991–92	York C (loan)	0	0
1992–93	Sheffield W	0	0
1993–94	Sheffield W	0	0
1993–94	Oldham Ath (loan)	2	0
1993–94	Portsmouth (loan)	0	0
1994–95	Sheffield W	0	0
1994–95	Oxford U (loan)	6	0
1995–96	Sheffield W	0	0
1995–96	Lincoln C (loan)	5	0
1995–96	Hartlepool U (loan)	1	0
1995–96	Rochdale (loan)	14	0
1996–97	Dundee U	4	0
1996–97	Sheffield U	0	0
1997–98	Rochdale	19	0
1998–99	Rochdale	0	0
Total:		**51**	**0**

KHARINE, Dmitri — Goalkeeper

H: 6 2 W: 13 11 b.Moscow 16-8-68

Honours: USSR Youth, Under-21, 15 full caps, Russia 22 full caps.

1984	Torpedo Moscow	1	0
1985	Torpedo Moscow	10	0
1986	Torpedo Moscow	25	0
1987	Torpedo Moscow	27	0
1988	Dynamo Moscow	19	0
1989	Dynamo Moscow	20	0
1990	Dynamo Moscow	1	0
1991	CSKA Moscow	11	0
1992	CSKA Moscow	23	0
1992–93	Chelsea	5	0
1993–94	Chelsea	40	0
1994–95	Chelsea	31	0
1995–96	Chelsea	26	0
1996–97	Chelsea	5	0
1997–98	Chelsea	10	0
1998–99	Chelsea	1	0
Total:		**255**	**0**

KIDD, Ryan — Defender

H: 5 11 W: 10 08 b.Radcliffe 16-10-71

Source: Trainee.

1990–91	Port Vale	0	0
1991–92	Port Vale	1	0
1992–93	Preston NE	15	0
1993–94	Preston NE	36	1
1994–95	Preston NE	32	3
1995–96	Preston NE	30	0
1996–97	Preston NE	35	0
1997–98	Preston NE	33	2
1998–99	Preston NE	28	3
Total:		**210**	**9**

KIELY, Dean — Goalkeeper

H: 6 0 W: 12 13 b.Salford 10-10-70

Source: WBA School. *Honours:* England Schools, FA Schools, Youth.

1987–88	Coventry C	0	0
1988–89	Coventry C	0	0
1989–90	Coventry C	0	0
1989–90	Ipswich T (loan)	0	0
1989–90	York C (loan)	0	0
1990–91	York C	17	0
1991–92	York C	21	0
1992–93	York C	40	0
1993–94	York C	46	0
1994–95	York C	46	0
1995–96	York C	40	0
1996–97	Bury	46	0
1997–98	Bury	46	0
1998–99	Bury	45	0
Total:		**347**	**0**

KILBANE, Kevin — Forward

H: 6 0 W: 12 07 b.Preston 1-2-77

Source: Trainee. *Honours:* Eire Under-21, 5 full caps.

1993–94	Preston NE	0	0
1994–95	Preston NE	0	0
1995–96	Preston NE	11	1
1996–97	Preston NE	36	2
1997–98	WBA	43	4
1998–99	WBA	44	6
Total:		**134**	**13**

KILFORD, Ian — Midfield

H: 5 10 W: 11 03 b.Bristol 6-10-73

Source: Trainee.

1991–92	Nottingham F	0	0
1992–93	Nottingham F	0	0
1993–94	Nottingham F	1	0
1993–94	Wigan Ath (loan)	8	3
1994–95	Wigan Ath	35	5
1995–96	Wigan Ath	25	3
1996–97	Wigan Ath	35	8
1997–98	Wigan Ath	30	10
1998–99	Wigan Ath	23	0
Total:		**157**	**29**

KILLEN, Chris — Forward

H: 5 11 W: 11 03 b.Wellington 8-10-81

Source: Miramar R.

1998–99	Manchester C	0	0

KILTY, Mark — Midfield

b.Sunderland 24-6-81

Source: Trainee.

1998–99	Darlington	2	0
Total:		**2**	**0**

KIMBLE, Alan — Defender

H: 5 10 W: 12 04 b.Poole 6-8-66

1984–85	Charlton Ath	6	0
1985–86	Charlton Ath	0	0
1985–86	Exeter C (loan)	1	0
1986–87	Cambridge U	35	0
1987–88	Cambridge U	41	2
1988–89	Cambridge U	45	6
1989–90	Cambridge U	44	8
1990–91	Cambridge U	43	4
1991–92	Cambridge U	45	0
1992–93	Cambridge U	46	4
1993–94	Wimbledon	14	0
1994–95	Wimbledon	26	0
1995–96	Wimbledon	31	0
1996–97	Wimbledon	31	0
1997–98	Wimbledon	25	0
1998–99	Wimbledon	26	0
Total:		**459**	**24**

KINDER, Vladimir — Defender

H: 5 9 W: 12 03 b.Bratislava 9-3-69

Source: Karlovy Vary. *Honours:* Czech Republic 1 full cap, Slovakia 38 full caps, 1 goal.

1990–91	Slovan Bratislava	10	2
1991–92	Slovan Bratislava	29	2
1992–93	Slovan Bratislava	29	5
1993–94	Slovan Bratislava	31	3
1994–95	Slovan Bratislava	26	4
1995–96	Slovan Bratislava	23	3
1996–97	Slovan Bratislava	13	3
1996–97	Middlesbrough	6	1
1997–98	Middlesbrough	26	2
1998–99	Middlesbrough	5	2
Total:		**198**	**27**

KING, Christopher — Defender

H: 5 11 W: 10 12 b.Sheffield 1-10-79

Source: Trainee.

1998–99	Sheffield W	0	0

KING, Ledley — Defender

H: 6 2 W: 13 08 b.London 12-10-80

Source: Trainee. *Honours:* England Youth.

1998–99	Tottenham H	1	0
Total:		**1**	**0**

KING, Marlon — Forward

H: 6 1 W: 12 03 b.Dulwich 26-4-80

Source: Trainee.

1998–99	Barnet	22	6
Total:		**22**	**6**

KING, Phil — Defender

H: 5 11 W: 12 07 b.Bristol 28-12-67

Source: Apprentice. *Honours:* England B.

1984–85	Exeter C	16	0
1985–86	Exeter C	11	0
1986–87	Torquay U	24	3
1986–87	Swindon T	21	0
1987–88	Swindon T	44	1
1988–89	Swindon T	37	2
1989–90	Swindon T	14	1
1989–90	Sheffield W	25	0
1990–91	Sheffield W	43	0
1991–92	Sheffield W	39	1
1992–93	Sheffield W	12	1
1993–94	Sheffield W	10	0
1993–94	Notts Co (loan)	6	0
1994–95	Aston Villa	16	0
1995–96	Aston Villa	0	0
1995–96	WBA (loan)	4	0
1996–97	Aston Villa	0	0
1996–97	Swindon T	5	0
1997–98	Swindon T	0	0
1997–98	Blackpool (loan)	6	0
1998–99	Swindon T	0	0
1998–99	Brighton & HA	3	0
Total:		**336**	**9**

KING, Stuart — Midfield

b.Derry 20-3-81

Source: Trainee.

1998–99	Preston NE	0	0

KINKLADZE, Georgiou — Midfield

H: 5 8 W: 10 09 b.Tbilisi 6-7-73

Source: Dynamo Tbilisi. *Honours:* Georgia 26 full caps, 5 goals.

1995–96	Manchester C	37	4
1996–97	Manchester C	39	12
1997–98	Manchester C	30	4
1998–99	Manchester C	0	0
Total:		**106**	**20**

KINSELLA, Mark — Midfield

H: 5 9 W: 11 05 b.Dublin 12-8-72

Source: Home Farm. *Honours:* Eire 9 full caps.

1989–90	Colchester U	6	0
1990–91	Colchester U	0	0
1991–92	Colchester U	0	0
1992–93	Colchester U	38	6
1993–94	Colchester U	42	8
1994–95	Colchester U	42	6
1995–96	Colchester U	45	5
1996–97	Colchester U	7	2
1996–97	Charlton Ath	37	6
1997–98	Charlton Ath	46	6
1998–99	Charlton Ath	38	2
Total:		**301**	**41**

KIPPE, Frode — Defender

b.Oslo 17-1-78

1997	Lillestrom	9	0
1998	Lillestrom	25	2
1998–99	Liverpool	0	0
Total:		**34**	**2**

KIRIAKOV, Ilian — Midfield

H: 5 5 W: 11 09 b.Pavlikeni 4-8-67

Source: Etur. *Honours:* Bulgaria 57 full caps.

1991–92	La Coruna	36	3
1992–93	La Coruna	3	0
From Merida.			
1994–95	CSKA Sofia	18	0
1994–95	Etur	8	3
1995–96	Anorthosis	19	8
1996–97	Aberdeen	27	1
1997–98	Aberdeen	15	0
1998–99	Aberdeen	22	0
Total:		**148**	**15**

KIRK, Andy — Forward

b.Belfast 29-5-79

Honours: Northern Ireland Under-21.

1995–96	Glentoran	1	1
1996–97	Glentoran	25	8
1997–98	Glentoran	25	9
1998–99	Hearts	5	0
Total:		**56**	**18**

KIRKLAND, Christopher — Goalkeeper

H: 6 3 W: 11 07 b.Leicester 2-5-81

Source: Trainee. *Honours:* England Youth.

1997–98	Coventry C	0	0
1998–99	Coventry C	0	0

KITE, Phil — Goalkeeper

H: 6 2 W: 15 04 b.Bristol 26-10-62

Source: Apprentice. *Honours:* England Youth.

1980–81	Bristol R	4	0
1981–82	Bristol R	27	0
1982–83	Bristol R	46	0
1983–84	Bristol R	19	0
1983–84	Tottenham H (loan)	0	0
1984–85	Southampton	1	0
1985–86	Southampton	3	0
1985–86	Middlesbrough (loan)	2	0
1986–87	Gillingham	17	0
1987–88	Gillingham	26	0
1988–89	Gillingham	27	0
1989–90	Bournemouth	7	0
1990–91	Sheffield U	7	0
1991–92	Sheffield U	4	0
1991–92	Mansfield T (loan)	11	0
1992–93	Sheffield U	0	0
1992–93	Plymouth Arg (loan)	2	0
1992–93	Rotherham U (loan)	1	0
1992–93	Crewe Alex (loan)	5	0
1992–93	Stockport Co (loan)	5	0
1993–94	Cardiff C	18	0
1994–95	Bristol C	2	0
1995–96	Bristol C	4	0
1996–97	Bristol R	0	0
1997–98	Bristol R	0	0
1998–99	Bristol R	0	0
Total:		**238**	**0**

KITSON, Paul — Forward

H: 5 11 W: 10 12 b.Murton 9-1-71

Source: Trainee. *Honours:* England Under-21.

1988–89	Leicester C	0	0
1989–90	Leicester C	13	0
1990–91	Leicester C	7	0
1991–92	Leicester C	30	6

1991–92	Derby Co	12	4
1992–93	Derby Co	44	17
1993–94	Derby Co	41	13
1994–95	Derby Co	8	2
1994–95	Newcastle U	26	8
1995–96	Newcastle U	7	2
1996–97	Newcastle U	3	0
1996–97	West Ham U	14	8
1997–98	West Ham U	13	4
1998–99	West Ham U	17	3
Total:		**235**	**67**

KIWOMYA, Chris — Forward

H: 5 9 W: 10 07 b.Huddersfield 2-12-69

Source: Trainee.

1986–87	Ipswich T	0	0
1987–88	Ipswich T	0	0
1988–89	Ipswich T	26	2
1989–90	Ipswich T	29	5
1990–91	Ipswich T	37	10
1991–92	Ipswich T	43	16
1992–93	Ipswich T	38	10
1993–94	Ipswich T	37	5
1994–95	Ipswich T	15	3
1994–95	Arsenal	14	3
1995–96	Arsenal	0	0
1996–97	Arsenal	0	0
1996–97	Le Havre (loan)	7	0
1997–98	Arsenal	0	0
1998–99	QPR	16	6
Total:		**262**	**60**

KLOS, Stefan — Goalkeeper

H: 5 11 W: 13 06 b.Germany 16-8-71

Source: Eving-Lindenhorst, Eintracht Dortmund.

1990–91	Borussia Dortmund	2	0
1991–92	Borussia Dortmund	31	0
1992–93	Borussia Dortmund	34	0
1993–94	Borussia Dortmund	34	0
1994–95	Borussia Dortmund	34	0
1995–96	Borussia Dortmund	33	0
1996–97	Borussia Dortmund	34	0
1997–98	Borussia Dortmund	34	0
1998–99	Rangers	18	0
Total:		**254**	**0**

KNARVIK, Tommy — Midfield

H: 5 8 W: 11 00 b.Bergen 1-11-79

Source: Skjerjard.

1996–97	Leeds U	0	0
1997–98	Leeds U	0	0
1998–99	Leeds U	0	0

KNIGHT, Alan — Goalkeeper

H: 6 1 W: 13 11 b.Balham 3-7-61

Source: Apprentice. *Honours:* England Youth, Under-21.

1977–78	Portsmouth	1	0
1978–79	Portsmouth	0	0
1979–80	Portsmouth	8	0
1980–81	Portsmouth	1	0
1981–82	Portsmouth	45	0
1982–83	Portsmouth	46	0
1983–84	Portsmouth	42	0
1984–85	Portsmouth	42	0
1985–86	Portsmouth	38	0
1986–87	Portsmouth	42	0
1987–88	Portsmouth	36	0
1988–89	Portsmouth	32	0
1989–90	Portsmouth	46	0
1990–91	Portsmouth	22	0
1991–92	Portsmouth	45	0
1992–93	Portsmouth	46	0
1993–94	Portsmouth	43	0
1994–95	Portsmouth	43	0
1995–96	Portsmouth	42	0
1996–97	Portsmouth	22	0
1997–98	Portsmouth	20	0
1998–99	Portsmouth	20	0
Total:		**682**	**0**

KNIGHT, Paul — Forward

H: 5 7 W: 10 07 b.Dublin 16-10-80

Source: Trainee.

1997–98	Newcastle U	0	0
1998–99	Newcastle U	0	0

KNIGHT, Richard — Goalkeeper

H: 6 1 W: 14 00 b.Burton 3-8-79

Source: Burton Alb. *Honours:* England Youth.

1997–98	Derby Co	0	0
1998–99	Derby Co	0	0
1998–99	Carlisle U (loan)	6	0
Total:		**6**	**0**

KNIGHT, Zatyiah — Midfield

b.Solihull 2-5-80

1998–99	Fulham	0	0

KNILL, Alan — Defender

H: 6 4 W: 13 00 b.Slough 8-10-64

Source: Apprentice. *Honours:* Wales Youth, 1 full cap.

1982–83	Southampton	0	0
1983–84	Southampton	0	0

1984–85	Halifax T	44	1
1985–86	Halifax T	33	2
1986–87	Halifax T	41	3
1987–88	Swansea C	46	1
1988–89	Swansea C	43	2
1989–90	Bury	43	1
1990–91	Bury	20	1
1991–92	Bury	35	1
1992–93	Bury	38	5
1993–94	Bury	8	0
1993–94	Cardiff C (loan)	4	0
1993–94	Scunthorpe U	25	1
1994–95	Scunthorpe U	39	4
1995–96	Scunthorpe U	38	3
1996–97	Scunthorpe U	29	0
1997–98	Rotherham U	38	3
1998–99	Rotherham U	36	3
Total:		**560**	**31**

KNOWLES, Darren — Defender

H: 5 6 W: 11 01 b.Sheffield 8-10-70

Source: Trainee.

1989–90	Sheffield U	0	0
1989–90	Stockport Co	9	0
1990–91	Stockport Co	12	0
1991–92	Stockport Co	31	0
1992–93	Stockport Co	11	0
1993–94	Scarborough	42	1
1994–95	Scarborough	39	0
1995–96	Scarborough	46	1
1996–97	Scarborough	17	0
1996–97	Hartlepool U	7	0
1997–98	Hartlepool U	46	1
1998–99	Hartlepool U	46	0
Total:		**306**	**3**

KONCHESKY, Paul — Defender

H: 5 10 W: 10 05 b.Barking 15-5-81

Source: Trainee. *Honours:* England Youth.

1997–98	Charlton Ath	3	0
1998–99	Charlton Ath	2	0
Total:		**5**	**0**

KONDE, Oumar — Midfield

H: 6 2 W: 13 00 b.Basle 19-8-79

Source: Binningen.

1995–96	Basle	7	0
1996–97	Basle	16	0
1997–98	Basle	12	0
1998–99	Blackburn R	0	0
Total:		**35**	**0**

KONJIC, Muhamed — Defender

H: 6 3 W: 13 00 b.Tulsa 14-5-70

1990–91	Tuzla	3	0
1991–92	Tuzla	5	0
1992–93	Belisce	18	0
1993–94	Zagreb	29	3
1994–95	Zagreb	19	1
1995–96	Zagreb	15	1
1996–97	Zurich	29	2
1997–98	Zurich	7	3
1997–98	Monaco	19	0
1998–99	Monaco	18	2
1998–99	Coventry C	4	0
Total:		**166**	**12**

KOOGI, Anders — Midfield

H: 5 10 W: 10 11 b.Roskilde 8-9-79

Source: Trainee.

1997–98	Peterborough U	0	0
1998–99	Peterborough U	1	0
Total:		**1**	**0**

KOORDES, Rogier — Midfield

H: 6 1 W: 13 06 b.Holland 13-6-72

1996–97	Telstar	12	0
1996–97	Port Vale	13	0
1997–98	Port Vale	10	0
1998–99	Port Vale	15	0
Total:		**50**	**0**

KORSTEN, Willem — Forward

H: 6 4 W: 13 04 b.Boxtel 21-1-75

1992–93	NEC	4	0
1993–94	Vitesse	22	3
1994–95	Vitesse	18	6
1995–96	Vitesse	1	1
1996–97	Vitesse	12	1
1997–98	Vitesse	17	1
1998–99	Vitesse	1	0
1998–99	Leeds U	7	2
Total:		**82**	**14**

KOTYLO, Krystof — Midfield

H: 5 10 W: 11 02 b.Sheffield 28-9-77

Source: School.

1996–97	Sheffield W	0	0
1997–98	Sheffield W	0	0
1998–99	Sheffield W	0	0

KOUMAS, Jason — Midfield

H: 5 10 W: 11 06 b.Wrexham 25-9-79

Source: Trainee.

1997–98	Tranmere R	0	0
1998–99	Tranmere R	23	3
Total:		**23**	**3**

KOZLUK, Robert — Defender

H: 5 8 W: 10 12 b.Sutton-in-Ashfield 5-8-77

Source: Trainee. *Honours:* England Under-21.

1995–96	Derby Co	0	0
1996–97	Derby Co	0	0
1997–98	Derby Co	9	0
1998–99	Derby Co	7	0
1998–99	Sheffield U	10	0
Total:		**26**	**0**

KRIZAN, Ales — Defender

H: 5 9 W: 12 09 b.Maribor 25-7-71

Honours: Slovenia 24 full caps.

1992–93	Branik Maribor	34	0
1993–94	Branik Maribor	28	0
1994–95	Branik Maribor	29	0
1995–96	Branik Maribor	33	0
1996–97	Branik Maribor	35	0
1997–98	Barnsley	12	0
1998–99	Barnsley	1	0
Total:		**172**	**0**

KROMHEER, Elroy — Defender

H: 6 4 W: 12 07 b.Amsterdam 15-1-70

1989–90	Volendam	19	2
1990–91	Volendam	23	1
1991–92	Volendam	30	3
1992–93	Motherwell	12	0
1993–94	Motherwell	0	0
1993–94	Volendam	13	1
1994–95	Volendam	12	0
1995–96	Volendam	28	1
1996–97	Zwolle	30	5
1998–99	Reading	11	0
Total:		**178**	**13**

KUBICKI, Dariusz — Defender

H: 5 10 W: 12 05 b.Kozuchow 6-6-63

Source: Mielec, Zastra, Legia Warsaw. *Honours:* Poland 46 full caps, 1 goal.

1991–92	Aston Villa	23	0
1992–93	Aston Villa	0	0
1993–94	Aston Villa	2	0
1993–94	Sunderland (loan)	15	0
1994–95	Sunderland	46	0
1995–96	Sunderland	46	0
1996–97	Sunderland	29	0
1997–98	Wolverhampton W	12	0
1997–98	Tranmere R (loan)	12	0
1998–99	Carlisle U	7	0
1998–99	Darlington	3	0
Total:		**195**	**0**

KUIPERS, Michels — Goalkeeper

H: 6 2 W: 14 03 b.Amsterdam 26-6-74

1998–99	Bristol R	1	0
Total:		**1**	**0**

KULCSAR, George — Midfield

H: 6 1 W: 13 08 b.Budapest 12-8-67

1992–93	Antwerp	4	0
1993–94	Antwerp	8	0
1994–95	Antwerp	25	1
1995–96	Antwerp	12	0
1996–97	Antwerp	17	0
1996–97	Bradford C	9	0
1997–98	Bradford C	17	1
1997–98	QPR	12	0
1998–99	QPR	17	1
Total:		**121**	**3**

KVAL, Frank — Goalkeeper

H: 6 0 W: 13 00 b.Bergen 17-7-74

1998–99	Burnley	0	0

KVARME, Bjorn — Defender

H: 5 11 W: 12 04 b.Trondheim 17-6-72

Honours: Norway 1 full cap.

1991	Rosenborg	9	1
1992	Rosenborg	5	0
1993	Rosenborg	17	0
1994	Rosenborg	22	1
1995	Rosenborg	23	0
1996	Rosenborg	12	0
1996–97	Liverpool	15	0
1997–98	Liverpool	23	0
1998–99	Liverpool	7	0
Total:		**133**	**2**

KYD, Michael — Forward

H: 5 8 W: 12 08 b.Hackney 21-5-77

Source: Trainee.

1994–95	Cambridge U	19	1
1995–96	Cambridge U	9	1
1996–97	Cambridge U	28	7
1997–98	Cambridge U	38	11
1998–99	Cambridge U	12	0
Total:		**106**	**20**

KYLE, Kevin — Forward

H: 5 8 W: 12 00 b.Stranraer 7-6-81

1998–99	Sunderland	0	0

KYZERIDIS, Nicos — Midfield

H: 5 6 W: 11 07 b.Salonika 20-4-71

1993–94	Naoussa	24	2
1994–95	Naoussa*	0	0
1995–96	Paniliakos	21	3
1996–97	Paniliakos	27	5
1997–98	Paniliakos	34	9
1998–99	Portsmouth	4	0
Total:		**110**	**19**

L'HELGOUALCH, Cyrille — Defender

b.Saint Nazaire 25-9-70

1998–99	Mansfield T	4	1
Total:		**4**	**1**

LACEY, Damien — Defender

H: 5 9 W: 11 03 b.Bridgend 3-8-77

Source: Trainee.

1996–97	Swansea C	10	0
1997–98	Swansea C	22	1
1998–99	Swansea C	12	0
Total:		**44**	**1**

LAGAN, Brian — Midfield

H: 5 5 W: 10 00 b.Magherafelt 3-10-80

Source: Trainee.

1997–98	Leeds U	0	0
1998–99	Leeds U	0	0

LAKE, Craig — Defender

H: 5 11 W: 10 02 b.Stockton 10-2-80

Source: Trainee.

1998–99	Hartlepool U	0	0

LAMB, Kris — Midfield

H: 5 10 W: 10 10 b.Gateshead 22-9-79

Source: Trainee.

1998–99	Sunderland	0	0

LAMBERT, James — Midfield

H: 5 7 W: 11 02 b.Henley 14-9-73

Source: School.

1992–93	Reading	27	3
1993–94	Reading	6	0
1994–95	Reading	11	1
1995–96	Reading	15	4
1996–97	Reading	31	5
1997–98	Reading	34	3
1998–99	Reading	1	0
1998–99	Walsall (loan)	6	0
Total:		**131**	**16**

LAMBERT, Paul — Midfield

H: 5 11 W: 9 10 b.Glasgow 7-8-69

Source: Linwood Rangers BC. *Honours:* Scotland Under-21, 20 full caps.

1985–86	St Mirren	1	0
1986–87	St Mirren	36	2
1987–88	St Mirren	36	2
1988–89	St Mirren	16	2
1989–90	St Mirren	25	3
1990–91	St Mirren	31	2
1991–92	St Mirren	40	2
1992–93	St Mirren	39	1
1993–94	St Mirren	3	0
1993–94	Motherwell	32	3
1994–95	Motherwell	36	1
1995–96	Motherwell	35	2
1996–97	Borussia Dortmund	31	1
1997–98	Borussia Dortmund	13	0
1997–98	Celtic	26	2
1998–99	Celtic	33	1
Total:		**433**	**24**

LAMBOURDE, Bernard — Defender

H: 6 1 W: 12 06 b.Pointe-A-Pitre 11-5-71

1991–92	Cannes	2	0
1992–93	Cannes	5	0
1993–94	Cannes	6	1

1994–95	Angers	36	1
1995–96	Cannes	28	1
1996–97	Bordeaux	28	1
1997–98	Chelsea	7	0
1998–99	Chelsea	17	0
Total:		**129**	**4**

LAMEY, Nathan — Forward

b.Leeds 14-10-80

Source: Trainee.

1997–98	Wolverhampton W	0	0
1998–99	Wolverhampton W	0	0

LAMPARD, Frank — Midfield

H: 6 0 W: 11 12 b.Romford 20-6-78

Source: Trainee. *Honours:* England Youth, Under-21, B.

1994–95	West Ham U	0	0
1995–96	West Ham U	2	0
1995–96	Swansea C (loan)	9	1
1996–97	West Ham U	13	0
1997–98	West Ham U	31	4
1998–99	West Ham U	38	5
Total:		**93**	**10**

LANCASHIRE, Graham — Forward

H: 5 9 W: 12 04 b.Blackpool 19-10-72

Source: Trainee.

1990–91	Burnley	1	0
1991–92	Burnley	25	8
1992–93	Burnley	3	0
1992–93	Halifax T (loan)	2	0
1993–94	Burnley	1	0
1993–94	Chester C (loan)	11	7
1994–95	Burnley	1	0
1994–95	Preston NE	17	0
1995–96	Preston NE	6	2
1995–96	Wigan Ath	5	3
1996–97	Wigan Ath	24	9
1997–98	Wigan Ath	1	0
1997–98	Rochdale	27	9
1998–99	Rochdale	11	3
Total:		**135**	**41**

LANCASTER, Martin — Defender

H: 6 0 W: 12 07 b.Wigan 10-11-80

Source: Trainee.

1998–99	Chester C	11	0
Total:		**11**	**0**

LANDON, Richard — Forward

H: 6 2 W: 13 10 b.Worthing 22-3-70

Source: Bedworth U.

1993–94	Plymouth Arg	6	5
1994–95	Plymouth Arg	24	7
1995–96	Stockport Co	11	5
1996–97	Stockport Co	2	0
1996–97	Rotherham U (loan)	8	0
1997–98	Macclesfield T	18	7
1998–99	Macclesfield T	14	2
Total:		**83**	**26**

LANGAN, Kevin — Defender

H: 5 11 W: 11 02 b.Jersey 7-4-78

Source: Trainee.

1996–97	Bristol C	0	0
1997–98	Bristol C	3	0
1998–99	Bristol C	1	0
Total:		**4**	**0**

LANGFIELD, James — Goalkeeper

H: 6 4 W: 13 00 b.Paisley 22-12-79

Source: Glasgow City BC.

1996–97	Dundee	0	0
1997–98	Dundee	0	0
1998–99	Dundee	2	0
Total:		**2**	**0**

LANGLEY, Richard — Midfield

H: 5 10 W: 11 04 b.London 27-12-79

Source: Trainee. *Honours:* England Youth.

1996–97	QPR	0	0
1997–98	QPR	0	0
1998–99	QPR	8	1
Total:		**8**	**1**

LANGSTON, Matthew — Midfield

b.Brighton 2-4-81

Source: Trainee.

1998–99	Watford	0	0

LANNS, Jason — Defender

H: 5 8 W: 10 07 b.Birmingham 2-11-81

Source: Birmingham C Trainee.

1998–99	Leeds U	0	0

LARKIN, Colin — Midfield

b.Dundalk 27-4-82

Source: Trainee.

1998–99	Wolverhampton W	0	0

LARKIN, James — Goalkeeper

b.Canada 23-10-75

1997–98	Cambridge U	1	0
1997–98	Walsall	0	0
1998–99	Walsall	0	0
Total:		**1**	**0**

LARSSON, Henrik — Forward

H: 5 10 W: 11 11 b.Sweden 20-9-71

Source: Helsingborg. *Honours:* Sweden 42 full caps, 9 goals.

1993–94	Feyenoord	15	1
1994–95	Feyenoord	23	8
1995–96	Feyenoord	32	10
1996–97	Feyenoord	31	7
1997–98	Celtic	35	16
1998–99	Celtic	35	29
Total:		**171**	**71**

LARUSSON, Bjarni — Midfield

b.Iceland 11-3-76

1993	IBV	4	0
1994	IBV	15	0
1995	IBV	13	1
1996	IBV	15	2
1997	IBV	13	2
1997–98	Hibernian	7	1
1998–99	Hibernian	0	0
1998–99	Walsall	36	3
Total:		**103**	**9**

LATAPY, Russell — Midfield

H: 5 6 W: 10 05 b.Trinidad 2-8-68

Source: Academica. *Honours:* Trinidad & Tobago full caps.

1994–95	Porto	14	1
1995–96	Porto	26	5
1996–97	Boavista	21	0
1997–98	Boavista	19	1
1998–99	Hibernian	23	6
Total:		**103**	**13**

LAUCHLAN, James — Midfield

H: 6 1 W: 10 13 b.Glasgow 2-2-77

Source: Highbury BC. *Honours:* Scotland Under-21.

1993–94	Kilmarnock	1	0
1994–95	Kilmarnock	2	0
1995–96	Kilmarnock	5	0
1996–97	Kilmarnock	10	0
1997–98	Kilmarnock	22	0
1998–99	Kilmarnock	14	0
Total:		**54**	**0**

LAUDRUP, Brian — Forward

H: 6 0 W: 13 02 b.Vienna 22-2-69

Honours: Denmark 82 full caps, 21 goals.

1986	Brondby	2	0
1987	Brondby	24	11
1988	Brondby	12	0
1989	Brondby	11	2
1989–90	Uerdingen	34	6
1990–91	Bayern Munich	33	9
1991–92	Bayern Munich	20	2
1992–93	Fiorentina	31	5
1993–94	AC Milan	9	1
1994–95	Rangers	33	10
1995–96	Rangers	22	2
1996–97	Rangers	33	16
1997–98	Rangers	28	5
1998–99	Chelsea	7	0
Total:		**299**	**69**

LAUNDERS, Brian — Midfield

H: 5 8 W: 11 10 b.Dublin 8-1-76

Source: Trainee. *Honours:* Eire Under-21.

1993–94	Crystal Palace	0	0
1994–95	Crystal Palace	2	0
1995–96	Crystal Palace	2	0
1995–96	Oldham Ath (loan)	0	0
1996–97	Crewe Alex	9	0
From Veendam.			
1998–99	Derby Co	1	0
1998–99	Colchester U (loan)	1	0
Total:		**15**	**0**

LAURSEN, Jacob — Defender

H: 5 11 W: 12 11 b.Vejle 6-10-71

Honours: Denmark 22 full caps.

1990	Vejle	20	0
1990–91	Vejle	18	0
1991–92	Vejle	17	1
1992–93	Silkeborg	32	0
1993–94	Silkeborg	30	1
1994–95	Silkeborg	31	3
1995–96	Silkeborg	32	4

1996–97	Derby Co	36	1
1997–98	Derby Co	28	1
1998–99	Derby Co	37	0
Total:		**281**	**11**

LAVETY, Barry — Forward

H: 6 0 W: 12 02 b.Johnstone 21-8-74

Source: Gleniffer Thistle. *Honours:* Scotland Under-21.

1991–92	St Mirren	5	2
1992–93	St Mirren	42	18
1993–94	St Mirren	42	10
1994–95	St Mirren	31	7
1995–96	St Mirren	29	11
1996–97	Hibernian	10	0
1997–98	Hibernian	26	7
1998–99	Hibernian	26	2
Total:		**211**	**57**

LAVIN, Gerard — Defender

H: 5 10 W: 11 00 b.Corby 5-2-74

Source: Trainee. *Honours:* Scotland Under-21.

1991–92	Watford	1	0
1992–93	Watford	28	0
1993–94	Watford	46	3
1994–95	Watford	35	0
1995–96	Watford	16	0
1995–96	Millwall	20	0
1996–97	Millwall	9	0
1997–98	Millwall	7	0
1998–99	Millwall	38	0
Total:		**200**	**3**

LAW, Brian — Defender

H: 6 2 W: 13 07 b.Merthyr 1-1-70

Source: Apprentice. *Honours:* Wales Under-21, 1 full cap.

1987–88	QPR	1	0
1988–89	QPR	6	0
1989–90	QPR	10	0
1990–91	QPR	3	0
1991–92	QPR	0	0
1992–93	QPR	0	0
1993–94	QPR	0	0
1994–95	Wolverhampton W	17	0
1995–96	Wolverhampton W	7	1
1996–97	Wolverhampton W	7	0
1997–98	Millwall	40	4
1998–99	Millwall	5	0
Total:		**96**	**5**

LAWES, Russell — Defender

H: 5 10 W: 11 00 b.Bedford 16-1-80

Source: Trainee.

1998–99	Luton T	0	0

LAWLESS, Michael — Midfield

H: 5 6 W: 10 13 b.Dublin 15-8-81

Source: Trainee.

1998–99	Blackburn R	0	0

LAWRENCE, Jamie — Midfield

H: 6 0 W: 12 06 b.Balham 8-3-70

Source: Cowes.

1993–94	Sunderland	4	0
1993–94	Doncaster R	9	1
1994–95	Doncaster R	16	2
1994–95	Leicester C	17	1
1995–96	Leicester C	15	0
1996–97	Leicester C	15	0
1997–98	Bradford C	43	3
1998–99	Bradford C	35	2
Total:		**154**	**9**

LAWRENCE, Matthew — Defender

H: 6 1 W: 12 12 b.Northampton 19-6-74

Source: Grays Ath. *Honours:* England Schools.

1995–96	Wycombe W	3	0
1996–97	Wycombe W	13	1
1996–97	Fulham	15	0
1997–98	Fulham	43	0
1998–99	Fulham	1	0
1998–99	Wycombe W	34	2
Total:		**109**	**3**

LAWS, Brian — Defender

H: 5 9 W: 12 04 b.Wallsend 14-10-61

Source: Apprentice. *Honours:* England B.

1979–80	Burnley	1	0
1980–81	Burnley	42	2
1981–82	Burnley	44	6
1982–83	Burnley	38	4
1983–84	Huddersfield T	31	0
1984–85	Huddersfield T	25	1
1984–85	Middlesbrough	11	1
1985–86	Middlesbrough	42	2
1986–87	Middlesbrough	26	8
1987–88	Middlesbrough	28	1
1988–89	Nottingham F	22	1
1989–90	Nottingham F	38	3
1990–91	Nottingham F	32	0
1991–92	Nottingham F	15	0
1992–93	Nottingham F	33	0
1993–94	Nottingham F	7	0
1994–95	Nottingham F	0	0
1994–95	Grimsby T	16	1
1995–96	Grimsby T	27	1
1996–97	Grimsby T	3	0
1996–97	Darlington	10	0

1996–97	Scunthorpe U	4	0
1997–98	Scunthorpe U	14	0
1998–99	Scunthorpe U	0	0
Total:		**509**	**31**

LAWSON, Ian — Forward

H: 5 11 W: 11 00 b.Huddersfield 4-11-77

Source: Trainee.

1994–95	Huddersfield T	0	0
1995–96	Huddersfield T	0	0
1996–97	Huddersfield T	18	3
1997–98	Huddersfield T	18	0
1998–99	Huddersfield T	6	2
1998–99	Blackpool (loan)	9	3
Total:		**51**	**8**

LAYCOCK, David — Midfield

H: 5 10 W: 10 07 b.Hull 1-10-80

Source: Trainee.

1998–99	Manchester C	0	0

LAZARIDIS, Stan — Defender

H: 5 9 W: 12 00 b.Perth 16-8-72

Source: West Adelaide. *Honours:* Australia full caps.

1995–96	West Ham U	4	0
1996–97	West Ham U	22	1
1997–98	West Ham U	28	2
1998–99	West Ham U	15	0
Total:		**69**	**3**

LE GEYT, Sinclair — Midfield

b.Port Elizabeth 10-7-80

1998–99	Derby Co	0	0

LE SAUX, Graeme — Defender

H: 5 10 W: 11 09 b.Jersey 17-10-68

Source: St Pauls. *Honours:* England Under-21, B, 35 full caps, 1 goal.

1987–88	Chelsea	0	0
1988–89	Chelsea	1	0
1989–90	Chelsea	7	1
1990–91	Chelsea	28	4
1991–92	Chelsea	40	3
1992–93	Chelsea	14	0
1992–93	Blackburn R	9	0
1993–94	Blackburn R	41	2
1994–95	Blackburn R	39	3
1995–96	Blackburn R	14	1
1996–97	Blackburn R	26	1
1997–98	Chelsea	26	1
1998–99	Chelsea	31	0
Total:		**276**	**16**

LE TISSIER, Matthew — Forward

H: 6 0 W: 14 01 b.Guernsey 14-10-68

Source: Trainee. *Honours:* England Youth, B, 8 full caps.

1986–87	Southampton	24	6
1987–88	Southampton	19	0
1988–89	Southampton	28	9
1989–90	Southampton	35	20
1990–91	Southampton	35	19
1991–92	Southampton	32	6
1992–93	Southampton	40	15
1993–94	Southampton	38	25
1994–95	Southampton	41	20
1995–96	Southampton	34	7
1996–97	Southampton	31	13
1997–98	Southampton	26	11
1998–99	Southampton	30	7
Total:		**413**	**158**

LEABURN, Carl — Forward

H: 6 3 W: 13 00 b.Lewisham 30-3-69

Source: Apprentice. *Honours:* England Youth.

1986–87	Charlton Ath	3	1
1987–88	Charlton Ath	12	0
1988–89	Charlton Ath	32	2
1989–90	Charlton Ath	13	0
1989–90	Northampton T (loan)	9	0
1990–91	Charlton Ath	20	1
1991–92	Charlton Ath	39	11
1992–93	Charlton Ath	39	5
1993–94	Charlton Ath	39	10
1994–95	Charlton Ath	27	3
1995–96	Charlton Ath	40	9
1996–97	Charlton Ath	44	8
1997–98	Charlton Ath	14	3
1997–98	Wimbledon	16	4
1998–99	Wimbledon	22	0
Total:		**369**	**57**

LEADBITTER, Chris — Midfield

H: 5 9 W: 10 06 b.Middlesbrough 17-10-67

Source: Apprentice.

1985–86	Grimsby T	0	0
1986–87	Hereford U	6	0
1987–88	Hereford U	30	1
1988–89	Cambridge U	31	6
1989–90	Cambridge U	43	4
1990–91	Cambridge U	39	1
1991–92	Cambridge U	25	1
1992–93	Cambridge U	38	6
1993–94	Bournemouth	27	0
1994–95	Bournemouth	27	3
1995–96	Plymouth Arg	33	1
1996–97	Plymouth Arg	19	0
1997–98	Torquay U	26	1
1998–99	Torquay U	37	1
Total:		**381**	**25**

LEAH, John — Midfield

H: 5 9 W: 12 00 b.Shrewsbury 3-8-78

Source: Newtown.

1998–99	Darlington	7	1
Total:		**7**	**1**

LEANING, Andy — Goalkeeper

H: 6 2 W: 13 00 b.York 18-5-63

Source: Rowntree Mackintosh.

1984–85	York C	0	0
1985–86	York C	30	0
1986–87	York C	39	0
1987–88	Sheffield U	21	0
1988–89	Sheffield U	0	0
1988–89	Bristol C	6	0
1989–90	Bristol C	19	0
1990–91	Bristol C	29	0
1991–92	Bristol C	20	0
1992–93	Bristol C	1	0
1993–94	Bristol C	0	0
1993–94	Lincoln C	8	0
1994–95	Lincoln C	21	0
1995–96	Lincoln C	7	0
1996–97	Lincoln C	0	0
1996–97	Chesterfield	9	0
1997–98	Chesterfield	5	0
1998–99	Chesterfield	2	0
Total:		**217**	**0**

LEBOEUF, Franck — Defender

H: 6 0 W: 12 00 b.Marseille 22-1-68

Honours: France 22 full caps, 3 goals.

1986–87	Hyeres	14	1
1986–87	Meaux	12	3
1987–88	Meaux	27	0
1988–89	Laval	21	0
1989–90	Laval	32	1
1990–91	Laval	16	9
1990–91	Strasbourg	17	9
1991–92	Strasbourg	31	11
1992–93	Strasbourg	36	12
1993–94	Strasbourg	36	6
1994–95	Strasbourg	34	7
1995–96	Strasbourg	35	4
1996–97	Chelsea	26	6
1997–98	Chelsea	32	5
1998–99	Chelsea	33	4
Total:		**402**	**78**

LEE, Alan — Forward

H: 6 2 W: 13 09 b.Galway 21-8-78

Source: Trainee. *Honours:* Eire Under-21.

1995–96	Aston Villa	0	0
1996–97	Aston Villa	0	0
1997–98	Aston Villa	0	0
1998–99	Aston Villa	0	0
1998–99	Torquay U (loan)	7	2
1998–99	Port Vale (loan)	11	2
Total:		**18**	**4**

LEE, Christian — Forward

H: 6 2 W: 11 07 b.Aylesbury 8-10-76

Source: Doncaster R.

1995–96	Northampton T	5	0
1996–97	Northampton T	29	7
1997–98	Northampton T	6	0
1998–99	Northampton T	19	1
Total:		**59**	**8**

LEE, David — Forward

H: 5 7 W: 11 01 b.Whitefield 5-11-67

Source: Blackburn Schools.

1984–85	Bury	0	0
1985–86	Bury	1	0
1986–87	Bury	30	4
1987–88	Bury	40	3
1988–89	Bury	45	4
1989–90	Bury	45	8
1990–91	Bury	45	15
1991–92	Bury	2	1
1991–92	Southampton	19	0
1992–93	Southampton	1	0
1992–93	Bolton W	32	5
1993–94	Bolton W	41	5
1994–95	Bolton W	39	4
1995–96	Bolton W	18	1
1996–97	Bolton W	25	2
1997–98	Wigan Ath	43	5
1998–99	Wigan Ath	36	6
Total:		**462**	**63**

LEE, David — Defender

H: 6 3 W: 14 10 b.Kingswood 26-11-69

Source: Trainee. *Honours:* England Youth, Under-21.

1988–89	Chelsea	20	4
1989–90	Chelsea	30	1
1990–91	Chelsea	21	1
1991–92	Chelsea	1	0
1991–92	Reading (loan)	5	5
1991–92	Plymouth Arg (loan)	9	1
1992–93	Chelsea	25	2
1993–94	Chelsea	7	1
1994–95	Chelsea	14	0
1994–95	Portsmouth (loan)	5	0
1995–96	Chelsea	31	1
1996–97	Chelsea	1	1
1997–98	Chelsea	1	0
1997–98	Sheffield U (loan)	5	0
1998–99	Chelsea	0	0
1998–99	Bristol R	11	1
Total:		**186**	**18**

LEE, David — Midfield

H: 5 11 W: 11 08 b.Basildon 28-3-80

Source: Trainee.

1998–99	Tottenham H	0	0

LEE, Graeme — Defender

H: 6 2 W: 13 00 b.Middlesbrough 31-5-78

Source: Trainee.

1995–96	Hartlepool U	6	0
1996–97	Hartlepool U	24	0
1997–98	Hartlepool U	37	3
1998–99	Hartlepool U	24	3
Total:		**91**	**6**

LEE, Jason — Forward

H: 6 3 W: 13 03 b.Newham 9-5-71

Source: Trainee.

1989–90	Charlton Ath	1	0
1990–91	Charlton Ath	0	0
1990–91	Stockport Co (loan)	2	0
1990–91	Lincoln C	17	3
1991–92	Lincoln C	35	6
1992–93	Lincoln C	41	12
1993–94	Southend U	24	3
1993–94	Nottingham F	13	2
1994–95	Nottingham F	22	3
1995–96	Nottingham F	28	8
1996–97	Nottingham F	13	1
1996–97	Charlton Ath (loan)	8	3
1996–97	Grimsby T (loan)	7	1
1997–98	Watford	36	10
1998–99	Watford	1	1
1998–99	Chesterfield	22	1
Total:		**270**	**54**

LEE, Martyn — Midfield

H: 5 7 W: 9 00 b.Guilford 10-9-80

Source: Trainee.

1998–99	Wycombe W	3	0
Total:		**3**	**0**

LEE, Matt — Defender

H: 5 10 W: 11 00 b.Farnborough 13-5-79

Source: Trainee.

1996–97	Charlton Ath	0	0
1997–98	Charlton Ath	0	0
1998–99	Charlton Ath	0	0

LEE, Robert — Midfield

H: 5 10 W: 11 03 b.Hornchurch 1-2-66

Source: Hornchurch. *Honours:* England Under-21, 21 full caps, 2 goals.

1983–84	Charlton Ath	11	4
1984–85	Charlton Ath	39	10
1985–86	Charlton Ath	35	8
1986–87	Charlton Ath	33	3
1987–88	Charlton Ath	23	2
1988–89	Charlton Ath	31	5
1989–90	Charlton Ath	37	1
1990–91	Charlton Ath	43	13
1991–92	Charlton Ath	39	12
1992–93	Charlton Ath	7	1
1992–93	Newcastle U	36	10
1993–94	Newcastle U	41	7
1994–95	Newcastle U	35	9
1995–96	Newcastle U	36	8
1996–97	Newcastle U	33	5
1997–98	Newcastle U	28	4
1998–99	Newcastle U	26	0
Total:		**533**	**102**

LEESE, Lars — Goalkeeper

H: 6 5 W: 14 07 b.Cologne 18-8-69

Source: Leverkusen.

1997–98	Barnsley	9	0
1998–99	Barnsley	8	0
Total:		**17**	**0**

LEGG, Andy — Midfield

H: 5 8 W: 10 12 b.Swansea 28-7-66

Source: Briton Ferry. *Honours:* Wales 5 full caps.

1988–89	Swansea C	6	0
1989–90	Swansea C	26	3
1990–91	Swansea C	39	5
1991–92	Swansea C	46	9
1992–93	Swansea C	46	12
1993–94	Notts Co	30	2
1994–95	Notts Co	34	3
1995–96	Notts Co	25	4
1995–96	Birmingham C	12	1
1996–97	Birmingham C	33	4
1997–98	Birmingham C	0	0
1997–98	Ipswich T (loan)	6	1
1997–98	Reading	10	0
1998–99	Reading	2	0
1998–99	Peterborough U (loan)	5	0
1998–99	Cardiff C	24	2
Total:		**344**	**46**

LEGGATT, Philip — Midfield

H: 5 8 W: 10 04 b.Harlow 7-10-78

Source: Trainee.

1997–98	Southend U	0	0
1998–99	Southend U	0	0

LEHMANN, Dirk — Forward

H: 6 0 W: 11 06 b.Aachen 16-8-71

Source: Energie Cottbus.

1998–99	Fulham	26	2
Total:		**26**	**2**

LEHTINEN, Ville — Midfield

H: 5 11 W: 11 10 b.Toijala 17-12-78

Honours: Finland Under-21.

1996	JJK	22	1
1997	HJK Helsinki	2	0
1997–98	Sheffield U	0	0
1998–99	Sheffield U	0	0
Total:		**24**	**1**

LEIGHTON, Jim — Goalkeeper

H: 6 1 W: 12 09 b.Johnstone 24-7-58

Source: Dalry Thistle. *Honours:* Scotland Under-21, 91 full caps.

1978–79	Aberdeen	11	0
1979–80	Aberdeen	1	0
1980–81	Aberdeen	35	0
1981–82	Aberdeen	36	0
1982–83	Aberdeen	35	0
1983–84	Aberdeen	36	0
1984–85	Aberdeen	34	0
1985–86	Aberdeen	26	0
1986–87	Aberdeen	42	0
1987–88	Aberdeen	44	0
1988–89	Manchester U	38	0
1989–90	Manchester U	35	0
1990–91	Manchester U	0	0
1990–91	Arsenal (loan)	0	0
1991–92	Manchester U	0	0
1991–92	Reading (loan)	8	0
1991–92	Dundee	13	0
1992–93	Dundee	8	0
1992–93	Sheffield U (loan)	0	0
1993–94	Hibernian	44	0
1994–95	Hibernian	36	0
1995–96	Hibernian	36	0
1996–97	Hibernian	35	0
1997–98	Aberdeen	34	0
1998–99	Aberdeen	22	0
Total:		**609**	**0**

LEITCH, Scott — Midfield

H: 5 10 W: 12 00 b.Motherwell 6-10-69

Source: Shettleston Jun.

1990–91	Dunfermline Ath	14	3
1991–92	Dunfermline Ath	33	4
1992–93	Dunfermline Ath	42	9
1993–94	Hearts	28	2
1994–95	Hearts	21	0
1995–96	Hearts	6	0
1995–96	Swindon T	7	0
1996–97	Swindon T	36	0
1997–98	Swindon T	26	1
1998–99	Swindon T	24	0
Total:		**237**	**19**

LENAGH, Steve — Defender

H: 5 11 W: 10 09 b.Durham 21-3-79

Source: Sheffield W Trainee.

1997–98	Chesterfield	3	0
1998–99	Chesterfield	10	1
Total:		**13**	**1**

LENNON, Anthony — Midfield

b.Leeds 16-5-82

Source: Trainee.

1998–99	Leeds U	0	0

LENNON, Neil — Midfield

H: 5 9 W: 13 02 b.Lurgan 25-6-71

Source: Trainee. *Honours:* Northern Ireland Under-21, 27 full caps, 2 goals.

1987–88	Manchester C	1	0
1988–89	Manchester C	0	0
1989–90	Manchester C	0	0
1990–91	Crewe Alex	34	3
1991–92	Crewe Alex	0	0
1992–93	Crewe Alex	24	0
1993–94	Crewe Alex	33	4
1994–95	Crewe Alex	31	6
1995–96	Crewe Alex	25	2
1995–96	Leicester C	15	1
1996–97	Leicester C	35	1
1997–98	Leicester C	37	2
1998–99	Leicester C	37	1
Total:		**272**	**20**

LEONARD, Mark — Forward

H: 6 1 W: 13 03 b.Whiston 27-9-62

Source: Witton Alb. *Honours:* England Schools.

1981–82	Everton	0	0
1982–83	Everton	0	0

1982–83	Tranmere R (loan)	7	0
1983–84	Crewe Alex	38	10
1984–85	Crewe Alex	16	5
1984–85	Stockport Co	23	4
1985–86	Stockport Co	44	20
1986–87	Stockport Co	6	0
1986–87	Bradford C	24	3
1987–88	Bradford C	28	10
1988–89	Bradford C	44	7
1989–90	Bradford C	24	5
1990–91	Bradford C	18	4
1991–92	Bradford C	19	0
1991–92	Rochdale	9	1
1992–93	Preston NE	22	1
1993–94	Chester C	32	8
1994–95	Chester C	0	0
1994–95	Wigan Ath	29	5
1995–96	Wigan Ath	35	7
1996–97	Rochdale	39	4
1997–98	Rochdale	33	2
1998–99	Rochdale	8	0
Total:		**498**	**96**

LEONHARDSEN, Oyvind — Midfield

H: 5 10 W: 11 02 b.Kristiansund 17-8-70

Source: Clausenengen. *Honours:* Norway 61 full caps, 14 goals.

1989	Molde	22	5
1990	Molde	21	2
1991	Molde	21	2
1992	Rosenborg	22	6
1993	Rosenborg	19	6
1994	Rosenborg	22	8
1994–95	Wimbledon	20	4
1995–96	Wimbledon	29	4
1996–97	Wimbledon	27	5
1997–98	Liverpool	28	6
1998–99	Liverpool	9	1
Total:		**240**	**49**

LEONI, Stephane — Defender

H: 5 9 W: 13 00 b.Metz 1-9-76

1998–99	Bristol R	30	0
Total:		**30**	**0**

LESCOTT, Aaron — Midfield

H: 5 8 W: 10 09 b.Birmingham 2-12-78

Source: Trainee. *Honours:* England Schools.

1996–97	Aston Villa	0	0
1997–98	Aston Villa	0	0
1998–99	Aston Villa	0	0

LESTER, Jack — Forward

H: 5 10 W: 11 10 b.Sheffield 8-10-75

Source: Trainee. *Honours:* England Schools.

1994–95	Grimsby T	7	0
1995–96	Grimsby T	5	0
1996–97	Grimsby T	22	5
1996–97	Doncaster R (loan)	11	1
1997–98	Grimsby T	40	4
1998–99	Grimsby T	33	4
Total:		**118**	**14**

LEVER, Mark — Defender

H: 6 3 W: 14 00 b.Beverley 29-3-70

Source: Trainee.

1987–88	Grimsby T	1	0
1988–89	Grimsby T	37	2
1989–90	Grimsby T	38	2
1990–91	Grimsby T	40	2
1991–92	Grimsby T	36	0
1992–93	Grimsby T	14	1
1993–94	Grimsby T	22	0
1994–95	Grimsby T	31	0
1995–96	Grimsby T	24	1
1996–97	Grimsby T	21	0
1997–98	Grimsby T	38	0
1998–99	Grimsby T	24	0
Total:		**326**	**8**

LEWIS, Mickey — Midfield

H: 5 8 W: 12 04 b.Birmingham 15-2-65

Source: School. *Honours:* England Youth.

1981–82	WBA	4	0
1982–83	WBA	5	0
1983–84	WBA	14	0
1984–85	WBA	1	0
1984–85	Derby Co	22	0
1985–86	Derby Co	5	1
1986–87	Derby Co	0	0
1987–88	Derby Co	16	0
1988–89	Oxford U	36	0
1989–90	Oxford U	45	1
1990–91	Oxford U	34	1
1991–92	Oxford U	40	4
1992–93	Oxford U	41	0
1993–94	Oxford U	46	0
1994–95	Oxford U	39	1
1995–96	Oxford U	19	0
1996–97	Oxford U	0	0
1997–98	Oxford U	0	0
1998–99	Oxford U	0	0
Total:		**367**	**8**

LEWIS, Neil — Defender

H: 5 8 W: 10 05 b.Wolverhampton 28-6-74

Source: Trainee.

1992–93	Leicester C	7	0
1993–94	Leicester C	24	0
1994–95	Leicester C	16	0
1995–96	Leicester C	14	1
1996–97	Leicester C	6	0
1997–98	Peterborough U	34	0
1998–99	Peterborough U	0	0
Total:		**101**	**1**

LIBURD, Richard — Defender

H: 5 9 W: 11 01 b.Nottingham 26-9-73

Source: Forest Ath.

1992–93	Middlesbrough	0	0
1993–94	Middlesbrough	41	1
1994–95	Bradford C	9	1
1995–96	Bradford C	33	1
1996–97	Bradford C	36	1
1997–98	Bradford C	0	0
1997–98	Carlisle U	9	0
1998–99	Notts Co	35	1
Total:		**163**	**5**

LIDDELL, Andy — Forward

H: 5 6 W: 11 06 b.Leeds 28-6-73

Source: Trainee. *Honours:* Scotland Under-21.

1990–91	Barnsley	0	0
1991–92	Barnsley	1	0
1992–93	Barnsley	21	2
1993–94	Barnsley	22	1
1994–95	Barnsley	39	13
1995–96	Barnsley	43	9
1996–97	Barnsley	38	8
1997–98	Barnsley	26	1
1998–99	Barnsley	8	0
1998–99	Wigan Ath	28	10
Total:		**226**	**44**

LIDDLE, Craig — Defender

H: 5 11 W: 12 07 b.Chester-le-Street 21-10-71

Source: Blyth Spartans.

1994–95	Middlesbrough	1	0
1995–96	Middlesbrough	13	0
1996–97	Middlesbrough	5	0
1997–98	Middlesbrough	6	0
1997–98	Darlington (loan)	15	0
1998–99	Darlington	44	3
Total:		**84**	**3**

LIGHTBOURNE, Kyle — Forward

H: 6 2 W: 12 00 b.Bermuda 29-9-68

Honours: Bermuda full caps.

1992–93	Scarborough	19	3
1993–94	Scarborough	0	0
1993–94	Walsall	35	7
1994–95	Walsall	42	23
1995–96	Walsall	43	15
1996–97	Walsall	45	20
1997–98	Coventry C	7	0
1997–98	Fulham (loan)	4	2
1997–98	Stoke C	13	2
1998–99	Stoke C	36	7
Total:		**244**	**79**

LIGHTFOOT, Chris — Defender

H: 6 1 W: 12 00 b.Penketh 1-4-70

Source: Trainee.

1987–88	Chester C	16	1
1988–89	Chester C	36	7
1989–90	Chester C	40	1
1990–91	Chester C	37	2
1991–92	Chester C	44	5
1992–93	Chester C	39	2
1993–94	Chester C	37	11
1994–95	Chester C	28	3
1995–96	Wigan Ath	14	1
1995–96	Crewe Alex	6	0
1996–97	Crewe Alex	25	0
1997–98	Crewe Alex	13	1
1998–99	Crewe Alex	22	2
Total:		**357**	**36**

LILLEY, Derek — Forward

H: 5 10 W: 12 08 b.Paisley 9-2-74

Source: Everton BC.

1991–92	Morton	25	3
1992–93	Morton	22	4
1993–94	Morton	38	5
1994–95	Morton	35	16
1995–96	Morton	35	14
1996–97	Morton	25	15
1996–97	Leeds U	6	0
1997–98	Leeds U	13	1
1998–99	Leeds U	2	0
1998–99	Bury (loan)	5	1
1998–99	Hearts (loan)	4	1
Total:		**210**	**60**

LINCOLN, Greg — Midfield

b.Cheshunt 23-3-80

Source: Trainee. *Honours:* England Youth.

1998–99	Arsenal	0	0

LING, Martin — Midfield

H: 5 7 W: 10 08 b.West Ham 15-7-66

Source: Apprentice.

1983–84	Exeter C	29	0
1984–85	Exeter C	42	6
1985–86	Exeter C	45	8
1986–87	Swindon T	2	0
1986–87	Southend U	24	8
1987–88	Southend U	42	7
1988–89	Southend U	44	6
1989–90	Southend U	25	10
1990–91	Southend U	3	0
1990–91	Mansfield T (loan)	3	0
1990–91	Swindon T (loan)	1	0
1991–92	Swindon T	21	3
1992–93	Swindon T	43	3
1993–94	Swindon T	33	1
1994–95	Swindon T	36	3
1995–96	Swindon T	16	0
1996–97	Leyton Orient	44	1
1997–98	Leyton Orient	46	2
1998–99	Leyton Orient	44	4
Total:		**543**	**62**

LINIGHAN, Andy — Defender

H: 6 4 W: 13 10 b.Hartlepool 18-6-62

Source: Smiths BC. *Honours:* England B.

1980–81	Hartlepool U	6	0
1981–82	Hartlepool U	17	0
1982–83	Hartlepool U	45	3
1983–84	Hartlepool U	42	1
1984–85	Leeds U	42	2
1985–86	Leeds U	24	1
1985–86	Oldham Ath	15	1
1986–87	Oldham Ath	40	3
1987–88	Oldham Ath	32	2
1987–88	Norwich C	12	2
1988–89	Norwich C	37	4
1989–90	Norwich C	37	2
1990–91	Arsenal	10	0
1991–92	Arsenal	17	0
1992–93	Arsenal	21	2
1993–94	Arsenal	21	0
1994–95	Arsenal	20	2
1995–96	Arsenal	18	0
1996–97	Arsenal	11	1
1996–97	Crystal Palace	19	2
1997–98	Crystal Palace	26	0
1998–99	Crystal Palace	20	0
1998–99	QPR (loan)	7	0
Total:		**539**	**28**

LINIGHAN, Brian — Defender

H: 6 4 W: 11 04 b.Hartlepool 2-11-73

Source: Trainee.

1992–93	Sheffield W	0	0
1993–94	Sheffield W	1	0
1994–95	Sheffield W	0	0
1995–96	Sheffield W	0	0
1996–97	Sheffield W	0	0
1997–98	Bury	0	0
1998–99	Bury	0	0
Total:		**1**	**0**

LINIGHAN, David — Defender

H: 6 2 W: 13 12 b.Hartlepool 9-1-65

Source: Local.

1981–82	Hartlepool U	6	0
1982–83	Hartlepool U	6	1
1983–84	Hartlepool U	23	1
1984–85	Hartlepool U	17	2
1984–85	Leeds U (loan)	0	0
1985–86	Hartlepool U	39	1
1986–87	Derby Co	0	0
1986–87	Shrewsbury T	24	0
1987–88	Shrewsbury T	41	1
1988–89	Ipswich T	41	2
1989–90	Ipswich T	41	0
1990–91	Ipswich T	45	3
1991–92	Ipswich T	36	3
1992–93	Ipswich T	42	1
1993–94	Ipswich T	38	3
1994–95	Ipswich T	32	0
1995–96	Ipswich T	2	0
1995–96	Blackpool	29	4
1996–97	Blackpool	42	1
1997–98	Blackpool	29	0
1998–99	Dunfermline Ath	1	0
1998–99	Mansfield T	10	0
Total:		**544**	**23**

LINTON, Des — Defender

H: 6 1 W: 13 10 b.Birmingham 5-9-71

Source: Trainee.

1989–90	Leicester C	2	0
1990–91	Leicester C	8	0
1991–92	Leicester C	1	0
1991–92	Luton T	3	0
1992–93	Luton T	20	1
1993–94	Luton T	33	0
1994–95	Luton T	10	0
1995–96	Luton T	10	0
1996–97	Luton T	7	0
1996–97	Peterborough U	8	0
1997–98	Peterborough U	30	0
1998–99	Peterborough U	8	0
1998–99	Swindon T (loan)	8	0
Total:		**148**	**1**

LISBIE, Kevin — Forward

H: 5 9 W: 11 00 b.Hackney 17-10-78

Source: Trainee. *Honours:* England Youth.

1996–97	Charlton Ath	25	1
1997–98	Charlton Ath	17	1
1998–99	Charlton Ath	1	0
1998–99	Gillingham (loan)	7	4
Total:		**50**	**6**

LITTLE, Colin — Forward

H: 5 10 W: 11 00 b.Wythenshaw 4-11-72

Source: Hyde U.

1995–96	Crewe Alex	12	1
1996–97	Crewe Alex	17	0
1997–98	Crewe Alex	40	13
1998–99	Crewe Alex	37	10
Total:		**106**	**24**

LITTLE, Glen — Midfield

H: 6 3 W: 13 00 b.Wimbledon 15-10-75

Source: Trainee.

1994–95	Crystal Palace	0	0
1995–96	Crystal Palace	0	0
1996–97	Glentoran	6	2
1996–97	Burnley	9	0
1997–98	Burnley	24	4
1998–99	Burnley	34	5
Total:		**73**	**11**

LITTLEJOHN, Adrian — Midfield

H: 5 10 W: 11 00 b.Wolverhampton 26-9-71

Source: WBA Trainee.

1989–90	Walsall	11	0
1990–91	Walsall	33	1
1991–92	Sheffield U	7	0
1992–93	Sheffield U	27	8
1993–94	Sheffield U	19	3
1994–95	Sheffield U	16	1
1995–96	Plymouth Arg	42	17
1996–97	Plymouth Arg	37	6
1997–98	Plymouth Arg	31	6
1997–98	Oldham Ath	5	3
1998–99	Oldham Ath	16	2
1998–99	Bury	20	1
Total:		**264**	**48**

LIVERMORE, David — Defender

b.Edmonton 20-5-80

Source: Trainee.

1998–99	Arsenal	0	0

LIVETT, Simon — Midfield

H: 5 10 W: 12 07 b.Plaistow 8-1-69

Source: Trainee.

1986–87	West Ham U	0	0
1987–88	West Ham U	0	0
1988–89	West Ham U	0	0
1989–90	West Ham U	0	0
1990–91	West Ham U	1	0
1991–92	West Ham U	0	0
1992–93	West Ham U	0	0
1992–93	Leyton Orient	23	0
1993–94	Leyton Orient	1	0
1993–94	Cambridge U	10	0
1994–95	Cambridge U	2	0
1995–96	Cambridge U	0	0
1996–97	Cambridge U	0	0
1997–98	Cambridge U	0	0
From Billericay T.			
1998–99	Southend U	23	1
Total:		**60**	**1**

LIVINGSTONE, Steve — Forward

H: 6 1 W: 14 00 b.Middlesbrough 8-9-68

Source: Trainee.

1986–87	Coventry C	3	0
1987–88	Coventry C	4	0
1988–89	Coventry C	1	0
1989–90	Coventry C	13	3
1990–91	Coventry C	10	2
1990–91	Blackburn R	18	9
1991–92	Blackburn R	10	1
1992–93	Blackburn R	2	0
1992–93	Chelsea	1	0
1993–94	Chelsea	0	0
1993–94	Port Vale (loan)	5	0
1993–94	Grimsby T	27	3
1994–95	Grimsby T	34	8
1995–96	Grimsby T	38	11
1996–97	Grimsby T	32	6
1997–98	Grimsby T	41	5
1998–99	Grimsby T	23	0
Total:		**262**	**48**

LJUNGBERG, Frederik — Midfield

b.Sweden 16-4-77

Honours: Sweden 10 full caps, 2 goals.

1994	Halmstad	1	0
1995	Halmstad	16	1
1996	Halmstad	20	2
1997	Halmstad	24	5
1998	Halmstad	18	2
1998–99	Arsenal	16	1
Total:		**95**	**11**

LLEWELLYN, Chris — Forward

H: 6 0 W: 11 07 b.Merthyr 28-8-79

Source: Trainee. *Honours:* Wales Under-21, B, 2 full caps.

1996–97	Norwich C	0	0
1997–98	Norwich C	15	4
1998–99	Norwich C	31	2
Total:		**46**	**6**

LLOYD, Kevin — Defender

H: 6 0 W: 12 03 b.Llanidloes 26-9-70

Source: Caersws.

1994–95	Hereford U	24	3
1995–96	Hereford U	27	0
1996–97	Cardiff C	31	1
1997–98	Cardiff C	2	0
1998–99	Oldham Ath	0	0
1998–99	Plymouth Arg	0	0
Total:		**84**	**4**

LLOYD, Neil — Forward

H: 5 10 W: 11 08 b.Knowsley 19-7-79

Source: Trainee.

1998–99	Wigan Ath	0	0

LOCK, Tony — Forward

H: 6 0 W: 12 04 b.Harlow 3-9-76

Source: Trainee.

1994–95	Colchester U	3	1
1995–96	Colchester U	0	0
1996–97	Colchester U	6	1
1997–98	Colchester U	32	6
1998–99	Colchester U	23	1
Total:		**64**	**9**

LOCKE, Adam — Midfield

H: 5 11 W: 12 07 b.Croydon 20-8-70

Source: Trainee.

1988–89	Crystal Palace	0	0
1989–90	Crystal Palace	0	0
1990–91	Southend U	28	4
1991–92	Southend U	10	0
1992–93	Southend U	27	0
1993–94	Southend U	8	0
1993–94	Colchester U (loan)	4	0
1994–95	Colchester U	22	1
1995–96	Colchester U	25	3
1996–97	Colchester U	32	4
1997–98	Bristol C	37	1
1998–99	Bristol C	28	3
Total:		**221**	**16**

LOCKE, Gary — Midfield

H: 5 8 W: 10 07 b.Edinburgh 16-6-75

Source: Whitehill Welfare. *Honours:* Scotland Under-21.

1992–93	Hearts	1	0
1993–94	Hearts	33	0
1994–95	Hearts	9	0
1995–96	Hearts	29	4
1996–97	Hearts	11	0
1997–98	Hearts	21	0
1998–99	Hearts	25	1
Total:		**129**	**5**

LOCKWOOD, Adam — Defender

H: 5 11 W: 11 08 b.Wakefield 26-10-81

Source: Trainee.

1998–99	Reading	0	0

LOCKWOOD, Matt — Defender

H: 5 9 W: 10 12 b.Rochford 17-10-76

Source: Trainee.

1994–95	QPR	0	0
1995–96	QPR	0	0
1996–97	Bristol R	39	1
1997–98	Bristol R	24	0
1998–99	Leyton Orient	37	3
Total:		**100**	**4**

LOGAN, Richard — Midfield

H: 6 0 W: 13 03 b.Barnsley 24-5-69

Source: Gainsborough T.

1993–94	Huddersfield T	16	0
1994–95	Huddersfield T	27	1
1995–96	Huddersfield T	2	0
1995–96	Plymouth Arg	31	4
1996–97	Plymouth Arg	28	4
1997–98	Plymouth Arg	27	4
1998–99	Scunthorpe U	41	6
Total:		**172**	**19**

LOGAN, Richard — Forward

H: 6.0 W: 12 05 b.Bury St Edmunds 4-1-82

Source: Trainee. *Honours:* England Schools.

1998–99	Ipswich T	2	0
Total:		**2**	**0**

LOMAS, Jamie — Midfield

H: 5 11 W: 10 09 b.Chesterfield 18-10-77

Source: Trainee.

1996–97	Chesterfield	2	0
1997–98	Chesterfield	4	0
1998–99	Chesterfield	7	0
Total:		**13**	**0**

LOMAS, Steve — Midfield

H: 6 0 W: 12 08 b.Hanover 18-1-74

Source: Trainee. *Honours:* Northern Ireland 30 full caps, 2 goals.

1991–92	Manchester C	0	0
1992–93	Manchester C	0	0
1993–94	Manchester C	23	0
1994–95	Manchester C	20	2
1995–96	Manchester C	33	3
1996–97	Manchester C	35	3
1996–97	West Ham U	7	0
1997–98	West Ham U	33	2
1998–99	West Ham U	30	1
Total:		**181**	**11**

LOMAX, Michael — Defender

H: 5 10 W: 10 12 b.Whithington 7-12-79

1998–99	Macclesfield T	1	0
Total:		**1**	**0**

LOMBARDI, Gustavo — Defender

H: 5 10 W: 11 05 b.Buenos Aires 10-9-75

Source: River Plate.

1998–99	Middlesbrough	0	0

LOMBARDO, Attilio — Midfield

H: 5 11 W: 11 07 b.St. Maria La Fossa 6-1-66

Honours: Italy 18 full caps, 3 goals.

1983–84	Pergocrema	7	2
1984–85	Pergocrema	31	7
1985–86	Cremonese	31	4
1986–87	Cremonese	36	3
1987–88	Cremonese	37	5
1988–89	Cremonese	37	5
1989–90	Sampdoria	34	7
1990–91	Sampdoria	32	3
1991–92	Sampdoria	34	4
1992–93	Sampdoria	34	6
1993–94	Sampdoria	34	8
1994–95	Sampdoria	33	6
1995–96	Juventus	13	2
1996–97	Juventus	22	0
1997–98	Crystal Palace	24	5
1998–99	Crystal Palace	19	3
Total:		**458**	**70**

LONERGAN, Darren — Defender

H: 6 0 W: 13 04 b.Cork 28-1-74

Source: Waterford.

1994–95	Oldham Ath	0	0
1995–96	Oldham Ath	2	0
1996–97	Oldham Ath	0	0
1997–98	Bury	0	0
1998–99	Macclesfield T	0	0
Total:		**2**	**0**

LONGWORTH, Steve — Forward

H: 5 9 W: 11 00 b.Leyland 6-2-80

Source: Trainee.

1997–98	Blackpool	2	0
1998–99	Blackpool	0	0
Total:		**2**	**0**

LOPEZ, Rik — Forward

H: 5 10 W: 11 04 b.Northwick Park 25-12-79

Source: Arsenal Trainee.

1996–97	QPR	0	0
1997–98	QPR	0	0
1998–99	QPR	0	0

LORMOR, Tony — Forward

H: 6 2 W: 13 13 b.Ashington 29-10-70

Source: Trainee.

1987–88	Newcastle U	5	2
1988–89	Newcastle U	3	1
1988–89	Norwich C (loan)	0	0
1989–90	Newcastle U	0	0
1989–90	Lincoln C	21	8
1990–91	Lincoln C	34	12
1991–92	Lincoln C	35	9
1992–93	Lincoln C	0	0
1993–94	Lincoln C	10	1
1994–95	Peterborough U	5	0
1994–95	Chesterfield	23	10
1995–96	Chesterfield	41	13
1996–97	Chesterfield	36	8
1997–98	Chesterfield	13	4
1997–98	Preston NE	12	3
1997–98	Notts Co (loan)	7	0
1998–99	Mansfield T	41	11
Total:		**286**	**82**

LOUGH, Lee — Midfield

H: 5 10 W: 12 06 b.London 18-7-79

Source: Ashford T.

1998–99	Luton T	0	0

LOUGHLIN, Paul — Midfield

b.Dublin 5-10-81

Source: Stella Maris.

1998–99	Wolverhampton W	0	0

LOUGHRAN, Anthony — Defender

H: 6 0 W: 11 12 b.Liverpool 11-11-81

Source: Trainee.

1998–99	Leeds U	0	0

LOUGHRAN, Kieran — Midfield

H: 5 10 W: 10 05 b.Ballymena 26-8-80

Source: Trainee.

1998–99	Crystal Palace	0	0

LOUIS-JEAN, Mathieu — Defender

H: 5 9 W: 10 08 b.Mont-St-Aignan 22-2-76

1993–94	Le Havre	7	0
1994–95	Le Havre	9	0
1995–96	Le Havre	15	0
1996–97	Le Havre	31	0
1997–98	Le Havre	16	0
1998–99	Nottingham F	16	0
Total:		**94**	**0**

LOVE, Andrew — Goalkeeper

H: 6 1 W: 14 00 b.Grimsby 28-3-79

Source: Trainee.

1996–97	Grimsby T	3	0
1997–98	Grimsby T	0	0
1998–99	Grimsby T	9	0
Total:		**12**	**0**

LOVELESS, Ian — Goalkeeper

H: 6 2 W: 14 05 b.Cardiff 1-11-79

Source: Trainee.

1998–99	Cardiff C	0	0

LOVELL, Stephen — Forward

b.Amersham 6-12-80

Source: Trainee.

1998–99	Bournemouth	7	0
Total:		**7**	**0**

LOVELL, Stuart — Forward

H: 5 10 W: 12 03 b.Sydney 9-1-72

Source: Trainee.

1990–91	Reading	30	2
1991–92	Reading	24	4
1992–93	Reading	22	8
1993–94	Reading	45	20
1994–95	Reading	30	11
1995–96	Reading	35	7
1996–97	Reading	26	5
1997–98	Reading	15	1
1998–99	Hibernian	31	11
Total:		**258**	**69**

LOVELOCK, Andrew — Forward

H: 6 0 W: 12 08 b.Swindon 20-12-76

Source: Trainee.

1993–94	Coventry C	0	0
1994–95	Coventry C	0	0
1995–96	Coventry C	0	0
1996–97	Coventry C	0	0
1997–98	Coventry C	0	0
From Southam U			
1998–99	Crewe Alex	0	0

LOVERING, Paul — Defender

H: 5 10 W: 10 00 b.Glasgow 25-11-75

Source: Blackburn Juniors.

1994–95	Clydebank	3	0
1995–96	Clydebank	21	1
1996–97	Clydebank	26	0
1997–98	Clydebank	32	4
1998–99	Hibernian	17	1
Total:		**99**	**6**

LOW, Josh — Midfield

H: 6 0 W: 14 00 b.Bristol 15-2-79

Source: Trainee. *Honours:* Wales Under-21.

1995–96	Bristol R	1	0
1996–97	Bristol R	3	0
1997–98	Bristol R	10	0
1998–99	Bristol R	8	0
Total:		**22**	**0**

LOWE, David — Forward

H: 5 10 W: 11 10 b.Liverpool 30-8-65

Source: Apprentice. *Honours:* England Youth, Under-21.

1982–83	Wigan Ath	28	6
1983–84	Wigan Ath	40	8
1984–85	Wigan Ath	29	5
1985–86	Wigan Ath	46	5
1986–87	Wigan Ath	45	16
1987–88	Ipswich T	41	17
1988–89	Ipswich T	32	6
1989–90	Ipswich T	34	13
1990–91	Ipswich T	13	0
1991–92	Ipswich T	14	1
1991–92	Port Vale (loan)	9	2
1992–93	Leicester C	32	11
1993–94	Leicester C	5	0
1993–94	Port Vale (loan)	19	5
1994–95	Leicester C	29	8
1995–96	Leicester C	28	3

1995–96	Wigan Ath	7	3
1996–97	Wigan Ath	42	6
1997–98	Wigan Ath	43	16
1998–99	Wigan Ath	16	1
Total:		**552**	**132**

LOWNDES, Nathan — Forward

H: 5 11 W: 10 11 b.Salford 2-6-77

Source: Trainee.

1994–95	Leeds U	0	0
1995–96	Leeds U	0	0
1995–96	Watford	0	0
1996–97	Watford	3	0
1997–98	Watford	4	0
1998–99	St Johnstone	29	2
Total:		**36**	**2**

LUA-LUA, Lomano — Forward

b.Zaire 28-12-80

1998–99	Colchester U	13	1
Total:		**13**	**1**

LUCAS, David — Goalkeeper

H: 6 1 W: 11 06 b.Preston 23-11-77

Source: Trainee. *Honours:* England Youth.

1995–96	Preston NE	1	0
1995–96	Darlington (loan)	6	0
1996–97	Preston NE	2	0
1996–97	Darlington (loan)	7	0
1996–97	Scunthorpe U (loan)	6	0
1997–98	Preston NE	6	0
1998–99	Preston NE	31	0
Total:		**59**	**0**

LUCAS, Richard — Defender

H: 5 10 W: 12 06 b.Chapeltown 22-9-70

Source: Trainee.

1989–90	Sheffield U	0	0
1990–91	Sheffield U	9	0
1991–92	Sheffield U	1	0
1992–93	Sheffield U	0	0
1992–93	Preston NE	26	0
1993–94	Preston NE	24	0
1994–95	Preston NE	0	0
1994–95	Lincoln C (loan)	4	0
1994–95	Preston NE	0	0
1995–96	Scarborough	44	0
1995–96	Scarborough	44	0
1996–97	Scarborough	28	0
1996–97	Hartlepool U	7	0
1997–98	Hartlepool U	42	2
1998–99	Halifax T	36	0
Total:		**265**	**2**

LUCKETTI, Chris — Defender

H: 6 2 W: 13 06 b.Littleborough 28-9-71

Source: Trainee.

1988–89	Rochdale	1	0
1989–90	Rochdale	0	0
1990–91	Stockport Co	0	0
1991–92	Halifax T	36	0
1992–93	Halifax T	42	2
1993–94	Bury	27	1
1994–95	Bury	39	3
1995–96	Bury	42	1
1996–97	Bury	38	0
1997–98	Bury	46	2
1998–99	Bury	43	1
Total:		**314**	**10**

LUDDEN, Dominic — Defender

H: 5 7 W: 10 09 b.Basildon 30-3-74

Source: Trainee. *Honours:* England Schools.

1992–93	Leyton Orient	24	1
1993–94	Leyton Orient	34	0
1994–95	Watford	1	0
1995–96	Watford	12	0
1996–97	Watford	20	0
1997–98	Watford	0	0
1998–99	Preston NE	32	0
Total:		**123**	**1**

LUDLAM, Ryan — Midfield

H: 5 9 W: 11 00 b.Carlisle 12-5-79

Source: Trainee.

1997–98	Sheffield U	0	0
1998–99	Sheffield U	0	0

LUKIC, John — Goalkeeper

H: 6 4 W: 13 07 b.Chesterfield 11-12-60

Source: Apprentice. *Honours:* England Youth, Under-21, B.

1978–79	Leeds U	0	0
1979–80	Leeds U	33	0
1980–81	Leeds U	42	0
1981–82	Leeds U	42	0
1982–83	Leeds U	29	0
1983–84	Arsenal	4	0
1984–85	Arsenal	27	0
1985–86	Arsenal	40	0
1986–87	Arsenal	36	0
1987–88	Arsenal	40	0
1988–89	Arsenal	38	0
1989–90	Arsenal	38	0
1990–91	Leeds U	38	0
1991–92	Leeds U	42	0
1992–93	Leeds U	39	0
1993–94	Leeds U	20	0

1994–95	Leeds U	42	0
1995–96	Leeds U	28	0
1996–97	Arsenal	15	0
1997–98	Arsenal	0	0
1998–99	Arsenal	0	0
Total:		**593**	**0**

LUMSDON, Chris — Midfield

H: 5 11 W: 10 03 b.Newcastle 15-12-79

Source: Trainee.

1997–98	Sunderland	1	0
1998–99	Sunderland	0	0
Total:		**1**	**0**

LUNDEKVAM, Claus — Defender

H: 6 3 W: 13 03 b.Austevoll 22-2-73

Honours: Norway 6 full caps.

1993	Brann	3	0
1994	Brann	20	0
1995	Brann	14	0
1996	Brann	16	1
1996–97	Southampton	29	0
1997–98	Southampton	31	0
1998–99	Southampton	33	0
Total:		**146**	**1**

LUNDIN, Paul — Goalkeeper

H: 6 4 W: 14 00 b.Osby 21-11-64

1989	Osters*	0	0
1990	Osters	24	0
1991	Osters	18	0
1992	Osters	27	0
1993	Osters	25	0
1994	Osters	24	0
1995	Osters	26	0
1996	Umea	7	0
1997	Osters	23	0
1998	Osters	15	0
1998–99	Oxford U	7	0
Total:		**196**	**0**

LUNT, Kenny — Midfield

H: 5 10 W: 10 00 b.Runcorn 20-11-79

Source: Trainee. *Honours:* England Schools, Youth.

1997–98	Crewe Alex	41	2
1998–99	Crewe Alex	18	1
Total:		**59**	**3**

LUSARDI, Mario — Forward

H: 5 9 W: 10 02 b.Islington 27-9-79

Source: Trainee.

1996–97	QPR	0	0
1997–98	QPR	0	0
1998–99	QPR	0	0

LYDIATE, Jason — Defender

H: 6 0 W: 13 00 b.Manchester 29-10-71

Source: Trainee.

1989–90	Manchester U	0	0
1990–91	Manchester U	0	0
1991–92	Manchester U	0	0
1991–92	Bolton W	1	0
1992–93	Bolton W	6	0
1993–94	Bolton W	5	0
1994–95	Bolton W	18	0
1994–95	Blackpool	11	0
1995–96	Blackpool	32	1
1996–97	Blackpool	20	0
1997–98	Blackpool	23	1
1998–99	Scarborough	27	1
1998–99	Rochdale (loan)	14	1
Total:		**157**	**4**

LYNCH, Damien — Defender

H: 5 10 W: 11 00 b.Dublin 31-7-79

1996–97	Leeds U	0	0
1997–98	Leeds U	0	0
1998–99	Leeds U	0	0

LYNCH, Finbar — Forward

H: 5 8 W: 10 01 b.Dublin 24-1-82

1998–99	Sunderland	0	0

LYONS, Michael — Midfield

b.Derby 24-7-81

Source: Trainee. *Honours:* England Youth.

1998–99	Derby Co	0	0

LYTTLE, Des — Defender

H: 5 8 W: 13 02 b.Wolverhampton 24-9-71

Source: Worcester C.

1992–93	Swansea C	46	1
1993–94	Nottingham F	37	1
1994–95	Nottingham F	38	0
1995–96	Nottingham F	33	1
1996–97	Nottingham F	32	1

1997–98	Nottingham F	35	0
1998–99	Nottingham F	10	0
1998–99	Port Vale (loan)	7	0
Total:		**238**	**4**

LYTTLE, Gerard — Defender

H: 5 7 W: 11 01 b.Belfast 27-11-77

Source: Star of the Sea. *Honours:* Northern Ireland Under-21.

1997–98	Celtic	0	0
1998–99	Peterborough U	0	0

MACDIARMID, Philip — Midfield

b.Liverpool 17-6-80

Source: Swindon T Trainee.

1998–99	Bristol C	0	0
1998–99	Exeter C	0	0

MACDONALD, Billy — Forward

H: 5 7 W: 11 00 b.Irvine 17-9-76

Source: Rangers 'S' Form.

1994–95	WBA	0	0
1995–96	Partick T	17	1
1996–97	Partick T	15	1
1997–98	Partick T	26	0
1998–99	Dunfermline Ath	1	0
Total:		**59**	**2**

MACDONALD, Charles — Forward

H: 5 9 W: 11 00 b.Southwark 13-2-81

Source: Trainee.

1998–99	Charlton Ath	0	0

MACDONALD, Gary — Midfield

H: 6 1 W: 12 00 b.Germany 25-10-79

1998–99	Portsmouth	0	0

MACDONALD, James — Midfield

H: 6 0 W: 12 05 b.Inverness 21-2-79

Source: Trainee. *Honours:* Scotland Schools.

1995–96	Arsenal	0	0
1996–97	Arsenal	0	0
1997–98	Arsenal	0	0
1998–99	Arsenal	0	0

MACKAY, Malcolm — Defender

H: 6 3 W: 13 06 b.Bellshill 19-2-72

Source: Queen's Park Youth.

1990–91	Queen's Park	10	0
1991–92	Queen's Park	27	3
1992–93	Queen's Park	33	3
1993–94	Celtic	0	0
1994–95	Celtic	1	0
1995–96	Celtic	11	1
1996–97	Celtic	20	1
1997–98	Celtic	4	1
1998–99	Celtic	1	1
1998–99	Norwich C	27	1
Total:		**134**	**11**

MACKENZIE, Chris — Goalkeeper

H: 6 0 W: 12 06 b.Northampton 14-5-72

Source: Corby T.

1994–95	Hereford U	22	0
1995–96	Hereford U	38	1
1996–97	Hereford U	0	0
1997–98	Leyton Orient	4	0
1998–99	Leyton Orient	26	0
Total:		**90**	**1**

MACKENZIE, Neil — Midfield

H: 6 2 W: 12 05 b.Birmingham 15-4-76

1996–97	Stoke C	22	1
1997–98	Stoke C	12	0
1998–99	Stoke C	6	0
1998–99	Cambridge U (loan)	4	1
Total:		**44**	**2**

MACPHERSON, Angus — Defender

H: 5 11 W: 10 04 b.Glasgow 11-10-68

Source: Rangers 'S' Form.

1988–89	Rangers	0	0
1989–90	Rangers	0	0
1989–90	Exeter C (loan)	11	1
1990–91	Kilmarnock	11	0
1991–92	Kilmarnock	43	3
1992–93	Kilmarnock	40	5
1993–94	Kilmarnock	43	2
1994–95	Kilmarnock	33	1
1995–96	Kilmarnock	35	1
1996–97	Kilmarnock	33	1
1997–98	Kilmarnock	25	0
1998–99	Kilmarnock	31	1
Total:		**305**	**15**

MACARI, Paul — Forward

H: 5 8 W: 11 06 b.Manchester 23-8-76

Source: Trainee.

1993–94	Stoke C	0	0
1994–95	Stoke C	0	0
1995–96	Stoke C	0	0
1996–97	Stoke C	0	0
1997–98	Stoke C	3	0
1998–99	Sheffield U	0	0
Total:		**3**	**0**

MACAULEY, Steve — Defender

H: 6 1 W: 12 03 b.Lytham 4-3-69

Source: Fleetwood T.

1991–92	Crewe Alex	9	1
1992–93	Crewe Alex	25	3
1993–94	Crewe Alex	17	3
1994–95	Crewe Alex	43	4
1995–96	Crewe Alex	29	7
1996–97	Crewe Alex	42	2
1997–98	Crewe Alex	0	0
1998–99	Crewe Alex	20	1
Total:		**185**	**21**

MACKEN, Jonathan — Forward

H: 5 10 W: 12 00 b.Manchester 7-9-77

Source: Trainee. *Honours:* England Youth.

1996–97	Manchester U	0	0
1997–98	Preston NE	29	6
1998–99	Preston NE	42	8
Total:		**71**	**14**

MACKLIN, Gareth — Defender

H: 5 8 W: 10 06 b.Belfast 27-8-80

Source: Trainee.

1997–98	Newcastle U	0	0
1998–99	Newcastle U	0	0

MADAR, Mikael — Forward

H: 6 1 W: 13 01 b.Paris 8-5-68

Source: Paris FC, Laval. *Honours:* France 3 full caps, 1 goal.

1989–90	Sochaux	7	0
1990–91	Sochaux	18	4
1991–92	Sochaux	21	2
1992–93	Cannes	27	16
1993–94	Cannes	27	10
1994–95	Monaco	23	6
1995–96	Monaco	29	8
1996–97	La Coruna	17	3
1997–98	La Coruna	7	1
1997–98	Everton	17	6
1998–99	Everton	2	0
Total:		**195**	**56**

MADDISON, Lee — Defender

H: 6 0 W: 12 10 b.Bristol 5-10-72

Source: Trainee.

1991–92	Bristol R	10	0
1992–93	Bristol R	12	0
1993–94	Bristol R	37	0
1994–95	Bristol R	14	0
1995–96	Bristol R	0	0
1995–96	Northampton T	21	0
1996–97	Northampton T	34	0
1997–98	Dundee	24	1
1998–99	Dundee	21	0
Total:		**173**	**1**

MADDISON, Neil — Midfield

H: 5 10 W: 11 10 b.Darlington 2-10-69

Source: Trainee.

1987–88	Southampton	0	0
1988–89	Southampton	5	2
1989–90	Southampton	2	0
1990–91	Southampton	4	0
1991–92	Southampton	6	0
1992–93	Southampton	37	4
1993–94	Southampton	41	7
1994–95	Southampton	35	3
1995–96	Southampton	15	1
1996–97	Southampton	18	1
1997–98	Southampton	6	1
1997–98	Middlesbrough	22	4
1998–99	Middlesbrough	21	0
Total:		**212**	**23**

MADDIX, Danny — Defender

H: 5 11 W: 12 00 b.Ashford 11-10-67

Source: Apprentice.

1985–86	Tottenham H	0	0
1986–87	Tottenham H	0	0
1986–87	Southend U (loan)	2	0
1987–88	QPR	9	0
1988–89	QPR	33	2
1989–90	QPR	32	3
1990–91	QPR	32	1
1991–92	QPR	19	0
1992–93	QPR	14	0
1993–94	QPR	0	0
1994–95	QPR	27	1
1995–96	QPR	22	0
1996–97	QPR	25	0
1997–98	QPR	25	1
1998–99	QPR	37	4
Total:		**277**	**12**

MAGEE, Darren — Midfield

H: 5 10 W: 12 00 b.Glasgow 14-4-77

Source: Milngavie W.

1997–98	Dundee	17	0
1998–99	Dundee	2	0
Total:		**19**	**0**

MAGILTON, Jim — Midfield

H: 6 0 W: 14 00 b.Belfast 6-5-69

Source: Apprentice. *Honours:* Northern Ireland Under-21, 39 full caps, 5 goals. Football League.

1986–87	Liverpool	0	0
1987–88	Liverpool	0	0
1988–89	Liverpool	0	0
1989–90	Liverpool	0	0
1990–91	Liverpool	0	0
1990–91	Oxford U	37	6
1991–92	Oxford U	44	12
1992–93	Oxford U	40	11
1993–94	Oxford U	29	5
1993–94	Southampton	15	0
1994–95	Southampton	42	6
1995–96	Southampton	31	3
1996–97	Southampton	37	4
1997–98	Southampton	5	0
1997–98	Sheffield W	21	1
1998–99	Sheffield W	6	0
1998–99	Ipswich T	19	3
Total:		**326**	**51**

MAHE, Stephane — Defender

H: 5 11 W: 11 11 b.Puteaux 23-9-68

1988–89	Auxerre	1	0
1989–90	Auxerre	0	0
1990–91	Auxerre	6	0
1991–92	Auxerre	34	1
1992–93	Auxerre	21	0
1993–94	Auxerre	32	2
1994–95	Auxerre	29	0
1995–96	Paris St Germain	23	0
1996–97	Rennes	33	0
1997–98	Celtic	23	0
1998–99	Celtic	24	0
Total:		**226**	**3**

MAHER, Kevin — Midfield

H: 5 11 W: 12 08 b.Ilford 17-10-76

Source: Trainee.

1995–96	Tottenham H	0	0
1996–97	Tottenham H	0	0
1997–98	Tottenham H	0	0
1997–98	Southend U	18	1
1998–99	Southend U	34	4
Total:		**52**	**5**

MAHER, Shaun — Defender

H: 6 2 W: 12 03 b.Dublin 10-6-78

Source: Bohemians.

1997–98	Fulham	0	0
1998–99	Fulham	0	0

MAHON, Alan — Midfield

H: 5 9 W: 11 05 b.Dublin 4-4-78

Source: Crumplin U. *Honours:* Eire Under-21.

1994–95	Tranmere R	0	0
1995–96	Tranmere R	2	0
1996–97	Tranmere R	25	2
1997–98	Tranmere R	18	1
1998–99	Tranmere R	39	6
Total:		**84**	**9**

MAHON, Gavin — Midfield

H: 5 11 W: 12 07 b.Birmingham 2-1-77

Source: Trainee.

1995–96	Wolverhampton W	0	0
1996–97	Hereford U	11	1
1997–98	Hereford U	0	0
1998–99	Hereford U	0	0
1998–99	Brentford	29	4
Total:		**40**	**5**

MAHONEY-JOHNSON, Michael — Forward

H: 5 10 W: 12 10 b.Paddington 6-11-76

Source: Trainee.

1994–95	QPR	0	0
1995–96	QPR	0	0
1996–97	QPR	2	0
1996–97	Wycombe W (loan)	4	2
1997–98	QPR	1	0
1997–98	Brighton & HA (loan)	4	0
1998–99	QPR	0	0
Total:		**11**	**2**

MAHOOD, Alan — Midfield

H: 5 8 W: 10 10 b.Kilwinning 26-3-73

Source: Bonnyton Th.

1990–91	Morton	8	0
1990–91	Nottingham F	0	0
1991–92	Morton	5	0
1992–93	Morton	17	6
1993–94	Morton	12	3
1994–95	Morton	21	1
1995–96	Morton	31	4
1996–97	Morton	27	3
1997–98	Morton	24	6
1998–99	Kilmarnock	28	2
Total:		**173**	**25**

MAIN, Alan — Goalkeeper

H: 5 11 W: 12 03 b.Elgin 5-12-67

Source: Elgin City. *Honours:* Scotland Under-21, B.

1986–97	Dundee U	2	0
1987–88	Dundee U	8	0
1988–89	Dundee U	0	0
1988–89	Cowdenbeath (loan)	3	0
1988–89	East Stirling (loan)	2	0
1989–90	Dundee U	27	0
1990–91	Dundee U	31	0
1991–92	Dundee U	17	0
1992–93	Dundee U	43	0
1993–94	Dundee U	18	0
1994–95	Dundee U	6	0
1994–95	St Johnstone	17	0
1995–96	St Johnstone	34	0
1996–97	St Johnstone	34	0
1997–98	St Johnstone	34	0
1998–99	St Johnstone	34	0
Total:		**310**	**0**

MAINWARING, Carl — Forward

H: 5 11 W: 12 07 b.Swansea 15-3-80

Source: Trainee.

1997–98	Swansea C	3	0
1998–99	Swansea C	0	0
Total:		**3**	**0**

MAKEL, Lee — Midfield

H: 5 9 W: 11 05 b.Sunderland 11-1-73

Source: Trainee.

1990–91	Newcastle U	3	0
1991–92	Newcastle U	9	1
1992–93	Blackburn R	1	0
1993–94	Blackburn R	2	0
1994–95	Blackburn R	0	0
1995–96	Blackburn R	3	0
1995–96	Huddersfield T	33	2
1996–97	Huddersfield T	19	3
1997–98	Huddersfield T	13	0
1997–98	Hearts	5	0
1998–99	Hearts	14	1
Total:		**102**	**7**

MAKIN, Chris — Defender

H: 5 10 W: 12 10 b.Manchester 8-5-73

Source: Trainee. *Honours:* England Schools, Under-21.

1991–92	Oldham Ath	0	0
1992–93	Oldham Ath	0	0
1992–93	Wigan Ath (loan)	15	2
1993–94	Oldham Ath	27	1
1994–95	Oldham Ath	28	1
1995–96	Oldham Ath	39	2
1996–97	Marseille	29	0
1997–98	Sunderland	25	0
1998–99	Sunderland	38	0
Total:		**201**	**6**

MALEY, Mark — Defender

H: 5 8 W: 12 00 b.Newcastle 26-1-81

Source: Trainee. *Honours:* England Schools, Youth.

1997–98	Sunderland	0	0
1998–99	Sunderland	0	0

MALKIN, Chris — Forward

H: 6 3 W: 12 09 b.Hoylake 4-6-67

Source: Stork, Overpool.

1987–88	Tranmere R	5	0
1988–89	Tranmere R	20	4
1989–90	Tranmere R	40	18
1990–91	Tranmere R	25	4
1991–92	Tranmere R	35	3
1992–93	Tranmere R	36	7
1993–94	Tranmere R	28	8
1994–95	Tranmere R	43	16
1995–96	Millwall	43	11
1996–97	Millwall	9	3
1996–97	Blackpool	15	3
1997–98	Blackpool	20	2
1998–99	Blackpool	29	1
Total:		**348**	**80**

MALPAS, Maurice — Defender

H: 5 8 W: 10 11 b.Dunfermline 3-8-62

Source: 'S' Form. *Honours:* Scotland Schools, Youth, Under-21, 55 full caps.

1979–80	Dundee U	0	0
1980–81	Dundee U	0	0
1981–82	Dundee U	19	0
1982–83	Dundee U	34	1
1983–84	Dundee U	34	2
1984–85	Dundee U	35	2
1985–86	Dundee U	36	2
1986–87	Dundee U	36	0
1987–88	Dundee U	44	0
1988–89	Dundee U	36	1
1989–90	Dundee U	30	2
1990–91	Dundee U	36	1
1991–92	Dundee U	44	3
1992–93	Dundee U	37	0
1993–94	Dundee U	35	0
1994–95	Dundee U	31	2
1995–96	Dundee U	30	2
1996–97	Dundee U	26	1
1997–98	Dundee U	31	1
1998–99	Dundee U	31	0
Total:		**605**	**20**

MANN, Neil — Midfield

H: 5 10 W: 12 01 b.Nottingham 19-11-72

Source: Notts Co, Spalding U, Grantham T.

1993–94	Hull C	5	0
1994–95	Hull C	31	2
1995–96	Hull C	38	1
1996–97	Hull C	32	2
1997–98	Hull C	34	3
1998–99	Hull C	20	1
Total:		**160**	**9**

MANNINGER, Alex — Goalkeeper

H: 6 2 W: 13 03 b.Salzburg 4-6-77

Honours: Austria Under-21.

1995–96	Vorwaerts Steyr	5	0
1995–96	Salzburg	1	0
1996–97	Graz	23	0
1997–98	Arsenal	7	0
1998–99	Arsenal	6	0
Total:		**42**	**0**

MANNION, Sean — Midfield

H: 5 8 W: 11 05 b.Dublin 3-3-80

Source: Stella Maris.

1997–98	Stockport Co	0	0
1998–99	Stockport Co	1	0
Total:		**1**	**0**

MANUEL, Billy — Midfield

H: 5 8 W: 12 00 b.Hackney 28-6-69

Source: Apprentice.

1987–88	Tottenham H	0	0
1988–89	Tottenham H	0	0
1988–89	Gillingham	17	1
1989–90	Gillingham	32	4
1990–91	Gillingham	38	0
1991–92	Brentford	35	0
1992–93	Brentford	41	1
1993–94	Brentford	18	0
1994–95	Cambridge U	10	0
1994–95	Peterborough U	14	1
1995–96	Peterborough U	13	1
1995–96	Gillingham	10	0
1996–97	Gillingham	11	0
1997–98	Barnet	17	0
1998–99	Barnet	12	1
Total:		**268**	**9**

MARCELLE, Clint — Midfield

H: 5 5 W: 9 09 b.Port of Spain 9-11-68

Source: Vitoria Setubal, Rio Ave. *Honours:* Trinidad & Tobago 30 full caps.

1994–95	Falgueiras	30	3
1995–96	Falgueiras	21	0
1996–97	Barnsley	40	8
1997–98	Barnsley	20	0
1998–99	Barnsley	9	0
Total:		**120**	**11**

MARCELO — Forward

H: 6 0 W: 13 08 b.Niteroi 11-10-69

Source: Alaves.

1997–98	Sheffield U	21	6
1998–99	Sheffield U	35	16
Total:		**56**	**22**

MARCOLIN, Dario — Midfield

H: 5 10 W: 11 07 b.Brescia 28-10-71

1989–90	Cremonese	4	1
1990–91	Cremonese	23	1
1991–92	Cremonese	33	3
1992–93	Lazio	15	0
1993–94	Lazio	4	0
1993–94	Cagliari	18	0
1994–95	Genoa	22	2
1995–96	Lazio	20	0
1996–97	Lazio	13	0
1997–98	Lazio	18	2
1998–99	Blackburn R	10	1
Total:		**180**	**10**

MARDON, Paul — Defender

H: 6 0 W: 11 10 b.Bristol 14-9-69

Source: Trainee. *Honours:* Wales 1 full cap.

1987–88	Bristol C	8	0
1988–89	Bristol C	20	0
1989–90	Bristol C	7	0
1990–91	Bristol C	7	0
1990–91	Doncaster R (loan)	3	0
1991–92	Birmingham C	35	0
1992–93	Birmingham C	21	0
1993–94	Birmingham C	8	0
1993–94	WBA	22	1
1994–95	WBA	28	1
1995–96	WBA	39	0
1996–97	WBA	14	0
1997–98	WBA	18	1
1998–99	WBA	18	0
1998–99	Oldham Ath (loan)	12	3
Total:		**260**	**6**

MARESCA, Enzo — Midfield

H: 5 11 W: 12 00 b.Salerno 10-2-80

1998–99	WBA	22	2
Total:		**22**	**2**

MARGAS, Javier — Defender

b.Chile 10-5-69

Source: Colo-Colo, America (Mexico), Univ Catolica. *Honours:* Chile 55 full caps, 4 goals.

1998–99	West Ham U	3	0
Total:		**3**	**0**

MARGETSON, Martyn — Goalkeeper

H: 6 0 W: 14 00 b.West Neath 8-9-71

Source: Trainee. *Honours:* Wales Under-21.

1990–91	Manchester C	2	0
1991–92	Manchester C	3	0
1992–93	Manchester C	1	0
1993–94	Manchester C	0	0
1993–94	Bristol R (loan)	3	0
1993–94	Bolton W (loan)	0	0
1994–95	Manchester C	0	0
1994–95	Luton T (loan)	0	0
1995–96	Manchester C	0	0
1996–97	Manchester C	17	0
1997–98	Manchester C	28	0
1998–99	Southend U	32	0
Total:		**86**	**0**

MARIC, Silvio — Midfield

H: 5 10 W: 11 02 b.Zagreb 20-3-75

Source: Croatia Zagreb. *Honours:* Croatia 16 full caps.

1998–99	Newcastle U	10	0
Total:		**10**	**0**

MARKER, Nicky — Defender

H: 6 0 W: 13 00 b.Exeter 3-5-65

Source: Apprentice.

1981–82	Exeter C	14	1
1982–83	Exeter C	18	1
1983–84	Exeter C	31	0
1984–85	Exeter C	45	0
1985–86	Exeter C	40	0
1986–87	Exeter C	43	1
1987–88	Exeter C	11	0
1987–88	Plymouth Arg	26	1
1988–89	Plymouth Arg	43	6
1989–90	Plymouth Arg	43	1
1990–91	Plymouth Arg	39	2
1991–92	Plymouth Arg	44	1
1992–93	Plymouth Arg	7	2
1992–93	Blackburn R	15	0
1993–94	Blackburn R	23	0
1994–95	Blackburn R	0	0
1995–96	Blackburn R	9	1
1996–97	Blackburn R	7	0
1997–98	Sheffield U	43	2
1998–99	Sheffield U	18	3
1998–99	Plymouth Arg (loan)	4	0
Total:		**523**	**22**

MARKEY, Brendan — Forward

H: 5 10 W: 12 00 b.Dublin 19-5-76

Source: Bohemians.

1995–96	Millwall	0	0
1996–97	Millwall	0	0
1997–98	Millwall	0	0
1998–99	Millwall	0	0

MARKSTEDT, Peter — Defender

H: 6 2 W: 13 05 b.Vasteras 11-1-72

1997	Vasteras	23	4
1997–98	Barnsley	7	0
1998–99	Barnsley	2	0
Total:		**32**	**4**

MARRIOTT, Alan — Goalkeeper

H: 6 1 W: 12 05 b.Bedford 3-9-78

Source: Trainee.

1997–98	Tottenham H	0	0
1998–99	Tottenham H	0	0

MARRIOTT, Andy — Goalkeeper

H: 6 2 W: 10 10 b.Sutton-in-Ashfield 11-10-70

Source: Trainee. *Honours:* England Schools, FA Schools, Youth, Under-21, Wales 5 full caps.

1988–89	Arsenal	0	0
1989–90	Nottingham F	0	0
1989–90	WBA (loan)	3	0
1989–90	Blackburn R (loan)	2	0
1989–90	Colchester U (loan)	10	0
1990–91	Nottingham F	0	0
1991–92	Nottingham F	6	0
1991–92	Burnley (loan)	15	0
1992–93	Nottingham F	5	0
1993–94	Nottingham F	0	0
1993–94	Wrexham	36	0
1994–95	Wrexham	46	0
1995–96	Wrexham	46	0
1996–97	Wrexham	43	0
1997–98	Wrexham	42	0
1998–99	Wrexham	0	0
1998–99	Sunderland	1	0
Total:		**255**	**0**

MARSDEN, Chris — Midfield

H: 6 0 W: 12 07 b.Sheffield 3-10-69

Source: Trainee.

1986–87	Sheffield U	0	0
1987–88	Sheffield U	16	1
1988–89	Huddersfield T	14	1
1989–90	Huddersfield T	32	2
1990–91	Huddersfield T	43	5
1991–92	Huddersfield T	23	1
1992–93	Huddersfield T	7	0
1993–94	Huddersfield T	2	0
1993–94	Coventry C (loan)	7	0
1993–94	Wolverhampton W	8	0
1994–95	Wolverhampton W	0	0
1994–95	Notts Co	7	0
1995–96	Notts Co	3	0
1995–96	Stockport Co	20	1
1996–97	Stockport Co	35	2
1997–98	Stockport Co	10	0
1997–98	Birmingham C	32	1
1998–99	Birmingham C	20	2
1998–99	Southampton	14	2
Total:		**293**	**18**

MARSH, Chris — Defender

H: 5 10 W: 13 04 b.Dudley 14-1-70

Source: Trainee.

1987–88	Walsall	3	0
1988–89	Walsall	13	0
1989–90	Walsall	9	0
1990–91	Walsall	23	2
1991–92	Walsall	37	1
1992–93	Walsall	33	3
1993–94	Walsall	39	4
1994–95	Walsall	38	9
1995–96	Walsall	41	2
1996–97	Walsall	30	0
1997–98	Walsall	36	0
1998–99	Walsall	43	2
Total:		**345**	**23**

MARSH, Simon — Defender

H: 5 11 W: 12 00 b.Ealing 29-1-77

Source: Trainee. *Honours:* England Under-21.

1994–95	Oxford U	8	0
1995–96	Oxford U	5	0
1996–97	Oxford U	8	1
1997–98	Oxford U	14	0
1998–99	Oxford U	21	2
1998–99	Birmingham C	7	0
Total:		**63**	**3**

MARSHALL, Andy — Goalkeeper

H: 6 2 W: 14 00 b.Bury 14-4-75

Source: Trainee. *Honours:* England Under-21.

1993–94	Norwich C	0	0
1994–95	Norwich C	21	0
1995–96	Norwich C	3	0
1996–97	Norwich C	7	0
1996–97	Bournemouth (loan)	11	0
1996–97	Gillingham (loan)	5	0
1997–98	Norwich C	42	0
1998–99	Norwich C	37	0
Total:		**126**	**0**

MARSHALL, Ben — Midfield

H: 6 0 W: 12 00 b.Sutton 5-9-79

Source: Trainee.

1997–98	Notts Co	0	0
1998–99	Notts Co	0	0

MARSHALL, Dwight — Forward

H: 6 1 W: 11 02 b.Lucea 3-10-65

Source: Grays Ath.

1991–92	Plymouth Arg	44	14
1992–93	Plymouth Arg	24	1
1992–93	Middlesbrough (loan)	3	0
1993–94	Plymouth Arg	31	12
1994–95	Luton T	45	11
1995–96	Luton T	26	9
1996–97	Luton T	24	4
1997–98	Luton T	29	3
1998–99	Luton T	4	1
1998–99	Plymouth Arg	28	12
Total:		**258**	**67**

MARSHALL, Gordon — Goalkeeper

H: 6 2 W: 12 00 b.Edinburgh 19-4-64

Source: School. *Honours:* Scotland 1 full cap.

1982–83	East Stirling	15	0
1982–83	East Fife	10	0
1983–84	East Fife	34	0
1984–85	East Fife	39	0
1985–86	East Fife	39	0
1986–87	East Fife	36	0
1986–87	Falkirk	10	0
1987–88	Falkirk	44	0
1988–89	Falkirk	39	0
1989–90	Falkirk	39	0
1990–91	Falkirk	39	0
1991–92	Celtic	25	0
1992–93	Celtic	11	0
1993–94	Celtic	1	0
1993–94	Stoke C (loan)	10	0
1994–95	Celtic	16	0

1995–96	Celtic	36	0
1996–97	Celtic	11	0
1997–98	Celtic	1	0
1997–98	Kilmarnock	12	0
1998–99	Kilmarnock	36	0
Total:		**503**	**0**

MARSHALL, Ian — Forward

H: 6 2 W: 13 09 b.Liverpool 20-3-66

Source: Apprentice.

1983–84	Everton	0	0
1984–85	Everton	0	0
1985–86	Everton	9	0
1986–87	Everton	2	1
1987–88	Everton	4	0
1987–88	Oldham Ath	10	0
1988–89	Oldham Ath	41	4
1989–90	Oldham Ath	25	3
1990–91	Oldham Ath	26	17
1991–92	Oldham Ath	41	10
1992–93	Oldham Ath	27	2
1993–94	Ipswich T	29	10
1994–95	Ipswich T	18	3
1995–96	Ipswich T	35	19
1996–97	Ipswich T	2	0
1996–97	Leicester C	28	8
1997–98	Leicester C	24	7
1998–99	Leicester C	10	3
Total:		**331**	**87**

MARSHALL, John — Defender

H: 5 10 W: 12 04 b.Surrey 18-8-64

Source: Apprentice.

1982–83	Fulham	0	0
1983–84	Fulham	25	0
1984–85	Fulham	32	1
1985–86	Fulham	42	3
1986–87	Fulham	29	4
1987–88	Fulham	25	2
1988–89	Fulham	41	7
1989–90	Fulham	36	4
1990–91	Fulham	35	2
1991–92	Fulham	41	0
1992–93	Fulham	41	2
1993–94	Fulham	21	1
1994–95	Fulham	27	2
1995–96	Fulham	16	0
1996–97	Fulham	0	0
1997–98	Fulham	0	0
1998–99	Fulham	0	0
Total:		**411**	**28**

MARSHALL, Lee — Midfield

H: 5 10 W: 10 08 b.Nottingham 1-8-75

Source: Trainee.

1992–93	Nottingham F	0	0
1993–94	Nottingham F	0	0
From Grantham T			
1994–95	Stockport Co	1	0
1995–96	Stockport Co	0	0
From Eastwood T.			
1997–98	Scunthorpe U	21	1
1998–99	Scunthorpe U	19	1
Total:		**41**	**2**

MARSHALL, Lee — Midfield

H: 6 2 W: 12 06 b.Islington 21-1-79

Source: Enfield. *Honours:* England Under-21.

1996–97	Norwich C	0	0
1997–98	Norwich C	4	0
1998–99	Norwich C	44	3
Total:		**48**	**3**

MARSHALL, Scott — Defender

H: 6 1 W: 12 13 b.Edinburgh 1-5-73

Source: Trainee. *Honours:* Scotland Under-21.

1992–93	Arsenal	2	0
1993–94	Arsenal	0	0
1993–94	Rotherham U (loan)	10	1
1993–94	Oxford U (loan)	0	0
1994–95	Arsenal	0	0
1994–95	Sheffield U (loan)	17	0
1995–96	Arsenal	11	1
1996–97	Arsenal	8	0
1997–98	Arsenal	3	0
1998–99	Southampton	2	0
1998–99	Celtic	2	0
Total:		**55**	**2**

MARSHALL, Shaun — Goalkeeper

H: 6 2 W: 12 12 b.Fakenham 3-10-78

Source: Trainee.

1996–97	Cambridge U	1	0
1997–98	Cambridge U	2	0
1998–99	Cambridge U	19	0
Total:		**22**	**0**

MARTIN, Alan — Defender

H: 5 10 W: 11 05 b.Dublin 21-11-81

Source: Trainee.

1998–99	Leeds U	0	0

MARTIN, Andrew — Forward

H: 6 0 W: 10 12 b.Cardiff 28-2-80

Source: Trainee. *Honours:* Wales Under-21.

1996–97	Crystal Palace	0	0
1997–98	Crystal Palace	0	0
1998–99	Crystal Palace	3	0
Total:		**3**	**0**

MARTIN, Brian — Midfield

H: 6 0 W: 13 00 b.Bellshill 24-2-63

Source: Shotts Bon-Accord. *Honours:* Scotland 2 full caps.

1985–86	Falkirk	25	1
1986–87	Falkirk	34	1
1986–87	Hamilton A	7	0
1987–88	Hamilton A	23	0
1987–88	St Mirren	12	1
1988–89	St Mirren	34	2
1989–90	St Mirren	35	2
1990–91	St Mirren	31	2
1991–92	St Mirren	17	2
1991–92	Motherwell	25	0
1992–93	Motherwell	44	3
1993–94	Motherwell	43	2
1994–95	Motherwell	32	2
1995–96	Motherwell	33	2
1996–97	Motherwell	34	0
1997–98	Motherwell	26	1
1998–99	Motherwell	0	0
Total:		**455**	**21**

MARTIN, Craig — Midfield

H: 6 2 W: 11 07 b.Uphall 10-11-78

Source: Links U.

1997–98	Dunfermline Ath	0	0
1998–99	Dunfermline Ath	3	0
Total:		**3**	**0**

MARTIN, Jae — Midfield

H: 5 11 W: 11 00 b.London 5-2-76

Source: Trainee.

1992–93	Southend U	0	0
1993–94	Southend U	4	0
1994–95	Southend U	4	0
1994–95	Leyton Orient (loan)	4	0
1995–96	Birmingham C	7	0
1996–97	Birmingham C	0	0
1996–97	Lincoln C	34	4
1997–98	Lincoln C	7	1
1998–99	Peterborough U	4	0
Total:		**64**	**5**

MARTIN, John — Midfield

H: 5 5 W: 10 00 b.Bethnal Green 15-7-81

Source: Trainee.

1997–98	Leyton Orient	1	0
1998–99	Leyton Orient	1	0
Total:		**2**	**0**

MARTIN, Kevin — Goalkeeper

H: 6 1 W: 12 05 b.Bromsgrove 22-6-76

Source: Trainee.

1994–95	Scarborough	3	0
1995–96	Scarborough	0	0
1996–97	Scarborough	3	0
1997–98	Scarborough	17	0
1998–99	Scarborough	0	0
Total:		**23**	**0**

MARTIN, Lee — Goalkeeper

H: 6 0 W: 13 00 b.Huddersfield 9-9-68

Source: Trainee. *Honours:* England Schools.

1987–88	Huddersfield T	18	0
1988–89	Huddersfield T	0	0
1989–90	Huddersfield T	25	0
1990–91	Huddersfield T	4	0
1991–92	Huddersfield T	7	0
1992–93	Blackpool	24	0
1993–94	Blackpool	43	0
1994–95	Blackpool	31	0
1995–96	Blackpool	0	0
1995–96	Bradford C (loan)	0	0
1996–97	Blackpool	0	0
1996–97	Rochdale	0	0
1997–98	Rochdale	0	0
1998–99	Halifax T	37	0
Total:		**189**	**0**

MARTINDALE, Gary — Forward

H: 6 1 W: 11 13 b.Liverpool 24-6-71

Source: Burscough.

1993–94	Bolton W	0	0
1994–95	Bolton W	0	0
1995–96	Peterborough U	31	15
1995–96	Notts Co	16	6
1996–97	Notts Co	28	6
1996–97	Mansfield T (loan)	5	2
1997–98	Notts Co	22	1
1997–98	Rotherham U	8	2
1998–99	Rotherham U	10	2
Total:		**120**	**34**

MARTINEZ, Roberto — Midfield

H: 5 11 W: 12 03 b.Balaguer 13-7-73

Source: Balaguer.

1995–96	Wigan Ath	42	9
1996–97	Wigan Ath	43	4
1997–98	Wigan Ath	33	1
1998–99	Wigan Ath	10	0
Total:		**128**	**14**

MARTYN, Nigel — Goalkeeper

H: 6 2 W: 14 10 b.St Austell 11-8-66

Source: St Blazey. *Honours:* England Under-21, B, 9 full caps.

1987–88	Bristol R	39	0
1988–89	Bristol R	46	0
1989–90	Bristol R	16	0
1989–90	Crystal Palace	25	0
1990–91	Crystal Palace	38	0
1991–92	Crystal Palace	38	0
1992–93	Crystal Palace	42	0
1993–94	Crystal Palace	46	0
1994–95	Crystal Palace	37	0
1995–96	Crystal Palace	46	0
1996–97	Leeds U	37	0
1997–98	Leeds U	37	0
1998–99	Leeds U	34	0
Total:		**481**	**0**

MASKELL, Craig — Forward

H: 5 10 W: 11 10 b.Aldershot 10-4-68

Source: Apprentice. *Honours:* Football League.

1985–86	Southampton	2	1
1986–87	Southampton	4	0
1986–87	Swindon T (loan)	0	0
1987–88	Southampton	0	0
1988–89	Huddersfield T	46	28
1989–90	Huddersfield T	41	15
1990–91	Reading	38	10
1991–92	Reading	34	16
1992–93	Swindon T	33	19
1993–94	Swindon T	14	3
1993–94	Southampton	10	1
1994–95	Southampton	6	0
1995–96	Southampton	1	0
1995–96	Bristol C (loan)	5	1
1995–96	Brighton & HA	15	4
1996–97	Brighton & HA	37	14
1997–98	Brighton & HA	17	2
From Happy Valley.			
1997–98	Leyton Orient	8	2
1998–99	Leyton Orient	15	0
Total:		**326**	**116**

MASON, Gary — Midfield

H: 5 8 W: 10 01 b.Edinburgh 15-10-79

Source: Trainee. *Honours:* Scotland Under-21.

1996–97	Manchester C	0	0
1997–98	Manchester C	0	0
1998–99	Manchester C	19	0
Total:		**19**	**0**

MASON, Michael — Forward

H: 5 9 W: 11 11 b.Walsall 7-8-79

1998–99	Macclesfield T	0	0

MASON, Paul — Midfield

H: 5 9 W: 12 01 b.Liverpool 3-9-63

Source: Groningen.

1988–89	Aberdeen	28	4
1989–90	Aberdeen	34	9
1990–91	Aberdeen	26	3
1991–92	Aberdeen	31	7
1992–93	Aberdeen	39	4
1993–94	Ipswich T	22	3
1994–95	Ipswich T	21	3
1995–96	Ipswich T	26	7
1996–97	Ipswich T	43	12
1997–98	Ipswich T	1	0
1998–99	Ipswich T	0	0
Total:		**271**	**52**

MASTERS, Neil — Defender

H: 6 1 W: 14 02 b.Lisburn 25-5-72

Source: Trainee.

1992–93	Bournemouth	20	0
1993–94	Bournemouth	18	2
1993–94	Wolverhampton W	4	0
1994–95	Wolverhampton W	5	0
1995–96	Wolverhampton W	3	0
1996–97	Wolverhampton W	0	0
1996–97	Gillingham	0	0
1997–98	Gillingham	11	0
1998–99	Gillingham	0	0
Total:		**61**	**2**

MATERAZZI, Marco — Defender

H: 6 4 W: 14 00 b.Perugia 19-8-73

1990–91	Messina	0	0
Tor di Quinto			
1993–94	Marsala	25	4
1994–95	Trapani	13	2
1995–96	Perugia	1	0

1996–97	Carpi	18	7
1996–97	Perugia	14	2
1997–98	Perugia	32	5
1998–99	Everton	27	1
Total:		**130**	**21**

MATHIE, Alex — Forward

H: 5 10 W: 11 13 b.Bathgate 20-12-68

Source: Celtic BC.

1987–88	Celtic	0	0
1988–89	Celtic	1	0
1989–90	Celtic	6	0
1990–91	Celtic	4	0
1991–92	Morton	42	18
1992–93	Morton	32	13
1992–93	Port Vale (loan)	3	0
1993–94	Newcastle U	16	3
1994–95	Newcastle U	9	1
1994–95	Ipswich T	13	2
1995–96	Ipswich T	39	18
1996–97	Ipswich T	12	4
1997–98	Ipswich T	37	13
1998–99	Ipswich T	8	1
1998–99	Dundee U	22	1
Total:		**244**	**74**

MATIAS, Pedro — Forward

H: 6 0 W: 12 00 b.Madrid 11-10-73

1998–99	Logrones	12	0
1998–99	Macclesfield T	22	2
Total:		**34**	**2**

MATTEO, Dominic — Defender

H: 6 1 W: 11 10 b.Dumfries 24-4-74

Source: Trainee. *Honours:* England Youth, Under-21, B.

1992–93	Liverpool	0	0
1993–94	Liverpool	11	0
1994–95	Liverpool	7	0
1994–95	Sunderland (loan)	1	0
1995–96	Liverpool	5	0
1996–97	Liverpool	26	0
1997–98	Liverpool	26	0
1998–99	Liverpool	20	1
Total:		**96**	**1**

MATTHAEI, Rob — Midfield

H: 5 8 W: 11 07 b.Amsterdam 20-9-66

1985–86	Haarlem	30	1
1986–87	Haarlem	31	3
1987–88	Haarlem	33	5
1988–89	Haarlem	32	2
1989–90	Haarlem	20	0
1990–91	Haarlem	0	0
1990–91	De Graafschap	12	1
1991–92	De Graafschap	25	0
1992–93	De Graafschap	32	0
1993–94	De Graafschap	29	1
1994–95	De Graafschap	30	1
1995–96	De Graafschap	26	0
1996–97	Volendam	22	0
1997–98	Volendam	29	0
1998–99	Motherwell	17	0
Total:		**368**	**14**

MATTHEW, Damian — Midfield

H: 5 11 W: 10 10 b.Islington 23-9-70

Source: Trainee. *Honours:* England Under-21.

1989–90	Chelsea	2	0
1990–91	Chelsea	8	0
1991–92	Chelsea	7	0
1992–93	Chelsea	4	0
1992–93	Luton T (loan)	5	0
1993–94	Chelsea	0	0
1993–94	Crystal Palace	12	1
1994–95	Crystal Palace	4	0
1995–96	Crystal Palace	8	0
1995–96	Bristol R (loan)	8	0
1996–97	Burnley	32	6
1997–98	Burnley	27	1
1998–99	Northampton T	1	0
Total:		**118**	**8**

MATTHEWS, Lee — Forward

H: 6 2 W: 13 05 b.Middlesbrough 6-1-79

Source: Trainee. *Honours:* England Youth.

1995–96	Leeds U	0	0
1996–97	Leeds U	0	0
1997–98	Leeds U	3	0
1998–99	Leeds U	0	0
1998–99	Notts Co (loan)	5	0
Total:		**8**	**0**

MATTHEWS, Rob — Forward

H: 6 0 W: 12 05 b.Slough 14-10-70

Source: Loughborough Univ. *Honours:* England Schools.

1991–92	Notts Co	5	3
1992–93	Notts Co	8	2
1993–94	Notts Co	12	3
1994–95	Notts Co	18	3
1994–95	Luton T	11	0
1995–96	Luton T	0	0
1995–96	York C	17	1
1995–96	Bury	16	4
1996–97	Bury	27	5
1997–98	Bury	15	0
1998–99	Bury	16	2
1998–99	Stockport Co	23	2
Total:		**168**	**25**

MATTIS, Dwayne — Midfield

H: 6 1 W: 10 09 b.Huddersfield 31-7-81

Source: Trainee.

1998–99	Huddersfield T	2	0
Total:		**2**	**0**

MATTSSON, Jesper — Defender

H: 6 1 W: 13 01 b.Visby 18-4-68

1994	Hacken	24	3
1995	Halmstad	25	0
1996	Halmstad	24	1
1997	Halmstad	26	4
1998	Halmstad	26	3
1998–99	Nottingham F	6	0
Total:		**131**	**11**

MAUGE, Ronnie — Midfield

H: 5 10 W: 10 06 b.Islington 10-3-69

Source: Trainee.

1987–88	Charlton Ath	0	0
1988–89	Fulham	13	0
1989–90	Fulham	37	2
1990–91	Bury	29	6
1991–92	Bury	22	0
1991–92	Manchester C (loan)	0	0
1992–93	Bury	13	1
1993–94	Bury	26	3
1994–95	Bury	18	0
1995–96	Plymouth Arg	37	7
1996–97	Plymouth Arg	35	3
1997–98	Plymouth Arg	31	1
1998–99	Plymouth Arg	32	3
Total:		**293**	**26**

MAURO — Midfield

H: 6 1 W: 12 12 b.Portugal 16-6-76

Source: Casapia.

1997–98	Tranmere R	0	0
1998–99	Tranmere R	0	0

MAUTONE, Steve — Goalkeeper

H: 6 2 W: 13 02 b.Myrtleford 10-8-70

Source: Canberra Cosmos.

1995–96	West Ham U	0	0
1996–97	West Ham U	1	0
1996–97	Crewe Alex (loan)	3	0
1996–97	Reading	15	0
1997–98	Reading	14	0
1998–99	Reading	0	0
Total:		**33**	**0**

MAVRAK, Darko — Midfield

b.Mostar 19-1-69

1996	Norrkoping	13	0
1997	Norrkoping	13	1
1998–99	Walsall	13	2
Total:		**39**	**3**

MAWSON, Craig — Goalkeeper

H: 6 2 W: 13 04 b.Keighley 16-5-79

Source: Trainee.

1997–98	Burnley	0	0
1998–99	Burnley	0	0

MAXWELL, Leyton — Midfield

H: 5 8 W: 11 00 b.St Asaph 3-10-79

Source: Trainee. *Honours:* Wales Under-21.

1997–98	Liverpool	0	0
1998–99	Liverpool	0	0

MAY, David — Defender

H: 6 0 W: 13 05 b.Oldham 24-6-70

Source: Trainee.

1988–89	Blackburn R	1	0
1989–90	Blackburn R	17	0
1990–91	Blackburn R	19	1
1991–92	Blackburn R	12	0
1992–93	Blackburn R	34	1
1993–94	Blackburn R	40	1
1994–95	Manchester U	19	2
1995–96	Manchester U	16	1
1996–97	Manchester U	29	3
1997–98	Manchester U	9	0
1998–99	Manchester U	6	0
Total:		**202**	**9**

MAY, Edward — Forward

H: 5 7 W: 10 03 b.Edinburgh 30-8-67

Source: Hutchison Vale BC. *Honours:* Scotland Youth, Under-21.

1983–84	Dundee U	0	0
1984–85	Dundee U	0	0
1984–85	Hibernian	0	0
1985–86	Hibernian	19	1
1986–87	Hibernian	30	5
1987–88	Hibernian	35	2
1988–89	Hibernian	25	2
1989–90	Brentford	30	8
1990–91	Brentford	17	2
1990–91	Falkirk	13	6
1991–92	Falkirk	36	9

1992–93	Falkirk	42	6
1993–94	Falkirk	38	9
1994–95	Falkirk	24	2
1994–95	Motherwell	10	2
1995–96	Motherwell	28	1
1996–97	Motherwell	34	2
1997–98	Motherwell	25	0
1998–99	Motherwell	12	0
Total:		**418**	**57**

MAYBURY, Alan — Defender

H: 5 9 W: 10 04 b.Dublin 8-8-78

Source: Trainee. *Honours:* Eire 2 full caps.

1995–96	Leeds U	1	0
1996–97	Leeds U	0	0
1997–98	Leeds U	12	0
1998–99	Leeds U	0	0
1998–99	Reading (loan)	8	0
Total:		**21**	**0**

MAYER, Andreas — Midfield

H: 5 10 W: 12 01 b.Burgau 13-9-72

Source: Rofingen, Augsburg.

1992–93	Bayern Munich	0	0
1993–94	St Pauli	0	0
1994–95	St Pauli	0	0
1995–96	St Pauli	0	0
1995	Stabaek	7	1
1996	Stabaek	24	6
1997	Stabaek	12	1
1997	Rosenborg	7	0
1998–99	Aberdeen	13	2
Total:		**63**	**10**

MAYLETT, Bradley — Forward

b.Manchester 24-12-80

Source: Trainee.

1998–99	Burnley	17	0
Total:		**17**	**0**

MAYO, Kerry — Defender

H: 5 8 W: 11 07 b.Cuckfield 21-9-77

Source: Trainee.

1996–97	Brighton & HA	24	0
1997–98	Brighton & HA	44	6
1998–99	Brighton & HA	25	1
Total:		**93**	**7**

MAZZARELLA, Paul — Midfield

H: 6 0 W: 11 05 b.Wrexham 8-8-80

Source: Trainee.

1998–99	Wrexham	0	0

McALINDON, Gareth — Forward

H: 5 9 W: 11 10 b.Hexham 6-4-77

Source: Newcastle U Trainee.

1995–96	Carlisle U	3	0
1996–97	Carlisle U	12	2
1997–98	Carlisle U	28	3
1998–99	Carlisle U	16	0
Total:		**59**	**5**

McALLISTER, Brian — Defender

H: 5 11 W: 12 05 b.Glasgow 30-11-70

Source: Trainee. *Honours:* Scotland 3 full caps.

1988–89	Wimbledon	0	0
1989–90	Wimbledon	3	0
1990–91	Wimbledon	0	0
1990–91	Plymouth Arg (loan)	8	0
1991–92	Wimbledon	10	0
1992–93	Wimbledon	27	0
1993–94	Wimbledon	13	0
1994–95	Wimbledon	0	0
1995–96	Wimbledon	2	0
1995–96	Crewe Alex (loan)	13	1
1996–97	Wimbledon	23	0
1997–98	Wimbledon	7	0
1998–99	Wimbledon	0	0
Total:		**106**	**1**

McALLISTER, Gary — Midfield

H: 6 1 W: 11 11 b.Motherwell 25-12-64

Source: Fir Park BC. *Honours:* Scotland Under-21, B, 57 full caps, 5 goals.

1981–82	Motherwell	1	0
1982–83	Motherwell	1	0
1983–84	Motherwell	21	0
1984–85	Motherwell	35	6
1985–86	Motherwell	1	0
1985–86	Leicester C	31	7
1986–87	Leicester C	39	10
1987–88	Leicester C	42	9
1988–89	Leicester C	46	11
1989–90	Leicester C	43	10
1990–91	Leeds U	38	2
1991–92	Leeds U	42	5
1992–93	Leeds U	32	5
1993–94	Leeds U	42	8
1994–95	Leeds U	41	6
1995–96	Leeds U	36	5
1996–97	Coventry C	38	6
1997–98	Coventry C	14	0
1998–99	Coventry C	29	3
Total:		**572**	**93**

McALPINE, Joseph — Defender

b.Glasgow 12-9-81

1997–98	Everton	0	0
1998–99	Everton	0	0

McANESPIE, Kieran — Forward

H: 5 8 W: 10 13 b.Gosport 11-9-79

Source: St Johnstone BC. *Honours:* Scotland Under-17, Under-21.

1995–96	St Johnstone	0	0
1996–97	St Johnstone	9	2
1997–98	St Johnstone	3	0
1998–99	St Johnstone	18	2
Total:		**30**	**4**

McANESPIE, Steve — Defender

H: 5 9 W: 10 08 b.Kilmarnock 1-2-72

Source: Vasterhauringe.

1993–94	Raith R	3	0
1994–95	Raith R	34	0
1995–96	Raith R	3	0
1995–96	Bolton W	9	0
1996–97	Bolton W	13	0
1997–98	Bolton W	2	0
1997–98	Fulham	4	0
1997–98	Bradford C (loan)	7	0
1998–99	Fulham	3	0
Total:		**78**	**0**

McAREAVEY, Paul — Midfield

b.Belfast 3-12-80

Source: Trainee.

1997–98	Swindon T	1	0
1998–99	Swindon T	1	0
Total:		**2**	**0**

McAREE, Rod — Midfield

H: 5 7 W: 11 00 b.Dungannon 10-8-74

Source: Trainee.

1991–92	Liverpool	0	0
1992–93	Liverpool	0	0
1993–94	Liverpool	0	0
1994–95	Bristol C	6	0
1995–96	Bristol C	0	0
1995–96	Fulham	17	2
1996–97	Fulham	9	1
1997–98	Fulham	2	0
1998–99	Fulham	0	0
Total:		**34**	**3**

McARTHUR, Duncan — Midfield

b.Brighton 6-5-81

Source: Trainee.

1998–99	Brighton & HA	3	0
Total:		**3**	**0**

McATEER, Jason — Midfield

H: 5 11 W: 11 10 b.Birkenhead 18-6-71

Source: Marine. *Honours:* Eire B, 30 full caps, 1 goal.

1991–92	Bolton W	0	0
1992–93	Bolton W	21	0
1993–94	Bolton W	46	3
1994–95	Bolton W	43	5
1995–96	Bolton W	4	0
1995–96	Liverpool	29	0
1996–97	Liverpool	37	1
1997–98	Liverpool	21	2
1998–99	Liverpool	13	0
1998–99	Blackburn R	13	1
Total:		**227**	**12**

McAULEY, Sean — Defender

H: 5 11 W: 12 02 b.Sheffield 23-6-72

Source: Trainee. *Honours:* Scotland Under-21.

1991–92	Manchester U	0	0
1992–93	St Johnstone	26	0
1993–94	St Johnstone	28	0
1994–95	St Johnstone	8	0
1994–95	Chesterfield (loan)	1	1
1995–96	Hartlepool U	46	0
1996–97	Hartlepool U	38	1
1996–97	Scunthorpe U	9	0
1997–98	Scunthorpe U	35	1
1998–99	Scunthorpe U	17	0
1998–99	Scarborough (loan)	7	0
Total:		**215**	**3**

McAVOY, Andy — Midfield

H: 6 0 W: 12 00 b.Middlesbrough 28-8-79

Source: Trainee.

1997–98	Blackburn R	0	0
1998–99	Blackburn R	0	0

McAVOY, Larry — Defender

H: 5 8 W: 11 00 b.Lambeth 7-9-79

Source: Trainee.

1998–99	Cambridge U	1	0
Total:		**1**	**0**

McBRIDE, John Paul — Midfield

H: 5 10 W: 10 02 b.Hamilton 28-11-78

Source: Celtic BC. *Honours:* Scotland Under-21.

1995–96	Celtic	0	0
1996–97	Celtic	2	0
1997–98	Celtic	0	0
1998–99	Celtic	1	0
1998–99	St Johnstone	3	0
Total:		**6**	**0**

McCALL, Steve — Midfield

H: 5 11 W: 12 10 b.Carlisle 15-10-60

Source: Apprentice. *Honours:* England Youth, Under-21, B.

1978–79	Ipswich T	0	0
1979–80	Ipswich T	10	0
1980–81	Ipswich T	31	1
1981–82	Ipswich T	42	1
1982–83	Ipswich T	42	4
1983–84	Ipswich T	42	1
1984–85	Ipswich T	31	0
1985–86	Ipswich T	33	0
1986–87	Ipswich T	26	0
1987–88	Sheffield W	5	0
1988–89	Sheffield W	2	0
1989–90	Sheffield W	3	0
1989–90	Carlisle U (loan)	6	0
1990–91	Sheffield W	19	2
1991–92	Sheffield W	0	0
1991–92	Plymouth Arg	9	1
1992–93	Plymouth Arg	35	1
1993–94	Plymouth Arg	45	2
1994–95	Plymouth Arg	7	1
1995–96	Plymouth Arg	4	0
1996–97	Torquay U	24	1
1997–98	Torquay U	27	1
1998–99	Plymouth Arg	17	0
Total:		**460**	**16**

McCALL, Stuart — Midfield

H: 5 9 W: 11 04 b.Leeds 10-6-64

Source: Apprentice. *Honours:* Scotland Under-21, 40 full caps, 1 goal.

1982–83	Bradford C	28	4
1983–84	Bradford C	46	5
1984–85	Bradford C	46	8
1985–86	Bradford C	38	4
1986–87	Bradford C	36	7
1987–88	Bradford C	44	9
1988–89	Everton	33	0
1989–90	Everton	37	3
1990–91	Everton	33	3
1991–92	Rangers	36	1
1992–93	Rangers	36	5
1993–94	Rangers	34	3
1994–95	Rangers	30	2
1995–96	Rangers	21	3
1996–97	Rangers	7	0
1997–98	Rangers	30	0
1998–99	Bradford C	43	3
Total:		**578**	**60**

McCAMMON, Mark — Forward

H: 6 2 W: 12 00 b.Barnet 7-8-78

1997–98	Cambridge U	2	0
1998–99	Cambridge U	2	0
1998–99	Charlton Ath	0	0
Total:		**4**	**0**

McCANN, Gavin — Midfield

H: 5 11 W: 11 00 b.Blackpool 10-1-78

Source: Trainee.

1995–96	Everton	0	0
1996–97	Everton	0	0
1997–98	Everton	11	0
1998–99	Everton	0	0
1998–99	Sunderland	11	0
Total:		**22**	**0**

McCANN, Grant — Midfield

b.Belfast 14-4-80

Source: Trainee. *Honours:* Northern Ireland Youth.

1998–99	West Ham U	0	0

McCANN, Neil — Forward

H: 5 10 W: 10 00 b.Greenock 11-8-74

Source: Port Glasgow BC. *Honours:* Scotland Under-21, B, 2 full caps.

1992–93	Dundee	3	0
1993–94	Dundee	22	1
1994–95	Dundee	32	2
1995–96	Dundee	22	2
1996–97	Hearts	30	5
1997–98	Hearts	35	10
1998–99	Hearts	8	3
1998–99	Rangers	19	5
Total:		**171**	**28**

McCANN, Peter — Defender

H: 5 6 W: 10 13 b.Dublin 18-8-81

Source: Trainee.

1998–99	Blackburn R	0	0

McCANN, Tim — Midfield

H: 5 9 W: 11 05 b.Belfast 22-3-80

Source: Trainee.

1998–99	Leicester C	0	0

McCARTHY, Jon — Midfield

H: 5 9 W: 11 05 b.Middlesbrough 18-8-70

Honours: Northern Ireland 12 full caps.

1987–88	Hartlepool U	1	0
From Shepshed			
1990–91	York C	27	2
1991–92	York C	42	6
1992–93	York C	42	7
1993–94	York C	44	7
1994–95	York C	44	9
1995–96	Port Vale	45	7
1996–97	Port Vale	45	4
1997–98	Port Vale	4	0
1997–98	Birmingham C	41	4
1998–99	Birmingham C	43	0
Total:		**378**	**46**

McCARTHY, Paul — Defender

H: 5 10 W: 13 10 b.Cork 4-8-71

Source: Trainee. *Honours:* Eire Youth, Under-21.

1989–90	Brighton & HA	3	0
1990–91	Brighton & HA	21	0
1991–92	Brighton & HA	20	0
1992–93	Brighton & HA	30	0
1993–94	Brighton & HA	37	3
1994–95	Brighton & HA	37	2
1995–96	Brighton & HA	33	1
1996–97	Wycombe W	40	0
1997–98	Wycombe W	31	1
1998–99	Wycombe W	29	1
Total:		**281**	**8**

McCARTHY, Sean — Forward

H: 6 1 W: 12 05 b.Bridgend 12-9-67

Source: Bridgend. *Honours:* Wales B.

1985–86	Swansea C	22	3
1986–87	Swansea C	44	14
1987–88	Swansea C	25	8
1988–89	Plymouth Arg	38	8
1989–90	Plymouth Arg	32	11
1990–91	Bradford C	42	13
1991–92	Bradford C	29	16
1992–93	Bradford C	42	17
1993–94	Bradford C	18	14
1993–94	Oldham Ath	20	4
1994–95	Oldham Ath	39	18
1995–96	Oldham Ath	35	10
1996–97	Oldham Ath	21	3
1997–98	Oldham Ath	25	7
1997–98	Bristol C (loan)	7	1
1998–99	Plymouth Arg	16	3
Total:		**455**	**150**

McCARTNEY, George — Defender

H: 6 0 W: 12 06 b.Belfast 29-4-81

Source: Trainee.

1998–99	Sunderland	0	0

McCHRYSTAL, Brian — Defender

H: 6 3 W: 13 01 b.Dundalk 20-1-81

Source: Bellurgan U.

1998–99	Leeds U	0	0

McCLAIR, Brian — Forward

H: 5 10 W: 12 12 b.Airdrie 8-12-63

Source: Apprentice. *Honours:* Scotland Youth, Under-21, B, 30 full caps, 2 goals.

1980–81	Aston Villa	0	0
1981–82	Motherwell	11	4
1982–83	Motherwell	28	11
1983–84	Celtic	35	23
1984–85	Celtic	32	19
1985–86	Celtic	34	22
1986–87	Celtic	44	35
1987–88	Manchester U	40	24
1988–89	Manchester U	38	10
1989–90	Manchester U	37	5
1990–91	Manchester U	36	13
1991–92	Manchester U	42	18
1992–93	Manchester U	42	9
1993–94	Manchester U	26	1
1994–95	Manchester U	40	5
1995–96	Manchester U	22	3
1996–97	Manchester U	19	0
1997–98	Manchester U	13	0
1998–99	Manchester U	0	0
1998–99	Motherwell	11	0
Total:		**550**	**202**

McCLARE, Sean — Midfield

H: 5 11 W: 11 08 b.Rotherham 12-1-78

Source: Trainee. *Honours:* Eire Under-21.

1996–97	Barnsley	0	0
1997–98	Barnsley	0	0
1998–99	Barnsley	30	3
Total:		**30**	**3**

McCLEN, Jamie — Midfield

H: 5 8 W: 10 07 b.Newcastle 13-5-79

Source: Trainee.

1997–98	Newcastle U	0	0
1998–99	Newcastle U	1	0
Total:		**1**	**0**

McCLUSKEY, Stuart — Defender

H: 5 11 W: 10 03 b.Bellshill 29-10-77

Source: 'S' Form. *Honours:* Scotland Under-18, Under-21.

1994–95	St Johnstone	2	0
1995–96	St Johnstone	2	0
1996–97	St Johnstone	10	1
1997–98	St Johnstone	18	1
1998–99	St Johnstone	7	0
Total:		**39**	**2**

McCOIST, Ally — Forward

H: 5 10 W: 12 00 b.Bellshill 24-9-62

Source: Fir Park BC. *Honours:* Scotland Youth, Under-21, 61 full caps, 19 goals.

1978–79	St Johnstone	4	0
1979–80	St Johnstone	15	0
1980–81	St Johnstone	38	22
1981–82	Sunderland	28	2
1982–83	Sunderland	28	6
1983–84	Rangers	30	9
1984–85	Rangers	25	12
1985–86	Rangers	33	24
1986–87	Rangers	44	33
1987–88	Rangers	40	31
1988–89	Rangers	19	9
1989–90	Rangers	34	14
1990–91	Rangers	26	11
1991–92	Rangers	38	34
1992–93	Rangers	34	34
1993–94	Rangers	21	7
1994–95	Rangers	9	1
1995–96	Rangers	25	16
1996–97	Rangers	25	10
1997–98	Rangers	15	5
1998–99	Kilmarnock	26	7
Total:		**557**	**287**

McCONALOGUE, Stephen — Forward

H: 5 9 W: 10 06 b.Glasgow 16-6-81

Source: Dundee U BC.

1998–99	Dundee U	1	0
Total:		**1**	**0**

McCONDICHIE, Andrew — Goalkeeper

H: 5 10 W: 11 09 b.Glasgow 21-8-77

Source: Celtic BC.

1995–96	Celtic	0	0
1996–97	Celtic	0	0
1997–98	Celtic	0	0
1998–99	Celtic	1	0
Total:		**1**	**0**

McCONNELL, Barry — Forward

H: 5 11 W: 10 03 b.Exeter 1-1-77

Source: Trainee.

1995–96	Exeter C	8	0
1996–97	Exeter C	34	0
1997–98	Exeter C	16	6
1998–99	Exeter C	22	5
Total:		**80**	**11**

McCORMICK, Stephen — Forward

H: 6 4 W: 11 04 b.Dumbarton 14-8-69

Source: Yoker Ath.

1993–94	Queen's Park	36	7
1994–95	Queen's Park	22	8
1995–96	Stirling A	33	25
1996–97	Stirling A	31	8
1997–98	Stirling A	8	0
1997–98	Dundee	14	5
1998–99	Dundee	1	0
1998–99	Leyton Orient (loan)	4	0
Total:		**149**	**53**

McCULLOCH, Lee — Midfield

H: 5 11 W: 12 05 b.Bellshill 14-5-78

Source: Cumbernauld U. *Honours:* Scotland Under-18, Under-21.

1995–96	Motherwell	1	0
1996–97	Motherwell	15	0
1997–98	Motherwell	25	2
1998–99	Motherwell	26	3
Total:		**67**	**5**

McCULLOCH, Scott — Defender

H: 6 0 W: 13 04 b.Cumnock 29-11-75

Source: Rangers BC.

1992–93	Rangers	0	0
1993–94	Rangers	0	0
1994–95	Hamilton A	8	1
1995–96	Hamilton A	10	1
1996–97	Hamilton A	24	1
1997–98	Hamilton A	15	1
1997–98	Dunfermline Ath	18	0
1998–99	Dunfermline Ath	19	1
Total:		**94**	**5**

McCULLOCH, Stephen — Defender

H: 6 1 W: 11 09 b.Irvine 3-4-81

Source: Maybole Am.

1998–99	Dundee U	9	0
Total:		**9**	**0**

McCUTCHEON, Gary — Forward

H: 5 4 W: 9 11 b.Dumfries 8-10-78

Source: Kilmarnock BC.

1995–96	Kilmarnock	0	0
1996–97	Kilmarnock	0	0
1997–98	Kilmarnock	1	0
1998–99	Kilmarnock	13	2
Total:		**14**	**2**

McDERMOTT, Alan — Defender

H: 6 1 W: 11 13 b.Dublin 22-1-82

Source: Trainee.

1998–99	Manchester U	0	0

McDERMOTT, Andy — Defender

H: 5 9 W: 11 03 b.Sydney 24-3-77

Source: Australian Institute of Sport.

1995–96	QPR	0	0
1996–97	QPR	6	2
1996–97	WBA	6	0
1997–98	WBA	13	0
1998–99	WBA	20	0
Total:		**45**	**2**

McDERMOTT, John — Defender

H: 5 7 W: 11 02 b.Middlesbrough 3-2-69

Source: Trainee.

1986–87	Grimsby T	13	0
1987–88	Grimsby T	28	0
1988–89	Grimsby T	38	1
1989–90	Grimsby T	39	0
1990–91	Grimsby T	43	0
1991–92	Grimsby T	39	1
1992–93	Grimsby T	38	2
1993–94	Grimsby T	26	0
1994–95	Grimsby T	12	0
1995–96	Grimsby T	28	1
1996–97	Grimsby T	29	1
1997–98	Grimsby T	41	1
1998–99	Grimsby T	37	0
Total:		**411**	**7**

McDERMOTT, Wayne — Midfield

b.Liverpool 30-10-79

Source: Trainee.

1998–99	Everton	0	0

McDONALD, Alan — Defender

H: 6 3 W: 13 10 b.Belfast 12-10-63

Source: Apprentice. *Honours:* Northern Ireland Youth, 52 full caps, 3 goals.

1981–82	QPR	0	0
1982–83	QPR	0	0
1982–83	Charlton Ath (loan)	9	0
1983–84	QPR	5	0
1984–85	QPR	16	1
1985–86	QPR	42	0
1986–87	QPR	39	4
1987–88	QPR	36	3
1988–89	QPR	30	0
1989–90	QPR	34	0
1990–91	QPR	17	0
1991–92	QPR	28	0
1992–93	QPR	39	0
1993–94	QPR	12	1
1994–95	QPR	39	1
1995–96	QPR	26	1
1996–97	QPR	39	2
1997–98	Swindon T	33	1
1998–99	Swindon T	0	0
Total:		**444**	**14**

McDONALD, Chris — Defender

H: 6 0 W: 13 04 b.Edinburgh 14-10-75

Source: Trainee.

1993–94	Arsenal	0	0
1994–95	Arsenal	0	0
1995–96	Arsenal	0	0
1996–97	Hartlepool U	9	0
1997–98	Hartlepool U	6	0
1998–99	Hartlepool U	5	0
Total:		**20**	**0**

McDONALD, Jamie — Midfield

b.Luton 29-1-80

Source: Trainee.

1996–97	Derby Co	0	0
1997–98	Derby Co	0	0
1998–99	Derby Co	0	0

McDONALD, Martin — Midfield

H: 5 11 W: 11 12 b.Irvine 4-12-73

Source: Macclesfield T, Southport.

1996–97	Doncaster R	33	2

1997–98	Doncaster R	15	2
1997–98	Macclesfield T	22	1
1998–99	Macclesfield T	23	2
Total:		**93**	**7**

McDONALD, Neil — Defender

H: 6 0 W: 13 10 b.Wallsend 2-11-65

Source: Wallsend BC. *Honours:* England Schools, Youth, Under-21.

1982–83	Newcastle U	24	4
1983–84	Newcastle U	12	0
1984–85	Newcastle U	36	6
1985–86	Newcastle U	28	4
1986–87	Newcastle U	40	7
1987–88	Newcastle U	40	3
1988–89	Everton	25	1
1989–90	Everton	31	1
1990–91	Everton	29	2
1991–92	Everton	5	0
1991–92	Oldham Ath	17	1
1992–93	Oldham Ath	4	0
1993–94	Oldham Ath	3	0
1994–95	Bolton W	4	0
1995–96	Bolton W	0	0
1995–96	Preston NE	11	0
1996–97	Preston NE	22	0
1997–98	Preston NE	0	0
1998–99	Preston NE	0	0
Total:		**331**	**29**

McDOUGALD, Junior — Forward

H: 5 9 W: 11 00 b.Big Spring 12-1-75

Source: Trainee.

1993–94	Tottenham H	0	0
1994–95	Brighton & HA	41	10
1995–96	Brighton & HA	37	4
1995–96	Chesterfield (loan)	9	3
1996–97	Rotherham U	18	2
1997–98	Rotherham U	0	0
1998–99	Millwall	1	0
1998–99	Leyton Orient	8	0
Total:		**114**	**19**

McFARLANE, Andy — Forward

H: 6 3 W: 12 08 b.Wolverhampton 30-11-66

Source: Cradley T.

1990–91	Portsmouth	0	0
1991–92	Portsmouth	2	0
1992–93	Swansea C	24	5
1993–94	Swansea C	28	3
1994–95	Swansea C	3	0
1995–96	Scunthorpe U	46	16
1996–97	Scunthorpe U	14	3
1996–97	Torquay U	19	3
1997–98	Torquay U	22	5
1998–99	Torquay U	15	3
Total:		**173**	**38**

McFLYNN, Terry — Midfield

H: 5 9 W: 10 05 b.Magherafelt 27-3-81

Source: Trainee.

1997–98	QPR	0	0
1998–99	QPR	0	0

McGAVIN, Steve — Forward

H: 5 11 W: 12 07 b.North Walsham 24-1-69

Source: Sudbury T.

1990–91	Colchester U	0	0
1991–92	Colchester U	0	0
1992–93	Colchester U	37	9
1993–94	Colchester U	21	8
1993–94	Birmingham C	8	1
1994–95	Birmingham C	15	1
1994–95	Wycombe W	12	2
1995–96	Wycombe W	31	2
1996–97	Wycombe W	35	9
1997–98	Wycombe W	37	2
1998–99	Wycombe W	5	0
1998–99	Southend U	11	0
Total:		**212**	**34**

McGEOUGH, David — Midfield

b.Drogheda 10-11-80

1998–99	Stoke C	0	0

McGHEE, David — Defender

H: 5 11 W: 12 05 b.Sussex 19-6-76

Source: Trainee.

1994–95	Brentford	7	1
1995–96	Brentford	36	5
1996–97	Brentford	45	1
1997–98	Brentford	29	1
1998–99	Brentford	0	0
Total:		**117**	**8**

McGIBBON, Pat — Defender

H: 6 2 W: 14 01 b.Lurgan 6-9-73

Source: Portadown. *Honours:* Northern Ireland Under-21, 6 full caps.

1992–93	Manchester U	0	0
1993–94	Manchester U	0	0
1994–95	Manchester U	0	0
1995–96	Manchester U	0	0
1996–97	Manchester U	0	0
1996–97	Swansea C (loan)	1	0

1996–97	Wigan Ath (loan)	10	1
1997–98	Wigan Ath	35	0
1998–99	Wigan Ath	36	5
Total:		**82**	**6**

McGILL, Brendan — Midfield

H: 5 9 W: 10 05 b.Dublin 22-3-81

1998–99	Sunderland	0	0

McGILL, Derek — Forward

H: 5 11 W: 11 04 b.Lanark 14-10-75

1992–93	Dunfermline Ath	0	0
1993–94	Hamilton A	16	3
1994–95	Hamilton A	7	1
1995–96	Falkirk	0	0
1996–97	Raith R	9	0
1997–98	Raith R	0	0
1998–99	Raith R	0	0
1998–99	Port Vale	3	0
Total:		**35**	**4**

McGINLAY, John — Forward

H: 5 10 W: 12 02 b.Inverness 8-4-64

Source: Elgin C. *Honours:* Scotland 13 full caps, 4 goals.

1988–89	Shrewsbury T	16	5
1989–90	Shrewsbury T	44	22
1990–91	Bury	25	9
1990–91	Millwall	2	0
1991–92	Millwall	25	8
1992–93	Millwall	7	2
1992–93	Bolton W	34	16
1993–94	Bolton W	39	25
1994–95	Bolton W	37	16
1995–96	Bolton W	32	6
1996–97	Bolton W	43	24
1997–98	Bolton W	7	0
1997–98	Bradford C	17	3
1998–99	Bradford C	0	0
1998–99	Oldham Ath	7	1
Total:		**335**	**137**

McGINLAY, Pat — Midfield

H: 5 10 W: 10 10 b.Glasgow 30-5-67

Source: Scottish Junior.

1985–86	Blackpool	0	0
1986–87	Blackpool	12	1
1987–88	Hibernian	0	0
1988–89	Hibernian	2	0
1989–90	Hibernian	28	3
1990–91	Hibernian	32	1
1991–92	Hibernian	43	9
1992–93	Hibernian	40	10
1993–94	Celtic	41	10
1994–95	Celtic	8	1
1994–95	Hibernian	24	7
1995–96	Hibernian	31	5
1996–97	Hibernian	29	6
1997–98	Hibernian	33	4
1998–99	Hibernian	30	12
Total:		**353**	**69**

McGINTY, Brian — Midfield

H: 6 1 W: 12 01 b.East Kilbride 10-12-76

Source: Rangers BC.

1993–94	Rangers	0	0
1994–95	Rangers	1	0
1995–96	Rangers	2	0
1996–97	Rangers	0	0
1997–98	Rangers	0	0
1997–98	Hull C	21	2
1998–99	Hull C	32	4
Total:		**56**	**6**

McGLEISH, Scott — Forward

H: 5 10 W: 11 07 b.Camden Town 10-2-74

Source: Edgware T.

1994–95	Charlton Ath	6	0
1994–95	Leyton Orient (loan)	6	1
1995–96	Peterborough U	12	0
1995–96	Colchester U (loan)	15	6
1996–97	Peterborough U	1	0
1996–97	Cambridge U (loan)	10	7
1996–97	Leyton Orient	28	7
1997–98	Leyton Orient	8	0
1997–98	Barnet	37	13
1998–99	Barnet	36	8
Total:		**159**	**42**

McGLINCHEY, Brian — Defender

H: 5 8 W: 10 05 b.Derry 26-10-77

Source: Trainee. *Honours:* Northern Ireland Under-21.

1995–96	Manchester C	0	0
1996–97	Manchester C	0	0
1997–98	Manchester C	0	0
1998–99	Port Vale	15	1
Total:		**15**	**1**

McGOLDRICK, Eddie — Midfield

H: 5 10 W: 11 07 b.London 30-4-65

Source: Nuneaton Bor, Kettering T. *Honours:* Eire 15 full caps.

1986–87	Northampton T	39	5
1987–88	Northampton T	46	2
1988–89	Northampton T	22	2
1988–89	Crystal Palace	21	0
1989–90	Crystal Palace	22	0
1990–91	Crystal Palace	26	0

McGorry, Brian

1991–92	Crystal Palace	36	3
1992–93	Crystal Palace	42	8
1993–94	Arsenal	26	0
1994–95	Arsenal	11	0
1995–96	Arsenal	1	0
1996–97	Arsenal	0	0
1996–97	Manchester C	33	0
1997–98	Manchester C	7	0
1997–98	Stockport Co (loan)	2	0
1998–99	Manchester C	0	0
Total:		**334**	**20**

McGORRY, Brian — Midfield

H: 5 10 W: 12 08 b.Liverpool 16-4-70

Source: Weymouth.

1991–92	Bournemouth	8	0
1992–93	Bournemouth	37	8
1993–94	Bournemouth	16	3
1993–94	Peterborough U	18	3
1994–95	Peterborough U	34	3
1995–96	Peterborough U	0	0
1995–96	Wycombe W	4	0
1995–96	Cardiff C (loan)	7	0
1996–97	Wycombe W	0	0
1996–97	Hereford U	7	1
From Hereford U.			
1998–99	Torquay U	34	1
Total:		**165**	**19**

McGOVERN, Brendan — Midfield

H: 5 10 W: 12 07 b.Camborne 9-2-80

Source: Trainee.

1998–99	Plymouth Arg	2	0
Total:		**2**	**0**

McGOVERN, Brian — Defender

b.Dublin 28-4-80

Honours: Eire Youth.

1997–98	Arsenal	0	0
1998–99	Arsenal	0	0

McGOWAN, Gavin — Defender

H: 5 10 W: 12 06 b.Blackheath 16-1-76

Source: Trainee. *Honours:* England Schools, Youth.

1992–93	Arsenal	2	0
1993–94	Arsenal	0	0
1994–95	Arsenal	1	0
1995–96	Arsenal	1	0
1996–97	Arsenal	1	0
1996–97	Luton T (loan)	2	0
1997–98	Arsenal	1	0
1997–98	Luton T (loan)	8	0
1998–99	Luton T	31	0
Total:		**47**	**0**

McGOWAN, Jamie — Defender

H: 6 0 W: 11 01 b.Morecambe 5-12-70

Source: Morecambe.

1992–93	Dundee	21	1
1993–94	Dundee	14	0
1993–94	Falkirk	9	2
1994–95	Falkirk	31	1
1995–96	Falkirk	29	1
1996–97	Falkirk	29	2
1997–98	Falkirk	33	2
1998–99	Motherwell	32	1
Total:		**198**	**10**

McGOWNE, Kevin — Defender

H: 6 0 W: 12 03 b.Kilmarnock 16-12-69

Source: Hurlford Utd.

1988–89	St Mirren	0	0
1989–90	St Mirren	2	0
1990–91	St Mirren	10	0
1991–92	St Mirren	36	0
1992–93	St Johnstone	26	0
1993–94	St Johnstone	41	0
1994–95	St Johnstone	30	1
1995–96	St Johnstone	23	2
1996–97	St Johnstone	2	0
1996–97	Kilmarnock	31	0
1997–98	Kilmarnock	26	0
1998–99	Kilmarnock	32	4
Total:		**259**	**7**

McGREAL, John — Defender

H: 6 1 W: 11 06 b.Birkenhead 2-6-72

Source: Trainee.

1990–91	Tranmere R	3	0
1991–92	Tranmere R	0	0
1992–93	Tranmere R	0	0
1993–94	Tranmere R	15	1
1994–95	Tranmere R	43	0
1995–96	Tranmere R	32	0
1996–97	Tranmere R	24	0
1997–98	Tranmere R	42	0
1998–99	Tranmere R	36	0
Total:		**195**	**1**

McGREGOR, Mark — Defender

H: 5 10 W: 11 05 b.Chester 16-2-77

Source: Trainee.

1994–95	Wrexham	1	0
1995–96	Wrexham	32	1
1996–97	Wrexham	38	1
1997–98	Wrexham	42	2
1998–99	Wrexham	43	1
Total:		**156**	**5**

McGREGOR, Paul — Forward

H: 5 10 W: 11 06 b.Liverpool 17-12-74

Source: Trainee.

1991–92	Nottingham F	0	0
1992–93	Nottingham F	0	0
1993–94	Nottingham F	0	0
1994–95	Nottingham F	11	1
1995–96	Nottingham F	14	2
1996–97	Nottingham F	5	0
1997–98	Nottingham F	0	0
1998–99	Nottingham F	0	0
1998–99	Carlisle U (loan)	10	3
1998–99	Preston NE	4	0
Total:		**44**	**6**

McGROARTY, Chris — Midfield

b.Bellshill 6-2-81

Source: Rosyth Rec.

1998–99	Dunfermline Ath	4	0
Total:		**4**	**0**

McGUCKIN, Ian — Defender

H: 6 2 W: 14 02 b.Middlesbrough 24-4-73

Source: Trainee.

1991–92	Hartlepool U	7	0
1992–93	Hartlepool U	14	1
1993–94	Hartlepool U	35	2
1994–95	Hartlepool U	34	3
1995–96	Hartlepool U	40	2
1996–97	Hartlepool U	22	0
1997–98	Fulham	0	0
1998–99	Fulham	0	0
1998–99	Hartlepool U (loan)	8	0
Total:		**160**	**8**

McHUGH, Frazer — Midfield

b.Nottingham 14-7-81

Source: Trainee.

1998–99	Swindon T	1	0
Total:		**1**	**0**

McINALLY, Jim — Midfield

H: 6 0 W: 12 00 b.Glasgow 19-2-64

Source: Celtic BC. *Honours:* Scottish Youth, Under-21. 10 full caps.

1982–83	Celtic	1	0
1983–84	Celtic	0	0
1983–84	Dundee (loan)	11	2
1984–85	Nottingham F	24	0
1985–86	Nottingham F	12	0
1985–86	Coventry C	5	0
1986–87	Dundee U	32	1
1987–88	Dundee U	36	2
1988–89	Dundee U	29	1
1989–90	Dundee U	35	3
1990–91	Dundee U	33	1
1991–92	Dundee U	32	4
1992–93	Dundee U	32	0
1993–94	Dundee U	31	0
1994–95	Dundee U	24	0
1995–96	Raith R	25	0
1996–97	Raith R	4	0
1996–97	Dundee U	16	1
1997–98	Dundee	32	1
1998–99	Dundee	15	0
Total:		**429**	**16**

McINDOE, Michael — Midfield

H: 5 8 W: 10 06 b.Edinburgh 2-12-79

Source: Trainee.

1997–98	Luton T	0	0
1998–99	Luton T	22	0
Total:		**22**	**0**

McINNES, Derek — Midfield

H: 5 7 W: 11 04 b.Paisley 5-7-71

Source: Gleniffer Th.

1987–88	Greenock Morton	2	0
1988–89	Greenock Morton	29	1
1989–90	Greenock Morton	23	1
1990–91	Greenock Morton	31	3
1991–92	Greenock Morton	42	7
1992–93	Greenock Morton	40	2
1993–94	Greenock Morton	16	1
1994–95	Greenock Morton	26	3
1995–96	Greenock Morton	12	1
1995–96	Rangers	6	0
1996–97	Rangers	21	1
1997–98	Rangers	0	0
1998–99	Rangers	7	0
1998–99	Stockport Co (loan)	13	0
Total:		**268**	**20**

McINTOSH, Martin — Defender

H: 6 3 W: 12 05 b.East Kilbride 19-3-71

Honours: Scotland B.

1988–89	St Mirren	2	0
1989–90	St Mirren	2	0
1990–91	St Mirren	0	0
1991–92	Clydebank	28	5
1992–93	Clydebank	33	4
1993–94	Clydebank	4	1
1993–94	Hamilton A	13	2
1994–95	Hamilton A	30	2
1995–96	Hamilton A	23	1
1996–97	Hamilton A	33	7

1997–98	Stockport Co	38	2
1998–99	Stockport Co	41	3
Total:		**247**	**27**

McINTYRE, Jim — Forward

H: 5 11 W: 12 00 b.Alexandria 24-5-72

Source: Duntocher Boys. *Honours:* Scotland B.

1991–92	Bristol C	1	0
1992–93	Bristol C	0	0
1992–93	Exeter C (loan)	15	3
1993–94	Airdrieonians	13	0
1994–95	Airdrieonians	12	1
1995–96	Airdrieonians	29	9
1995–96	Kilmarnock	7	2
1996–97	Kilmarnock	31	6
1997–98	Kilmarnock	8	1
1997–98	Reading	6	0
1998–99	Reading	32	6
Total:		**154**	**28**

McINTYRE, Kevin — Midfield

H: 6 0 W: 11 10 b.Liverpool 23-12-77

Source: Trainee.

1996–97	Tranmere R	0	0
1997–98	Tranmere R	2	0
1998–99	Tranmere R	0	0
Total:		**2**	**0**

McKAY, Matthew — Midfield

H: 6 0 W: 11 08 b.Warrington 21-1-81

Source: Trainee.

1997–98	Chester C	5	0
1997–98	Everton	0	0
1998–99	Everton	0	0
Total:		**5**	**0**

McKEEVER, Mark — Midfield

H: 5 9 W: 11 08 b.Derry 16-11-78

Source: Trainee. *Honours:* Eire Under-21.

1996–97	Peterborough U	3	0
1996–97	Sheffield W	0	0
1997–98	Sheffield W	0	0
1998–99	Sheffield W	3	0
1998–99	Bristol R (loan)	7	0
1998–99	Reading (loan)	7	2
Total:		**20**	**2**

McKENNA, Paul — Midfield

H: 5 8 W: 11 11 b.Chorley 20-10-77

Source: Trainee.

1995–96	Preston NE	0	0
1996–97	Preston NE	5	1
1997–98	Preston NE	5	0
1998–99	Preston NE	36	0
Total:		**46**	**1**

McKENZIE, Leon — Forward

H: 5 10 W: 10 03 b.Croydon 17-5-78

Source: Trainee.

1995–96	Crystal Palace	12	0
1996–97	Crystal Palace	21	2
1997–98	Crystal Palace	3	0
1997–98	Fulham (loan)	3	0
1998–99	Crystal Palace	16	1
1998–99	Peterborough U (loan)	14	8
Total:		**69**	**11**

McKENZIE, Mat — Defender

H: 6 0 W: 13 00 b.Sheffield 3-4-79

Source: Dunkerque.

1998–99	Grimsby T	0	0

McKENZIE, Roderick — Goalkeeper

H: 6 0 W: 12 00 b.Bellshill 8-8-75

Source: Mill Utd. *Honours:* Scotland Under-21.

1993–94	Hearts	0	0
1994–95	Hearts	0	0
1995–96	Stenhousemuir	36	0
1996–97	Hearts	3	0
1997–98	Hearts	4	0
1998–99	Hearts	10	0
Total:		**53**	**0**

McKINLAY, Billy — Midfield

H: 5 8 W: 11 06 b.Glasgow 22-4-69

Source: Hamilton Th. *Honours:* Scotland Under-21, B, 29 full caps, 4 goals.

1986–87	Dundee U	3	0
1987–88	Dundee U	12	1
1988–89	Dundee U	30	1
1989–90	Dundee U	13	0
1990–91	Dundee U	34	2
1991–92	Dundee U	22	1
1992–93	Dundee U	37	1
1993–94	Dundee U	39	9
1994–95	Dundee U	27	4
1995–96	Dundee U	5	4
1995–96	Blackburn R	19	2
1996–97	Blackburn R	25	1
1997–98	Blackburn R	30	0
1998–99	Blackburn R	16	0
Total:		**312**	**26**

McKINLAY, Tosh — Defender

H: 5 7 W: 10 03 b.Glasgow 3-12-64

Source: Celtic BC. *Honours:* Scotland Youth, Under-21, B, 22 full caps.

1981–82	Dundee	0	0
1982–83	Dundee	1	0
1983–84	Dundee	36	3
1984–85	Dundee	34	3
1985–86	Dundee	22	0
1986–87	Dundee	32	2
1987–88	Dundee	19	0
1988–89	Dundee	18	0
1988–89	Hearts	17	1
1989–90	Hearts	29	1
1990–91	Hearts	33	2
1991–92	Hearts	39	2
1992–93	Hearts	34	0
1993–94	Hearts	43	0
1994–95	Hearts	11	0
1994–95	Celtic	17	0
1995–96	Celtic	32	0
1996–97	Celtic	27	0
1997–98	Celtic	5	0
1997–98	Stoke C (loan)	3	0
1998–99	Celtic	18	0
Total:		**470**	**14**

McKINNON, Ray — Midfield

H: 5 10 W: 11 08 b.Dundee 5-8-70

Source: 'S' Form. *Honours:* Scotland Under-21.

1987–88	Dundee U	0	0
1988–89	Dundee U	1	0
1989–90	Dundee U	10	0
1990–91	Dundee U	17	2
1991–92	Dundee U	25	4
1992–93	Nottingham F	6	1
1993–94	Nottingham F	0	0
1993–94	Aberdeen	5	0
1994–95	Aberdeen	20	0
1995–96	Aberdeen	1	0
1995–96	Dundee U	9	0
1996–97	Dundee U	26	6
1997–98	Dundee U	9	0
1998–99	Luton T	30	2
Total:		**159**	**15**

McKINNON, Rob — Defender

H: 5 11 W: 11 01 b.Glasgow 31-7-66

Source: Rutherglen Glencairn. *Honours:* Scotland 3 full caps.

1984–85	Newcastle U	0	0
1985–86	Newcastle U	1	0
1986–87	Hartlepool U	45	0
1987–88	Hartlepool U	42	2
1988–89	Hartlepool U	46	2
1989–90	Hartlepool U	46	1
1990–91	Hartlepool U	45	1
1990–91	Manchester U (loan)	0	0
1991–92	Hartlepool U	23	1
1991–92	Motherwell	16	1
1992–93	Motherwell	35	0
1993–94	Motherwell	42	4
1994–95	Motherwell	32	3
1995–96	Motherwell	27	0
1996–97	Twente	24	0
1997–98	Twente	26	1
1998–99	Hearts	16	0
1998–99	Hartlepool U (loan)	7	0
Total:		**473**	**16**

McLAREN, Andy — Midfield

H: 5 10 W: 10 06 b.Glasgow 5-6-73

Source: Rangers Amateur BC. *Honours:* Scotland Under-21.

1989–90	Dundee U	0	0
1990–91	Dundee U	0	0
1991–92	Dundee U	13	0
1992–93	Dundee U	5	0
1993–94	Dundee U	27	1
1994–95	Dundee U	20	0
1995–96	Dundee U	31	3
1996–97	Dundee U	34	4
1997–98	Dundee U	27	4
1998–99	Dundee U	8	0
1998–99	Reading	7	1
Total:		**172**	**13**

McLAREN, Paul — Midfield

H: 6 1 W: 13 00 b.High Wycombe 17-11-76

Source: Trainee.

1993–94	Luton T	1	0
1994–95	Luton T	0	0
1995–96	Luton T	12	1
1996–97	Luton T	24	0
1997–98	Luton T	43	0
1998–99	Luton T	23	0
Total:		**103**	**1**

McLAUGHLIN, Brian — Midfield

H: 5 4 W: 8 07 b.Bellshill 14-5-74

Source: Giffnock N. *Honours:* Scotland Under-21.

1992–93	Celtic	0	0
1993–94	Celtic	8	0
1994–95	Celtic	21	0
1995–96	Celtic	26	4
1996–97	Celtic	20	1
1997–98	Celtic	0	0
1997–98	Airdrieonians (loan)	0	0
1998–99	Celtic	0	0
1998–99	Dundee U	3	0
Total:		**78**	**5**

McLEAN, Ian — Defender

H: 5 10 W: 11 04 b.Leeds 13-9-78

Source: Trainee.

1997–98	Bradford C	0	0
1998–99	Oldham Ath	5	0
Total:		**5**	**0**

McLEARY, Alan — Defender

H: 5 11 W: 11 09 b.Lambeth 6-10-64

Source: Apprentice. *Honours:* England Youth, Under-21, B.

1981–82	Millwall	0	0
1982–83	Millwall	3	1
1983–84	Millwall	30	0
1984–85	Millwall	21	0
1985–86	Millwall	35	3
1986–87	Millwall	42	0
1987–88	Millwall	31	0
1988–89	Millwall	38	1
1989–90	Millwall	31	0
1990–91	Millwall	42	0
1991–92	Millwall	28	0
1992–93	Millwall	6	0
1992–93	Sheffield U (loan)	3	0
1992–93	Wimbledon (loan)	4	0
1993–94	Charlton Ath	44	3
1994–95	Charlton Ath	22	0
1995–96	Bristol C	31	0
1996–97	Bristol C	3	0
1996–97	Millwall	15	0
1997–98	Millwall	19	0
1998–99	Millwall	2	0
Total:		**450**	**8**

McLEOD, Allan — Defender

b.Islington 19-4-80

Source: Trainee.

1998–99	Arsenal	0	0

McLEOD, Kevin — Midfield

H: 5 11 W: 11 00 b.Liverpool 12-9-80

Source: Trainee.

1998–99	Everton	0	0

McLOUGHLIN, Alan — Midfield

H: 5 8 W: 10 10 b.Manchester 20-4-67

Source: Local. *Honours:* Eire B, 39 full caps, 2 goals.

1984–85	Manchester U	0	0
1985–86	Manchester U	0	0
1986–87	Swindon T	9	0
1986–87	Torquay U	16	1
1987–88	Torquay U	8	3
1987–88	Swindon T	8	0
1988–89	Swindon T	26	3
1989–90	Swindon T	46	12
1990–91	Swindon T	17	4
1990–91	Southampton	22	1
1991–92	Southampton	2	0
1991–92	Aston Villa (loan)	0	0
1991–92	Portsmouth	14	2
1992–93	Portsmouth	46	9
1993–94	Portsmouth	38	6
1994–95	Portsmouth	38	6
1995–96	Portsmouth	40	10
1996–97	Portsmouth	36	5
1997–98	Portsmouth	37	4
1998–99	Portsmouth	41	7
Total:		**444**	**73**

McMAHON, David — Forward

H: 6 1 W: 11 05 b.Dublin 17-1-81

Source: Trainee.

1997–98	Newcastle U	0	0
1998–99	Newcastle U	0	0

McMAHON, Gerry — Forward

H: 5 11 W: 11 13 b.Belfast 29-12-73

Source: Glenavon. *Honours:* Northern Ireland Under-21, 17 full caps, 2 goals.

1992–93	Tottenham H	0	0
1993–94	Tottenham H	0	0
1994–95	Tottenham H	2	0
1994–95	Barnet (loan)	10	2
1995–96	Tottenham H	14	0
1996–97	Tottenham H	0	0
1996–97	Stoke C	35	3
1997–98	Stoke C	17	0
1997–98	St Johnstone	10	0
1998–99	St Johnstone	19	1
Total:		**107**	**6**

McMAHON, Sam — Midfield

H: 5 10 W: 11 09 b.Newark 10-2-76

Source: Trainee.

1994–95	Leicester C	1	0
1995–96	Leicester C	3	1
1996–97	Leicester C	0	0
1997–98	Leicester C	1	0
1998–99	Leicester C	0	0
1998–99	Cambridge U	3	0
Total:		**8**	**1**

McMANAMAN, Steve — Midfield

H: 6 0 W: 10 06 b.Liverpool 11-2-72

Source: School. *Honours:* England Youth, Under-21, 24 full caps.

1989–90	Liverpool	0	0

1990–91	Liverpool	2	0
1991–92	Liverpool	30	5
1992–93	Liverpool	31	4
1993–94	Liverpool	30	2
1994–95	Liverpool	40	7
1995–96	Liverpool	38	6
1996–97	Liverpool	37	7
1997–98	Liverpool	36	11
1998–99	Liverpool	28	4
Total:		**272**	**46**

McMANUS, Tom — Forward

H: 5 9 W: 10 02 b.Glasgow 28-2-81

Source: S Form.

1997–98	Hibernian	0	0
1998–99	Hibernian	1	0
Total:		**1**	**0**

McMENAMIN, Chris — Defender

H: 5 10 W: 11 10 b.Donegal 27-12-73

Source: Hitchin T.

1996–97	Coventry C	0	0
1997–98	Peterborough U	28	0
1998–99	Peterborough U	5	0
Total:		**33**	**0**

McMILLAN, Andy — Defender

H: 5 11 W: 11 09 b.Bloemfontein 22-6-68

1987–88	York C	22	0
1988–89	York C	2	0
1989–90	York C	25	0
1990–91	York C	45	1
1991–92	York C	41	1
1992–93	York C	42	0
1993–94	York C	46	0
1994–95	York C	43	1
1995–96	York C	46	1
1996–97	York C	46	0
1997–98	York C	30	1
1998–99	York C	33	0
Total:		**421**	**5**

McMILLAN, Stephen — Midfield

H: 5 10 W: 11 00 b.Edinburgh 19-1-76

Source: Troon Juniors. *Honours:* Scotland Under-21.

1993–94	Motherwell	1	0
1994–95	Motherwell	3	0
1995–96	Motherwell	12	0
1996–97	Motherwell	16	0
1997–98	Motherwell	34	1
1998–99	Motherwell	30	2
Total:		**96**	**3**

McNAB, Joe — Midfield

H: 5 4 W: 9 00 b.Brighton 29-10-80

Source: Manchester C Trainee.

1998–99	Portsmouth	0	0

McNAB, Neil — Midfield

H: 5 6 W: 10 03 b.Brighton 29-10-80

Source: Manchester C Trainee.

1998–99	Portsmouth	0	0

McNALLY, Mark — Defender

H: 5 11 W: 12 02 b.Bellshill 10-3-71

Source: Celtic BC. *Honours:* Scotland Under-21.

1987–88	Celtic	0	0
1988–89	Celtic	0	0
1989–90	Celtic	0	0
1990–91	Celtic	19	0
1991–92	Celtic	25	1
1992–93	Celtic	27	0
1993–94	Celtic	32	2
1994–95	Celtic	20	0
1995–96	Southend U	20	2
1996–97	Southend U	34	0
1996–97	Stoke C	3	0
1997–98	Stoke C	4	0
1998–99	Dundee U	5	0
Total:		**189**	**5**

McNAMARA, Jackie — Midfield

H: 5 8 W: 9 07 b.Glasgow 24-10-73

Source: Gairdoch U. *Honours:* Scotland B, Under-21, 9 full caps.

1991–92	Dunfermline Ath	0	0
1992–93	Dunfermline Ath	3	0
1993–94	Dunfermline Ath	39	0
1994–95	Dunfermline Ath	30	2
1995–96	Dunfermline Ath	7	1
1995–96	Celtic	26	1
1996–97	Celtic	30	1
1997–98	Celtic	31	2
1998–99	Celtic	16	0
Total:		**182**	**7**

McNAMARA, Niall — Forward

H: 5 11 W: 11 09 b.Eire 26-1-82

Source: Trainee.

1998–99	Nottingham F	0	0

McNAMEE, David — Defender

H: 5 11 W: 10 07 b.Glasgow 10-10-80

Source: St Mirren BC.

1998–99	St Mirren	31	0
1998–99	Blackburn R	0	0
Total:		**31**	**0**

McNAUGHTON, Michael — Defender

H: 6 2 W: 14 00 b.Blackpool 29-1-80

Source: Trainee.

1998–99	Scarborough	31	1
Total:		**31**	**1**

McNEIL, Martin — Defender

b.Rutherglen 28-9-80

Source: Trainee.

1998–99	Cambridge U	6	0
Total:		**6**	**0**

McNIVEN, David — Forward

H: 5 10 W: 12 00 b.Leeds 27-5-78

Source: Trainee.

1995–96	Oldham Ath	0	0
1996–97	Oldham Ath	8	0
1997–98	Oldham Ath	8	1
1998–99	Oldham Ath	6	0
Total:		**22**	**1**

McNIVEN, Scott — Defender

H: 5 10 W: 10 08 b.Leeds 27-5-78

Source: Trainee. *Honours:* Scotland Under-21.

1994–95	Oldham Ath	1	0
1995–96	Oldham Ath	15	0
1996–97	Oldham Ath	12	0
1997–98	Oldham Ath	32	1
1998–99	Oldham Ath	37	1
Total:		**97**	**2**

McPHAIL, Stephen — Midfield

H: 5 10 W: 11 06 b.London 9-12-79

Source: Trainee. *Honours:* Eire Under-21.

1996–97	Leeds U	0	0
1997–98	Leeds U	4	0
1998–99	Leeds U	17	0
Total:		**21**	**0**

McPHEE, Gary — Forward

H: 6 0 W: 12 00 b.Glasgow 18-4-80

1998–99	Coventry C	0	0

McPHEE, Stephen — Midfield

H: 5 7 W: 10 08 b.Glasgow 5-6-81

1998–99	Coventry C	0	0

McPHERSON, David — Defender

H: 6 3 W: 11 11 b.Paisley 28-1-64

Source: Gartcosh United. *Honours:* Scotland Youth, Under-21 B, 27 full caps.

1980–81	Rangers	0	0
1981–82	Rangers	0	0
1982–83	Rangers	18	1
1983–84	Rangers	36	2
1984–85	Rangers	31	0
1985–86	Rangers	34	5
1986–87	Rangers	42	7
1987–88	Rangers	44	4
1988–89	Hearts	32	4
1989–90	Hearts	35	4
1990–91	Hearts	34	2
1991–92	Hearts	44	2
1992–93	Rangers	34	2
1993–94	Rangers	28	1
1994–95	Rangers	9	0
1994–95	Hearts	23	2
1995–96	Hearts	26	1
1996–97	Hearts	26	1
1997–98	Hearts	13	3
1998–99	Hearts	18	0
Total:		**527**	**41**

McPHERSON, Keith — Defender

H: 5 11 W: 11 10 b.Greenwich 11-9-63

Source: Apprentice.

1981–82	West Ham U	0	0
1982–83	West Ham U	0	0
1983–84	West Ham U	0	0
1984–85	West Ham U	1	0
1985–86	West Ham U	0	0
1985–86	Cambridge U (loan)	11	1
1985–86	Northampton T	20	0
1986–87	Northampton T	46	5
1987–88	Northampton T	32	0
1988–89	Northampton T	41	2
1989–90	Northampton T	43	1
1990–91	Reading	46	3
1991–92	Reading	44	1
1992–93	Reading	44	1

1993–94	Reading	20	1
1994–95	Reading	23	0
1995–96	Reading	16	0
1996–97	Reading	39	2
1997–98	Reading	24	0
1998–99	Reading	15	0
1998–99	Brighton & HA	10	0
Total:		**475**	**17**

McQUADE, John — Forward

H: 5 8 W: 12 02 b.Glasgow 8-7-70

1998–99	Port Vale	3	0
Total:		**3**	**0**

McQUILKEN, James — Defender

H: 5 9 W: 10 07 b.Glasgow 3-10-74

Source: Giffnock North.

1992–93	Celtic	1	0
1993–94	Celtic	0	0
1994–95	Celtic	0	0
1995–96	Celtic	4	0
1995–96	Dundee U	9	0
1996–97	Dundee U	9	0
1996–97	Hibernian	9	0
1997–98	Hibernian	1	0
1998–99	Dundee U	0	0
Total:		**33**	**0**

McQUILLAN, John — Defender

H: 5 10 W: 11 07 b.Stranraer 20-7-70

Source: Stranraer schools.

1986–87	Stranraer	0	0
1987–88	Dundee	0	0
1988–89	Dundee	0	0
1989–90	Dundee	2	0
1990–91	Dundee	14	1
1991–92	Dundee	40	3
1992–93	Dundee	29	0
1993–94	Dundee	34	0
1994–95	Dundee	32	0
1995–96	St Johnstone	25	2
1996–97	St Johnstone	32	0
1997–98	St Johnstone	34	1
1998–99	St Johnstone	28	1
Total:		**270**	**8**

McSHEFFREY, Gary — Forward

b.Coventry 13-8-81

Source: Trainee.

1998–99	Coventry C	1	0
Total:		**1**	**0**

McSKIMMING, Shaun — Defender

H: 5 11 W: 10 08 b.Stranraer 29-5-70

Source: School.

1986–87	Stranraer	0	0
1987–88	Dundee	0	0
1988–89	Dundee	0	0
1989–90	Dundee	7	0
1990–91	Dundee	16	3
1991–92	Kilmarnock	30	1
1992–93	Kilmarnock	35	5
1993–94	Kilmarnock	40	3
1994–95	Kilmarnock	8	0
1994–95	Motherwell	14	2
1995–96	Motherwell	15	1
1996–97	Motherwell	23	4
1997–98	Motherwell	12	0
1998–99	Dundee	29	2
Total:		**229**	**21**

McSPORRAN, Jermaine — Forward

H: 5 7 W: 10 12 b.Manchester 1-1-77

1998–99	Wycombe W	26	4
Total:		**26**	**4**

McSWEGAN, Gary — Forward

H: 5 8 W: 10 09 b.Glasgow 24-9-70

Source: Rangers Amateur BC.

1986–87	Rangers	0	0
1987–88	Rangers	1	0
1988–89	Rangers	1	0
1989–90	Rangers	0	0
1990–91	Rangers	3	0
1991–92	Rangers	4	0
1992–93	Rangers	9	4
1993–94	Notts Co	37	15
1994–95	Notts Co	22	6
1995–96	Notts Co	3	0
1995–96	Dundee U	25	17
1996–97	Dundee U	31	7
1997–98	Dundee U	31	5
1998–99	Dundee U	5	3
1998–99	Hearts	21	7
Total:		**193**	**64**

McVEIGH, Paul — Forward

H: 5 6 W: 10 05 b.Belfast 6-12-77

Source: Trainee. *Honours:* Northern Ireland Under-21, 1 full cap.

1995–96	Tottenham H	0	0
1996–97	Tottenham H	3	1
1997–98	Tottenham H	0	0
1998–99	Tottenham H	0	0
Total:		**3**	**1**

MEACCI, Francesco — Midfield

b.Florence 19-9-79

1998–99	Sheffield U	0	0

MEAD, Billy — Defender

b.London 7-1-81

1998–99	Millwall	0	0

MEAKER, Michael — Midfield

H: 5 11 W: 12 12 b.Greenford 18-8-71

Source: Trainee. *Honours:* Wales Under-21.

1989–90	QPR	0	0
1990–91	QPR	8	0
1991–92	QPR	1	0
1991–92	Plymouth Arg (loan)	4	0
1992–93	QPR	3	0
1993–94	QPR	14	1
1994–95	QPR	8	0
1995–96	Reading	21	0
1996–97	Reading	25	1
1997–98	Reading	21	1
1998–99	Bristol R	20	2
Total:		**125**	**5**

MEAN, Scott — Midfield

H: 5 11 W: 13 08 b.Crawley 13-12-73

Source: Trainee.

1992–93	Bournemouth	15	1
1993–94	Bournemouth	5	0
1994–95	Bournemouth	40	6
1995–96	Bournemouth	14	1
1996–97	Bournemouth	0	0
1996–97	West Ham U	0	0
1997–98	West Ham U	3	0
1998–99	West Ham U	0	0
1998–99	Port Vale (loan)	1	0
Total:		**78**	**8**

MEECHAN, Alex — Forward

b.Plymouth 29-1-80

Source: Trainee.

1997–98	Swindon T	1	0
1998–99	Bristol C	1	0
Total:		**2**	**0**

MELAUGH, Gavin — Midfield

H: 5 7 W: 9 07 b.Derry 9-7-81

Source: Trainee.

1998–99	Aston Villa	0	0

MELDRUM, Colin — Goalkeeper

H: 5 10 W: 13 04 b.Kilmarnock 26-11-75

Source: Kilwinning Rangers. *Honours:* Scotland Under-21.

1993–94	Kilmarnock	0	0
1994–95	Kilmarnock	40	0
1995–96	Kilmarnock	1	0
1996–97	Kilmarnock	6	0
1997–98	Kilmarnock	11	0
1998–99	Kilmarnock	0	0
Total:		**58**	**0**

MELLON, Micky — Defender

H: 5 10 W: 12 11 b.Paisley 18-3-72

Source: Trainee.

1989–90	Bristol C	9	0
1990–91	Bristol C	0	0
1991–92	Bristol C	16	0
1992–93	Bristol C	10	1
1992–93	WBA	17	3
1993–94	WBA	21	2
1994–95	WBA	7	1
1994–95	Blackpool	26	4
1995–96	Blackpool	45	6
1996–97	Blackpool	43	4
1997–98	Blackpool	10	0
1997–98	Tranmere R	33	2
1998–99	Tranmere R	24	1
1998–99	Burnley	20	2
Total:		**281**	**26**

MELTON, Steve — Midfield

H: 5 11 W: 12 03 b.Lincoln 3-10-78

Source: Trainee.

1995–96	Nottingham F	0	0
1996–97	Nottingham F	0	0
1997–98	Nottingham F	0	0
1998–99	Nottingham F	1	0
Total:		**1**	**0**

MELVILLE, Andy — Defender

H: 6 1 W: 12 06 b.Swansea 29-11-68

Source: School. *Honours:* Wales Under-21, B, 34 full caps, 3 goals.

1985–86	Swansea C	5	0
1986–87	Swansea C	42	3
1987–88	Swansea C	37	4
1988–89	Swansea C	45	10

1989–90	Swansea C	46	5
1990–91	Oxford U	46	3
1991–92	Oxford U	45	4
1992–93	Oxford U	44	6
1993–94	Sunderland	44	2
1994–95	Sunderland	36	3
1995–96	Sunderland	40	4
1996–97	Sunderland	30	2
1997–98	Sunderland	10	1
1997–98	Bradford C (loan)	6	1
1998–99	Sunderland	44	2
Total:		**520**	**50**

MENDES, Junior — Midfield

H: 5 8 W: 10 00 b.Balham 15-9-76

Source: Trainee.

1995–96	Chelsea	0	0
1996–97	Chelsea	0	0
1997–98	Chelsea	0	0
1998–99	St Mirren	22	4
1998–99	Carlisle U (loan)	6	1
Total:		**28**	**5**

MENDEZ, Alberto — Midfield

H: 5 11 W: 11 09 b.Nuremberg 24-10-74

Source: FC Feucht.

1997–98	Arsenal	3	0
1998–99	Arsenal	1	0
Total:		**4**	**0**

MENDONCA, Clive — Forward

H: 5 10 W: 10 07 b.Islington 9-9-68

Source: Apprentice.

1986–87	Sheffield U	2	0
1987–88	Sheffield U	11	4
1987–88	Doncaster R (loan)	2	0
1987–88	Rotherham U	8	2
1988–89	Rotherham U	10	1
1989–90	Rotherham U	32	14
1990–91	Rotherham U	34	10
1991–92	Sheffield U	10	1
1991–92	Grimsby T (loan)	10	3
1992–93	Grimsby T	42	10
1993–94	Grimsby T	39	14
1994–95	Grimsby T	22	11
1995–96	Grimsby T	8	4
1996–97	Grimsby T	45	17
1997–98	Charlton Ath	40	23
1998–99	Charlton Ath	25	8
Total:		**340**	**122**

MERCER, Billy — Goalkeeper

H: 6 1 W: 11 00 b.Liverpool 22-5-69

Source: Trainee.

1987–88	Liverpool	0	0
1988–89	Liverpool	0	0
1988–89	Rotherham U	0	0
1989–90	Rotherham U	2	0
1990–91	Rotherham U	13	0
1991–92	Rotherham U	35	0
1992–93	Rotherham U	36	0
1993–94	Rotherham U	17	0
1994–95	Rotherham U	1	0
1994–95	Sheffield U	3	0
1994–95	Nottingham F (loan)	0	0
1995–96	Sheffield U	1	0
1995–96	Chesterfield	34	0
1996–97	Chesterfield	35	0
1997–98	Chesterfield	36	0
1998–99	Chesterfield	44	0
Total:		**257**	**0**

MERINO, Carlos — Midfield

H: 5 8 W: 10 04 b.Bilbao 15-3-80

Source: Urdaneta.

1997–98	Nottingham F	0	0
1998–99	Nottingham F	0	0

MERSON, Paul — Forward

H: 6 0 W: 13 02 b.Northolt 20-3-68

Source: Apprentice. *Honours:* England Youth, Under-21, B, 21 full caps, 3 goals.

1985–86	Arsenal	0	0
1986–87	Arsenal	7	3
1986–87	Brentford (loan)	7	0
1987–88	Arsenal	15	5
1988–89	Arsenal	37	10
1989–90	Arsenal	29	7
1990–91	Arsenal	37	13
1991–92	Arsenal	42	12
1992–93	Arsenal	33	6
1993–94	Arsenal	33	7
1994–95	Arsenal	24	4
1995–96	Arsenal	38	5
1996–97	Arsenal	32	6
1997–98	Middlesbrough	45	11
1998–99	Middlesbrough	3	0
1998–99	Aston Villa	26	5
Total:		**408**	**94**

MESSER, Gary — Forward

H: 6 1 W: 13 00 b.Consett 22-9-79

Source: Trainee.

1996–97	Doncaster R	1	0

1997–98	Doncaster R	13	1
1998–99	Bury	0	0
Total:		**14**	**1**

MICHELS, Jan — Midfield

H: 5 8 W: 12 01 b.Deventer 8-9-70

1990–91	Zwolle	2	0
1991–92	Zwolle	32	2
1992–93	Go Ahead	14	0
1993–94	Go Ahead	29	0
1994–95	Go Ahead	33	3
1995–96	Go Ahead	32	2
1996–97	Go Ahead	31	3
1997–98	Go Ahead*	0	0
1998–99	Motherwell	10	0
Total:		**183**	**10**

MIDDLETON, Craig — Midfield

H: 5 11 W: 12 00 b.Nuneaton 10-9-70

Source: Trainee.

1989–90	Coventry C	1	0
1990–91	Coventry C	0	0
1991–92	Coventry C	1	0
1992–93	Coventry C	1	0
1993–94	Cambridge U	19	2
1994–95	Cambridge U	0	0
1995–96	Cambridge U	40	8
1996–97	Cardiff C	41	4
1997–98	Cardiff C	33	0
1998–99	Cardiff C	35	4
Total:		**171**	**18**

MIDDLETON, Darren — Forward

H: 6 1 W: 11 13 b.Lichfield 28-12-78

Source: Trainee.

1995–96	Aston Villa	0	0
1996–97	Aston Villa	0	0
1997–98	Aston Villa	0	0
1998–99	Aston Villa	0	0
1998–99	Wolverhampton W	0	0

MIDDLETON, James — Defender

H: 6 1 W: 10 10 b.Stockton 2-10-79

Source: Trainee.

1998–99	Middlesbrough	0	0

MIDGLEY, Craig — Forward

H: 5 7 W: 11 00 b.Bradford 24-5-76

Source: Trainee.

1994–95	Bradford C	3	0
1995–96	Bradford C	5	1
1995–96	Scarborough (loan)	16	1
1996–97	Bradford C	1	0
1996–97	Scarborough (loan)	6	2
1997–98	Bradford C	2	0
1997–98	Darlington (loan)	1	0
1997–98	Hartlepool U	9	3
1998–99	Hartlepool U	29	7
Total:		**72**	**14**

MIDGLEY, Neil — Forward

H: 5 11 W: 11 08 b.Cambridge 21-10-78

Source: Trainee.

1997–98	Ipswich T	0	0
1998–99	Ipswich T	0	0

MIGLIORANZI, Stefani — Midfield

H: 6 0 W: 11 12 b.Pacos de Caldas 20-9-77

Source: St Johns Univ.

1998–99	Portsmouth	7	0
Total:		**7**	**0**

MIKE, Leon — Forward

H: 6 0 W: 12 02 b.Manchester 4-9-81

Source: Scholarship. *Honours:* England Schools, Youth.

1998–99	Manchester C	0	0

MIKLOSKO, Ludek — Goalkeeper

H: 6 5 W: 14 00 b.Protesov 9-12-61

Source: Banik Ostrava. *Honours:* Czech Republic 42 full caps.

1989–90	West Ham U	18	0
1990–91	West Ham U	46	0
1991–92	West Ham U	36	0
1992–93	West Ham U	46	0
1993–94	West Ham U	42	0
1994–95	West Ham U	42	0
1995–96	West Ham U	36	0
1996–97	West Ham U	36	0
1997–98	West Ham U	13	0
1998–99	West Ham U	0	0
1998–99	QPR	31	0
Total:		**346**	**0**

MILBOURNE, Ian — Forward

H: 5 9 W: 11 02 b.Hexham 21-1-79

Source: Trainee.

1997–98	Newcastle U	0	0
1998–99	Scarborough	16	0
Total:		**16**	**0**

MILDENHALL, Steve — Goalkeeper

H: 6 4 W: 14 01 b.Swindon 13-5-78

Source: Trainee.

1996–97	Swindon T	1	0
1997–98	Swindon T	4	0
1998–99	Swindon T	0	0
Total:		**5**	**0**

MILES, John — Forward

b.Fazackerley 28-9-81

Source: Trainee.

1998–99	Liverpool	0	0

MILLAR, Marc — Forward

H: 5 9 W: 10 12 b.Dundee 10-4-69

Source: Riverside Ath.

1991–92	Brechin C	17	1
1992–93	Brechin C	31	11
1993–94	Brechin C	39	10
1994–95	Brechin C	8	1
1994–95	Dunfermline Ath	24	2
1995–96	Dunfermline Ath	24	5
1996–97	Dunfermline Ath	23	6
1997–98	Dunfermline Ath	12	2
1998–99	Dunfermline Ath	21	1
Total:		**199**	**39**

MILLEN, Keith — Defender

H: 6 2 W: 13 00 b.Croydon 26-9-66

Source: Juniors.

1984–85	Brentford	17	0
1985–86	Brentford	32	2
1986–87	Brentford	39	2
1987–88	Brentford	40	3
1988–89	Brentford	36	3
1989–90	Brentford	32	0
1990–91	Brentford	32	2
1991–92	Brentford	34	1
1992–93	Brentford	43	4
1993–94	Brentford	0	0
1993–94	Watford	10	0
1994–95	Watford	31	1
1995–96	Watford	33	0
1996–97	Watford	42	2
1997–98	Watford	38	1
1998–99	Watford	11	1
Total:		**470**	**22**

MILLER, Alan — Goalkeeper

H: 6 3 W: 14 06 b.Epping 29-3-70

Source: Trainee. *Honours:* England Schools, FA Schools, Under-21.

1987–88	Arsenal	0	0
1988–89	Arsenal	0	0
1988–89	Plymouth Arg (loan)	13	0
1989–90	Arsenal	0	0
1990–91	Arsenal	0	0
1991–92	Arsenal	0	0
1991–92	WBA (loan)	3	0
1991–92	Birmingham C (loan)	15	0
1992–93	Arsenal	4	0
1993–94	Arsenal	4	0
1994–95	Middlesbrough	41	0
1995–96	Middlesbrough	6	0
1996–97	Middlesbrough	10	0
1996–97	Huddersfield T (loan)	0	0
1996–97	Grimsby T (loan)	3	0
1996–97	WBA	12	0
1997–98	WBA	41	0
1998–99	WBA	20	0
Total:		**172**	**0**

MILLER, Charlie — Forward

H: 5 9 W: 10 08 b.Glasgow 18-3-76

Source: Rangers BC. *Honours:* Scotland Under-21.

1992–93	Rangers	0	0
1993–94	Rangers	3	0
1994–95	Rangers	21	3
1995–96	Rangers	23	3
1996–97	Rangers	13	1
1997–98	Rangers	7	0
1998–99	Rangers	16	3
1998–99	Leicester C (loan)	4	0
Total:		**87**	**10**

MILLER, Colin — Defender

H: 5 7 W: 12 02 b.Lanark 4-10-64

Source: Toronto Blizzard. *Honours:* Canada 51 full caps.

1985–86	Rangers	2	0
1986–87	Doncaster R	20	2
1987–88	Doncaster R	41	1
From Hamilton Steelers			
1988–89	Hamilton A	21	0
1989–90	Hamilton A	37	1
1990–91	Hamilton A	37	0
1991–92	Hamilton A	43	1
1992–93	Hamilton A	29	3
1993–94	Hamilton A	31	0
1993–94	St Johnstone	12	0
1994–95	St Johnstone	12	0
1994–95	Hearts	16	1
1995–96	Hearts	3	0
1995–96	Dunfermline Ath	25	0

1996–97	Dunfermline Ath	22	0
1997–98	Dunfermline Ath	15	0
1998–99	Dunfermline Ath	0	0
Total:		**366**	**9**

MILLER, Greg — Midfield

H: 5 7 W: 10 00 b.Glasgow 1-4-76

Source: Hutcheson Vale BC.

1994–95	Hibernian	0	0
1995–96	Hibernian	3	0
1996–97	Hibernian	6	0
1997–98	Hibernian	3	1
1998–99	Motherwell	4	0
Total:		**16**	**1**

MILLER, Joe — Forward

H: 5 8 W: 9 12 b.Glasgow 8-12-67

Source: 'S' Form. *Honours:* Scotland Schools, Youth, Under-21.

1984–85	Aberdeen	1	0
1985–86	Aberdeen	18	3
1986–87	Aberdeen	27	6
1987–88	Aberdeen	14	4
1987–88	Celtic	27	3
1988–89	Celtic	22	8
1989–90	Celtic	24	5
1990–91	Celtic	30	8
1991–92	Celtic	26	2
1992–93	Celtic	23	2
1993–94	Aberdeen	27	4
1994–95	Aberdeen	27	0
1995–96	Aberdeen	31	9
1996–97	Aberdeen	30	4
1997–98	Aberdeen	29	1
1998–99	Dundee U	24	2
Total:		**380**	**61**

MILLER, Kenneth — Forward

H: 5 9 W: 10 09 b.Edinburgh 23-12-79

Source: Hutchison Vale.

1996–97	Hibernian	0	0
1997–98	Hibernian	7	0
1998–99	Hibernian	7	1
Total:		**14**	**1**

MILLER, Kevin — Goalkeeper

H: 6 1 W: 13 00 b.Falmouth 15-3-69

Source: Newquay.

1988–89	Exeter C	3	0
1989–90	Exeter C	28	0
1990–91	Exeter C	46	0
1991–92	Exeter C	42	0
1992–93	Exeter C	44	0
1993–94	Birmingham C	24	0
1994–95	Watford	44	0
1995–96	Watford	42	0
1996–97	Watford	42	0
1997–98	Crystal Palace	38	0
1998–99	Crystal Palace	28	0
Total:		**381**	**0**

MILLER, Paul — Midfield

H: 6 0 W: 11 07 b.Bisley 31-1-68

Source: Trainee.

1987–88	Wimbledon	5	0
1987–88	Newport Co (loan)	6	2
1988–89	Wimbledon	18	5
1989–90	Wimbledon	15	2
1989–90	Bristol C (loan)	3	0
1990–91	Wimbledon	1	0
1991–92	Wimbledon	22	2
1992–93	Wimbledon	19	1
1993–94	Wimbledon	0	0
1994–95	Bristol R	42	16
1995–96	Bristol R	38	4
1996–97	Bristol R	25	2
1997–98	Lincoln C	24	2
1998–99	Lincoln C	32	2
Total:		**250**	**38**

MILLER, Robert — Midfield

H: 5 8 W: 11 00 b.Bedford 28-3-80

Source: West Ham U Trainee.

1998–99	Coventry C	0	0

MILLER, Tommy — Defender

H: 6 1 W: 12 00 b.Easington 8-1-79

Source: Trainee.

1997–98	Hartlepool U	13	1
1998–99	Hartlepool U	34	4
Total:		**47**	**5**

MILLER, William — Defender

H: 5 8 W: 10 06 b.Edinburgh 1-11-69

Source: Edina Hibs BC. *Honours:* Scotland Under-21.

1989–90	Hibernian	11	0
1990–91	Hibernian	25	1
1991–92	Hibernian	30	0
1992–93	Hibernian	34	0
1993–94	Hibernian	37	0
1994–95	Hibernian	34	0
1995–96	Hibernian	13	0
1996–97	Hibernian	31	0
1997–98	Hibernian	31	1
1998–99	Dundee	26	0
Total:		**272**	**2**

MILLIGAN, Jamie — Forward

b.Blackpool 3-1-80

Source: Trainee. *Honours:* England Youth.

1997–98	Everton	0	0
1998–99	Everton	3	0
Total:		**3**	**0**

MILLIGAN, Mike — Midfield

H: 5 10 W: 11 06 b.Manchester 20-2-67

Source: Trainee. *Honours:* Eire Under-21, B, 1 full cap.

1984–85	Oldham Ath	0	0
1985–86	Oldham Ath	5	1
1986–87	Oldham Ath	38	2
1987–88	Oldham Ath	39	1
1988–89	Oldham Ath	39	6
1989–90	Oldham Ath	41	7
1990–91	Everton	17	1
1991–92	Oldham Ath	36	3
1992–93	Oldham Ath	42	3
1993–94	Oldham Ath	39	0
1994–95	Norwich C	26	2
1995–96	Norwich C	28	2
1996–97	Norwich C	37	1
1997–98	Norwich C	20	0
1998–99	Norwich C	2	0
Total:		**409**	**29**

MILLS, Danny — Midfield

H: 5 11 W: 11 07 b.Sidcup 13-2-75

Source: Trainee.

1993–94	Charlton Ath	0	0
1994–95	Charlton Ath	0	0
1995–96	Barnet	19	0
1996–97	Barnet	2	0
1997–98	Barnet	6	0
1998–99	Brighton & HA	2	0
Total:		**29**	**0**

MILLS, Danny — Defender

H: 5 11 W: 11 09 b.Norwich 18-5-77

Source: Trainee. *Honours:* England Youth, Under-21.

1994–95	Norwich C	0	0
1995–96	Norwich C	14	0
1996–97	Norwich C	32	0
1997–98	Norwich C	20	0
1997–98	Charlton Ath	9	1
1998–99	Charlton Ath	36	2
Total:		**111**	**3**

MILLS, Lee — Forward

H: 6 2 W: 12 09 b.Mexborough 10-7-70

Source: Stocksbridge PS.

1992–93	Wolverhampton W	0	0
1993–94	Wolverhampton W	14	1
1994–95	Wolverhampton W	11	1
1994–95	Derby Co	16	7
1995–96	Port Vale	32	8
1996–97	Port Vale	35	13
1997–98	Port Vale	42	14
1998–99	Bradford C	44	23
Total:		**194**	**67**

MILLS, Leon — Midfield

H: 5 11 W: 11 10 b.Manchester 17-11-79

Source: Manchester U Trainee.

1998–99	Wigan Ath	0	0

MILNER, Jonathan — Forward

H: 5 8 W: 11 07 b.Mansfield 30-3-81

Source: Trainee.

1997–98	Mansfield T	7	0
1998–99	Mansfield T	0	0
Total:		**7**	**0**

MILOSEVIC, Savo — Forward

H: 6 1 W: 13 08 b.Bijelina 2-9-73

Honours: Yugoslavia 28 full caps, 16 goals.

1992–93	Partizan Belgrade	31	14
1993–94	Partizan Belgrade	32	20
1994–95	Partizan Belgrade	35	30
1995–96	Aston Villa	37	12
1996–97	Aston Villa	30	9
1997–98	Aston Villa	23	7
1998–99	Aston Villa	0	0
Total:		**188**	**92**

MIMMS, Bobby — Goalkeeper

H: 6 2 W: 14 01 b.York 12-10-63

Source: Halifax T Apprentice. *Honours:* England Under-21.

1981–82	Rotherham U	2	0
1982–83	Rotherham U	13	0
1983–84	Rotherham U	22	0
1984–85	Rotherham U	46	0
1985–86	Everton	10	0
1985–86	Notts Co (loan)	2	0
1986–87	Everton	11	0
1986–87	Sunderland (loan)	4	0
1986–87	Blackburn R (loan)	6	0
1987–88	Everton	8	0
1987–88	Manchester C (loan)	3	0

1987–88	Tottenham H	13	0
1988–89	Tottenham H	20	0
1989–90	Tottenham H	4	0
1989–90	Aberdeen (loan)	6	0
1990–91	Tottenham H	0	0
1990–91	Blackburn R	22	0
1991–92	Blackburn R	45	0
1992–93	Blackburn R	42	0
1993–94	Blackburn R	13	0
1994–95	Blackburn R	4	0
1995–96	Blackburn R	2	0
1996–97	Crystal Palace	1	0
1996–97	Preston NE	27	0
1997–98	Rotherham U	43	0
1998–99	Rotherham U	0	0
1998–99	York C	35	0
Total:		**404**	**0**

MINTO, Scott — Defender

H: 5 10 W: 12 04 b.Cheshire 6-8-71

Source: Trainee. *Honours:* England Youth, Under-21.

1988–89	Charlton Ath	3	0
1989–90	Charlton Ath	23	2
1990–91	Charlton Ath	43	1
1991–92	Charlton Ath	33	1
1992–93	Charlton Ath	36	1
1993–94	Charlton Ath	42	2
1994–95	Chelsea	19	0
1995–96	Chelsea	10	0
1996–97	Chelsea	25	4
1997–98	Benfica	21	0
1998–99	Benfica	10	0
1998–99	West Ham U	15	0
Total:		**280**	**11**

MINTON, Jeffrey — Midfield

H: 5 6 W: 11 11 b.Hackney 28-12-73

Source: Trainee.

1991–92	Tottenham H	2	1
1992–93	Tottenham H	0	0
1993–94	Tottenham H	0	0
1994–95	Brighton & HA	39	5
1995–96	Brighton & HA	39	8
1996–97	Brighton & HA	25	3
1997–98	Brighton & HA	36	6
1998–99	Brighton & HA	35	9
Total:		**176**	**32**

MIOTTO, Simon — Goalkeeper

H: 6 1 W: 13 03 b.Tasmania 5-9-69

Source: Riverside Olympic.

1994–95	Blackpool	0	0
1995–96	Blackpool	0	0
1996–97	Blackpool	0	0
1997–98	Blackpool	0	0
1998–99	Hartlepool U	5	0
Total:		**5**	**0**

MIRANKOV, Alex — Defender

H: 6 2 W: 13 00 b.Grenoble 2-12-67

1998–99	Scarborough	22	4
1998–99	Hibernian	10	1
Total:		**32**	**5**

MISKELLY, David — Goalkeeper

H: 6 0 W: 12 02 b.Ards 3-9-79

Source: Trainee.

1997–98	Oldham Ath	0	0
1998–99	Oldham Ath	1	0
Total:		**1**	**0**

MITCHELL, Alistair — Forward

H: 5 7 W: 11 00 b.Kirkcaldy 3-12-68

Source: Ballingry Rovers. *Honours:*

1988–89	East Fife	18	4
1989–90	East Fife	35	12
1990–91	East Fife	34	7
1991–92	Kilmarnock	42	10
1992–93	Kilmarnock	32	6
1993–94	Kilmarnock	34	5
1994–95	Kilmarnock	35	4
1995–96	Kilmarnock	30	3
1996–97	Kilmarnock	30	3
1997–98	Kilmarnock	33	4
1998–99	Kilmarnock	32	4
Total:		**355**	**62**

MITCHELL, Graham — Defender

H: 6 1 W: 13 01 b.Shipley 16-2-68

Source: Apprentice.

1986–87	Huddersfield T	17	0
1987–88	Huddersfield T	29	1
1988–89	Huddersfield T	34	0
1989–90	Huddersfield T	37	1
1990–91	Huddersfield T	46	0
1991–92	Huddersfield T	43	0
1992–93	Huddersfield T	4	0
1993–94	Huddersfield T	22	0
1993–94	Bournemouth (loan)	4	0
1994–95	Huddersfield T	12	0
1994–95	Bradford C	26	0
1995–96	Bradford C	33	1
1996–97	Bradford C	6	0
1996–97	Raith R	20	0
1997–98	Raith R	3	0
1998–99	Cardiff C	46	0
Total:		**382**	**3**

MITCHELL, Ross — Midfield

H: 5 11 W: 10 13 b.Halifax 24-8-78

Source: Trainee.

1997–98	Leicester C	0	0
1998–99	Leicester C	0	0

MJALLBY, Johan — Midfield

H: 6 1 W: 13 06 b.Sweden 9-2-71

Honours: Sweden 11 full caps, 1 goal.

1989	AIK Stockholm	1	0
1990	AIK Stockholm	14	0
1991	AIK Stockholm	26	0
1992	AIK Stockholm	0	0
1993	AIK Stockholm	7	0
1994	AIK Stockholm	23	0
1995	AIK Stockholm	19	0
1996	AIK Stockholm	23	5
1997	AIK Stockholm	7	1
1998–99	Celtic	17	1
Total:		**137**	**7**

MOHAN, Nicky — Defender

H: 6 0 W: 13 07 b.Middlesbrough 6-10-70

Source: Trainee.

1987–88	Middlesbrough	0	0
1988–89	Middlesbrough	6	0
1989–90	Middlesbrough	22	0
1990–91	Middlesbrough	0	0
1991–92	Middlesbrough	27	2
1992–93	Middlesbrough	18	2
1992–93	Hull C (loan)	5	1
1993–94	Middlesbrough	26	0
1994–95	Leicester C	23	0
1995–96	Bradford C	39	4
1996–97	Bradford C	44	0
1997–98	Bradford C	0	0
1997–98	Wycombe W	33	0
1998–99	Wycombe W	25	2
1998–99	Stoke C	15	0
Total:		**283**	**11**

MOILANEN, Teuvo — Goalkeeper

H: 6 5 W: 12 06 b.Oulu 12-12-73

Honours: Finland Under-21, 2 full caps.

1990	Ilves	3	0
1991	Ilves	7	0
1992	Ilves	29	0
1993	Ilves	5	0
1994	Ilves	19	0
1995	Jaro	26	0
1995–96	Preston NE	2	0
1996–97	Preston NE	4	0
1996–97	Scarborough (loan)	4	0
1996–97	Darlington (loan)	16	0
1997–98	Preston NE	40	0
1998–99	Preston NE	15	0
Total:		**170**	**0**

MOLDOVAN, Viorel — Forward

H: 5 9 W: 11 08 b.Bistrita 8-7-72

Honours: Romania 27 full caps, 16 goals.

1990–91	Gloria	30	9
1991–92	Gloria	26	6
1992–93	Gloria	28	7
1993–94	Dynamo Bucharest	29	9
1994–95	Dynamo Bucharest	31	10
1995–96	Neuchatel Xamax	32	19
1996–97	Grasshoppers	32	27
1997–98	Grasshoppers	19	17
1997–98	Coventry C	10	1
1998–99	Coventry C	0	0
Total:		**237**	**105**

MOLENAAR, Robert — Defender

H: 6 2 W: 14 09 b.Zaandam 27-2-69

1992–93	Volendam	28	2
1993–94	Volendam	27	1
1994–95	Volendam	31	0
1995–96	Volendam	21	0
1996–97	Volendam	17	0
1996–97	Leeds U	12	1
1997–98	Leeds U	22	2
1998–99	Leeds U	17	2
Total:		**175**	**8**

MOLS, Tonny — Midfield

H: 5 11 W: 11 09 b.Eeklo 8-1-69

1991–92	FC Brugge	3	0
1992–93	Molenbeek	20	0
1993–94	Lokeren*	0	0
1994–95	Lokeren*	0	0
1995–96	Lokeren*	0	0
1996–97	Lokeren	32	0
1997–98	Lokeren	10	0
1998–99	Dundee U	11	0
Total:		**76**	**0**

MONCUR, John — Midfield

H: 5 7 W: 9 10 b.Mile End 22-9-66

Source: Apprentice.

1984–85	Tottenham H	0	0
1985–86	Tottenham H	0	0
1986–87	Tottenham H	1	0
1986–87	Cambridge U (loan)	4	0
1986–87	Doncaster R (loan)	4	0

1987–88	Tottenham H	5	0
1988–89	Tottenham H	1	0
1988–89	Portsmouth (loan)	7	0
1989–90	Tottenham H	5	1
1989–90	Brentford (loan)	5	1
1990–91	Tottenham H	9	0
1991–92	Ipswich T (loan)	6	0
1991–92	Nottingham F (loan)	0	0
1991–92	Swindon T	3	0
1992–93	Swindon T	14	1
1993–94	Swindon T	41	4
1994–95	West Ham U	30	2
1995–96	West Ham U	20	0
1996–97	West Ham U	27	2
1997–98	West Ham U	20	1
1998–99	West Ham U	14	0
Total:		**216**	**12**

MONINGTON, Mark — Defender

H: 6 1 W: 13 07 b.Mansfield 21-10-70

Source: School.

1988–89	Burnley	8	1
1989–90	Burnley	13	0
1990–91	Burnley	0	0
1991–92	Burnley	12	1
1992–93	Burnley	31	2
1993–94	Burnley	20	1
1994–95	Burnley	0	0
1994–95	Rotherham U	25	2
1995–96	Rotherham U	11	0
1996–97	Rotherham U	28	0
1997–98	Rotherham U	15	1
1998–99	Rochdale	37	3
Total:		**200**	**11**

MONK, Gary — Defender

H: 6 1 W: 13 05 b.Bedford 6-3-79

Source: Trainee.

1995–96	Torquay U	5	0
1996–97	Southampton	0	0
1997–98	Southampton	0	0
1998–99	Southampton	4	0
1998–99	Torquay U (loan)	6	0
Total:		**15**	**0**

MONKHOUSE, Andy — Forward

H: 6 0 W: 13 09 b.Leeds 23-10-80

Source: Trainee.

1998–99	Rotherham U	5	1
Total:		**5**	**1**

MONKOU, Ken — Defender

H: 6 3 W: 14 11 b.Surinam 29-11-64

Source: Feyenoord. *Honours:* Holland Under-21.

1988–89	Chelsea	2	0
1989–90	Chelsea	34	1
1990–91	Chelsea	27	1
1991–92	Chelsea	31	0
1992–93	Chelsea	0	0
1992–93	Southampton	33	1
1993–94	Southampton	35	4
1994–95	Southampton	31	1
1995–96	Southampton	32	2
1996–97	Southampton	13	0
1997–98	Southampton	32	1
1998–99	Southampton	22	1
Total:		**292**	**12**

MONTGOMERIE, Ray — Defender

H: 5 8 W: 11 07 b.Irvine 17-4-61

Source: Saltcoats Vic.

1980–81	Newcastle U	0	0
1981–82	Dumbarton	20	5
1982–83	Dumbarton	25	2
1983–84	Dumbarton	39	1
1984–85	Dumbarton	6	0
1985–86	Dumbarton	24	0
1986–87	Dumbarton	35	0
1987–88	Dumbarton	31	0
1988–89	Kilmarnock	31	2
1989–90	Kilmarnock	35	3
1990–91	Kilmarnock	37	0
1991–92	Kilmarnock	30	1
1992–93	Kilmarnock	42	0
1993–94	Kilmarnock	42	0
1994–95	Kilmarnock	12	0
1995–96	Kilmarnock	14	0
1996–97	Kilmarnock	21	1
1997–98	Kilmarnock	27	0
1998–99	Kilmarnock	22	0
Total:		**493**	**15**

MOODY, Paul — Forward

H: 6 3 W: 14 08 b.Portsmouth 13-6-67

Source: Waterlooville.

1991–92	Southampton	4	0
1992–93	Southampton	3	0
1992–93	Reading (loan)	5	1
1993–94	Southampton	5	0
1993–94	Oxford U	15	8
1994–95	Oxford U	41	20
1995–96	Oxford U	42	17
1996–97	Oxford U	38	4
1997–98	Fulham	33	15
1998–99	Fulham	7	4
Total:		**193**	**69**

MOONEY, Gerard — Defender

H: 5 9 W: 11 00 b.Glasgow 28-8-80

Source: Trainee.

1997–98	Coventry C	0	0
1998–99	Coventry C	0	0

MOONEY, Tommy — Defender

H: 5 11 W: 13 10 b.Teesside North 11-8-71

Source: Trainee.

1989–90	Aston Villa	0	0
1990–91	Scarborough	27	13
1991–92	Scarborough	40	8
1992–93	Scarborough	40	9
1993–94	Southend U	14	5
1993–94	Watford (loan)	10	2
1994–95	Watford	29	3
1995–96	Watford	42	6
1996–97	Watford	37	13
1997–98	Watford	45	6
1998–99	Watford	36	9
Total:		**320**	**74**

MOORE, Alan — Midfield

H: 5 10 W: 11 02 b.Dublin 25-11-74

Source: Rivermount. *Honours:* Eire Under-21, 8 full caps.

1991–92	Middlesbrough	0	0
1992–93	Middlesbrough	2	0
1993–94	Middlesbrough	42	10
1994–95	Middlesbrough	37	4
1995–96	Middlesbrough	12	0
1996–97	Middlesbrough	17	0
1997–98	Middlesbrough	4	0
1998–99	Middlesbrough	4	0
1998–99	Barnsley (loan)	5	0
Total:		**123**	**14**

MOORE, Craig — Defender

H: 6 1 W: 12 00 b.Canterbury, Australia 12-12-75

Source: Australian Institute of Sport.

1993–94	Rangers	1	0
1994–95	Rangers	21	2
1995–96	Rangers	11	1
1996–97	Rangers	23	1
1997–98	Rangers	10	0
1998–99	Rangers	8	1
1998–99	Crystal Palace	23	3
Total:		**97**	**8**

MOORE, Darren — Defender

H: 6 3 W: 15 08 b.Birmingham 22-4-74

Source: Trainee.

1991–92	Torquay U	5	1
1992–93	Torquay U	31	2
1993–94	Torquay U	37	2
1994–95	Torquay U	30	3
1995–96	Doncaster R	35	2
1996–97	Doncaster R	41	5
1997–98	Bradford C	18	0
1998–99	Bradford C	44	3
Total:		**241**	**18**

MOORE, Ian — Forward

H: 5 11 W: 12 02 b.Birkenhead 26-8-76

Source: Trainee. *Honours:* England Youth, Under-21.

1994–95	Tranmere R	1	0
1995–96	Tranmere R	36	9
1996–97	Tranmere R	21	3
1996–97	Bradford C (loan)	6	0
1996–97	Nottingham F	5	0
1997–98	Nottingham F	10	1
1997–98	West Ham U (loan)	1	0
1998–99	Stockport Co	38	3
Total:		**118**	**16**

MOORE, Neil — Defender

H: 6 1 W: 12 07 b.Liverpool 21-9-72

Source: Trainee.

1991–92	Everton	0	0
1992–93	Everton	1	0
1993–94	Everton	4	0
1994–95	Everton	0	0
1994–95	Blackpool (loan)	7	0
1994–95	Oldham Ath (loan)	5	0
1995–96	Everton	0	0
1995–96	Carlisle U (loan)	13	0
1995–96	Rotherham U (loan)	11	0
1996–97	Everton	0	0
1996–97	Norwich C	2	0
1997–98	Burnley	40	3
1998–99	Burnley	12	0
Total:		**95**	**3**

MORALEE, Jamie — Forward

H: 5 11 W: 11 00 b.Wandsworth 2-12-71

Source: Trainee.

1989–90	Crystal Palace	0	0
1990–91	Crystal Palace	0	0
1991–92	Crystal Palace	6	0
1992–93	Crystal Palace	0	0
1992–93	Millwall	37	15
1993–94	Millwall	30	4
1994–95	Watford	24	4
1995–96	Watford	25	3
1996–97	Crewe Alex	7	0
1997–98	Crewe Alex	9	0
1998–99	Brighton & HA	31	3
Total:		**169**	**29**

MORAN, Andy — Forward

H: 5 11 W: 11 02 b.Wigan 7-10-79

Source: Trainee.

1997–98	Tranmere R	0	0
1998–99	Tranmere R	0	0

MORAVCIK, Lubomir — Midfield

H: 5 6 W: 11 07 b.Nitra 22-6-65

Source: Plastika Nitra. *Honours:* Czechoslovakia 42 caps, 6 goals. Slovakia 28 caps, 5 goals.

1990–91	St Etienne	37	7
1991–92	St Etienne	32	4
1992–93	St Etienne	34	5
1993–94	St Etienne	33	4
1994–95	St Etienne	27	4
1995–96	St Etienne	34	7
1996–97	Bastia	21	6
1997–98	Bastia	12	2
1998–99	Celtic	14	6
Total:		**244**	**45**

MORGAN, Alan — Defender

H: 5 9 W: 11 00 b.Aberystwyth 2-11-73

Source: Trainee. *Honours:* Wales Under-21.

1991–92	Tranmere R	0	0
1992–93	Tranmere R	0	0
1993–94	Tranmere R	0	0
1994–95	Tranmere R	0	0
1995–96	Tranmere R	4	1
1996–97	Tranmere R	1	0
1997–98	Tranmere R	19	0
1998–99	Tranmere R	6	0
Total:		**30**	**1**

MORGAN, Chris — Defender

H: 6 1 W: 12 08 b.Barnsley 9-11-77

Source: Trainee.

1996–97	Barnsley	0	0
1997–98	Barnsley	11	0
1998–99	Barnsley	19	0
Total:		**30**	**0**

MORGAN, Paul — Defender

H: 6 0 W: 11 03 b.Belfast 23-10-78

Source: Trainee. *Honours:* Northern Ireland Under-21.

1997–98	Preston NE	0	0
1998–99	Preston NE	0	0

MORGAN, Simon — Defender

H: 5 10 W: 12 05 b.Birmingham 5-9-66

Source: Trainee. *Honours:* England Under-21.

1984–85	Leicester C	0	0
1985–86	Leicester C	30	0
1986–87	Leicester C	41	1
1987–88	Leicester C	40	0
1988–89	Leicester C	32	0
1989–90	Leicester C	17	2
1990–91	Leicester C	0	0
1990–91	Fulham	32	0
1991–92	Fulham	36	3
1992–93	Fulham	39	8
1993–94	Fulham	37	6
1994–95	Fulham	42	11
1995–96	Fulham	41	6
1996–97	Fulham	44	8
1997–98	Fulham	19	1
1998–99	Fulham	34	5
Total:		**484**	**51**

MORGAN, Steve — Defender

H: 6 0 W: 13 00 b.Oldham 19-9-68

Source: Apprentice. *Honours:* England Youth.

1985–86	Blackpool	5	0
1986–87	Blackpool	11	0
1987–88	Blackpool	46	6
1988–89	Blackpool	44	3
1989–90	Blackpool	38	1
1990–91	Plymouth Arg	40	3
1991–92	Plymouth Arg	45	2
1992–93	Plymouth Arg	36	1
1993–94	Coventry C	40	2
1994–95	Coventry C	28	0
1995–96	Coventry C	0	0
1995–96	Bristol R (loan)	5	0
1996–97	Wigan Ath	23	1
1997–98	Wigan Ath	13	1
1997–98	Bury (loan)	5	0
1998–99	Burnley	17	0
Total:		**396**	**20**

MORLEY, Ben — Defender

H: 5 9 W: 10 11 b.Hull 22-12-80

Source: Trainee.

1997–98	Hull C	8	0
1998–99	Hull C	12	0
Total:		**20**	**0**

MORLEY, David — Defender

H: 6 2 W: 13 02 b.St Helens 25-9-77

Source: Trainee.

1995–96	Manchester C	0	0

1996–97	Manchester C	0	0
1997–98	Manchester C	3	1
1997–98	Ayr U (loan)	4	0
1998–99	Manchester C	0	0
1998–99	Southend U	27	0
Total:		**34**	**1**

MORLEY, Neil — Midfield

H: 5 8 W: 10 02 b.Warrington 16-11-78

Source: Trainee.

1996–97	Manchester C	0	0
1997–98	Manchester C	0	0
1998–99	Manchester C	0	0

MORLEY, Trevor — Forward

H: 5 11 W: 12 01 b.Nottingham 20-3-61

Source: Derby Co, Corby T, Nuneaton Bor.

1985–86	Northampton T	43	13
1986–87	Northampton T	37	16
1987–88	Northampton T	27	10
1987–88	Manchester C	15	4
1988–89	Manchester C	40	12
1989–90	Manchester C	17	2
1989–90	West Ham U	19	10
1990–91	West Ham U	38	12
1991–92	West Ham U	24	2
1992	Brann	8	4
1992–93	West Ham U	41	20
1993	Brann	6	1
1993–94	West Ham U	42	13
1994–95	West Ham U	14	0
1995	Brann	7	4
1995–96	Reading	17	4
1996–97	Reading	37	22
1997–98	Reading	23	5
1998–99	Reading	0	0
Total:		**455**	**154**

MORRELL, Andy — Forward

H: 5 11 W: 11 06 b.Doncaster 28-9-74

1998–99	Wrexham	7	0
Total:		**7**	**0**

MORRIS, Andy — Forward

H: 6 4 W: 14 07 b.Sheffield 17-11-67

Source: School.

1984–85	Rotherham U	1	0
1985–86	Rotherham U	0	0
1986–87	Rotherham U	6	0
1987–88	Rotherham U	0	0
1987–88	Chesterfield	10	0
1988–89	Chesterfield	42	9
1989–90	Chesterfield	43	4
1990–91	Chesterfield	15	4
1991–92	Chesterfield	8	2
1991–92	Exeter C (loan)	7	2
1992–93	Chesterfield	40	10
1993–94	Chesterfield	34	11
1994–95	Chesterfield	26	6
1995–96	Chesterfield	16	5
1996–97	Chesterfield	27	4
1997–98	Chesterfield	4	1
1998–99	Chesterfield	1	0
1998–99	Rochdale	25	7
Total:		**305**	**65**

MORRIS, Jody — Midfield

H: 5 5 W: 10 11 b.Hammersmith 22-12-78

Source: Trainee. *Honours:* England Schools, Youth, Under-21.

1995–96	Chelsea	1	0
1996–97	Chelsea	12	0
1997–98	Chelsea	12	1
1998–99	Chelsea	18	1
Total:		**43**	**2**

MORRIS, Lee — Forward

H: 5 10 W: 10 06 b.Driffield 30-4-80

Source: Trainee. *Honours:* England Youth.

1997–98	Sheffield U	5	0
1998–99	Sheffield U	20	6
Total:		**25**	**6**

MORRISH, Adam — Midfield

b.Greenwich 28-6-80

Source: Trainee.

1998–99	Southend U	0	0

MORRISON, Andy — Defender

H: 5 11 W: 12 12 b.Inverness 30-7-70

Source: Trainee.

1987–88	Plymouth Arg	1	0
1988–89	Plymouth Arg	2	0
1989–90	Plymouth Arg	19	1
1990–91	Plymouth Arg	32	2
1991–92	Plymouth Arg	30	3
1992–93	Plymouth Arg	29	0
1993–94	Blackburn R	5	0
1994–95	Blackburn R	0	0
1994–95	Blackpool	18	0
1995–96	Blackpool	29	3
1996–97	Huddersfield T	10	1
1997–98	Huddersfield T	23	1
1998–99	Huddersfield T	12	0
1998–99	Manchester C	22	4
Total:		**232**	**15**

MORRISON, Clinton — Forward

H: 6 1 W: 11 02 b.Tooting 14-5-79

Source: Trainee.

1996–97	Crystal Palace	0	0
1997–98	Crystal Palace	1	1
1998–99	Crystal Palace	37	12
Total:		**38**	**13**

MORRISON, Dave — Midfield

H: 5 11 W: 12 10 b.Waltham Forest 30-11-74

Source: Chelmsford C.

1993–94	Peterborough U	0	0
1994–95	Peterborough U	42	8
1995–96	Peterborough U	24	2
1996–97	Peterborough U	11	2
1996–97	Leyton Orient	8	0
1997–98	Leyton Orient	2	0
1998–99	Leyton Orient	23	3
Total:		**110**	**15**

MORRISON, Owen — Forward

b.Derry 8-12-81

Source: Trainee.

1998–99	Sheffield W	1	0
Total:		**1**	**0**

MORRISON, Peter — Midfield

H: 5 11 W: 10 00 b.Manchester 29-6-80

Source: Trainee.

1998–99	Bolton W	0	0

MORRISON, Scott — Midfield

b.Bristol 1-8-80

Source: Trainee.

1998–99	Bristol C	0	0

MORRISSEY, John — Forward

H: 5 8 W: 11 09 b.Liverpool 8-3-65

Source: Apprentice. *Honours:* England Youth.

1982–83	Everton	0	0
1983–84	Everton	0	0
1984–85	Everton	1	0
1985–86	Wolverhampton W	10	1
1985–86	Tranmere R	32	5
1986–87	Tranmere R	38	7
1987–88	Tranmere R	39	4
1988–89	Tranmere R	42	4
1989–90	Tranmere R	27	4
1990–91	Tranmere R	40	9
1991–92	Tranmere R	40	5
1992–93	Tranmere R	43	5
1993–94	Tranmere R	25	1
1994–95	Tranmere R	36	3
1995–96	Tranmere R	16	0
1996–97	Tranmere R	31	1
1997–98	Tranmere R	37	2
1998–99	Tranmere R	24	0
Total:		**481**	**51**

MORROW, Andrew — Forward

H: 5 8 W: 9 07 b.Bangor 5-10-80

Source: Trainee.

1998–99	Northampton T	0	0

MORROW, Steve — Defender

H: 6 0 W: 11 03 b.Bangor 2-7-70

Source: Trainee. *Honours:* Northern Ireland Youth, Under-23, 37 full caps, 1 goal.

1987–88	Arsenal	0	0
1988–89	Arsenal	0	0
1989–90	Arsenal	0	0
1990–91	Reading (loan)	10	0
1991–92	Arsenal	2	0
1991–92	Watford (loan)	8	0
1991–92	Reading (loan)	3	0
1991–92	Barnet (loan)	1	0
1992–93	Arsenal	16	0
1993–94	Arsenal	11	0
1994–95	Arsenal	15	1
1995–96	Arsenal	4	0
1996–97	Arsenal	14	0
1996–97	QPR	5	1
1997–98	QPR	31	1
1998–99	QPR	24	0
Total:		**144**	**3**

MORSE, Peter — Midfield

b.Stoke 5-3-79

Source: Trainee.

1997–98	Crewe Alex	0	0
1998–99	Crewe Alex	0	0

MORTIMER, Paul — Midfield

H: 5 11 W: 11 03 b.Kensington 8-5-68

Source: Fulham Apprentice. *Honours:* England Under-21.

1987–88	Charlton Ath	12	0
1988–89	Charlton Ath	33	5
1989–90	Charlton Ath	36	5
1990–91	Charlton Ath	32	7
1991–92	Aston Villa	12	1
1991–92	Crystal Palace	21	2
1992–93	Crystal Palace	1	0
1992–93	Brentford (loan)	6	0
1993–94	Crystal Palace	0	0

1994–95	Charlton Ath	26	4
1995–96	Charlton Ath	19	5
1996–97	Charlton Ath	11	1
1997–98	Charlton Ath	13	4
1998–99	Charlton Ath	17	1
Total:		**239**	**35**

MOSES, Adrian — Defender

H: 6 0 W: 12 07 b.Doncaster 4-5-75

Source: School. *Honours:* England Under-21.

1993–94	Barnsley	0	0
1994–95	Barnsley	4	0
1995–96	Barnsley	24	1
1996–97	Barnsley	28	2
1997–98	Barnsley	35	0
1998–99	Barnsley	34	0
Total:		**125**	**3**

MOSES, Jerry — Midfield

H: 5 9 W: 11 05 b.Kampala 22-2-81

1998–99	Luton T	0	0

MOSS, Darren — Midfield

H: 5 10 W: 11 00 b.Wrexham 24-5-81

Source: Trainee.

1998–99	Chester C	7	0
Total:		**7**	**0**

MOSS, Neil — Goalkeeper

H: 6 2 W: 13 07 b.New Milton 10-5-75

Source: Trainee.

1992–93	Bournemouth	1	0
1993–94	Bournemouth	6	0
1994–95	Bournemouth	8	0
1995–96	Bournemouth	7	0
1995–96	Southampton	0	0
1996–97	Southampton	3	0
1997–98	Southampton	0	0
1997–98	Gillingham (loan)	10	0
1998–99	Southampton	7	0
Total:		**42**	**0**

MOSS, Paul — Defender

H: 5 11 W: 12 10 b.Easington 4-5-80

Source: Trainee.

1998–99	Hartlepool U	0	0

MOUNTFIELD, Derek — Defender

H: 6 1 W: 13 08 b.Liverpool 2-11-62

Source: Apprentice. *Honours:* England Under-21, B.

1980–81	Tranmere R	5	0
1981–82	Tranmere R	21	1
1982–83	Everton	1	0
1983–84	Everton	31	3
1984–85	Everton	37	10
1985–86	Everton	15	3
1986–87	Everton	13	3
1987–88	Everton	9	0
1988–89	Aston Villa	24	1
1989–90	Aston Villa	32	4
1990–91	Aston Villa	32	4
1991–92	Aston Villa	2	0
1991–92	Wolverhampton W	28	1
1992–93	Wolverhampton W	36	2
1993–94	Wolverhampton W	19	1
1994–95	Carlisle U	31	3
1995–96	Carlisle U	0	0
1995–96	Northampton T	4	0
1995–96	Walsall	28	1
1996–97	Walsall	42	0
1997–98	Walsall	27	1
From Bromsgrove R.			
1998–99	Scarborough	6	0
Total:		**443**	**38**

MOWBRAY, Tony — Defender

H: 6 1 W: 13 07 b.Saltburn 22-11-63

Source: Apprentice. *Honours:* England B.

1981–82	Middlesbrough	0	0
1982–83	Middlesbrough	26	0
1983–84	Middlesbrough	35	1
1984–85	Middlesbrough	40	2
1985–86	Middlesbrough	35	4
1986–87	Middlesbrough	46	7
1987–88	Middlesbrough	44	3
1988–89	Middlesbrough	37	3
1989–90	Middlesbrough	28	2
1990–91	Middlesbrough	40	3
1991–92	Middlesbrough	17	0
1991–92	Celtic	15	2
1992–93	Celtic	26	2
1993–94	Celtic	22	1
1994–95	Celtic	15	1
1995–96	Ipswich T	19	2
1996–97	Ipswich T	8	0
1997–98	Ipswich T	25	0
1998–99	Ipswich T	40	2
Total:		**518**	**35**

MOYES, David — Defender

H: 6 1 W: 12 12 b.Glasgow 25-4-63

Source: Drumchapel Amateur.

1980–81	Celtic	0	0
1981–82	Celtic	19	0
1982–83	Celtic	5	0
1983–84	Celtic	0	0
1983–84	Cambridge U	30	0
1984–85	Cambridge U	40	1
1985–86	Cambridge U	9	0
1985–86	Bristol C	27	2
1986–87	Bristol C	41	3
1987–88	Bristol C	15	1
1987–88	Shrewsbury T	17	2
1988–89	Shrewsbury T	33	1
1989–90	Shrewsbury T	46	8
1990–91	Dunfermline Ath	35	7
1991–92	Dunfermline Ath	39	5
1992–93	Dunfermline Ath	30	1
1993–94	Dunfermline Ath	1	0
1993–94	Hamilton A	5	0
1993–94	Preston NE	29	4
1994–95	Preston NE	38	4
1995–96	Preston NE	41	3
1996–97	Preston NE	26	4
1997–98	Preston NE	9	0
1998–99	Preston NE	0	0
Total:		**535**	**46**

MUGGLETON, Carl — Goalkeeper

H: 6 2 W: 13 03 b.Leicester 13-9-68

Source: Apprentice. *Honours:* England Under-21.

1986–87	Leicester C	0	0
1987–88	Leicester C	0	0
1987–88	Chesterfield (loan)	17	0
1987–88	Blackpool (loan)	2	0
1988–89	Leicester C	3	0
1988–89	Hartlepool U (loan)	8	0
1989–90	Leicester C	0	0
1989–90	Stockport Co (loan)	4	0
1990–91	Leicester C	22	0
1990–91	Liverpool (loan)	0	0
1991–92	Leicester C	4	0
1992–93	Leicester C	17	0
1993–94	Leicester C	0	0
1993–94	Stoke C (loan)	6	0
1993–94	Sheffield U (loan)	0	0
1993–94	Celtic	12	0
1994–95	Stoke C	24	0
1995–96	Stoke C	6	0
1995–96	Rotherham U (loan)	6	0
1995–96	Sheffield U (loan)	1	0
1996–97	Stoke C	33	0
1997–98	Stoke C	34	0
1998–99	Stoke C	40	0
Total:		**239**	**0**

MUIR, Karl — Defender

b.North Shields 4-9-79

Source: Trainee.

1998–99	Newcastle U	0	0

MULHULLAND, Brian — Defender

b.Alexandria 22-8-81

Source: Trainee.

1998–99	Aston Villa	0	0

MULLIN, John — Forward

H: 6 0 W: 11 05 b.Bury 11-8-75

Source: School.

1992–93	Burnley	0	0
1993–94	Burnley	6	1
1994–95	Burnley	12	1
1995–96	Sunderland	10	1
1996–97	Sunderland	10	1
1997–98	Sunderland	6	0
1997–98	Preston NE (loan)	7	0
1997–98	Burnley (loan)	6	0
1998–99	Sunderland	9	2
Total:		**66**	**6**

MULLINS, Hayden — Midfield

H: 6 0 W: 11 12 b.Reading 27-3-79

Source: Trainee. *Honours:* England Under-21.

1996–97	Crystal Palace	0	0
1997–98	Crystal Palace	0	0
1998–99	Crystal Palace	40	5
Total:		**40**	**5**

MULRYNE, Philip — Midfield

H: 5 8 W: 11 02 b.Belfast 1-1-78

Source: Trainee. *Honours:* Northern Ireland Under-21, 8 full caps, 1 goal.

1994–95	Manchester U	0	0
1995–96	Manchester U	0	0
1996–97	Manchester U	0	0
1997–98	Manchester U	1	0
1998–99	Manchester U	0	0
1998–99	Norwich C	7	2
Total:		**8**	**2**

MUNROE, Karl — Defender

H: 6 0 W: 10 08 b.Manchester 23-9-79

Source: Trainee.

1997–98	Swansea C	1	0
1998–99	Swansea C	0	0
Total:		**1**	**0**

MUNTASSER, Jehad — Midfield

H: 5 10 W: 9 11 b.Tripoli 26-7-78

Source: Atalanta, Prosesto.

1997–98	Arsenal	0	0
1997–98	Bristol C	0	0
1998–99	Bristol C	0	0

MURDOCK, Colin — Defender

H: 6 1 W: 12 00 b.Ballymena 2-7-75

Source: Trainee.

1992–93	Manchester U	0	0
1993–94	Manchester U	0	0
1994–95	Manchester U	0	0
1995–96	Manchester U	0	0
1996–97	Manchester U	0	0
1997–98	Preston NE	27	1
1998–99	Preston NE	33	1
Total:		**60**	**2**

MURIE, David — Defender

H: 5 8 W: 10 04 b.Edinburgh 2-8-76

Source: Tynecastle BC.

1992–93	Hearts	0	0
1993–94	Hearts	0	0
1994–95	Hearts	0	0
1995–96	Hearts	0	0
1996–97	Hearts	7	0
1997–98	Hearts	1	0
1998–99	Hearts	4	0
Total:		**12**	**0**

MURPHY, Brendan — Goalkeeper

H: 5 11 W: 11 12 b.Wexford 19-8-75

Source: Bradford C Trainee. *Honours:* Eire Under-21.

1994–95	Wimbledon	0	0
1995–96	Wimbledon	0	0
1996–97	Wimbledon	0	0
1997–98	Wimbledon	0	0
1998–99	Wimbledon	0	0

MURPHY, Danny — Midfield

H: 5 9 W: 10 08 b.Chester 18-3-77

Source: Trainee. *Honours:* England Schools, Youth, Under-21.

1993–94	Crewe Alex	12	2
1994–95	Crewe Alex	35	5
1995–96	Crewe Alex	42	10
1996–97	Crewe Alex	45	10
1997–98	Liverpool	16	0
1998–99	Liverpool	1	0
1998–99	Crewe Alex (loan)	16	1
Total:		**167**	**28**

MURPHY, Ged — Defender

H: 5 10 W: 11 03 b.Manchester 19-12-78

Source: Trainee.

1996–97	Oldham Ath	0	0
1997–98	Oldham Ath	0	0
1998–99	Oldham Ath	0	0

MURPHY, Jamie — Defender

H: 6 1 W: 13 00 b.Manchester 25-2-73

Source: Trainee.

1991–92	Blackpool	0	0
1992–93	Blackpool	33	0
1993–94	Blackpool	16	0
1994–95	Blackpool	6	1
1995–96	Blackpool	0	0
1995–96	Doncaster R	23	0
1996–97	Doncaster R	31	0
1997–98	Cambridge U	0	0
1998–99	Halifax T	23	1
Total:		**132**	**2**

MURPHY, John — Forward

H: 6 1 W: 14 00 b.Whiston 18-10-76

Source: Trainee.

1994–95	Chester C	5	0
1995–96	Chester C	18	3
1996–97	Chester C	11	1
1997–98	Chester C	27	4
1998–99	Chester C	42	12
Total:		**103**	**20**

MURPHY, Leroy — Midfield

b.Birmingham 26-12-78

Source: Trainee.

1997–98	Derby Co	0	0
1998–99	Derby Co	0	0

MURPHY, Matt — Midfield

H: 6 0 W: 12 02 b.Northampton 20-8-71

Source: Corby T.

1992–93	Oxford U	2	0
1993–94	Oxford U	0	0
1994–95	Oxford U	22	7
1995–96	Oxford U	34	5
1996–97	Oxford U	30	3
1997–98	Oxford U	29	2
1997–98	Scunthorpe U (loan)	3	0
1998–99	Oxford U	43	4
Total:		**163**	**21**

MURPHY, Neil — Defender

H: 5 9 W: 11 00 b.Liverpool 19-5-80

Source: Trainee. *Honours:* England Youth.

1997–98	Liverpool	0	0
1998–99	Liverpool	0	0

MURPHY, Peter — Defender

H: 5 10 W: 12 03 b.Dublin 27-10-80

Source: Trainee.

1998–99	Blackburn R	0	0

MURPHY, Shaun — Defender

H: 6 1 W: 12 00 b.Sydney 5-5-70

Source: Perth Italia.

1992–93	Notts Co	8	1
1993–94	Notts Co	11	1
1994–95	Notts Co	35	0
1995–96	Notts Co	39	3
1996–97	Notts Co	16	0
1996–97	WBA	17	2
1997–98	WBA	17	1
1998–99	WBA	37	4
Total:		**180**	**12**

MURPHY, Stephen — Midfield

H: 5 11 W: 11 06 b.Dublin 5-4-78

Source: Belvedere. *Honours:* Eire Youth.

1994–95	Huddersfield T	0	0
1995–96	Huddersfield T	0	0
1996–97	Huddersfield T	0	0
1997–98	Huddersfield T	0	0
1998–99	Halifax T	12	0
Total:		**12**	**0**

MURRAY, Adam — Midfield

H: 5 9 W: 10 00 b.Birmingham 30-9-81

Source: Trainee.

1998–99	Derby Co	4	0
Total:		**4**	**0**

MURRAY, Frederick — Midfield

b.Clonmel 22-5-82

Source: Trainee.

1998–99	Blackburn R	0	0

MURRAY, Grant — Midfield

H: 5 10 W: 12 00 b.Edinburgh 29-8-75

Source: Bonnyrigg Rose.

1995–96	Hearts	0	0
1996–97	Hearts	4	0
1997–98	Hearts	10	0
1998–99	Hearts	21	0
Total:		**35**	**0**

MURRAY, Matthew — Goalkeeper

H: 6 4 W: 13 11 b.Solihull 2-5-81

Source: Trainee. *Honours:* England Youth.

1997–98	Wolverhampton W	0	0
1998–99	Wolverhampton W	0	0

MURRAY, Neil — Midfield

H: 5 9 W: 10 10 b.Bellshill 21-2-73

Source: Rangers Amateur. *Honours:* Scotland Under-21.

1989–90	Rangers	0	0
1990–91	Rangers	0	0
1991–92	Rangers	0	0
1992–93	Rangers	16	0
1993–94	Rangers	22	0
1994–95	Rangers	20	1
1995–96	Rangers	5	0
From Lorient.			
1998–99	Dundee U	3	0
Total:		**66**	**1**

MURRAY, Paul — Midfield

H: 5 8 W: 10 05 b.Carlisle 31-8-76

Source: Trainee. *Honours:* England Youth, Under-21, B.

1993–94	Carlisle U	8	0
1994–95	Carlisle U	5	0
1995–96	Carlisle U	28	1
1995–96	QPR	1	0
1996–97	QPR	32	5
1997–98	QPR	32	1
1997–98	QPR	0	0
1998–99	QPR	39	1
Total:		**145**	**8**

MURRAY, Scott — Midfield

H: 5 8 W: 11 00 b.Aberdeen 26-5-74

Source: Fraserburgh.

1993–94	Aston Villa	0	0
1994–95	Aston Villa	0	0
1995–96	Aston Villa	3	0
1996–97	Aston Villa	1	0
1997–98	Aston Villa	0	0

1997–98	Bristol C	23	0
1998–99	Bristol C	32	3
Total:		**59**	**3**

MURRAY, Shaun — Midfield

H: 5 8 W: 11 02 b.Newcastle 7-12-70

Source: Trainee. *Honours:* England Schools, Youth.

1987–88	Tottenham H	0	0
1988–89	Tottenham H	0	0
1989–90	Portsmouth	0	0
1990–91	Portsmouth	25	1
1991–92	Portsmouth	2	0
1992–93	Portsmouth	7	0
1993–94	Portsmouth	0	0
1993–94	Millwall (loan)	0	0
1993–94	Scarborough	29	5
1994–95	Bradford C	41	5
1995–96	Bradford C	34	2
1996–97	Bradford C	17	1
1997–98	Bradford C	38	0
1998–99	Notts Co	35	3
Total:		**228**	**17**

MURTY, Graeme — Midfield

H: 5 10 W: 11 10 b.Saltburn 13-11-74

Source: Trainee.

1992–93	York C	0	0
1993–94	York C	1	0
1994–95	York C	20	2
1995–96	York C	35	2
1996–97	York C	27	2
1997–98	York C	34	1
1998–99	Reading	9	0
Total:		**126**	**7**

MUSCAT, Kevin — Defender

H: 5 11 W: 11 07 b.Crawley 7-8-73

Source: South Melbourne.

1996–97	Crystal Palace	44	2
1997–98	Crystal Palace	9	0
1997–98	Wolverhampton W	24	3
1998–99	Wolverhampton W	37	4
Total:		**114**	**9**

MUSSELWHITE, Paul — Goalkeeper

H: 6 2 W: 14 04 b.Portsmouth 22-12-68

1987–88	Portsmouth	0	0
1988–89	Scunthorpe U	41	0
1989–90	Scunthorpe U	29	0
1990–91	Scunthorpe U	38	0
1991–92	Scunthorpe U	24	0
1992–93	Port Vale	41	0
1993–94	Port Vale	46	0
1994–95	Port Vale	44	0
1995–96	Port Vale	39	0
1996–97	Port Vale	33	0
1997–98	Port Vale	41	0
1998–99	Port Vale	38	0
Total:		**414**	**0**

MUSTAFA, Tarkan — Defender

H: 5 10 W: 11 07 b.London 28-8-73

Source: Kettering T.

1997–98	Barnet	11	0
1998–99	Barnet	0	0
Total:		**11**	**0**

MUSTOE, Neil — Midfield

H: 5 8 W: 12 00 b.Gloucester 5-11-76

Source: Trainee.

1995–96	Manchester U	0	0
1996–97	Manchester U	0	0
1997–98	Manchester U	0	0
1998–99	Cambridge U	34	3
Total:		**34**	**3**

MUSTOE, Robbie — Midfield

H: 6 0 W: 12 03 b.Oxford 28-8-68

1986–87	Oxford U	3	0
1987–88	Oxford U	17	0
1988–89	Oxford U	33	3
1989–90	Oxford U	38	7
1990–91	Middlesbrough	41	4
1991–92	Middlesbrough	30	2
1992–93	Middlesbrough	23	1
1993–94	Middlesbrough	38	2
1994–95	Middlesbrough	27	3
1995–96	Middlesbrough	21	1
1996–97	Middlesbrough	31	3
1997–98	Middlesbrough	32	3
1998–99	Middlesbrough	33	4
Total:		**367**	**33**

MYERS, Andy — Defender

H: 5 10 W: 13 11 b.Hounslow 3-11-73

Source: Trainee. *Honours:* England Schools, Youth, Under-21.

1990–91	Chelsea	3	0
1991–92	Chelsea	11	1
1992–93	Chelsea	3	0
1993–94	Chelsea	6	0
1994–95	Chelsea	10	0
1995–96	Chelsea	20	0
1996–97	Chelsea	18	1
1997–98	Chelsea	12	0
1998–99	Chelsea	1	0
Total:		**84**	**2**

MYHRE, Thomas — Goalkeeper

H: 6 2 W: 13 00 b.Sarpsborg 16-10-73

Honours: Norway 5 full caps.

1993	Viking	22	0
1994	Viking	22	0
1995	Viking	24	0
1996	Viking	0	0
1997	Viking	26	0
1997–98	Everton	22	0
1998–99	Everton	38	0
Total:		**154**	**0**

NAISBETT, Philip — Goalkeeper

b.Easington 2-1-79

Source: Trainee.

1996–97	Sunderland	0	0
1997–98	Sunderland	0	0
1998–99	Sunderland	0	0
1998–99	Scarborough	2	0
Total:		**2**	**0**

NAISBITT, Daniel — Goalkeeper

H: 6 1 W: 11 12 b.Bishop Auckland 25-11-78

Source: From Trainee.

1997–98	Walsall	0	0
1998–99	Walsall	0	0

NASH, Carlo — Goalkeeper

H: 6 5 W: 14 01 b.Bolton 13-9-73

Source: Clitheroe.

1996–97	Crystal Palace	21	0
1997–98	Crystal Palace	0	0
1998–99	Stockport Co	43	0
Total:		**64**	**0**

NASH, Marc — Forward

H: 5 9 W: 11 07 b.Newcastle 13-5-78

Source: Benfield Park.

1997–98	Hartlepool U	1	0
1998–99	Hartlepool U	0	0
Total:		**1**	**0**

NAVARRO, Alan — Defender

b.Liverpool 31-5-81

Source: Trainee.

1998–99	Liverpool	0	0

NAYLOR, Gavin — Midfield

H: 5 6 W: 11 01 b.Hartlepool 30-5-79

Source: Trainee.

1997–98	Manchester U	0	0
1998–99	Middlesbrough	0	0

NAYLOR, Glenn — Forward

H: 5 10 W: 11 10 b.York 11-8-72

Source: Trainee.

1989–90	York C	1	0
1990–91	York C	20	5
1991–92	York C	21	8
1992–93	York C	4	0
1993–94	York C	10	1
1994–95	York C	29	9
1995–96	York C	25	7
1995–96	Darlington (loan)	4	1
1996–97	York C	1	0
1996–97	Darlington	37	11
1997–98	Darlington	42	8
1998–99	Darlington	42	9
Total:		**236**	**59**

NAYLOR, Lee — Defender

H: 5 8 W: 11 08 b.Bloxwich 19-3-80

Source: Trainee. *Honours:* England Youth.

1997–98	Wolverhampton W	16	0
1998–99	Wolverhampton W	23	1
Total:		**39**	**1**

NAYLOR, Martyn — Defender

H: 5 9 W: 10 02 b.Walsall 2-8-77

Source: Hereford U Trainee, Telford U.

1997–98	Shrewsbury T	2	0
1998–99	Shrewsbury T	0	0
Total:		**2**	**0**

NAYLOR, Richard — Forward

H: 6 0 W: 13 07 b.Leeds 28-2-77

Source: Trainee.

1995–96	Ipswich T	0	0
1996–97	Ipswich T	27	4
1997–98	Ipswich T	5	2
1998–99	Ipswich T	30	5
Total:		**62**	**11**

NAYLOR, Stuart — Goalkeeper

H: 6 4 W: 14 01 b.Wetherby 6-12-62

Source: Yorkshire Amateur. *Honours:* England Youth, B.

1980–81	Lincoln C	0	0

1981–82	Lincoln C	3	0
1982–83	Lincoln C	1	0
1982–83	Peterborough U (loan)	8	0
1983–84	Lincoln C	0	0
1983–84	Crewe Alex (loan)	38	0
1984–85	Crewe Alex (loan)	17	0
1984–85	Lincoln C	25	0
1985–86	Lincoln C	20	0
1985–86	WBA	12	0
1986–87	WBA	42	0
1987–88	WBA	35	0
1988–89	WBA	44	0
1989–90	WBA	39	0
1990–91	WBA	28	0
1991–92	WBA	34	0
1992–93	WBA	32	0
1993–94	WBA	20	0
1994–95	WBA	42	0
1995–96	WBA	27	0
1996–97	Bristol C	35	0
1997–98	Bristol C	2	0
1998–99	Bristol C	0	0
1998–99	Mansfield T (loan)	6	0
Total:		**510**	**0**

NAYLOR, Tony — Forward

H: 5 7 W: 10 07 b.Manchester 29-3-68

Source: Droylsden.

1989–90	Crewe Alex	2	0
1990–91	Crewe Alex	14	1
1991–92	Crewe Alex	34	15
1992–93	Crewe Alex	35	16
1993–94	Crewe Alex	37	13
1994–95	Port Vale	33	9
1995–96	Port Vale	39	11
1996–97	Port Vale	43	17
1997–98	Port Vale	38	10
1998–99	Port Vale	22	4
Total:		**297**	**96**

NAYSMITH, Gary — Forward

H: 5 7 W: 11 08 b.Edinburgh 16-11-78

Source: Whitehill Welfare Colts. *Honours:* Scotland Under-18, Under-21.

1995–96	Hearts	1	0
1996–97	Hearts	10	0
1997–98	Hearts	16	2
1998–99	Hearts	26	0
Total:		**53**	**2**

NDAH, George — Forward

H: 6 1 W: 11 04 b.Dulwich 23-12-74

Source: Trainee.

1992–93	Crystal Palace	13	0
1993–94	Crystal Palace	1	0
1994–95	Crystal Palace	12	1
1995–96	Crystal Palace	23	4
1995–96	Bournemouth (loan)	12	2
1996–97	Crystal Palace	26	3
1997–98	Crystal Palace	3	0
1997–98	Gillingham (loan)	4	0
1997–98	Swindon T	14	2
1998–99	Swindon T	41	11
Total:		**149**	**23**

NDLOVU, Peter — Forward

H: 5 8 W: 10 02 b.Zimbabwe 25-2-73

Source: Highlanders. *Honours:* Zimbabwe 37 full caps.

1991–92	Coventry C	23	2
1992–93	Coventry C	32	7
1993–94	Coventry C	40	11
1994–95	Coventry C	30	11
1995–96	Coventry C	32	5
1996–97	Coventry C	20	1
1997–98	Birmingham C	39	9
1998–99	Birmingham C	43	10
Total:		**259**	**56**

NEAL, Ashley — Defender

H: 6 1 W: 14 10 b.Northampton 16-12-74

Source: Trainee.

1992–93	Liverpool	0	0
1993–94	Liverpool	0	0
1994–95	Liverpool	0	0
1995–96	Liverpool	0	0
1996–97	Liverpool	0	0
1996–97	Brighton & HA (loan)	8	0
1996–97	Huddersfield T	0	0
1996–97	Peterborough U	4	0
1997–98	Peterborough U	4	0
1998–99	Peterborough U	0	0
Total:		**16**	**0**

NEAL, Lewis — Midfield

b.Leicester 14-7-81

1998–99	Stoke C	0	0

NEIL, Gary — Forward

H: 6 0 W: 12 10 b.Glasgow 16-8-78

Source: Trainee.

1997–98	Leicester C	0	0
1998–99	Leicester C	0	0
1998–99	Torquay U (loan)	7	0
Total:		**7**	**0**

NEIL, Jim — Defender

H: 5 8 W: 12 01 b.Bury St Edmunds 28-2-76

Source: Trainee.

1994–95	Grimsby T	0	0
1995–96	Grimsby T	1	0
1996–97	Grimsby T	1	0
1997–98	Scunthorpe U	7	0
1998–99	Scunthorpe U	0	0
Total:		**9**	**0**

NEILL, Lucas — Midfield

H: 6 1 W: 12 00 b.Sydney 9-3-78

Source: NSW Soccer Academy. *Honours:* Australia Youth, full caps.

1995–96	Millwall	13	0
1996–97	Millwall	39	3
1997–98	Millwall	6	0
1998–99	Millwall	35	6
Total:		**93**	**9**

NEILSON, Alan — Defender

H: 5 11 W: 12 08 b.Wegburg 26-9-72

Source: Trainee. *Honours:* Wales Under-21, 5 full caps.

1990–91	Newcastle U	3	0
1991–92	Newcastle U	16	1
1992–93	Newcastle U	3	0
1993–94	Newcastle U	14	0
1994–95	Newcastle U	6	0
1995–96	Southampton	18	0
1996–97	Southampton	29	0
1997–98	Southampton	8	0
1997–98	Fulham	17	0
1998–99	Fulham	4	1
Total:		**118**	**2**

NELSON, Fernando — Defender

H: 5 11 W: 11 08 b.Oporto 5-11-71

Honours: Portugal 6 full caps.

1991–92	Sporting	2	0
1992–93	Sporting	15	0
1993–94	Sporting	33	1
1994–95	Sporting	33	1
1995–96	Sporting	32	1
1996–97	Aston Villa	34	0
1997–98	Aston Villa	25	0
1998–99	Aston Villa	0	0
Total:		**174**	**3**

NETHERCOTT, Stuart — Defender

H: 6 0 W: 13 08 b.Ilford 21-3-73

Source: Trainee. *Honours:* England Under-21.

1991–92	Tottenham H	0	0
1991–92	Maidstone U (loan)	13	1
1991–92	Barnet (loan)	3	0
1992–93	Tottenham H	5	0
1993–94	Tottenham H	10	0
1994–95	Tottenham H	17	0
1995–96	Tottenham H	13	0
1996–97	Tottenham H	9	0
1997–98	Tottenham H	0	0
1997–98	Millwall	10	0
1998–99	Millwall	37	2
Total:		**117**	**3**

NEVILLE, Gary — Defender

H: 5 11 W: 12 07 b.Bury 18-2-75

Source: Trainee. *Honours:* England Youth, 32 full caps.

1992–93	Manchester U	0	0
1993–94	Manchester U	1	0
1994–95	Manchester U	18	0
1995–96	Manchester U	31	0
1996–97	Manchester U	31	1
1997–98	Manchester U	34	0
1998–99	Manchester U	34	1
Total:		**149**	**2**

NEVILLE, Philip — Defender

H: 5 11 W: 11 11 b.Bury 21-1-77

Source: Trainee. *Honours:* England Schools, Youth, Under-21, 17 full caps.

1994–95	Manchester U	2	0
1995–96	Manchester U	24	0
1996–97	Manchester U	18	0
1997–98	Manchester U	30	1
1998–99	Manchester U	28	0
Total:		**102**	**1**

NEVIN, Pat — Forward

H: 5 6 W: 11 09 b.Glasgow 6-9-63

Source: Gartcosh U. *Honours:* Scotland Youth, Under-21, B, 28 full caps, 5 goals.

1981–82	Clyde	34	12
1982–83	Clyde	39	5
1983–84	Chelsea	38	14
1984–85	Chelsea	41	4
1985–86	Chelsea	40	7
1986–87	Chelsea	37	5
1987–88	Chelsea	37	6
1988–89	Everton	25	2
1989–90	Everton	30	4
1990–91	Everton	37	8
1991–92	Everton	17	2
1991–92	Tranmere R (loan)	8	0
1992–93	Tranmere R	43	13
1993–94	Tranmere R	45	8
1994–95	Tranmere R	44	4
1995–96	Tranmere R	40	3

1996–97	Tranmere R	21	2
1997–98	Kilmarnock	31	5
1998–99	Kilmarnock	3	1
1998–99	Motherwell	30	0
Total:		**640**	**105**

NEVLAND, Erik — Forward

H: 5 10 W: 11 12 b.Stavanger 10-11-77

1996	Viking	1	0
1997	Viking	13	5
1997–98	Manchester U	1	0
1998–99	Manchester U	0	0
Total:		**15**	**5**

NEWBY, John — Forward

H: 6 0 W: 12 00 b.Warrington 28-11-78

Source: Trainee.

1998–99	Liverpool	0	0

NEWBY, Keith — Midfield

H: 5 8 W: 11 00 b.Grimsby 27-9-79

Source: Trainee.

1998–99	Cambridge U	0	0

NEWELL, Justin — Forward

H: 6 1 W: 10 07 b.Germany 8-2-80

Source: Trainee.

1997–98	Torquay U	1	0
1998–99	Torquay U	0	0
Total:		**1**	**0**

NEWELL, Mike — Forward

H: 6 0 W: 13 00 b.Liverpool 27-1-65

Source: Liverpool Amateur. *Honours:* England Under-21, B.

1983–84	Crewe Alex	3	0
1983–84	Wigan Ath	9	0
1984–85	Wigan Ath	39	9
1985–86	Wigan Ath	24	16
1985–86	Luton T	16	6
1986–87	Luton T	42	12
1987–88	Luton T	5	0
1987–88	Leicester C	36	8
1988–89	Leicester C	45	13
1989–90	Everton	26	7
1990–91	Everton	29	7
1991–92	Everton	13	1
1991–92	Blackburn R	20	6
1992–93	Blackburn R	40	13
1993–94	Blackburn R	28	6
1994–95	Blackburn R	12	0
1995–96	Blackburn R	30	3
1996–97	Birmingham C	15	1
1996–97	West Ham U (loan)	7	0
1996–97	Bradford C (loan)	7	0
1997–98	Aberdeen	21	4
1998–99	Aberdeen	23	2
1998–99	Crewe Alex	4	0
Total:		**494**	**114**

NEWELL, Paul — Goalkeeper

H: 6 1 W: 14 07 b.Woolwich 23-2-69

Source: Trainee.

1987–88	Southend U	13	0
1988–89	Southend U	2	0
1989–90	Southend U	0	0
1990–91	Leyton Orient	8	0
1991–92	Leyton Orient	10	0
1992–93	Leyton Orient	3	0
1992–93	Colchester U (loan)	14	0
1993–94	Leyton Orient	40	0
1994–95	Barnet	15	0
1995–96	Barnet	1	0
1995–96	Darlington	21	0
1996–97	Darlington	20	0
1997–98	Colchester U	0	0
1997–98	Northampton T	0	0
1998–99	Northampton T	0	0
Total:		**147**	**0**

NEWHOUSE, Aidan — Forward

H: 6 2 W: 13 10 b.Wallasey 23-5-72

Source: Trainee. *Honours:* England Youth.

1987–88	Chester C	1	0
1988–89	Chester C	25	2
1989–90	Chester C	18	4
1989–90	Wimbledon	2	0
1990–91	Wimbledon	8	1
1991–92	Wimbledon	12	1
1992–93	Wimbledon	1	0
1993–94	Wimbledon	0	0
1993–94	Tranmere R (loan)	0	0
1993–94	Port Vale (loan)	2	0
1994–95	Wimbledon	0	0
1994–95	Portsmouth (loan)	6	1
1995–96	Wimbledon	0	0
1995–96	Torquay U (loan)	4	2
1996–97	Wimbledon	0	0
1997–98	Fulham	8	1
1997–98	Swansea C	8	0
1998–99	Swansea C	6	0
Total:		**101**	**12**

NEWMAN, Ricky — Midfield

H: 5 10 W: 12 06 b.Guildford 5-8-70

Source: Trainee.

1987–88	Crystal Palace	0	0

1988–89	Crystal Palace	0	0
1989–90	Crystal Palace	0	0
1990–91	Crystal Palace	0	0
1991–92	Crystal Palace	0	0
1991–92	Maidstone U (loan)	10	1
1992–93	Crystal Palace	2	0
1993–94	Crystal Palace	11	0
1994–95	Crystal Palace	35	3
1995–96	Millwall	36	1
1996–97	Millwall	41	3
1997–98	Millwall	35	1
1998–99	Millwall	24	0
Total:		**194**	**9**

NEWMAN, Rob — Defender

H: 6 1 W: 13 10 b.Bradford-on-Avon 13-12-63

Source: Apprentice.

1981–82	Bristol C	21	3
1982–83	Bristol C	43	3
1983–84	Bristol C	30	1
1984–85	Bristol C	34	3
1985–86	Bristol C	39	3
1986–87	Bristol C	45	6
1987–88	Bristol C	44	11
1988–89	Bristol C	46	6
1989–90	Bristol C	46	8
1990–91	Bristol C	46	8
1991–92	Norwich C	41	7
1992–93	Norwich C	18	2
1993–94	Norwich C	32	2
1994–95	Norwich C	32	1
1995–96	Norwich C	23	1
1996–97	Norwich C	44	1
1997–98	Norwich C	15	0
1997–98	Motherwell (loan)	11	0
1997–98	Wigan Ath (loan)	8	0
1998–99	Southend U	36	7
Total:		**654**	**73**

NEWSOME, Jon — Defender

H: 6 3 W: 13 10 b.Sheffield 6-9-70

Source: Trainee.

1989–90	Sheffield W	6	0
1990–91	Sheffield W	1	0
1991–92	Leeds U	10	2
1992–93	Leeds U	37	0
1993–94	Leeds U	29	1
1994–95	Norwich C	35	3
1995–96	Norwich C	27	4
1995–96	Sheffield W	8	1
1996–97	Sheffield W	10	1
1997–98	Sheffield W	25	2
1998–99	Sheffield W	5	0
1998–99	Bolton W (loan)	6	0
Total:		**199**	**14**

NEWTON, Chris — Midfield

H: 6 0 W: 11 02 b.Leeds 5-11-79

Source: Huddersfield T Schoolboy.

1998–99	Halifax T	14	1
Total:		**14**	**1**

NEWTON, Eddie — Midfield

H: 6 0 W: 12 11 b.Hammersmith 13-12-71

Source: Trainee. *Honours:* England Under-21.

1990–91	Chelsea	0	0
1991–92	Chelsea	1	1
1991–92	Cardiff C (loan)	18	4
1992–93	Chelsea	34	5
1993–94	Chelsea	36	0
1994–95	Chelsea	30	1
1995–96	Chelsea	24	1
1996–97	Chelsea	15	0
1997–98	Chelsea	18	0
1998–99	Chelsea	7	0
Total:		**183**	**12**

NEWTON, Shaun — Forward

H: 5 8 W: 11 00 b.Camberwell 20-8-75

Source: Trainee. *Honours:* England Under-21.

1992–93	Charlton Ath	2	0
1993–94	Charlton Ath	19	2
1994–95	Charlton Ath	26	0
1995–96	Charlton Ath	41	5
1996–97	Charlton Ath	43	3
1997–98	Charlton Ath	41	5
1998–99	Charlton Ath	16	0
Total:		**188**	**15**

NGONGE, Michel — Forward

H: 6 0 W: 12 08 b.Huy 10-1-67

1995–96	Harelbeke	31	14
1996–97	Samsunspor	25	0
1997–98	Samsunspor	27	1
1998–99	Watford	22	4
Total:		**105**	**19**

NICHOLAS, Steven — Forward

H: 5 8 W: 10 02 b.Stirling 8-7-81

Source: Riverside BC.

1997–98	Stirling A	7	0
1998–99	Motherwell	7	1
Total:		**14**	**1**

NICHOLLS, Kevin — Midfield

H: 5 11 W: 11 12 b.Newham 2-1-79

Source: Trainee. *Honours:* England Youth.

1995–96	Charlton Ath	0	0
1996–97	Charlton Ath	6	1
1997–98	Charlton Ath	6	0
1998–99	Charlton Ath	0	0
1998–99	Brighton & HA (loan)	4	1
Total:		**16**	**2**

NICHOLLS, Mark — Forward

H: 5 10 W: 10 04 b.Hillingdon 30-5-77

Source: Trainee.

1995–96	Chelsea	0	0
1996–97	Chelsea	8	0
1997–98	Chelsea	19	3
1998–99	Chelsea	9	0
Total:		**36**	**3**

NICHOLS, Jon — Defender

H: 6 0 W: 11 10 b.Plymouth 10-9-80

Source: Trainee.

1998–99	Torquay U	6	0
Total:		**6**	**0**

NICHOLSON, Barry — Midfield

H: 5 8 W: 10 11 b.Dumfries 24-8-78

Source: Rangers SABC.

1995–96	Rangers	0	0
1996–97	Rangers	0	0
1997–98	Rangers	0	0
1998–99	Rangers	6	0
Total:		**6**	**0**

NICHOLSON, Kevin — Defender

H: 5 8 W: 11 05 b.Derby 2-10-80

Source: Trainee. *Honours:* England Schools.

1997–98	Sheffield W	0	0
1998–99	Sheffield W	0	0

NICHOLSON, Shane — Defender

H: 5 10 W: 11 10 b.Newark 3-6-70

Source: Trainee.

1986–87	Lincoln C	7	0
1987–88	Lincoln C	0	0
1988–89	Lincoln C	34	1
1989–90	Lincoln C	23	0
1990–91	Lincoln C	40	4
1991–92	Lincoln C	29	1
1991–92	Derby Co	0	0
1992–93	Derby Co	17	0
1993–94	Derby Co	22	1
1994–95	Derby Co	15	0
1995–96	Derby Co	20	0
1995–96	WBA	18	0
1996–97	WBA	18	0
1997–98	WBA	16	0
1998–99	Chesterfield	24	0
Total:		**283**	**7**

NIELSEN, Allan — Midfield

H: 5 8 W: 11 02 b.Esbjerg 13-3-71

Source: Esbjerg. *Honours:* Denmark Under-21, 29 full caps, 6 goals.

1988–89	Bayern Munich	0	0
1989–90	Bayern Munich	0	0
1990–91	Bayern Munich	1	0
1991–92	Sion	0	0
1991–92	Odense	8	2
1992–93	Odense	30	4
1993–94	Odense	17	3
1993–94	FC Copenhagen	8	0
1994–95	FC Copenhagen	18	3
1994–95	Brondby	10	3
1995–96	Brondby	28	6
1996–97	Brondby	4	2
1996–97	Tottenham H	29	6
1997–98	Tottenham H	26	3
1998–99	Tottenham H	28	3
Total:		**207**	**35**

NIELSEN, John — Midfield

H: 5 9 W: 11 12 b.Aarhus 7-4-72

1995–96	Ikast	19	0
1996–97	Southend U	24	3
1997–98	Southend U	5	0
1998–99	Southend U	0	0
Total:		**48**	**3**

NIELSEN, Jorgen — Goalkeeper

H: 6 0 W: 13 00 b.Nykobing 6-5-71

1993–94	Naestved	2	0
1994–95	Naestved	0	0
1995–96	Hvidovre*	0	0
1996–97	Liverpool	0	0
1997–98	Liverpool	0	0
1998–99	Liverpool	0	0
1998–99	Wolverhampton W (loan)	0	0
Total:		**2**	**0**

NIEMI, Antti — Goalkeeper

H: 6 1 W: 14 00 b.Oulu 31-5-72

Honours: Finland 35 full caps.

1991	HJK Helsinki	2	0
1992	HJK Helsinki	27	0
1993	HJK Helsinki	24	0
1994	HJK Helsinki	24	0
1995	HJK Helsinki	24	0
1995–96	FC Copenhagen	17	0
1996–97	FC Copenhagen	30	0
1997–98	Rangers	5	0
1998–99	Rangers	7	0
Total:		**160**	**0**

NIESTROJ, Robert — Midfield

H: 5 10 W: 11 03 b.Oppeln 2-12-74

Source: Fortuna Dusseldorf.

1998–99	Wolverhampton W	5	0
Total:		**5**	**0**

NIGHTINGALE, Luke — Forward

H: 5 10 W: 12 05 b.Portsmouth 22-12-80

Source: Trainee.

1998–99	Portsmouth	19	3
Total:		**19**	**3**

NILSEN, Roger — Defender

H: 5 11 W: 12 06 b.Tromso 8-8-69

Source: Viking Stavanger. *Honours:* Norway 31 full caps, 3 goals.

1993–94	Sheffield U	22	0
1994–95	Sheffield U	33	0
1995–96	Sheffield U	39	0
1996–97	Sheffield U	33	0
1997–98	Sheffield U	22	0
1998–99	Sheffield U	17	0
1998–99	Tottenham H	3	0
Total:		**169**	**0**

NILSSON, Roland — Defender

H: 5 10 W: 11 10 b.Helsingborg 27-11-63

Honours: Sweden 102 full caps, 1 goal.

1981	Helsingborg	16	1
1982	Helsingborg	22	2
1983	IFK Gothenburg	13	1
1984	IFK Gothenburg	0	0
1985	IFK Gothenburg	22	1
1986	IFK Gothenburg	23	3
1987	IFK Gothenburg	23	2
1988	IFK Gothenburg	22	0
1989	IFK Gothenburg	21	0
1989–90	Sheffield W	20	0
1990–91	Sheffield W	22	0
1991–92	Sheffield W	39	1
1992–93	Sheffield W	32	1
1993–94	Sheffield W	38	0
1994	Helsingborg	17	0
1995	Helsingborg	16	1
1996	Helsingborg	25	4
1997	Helsingborg	6	1
1997–98	Coventry C	32	0
1998–99	Coventry C	28	0
Total:		**437**	**18**

NISH, Colin — Forward

H: 6 3 W: 11 08 b.Edinburgh 7-3-81

Source: Rosyth Rec.

1997–98	Dunfermline Ath	0	0
1998–99	Dunfermline Ath	2	0
Total:		**2**	**0**

NIVEN, Stuart — Midfield

H: 5 11 W: 12 08 b.Glasgow 24-12-78

Source: Trainee.

1996–97	Ipswich T	2	0
1997–98	Ipswich T	0	0
1998–99	Ipswich T	0	0
Total:		**2**	**0**

NIXON, Eric — Goalkeeper

H: 6 4 W: 14 00 b.Manchester 4-10-62

Source: Curzon Ashton.

1983–84	Manchester C	0	0
1984–85	Manchester C	0	0
1985–86	Manchester C	28	0
1986–87	Manchester C	5	0
1986–87	Wolverhampton W (loan)	16	0
1986–87	Bradford C (loan)	3	0
1986–87	Southampton (loan)	4	0
1986–87	Carlisle U (loan)	16	0
1987–88	Manchester C	25	0
1987–88	Tranmere R (loan)	8	0
1988–89	Tranmere R	45	0
1989–90	Tranmere R	46	0
1990–91	Tranmere R	43	0
1991–92	Tranmere R	46	0
1992–93	Tranmere R	45	0
1993–94	Tranmere R	42	0
1994–95	Tranmere R	41	0
1995–96	Tranmere R	0	0
1995–96	Blackpool (loan)	20	0
1996–97	Tranmere R	25	0
1996–97	Bradford C (loan)	12	0
1997–98	Stockport Co	43	0
1998–99	Stockport Co	0	0
1998–99	Wigan Ath (loan)	3	0
Total:		**516**	**0**

NKUBI, Isaac — Midfield

b.Uganda 5-3-81

Source: Vasteras.

1998–99	Aston Villa	0	0

NOEL-WILLIAMS, Gifton — Forward

H: 6 1 W: 13 09 b.Islington 21-1-80

Source: Trainee. *Honours:* England Youth.

1996–97	Watford	25	2
1997–98	Watford	38	7
1998–99	Watford	26	10
Total:		**89**	**19**

NOGAN, Kurt — Forward

H: 5 10 W: 11 01 b.Cardiff 9-9-70

Source: Trainee. *Honours:* Wales Under-21.

1989–90	Luton T	10	2
1990–91	Luton T	9	0
1991–92	Luton T	14	1
1992–93	Peterborough U	0	0
1992–93	Brighton & HA	30	20
1993–94	Brighton & HA	41	22
1994–95	Brighton & HA	26	7
1994–95	Burnley	15	3
1995–96	Burnley	46	20
1996–97	Burnley	31	10
1996–97	Preston NE	7	0
1997–98	Preston NE	22	5
1998–99	Preston NE	42	18
Total:		**293**	**108**

NOGAN, Lee — Forward

H: 5 8 W: 11 04 b.Cardiff 21-5-69

Source: Apprentice. *Honours:* Wales Under-21, B, 2 full caps.

1986–87	Oxford U	0	0
1986–87	Brentford (loan)	11	2
1987–88	Oxford U	3	0
1987–88	Southend U (loan)	6	1
1988–89	Oxford U	3	0
1989–90	Oxford U	4	0
1990–91	Oxford U	32	5
1991–92	Oxford U	22	5
1991–92	Watford	23	5
1992–93	Watford	42	11
1993–94	Watford	26	3
1993–94	Southend U (loan)	5	0
1994–95	Watford	14	7
1994–95	Reading	20	10
1995–96	Reading	39	10
1996–97	Reading	32	6
1996–97	Notts Co (loan)	6	0
1997–98	Grimsby T	36	8
1998–99	Grimsby T	38	2
Total:		**362**	**75**

NOLAN, Ian — Defender

H: 5 11 W: 12 02 b.Liverpool 9-7-70

Source: Preston NE Trainee, Northwich Vic, Marine. *Honours:* Northern Ireland 7 full caps.

1991–92	Tranmere R	34	1
1992–93	Tranmere R	14	0
1993–94	Tranmere R	40	0
1994–95	Sheffield W	42	3
1995–96	Sheffield W	29	0
1996–97	Sheffield W	38	1
1997–98	Sheffield W	27	0
1998–99	Sheffield W	0	0
Total:		**224**	**5**

NORRIS, Richard — Midfield

b.Birkenhead 5-1-78

Source: Marine.

1996–97	Crewe Alex	0	0
1997–98	Crewe Alex	0	0
1998–99	Crewe Alex	0	0

NOSWORTHY, Nayron — Midfield

H: 6 1 W: 12 07 b.London 11-10-80

Source: Trainee.

1998–99	Gillingham	3	0
Total:		**3**	**0**

NOTMAN, Alex — Forward

H: 5 7 W: 10 11 b.Edinburgh 10-12-79

Source: Trainee. *Honours:* Scotland Under-21.

1996–97	Manchester U	0	0
1997–98	Manchester U	0	0
1998–99	Manchester U	0	0
1998–99	Aberdeen (loan)	2	0
Total:		**2**	**0**

NOTTINGHAM, Steve — Defender

b.Peterborough 21-2-80

Source: Trainee.

1997–98	Scunthorpe U	1	0
1998–99	Scunthorpe U	0	0
Total:		**1**	**0**

NOWLAND, Adam — Forward

H: 5 11 W: 11 06 b.Preston 6-7-81

Source: Trainee.

1997–98	Blackpool	1	0
1998–99	Blackpool	37	2
Total:		**38**	**2**

NUGENT, Kevin — Forward

H: 6 2 W: 13 00 b.Edmonton 10-4-69

Source: Trainee. *Honours:* Eire Youth.

1987–88	Leyton Orient	11	3
1988–89	Leyton Orient	3	0
1989–90	Leyton Orient	11	0
1990–91	Leyton Orient	33	5
1991–92	Leyton Orient	36	12
1991–92	Plymouth Arg	4	0
1992–93	Plymouth Arg	45	11
1993–94	Plymouth Arg	39	14
1994–95	Plymouth Arg	37	7
1995–96	Plymouth Arg	6	0
1995–96	Bristol C	34	8
1996–97	Bristol C	36	6
1997–98	Cardiff C	4	0
1998–99	Cardiff C	41	15
Total:		**340**	**81**

NUMAN, Arthur — Defender

H: 5 8 W: 12 03 b.Heemskerk 14-12-69

Source: SV Beverwijk. *Honours:* Holland 35 full caps.

1987–88	Haarlem	7	1
1988–89	Haarlem	32	0
1989–90	Haarlem	32	2
1990–91	Haarlem	20	2
1990–91	Twente	20	4
1991–92	Twente	29	3
1992–93	PSV Eindhoven	24	5
1993–94	PSV Eindhoven	34	10
1994–95	PSV Eindhoven	32	6
1995–96	PSV Eindhoven	27	2
1996–97	PSV Eindhoven	31	2
1997–98	PSV Eindhoven	31	2
1998–99	Rangers	10	0
Total:		**329**	**39**

NYAMAH, Kofi — Defender

H: 5 10 W: 11 07 b.Islington 20-6-75

Source: Trainee.

1993–94	Cambridge U	14	2
1994–95	Cambridge U	9	0
1995–96	Cambridge U	0	0
1996–97	Cambridge U	0	0
From Kettering T.			
1996–97	Stoke C	7	0
1997–98	Stoke C	10	0
1998–99	Luton T	0	0
1998–99	Cambridge U	0	0
Total:		**40**	**2**

NYYSSONEN, Kai — Forward

H: 5 11 W: 11 10 b.Kuopio 10-6-72

1990	KuPS	1	0
1991	KuPS	25	5
1992	Haka	32	8
1993	Haka	18	4
1994	Haka	16	0
1995	Haka	22	1
1995–96	Molenbeek	13	3
1996–97	Molenbeek	28	3
1997–98	Molenbeek	5	0
From Cordoba			
1998–99	Motherwell	3	1
Total:		**163**	**25**

NZAMBA, Guy — Forward

b.Gabon 13-7-70

Source: Trieste.

1997–98	Southend U	1	0
1998–99	Southend U	0	0
Total:		**1**	**0**

O'BOYLE, George — Forward

H: 5 8 W: 11 09 b.Belfast 14-12-67

Source: Linfield. *Honours:* Northern Ireland 13 full caps, 1 goal.

1989–90	Dunfermline Ath	28	3
1990–91	Dunfermline Ath	16	6
1991–92	Dunfermline Ath	16	1
1992–93	Dunfermline Ath	3	2
1993–94	Dunfermline Ath	32	17
1994–95	St Johnstone	32	19
1995–96	St Johnstone	35	21
1996–97	St Johnstone	25	12
1997–98	St Johnstone	33	10
1998–99	St Johnstone	13	2
Total:		**233**	**93**

O'BRIEN, Andrew — Defender

H: 5 10 W: 10 06 b.Harrogate 29-6-79

Source: Trainee. *Honours:* England Youth, Under-21, Eire Under-21.

1996–97	Bradford C	22	2
1997–98	Bradford C	26	0
1998–99	Bradford C	31	0
Total:		**79**	**2**

O'BRIEN, Burton — Forward

H: 5 11 W: 10 07 b.South Africa 10-6-81

Source: S Form. *Honours:* Scotland Under-21.

1998–99	St Mirren	22	1
1998–99	Blackburn R	0	0
Total:		**22**	**1**

O'BRIEN, Carl — Midfield

H: 5 9 W: 10 10 b.Dublin 6-11-81

Source: Trainee.

1998–99	Leeds U	0	0

O'BRIEN, Chris — Midfield

b.Liverpool 13-1-82

Source: Trainee. *Honours:* England Schools.

1998–99	Liverpool	0	0

O'BRIEN, Kevin — Defender

H: 5 11 W: 11 08 b.Waterford 14-8-80

Source: Trainee. *Honours:* Eire Schools.

1998–99	Tottenham H	0	0

O'BRIEN, Liam — Midfield

H: 6 1 W: 11 10 b.Dublin 5-9-64

Source: Shamrock R. *Honours:* Eire Youth, 16 full caps.

1986–87	Manchester U	11	0
1987–88	Manchester U	17	2
1988–89	Manchester U	3	0
1988–89	Newcastle U	20	4
1989–90	Newcastle U	19	2
1990–91	Newcastle U	33	3
1991–92	Newcastle U	40	4
1992–93	Newcastle U	33	6
1993–94	Newcastle U	6	0
1993–94	Tranmere R	17	1
1994–95	Tranmere R	38	1
1995–96	Tranmere R	22	4
1996–97	Tranmere R	41	1
1997–98	Tranmere R	40	3
1998–99	Tranmere R	23	2
Total:		**363**	**33**

O'BRIEN, Michael — Midfield

b.Liverpool 25-9-79

Source: Trainee. *Honours:* England Schools.

1997–98	Everton	0	0
1998–99	Everton	0	0

O'BRIEN, Ronnie — Midfield

H: 5 10 W: 11 08 b.Dublin 15-1-79

Source: St Joseph's BC.

1997–98	Middlesbrough	0	0
1998–99	Middlesbrough	0	0

O'CALLAGHAN, Brian — Defender

H: 6 1 W: 12 12 b.Limerick 24-2-81

Source: Pike Rovers.

1998–99	Barnsley	0	0

O'CALLAGHAN, George — Midfield

H: 6 1 W: 10 05 b.Cork 5-9-79

Source: Trainee.

1998–99	Port Vale	4	0
Total:		**4**	**0**

O'CONNELL, Brendan — Midfield

H: 5 9 W: 12 01 b.London 12-11-66

1984–85	Portsmouth	0	0
1985–86	Portsmouth	0	0
1986–87	Exeter C	42	8
1987–88	Exeter C	39	11
1988–89	Burnley	43	13
1989–90	Burnley	21	4
1989–90	Huddersfield T (loan)	11	1
1989–90	Barnsley	11	2
1990–91	Barnsley	45	9
1991–92	Barnsley	36	4
1992–93	Barnsley	40	6
1993–94	Barnsley	38	6
1994–95	Barnsley	45	7
1995–96	Barnsley	25	1
1996–97	Charlton Ath	38	2
1997–98	Wigan Ath	17	5
1998–99	Wigan Ath	0	0
Total:		**451**	**79**

O'CONNOR, James — Midfield

H: 5 8 W: 11 00 b.Dublin 1-9-79

Source: Trainee.

1996–97	Stoke C	0	0
1997–98	Stoke C	0	0
1998–99	Stoke C	4	0
Total:		**4**	**0**

O'CONNOR, Jon — Defender

H: 6 0 W: 11 00 b.Darlington 29-10-76

Source: Trainee. *Honours:* England Youth, Under-21.

1993–94	Everton	0	0
1994–95	Everton	0	0
1995–96	Everton	4	0
1996–97	Everton	0	0
1997–98	Everton	1	0
1997–98	Sheffield U	2	0
1998–99	Sheffield U	2	0
Total:		**9**	**0**

O'CONNOR, Mark — Midfield

H: 5 8 W: 11 03 b.Rochdale 10-3-63

Source: Apprentice. *Honours:* Eire Under-21.

1980–81	QPR	0	0
1981–82	QPR	1	0
1982–83	QPR	2	0
1983–84	QPR	0	0
1983–84	Exeter C (loan)	38	1
1984–85	Bristol R	46	8
1985–86	Bristol R	34	2
1985–86	Bournemouth	9	1
1986–87	Bournemouth	43	7
1987–88	Bournemouth	37	2
1988–89	Bournemouth	33	2
1989–90	Bournemouth	6	0
1989–90	Gillingham	15	1
1990–91	Gillingham	41	3
1991–92	Gillingham	39	3
1992–93	Gillingham	21	1
1993–94	Bournemouth	45	3
1994–95	Bournemouth	13	0
1995–96	Gillingham	18	1
1996–97	Gillingham	22	0
1997–98	Gillingham	0	0
1998–99	Gillingham	0	0
Total:		**463**	**35**

O'CONNOR, Martin — Midfield

H: 5 8 W: 10 08 b.Walsall 10-12-67

Source: Bromsgrove R.

1992–93	Crystal Palace	0	0
1992–93	Walsall (loan)	10	1
1993–94	Crystal Palace	2	0
1993–94	Walsall	14	2
1994–95	Walsall	39	10
1995–96	Walsall	41	9
1996–97	Peterborough U	18	3
1996–97	Birmingham C	24	4
1997–98	Birmingham C	33	1
1998–99	Birmingham C	37	4
Total:		**218**	**34**

O'CONNOR, Richard — Forward

H: 5 9 W: 10 07 b.Wandsworth 30-8-78

Source: Trainee.

1996–97	Wimbledon	0	0
1997–98	Wimbledon	0	0
1998–99	Wimbledon	0	0

O'DONNELL, Phillip — Midfield

H: 5 10 W: 10 05 b.Bellshill 25-3-72

Source: X Form. *Honours:* Scotland Under-21, 1 full cap.

1990–91	Motherwell	12	0
1991–92	Motherwell	42	4
1992–93	Motherwell	32	4
1993–94	Motherwell	35	7
1994–95	Motherwell	3	0
1994–95	Celtic	27	6
1995–96	Celtic	15	3
1996–97	Celtic	19	2
1997–98	Celtic	14	2
1998–99	Celtic	15	2
Total:		**214**	**30**

O'DRISCOLL, Jerry — Forward

H: 6 0 W: 11 09 b.Aberdeen 4-4-78

Source: Crombie J.

1995–96	Dundee	5	1
1996–97	Dundee	21	10
1997–98	Dundee	13	1
1998–99	Dundee	1	0
Total:		**40**	**12**

O'GORMAN, Dave — Forward

H: 6 0 W: 13 00 b.Chester 20-6-72

Source: School.

1990–91	Wrexham	17	0
Hyde U, Northwich V, Barry T			
1997–98	Swansea C	34	5
1998–99	Swansea C	5	0
Total:		**56**	**5**

O'HALLORAN, Keith — Defender

H: 5 9 W: 11 06 b.Ireland 10-11-75

Source: Cherry Orchard.

1994–95	Middlesbrough	1	0
1995–96	Middlesbrough	3	0
1995–96	Scunthorpe U (loan)	7	0
1996–97	Middlesbrough	0	0
1996–97	Cardiff C (loan)	8	0
1996–97	St Johnstone	5	0
1997–98	St Johnstone	22	1
1998–99	St Johnstone	16	1
Total:		**62**	**2**

O'HANLON, Kelham — Goalkeeper

H: 6 1 W: 13 12 b.Saltburn 16-5-62

Source: Apprentice. *Honours:* Eire Under-21, 1 full cap.

1980–81	Middlesbrough	0	0
1981–82	Middlesbrough	0	0
1982–83	Middlesbrough	19	0
1983–84	Middlesbrough	30	0
1984–85	Middlesbrough	38	0
1985–86	Rotherham U	46	0
1986–87	Rotherham U	40	0
1987–88	Rotherham U	40	0
1988–89	Rotherham U	46	0
1989–90	Rotherham U	43	0
1990–91	Rotherham U	33	0
1991–92	Carlisle U	42	0
1992–93	Carlisle U	41	0
1993–94	Preston NE	23	0
1994–95	Dundee U	29	0
1995–96	Dundee U	1	0
1996–97	Dundee U	0	0
1996–97	Preston NE	13	0
1997–98	Preston NE	0	0
1998–99	Preston NE	0	0
Total:		**484**	**0**

O'KANE, John — Defender

H: 5 10 W: 12 06 b.Nottingham 15-11-74

Source: Trainee.

1992–93	Manchester U	0	0
1993–94	Manchester U	0	0
1994–95	Manchester U	0	0
1994–95	Wimbledon (loan)	0	0
1995–96	Manchester U	1	0
1996–97	Manchester U	1	0
1996–97	Bury (loan)	13	3
1997–98	Manchester U	0	0
1997–98	Bradford C (loan)	7	0
1997–98	Everton	12	0
1998–99	Everton	2	0
1998–99	Burnley (loan)	8	0
Total:		**44**	**3**

O'KEEFFE, Darren — Midfield

b.Dublin 29-8-78

Source: Trainee.

1995–96	Huddersfield T	0	0
1996–97	Huddersfield T	0	0
1997–98	Hull C	0	0
1998–99	Hull C	0	0

O'LEARY, Kristian — Defender

H: 6 0 W: 13 04 b.Port Talbot 30-8-77

Source: Trainee.

1995–96	Swansea C	1	0
1996–97	Swansea C	12	1
1997–98	Swansea C	29	0
1998–99	Swansea C	19	2
Total:		**61**	**3**

O'LOUGHLIN, John — Midfield

H: 5 8 W: 10 12 b.Letterkenny 31-1-79

Source: Bruncrana Hearts.

1997–98	Middlesbrough	0	0
1998–99	Middlesbrough	0	0

O'MARA, Paul — Defender

H: 5 9 W: 11 00 b.Dublin 23-11-80

Source: Trainee.

1997–98	Liverpool	0	0
1998–99	Liverpool	0	0

O'NEIL, John — Midfield

H: 5 7 W: 10 02 b.Bellshill 6-7-71

Source: Fir Park BC. *Honours:* Scotland Under-21.

1988–89	Dundee U	1	0
1989–90	Dundee U	10	0
1990–91	Dundee U	15	0
1991–92	Dundee U	12	0
1992–93	Dundee U	28	3
1993–94	Dundee U	12	1
1994–95	St Johnstone	27	3
1995–96	St Johnstone	34	6
1996–97	St Johnstone	29	3
1997–98	St Johnstone	30	5
1998–99	St Johnstone	33	2
Total:		**231**	**23**

O'NEILL, Jon — Forward

H: 5 11 W: 12 00 b.Glasgow 2-1-74

Source: Queen's Park BC.

1991–92	Queen's Park	25	6
1992–93	Queen's Park	27	6
1993–94	Queen's Park	39	18
1994–95	Celtic	1	0
1995–96	Bournemouth	6	0
1996–97	Bournemouth	18	1
1997–98	Bournemouth	43	3
1998–99	Bournemouth	24	3
Total:		**183**	**37**

O'NEILL, Keith — Forward

H: 6 2 W: 12 07 b.Dublin 16-2-76

Source: Trainee. *Honours:* Eire 12 full caps, 4 goals.

1994–95	Norwich C	1	0
1995–96	Norwich C	19	1
1996–97	Norwich C	26	6
1997–98	Norwich C	9	1
1998–99	Norwich C	18	1
1998–99	Middlesbrough	6	0
Total:		**79**	**9**

O'NEILL, Kris — Forward

H: 5 7 W: 10 10 b.Edinburgh 29-9-80

Source: Musselburgh J.

1998–99	Hearts	3	0
Total:		**3**	**0**

O'NEILL, Michael — Midfield

H: 5 11 W: 10 10 b.Portadown 5-7-69

Source: Coleraine. *Honours:* Northern Ireland Under-21, 31 full caps, 4 goals.

1987–88	Newcastle U	21	12
1988–89	Newcastle U	27	3
1989–90	Dundee U	18	5
1990–91	Dundee U	13	0
1991–92	Dundee U	8	4
1992–93	Dundee U	25	2
1993–94	Hibernian	36	3
1994–95	Hibernian	33	10
1995–96	Hibernian	29	6
1996–97	Coventry C	1	0
1997–98	Coventry C	4	0
1997–98	Reading (loan)	9	1
1998–99	Coventry C	0	0
1998–99	Wigan Ath	36	0
Total:		**260**	**46**

O'REGAN, Kieran — Midfield

H: 5 8 W: 10 12 b.Cork 9-11-63

Source: Tramore Ath.

1982–83	Brighton & HA	1	0
1983–84	Brighton & HA	31	1
1984–85	Brighton & HA	15	0
1985–86	Brighton & HA	15	1
1986–87	Brighton & HA	24	0
1987–88	Swindon T	26	1
1988–89	Huddersfield T	36	2
1989–90	Huddersfield T	37	3
1990–91	Huddersfield T	46	11
1991–92	Huddersfield T	39	4
1992–93	Huddersfield T	41	5
1993–94	WBA	25	2
1998–99	Halifax T	19	2
Total:		**355**	**32**

O'REILLY, Alex — Goalkeeper

b.Epping 15-9-79

Source: Trainee. *Honours:* Eire Youth, Under-21.

1998–99	West Ham U	0	0

O'SHEA, John — Defender

H: 6 3 W: 11 12 b.Waterford 30-4-81

Source: Waterford.

1998–99	Manchester U	0	0

O'SULLIVAN, Wayne — Midfield

H: 5 7 W: 10 11 b.Akrotiri 25-2-74

Source: Trainee.

1992–93	Swindon T	0	0
1993–94	Swindon T	0	0
1994–95	Swindon T	30	0
1995–96	Swindon T	34	3
1996–97	Swindon T	25	0
1997–98	Swindon T	0	0
1997–98	Cardiff C	43	2
1998–99	Cardiff C	42	2
Total:		**174**	**7**

OAKES, Andy — Goalkeeper

b.Crewe 11-1-77

1995–96	Bury	0	0
1996–97	Bury	0	0
1997–98	Bury	0	0
From Winsford U.			
1998–99	Hull C	19	0
Total:		**19**	**0**

OAKES, Michael — Goalkeeper

H: 6 2 W: 14 07 b.Northwich 30-10-73

Source: Trainee. *Honours:* England Under-21.

1991–92	Aston Villa	0	0
1992–93	Aston Villa	0	0
1993–94	Aston Villa	0	0
1993–94	Scarborough (loan)	1	0
1993–94	Tranmere R (loan)	0	0
1994–95	Aston Villa	0	0
1995–96	Aston Villa	0	0
1996–97	Aston Villa	20	0
1997–98	Aston Villa	8	0
1998–99	Aston Villa	23	0
Total:		**52**	**0**

OAKES, Scott — Midfield

H: 5 11 W: 11 12 b.Leicester 5-8-72

Source: Trainee.

1989–90	Leicester C	2	0
1990–91	Leicester C	0	0
1991–92	Leicester C	1	0
1991–92	Luton T	21	2
1992–93	Luton T	44	5
1993–94	Luton T	36	8
1994–95	Luton T	43	9
1995–96	Luton T	29	3
1996–97	Sheffield W	19	1
1997–98	Sheffield W	4	0
1998–99	Sheffield W	1	0
Total:		**200**	**28**

OAKES, Stefan — Midfield

H: 5 11 W: 12 04 b.Leicester 6-9-78

Source: Trainee.

1997–98	Leicester C	0	0
1998–99	Leicester C	3	0
Total:		**3**	**0**

OAKLEY, Matthew — Midfield

H: 5 10 W: 12 06 b.Peterborough 17-8-77

Source: Trainee. *Honours:* England Under-21.

1994–95	Southampton	1	0
1995–96	Southampton	10	0
1996–97	Southampton	28	3
1997–98	Southampton	33	1
1998–99	Southampton	22	2
Total:		**94**	**6**

OATWAY, Charlie — Midfield

H: 5 7 W: 10 10 b.Hammersmith 28-11-73

Source: Yeading.

1994–95	Cardiff C	30	0
1995–96	Cardiff C	2	0
1995–96	Torquay U	24	0
1996–97	Torquay U	41	1
1997–98	Torquay U	2	0
1997–98	Brentford	33	0
1998–99	Brentford	24	0
1998–99	Lincoln C (loan)	3	0
Total:		**159**	**1**

ODLUM, Gary — Defender

H: 5 11 W: 11 04 b.Beckenham 19-10-78

Source: Trainee.

1996–97	Wimbledon	0	0
1997–98	Wimbledon	0	0
1998–99	Wimbledon	0	0

ODUNSI, Leke — Midfield

b.Walworth 5-12-80

Source: Trainee.

1998–99	Millwall	3	0
Total:		**3**	**0**

OGRIZOVIC, Steve — Goalkeeper

H: 6 3 W: 15 00 b.Mansfield 12-9-57

Source: ONRYC.

1977–78	Chesterfield	16	0
1977–78	Liverpool	2	0
1978–79	Liverpool	0	0
1979–80	Liverpool	1	0
1980–81	Liverpool	1	0
1981–82	Liverpool	0	0
1982–83	Shrewsbury T	42	0
1983–84	Shrewsbury T	42	0
1984–85	Coventry C	42	0
1985–86	Coventry C	42	0
1986–87	Coventry C	42	1
1987–88	Coventry C	40	0
1988–89	Coventry C	38	0
1989–90	Coventry C	37	0
1990–91	Coventry C	37	0
1991–92	Coventry C	38	0
1992–93	Coventry C	33	0
1993–94	Coventry C	33	0
1994–95	Coventry C	33	0
1995–96	Coventry C	25	0
1996–97	Coventry C	38	0
1997–98	Coventry C	24	0
1998–99	Coventry C	2	0
Total:		**608**	**1**

OKAFOR, Samuel — Midfield

b.Xtian 17-3-82

1998–99	Colchester U	1	0
Total:		**1**	**0**

OLDFIELD, David — Midfield

H: 6 1 W: 13 04 b.Perth (Aus) 30-5-68

Source: Apprentice. *Honours:* England Under-21.

1986–87	Luton T	0	0
1987–88	Luton T	8	3
1988–89	Luton T	21	1
1988–89	Manchester C	11	3
1989–90	Manchester C	15	3
1989–90	Leicester C	20	5
1990–91	Leicester C	42	7
1991–92	Leicester C	41	4
1992–93	Leicester C	44	5
1993–94	Leicester C	27	4

1994–95	Leicester C	14	1
1994–95	Millwall (loan)	17	6
1995–96	Luton T	34	2
1996–97	Luton T	38	6
1997–98	Luton T	45	10
1998–99	Stoke C	46	6
Total:		**423**	**66**

OLIVER, Adam — Midfield

H: 5 9 W: 11 02 b.Sandwell 25-10-80

Source: Trainee. *Honours:* England Youth.

1998–99	WBA	1	0
Total:		**1**	**0**

OLIVER, Michael — Midfield

H: 5 10 W: 11 04 b.Middlesbrough 2-8-75

Source: Trainee.

1992–93	Middlesbrough	0	0
1993–94	Middlesbrough	0	0
1994–95	Stockport Co	13	0
1995–96	Stockport Co	9	1
1996–97	Darlington	39	9
1997–98	Darlington	39	2
1998–99	Darlington	36	1
Total:		**136**	**13**

OLOFSSON, Kjell — Forward

H: 6 2 W: 13 08 b.Gothenburg 23-7-65

1996	Moss	25	9
1996–97	Dundee U	25	12
1997–98	Dundee U	32	18
1998–99	Dundee U	34	7
Total:		**116**	**46**

OMOYIMNI, Emmanuel — Forward

H: 5 6 W: 10 07 b.Nigeria 28-12-77

Source: Trainee. *Honours:* England Schools.

1994–95	West Ham U	0	0
1995–96	West Ham U	0	0
1996–97	West Ham U	1	0
1996–97	Bournemouth (loan)	7	0
1997–98	West Ham U	5	2
1997–98	Dundee U (loan)	4	0
1998–99	West Ham U	3	0
1998–99	Leyton Orient (loan)	4	1
Total:		**24**	**3**

ONUORA, Iffy — Forward

H: 6 0 W: 13 01 b.Glasgow 28-7-67

Source: British Univ.

1989–90	Huddersfield T	20	3
1990–91	Huddersfield T	43	7
1991–92	Huddersfield T	41	8
1992–93	Huddersfield T	39	6
1993–94	Huddersfield T	22	6
1994–95	Mansfield T	14	7
1995–96	Mansfield T	14	1
1996–97	Gillingham	40	21
1997–98	Gillingham	22	2
1997–98	Swindon T	6	1
1998–99	Swindon T	43	20
Total:		**304**	**82**

ONWERE, Udo — Midfield

H: 6 0 W: 11 07 b.Hammersmith 9-11-71

Source: Trainee.

1990–91	Fulham	7	1
1991–92	Fulham	27	3
1992–93	Fulham	29	3
1993–94	Fulham	22	0
1994–95	Lincoln C	8	0
1995–96	Lincoln C	35	4
1996–97	Lincoln C	0	0
1996–97	Blackpool	9	0
1997–98	Barnet	17	0
1998–99	Barnet	19	2
Total:		**173**	**13**

OPARA, Chris-Santos — Forward

b.Oweri Imo State 21-12-81

1998–99	Colchester U	1	0
Total:		**1**	**0**

ORD, Richard — Defender

H: 6 2 W: 12 08 b.Murton 3-3-70

Source: Trainee. *Honours:* England Under-21.

1987–88	Sunderland	8	0
1988–89	Sunderland	34	1
1989–90	Sunderland	7	1
1989–90	York C (loan)	3	0
1990–91	Sunderland	14	0
1991–92	Sunderland	6	0
1992–93	Sunderland	24	0
1993–94	Sunderland	28	2
1994–95	Sunderland	33	0
1995–96	Sunderland	42	1
1996–97	Sunderland	33	2
1997–98	Sunderland	14	0
1998–99	QPR	0	0
Total:		**246**	**7**

ORLYGSSON, Toddy — Midfield

H: 5 11 W: 11 02 b.Odense 2-8-66

Source: FC Akureyi. *Honours:* Iceland 41 full caps, 7 goals.

1989–90	Nottingham F	12	1
1990–91	Nottingham F	0	0
1991–92	Nottingham F	5	0
1992–93	Nottingham F	20	1
1993–94	Stoke C	45	9
1994–95	Stoke C	38	7
1995–96	Stoke C	7	0
1995–96	Oldham Ath	16	0
1996–97	Oldham Ath	27	1
1997–98	Oldham Ath	11	0
1998–99	Oldham Ath	22	0
Total:		**203**	**19**

ORMEROD, Anthony — Midfield

H: 5 11 W: 12 00 b.Middlesbrough 31-3-79

Source: Trainee. *Honours:* England Youth.

1995–96	Middlesbrough	0	0
1996–97	Middlesbrough	0	0
1997–98	Middlesbrough	18	3
1998–99	Middlesbrough	0	0
1998–99	Carlisle U (loan)	5	0
Total:		**23**	**3**

ORMEROD, Brett — Forward

H: 5 11 W: 11 04 b.Blackburn 18-10-76

Source: Blackburn R Trainee, Accrington S.

1996–97	Blackpool	4	0
1997–98	Blackpool	9	2
1998–99	Blackpool	40	8
Total:		**53**	**10**

ORMEROD, Mark — Goalkeeper

H: 6 0 W: 11 06 b.Bournemouth 5-2-76

Source: Trainee.

1994–95	Brighton & HA	0	0
1995–96	Brighton & HA	0	0
1996–97	Brighton & HA	21	0
1997–98	Brighton & HA	30	0
1998–99	Brighton & HA	27	0
Total:		**78**	**0**

ORMSHAW, Gareth — Goalkeeper

H: 6 0 W: 12 10 b.Durban 8-7-79

Source: Ramblers.

1996–97	Crystal Palace	0	0
1997–98	Crystal Palace	0	0
1998–99	Crystal Palace	0	0

OSBORN, Mark — Midfield

b.Bletchley 18-6-81

Source: Trainee.

1998–99	Wycombe W	0	0

OSBORN, Simon — Midfield

H: 5 8 W: 11 04 b.New Addington 9-1-72

Source: Apprentice.

1989–90	Crystal Palace	0	0
1990–91	Crystal Palace	4	0
1991–92	Crystal Palace	14	2
1992–93	Crystal Palace	31	2
1993–94	Crystal Palace	6	1
1994–95	Reading	32	5
1995–96	QPR	9	1
1995–96	Wolverhampton W	21	2
1996–97	Wolverhampton W	35	5
1997–98	Wolverhampton W	24	2
1998–99	Wolverhampton W	37	2
Total:		**213**	**22**

OSBORNE, Tommy — Midfield

H: 5 8 W: 11 00 b.Dartford 5-9-79

Source: Trainee.

1998–99	Gillingham	0	0

OSMAN, Leon — Midfield

H: 5 8 W: 9 11 b.Billinge 17-5-81

Source: Trainee. *Honours:* England Schools, Youth.

1998–99	Everton	0	0

OSTENSTAD, Egil — Forward

H: 5 11 W: 13 00 b.Haugesund 2-1-72

Honours: Norway 17 full caps, 6 goals.

1990	Viking	10	1
1991	Viking	10	1
1992	Viking	20	1
1993	Viking	22	10
1994	Viking	21	6
1995	Viking	21	12
1996	Viking	24	23
1996–97	Southampton	30	9
1997–98	Southampton	29	11
1998–99	Southampton	34	7
Total:		**221**	**81**

OSTER, John — Forward

H: 5 9 W: 10 12 b.Boston 8-12-78

Source: Trainee. *Honours:* Wales Under-21, 2 full caps.

1996–97	Grimsby T	24	3

1997–98	Everton	31	1
1998–99	Everton	9	0
Total:		**64**	**4**

OSWIN, Matthew — Midfield

b.Grimsby 2-10-79

Source: Trainee.

1998–99	Grimsby T	0	0

OTTA, Walter — Midfield

b.Cordova 20-12-73

Source: Puerto Montt.

1998–99	Walsall	8	3
Total:		**8**	**3**

OVENDALE, Mark — Goalkeeper

H: 6 2 W: 13 10 b.Leicester 22-11-73

Source: Wisbech T.

1994–95	Northampton T	6	0
From Barry T.			
1997–98	Bournemouth	0	0
1998–99	Bournemouth	46	0
Total:		**52**	**0**

OVERMARS, Marc — Forward

H: 5 8 W: 11 04 b.Emst 29-3-73

Honours: Holland 50 full caps, 10 goals.

1990–91	Go Ahead	11	1
1991–92	Willem II	31	1
1992–93	Ajax	34	3
1993–94	Ajax	34	12
1994–95	Ajax	27	8
1995–96	Ajax	15	11
1996–97	Ajax	25	2
1997–98	Arsenal	32	12
1998–99	Arsenal	37	6
Total:		**246**	**56**

OWEN, Gareth — Midfield

H: 5 8 W: 12 00 b.Chester 21-10-71

Source: Trainee. *Honours:* Wales Under-21.

1989–90	Wrexham	13	0
1990–91	Wrexham	27	2
1991–92	Wrexham	36	7
1992–93	Wrexham	41	3
1993–94	Wrexham	27	3
1994–95	Wrexham	28	3
1995–96	Wrexham	19	2
1996–97	Wrexham	23	1
1997–98	Wrexham	40	7
1998–99	Wrexham	35	3
Total:		**289**	**31**

OWEN, Karl — Defender

H: 5 10 W: 10 06 b.Coventry 12-10-79

Source: Trainee.

1996–97	QPR	0	0
1997–98	QPR	0	0
1998–99	QPR	0	0

OWEN, Michael — Forward

H: 5 8 W: 11 00 b.Chester 14-12-79

Source: Trainee. *Honours:* England Schools, Youth, Under-21, 13 full caps, 4 goals.

1996–97	Liverpool	2	1
1997–98	Liverpool	36	18
1998–99	Liverpool	30	18
Total:		**68**	**37**

OWERS, Gary — Midfield

H: 5 11 W: 12 07 b.Newcastle 3-10-68

Source: Apprentice.

1986–87	Sunderland	0	0
1987–88	Sunderland	37	4
1988–89	Sunderland	38	3
1989–90	Sunderland	43	9
1990–91	Sunderland	38	1
1991–92	Sunderland	30	4
1992–93	Sunderland	33	1
1993–94	Sunderland	30	2
1994–95	Sunderland	19	1
1994–95	Bristol C	21	2
1995–96	Bristol C	37	2
1996–97	Bristol C	46	4
1997–98	Bristol C	22	1
1998–99	Notts Co	39	3
Total:		**433**	**37**

OWUSU, Ansah — Midfield

H: 5 11 W: 11 02 b.Hackney 22-11-79

Source: Trainee.

1998–99	Wimbledon	0	0

OWUSU, Lloyd — Forward

b.Slough 12-12-76

Source: Slough T.

1998–99	Brentford	46	22
Total:		**46**	**22**

PAATELAINEN, Mixu — Forward

H: 6 0 W: 13 10 b.Helsinki 3-2-67

Source: Valkeakosken Haka. *Honours:* Finland 65 full caps, 18 goals.

1987–88	Dundee U	19	9
1988–89	Dundee U	33	10
1989–90	Dundee U	31	7
1990–91	Dundee U	20	1
1991–92	Dundee U	30	6
1991–92	Aberdeen	6	1
1992–93	Aberdeen	33	16
1993–94	Aberdeen	36	6
1994–95	Bolton W	44	12
1995–96	Bolton W	15	1
1996–97	Bolton W	10	2
1997–98	Wolverhampton W	23	0
1998–99	Wolverhampton W	0	0
1998–99	Hibernian	26	12
Total:		**326**	**83**

PADOVANO, Michele — Forward

H: 5 10 W: 11 00 b.Turin 28-8-66

Honours: Italy 1 full cap.

1985–86	Asti	22	5
1986–87	Asti	2	0
1986–87	Cosenza	21	2
1987–88	Cosenza	21	7
1988–89	Cosenza	30	5
1989–90	Cosenza	31	11
1990–91	Pisa	30	11
1991–92	Napoli	27	7
1992–93	Genoa	27	9
1993–94	Reggiana	29	10
1994–95	Genoa	2	0
1994–95	Reggiana	19	7
1995–96	Juventus	21	4
1996–97	Juventus	20	8
1997–98	Juventus	1	0
1997–98	Crystal Palace	10	1
1998–99	Crystal Palace	2	0
Total:		**315**	**87**

PAGE, Robert — Defender

H: 6 0 W: 12 13 b.Llwynipia 3-9-74

Source: Trainee. *Honours:* Wales Under-21, 7 full caps.

1992–93	Watford	0	0
1993–94	Watford	4	0
1994–95	Watford	5	0
1995–96	Watford	19	0
1996–97	Watford	36	0
1997–98	Watford	41	0
1998–99	Watford	39	0
Total:		**144**	**0**

PAINTER, Rob — Forward

H: 5 10 W: 12 02 b.Wigan 26-1-71

Source: Trainee.

1987–88	Chester C	2	0
1988–89	Chester C	8	1
1989–90	Chester C	32	4
1990–91	Chester C	42	3
1991–92	Maidstone U	30	5
1991–92	Burnley	9	2
1992–93	Burnley	17	0
1993–94	Burnley	0	0
1993–94	Darlington	36	11
1994–95	Darlington	38	9
1995–96	Darlington	35	8
1996–97	Darlington	6	0
1996–97	Rochdale	27	7
1997–98	Rochdale	45	17
1998–99	Rochdale	40	6
Total:		**367**	**73**

PAKHAR (PAHARS), Marian — Forward

H: 5 8 W: 10 09 b.Latvia 5-8-76

Honours: Latvia 34 caps, 8 goals.

1994	Pardaugava Riga	17	3
1995	Skonto/Metals Riga	16	4
1995	Skonto Riga	9	8
1996	Skonto Riga	28	12
1997	Skonto Riga	22	5
1998	Skonto Riga	26	19
1998–99	Southampton	6	3
Total:		**124**	**54**

PALLISTER, Gary — Defender

H: 6 5 W: 15 02 b.Ramsgate 30-6-65

Source: Billingham T. *Honours:* England B, 22 full caps.

1984–85	Middlesbrough	0	0
1985–86	Middlesbrough	28	0
1985–86	Darlington (loan)	7	0
1986–87	Middlesbrough	44	1
1987–88	Middlesbrough	44	3
1988–89	Middlesbrough	37	1
1989–90	Middlesbrough	3	0
1989–90	Manchester U	35	3
1990–91	Manchester U	36	0
1991–92	Manchester U	40	1
1992–93	Manchester U	42	1
1993–94	Manchester U	41	1
1994–95	Manchester U	42	2
1995–96	Manchester U	21	1
1996–97	Manchester U	27	3
1997–98	Manchester U	33	0
1998–99	Middlesbrough	26	0
Total:		**506**	**17**

PALMER, Carlton — Midfield

H: 6 2 W: 13 00 b.Oldbury 5-12-65

Source: Trainee. *Honours:* England Under-21, B, 18 full caps, 1 goal.

1984–85	WBA	0	0
1985–86	WBA	20	0
1986–87	WBA	37	1
1987–88	WBA	38	3
1988–89	WBA	26	0
1988–89	Sheffield W	13	1
1989–90	Sheffield W	34	0
1990–91	Sheffield W	45	2
1991–92	Sheffield W	42	5
1992–93	Sheffield W	34	1
1993–94	Sheffield W	37	5
1994–95	Leeds U	39	3
1995–96	Leeds U	35	2
1996–97	Leeds U	28	0
1997–98	Leeds U	0	0
1997–98	Southampton	26	3
1998–99	Southampton	19	0
1998–99	Nottingham F	13	0
Total:		**486**	**26**

PALMER, Ryan — Defender

H: 6 1 W: 11 02 b.Dulwich 2-2-80

1998–99	Fulham	0	0

PALMER, Steve — Midfield

H: 6 1 W: 13 05 b.Brighton 31-3-68

Source: Cambridge Univ. *Honours:* England Schools.

1989–90	Ipswich T	5	0
1990–91	Ipswich T	23	1
1991–92	Ipswich T	23	0
1992–93	Ipswich T	7	0
1993–94	Ipswich T	36	1
1994–95	Ipswich T	12	0
1995–96	Ipswich T	5	0
1995–96	Watford	35	1
1996–97	Watford	41	2
1997–98	Watford	41	2
1998–99	Watford	41	2
Total:		**269**	**9**

PANAYI, James — Defender

H: 6 1 W: 13 12 b.Hammersmith 24-1-80

Source: Trainee.

1998–99	Watford	0	0

PARKER, Garry — Midfield

H: 6 0 W: 13 03 b.Oxford 7-9-65

Source: Apprentice. *Honours:* England Youth, Under-21, B.

1982–83	Luton T	1	0
1983–84	Luton T	13	2
1984–85	Luton T	20	1
1985–86	Luton T	8	0
1985–86	Hull C	12	0
1986–87	Hull C	38	0
1987–88	Hull C	34	8
1987–88	Nottingham F	2	0
1988–89	Nottingham F	22	7
1989–90	Nottingham F	37	6
1990–91	Nottingham F	36	3
1991–92	Nottingham F	6	1
1991–92	Aston Villa	25	1
1992–93	Aston Villa	37	9
1993–94	Aston Villa	19	2
1994–95	Aston Villa	14	1
1994–95	Leicester C	14	2
1995–96	Leicester C	40	3
1996–97	Leicester C	31	2
1997–98	Leicester C	22	3
1998–99	Leicester C	7	0
Total:		**438**	**51**

PARKER, Keigan — Forward

H: 5 7 W: 10 05 b.Livingston 8-6-82

Source: St Johnstone BC.

1998–99	St Johnstone	2	0
Total:		**2**	**0**

PARKER, Scott — Midfield

H: 5 9 W: 11 00 b.Lambeth 13-10-80

Source: Trainee. *Honours:* England Schools, Youth.

1997–98	Charlton Ath	3	0
1998–99	Charlton Ath	4	0
Total:		**7**	**0**

PARKIN, Brian — Goalkeeper

H: 6 4 W: 14 02 b.Birkenhead 12-10-65

Source: Local.

1982–83	Oldham Ath	0	0
1983–84	Oldham Ath	5	0
1984–85	Oldham Ath	1	0
1984–85	Crewe Alex (loan)	12	0
1985–86	Crewe Alex	39	0
1986–87	Crewe Alex	44	0
1987–88	Crewe Alex	3	0
1987–88	Crystal Palace (loan)	0	0
1988–89	Crystal Palace	19	0
1989–90	Crystal Palace	1	0
1989–90	Bristol R	30	0

1990–91	Bristol R	39	0
1991–92	Bristol R	43	0
1992–93	Bristol R	26	0
1993–94	Bristol R	43	0
1994–95	Bristol R	40	0
1995–96	Bristol R	20	0
1996–97	Wycombe W	24	0
1997–98	Wycombe W	1	0
1998–99	Wycombe W	0	0
1998–99	Notts Co	1	0
Total:		**391**	**0**

PARKIN, Jonathan — Forward

H: 6 4 W: 13 07 b.Barnsley 30-12-81

Source: Scholarship.

1998–99	Barnsley	2	0
Total:		**2**	**0**

PARKIN, Sam — Forward

H: 6 1 W: 12 06 b.Roehampton 14-3-81

Honours: England Schools.

1998–99	Chelsea	0	0

PARKIN, Steve — Defender

H: 5 6 W: 11 01 b.Mansfield 7-11-65

Source: Apprentice. *Honours:* England Schools, Youth, Under-21.

1982–83	Stoke C	2	0
1983–84	Stoke C	1	0
1984–85	Stoke C	13	1
1985–86	Stoke C	12	1
1986–87	Stoke C	38	0
1987–88	Stoke C	43	3
1988–89	Stoke C	4	0
1989–90	WBA	14	1
1990–91	WBA	25	1
1991–92	WBA	9	0
1992–93	Mansfield T	16	0
1993–94	Mansfield T	23	1
1994–95	Mansfield T	22	1
1995–96	Mansfield T	26	1
1996–97	Mansfield T	0	0
1997–98	Mansfield T	0	0
1998–99	Mansfield T	0	0
Total:		**248**	**10**

PARKINSON, Andy — Forward

H: 5 8 W: 10 12 b.Liverpool 27-5-79

Source: Liverpool Trainee.

1996–97	Tranmere R	0	0
1997–98	Tranmere R	18	1
1998–99	Tranmere R	29	2
Total:		**47**	**3**

PARKINSON, Gary — Defender

H: 5 10 W: 11 08 b.Middlesbrough 10-1-68

Source: Everton Amateur.

1985–86	Middlesbrough	0	0
1986–87	Middlesbrough	46	0
1987–88	Middlesbrough	38	0
1988–89	Middlesbrough	36	2
1989–90	Middlesbrough	41	2
1990–91	Middlesbrough	10	1
1991–92	Middlesbrough	27	0
1992–93	Middlesbrough	4	0
1992–93	Southend U (loan)	6	0
1992–93	Bolton W	2	0
1993–94	Bolton W	1	0
1993–94	Burnley	20	1
1994–95	Burnley	43	2
1995–96	Burnley	29	0
1996–97	Burnley	43	1
1997–98	Preston NE	45	5
1998–99	Preston NE	27	1
Total:		**418**	**15**

PARKINSON, Joe — Midfield

H: 6 0 W: 15 05 b.Eccles 11-6-71

Source: Trainee.

1988–89	Wigan Ath	12	1
1989–90	Wigan Ath	33	2
1990–91	Wigan Ath	25	0
1991–92	Wigan Ath	36	3
1992–93	Wigan Ath	13	0
1993–94	Bournemouth	30	1
1993–94	Everton	0	0
1994–95	Everton	34	0
1995–96	Everton	28	3
1996–97	Everton	28	0
1997–98	Everton	0	0
1998–99	Everton	0	0
Total:		**239**	**10**

PARKINSON, Phil — Midfield

H: 6 0 W: 12 09 b.Chorley 1-12-67

Source: Apprentice.

1985–86	Southampton	0	0
1986–87	Southampton	0	0
1987–88	Southampton	0	0
1987–88	Bury	8	1
1988–89	Bury	39	0
1989–90	Bury	22	2
1990–91	Bury	44	2
1991–92	Bury	32	0
1992–93	Reading	39	4
1993–94	Reading	42	3
1994–95	Reading	31	0
1995–96	Reading	42	0
1996–97	Reading	24	1

1997–98	Reading	37	0
1998–99	Reading	42	5
Total:		**402**	**18**

PARKS, Tony — Goalkeeper

H: 5 10 W: 11 05 b.Hackney 28-1-63

Source: Apprentice.

1980–81	Tottenham H	0	0
1981–82	Tottenham H	2	0
1982–83	Tottenham H	1	0
1983–84	Tottenham H	16	0
1984–85	Tottenham H	0	0
1985–86	Tottenham H	0	0
1986–87	Tottenham H	2	0
1986–87	Oxford U (loan)	5	0
1987–88	Tottenham H	16	0
1987–88	Gillingham (loan)	2	0
1988–89	Brentford	33	0
1989–90	Brentford	37	0
1990–91	Brentford	1	0
1990–91	QPR (loan)	0	0
1990–91	Fulham	2	0
1991–92	West Ham U	6	0
1992–93	Stoke C	2	0
1992–93	Falkirk	15	0
1993–94	Falkirk	41	0
1994–95	Falkirk	28	0
1995–96	Falkirk	28	0
1996–97	Blackpool	0	0
1997–98	Burnley	0	0
1997–98	Doncaster R (loan)	6	0
1998–99	Burnley	0	0
From Barrow			
1998–99	Scarborough	15	0
Total:		**258**	**0**

PARLOUR, Ray — Midfield

H: 5 10 W: 11 12 b.Romford 7-3-73

Source: Trainee. *Honours:* England Under-21, B, 3 full caps.

1990–91	Arsenal	0	0
1991–92	Arsenal	6	1
1992–93	Arsenal	21	1
1993–94	Arsenal	27	2
1994–95	Arsenal	30	0
1995–96	Arsenal	22	0
1996–97	Arsenal	30	2
1997–98	Arsenal	34	5
1998–99	Arsenal	35	6
Total:		**205**	**17**

PARRISH, Sean — Midfield

H: 5 10 W: 11 08 b.Wrexham 14-3-72

Source: Trainee.

1989–90	Shrewsbury T	2	0
1990–91	Shrewsbury T	1	0
From Telford U			
1994–95	Doncaster R	25	3
1995–96	Doncaster R	41	5
1996–97	Northampton T	39	8
1997–98	Northampton T	12	1
1998–99	Northampton T	33	1
Total:		**153**	**18**

PARSONS, Matthew — Defender

H: 6 1 W: 12 07 b.Truro 29-2-80

Source: Trainee.

1998–99	Plymouth Arg	0	0

PARTRIDGE, David — Midfield

b.Westminster 26-11-78

Source: Trainee.

1997–98	West Ham U	0	0
1998–99	West Ham U	0	0
1998–99	Dundee U	1	0
Total:		**1**	**0**

PARTRIDGE, Richie — Midfield

H: 5 8 W: 10 10 b.Dublin 12-9-80

Source: Trainee.

1998–99	Liverpool	0	0

PARTRIDGE, Scott — Forward

H: 5 9 W: 11 02 b.Leicester 13-10-74

Source: Trainee.

1992–93	Bradford C	4	0
1993–94	Bradford C	1	0
1993–94	Bristol C	9	4
1994–95	Bristol C	33	2
1995–96	Bristol C	9	1
1995–96	Torquay U (loan)	5	2
1995–96	Plymouth Arg (loan)	7	2
1995–96	Scarborough (loan)	7	0
1996–97	Bristol C	6	0
1996–97	Cardiff C	15	0
1997–98	Cardiff C	22	2
1997–98	Torquay U	5	0
1998–99	Torquay U	29	12
1998–99	Brentford	14	7
Total:		**166**	**32**

PASCOLO, Marco — Goalkeeper

H: 6 2 W: 14 04 b.Sion 2-5-66

Honours: Switzerland 44 full caps.

1986–87	Sion	1	0
1987–88	Sion	13	0
1988–89	Sion	3	1
1989–90	Neuchatel Xamax	18	0

1990–91	Neuchatel Xamax	34	0
1991–92	Servette	35	0
1992–93	Servette	36	0
1993–94	Servette	35	0
1994–95	Servette	22	0
1995–96	Servette	35	0
1996–97	Cagliari	14	0
1997–98	Nottingham F	5	0
1998–99	Nottingham F	0	0
Total:		**251**	**1**

PASCUAL, Bernard — Defender

H: 5 10 W: 11 12 b.Aubervilliers 10-4-67

Source: From Chantilly, Beauvais

1993–94	Le Havre	32	0
1994–95	Le Havre	26	0
1995–96	Le Havre	36	0
1996–97	Le Havre	15	0
1997–98	Le Havre	6	0
1998–99	Dundee U	16	0
Total:		**131**	**0**

PATERSON, James — Midfield

H: 5 11 W: 12 13 b.Bellshill 25-9-79

Source: Dundee U BC.

1996–97	Dundee U	0	0
1997–98	Dundee U	0	0
1998–99	Dundee U	15	0
Total:		**15**	**0**

PATERSON, Jamie — Midfield

H: 5 3 W: 10 02 b.Dumfries 26-4-73

Source: Trainee.

1990–91	Halifax T	6	1
1991–92	Halifax T	15	2
1992–93	Halifax T	23	2
1993–94	Halifax T	42	13
1994–95	Falkirk	4	0
1995–96	Scunthorpe U	26	2
1996–97	Scunthorpe U	29	0
1997–98	Scunthorpe U	0	0
1998–99	Halifax T	24	10
Total:		**169**	**30**

PATERSON, Scott — Defender

H: 5 11 W: 11 09 b.Aberdeen 13-5-72

Source: Cove Rangers.

1991–92	Liverpool	0	0
1992–93	Liverpool	0	0
1993–94	Liverpool	0	0
1994–95	Bristol C	3	0
1995–96	Bristol C	18	1
1996–97	Bristol C	19	0
1997–98	Bristol C	10	0
1997–98	Cardiff C (loan)	5	0
1998–99	Carlisle U	19	1
Total:		**74**	**2**

PATES, Bradley — Midfield

H: 5 9 W: 11 02 b.Burnley 21-12-79

1998–99	Macclesfield T	0	0

PATON, Eric — Midfield

H: 5 8 W: 11 11 b.Glasgow 1-8-78

Source: Hutchison Vale BC.

1994–95	Hibernian	0	0
1995–96	Hibernian	0	0
1996–97	Hibernian	0	0
1997–98	Hibernian	0	0
1998–99	Hibernian	4	0
Total:		**4**	**0**

PATTERSON, Andrew — Forward

H: 5 10 W: 10 04 b.Kirkaldy 26-11-80

Source: Trainee.

1997–98	Bradford C	0	0
1998–99	Bradford C	0	0

PATTERSON, Darren — Defender

H: 6 1 W: 12 10 b.Belfast 15-10-69

Source: Trainee. *Honours:* Northern Ireland Under-21, 17 full caps, 1 goal.

1988–89	WBA	0	0
1989–90	Wigan Ath	29	1
1990–91	Wigan Ath	28	4
1991–92	Wigan Ath	40	1
1992–93	Crystal Palace	0	0
1993–94	Crystal Palace	0	0
1994–95	Crystal Palace	22	1
1995–96	Luton T	23	0
1996–97	Luton T	10	0
1996–97	Preston NE (loan)	2	0
1997–98	Luton T	23	0
1998–99	Dundee U	19	0
Total:		**196**	**7**

PATTERSON, Mark — Midfield

H: 5 8 W: 11 07 b.Darwen 24-5-65

Source: Apprentice.

1983–84	Blackburn R	29	7
1984–85	Blackburn R	9	0
1985–86	Blackburn R	26	10
1986–87	Blackburn R	24	1
1987–88	Blackburn R	13	2
1988–89	Preston NE	42	15

Patterson, Mark

1989–90	Preston NE	13	4
1989–90	Bury	20	4
1990–91	Bury	22	6
1990–91	Bolton W	19	2
1991–92	Bolton W	36	2
1992–93	Bolton W	37	2
1993–94	Bolton W	35	1
1994–95	Bolton W	26	3
1995–96	Bolton W	16	1
1995–96	Sheffield U	21	2
1996–97	Sheffield U	35	1
1996–97	Southend U (loan)	4	0
1997–98	Sheffield U	18	1
1997–98	Bury	18	2
1998–99	Bury	13	0
1998–99	Blackpool (loan)	7	0
1998–99	Southend U	5	0
Total:		**488**	**66**

PATTERSON, Mark — Defender

H: 5 9 W: 12 04 b.Leeds 13-9-68

Source: Trainee.

1986–87	Carlisle U	6	0
1987–88	Carlisle U	16	0
1987–88	Derby Co	0	0
1988–89	Derby Co	1	0
1989–90	Derby Co	9	0
1990–91	Derby Co	11	1
1991–92	Derby Co	12	2
1992–93	Derby Co	18	0
1993–94	Plymouth Arg	41	0
1994–95	Plymouth Arg	38	3
1995–96	Plymouth Arg	43	0
1996–97	Plymouth Arg	12	0
1997–98	Plymouth Arg	0	0
1997–98	Gillingham	23	0
1998–99	Gillingham	42	2
Total:		**272**	**8**

PATTON, Aaron — Midfield

H: 5 7 W: 12 11 b.London 27-2-79

Source: Trainee.

1997–98	Wycombe W	1	0
1998–99	Wycombe W	0	0
Total:		**1**	**0**

PAUL, Mark — Forward

H: 5 6 W: 10 10 b.Peterborough 3-1-79

Source: Kings Lynn.

1998–99	Southampton	0	0

PAYNE, Derek — Midfield

H: 5 6 W: 10 08 b.Edgware 26-4-67

Source: Kingsbury T, Burnham, Hayes.

1991–92	Barnet	14	1
1992–93	Barnet	37	5
1993–94	Southend U	35	0
1994–95	Watford	24	0
1995–96	Watford	12	1
1996–97	Peterborough U	36	2
1997–98	Peterborough U	37	2
1998–99	Peterborough U	9	0
Total:		**204**	**11**

PAYNE, Steve — Defender

H: 5 11 W: 12 05 b.Castleford 1-8-75

Source: Trainee.

1993–94	Huddersfield T	0	0
1994–95	Huddersfield T	0	0
1995–96	Huddersfield T	0	0
1996–97	Huddersfield T	0	0
1997–98	Macclesfield T	39	0
1998–99	Macclesfield T	38	2
Total:		**77**	**2**

PAYTON, Andy — Forward

H: 5 9 W: 11 13 b.Burnley 23-10-67

Source: Apprentice.

1985–86	Hull C	0	0
1986–87	Hull C	2	0
1987–88	Hull C	21	2
1988–89	Hull C	28	4
1989–90	Hull C	39	17
1990–91	Hull C	43	25
1991–92	Hull C	10	7
1991–92	Middlesbrough	19	3
1992–93	Celtic	29	13
1993–94	Celtic	7	2
1993–94	Barnsley	25	12
1994–95	Barnsley	43	12
1995–96	Barnsley	40	17
1996–97	Huddersfield T	38	17
1997–98	Huddersfield T	5	0
1997–98	Burnley	19	9
1998–99	Burnley	40	19
Total:		**408**	**159**

PEACOCK, Darren — Defender

H: 6 1 W: 12 12 b.Bristol 3-2-68

Source: Apprentice.

1984–85	Newport Co	0	0
1985–86	Newport Co	18	0
1986–87	Newport Co	5	0
1987–88	Newport Co	5	0

1988–89	Hereford U	8	0
1989–90	Hereford U	36	3
1990–91	Hereford U	15	1
1990–91	QPR	19	0
1991–92	QPR	39	1
1992–93	QPR	38	2
1993–94	QPR	30	3
1993–94	Newcastle U	9	0
1994–95	Newcastle U	35	1
1995–96	Newcastle U	34	0
1996–97	Newcastle U	35	1
1997–98	Newcastle U	20	0
1998–99	Blackburn R	30	1
Total:		**376**	**13**

PEACOCK, Gavin — Midfield

H: 5 8 W: 11 08 b.Eltham 18-11-67

Source: Apprentice. *Honours:* England Schools, Youth, Football League.

1984–85	QPR	0	0
1985–86	QPR	0	0
1986–87	QPR	12	1
1987–88	QPR	5	0
1987–88	Gillingham	26	2
1988–89	Gillingham	44	9
1989–90	Bournemouth	41	4
1990–91	Bournemouth	15	4
1990–91	Newcastle U	27	7
1991–92	Newcastle U	46	16
1992–93	Newcastle U	32	12
1993–94	Chelsea	37	8
1994–95	Chelsea	38	4
1995–96	Chelsea	28	5
1996–97	Chelsea	0	0
1996–97	QPR	27	5
1997–98	QPR	39	9
1998–99	QPR	42	8
Total:		**459**	**94**

PEACOCK, Lee — Forward

H: 6 1 W: 13 12 b.Paisley 9-10-76

Source: Trainee.

1993–94	Carlisle U	1	0
1994–95	Carlisle U	7	0
1995–96	Carlisle U	22	2
1996–97	Carlisle U	44	9
1997–98	Carlisle U	2	0
1997–98	Mansfield T	32	5
1998–99	Mansfield T	45	17
Total:		**153**	**33**

PEACOCK, Richard — Midfield

H: 5 10 W: 11 05 b.Sheffield 29-10-72

Source: Sheffield FC.

1993–94	Hull C	11	1
1994–95	Hull C	37	5
1995–96	Hull C	45	7
1996–97	Hull C	40	4
1997–98	Hull C	27	2
1998–99	Hull C	14	2
1998–99	Lincoln C	10	0
Total:		**184**	**21**

PEAD, Craig — Midfield

H: 5 9 W: 11 06 b.Bromsgrove 15-9-81

Source: Trainee. *Honours:* England Youth.

1998–99	Coventry C	0	0

PEAKE, Jason — Midfield

H: 5 11 W: 12 13 b.Leicester 29-9-71

Source: Trainee. *Honours:* England Schools, Youth.

1989–90	Leicester C	0	0
1990–91	Leicester C	8	1
1991–92	Leicester C	0	0
1991–92	Hartlepool U (loan)	6	1
1992–93	Halifax T	33	1
1993–94	Rochdale	10	0
1994–95	Rochdale	39	2
1995–96	Rochdale	46	4
1996–97	Brighton & HA	30	1
1997–98	Brighton & HA	0	0
1997–98	Bury	6	0
1998–99	Rochdale	38	5
Total:		**216**	**15**

PEARCE, Andy — Defender

H: 6 4 W: 14 11 b.Bradford-on-Avon 20-4-66

Source: Halesowen T.

1990–91	Coventry C	11	1
1991–92	Coventry C	36	2
1992–93	Coventry C	24	1
1993–94	Sheffield W	32	3
1994–95	Sheffield W	34	0
1995–96	Sheffield W	3	0
1995–96	Wimbledon	7	0
1996–97	Wimbledon	0	0
1997–98	Wimbledon	0	0
1998–99	Wimbledon	0	0
Total:		**147**	**7**

PEARCE, Dennis — Defender

H: 5 9 W: 11 00 b.Wolverhampton 10-9-74

Source: Trainee.

1993–94	Aston Villa	0	0
1994–95	Aston Villa	0	0
1995–96	Wolverhampton W	5	0
1996–97	Wolverhampton W	4	0

1997–98	Notts Co	38	2
1998–99	Notts Co	33	1
Total:		**80**	**3**

PEARCE, Greg — Midfield

H: 5 9 W: 10 09 b.Bolton 26-5-80

Source: Trainee.

1997–98	Chesterfield	0	0
1998–99	Chesterfield	1	0
Total:		**1**	**0**

PEARCE, Ian — Defender

H: 6 3 W: 14 04 b.Bury St Edmunds 7-5-74

Source: School. *Honours:* England Youth, Under-21.

1990–91	Chelsea	1	0
1991–92	Chelsea	2	0
1992–93	Chelsea	1	0
1993–94	Chelsea	0	0
1993–94	Blackburn R	5	1
1994–95	Blackburn R	28	0
1995–96	Blackburn R	12	1
1996–97	Blackburn R	12	0
1997–98	Blackburn R	5	0
1997–98	West Ham U	30	1
1998–99	West Ham U	33	2
Total:		**129**	**5**

PEARCE, Stuart — Defender

H: 5 10 W: 12 06 b.Shepherd's Bush 24-4-62

Source: Wealdstone. *Honours:* England Under-21, 76 full caps, 4 goals.

1983–84	Coventry C	23	0
1984–85	Coventry C	28	4
1985–86	Nottingham F	30	1
1986–87	Nottingham F	39	6
1987–88	Nottingham F	34	5
1988–89	Nottingham F	36	6
1989–90	Nottingham F	34	5
1990–91	Nottingham F	33	11
1991–92	Nottingham F	30	5
1992–93	Nottingham F	23	2
1993–94	Nottingham F	42	6
1994–95	Nottingham F	36	8
1995–96	Nottingham F	31	3
1996–97	Nottingham F	33	5
1997–98	Newcastle U	25	0
1998–99	Newcastle U	12	0
Total:		**489**	**67**

PEARCEY, Jason — Goalkeeper

H: 6 1 W: 13 12 b.Leamington Spa 23-7-71

Source: Trainee.

1988–89	Mansfield T	1	0
1989–90	Mansfield T	5	0
1990–91	Mansfield T	4	0
1991–92	Mansfield T	22	0
1992–93	Mansfield T	33	0
1993–94	Mansfield T	9	0
1994–95	Mansfield T	3	0
1994–95	Grimsby T	3	0
1995–96	Grimsby T	2	0
1996–97	Grimsby T	40	0
1997–98	Grimsby T	4	0
1998–99	Brentford	17	0
Total:		**143**	**0**

PEARSON, Nigel — Defender

H: 6 1 W: 14 01 b.Nottingham 21-8-63

Source: Heanor T.

1981–82	Shrewsbury T	0	0
1982–83	Shrewsbury T	39	1
1983–84	Shrewsbury T	26	0
1984–85	Shrewsbury T	0	0
1985–86	Shrewsbury T	35	1
1986–87	Shrewsbury T	42	3
1987–88	Shrewsbury T	11	0
1987–88	Sheffield W	19	2
1988–89	Sheffield W	37	2
1989–90	Sheffield W	33	1
1990–91	Sheffield W	39	6
1991–92	Sheffield W	31	2
1992–93	Sheffield W	16	1
1993–94	Sheffield W	5	0
1994–95	Middlesbrough	33	3
1995–96	Middlesbrough	36	0
1996–97	Middlesbrough	18	0
1997–98	Middlesbrough	29	2
1998–99	Middlesbrough	0	0
Total:		**449**	**24**

PEDERSEN, Erik — Defender

b.Porsgrunn Norway 11-10-67

1995	Viking	23	2
1996	Viking	23	3
1996–97	Dundee U	25	0
1997–98	Dundee U	32	0
1998–99	Dundee U	6	0
Total:		**109**	**5**

PEDERSEN, Per — Forward

H: 5 11 W: 13 00 b.Aalborg 30-3-69

Honours: Denmark 7 full caps, 6 goals.

1987	Odense	8	0
1988	Odense	11	7
1989	Odense	3	1
1990	Odense	22	8
1991	Lyngby	18	9
1991–92	Lyngby	22	10

1992–93	Lyngby	14	6
1993–94	Lyngby	17	3
1994–95	Lyngby	25	10
1995–96	Odense	32	16
1996–97	Odense	17	11
1996–97	Blackburn R	11	1
1997–98	Blackburn R	0	0
1998–99	Blackburn R	0	0
Total:		**200**	**82**

PEDERSEN, Tore — Defender

b.Fredrikstad 29-9-69

Honours: Norway 41 full caps.

1990	IFK Gothenburg	18	0
1991	IFK Gothenburg	25	0
1992	IFK Gothenburg	21	0
1993	Brann	22	0
1993–94	Oldham Ath	10	0
1994	Brann	1	0
Sanfrecce			
1995–96	St Pauli	12	0
1996–97	St Pauli	25	0
1997–98	Blackburn R	5	0
1998–99	Blackburn R	0	0
Total:		**139**	**0**

PEER, Dean — Midfield

H: 6 2 W: 12 04 b.Stourbridge 8-8-69

Source: Trainee.

1986–87	Birmingham C	2	0
1987–88	Birmingham C	0	0
1988–89	Birmingham C	17	1
1989–90	Birmingham C	27	3
1990–91	Birmingham C	40	2
1991–92	Birmingham C	21	1
1992–93	Birmingham C	13	1
1992–93	Mansfield T (loan)	10	0
1993–94	Birmingham C	0	0
1993–94	Walsall	33	8
1994–95	Walsall	12	0
1995–96	Northampton T	42	1
1996–97	Northampton T	21	1
1997–98	Northampton T	30	2
1998–99	Northampton T	26	1
Total:		**294**	**21**

PELANTI, Simone — Midfield

b.Italy 21-1-81

Source: Fiorentina.

1998–99	Southampton	0	0

PEMBERTON, John — Defender

H: 5 11 W: 11 09 b.Oldham 18-11-64

Source: Chadderton.

1984–85	Rochdale	1	0
1984–85	Crewe Alex	6	0
1985–86	Crewe Alex	41	0
1986–87	Crewe Alex	43	0
1987–88	Crewe Alex	31	1
1987–88	Crystal Palace	2	0
1988–89	Crystal Palace	42	1
1989–90	Crystal Palace	34	1
1990–91	Sheffield U	21	0
1991–92	Sheffield U	20	0
1992–93	Sheffield U	19	0
1993–94	Sheffield U	8	0
1993–94	Leeds U	9	0
1994–95	Leeds U	27	0
1995–96	Leeds U	17	0
1996–97	Leeds U	0	0
1997–98	Crewe Alex	1	0
1998–99	Crewe Alex	0	0
Total:		**322**	**3**

PEMBERTON, Martin — Midfield

H: 5 11 W: 11 08 b.Bradford 1-2-76

Source: Trainee.

1994–95	Oldham Ath	0	0
1995–96	Oldham Ath	2	0
1996–97	Oldham Ath	3	0
1996–97	Doncaster R	9	1
1997–98	Doncaster R	26	1
1997–98	Scunthorpe U	6	0
1998–99	Hartlepool U	4	0
Total:		**50**	**2**

PEMBRIDGE, Mark — Midfield

H: 5 7 W: 12 03 b.Merthyr Tydfil 28-11-70

Source: Trainee. *Honours:* Wales Under-21, B, 33 full caps, 5 goals.

1989–90	Luton T	0	0
1990–91	Luton T	18	1
1991–92	Luton T	42	5
1992–93	Derby Co	42	8
1993–94	Derby Co	41	11
1994–95	Derby Co	27	9
1995–96	Sheffield W	25	1
1996–97	Sheffield W	34	6
1997–98	Sheffield W	34	4
1998–99	Sheffield W	0	0
Total:		**263**	**45**

PENDER, John — Defender

H: 6 2 W: 13 05 b.Luton 19-11-63

Source: Apprentice. *Honours:* Eire Youth, Under-21.

1981–82	Wolverhampton W	8	0
1982–83	Wolverhampton W	39	1
1983–84	Wolverhampton W	34	1
1984–85	Wolverhampton W	36	1
1985–86	Charlton Ath	38	0
1986–87	Charlton Ath	1	0
1987–88	Charlton Ath	2	0
1987–88	Bristol C	28	2
1988–89	Bristol C	45	1
1989–90	Bristol C	10	0
1990–91	Bristol C	0	0
1990–91	Burnley	40	0
1991–92	Burnley	39	3
1992–93	Burnley	44	4
1993–94	Burnley	42	1
1994–95	Burnley	5	0
1995–96	Burnley	1	0
1995–96	Wigan Ath	41	1
1996–97	Wigan Ath	29	0
1997–98	Rochdale	14	0
1998–99	Rochdale	0	0
Total:		**496**	**15**

PENNANT, Jermaine — Midfield

b.Nottingham 15-1-83

Honours: England Schools.

1998–99	Notts Co	0	0
1998–99	Arsenal	0	0

PENNEY, David — Midfield

H: 5 9 W: 12 04 b.Wakefield 17-8-64

Source: Pontefract.

1985–86	Derby Co	0	0
1986–87	Derby Co	1	0
1987–88	Derby Co	9	0
1988–89	Derby Co	9	0
1989–90	Oxford U	29	2
1990–91	Oxford U	9	1
1990–91	Swansea C (loan)	12	3
1991–92	Oxford U	23	4
1992–93	Oxford U	33	6
1993–94	Oxford U	16	2
1993–94	Swansea C (loan)	11	2
1994–95	Swansea C	35	5
1995–96	Swansea C	29	0
1996–97	Swansea C	44	13
1997–98	Cardiff C	34	5
1998–99	Cardiff C	1	0
Total:		**295**	**43**

PENNOCK, Adrian — Midfield

H: 6 1 W: 13 05 b.Ipswich 27-3-71

Source: Trainee.

1989–90	Norwich C	1	0
1990–91	Norwich C	0	0
1991–92	Norwich C	0	0
1992–93	Bournemouth	43	1
1993–94	Bournemouth	40	3
1994–95	Bournemouth	31	5
1995–96	Bournemouth	17	0
1996–97	Bournemouth	0	0
1996–97	Gillingham	26	2
1997–98	Gillingham	20	0
1998–99	Gillingham	40	0
Total:		**218**	**11**

PENRICE, Gary — Forward

H: 5 8 W: 12 10 b.Bristol 23-3-64

Source: Bristol C Apprentice.

1984–85	Bristol R	5	1
1985–86	Bristol R	39	5
1986–87	Bristol R	43	7
1987–88	Bristol R	46	18
1988–89	Bristol R	43	20
1989–90	Bristol R	12	3
1989–90	Watford	29	13
1990–91	Watford	14	5
1990–91	Aston Villa	12	0
1991–92	Aston Villa	8	1
1991–92	QPR	19	3
1992–93	QPR	15	6
1993–94	QPR	26	8
1994–95	QPR	19	3
1995–96	QPR	3	0
1995–96	Watford	7	1
1996–97	Watford	32	1
1997–98	Bristol R	40	5
1998–99	Bristol R	26	1
Total:		**438**	**101**

PEPPER, Carl — Defender

H: 5 11 W: 11 00 b.Darlington 26-7-80

Source: Trainee.

1998–99	Darlington	6	0
Total:		**6**	**0**

PEPPER, Nigel — Midfield

H: 5 10 W: 11 13 b.Rotherham 25-4-68

Source: Apprentice.

1985–86	Rotherham U	7	0
1986–87	Rotherham U	2	0
1987–88	Rotherham U	15	0
1988–89	Rotherham U	2	0

1989–90	Rotherham U	19	1
1990–91	York C	39	3
1991–92	York C	35	4
1992–93	York C	34	8
1993–94	York C	23	0
1994–95	York C	35	4
1995–96	York C	40	8
1996–97	York C	29	12
1996–97	Bradford C	11	5
1997–98	Bradford C	32	5
1998–99	Bradford C	9	1
1998–99	Aberdeen	10	0
Total:		**342**	**51**

PERCASSI, Luca — Midfield

H: 5 9 W: 11 00 b.Milan 25-8-80

1997–98	Atalanta	0	0
1998–99	Chelsea	0	0

PEREIRA, Mauro — Midfield

b.Lisbon 16-6-76

Source: Casa Pia.

1997–98	Tranmere R	0	0
1998–99	Tranmere R	0	0

PEREZ, Lionel — Goalkeeper

H: 5 11 W: 13 04 b.Bagnols Coze 24-4-67

1989–90	Nimes	3	0
1990–91	Nimes	34	0
1991–92	Nimes	38	0
1992–93	Nimes	36	0
1993–94	Bordeaux	9	0
1994–95	Bordeaux	7	0
1995–96	Bordeaux	0	0
1996–97	Sunderland	29	0
1997–98	Sunderland	46	0
1998–99	Newcastle U	0	0
Total:		**202**	**0**

PEREZ, Sebastian — Defender

H: 5 10 W: 12 00 b.Saint-Chamond 24-11-73

1993–94	St Etienne	12	0
1994–95	St Etienne	30	2
1995–96	St Etienne	13	0
1996–97	Bastia	34	7
1997–98	Bastia	29	3
1998–99	Blackburn R	5	1
Total:		**123**	**13**

PERKINS, Chris — Midfield

H: 5 11 W: 10 09 b.Nottingham 9-1-74

Source: Trainee.

1992–93	Mansfield T	5	0
1993–94	Mansfield T	3	0
1994–95	Chesterfield	18	0
1995–96	Chesterfield	22	0
1996–97	Chesterfield	30	0
1997–98	Chesterfield	43	2
1998–99	Chesterfield	34	1
Total:		**155**	**3**

PERKINS, Chris — Defender

H: 5 11 W: 12 11 b.Stepney 1-3-80

Source: Trainee.

1997–98	Southend U	5	0
1998–99	Southend U	0	0
Total:		**5**	**0**

PERON, Jean-Francois — Midfield

H: 5 8 W: 10 04 b.St Omer 11-10-65

Source: Monaco, Caen.

1997–98	Walsall	38	1
1998–99	Walsall	0	0
1998–99	Portsmouth	38	1
Total:		**76**	**2**

PERPETUINI, David — Midfield

H: 5 9 W: 10 07 b.Hitchin 26-9-79

Source: Trainee.

1997–98	Watford	0	0
1998–99	Watford	1	0
Total:		**1**	**0**

PERRETT, Russell — Defender

H: 6 2 W: 13 00 b.Barton-on-Sea 18-6-73

Source: AFC Lymington.

1995–96	Portsmouth	9	0
1996–97	Portsmouth	32	1
1997–98	Portsmouth	16	1
1998–99	Portsmouth	15	0
Total:		**72**	**2**

PERRY, Chris — Defender

H: 5 8 W: 10 08 b.Carshalton 26-4-73

Source: Trainee.

1991–92	Wimbledon	0	0
1992–93	Wimbledon	0	0
1993–94	Wimbledon	2	0
1994–95	Wimbledon	22	0

1995–96	Wimbledon	37	0
1996–97	Wimbledon	37	1
1997–98	Wimbledon	35	1
1998–99	Wimbledon	34	0
Total:		**167**	**2**

PERRY, Jason — Defender

H: 5 11 W: 11 12 b.Caerphilly 2-4-70

Source: Trainee. *Honours:* Wales Under-21, B, 1 full cap.

1986–87	Cardiff C	1	0
1987–88	Cardiff C	3	0
1988–89	Cardiff C	0	0
1989–90	Cardiff C	36	0
1990–91	Cardiff C	43	0
1991–92	Cardiff C	36	0
1992–93	Cardiff C	39	3
1993–94	Cardiff C	40	1
1994–95	Cardiff C	34	1
1995–96	Cardiff C	14	0
1996–97	Cardiff C	35	0
1997–98	Bristol R	25	0
1998–99	Lincoln C	12	0
1998–99	Hull C	8	0
Total:		**326**	**5**

PERRY, Mark — Midfield

H: 5 11 W: 12 09 b.Perivale 19-10-78

Source: Trainee. *Honours:* England Schools, Youth.

1995–96	QPR	0	0
1996–97	QPR	2	1
1997–98	QPR	8	0
1998–99	QPR	1	0
Total:		**11**	**1**

PERRY, Mark — Defender

H: 6 1 W: 11 00 b.Aberdeen 7-2-71

Source: Cove Rangers.

1988–89	Dundee U	0	0
1989–90	Dundee U	0	0
1990–91	Dundee U	0	0
1991–92	Dundee U	0	0
1992–93	Dundee U	18	1
1993–94	Dundee U	9	0
1994–95	Dundee U	9	0
1995–96	Dundee U	20	2
1996–97	Dundee U	35	0
1997–98	Dundee U	32	1
1998–99	Aberdeen	32	4
Total:		**155**	**8**

PERRY, Mark — Defender

H: 6 3 W: 14 03 b.Wordsley 19-11-78

Source: Trainee.

1997–98	Walsall	0	0
1998–99	Walsall	0	0

PESCHISOLIDO, Paul — Forward

H: 5 7 W: 11 02 b.Canada 25-5-71

Source: Toronto Blizzard. *Honours:* Canada full caps.

1992–93	Birmingham C	19	7
1993–94	Birmingham C	24	9
1994–95	Stoke C	40	13
1995–96	Stoke C	26	6
1995–96	Birmingham C	9	1
1996–97	WBA	37	15
1997–98	WBA	8	3
1997–98	Fulham	32	13
1998–99	Fulham	33	7
Total:		**228**	**74**

PETERS, Mark — Defender

H: 6 0 W: 11 03 b.St Asaph 6-7-72

Source: Trainee. *Honours:* Wales Under-21.

1991–92	Manchester C	0	0
1992–93	Norwich C	0	0
1993–94	Peterborough U	19	0
1994–95	Peterborough U	0	0
1994–95	Mansfield T	26	4
1995–96	Mansfield T	21	2
1996–97	Mansfield T	0	0
1997–98	Mansfield T	24	2
1998–99	Mansfield T	37	1
Total:		**127**	**9**

PETHICK, Robbie — Defender

H: 5 10 W: 12 07 b.Tavistock 8-9-70

Source: Weymouth.

1993–94	Portsmouth	18	0
1994–95	Portsmouth	44	1
1995–96	Portsmouth	38	0
1996–97	Portsmouth	35	0
1997–98	Portsmouth	44	2
1998–99	Portsmouth	10	0
1998–99	Bristol R	9	0
Total:		**198**	**3**

PETIT, Emmanuel — Midfield

H: 6 1 W: 12 07 b.Dieppe 22-9-70

Source: ES Arques. *Honours:* France 32 full caps, 3 goal.

1988–89	Monaco	9	0
1989–90	Monaco	28	0
1990–91	Monaco	27	1
1991–92	Monaco	28	0
1992–93	Monaco	25	1
1993–94	Monaco	28	0
1994–95	Monaco	25	1
1995–96	Monaco	23	1
1996–97	Monaco	29	0

1997–98	Arsenal	32	2
1998–99	Arsenal	27	4
Total:		**281**	**10**

PETRESCU, Dan — Defender

H: 5 10 W: 11 07 b.Bucharest 22-12-67

Honours: Romania 82 full caps, 12 goals.

1985–86	Steaua	2	0
1986–87	FC Olt (loan)	24	0
1987–88	Steaua	11	0
1988–89	Steaua	28	4
1989–90	Steaua	23	9
1990–91	Steaua	31	13
1991–92	Foggia	25	4
1992–93	Foggia	30	3
1993–94	Genoa	24	1
1994–95	Sheffield W	29	3
1995–96	Sheffield W	8	0
1995–96	Chelsea	24	2
1996–97	Chelsea	34	3
1997–98	Chelsea	31	5
1998–99	Chelsea	32	4
Total:		**356**	**51**

PETRIC, Gordan — Defender

H: 6 1 W: 12 03 b.Belgrade 30-7-69

Source: Partizan Belgrade. *Honours:* Yugoslavia full caps.

1993–94	Dundee U	27	1
1994–95	Dundee U	33	2
1995–96	Rangers	33	1
1996–97	Rangers	26	2
1997–98	Rangers	6	0
1998–99	Rangers	0	0
1998–99	Crystal Palace	18	1
Total:		**143**	**7**

PETRIE, Stewart — Forward

H: 5 10 W: 11 11 b.Dundee 27-2-70

Source: East Craigie.

1988–89	Forfar Ath	0	0
1989–90	Forfar Ath	0	0
1990–91	Forfar Ath	36	6
1991–92	Forfar Ath	41	7
1992–93	Forfar Ath	37	21
1993–94	Forfar Ath	3	0
1993–94	Dunfermline Ath	37	6
1994–95	Dunfermline Ath	33	14
1995–96	Dunfermline Ath	34	13
1996–97	Dunfermline Ath	28	3
1997–98	Dunfermline Ath	27	2
1998–99	Dunfermline Ath	30	2
Total:		**306**	**74**

PETTA, Bobby — Midfield

H: 5 7 W: 11 05 b.Rotterdam 6-8-74

1996–97	Ipswich T	6	0
1997–98	Ipswich T	32	7
1998–99	Ipswich T	32	2
Total:		**70**	**9**

PETTEFER, Carl — Midfield

H: 5 6 W: 10 11 b.Taplow 22-3-81

Source: Trainee.

1998–99	Portsmouth	0	0

PETTERSON, Andy — Goalkeeper

H: 6 2 W: 14 12 b.Fremantle 29-9-69

1988–89	Luton T	0	0
1988–89	Swindon T (loan)	0	0
1989–90	Luton T	0	0
1990–91	Luton T	0	0
1991–92	Luton T	0	0
1991–92	Ipswich T (loan)	0	0
1992–93	Luton T	14	0
1992–93	Ipswich T (loan)	1	0
1993–94	Luton T	5	0
1994–95	Charlton Ath	9	0
1994–95	Bradford C (loan)	3	0
1995–96	Charlton Ath	9	0
1995–96	Ipswich T (loan)	1	0
1995–96	Plymouth Arg (loan)	6	0
1995–96	Colchester U (loan)	5	0
1996–97	Charlton Ath	21	0
1997–98	Charlton Ath	23	0
1998–99	Charlton Ath	10	0
1998–99	Portsmouth (loan)	13	0
Total:		**120**	**0**

PETTINGER, Paul — Goalkeeper

H: 6 0 W: 13 00 b.Sheffield 1-10-75

Source: Barnsley. *Honours:* England Schools, Youth.

1992–93	Leeds U	0	0
1993–94	Leeds U	0	0
1994–95	Leeds U	0	0
1994–95	Torquay U (loan)	3	0
1995–96	Leeds U	0	0
1995–96	Rotherham U (loan)	1	0
1995–96	Gillingham	0	0
1996–97	Carlisle U	0	0
1997–98	Rotherham U	3	0
1998–99	Rotherham U	0	0
Total:		**7**	**0**

PETTY, Ben — Defender

H: 6 1 W: 13 03 b.Solihull 22-3-77

Source: Trainee.

1994–95	Aston Villa	0	0
1995–96	Aston Villa	0	0
1996–97	Aston Villa	0	0
1997–98	Aston Villa	0	0
1998–99	Aston Villa	0	0
1998–99	Stoke C	11	0
Total:		**11**	**0**

PHELAN, Mike — Defender

H: 5 11 W: 11 01 b.Nelson 24-9-62

Source: Apprentice. *Honours:* England Youth, 1 full cap.

1980–81	Burnley	16	2
1981–82	Burnley	23	1
1982–83	Burnley	42	3
1983–84	Burnley	44	2
1984–85	Burnley	43	1
1985–86	Norwich C	42	3
1986–87	Norwich C	40	4
1987–88	Norwich C	37	0
1988–89	Norwich C	37	2
1989–90	Manchester U	38	1
1990–91	Manchester U	33	1
1991–92	Manchester U	18	0
1992–93	Manchester U	11	0
1993–94	Manchester U	2	0
1994–95	WBA	20	0
1995–96	WBA	1	0
1996–97	Blackpool	0	0
1997–98	Blackpool	0	0
1997–98	Stockport Co	0	0
1998–99	Stockport Co	0	0
Total:		**447**	**20**

PHELAN, Terry — Defender

H: 5 8 W: 10 04 b.Manchester 16-3-67

Source: Trainee. *Honours:* Eire Youth, Under-21, Under-23, B, 38 full caps.

1984–85	Leeds U	0	0
1985–86	Leeds U	14	0
1986–87	Swansea C	45	0
1987–88	Wimbledon	30	0
1988–89	Wimbledon	29	0
1989–90	Wimbledon	34	0
1990–91	Wimbledon	29	0
1991–92	Wimbledon	37	1
1992–93	Wimbledon	0	0
1992–93	Manchester C	37	0
1993–94	Manchester C	30	1
1994–95	Manchester C	27	0
1995–96	Manchester C	9	0
1995–96	Chelsea	12	0
1996–97	Chelsea	3	0
1996–97	Everton	15	0
1997–98	Everton	9	0
1998–99	Everton	0	0
Total:		**360**	**2**

PHILLIPS, Dave — Defender

H: 5 9 W: 12 04 b.Wegberg 29-7-63

Source: Apprentice. *Honours:* Wales Under-21, 62 full caps, 2 goals.

1981–82	Plymouth Arg	8	1
1982–83	Plymouth Arg	23	8
1983–84	Plymouth Arg	42	6
1984–85	Manchester C	42	12
1985–86	Manchester C	39	1
1986–87	Coventry C	39	4
1987–88	Coventry C	35	2
1988–89	Coventry C	26	2
1989–90	Norwich C	38	4
1990–91	Norwich C	38	4
1991–92	Norwich C	34	1
1992–93	Norwich C	42	9
1993–94	Nottingham F	43	4
1994–95	Nottingham F	38	1
1995–96	Nottingham F	18	0
1996–97	Nottingham F	27	0
1997–98	Nottingham F	0	0
1997–98	Huddersfield T	29	2
1998–99	Huddersfield T	23	1
1998–99	Lincoln C	9	0
Total:		**593**	**62**

PHILLIPS, Gareth — Midfield

H: 5 7 W: 11 02 b.Church Village 19-8-79

Source: Trainee.

1996–97	Swansea C	1	0
1997–98	Swansea C	6	0
1998–99	Swansea C	1	0
Total:		**8**	**0**

PHILLIPS, Jimmy — Defender

H: 6 0 W: 12 07 b.Bolton 8-2-66

Source: Apprentice.

1983–84	Bolton W	1	0
1984–85	Bolton W	40	1
1985–86	Bolton W	33	1
1986–87	Bolton W	34	0
1986–87	Rangers	6	0
1987–88	Rangers	19	0
1988–89	Oxford U	45	5
1989–90	Oxford U	34	3
1989–90	Middlesbrough	12	0
1990–91	Middlesbrough	44	2
1991–92	Middlesbrough	43	2
1992–93	Middlesbrough	40	2
1993–94	Bolton W	42	0

1994–95	Bolton W	46	1
1995–96	Bolton W	37	0
1996–97	Bolton W	36	0
1997–98	Bolton W	22	1
1998–99	Bolton W	15	0
Total:		**549**	**18**

PHILLIPS, Kevin — Forward

H: 5 7 W: 11 00 b.Hitchin 25-7-73

Source: Baldock T. *Honours:* England B, 1 full cap.

1994–95	Watford	16	9
1995–96	Watford	27	11
1996–97	Watford	16	4
1997–98	Sunderland	43	29
1998–99	Sunderland	26	23
Total:		**128**	**76**

PHILLIPS, Lee — Forward

H: 5 10 W: 12 00 b.Penzance 16-9-80

Source: School.

1996–97	Plymouth Arg	2	0
1997–98	Plymouth Arg	10	0
1998–99	Plymouth Arg	15	1
Total:		**27**	**1**

PHILLIPS, Lee — Defender

H: 6 0 W: 12 10 b.Aberdare 18-3-79

Source: Trainee.

1996–97	Cardiff C	3	0
1997–98	Cardiff C	8	0
1998–99	Cardiff C	2	0
Total:		**13**	**0**

PHILLIPS, Martin — Midfield

H: 5 9 W: 10 03 b.Exeter 13-3-76

Source: Trainee.

1992–93	Exeter C	6	0
1993–94	Exeter C	9	0
1994–95	Exeter C	24	2
1995–96	Exeter C	13	3
1995–96	Manchester C	11	0
1996–97	Manchester C	4	0
1997–98	Manchester C	0	0
1997–98	Scunthorpe U (loan)	3	0
1997–98	Exeter C (loan)	8	0
1998–99	Manchester C	0	0
1998–99	Portsmouth	17	1
1998–99	Bristol R (loan)	2	0
Total:		**97**	**6**

PHILLIPS, Steve — Goalkeeper

H: 6 1 W: 12 07 b.Bath 6-5-78

Source: Paulton R.

1996–97	Bristol C	0	0
1997–98	Bristol C	0	0
1998–99	Bristol C	15	0
Total:		**15**	**0**

PHILLIPS, Wayne — Midfield

H: 5 11 W: 11 00 b.Bangor 15-12-70

Source: Trainee. *Honours:* Wales B.

1989–90	Wrexham	5	0
1990–91	Wrexham	28	0
1991–92	Wrexham	30	3
1992–93	Wrexham	15	0
1993–94	Wrexham	21	1
1994–95	Wrexham	18	1
1995–96	Wrexham	44	5
1996–97	Wrexham	26	5
1997–98	Wrexham	20	1
1997–98	Stockport Co	13	0
1998–99	Stockport Co	9	0
Total:		**229**	**16**

PHILLISKIRK, Tony — Forward

H: 6 2 W: 12 12 b.Sunderland 10-2-65

Source: Amateur. *Honours:* England Schools.

1983–84	Sheffield U	21	8
1984–85	Sheffield U	23	2
1985–86	Sheffield U	4	0
1986–87	Sheffield U	6	1
1986–87	Rotherham U (loan)	6	1
1987–88	Sheffield U	26	9
1988–89	Oldham Ath	10	1
1988–89	Preston NE	14	6
1989–90	Bolton W	45	18
1990–91	Bolton W	43	19
1991–92	Bolton W	43	12
1992–93	Bolton W	10	2
1992–93	Peterborough U	32	11
1993–94	Peterborough U	11	4
1993–94	Burnley	19	7
1994–95	Burnley	13	1
1995–96	Burnley	8	1
1995–96	Carlisle U (loan)	3	1
1995–96	Cardiff C	28	4
1996–97	Cardiff C	33	1
1997–98	Cardiff C	0	0
1997–98	Macclesfield T (loan)	10	1
1998–99	Oldham Ath	0	0
Total:		**408**	**110**

PHILPOTT, Lee — Midfield

H: 5 9 W: 11 08 b.Barnet 21-2-70

Source: Trainee.

1987–88	Peterborough U	1	0
1988–89	Peterborough U	3	0
1989–90	Cambridge U	42	5
1990–91	Cambridge U	45	5
1991–92	Cambridge U	31	5
1992–93	Cambridge U	16	2
1992–93	Leicester C	27	3
1993–94	Leicester C	19	0
1994–95	Leicester C	23	0
1995–96	Leicester C	6	0
1995–96	Blackpool	10	0
1996–97	Blackpool	26	3
1997–98	Blackpool	35	2
1998–99	Lincoln C	24	0
Total:		**308**	**25**

PICKERING, Ally — Defender

H: 5 9 W: 11 07 b.Manchester 22-6-67

Source: Buxton.

1989–90	Rotherham U	10	0
1990–91	Rotherham U	1	0
1991–92	Rotherham U	27	0
1992–93	Rotherham U	38	1
1993–94	Rotherham U	12	1
1993–94	Coventry C	4	0
1994–95	Coventry C	31	0
1995–96	Coventry C	30	0
1996–97	Stoke C	40	0
1997–98	Stoke C	42	1
1998–99	Stoke C	1	0
1998–99	Burnley	21	1
Total:		**257**	**4**

PIERCY, John — Midfield

H: 5 11 W: 11 12 b.Forest Gate 18-9-79

Source: Trainee. *Honours:* England Youth.

1998–99	Tottenham H	0	0

PILKINGTON, George — Defender

H: 5 11 W: 11 00 b.Rugeley 7-11-81

Source: Trainee. *Honours:* England Youth.

1998–99	Everton	0	0

PILKINGTON, Kevin — Goalkeeper

H: 6 1 W: 13 00 b.Hitchin 8-3-74

Source: Trainee. *Honours:* England Schools.

1992–93	Manchester U	0	0
1993–94	Manchester U	0	0
1994–95	Manchester U	1	0
1995–96	Manchester U	3	0
1995–96	Rochdale (loan)	6	0
1996–97	Manchester U	0	0
1996–97	Rotherham U (loan)	17	0
1997–98	Manchester U	2	0
1998–99	Manchester U	0	0
1998–99	Port Vale	8	0
Total:		**37**	**0**

PINAMONTE, Lorenzo — Forward

H: 6 3 W: 13 04 b.Foggia 9-5-78

Source: Foggia.

1998–99	Bristol C	1	1
Total:		**1**	**1**

PINAS, Brian — Midfield

H: 5 8 W: 10 12 b.Rotterdam 29-12-78

Source: Feyenoord.

1997–98	Newcastle U	0	0
1998–99	Newcastle U	0	0

PINNOCK, James — Forward

H: 5 9 W: 11 05 b.Dartford 1-8-78

Source: Trainee.

1996–97	Gillingham	2	0
1997–98	Gillingham	1	0
1998–99	Gillingham	4	0
Total:		**7**	**0**

PIRRI — Midfield

b.Caneas de Onis 10-11-70

1998–99	Merida	19	1
1998–99	Barnsley	2	0
Total:		**21**	**1**

PISTONE, Alessandro — Defender

H: 5 11 W: 11 05 b.Milan 27-7-75

1992–93	Vicenza	0	0
1993–94	Solbiatese	20	1
1994–95	Crevalcore	29	4
1995–96	Vicenza	6	0
1995–96	Internazionale	19	1
1996–97	Internazionale	26	0
1997–98	Newcastle U	28	0
1998–99	Newcastle U	3	0
Total:		**131**	**6**

PITTS, Matthew — Defender

H: 5 11 W: 12 06 b.Middlesbrough 25-12-79

Source: Trainee.

1998–99	Sunderland	0	0

PLACE, Damien — Midfield

H: 5 9 W: 10 07 b.Halifax 31-12-78

Source: Trainee.

1998–99	Halifax T	0	0

PLATT, Clive — Forward

H: 6 3 W: 13 04 b.Wolverhampton 27-10-77

Source: Trainee.

1995–96	Walsall	4	2
1996–97	Walsall	1	0
1997–98	Walsall	20	1
1998–99	Walsall	7	1
Total:		**32**	**4**

PLATT, David — Midfield

H: 5 10 W: 11 12 b.Chadderton 10-6-66

Source: Chadderton. *Honours:* England Under-21, B, 62 full caps, 27 goals.

1984–85	Manchester U	0	0
1984–85	Crewe Alex	22	5
1985–86	Crewe Alex	43	8
1986–87	Crewe Alex	43	23
1987–88	Crewe Alex	26	19
1987–88	Aston Villa	11	5
1988–89	Aston Villa	38	7
1989–90	Aston Villa	37	19
1990–91	Aston Villa	35	19
1991–92	Bari	29	11
1992–93	Juventus	16	3
1993–94	Sampdoria	29	9
1994–95	Sampdoria	26	8
1995–96	Arsenal	29	6
1996–97	Arsenal	28	4
1997–98	Arsenal	31	3
1998–99	Arsenal	0	0
Total:		**443**	**149**

PLATTS, Mark — Forward

H: 5 8 W: 11 12 b.Sheffield 23-5-79

Source: Trainee. *Honours:* England Schools, Youth.

1995–96	Sheffield W	2	0
1996–97	Sheffield W	0	0
1997–98	Sheffield W	0	0
1998–99	Sheffield W	0	0
1998–99	Torquay U	8	0
Total:		**10**	**0**

PLUCK, Colin — Defender

H: 6 0 W: 12 05 b.London 6-9-78

Source: Trainee.

1996–97	Watford	0	0
1997–98	Watford	1	0
1998–99	Watford	0	0
Total:		**1**	**0**

PLUMMER, Chris — Defender

H: 6 2 W: 12 12 b.Isleworth 12-10-76

Source: Trainee. *Honours:* England Youth, Under-21.

1994–95	QPR	0	0
1995–96	QPR	1	0
1996–97	QPR	5	0
1997–98	QPR	0	0
1998–99	QPR	10	0
Total:		**16**	**0**

PLUMMER, Dwayne — Forward

H: 5 9 W: 10 12 b.Bristol 12-5-78

Source: Trainee.

1995–96	Bristol C	11	0
1996–97	Bristol C	2	0
1997–98	Bristol C	1	0
1998–99	Bristol C	0	0
Total:		**14**	**0**

POINTON, Neil — Defender

H: 5 10 W: 12 11 b.Warsop Vale 28-11-64

Source: Apprentice.

1981–82	Scunthorpe U	5	0
1982–83	Scunthorpe U	46	1
1983–84	Scunthorpe U	45	1
1984–85	Scunthorpe U	46	0
1985–86	Scunthorpe U	17	0
1985–86	Everton	15	0
1986–87	Everton	12	1
1987–88	Everton	33	3
1988–89	Everton	23	0
1989–90	Everton	19	1
1990–91	Manchester C	35	1
1991–92	Manchester C	39	1
1992–93	Oldham Ath	34	3
1993–94	Oldham Ath	24	0
1994–95	Oldham Ath	32	0
1995–96	Oldham Ath	4	0
1995–96	Hearts	22	3
1996–97	Hearts	25	0
1997–98	Hearts	20	0
1998–99	Walsall	43	0
Total:		**539**	**15**

POLLITT, Mike — Goalkeeper

H: 6 3 W: 14 12 b.Farnworth 29-2-72

Source: Trainee.

1990–91	Manchester U	0	0
1990–91	Oldham Ath (loan)	0	0
1991–92	Bury	0	0
1992–93	Lincoln C	27	0
1993–94	Lincoln C	30	0
1994–95	Darlington	40	0
1995–96	Darlington	15	0
1995–96	Notts Co	0	0
1996–97	Notts Co	8	0
1997–98	Notts Co	2	0
1997–98	Oldham Ath (loan)	16	0
1997–98	Gillingham (loan)	6	0
1997–98	Brentford (loan)	5	0
1997–98	Sunderland	0	0
1998–99	Rotherham U	46	0
Total:		**195**	**0**

POLLOCK, Jamie — Midfield

H: 6 0 W: 13 03 b.Stockton 16-2-74

Source: Trainee. *Honours:* England Youth, Under-21.

1990–91	Middlesbrough	1	0
1991–92	Middlesbrough	26	1
1992–93	Middlesbrough	22	1
1993–94	Middlesbrough	34	9
1994–95	Middlesbrough	41	5
1995–96	Middlesbrough	31	1
1996–97	Osasuna	0	0
1996–97	Bolton W	20	4
1997–98	Bolton W	26	1
1997–98	Manchester C	8	1
1998–99	Manchester C	26	1
Total:		**235**	**24**

POLSTON, John — Defender

H: 5 11 W: 11 12 b.Walthamstow 10-6-68

Source: Apprentice. *Honours:* England Youth.

1985–86	Tottenham H	0	0
1986–87	Tottenham H	6	0
1987–88	Tottenham H	2	0
1988–89	Tottenham H	3	0
1989–90	Tottenham H	13	1
1990–91	Norwich C	27	4
1991–92	Norwich C	19	1
1992–93	Norwich C	34	1
1993–94	Norwich C	24	0
1994–95	Norwich C	38	0
1995–96	Norwich C	30	0
1996–97	Norwich C	31	2
1997–98	Norwich C	12	0
1998–99	Reading	4	0
Total:		**243**	**9**

POOLE, Gary — Defender

H: 6 0 W: 11 00 b.Stratford 11-9-67

Source: Arsenal Schoolboys.

1984–85	Tottenham H	0	0
1985–86	Tottenham H	0	0
1986–87	Tottenham H	0	0
1987–88	Cambridge U	42	0
1988–89	Cambridge U	1	0
From Barnet			
1991–92	Barnet	40	2
1992–93	Plymouth Arg	39	5
1993–94	Southend U	38	2
1994–95	Southend U	6	0
1994–95	Birmingham C	34	0
1995–96	Birmingham C	28	0
1996–97	Birmingham C	10	0
1996–97	Charlton Ath	16	1
1997–98	Charlton Ath	0	0
1998–99	Charlton Ath	0	0
Total:		**254**	**10**

POOLE, Kevin — Goalkeeper

H: 5 10 W: 11 11 b.Bromsgrove 21-7-63

Source: Apprentice.

1981–82	Aston Villa	0	0
1982–83	Aston Villa	0	0
1983–84	Aston Villa	0	0
1984–85	Aston Villa	7	0
1984–85	Northampton T (loan)	3	0
1985–86	Aston Villa	11	0
1986–87	Aston Villa	10	0
1987–88	Middlesbrough	1	0
1988–89	Middlesbrough	12	0
1989–90	Middlesbrough	21	0
1990–91	Middlesbrough	0	0
1990–91	Hartlepool U (loan)	12	0
1991–92	Leicester C	42	0
1992–93	Leicester C	19	0
1993–94	Leicester C	14	0
1994–95	Leicester C	36	0
1995–96	Leicester C	45	0
1996–97	Leicester C	7	0
1997–98	Birmingham C	1	0
1998–99	Birmingham C	36	0
Total:		**277**	**0**

POOM, Mart — Goalkeeper

H: 6 5 W: 13 05 b.Tallinn 3-2-72

Honours: Estonia 67 full caps.

1992–93	Flora Tallinn	11	0
1993–94	Flora Tallinn	11	0
1994–95	Portsmouth	0	0
1995–96	Portsmouth	4	0
1995–96	Flora Tallinn	7	0
1996–97	Portsmouth	0	0

1996–97	Flora Tallinn	12	0
1996–97	Derby Co	4	0
1997–98	Derby Co	36	0
1998–99	Derby Co	17	0
Total:		**102**	**0**

POPPLETON, David — Midfield

b.Doncaster 19-12-79

Source: Trainee.

1997–98	Everton	0	0
1998–99	Everton	0	0

PORFIRIO, Hugo — Midfield

H: 5 8 W: 10 05 b.Lisbon 28-9-73

Honours: Portugal 2 full caps.

1992–93	Sporting	2	0
1993–94	Sporting	9	0
1994–95	Sporting	0	0
1994–95	Tirsense (loan)	19	0
1995–96	Uniao Leiria (loan)	28	8
1996–97	West Ham U	23	2
1997–98	Santander	20	1
1998–99	Benfica	3	0
1998–99	Nottingham F	9	1
Total:		**113**	**12**

PORRINI, Sergio — Defender

H: 5 11 W: 12 04 b.Milan 8-11-68

1988–89	AC Milan	0	0
1989–90	Atalanta	8	1
1990–91	Atalanta	29	0
1991–92	Atalanta	30	0
1992–93	Atalanta	33	2
1993–94	Juventus	30	0
1994–95	Juventus	19	0
1995–96	Juventus	15	0
1996–97	Juventus	23	1
1997–98	Rangers	26	4
1998–99	Rangers	35	2
Total:		**248**	**10**

PORTEOUS, Andrew — Midfield

H: 5 11 W: 10 11 b.Edinburgh 13-9-79

Source: Trainee.

1996–97	Nottingham F	0	0
1997–98	Nottingham F	0	0
1997–98	Manchester C	0	0
1998–99	Manchester C	0	0

PORTER, Andy — Midfield

H: 5 9 W: 12 03 b.Holmes Chapel 17-9-68

Source: Trainee.

1986–87	Port Vale	1	0
1987–88	Port Vale	6	0
1988–89	Port Vale	14	1
1989–90	Port Vale	36	1
1990–91	Port Vale	40	0
1991–92	Port Vale	32	1
1992–93	Port Vale	17	1
1993–94	Port Vale	37	0
1994–95	Port Vale	44	3
1995–96	Port Vale	45	10
1996–97	Port Vale	44	4
1997–98	Port Vale	41	1
1998–99	Wigan Ath	16	1
Total:		**373**	**23**

PORTER, Christopher — Midfield

b.Sunderland 10-11-79

Source: Trainee.

1998–99	Sunderland	0	0

PORTER, Daniel — Midfield

b.Portsmouth 23-1-79

1997–98	Derby Co	0	0
1998–99	Derby Co	0	0

PORTER, Gary — Midfield

H: 5 6 W: 10 13 b.Sunderland 6-3-66

Source: Apprentice. *Honours:* England Youth, Under-21.

1983–84	Watford	2	0
1984–85	Watford	9	0
1985–86	Watford	8	1
1986–87	Watford	26	4
1987–88	Watford	40	3
1988–89	Watford	42	10
1989–90	Watford	32	4
1990–91	Watford	45	4
1991–92	Watford	44	8
1992–93	Watford	33	0
1993–94	Watford	43	9
1994–95	Watford	41	3
1995–96	Watford	29	1
1996–97	Watford	6	0
1997–98	Walsall	29	1
1998–99	Walsall	15	0
1998–99	Scarborough	13	0
Total:		**457**	**48**

PORTER, Graeme — Forward

H: 5 6 W: 10 00 b.Liverpool 24-11-81

Source: Trainee.

1998–99	Leeds U	0	0

POTTER, Danny — Goalkeeper

H: 5 11 W: 13 00 b.Ipswich 18-3-79

Source: Chelsea Trainee.

1997–98	Colchester U	0	0
1998–99	Exeter C	5	0
Total:		**5**	**0**

POTTER, Graham — Defender

H: 6 1 W: 11 12 b.Solihull 20-5-75

Source: Trainee. *Honours:* England Youth, Under-21.

1992–93	Birmingham C	18	2
1993–94	Birmingham C	7	0
1993–94	Wycombe W (loan)	3	0
1993–94	Stoke C	3	0
1994–95	Stoke C	1	0
1995–96	Stoke C	41	1
1996–97	Southampton	8	0
1996–97	WBA	6	0
1997–98	WBA	5	0
1997–98	Northampton T (loan)	4	0
1998–99	WBA	22	0
Total:		**118**	**3**

POTTER, Lee — Forward

H: 5 11 W: 12 10 b.Salford 3-9-78

Source: Trainee.

1997–98	Bolton W	0	0
1998–99	Bolton W	0	0

POTTS, Steve — Defender

H: 5 7 W: 10 11 b.Hartford (USA) 7-5-67

Source: Apprentice. *Honours:* England Youth.

1984–85	West Ham U	1	0
1985–86	West Ham U	1	0
1986–87	West Ham U	8	0
1987–88	West Ham U	8	0
1988–89	West Ham U	28	0
1989–90	West Ham U	32	0
1990–91	West Ham U	37	1
1991–92	West Ham U	34	0
1992–93	West Ham U	46	0
1993–94	West Ham U	41	0
1994–95	West Ham U	42	0
1995–96	West Ham U	34	0
1996–97	West Ham U	20	0
1997–98	West Ham U	23	0
1998–99	West Ham U	19	0
Total:		**374**	**1**

POUNEWATCHY, Stephane — Defender

H: 6 0 W: 15 00 b.Paris 10-2-68

1993–94	Martigues	29	1
1994–95	Martigues	15	1
1995–96	Gueugnon	30	0
1996–97	Carlisle U	42	1
1997–98	Carlisle U	39	2
1998–99	Dundee	3	0
1998–99	Port Vale	2	0
1998–99	Colchester U	15	1
Total:		**175**	**6**

POUNTNEY, Craig — Forward

H: 5 5 W: 9 00 b.Bromsgrove 23-11-79

Source: Trainee.

1997–98	Shrewsbury T	1	0
1998–99	Shrewsbury T	0	0
Total:		**1**	**0**

POUTON, Alan — Midfield

H: 6 0 W: 12 02 b.Newcastle 1-2-77

Source: Newcastle U Trainee.

1995–96	Oxford U	0	0
1995–96	York C	0	0
1996–97	York C	22	1
1997–98	York C	41	5
1998–99	York C	27	1
Total:		**90**	**7**

POWELL, Chris — Defender

H: 5 10 W: 11 07 b.Lambeth 8-9-69

Source: Trainee.

1987–88	Crystal Palace	0	0
1988–89	Crystal Palace	3	0
1989–90	Crystal Palace	0	0
1989–90	Aldershot (loan)	11	0
1990–91	Southend U	45	1
1991–92	Southend U	44	0
1992–93	Southend U	42	2
1993–94	Southend U	46	0
1994–95	Southend U	44	0
1995–96	Southend U	27	0
1995–96	Derby Co	19	0
1996–97	Derby Co	35	0
1997–98	Derby Co	37	1
1998–99	Charlton Ath	38	0
Total:		**391**	**4**

POWELL, Darren — Defender

b.Hammersmith 10-3-76

Source: Hampton.

1998–99	Brentford	33	2
Total:		**33**	**2**

POWELL, Darryl — Midfield

H: 6 0 W: 13 00 b.Lambeth 15-11-71

Source: Trainee. *Honours:* Jamaica 6 full caps, 1 goal.

1988–89	Portsmouth	3	0
1989–90	Portsmouth	0	0
1990–91	Portsmouth	8	0
1991–92	Portsmouth	36	6
1992–93	Portsmouth	23	0
1993–94	Portsmouth	28	5
1994–95	Portsmouth	34	5
1995–96	Derby Co	37	5
1996–97	Derby Co	33	1
1997–98	Derby Co	23	0
1998–99	Derby Co	33	0
Total:		**258**	**22**

POWELL, Gareth — Goalkeeper

H: 6 1 W: 12 00 b.Newcastle 23-3-80

Source: Trainee.

1998–99	Tranmere R	0	0

POWELL, Paul — Midfield

H: 5 8 W: 11 01 b.Wallingford 30-6-78

Source: Trainee.

1995–96	Oxford U	3	0
1996–97	Oxford U	0	0
1997–98	Oxford U	21	1
1998–99	Oxford U	44	3
Total:		**68**	**4**

POWELL, Vill — Forward

H: 5 11 W: 12 05 b.Sheffield 2-10-79

Source: Trainee.

1998–99	Sheffield W	0	0

POWER, Alan — Midfield

b.Dublin 18-9-80

Source: Trainee.

1998–99	Bolton W	0	0

POWER, Graeme — Defender

H: 5 11 W: 10 10 b.Northwick Park 7-3-77

Source: Trainee. *Honours:* England Schools, Youth.

1994–95	QPR	0	0
1995–96	QPR	0	0
1996–97	Bristol R	16	0
1997–98	Bristol R	10	0
1998–99	Exeter C	40	0
Total:		**66**	**0**

POWER, Lee — Forward

H: 6 0 W: 11 10 b.Lewisham 30-6-72

Source: Trainee. *Honours:* Eire Youth, Under-21, B.

1989–90	Norwich C	1	0
1990–91	Norwich C	16	3
1991–92	Norwich C	4	1
1992–93	Norwich C	18	6
1992–93	Charlton Ath (loan)	5	0
1993–94	Norwich C	5	0
1993–94	Sunderland (loan)	3	0
1993–94	Portsmouth (loan)	2	0
1993–94	Bradford C	3	2
1994–95	Bradford C	27	3
1994–95	Millwall (loan)	0	0
1995–96	Peterborough U	38	6
1996–97	Hibernian	6	1
1997–98	Hibernian	5	1
1998–99	Plymouth Arg	16	0
1998–99	Halifax T	18	4
Total:		**167**	**27**

POYET, Gustavo — Midfield

H: 6 1 W: 13 01 b.Montevideo 15-11-67

Source: River Plate, Grenoble, Bella Vista. *Honours:* Uruguay 13 full caps.

1990–91	Zaragoza	31	7
1991–92	Zaragoza	33	3
1992–93	Zaragoza	33	6
1993–94	Zaragoza	34	11
1994–95	Zaragoza	34	11
1995–96	Zaragoza	36	11
1996–97	Zaragoza	38	14
1997–98	Chelsea	14	4
1998–99	Chelsea	28	11
Total:		**281**	**78**

PREECE, Andy — Forward

H: 6 1 W: 12 00 b.Evesham 27-3-67

Source: Evesham U.

1988–89	Northampton T	1	0
From Worcester C			
1989–90	Wrexham	7	1
1990–91	Wrexham	34	4

1991–92	Wrexham	10	2
1991–92	Stockport Co	25	13
1992–93	Stockport Co	29	8
1993–94	Stockport Co	43	21
1994–95	Crystal Palace	20	4
1995–96	Blackpool	41	14
1996–97	Blackpool	41	10
1997–98	Blackpool	44	11
1998–99	Bury	39	3
Total:		**334**	**91**

PREECE, David — Midfield

H: 5 6 W: 11 01 b.Bridgnorth 28-5-63

Source: Apprentice. *Honours:* England B.

1980–81	Walsall	8	0
1981–82	Walsall	8	0
1982–83	Walsall	42	2
1983–84	Walsall	41	3
1984–85	Walsall	12	0
1984–85	Luton T	21	2
1985–86	Luton T	41	2
1986–87	Luton T	14	0
1987–88	Luton T	13	0
1988–89	Luton T	26	0
1989–90	Luton T	32	1
1990–91	Luton T	37	1
1991–92	Luton T	38	3
1992–93	Luton T	43	3
1993–94	Luton T	29	5
1994–95	Luton T	42	4
1995–96	Derby Co	13	1
1995–96	Birmingham C (loan)	6	0
1995–96	Swindon T (loan)	7	1
1996–97	Cambridge U	25	0
1997–98	Cambridge U	22	0
1998–99	Cambridge U	14	2
Total:		**534**	**30**

PREECE, David — Goalkeeper

H: 6 2 W: 11 11 b.Sunderland 26-8-76

Source: Trainee. *Honours:* England Under-18.

1994–95	Sunderland	0	0
1995–96	Sunderland	0	0
1996–97	Sunderland	0	0
1997–98	Darlington	45	0
1998–99	Darlington	46	0
Total:		**91**	**0**

PREECE, Roger — Midfield

H: 5 8 W: 10 13 b.Much Wenlock 9-6-69

Source: Coventry C Apprentice.

1986–87	Wrexham	7	2
1987–88	Wrexham	40	4
1988–89	Wrexham	31	5
1989–90	Wrexham	32	1
1990–91	Chester C	35	0
1991–92	Chester C	29	0
1992–93	Chester C	23	0
1993–94	Chester C	39	2
1994–95	Chester C	43	2
1995–96	Chester C	1	0
1996–97	Chester C	0	0
1997–98	Shrewsbury T	27	1
1998–99	Shrewsbury T	20	2
Total:		**327**	**19**

PRENDERGAST, Rory — Midfield

H: 5 8 W: 12 00 b.Pontefract 6-4-78

Source: Rochdale.

1995–96	Barnsley	0	0
1996–97	Barnsley	0	0
1997–98	Barnsley	0	0
1998–99	York C	3	0
1998–99	Oldham Ath	0	0
Total:		**3**	**0**

PRENDERVILLE, Barry — Defender

H: 6 0 W: 12 08 b.Dublin 16-10-76

Source: Trainee.

1994–95	Coventry C	0	0
1995–96	Coventry C	0	0
1996–97	Coventry C	0	0
1997–98	Coventry C	0	0
1998–99	Coventry C	0	0
1998–99	Hibernian (loan)	13	2
Total:		**13**	**2**

PRESSLEY, Steven — Defender

H: 6 0 W: 11 00 b.Elgin 11-10-73

1991–92	Rangers	1	0
1992–93	Rangers	8	0
1993–94	Rangers	23	0
1994–95	Rangers	2	1
1994–95	Coventry C	19	1
1995–96	Coventry C	0	0
1995–96	Dundee U	35	2
1996–97	Dundee U	36	2
1997–98	Dundee U	29	2
1998–99	Hearts	30	1
Total:		**183**	**9**

PRESSMAN, Kevin — Goalkeeper

H: 6 1 W: 15 05 b.Fareham 6-11-67

Source: Apprentice. *Honours:* England Schools, Youth, Under-21, B.

1985–86	Sheffield W	0	0
1986–87	Sheffield W	0	0
1987–88	Sheffield W	11	0

1988–89	Sheffield W	9	0
1989–90	Sheffield W	15	0
1990–91	Sheffield W	23	0
1991–92	Sheffield W	1	0
1991–92	Stoke C (loan)	4	0
1992–93	Sheffield W	3	0
1993–94	Sheffield W	32	0
1994–95	Sheffield W	34	0
1995–96	Sheffield W	30	0
1996–97	Sheffield W	38	0
1997–98	Sheffield W	36	0
1998–99	Sheffield W	15	0
Total:		**251**	**0**

PRESTON, Allan — Defender

H: 5 10 W: 11 04 b.Edinburgh 6-8-69

Source: Hutcheson Vale BC.

1985–86	Dundee U	0	0
1986–87	Dundee U	0	0
1987–88	Dundee U	2	0
1988–89	Dundee U	9	1
1989–90	Dundee U	8	0
1990–91	Dundee U	3	0
1991–92	Dundee U	2	0
1992–93	Hearts	21	2
1993–94	St Johnstone	9	0
1994–95	St Johnstone	26	2
1995–96	St Johnstone	27	2
1996–97	St Johnstone	32	1
1997–98	St Johnstone	35	1
1998–99	St Johnstone	15	0
Total:		**189**	**9**

PRICE, Jason — Defender

H: 6 0 W: 11 05 b.Aberdare 12-4-77

Source: Aberaman Ath. *Honours:* Wales Under-21.

1995–96	Swansea C	0	0
1996–97	Swansea C	2	0
1997–98	Swansea C	34	3
1998–99	Swansea C	28	4
Total:		**64**	**7**

PRICE, Ryan — Goalkeeper

H: 6 6 W: 14 00 b.Wolverhampton 13-3-70

Source: Stafford R.

1994–95	Birmingham C	0	0
1995–96	Birmingham C	0	0
1997–98	Macclesfield T	46	0
1998–99	Macclesfield T	42	0
Total:		**88**	**0**

PRIEST, Chris — Midfield

H: 5 10 W: 10 10 b.Leigh 18-10-73

Source: Trainee.

1992–93	Everton	0	0
1993–94	Everton	0	0
1994–95	Everton	0	0
1994–95	Chester C	24	1
1995–96	Chester C	39	13
1996–97	Chester C	32	2
1997–98	Chester C	37	6
1998–99	Chester C	35	4
Total:		**167**	**26**

PRIESTLEY, Phil — Goalkeeper

b.Wigan 30-3-76

Source: Atherton LR.

1998–99	Rochdale	1	0
Total:		**1**	**0**

PRIMUS, Linvoy — Defender

H: 6 0 W: 13 07 b.Forest Gate 14-9-73

Source: Trainee.

1992–93	Charlton Ath	4	0
1993–94	Charlton Ath	0	0
1994–95	Barnet	39	0
1995–96	Barnet	42	4
1996–97	Barnet	46	3
1997–98	Reading	36	1
1998–99	Reading	31	0
Total:		**198**	**8**

PRINGLE, Martin — Forward

H: 6 2 W: 12 00 b.Gothenburg 18-11-70

Source: Stenungsund.

1994	Helsingborg	21	3
1995	Helsingborg	22	7
1996	Helsingborg	21	5
1996–97	Benfica	15	3
1997–98	Benfica	14	2
1998–99	Benfica	12	1
1998–99	Charlton Ath	18	3
Total:		**123**	**24**

PRIOR, Spencer — Defender

H: 6 1 W: 13 00 b.Rochford 22-4-71

Source: Trainee.

1988–89	Southend U	14	1
1989–90	Southend U	15	1
1990–91	Southend U	19	0
1991–92	Southend U	42	1
1992–93	Southend U	45	0
1993–94	Norwich C	13	0

1994–95	Norwich C	17	0
1995–96	Norwich C	44	1
1996–97	Leicester C	34	0
1997–98	Leicester C	30	0
1998–99	Derby Co	34	1
Total:		**307**	**5**

PRITCHARD, David — Defender

H: 5 7 W: 12 00 b.Wolverhampton 27-5-72

Source: Telford U. *Honours:* Wales B.

1990–91	WBA	0	0
1991–92	WBA	5	0
1993–94	Bristol R	11	0
1994–95	Bristol R	43	0
1995–96	Bristol R	12	0
1996–97	Bristol R	26	0
1997–98	Bristol R	33	0
1998–99	Bristol R	12	0
Total:		**142**	**0**

PROCTOR, Michael — Forward

H: 5 11 W: 12 00 b.Sunderland 3-10-80

Source: Trainee.

1997–98	Sunderland	0	0
1998–99	Sunderland	0	0

PROKAS, Richard — Midfield

H: 5 9 W: 11 05 b.Penrith 22-1-76

Source: Trainee.

1994–95	Carlisle U	39	1
1995–96	Carlisle U	20	0
1996–97	Carlisle U	13	1
1997–98	Carlisle U	34	0
1998–99	Carlisle U	34	0
Total:		**140**	**2**

PRUDHOE, Mark — Goalkeeper

H: 6 0 W: 14 00 b.Washington 8-11-63

Source: Apprentice.

1981–82	Sunderland	0	0
1982–83	Sunderland	7	0
1983–84	Sunderland	0	0
1983–84	Hartlepool U (loan)	3	0
1984–85	Sunderland	0	0
1984–85	Birmingham C	1	0
1985–86	Walsall	16	0
1986–87	Walsall	10	0
1986–87	Doncaster R (loan)	5	0
1986–87	Sheffield W (loan)	0	0
1986–87	Grimsby T (loan)	8	0
1987–88	Walsall	0	0
1987–88	Hartlepool U (loan)	13	0
1987–88	Bristol C (loan)	3	0
1987–88	Carlisle U	22	0
1988–89	Carlisle U	12	0
1988–89	Darlington	12	0
1989–90	Darlington	0	0
1990–91	Darlington	46	0
1991–92	Darlington	46	0
1992–93	Darlington	42	0
1993–94	Stoke C	30	0
1994–95	Stoke C	0	0
1994–95	Peterborough U (loan)	6	0
1994–95	Liverpool (loan)	0	0
1995–96	Stoke C	39	0
1996–97	Stoke C	13	0
1996–97	York C (loan)	2	0
1997–98	Bradford C	8	0
1998–99	Bradford C	0	0
Total:		**344**	**0**

PRUNTY, Sean — Midfield

H: 5 9 W: 10 11 b.Dublin 10-7-80

Source: Belvedere.

1998–99	Middlesbrough	0	0

PRUTTON, David — Defender

H: 6 1 W: 11 06 b.Hull 12-9-81

Source: Trainee.

1998–99	Nottingham F	0	0

PRYERS, Lee — Defender

H: 5 6 W: 10 00 b.Bolton 23-2-80

Source: Trainee.

1998–99	Bolton W	0	0

PURCES, Stephen — Midfield

b.Essex 14-1-80

Source: Trainee.

1998–99	West Ham U	0	0

PURSE, Darren — Defender

H: 6 2 W: 13 08 b.Stepney 14-2-76

Source: Trainee. *Honours:* England Under-21.

1993–94	Leyton Orient	5	0
1994–95	Leyton Orient	38	3
1995–96	Leyton Orient	12	0
1996–97	Oxford U	31	1
1997–98	Oxford U	28	4
1997–98	Birmingham C	8	0
1998–99	Birmingham C	20	0
Total:		**142**	**8**

PURSER, Wayne — Forward

H: 5 9 W: 11 04 b.Basildon 13-4-80

Source: Trainee.

1996–97	QPR	0	0
1997–98	QPR	0	0
1998–99	QPR	0	0

QUAILEY, Brian — Forward

H: 6 1 W: 13 11 b.Leicester 21-3-78

Source: Nuneaton B.

1997–98	WBA	5	0
1998–99	WBA	2	0
1998–99	Exeter C (loan)	12	2
Total:		**19**	**2**

QUASHIE, Nigel — Midfield

H: 5 9 W: 12 08 b.Nunhead 20-7-78

Source: Trainee. *Honours:* England Youth, Under-21, B.

1995–96	QPR	11	0
1996–97	QPR	13	0
1997–98	QPR	33	3
1998–99	QPR	0	0
1998–99	Nottingham F	16	0
Total:		**73**	**3**

QUAYLE, Mark — Forward

H: 5 9 W: 11 04 b.Liverpool 2-10-78

Source: Trainee.

1995–96	Everton	0	0
1996–97	Everton	0	0
1997–98	Everton	0	0
1998–99	Notts Co	5	0
Total:		**5**	**0**

QUIGLEY, Michael — Midfield

H: 5 7 W: 11 04 b.Manchester 2-10-70

Source: Trainee.

1990–91	Manchester C	0	0
1991–92	Manchester C	5	0
1992–93	Manchester C	5	0
1993–94	Manchester C	2	0
1994–95	Manchester C	0	0
1994–95	Wrexham (loan)	4	0
1995–96	Hull C	13	1
1996–97	Hull C	29	1
1997–98	Hull C	9	1
1998–99	Hull C	0	0
Total:		**67**	**3**

QUINN, Alan — Forward

H: 5 9 W: 10 05 b.Dublin 13-6-79

1997–98	Sheffield W	1	0
1998–99	Sheffield W	1	0
Total:		**2**	**0**

QUINN, Andrew — Midfield

b.Halifax 1-9-79

1996–97	Leeds U	0	0
1997–98	Leeds U	0	0
1998–99	Leeds U	0	0

QUINN, Barry — Midfield

H: 6 0 W: 12 02 b.Dublin 9-5-79

Source: Trainee. *Honours:* Eire Under-21.

1996–97	Coventry C	0	0
1997–98	Coventry C	0	0
1998–99	Coventry C	7	0
Total:		**7**	**0**

QUINN, James — Forward

H: 6 1 W: 12 10 b.Coventry 15-12-74

Source: Trainee. *Honours:* Northern Ireland Under-21, 15 full caps, 1 goal.

1992–93	Birmingham C	4	0
1993–94	Blackpool	14	2
1993–94	Stockport Co (loan)	1	0
1994–95	Blackpool	41	9
1995–96	Blackpool	44	9
1996–97	Blackpool	38	13
1997–98	Blackpool	14	4
1997–98	WBA	13	2
1998–99	WBA	43	6
Total:		**212**	**45**

QUINN, Jimmy — Forward

H: 6 1 W: 13 10 b.Belfast 18-11-59

Source: Oswestry T. *Honours:* Northern Ireland 46 full caps, 12 goals.

1981–82	Swindon T	4	0
1982–83	Swindon T	13	3
1983–84	Swindon T	32	7
1984–85	Blackburn R	25	10

1985–86	Blackburn R	31	4
1986–87	Blackburn R	15	3
1986–87	Swindon T	22	9
1987–88	Swindon T	42	21
1988–89	Leicester C	31	6
1988–89	Bradford C	12	8
1989–90	Bradford C	23	6
1989–90	West Ham U	21	12
1990–91	West Ham U	26	6
1991–92	Bournemouth	43	19
1992–93	Reading	42	17
1993–94	Reading	46	35
1994–95	Reading	35	5
1995–96	Reading	35	11
1996–97	Reading	24	3
1997–98	Peterborough U	42	20
1998–99	Peterborough U	7	5
1998–99	Swindon T	0	0
Total:		**571**	**210**

QUINN, Niall — Forward

H: 6 4 W: 12 04 b.Dublin 6-10-66

Honours: Eire Youth, Under-21, Under-23, B, 69 full caps, 18 goals.

1983–84	Arsenal	0	0
1984–85	Arsenal	0	0
1985–86	Arsenal	12	1
1986–87	Arsenal	35	8
1987–88	Arsenal	11	2
1988–89	Arsenal	3	1
1989–90	Arsenal	6	2
1989–90	Manchester C	9	4
1990–91	Manchester C	38	20
1991–92	Manchester C	35	12
1992–93	Manchester C	39	9
1993–94	Manchester C	15	5
1994–95	Manchester C	35	8
1995–96	Manchester C	32	8
1996–97	Sunderland	12	2
1997–98	Sunderland	35	14
1998–99	Sunderland	39	18
Total:		**356**	**114**

QUINN, Robert — Midfield

H: 5 11 W: 11 02 b.Sidcup 8-11-76

Source: Trainee.

1994–95	Crystal Palace	0	0
1995–96	Crystal Palace	1	0
1996–97	Crystal Palace	21	1
1997–98	Crystal Palace	1	0
1998–99	Brentford	43	2
Total:		**66**	**3**

QUINN, Wayne — Midfield

H: 5 10 W: 11 11 b.Truro 19-11-76

Honours: England Under-21, B.

1994–95	Sheffield U	0	0
1995–96	Sheffield U	0	0
1996–97	Sheffield U	0	0
1997–98	Sheffield U	28	2
1998–99	Sheffield U	44	1
Total:		**72**	**3**

QUITONGO, Jose — Forward

H: 5 7 W: 10 07 b.Luanda 18-11-74

1995–96	Darlington	1	0
1995–96	Hamilton A	22	4
1996–97	Hamilton A	34	3
1997–98	Hamilton A	6	2
1997–98	Hearts	17	3
1998–99	Hearts	12	0
Total:		**92**	**12**

RACHEL, Adam — Goalkeeper

H: 5 11 W: 12 08 b.Birmingham 10-12-76

Source: Trainee.

1994–95	Aston Villa	0	0
1995–96	Aston Villa	0	0
1996–97	Aston Villa	0	0
1997–98	Aston Villa	0	0
1998–99	Aston Villa	1	0
Total:		**1**	**0**

RADEBE, Lucas — Defender

H: 6 1 W: 12 04 b.Johannesburg 12-4-69

Source: Kaiser Chiefs. *Honours:* South Africa 49 full caps, 1 goal.

1994–95	Leeds U	12	0
1995–96	Leeds U	13	0
1996–97	Leeds U	32	0
1997–98	Leeds U	27	0
1998–99	Leeds U	29	0
Total:		**113**	**0**

RADIGAN, Neil — Midfield

H: 5 9 W: 11 00 b.Middlesbrough 4-7-80

Source: Trainee.

1998–99	Scarborough	9	0
Total:		**9**	**0**

RADZKI, Lee — Midfield

b.Mansfield 14-11-78

Source: Trainee.

1995–96	Derby Co	0	0
1996–97	Derby Co	0	0
1997–98	Derby Co	0	0
1998–99	Derby Co	0	0

RAE, Alex — Midfield

H: 5 8 W: 11 08 b.Glasgow 30-9-69

Source: Bishopbriggs. *Honours:* Scotland Under-21, B.

1987–88	Falkirk	12	0
1988–89	Falkirk	37	12
1989–90	Falkirk	34	8
1990–91	Millwall	39	10
1991–92	Millwall	38	11
1992–93	Millwall	30	6
1993–94	Millwall	36	13
1994–95	Millwall	38	10
1995–96	Millwall	37	13
1996–97	Sunderland	23	2
1997–98	Sunderland	29	3
1998–99	Sunderland	15	2
Total:		**368**	**90**

RAE, Gavin — Defender

H: 5 11 W: 10 04 b.Aberdeen 28-11-77

Source: Hermes J. *Honours:* Scotland Under-21.

1995–96	Dundee	6	0
1996–97	Dundee	17	2
1997–98	Dundee	6	0
1998–99	Dundee	30	1
Total:		**59**	**3**

RAESIDE, Robert — Defender

H: 6 0 W: 11 10 b.South Africa 7-7-72

Source: From St Andrews University

1990–91	Raith R	14	0
1991–92	Raith R	13	0
1992–93	Raith R	10	0
1993–94	Raith R	0	0
1994–95	Raith R	10	0
1995–96	Raith R	8	1
1996–97	Dundee	34	4
1997–98	Dundee	11	0
1998–99	Dundee	21	0
Total:		**121**	**5**

RAINFORD, David — Midfield

H: 6 0 W: 12 04 b.Stepney 21-4-79

Source: Trainee.

1997–98	Colchester U	0	0
1998–99	Colchester U	1	0
1998–99	Scarborough (loan)	2	0
Total:		**3**	**0**

RAMAGE, Craig — Midfield

H: 5 9 W: 11 08 b.Derby 30-3-70

Source: Trainee. *Honours:* England Under-21.

1988–89	Derby Co	0	0
1988–89	Wigan Ath (loan)	10	2
1989–90	Derby Co	12	1
1990–91	Derby Co	17	1
1991–92	Derby Co	7	2
1992–93	Derby Co	1	0
1993–94	Derby Co	5	0
1993–94	Watford	13	0
1994–95	Watford	44	9
1995–96	Watford	36	15
1996–97	Watford	11	3
1996–97	Peterborough U (loan)	7	0
1997–98	Bradford C	32	1
1998–99	Bradford C	3	0
Total:		**198**	**34**

RAMASUT, Tom — Midfield

H: 5 10 W: 11 00 b.Cardiff 30-8-77

Honours: Wales Under-21, B.

1995–96	Norwich C	0	0
1996–97	Bristol R	11	0
1997–98	Bristol R	31	6
1998–99	Bristol R	0	0
1998–99	Cardiff C	0	0
Total:		**42**	**6**

RAMM, Daniel — Midfield

b.Norwich 21-9-79

Source: Trainee.

1998–99	Leicester C	0	0

RAMMELL, Andy — Forward

H: 6 1 W: 14 00 b.Nuneaton 10-2-67

Source: Atherstone U.

1989–90	Manchester U	0	0
1990–91	Barnsley	40	12
1991–92	Barnsley	37	8
1992–93	Barnsley	30	7
1993–94	Barnsley	34	6
1994–95	Barnsley	24	7
1995–96	Barnsley	20	4
1995–96	Southend U	7	2
1996–97	Southend U	36	9
1997–98	Southend U	26	2
1998–99	Walsall	39	18
Total:		**293**	**75**

RAMSAY, Douglas — Midfield

H: 5 11 W: 11 01 b.Irvine 26-4-79

Source: Bearsden BC.

1997–98	Motherwell	0	0
1998–99	Motherwell	4	1
Total:		**4**	**1**

RANDALL, Adrian — Midfield

H: 5 11 W: 12 04 b.Salisbury 10-11-68

Source: Apprentice. *Honours:* England Youth.

1985–86	Bournemouth	2	0
1986–87	Bournemouth	0	0
1987–88	Bournemouth	1	0
1988–89	Bournemouth	0	0
1988–89	Aldershot	37	2
1989–90	Aldershot	34	2
1990–91	Aldershot	36	8
1991–92	Aldershot	0	0
1991–92	Burnley	18	2
1992–93	Burnley	23	1
1993–94	Burnley	37	4
1994–95	Burnley	32	1
1995–96	Burnley	15	0
1995–96	York C	16	0
1996–97	York C	16	2
1996–97	Bury	19	3
1997–98	Bury	15	0
1998–99	Bury	0	0
Total:		**301**	**25**

RANKIN, Isiah — Forward

H: 5 10 W: 11 00 b.London 22-5-78

Source: Trainee.

1995–96	Arsenal	0	0
1996–97	Arsenal	0	0
1997–98	Arsenal	1	0
1997–98	Colchester U (loan)	11	5
1998–99	Bradford C	27	4
Total:		**39**	**9**

RANKINE, Mark — Midfield

H: 5 9 W: 11 06 b.Doncaster 30-9-69

Source: Trainee.

1987–88	Doncaster R	18	2
1988–89	Doncaster R	46	11
1989–90	Doncaster R	36	2
1990–91	Doncaster R	40	2
1991–92	Doncaster R	24	3
1991–92	Wolverhampton W	15	1
1992–93	Wolverhampton W	27	0
1993–94	Wolverhampton W	31	0
1994–95	Wolverhampton W	27	0
1995–96	Wolverhampton W	32	0
1996–97	Wolverhampton W	0	0
1996–97	Preston NE	23	0
1997–98	Preston NE	35	1
1998–99	Preston NE	42	3
Total:		**396**	**25**

RAPLEY, Kevin — Forward

H: 5 9 W: 10 08 b.Reading 21-9-77

Source: Trainee.

1996–97	Brentford	2	0
1997–98	Brentford	37	9
1998–99	Brentford	12	3
1998–99	Southend U (loan)	9	4
1998–99	Notts Co	16	2
Total:		**76**	**18**

RATCLIFFE, Simon — Midfield

H: 6 0 W: 12 13 b.Davyhulme 6-2-67

Source: Apprentice. *Honours:* England Schools, Youth.

1984–85	Manchester U	0	0
1985–86	Manchester U	0	0
1986–87	Manchester U	0	0
1987–88	Norwich C	9	0
1988–89	Norwich C	0	0
1988–89	Brentford	9	1
1989–90	Brentford	35	2
1990–91	Brentford	38	2
1991–92	Brentford	34	2
1992–93	Brentford	30	2
1993–94	Brentford	43	4
1994–95	Brentford	25	1
1995–96	Gillingham	41	3
1996–97	Gillingham	43	6
1997–98	Gillingham	21	1
1998–99	Gillingham	0	0
Total:		**328**	**24**

RAVEN, Paul — Defender

H: 6 1 W: 12 11 b.Salisbury 28-7-70

Source: School. *Honours:* England Schools, Youth.

1987–88	Doncaster R	17	3
1988–89	Doncaster R	35	1
1988–89	WBA	3	0
1989–90	WBA	7	0
1990–91	WBA	13	0
1991–92	WBA	7	1
1991–92	Doncaster R (loan)	7	0
1992–93	WBA	44	7
1993–94	WBA	34	1
1994–95	WBA	31	0
1995–96	WBA	40	4
1996–97	WBA	33	1
1997–98	WBA	8	0

1998–99	WBA	7	0
1998–99	Rotherham U (loan)	11	2
Total:		**297**	**20**

RAWLINSON, Mark — Midfield

H: 5 10 W: 11 04 b.Bolton 9-6-75

Source: Trainee.

1993–94	Manchester U	0	0
1994–95	Manchester U	0	0
1995–96	Bournemouth	19	0
1996–97	Bournemouth	25	2
1997–98	Bournemouth	25	0
1998–99	Bournemouth	7	0
Total:		**76**	**2**

RAYNOR, Paul — Midfield

H: 5 11 W: 12 03 b.Nottingham 29-4-66

Source: Apprentice.

1983–84	Nottingham F	0	0
1984–85	Nottingham F	3	0
1984–85	Bristol R (loan)	8	0
1985–86	Huddersfield T	30	5
1986–87	Huddersfield T	20	4
1986–87	Swansea C	12	1
1987–88	Swansea C	44	8
1988–89	Swansea C	26	5
1988–89	Wrexham (loan)	6	0
1989–90	Swansea C	40	6
1990–91	Swansea C	43	5
1991–92	Swansea C	26	2
1991–92	Cambridge U	8	0
1992–93	Cambridge U	41	2
1993–94	Preston NE	39	6
1994–95	Preston NE	38	3
1995–96	Preston NE	3	0
1995–96	Cambridge U	35	3
1996–97	Cambridge U	44	4
1997–98	Cambridge U	0	0
From Guang Deong			
1997–98	Leyton Orient	10	0
1998–99	Leyton Orient	5	0
Total:		**481**	**54**

REA, Simon — Defender

H: 6 1 W: 13 00 b.Coventry 20-9-76

Source: Trainee.

1994–95	Birmingham C	0	0
1995–96	Birmingham C	1	0
1996–97	Birmingham C	0	0
1997–98	Birmingham C	0	0
1998–99	Birmingham C	0	0
Total:		**1**	**0**

READ, Paul — Forward

H: 5 8 W: 12 06 b.Harlow 25-9-73

Source: Trainee. *Honours:* England Schools.

1991–92	Arsenal	0	0
1992–93	Arsenal	0	0
1993–94	Arsenal	0	0
1994–95	Arsenal	0	0
1994–95	Leyton Orient (loan)	11	0
1995–96	Arsenal	0	0
1995–96	Southend U (loan)	4	1
1996–97	Arsenal	0	0
1996–97	Wycombe W	13	4
1997–98	Wycombe W	28	4
1998–99	Wycombe W	16	1
Total:		**72**	**10**

READY, Karl — Defender

H: 6 1 W: 12 10 b.Neath 14-8-72

Source: Trainee. *Honours:* Wales Under-21, B, 5 full caps.

1990–91	QPR	0	0
1991–92	QPR	1	0
1992–93	QPR	3	0
1993–94	QPR	22	1
1994–95	QPR	13	1
1995–96	QPR	22	1
1996–97	QPR	29	0
1997–98	QPR	39	3
1998–99	QPR	41	2
Total:		**170**	**8**

REDFEARN, Neil — Midfield

H: 5 8 W: 12 00 b.Dewsbury 20-6-65

Source: Nottingham F Apprentice.

1982–83	Bolton W	10	0
1983–84	Bolton W	25	1
1983–84	Lincoln C (loan)	10	1
1984–85	Lincoln C	45	4
1985–86	Lincoln C	45	8
1986–87	Doncaster R	46	14
1987–88	Crystal Palace	42	8
1988–89	Crystal Palace	15	2
1988–89	Watford	12	2
1989–90	Watford	12	1
1989–90	Oldham Ath	17	2
1990–91	Oldham Ath	45	14
1991–92	Barnsley	36	4
1992–93	Barnsley	46	3
1993–94	Barnsley	46	12
1994–95	Barnsley	39	11
1995–96	Barnsley	45	14
1996–97	Barnsley	43	17
1997–98	Barnsley	37	10
1998–99	Charlton Ath	30	3
Total:		**646**	**131**

REDKNAPP, Jamie — Midfield

H: 6 0 W: 12 10 b.Barton-on-Sea 25-6-73

Source: Tottenham H Schoolboy, Bournemouth Trainee.
Honours: England Schools, Youth, B, Under-21, 14 full caps.

1989–90	Bournemouth	4	0
1990–91	Bournemouth	9	0
1990–91	Liverpool	0	0
1991–92	Liverpool	6	1
1992–93	Liverpool	29	2
1993–94	Liverpool	35	4
1994–95	Liverpool	41	3
1995–96	Liverpool	23	3
1996–97	Liverpool	23	2
1997–98	Liverpool	20	3
1998–99	Liverpool	34	8
Total:		**224**	**26**

REDMILE, Matthew — Defender

H: 6 4 W: 14 10 b.Nottingham 12-11-76

Source: Trainee.

1995–96	Notts Co	0	0
1996–97	Notts Co	23	2
1997–98	Notts Co	34	3
1998–99	Notts Co	41	1
Total:		**98**	**6**

REDMOND, Steve — Defender

H: 5 11 W: 13 00 b.Liverpool 2-11-67

Source: Apprentice. *Honours:* England Youth, Under-21.

1984–85	Manchester C	0	0
1985–86	Manchester C	9	0
1986–87	Manchester C	30	2
1987–88	Manchester C	44	0
1988–89	Manchester C	46	1
1989–90	Manchester C	38	0
1990–91	Manchester C	37	3
1991–92	Manchester C	31	1
1992–93	Oldham Ath	31	0
1993–94	Oldham Ath	33	1
1994–95	Oldham Ath	43	0
1995–96	Oldham Ath	40	1
1996–97	Oldham Ath	24	2
1997–98	Oldham Ath	34	0
1998–99	Bury	26	0
Total:		**466**	**11**

REED, Adam — Defender

H: 6 1 W: 11 00 b.Bishop Auckland 18-2-75

Source: Trainee.

1991–92	Darlington	1	0
1992–93	Darlington	0	0
1993–94	Darlington	13	0
1994–95	Darlington	38	1
1995–96	Blackburn R	0	0
1996–97	Blackburn R	0	0
1996–97	Darlington (loan)	14	0
1997–98	Blackburn R	0	0
1997–98	Rochdale (loan)	10	0
1998–99	Darlington	29	2
Total:		**105**	**3**

REED, John — Midfield

H: 5 10 W: 10 11 b.Rotherham 27-8-72

Source: Trainee.

1990–91	Sheffield U	0	0
1990–91	Scarborough (loan)	14	6
1991–92	Sheffield U	1	0
1991–92	Scarborough (loan)	6	0
1992–93	Sheffield U	0	0
1992–93	Darlington (loan)	10	2
1993–94	Sheffield U	0	0
1993–94	Mansfield T (loan)	13	2
1994–95	Sheffield U	12	2
1995–96	Sheffield U	2	0
1996–97	Sheffield U	0	0
1997–98	Sheffield U	0	0
1997–98	Blackpool	3	0
1998–99	Bury	0	0
Total:		**61**	**12**

REED, Martin — Defender

H: 5 11 W: 11 07 b.Scarborough 10-1-78

Source: Trainee.

1996–97	York C	2	0
1997–98	York C	22	0
1998–99	York C	12	0
Total:		**36**	**0**

REED, Matthew — Goalkeeper

H: 5 10 W: 11 10 b.Stanford-Le-Hope 7-4-80

Source: Trainee.

1997–98	Newcastle U	0	0
1998–99	Newcastle U	0	0

REES, Jason — Midfield

H: 5 5 W: 10 00 b.Aberdare 22-12-69

Source: Trainee. *Honours:* Wales Schools, Youth, Under-21, B, 1 full cap.

1988–89	Luton T	0	0
1989–90	Luton T	14	0
1990–91	Luton T	21	0
1991–92	Luton T	5	0
1992–93	Luton T	32	0
1993–94	Luton T	10	0
1993–94	Mansfield T (loan)	15	1
1994–95	Portsmouth	19	1
1995–96	Portsmouth	21	1

1996–97	Portsmouth	3	1
1996–97	Exeter C (loan)	7	0
1997–98	Cambridge U	20	0
1998–99	Exeter C	44	1
Total:		**211**	**5**

REESON, Nick — Midfield

b.Boston 5-5-80

Source: Trainee.

1997–98	Lincoln C	0	0
1998–99	Lincoln C	0	0

REEVE, Chris — Forward

H: 5 11 W: 11 05 b.Darlington 1-10-79

Source: Trainee.

1997–98	Middlesbrough	0	0
1998–99	Middlesbrough	0	0

REEVE, Daniel — Midfield

b.Pontefract 10-2-80

1998–99	Colchester U	0	0

REEVES, Alan — Defender

H: 6 0 W: 12 00 b.Birkenhead 19-11-67

Source: Heswall.

1988–89	Norwich C	0	0
1988–89	Gillingham (loan)	18	0
1989–90	Chester C	30	2
1990–91	Chester C	10	0
1991–92	Rochdale	34	3
1992–93	Rochdale	41	3
1993–94	Rochdale	41	3
1994–95	Rochdale	5	0
1994–95	Wimbledon	31	3
1995–96	Wimbledon	24	1
1996–97	Wimbledon	2	0
1997–98	Wimbledon	0	0
1998–99	Swindon T	24	2
Total:		**260**	**17**

REEVES, David — Forward

H: 6 0 W: 12 06 b.Birkenhead 19-11-67

Source: Heswall.

1986–87	Sheffield W	0	0
1986–87	Scunthorpe U (loan)	4	2
1987–88	Sheffield W	0	0
1987–88	Scunthorpe U (loan)	6	4
1987–88	Burnley (loan)	16	8
1988–89	Sheffield W	17	2
1989–90	Bolton W	41	10
1990–91	Bolton W	44	10
1991–92	Bolton W	35	8
1992–93	Bolton W	14	1
1992–93	Notts Co	9	2
1993–94	Notts Co	4	0
1993–94	Carlisle U	34	11
1994–95	Carlisle U	42	21
1995–96	Carlisle U	43	13
1996–97	Carlisle U	8	3
1996–97	Preston NE	34	11
1997–98	Preston NE	13	1
1997–98	Chesterfield	26	5
1998–99	Chesterfield	40	10
Total:		**430**	**122**

REGAN, Carl — Defender

b.Liverpool 9-9-80

Source: Trainee. *Honours:* England Youth.

1997–98	Everton	0	0
1998–99	Everton	0	0

REID, Alan — Forward

H: 5 8 W: 10 00 b.Paisley 21-10-80

Source: Renfrew Vic.

1998–99	Hibernian	1	0
Total:		**1**	**0**

REID, Brian — Defender

H: 6 3 W: 13 08 b.Paisley 15-6-70

1998–99	Burnley	31	3
Total:		**31**	**3**

REID, Paul — Midfield

H: 5 10 W: 10 12 b.Oldbury 19-1-68

Source: Apprentice.

1985–86	Leicester C	0	0
1986–87	Leicester C	6	0
1987–88	Leicester C	26	5
1988–89	Leicester C	45	6
1989–90	Leicester C	40	8
1990–91	Leicester C	33	2
1991–92	Leicester C	12	0
1991–92	Bradford C (loan)	7	0
1992–93	Bradford C	44	6
1993–94	Bradford C	38	9
1994–95	Huddersfield T	42	6
1995–96	Huddersfield T	13	0
1996–97	Huddersfield T	22	0
1996–97	Oldham Ath	9	1
1997–98	Oldham Ath	44	4
1998–99	Oldham Ath	40	1
Total:		**421**	**48**

REID, Paul — Defender

H: 6 2 W: 11 08 b.Carlisle 18-2-82

Source: Trainee.

1998–99	Carlisle U	0	0

REID, Shaun — Midfield

H: 5 8 W: 12 02 b.Huyton 13-10-65

Source: Local.

1983–84	Rochdale	17	0
1984–85	Rochdale	21	1
1985–86	Rochdale	8	0
1985–86	Preston NE (loan)	3	0
1986–87	Rochdale	41	1
1987–88	Rochdale	28	0
1988–89	Rochdale	18	2
1988–89	York C	24	2
1989–90	York C	25	4
1990–91	York C	29	0
1991–92	York C	28	1
1992–93	Rochdale	40	4
1993–94	Rochdale	39	3
1994–95	Rochdale	28	3
1995–96	Bury	21	0
1996–97	Bury	0	0
1996–97	Chester C	27	1
1997–98	Chester C	0	0
1998–99	Chester C	22	1
Total:		**419**	**23**

REID, Steven — Forward

H: 5 11 W: 11 10 b.Kingston 10-3-81

Source: Trainee. *Honours:* England Youth.

1997–98	Millwall	1	0
1998–99	Millwall	25	0
Total:		**26**	**0**

REILLY, Alan — Midfield

H: 5 11 W: 12 01 b.Dublin 22-8-80

Source: Trainee.

1998–99	Manchester C	0	0

REILLY, Mark — Midfield

H: 5 7 W: 11 00 b.Bellshill 3-3-69

Source: Wishaw Jun. *Honours:* Scotland B.

1988–89	Motherwell	0	0
1989–90	Motherwell	4	0
1990–91	Motherwell	0	0
1991–92	Kilmarnock	19	0
1992–93	Kilmarnock	19	3
1993–94	Kilmarnock	38	0
1994–95	Kilmarnock	32	0
1995–96	Kilmarnock	28	0
1996–97	Kilmarnock	33	2
1997–98	Kilmarnock	36	3
1998–99	Reading	6	0
1998–99	Kilmarnock	18	0
Total:		**233**	**8**

REINELT, Robbie — Forward

H: 5 11 W: 11 11 b.Epping 11-3-74

Source: Trainee.

1990–91	Aldershot	5	0
1991–92	Aldershot	0	0
1992–93	Gillingham	0	0
1993–94	Gillingham	25	1
1994–95	Gillingham	27	4
1994–95	Colchester U	5	0
1995–96	Colchester U	22	7
1996–97	Colchester U	21	3
1996–97	Brighton & HA	12	3
1997–98	Brighton & HA	32	4
1998–99	Leyton Orient	7	0
Total:		**156**	**22**

REMY, Christophe — Defender

H: 5 9 W: 12 06 b.Besancon 6-8-71

1992–93	Auxerre	1	0
1993–94	Auxerre	0	0
1994–95	Auxerre	8	0
1995–96	Auxerre	13	0
1996–97	Derby Co	0	0
1997–98	Oxford U	16	0
1998–99	Oxford U	12	1
Total:		**50**	**1**

RENNER, Victor — Forward

H: 6 0 W: 11 02 b.Sierra Leone 18-4-79

Source: Trainee.

1996–97	Wimbledon	0	0
1997–98	Wimbledon	0	0
1998–99	Wimbledon	0	0

RENNIE, David — Defender

H: 6 0 W: 13 00 b.Edinburgh 29-8-64

Source: Apprentice. *Honours:* Scotland Youth.

1982–83	Leicester C	0	0
1983–84	Leicester C	15	0
1984–85	Leicester C	3	1
1985–86	Leicester C	3	0
1985–86	Leeds U	16	2
1986–87	Leeds U	24	0
1987–88	Leeds U	28	2
1988–89	Leeds U	33	1
1989–90	Bristol C	45	4
1990–91	Bristol C	32	2

1991–92	Bristol C	27	2
1991–92	Birmingham C	17	2
1992–93	Birmingham C	18	2
1992–93	Coventry C	9	0
1993–94	Coventry C	34	1
1994–95	Coventry C	28	0
1995–96	Coventry C	11	2
1996–97	Northampton T	43	3
1997–98	Northampton T	5	0
1997–98	Peterborough U	18	0
1998–99	Peterborough U	9	0
Total:		**418**	**24**

RENNISON, Graham — Defender

H: 6 1 W: 12 00 b.Northallerton 2-10-78

Source: Trainee.

1997–98	York C	1	0
1998–99	York C	0	0
Total:		**1**	**0**

RENNISON, Shaun

b.Northallerton 23-11-80

Source: Trainee.

1998–99	Scarborough	15	1
Total:		**15**	**1**

RENSHAW, Ian — Defender

b.Chelmsford 14-4-78

1998–99	Scarborough	1	0
Total:		**1**	**0**

RENWICK, Michael — Defender

H: 5 9 W: 11 00 b.Edinburgh 29-2-76

Source: Hutchison Vale BC.

1994–95	Hibernian	1	0
1995–96	Hibernian	2	0
1996–97	Hibernian	9	0
1997–98	Hibernian	6	0
1998–99	Hibernian	16	0
Total:		**34**	**0**

REYNA, Claudio — Midfield

H: 5 9 W: 11 09 b.New Jersey 20-7-73

Source: Union County SC, Univ Virginia. *Honours:* USA 62 full caps, 7 goals.

1996–97	Leverkusen	5	0
1997–98	Wolfsburg	28	4
1998–99	Wolfsburg	20	2
1998–99	Rangers	6	0
Total:		**59**	**6**

RHODES, Andy — Goalkeeper

H: 6 0 W: 13 06 b.Doncaster 23-8-64

Source: Apprentice.

1982–83	Barnsley	0	0
1983–84	Barnsley	31	0
1984–85	Barnsley	5	0
1985–86	Barnsley	0	0
1985–86	Doncaster R	30	0
1986–87	Doncaster R	41	0
1987–88	Doncaster R	35	0
1987–88	Oldham Ath	11	0
1988–89	Oldham Ath	27	0
1989–90	Oldham Ath	31	0
1990–91	Dunfermline Ath	35	0
1991–92	Dunfermline Ath	44	0
1992–93	St Johnstone	44	0
1993–94	St Johnstone	44	0
1994–95	St Johnstone	19	0
1994–95	Bolton W (loan)	0	0
1995–96	Airdrieonians	16	0
1996–97	Airdrieonians	9	0
1997–98	Airdrieonians	4	0
1997–98	Scarborough	11	0
1998–99	Scarborough	0	0
Total:		**437**	**0**

RIBEIRO, Bruno — Midfield

H: 5 8 W: 12 07 b.Setubal 22-10-75

Honours: Portugal Under-21.

1994–95	Setubal	11	1
1995–96	Setubal	8	2
1996–97	Setubal	20	1
1997–98	Leeds U	29	3
1998–99	Leeds U	13	1
Total:		**81**	**8**

RICARD, Hamilton — Forward

H: 6 1 W: 13 12 b.Colombia 12-1-74

Source: Deportivo Cali.

1997–98	Middlesbrough	9	2
1998–99	Middlesbrough	36	15
Total:		**45**	**17**

RICCIO, Luigi — Defender

H: 5 8 W: 11 08 b.Naples 28-12-77

Source: Perugia.

1998–99	Rangers	1	0
Total:		**1**	**0**

RICHARD, Fabrice — Defender

b.Saintes 16-8-73

1998–99	Colchester U	10	0
Total:		**10**	**0**

RICHARDS, Dean — Defender

H: 6 2 W: 13 07 b.Bradford 9-6-74

Source: Trainee. *Honours:* England Under-21.

1991–92	Bradford C	7	1
1992–93	Bradford C	3	0
1993–94	Bradford C	46	2
1994–95	Bradford C	30	1
1994–95	Wolverhampton W (loan)	10	2
1995–96	Wolverhampton W	37	1
1996–97	Wolverhampton W	21	1
1997–98	Wolverhampton W	13	0
1998–99	Wolverhampton W	41	3
Total:		**208**	**11**

RICHARDS, Ian — Defender

H: 5 8 W: 11 04 b.Barnsley 5-10-79

Source: Trainee.

1997–98	Blackburn R	0	0
1998–99	Blackburn R	0	0

RICHARDS, Justin — Forward

H: 6 0 W: 11 10 b.Sandwell 16-10-80

Source: Trainee.

1998–99	WBA	1	0
Total:		**1**	**0**

RICHARDS, Tony — Forward

H: 6 0 W: 13 06 b.Newham 17-9-73

Source: West Ham U Trainee, Sudbury T.

1995–96	Cambridge U	19	1
1996–97	Cambridge U	23	4
1997–98	Leyton Orient	17	2
1998–99	Leyton Orient	29	7
Total:		**88**	**14**

RICHARDSON, Barry — Goalkeeper

H: 6 1 W: 12 01 b.Wallsend 5-8-69

Source: Trainee.

1987–88	Sunderland	0	0
1988–89	Scunthorpe U	0	0
1989–90	Scarborough	24	0
1990–91	Scarborough	6	0
1991–92	Northampton T	27	0
1992–93	Northampton T	42	0
1993–94	Northampton T	27	0
1994–95	Preston NE	17	0
1995–96	Preston NE	3	0
1995–96	Lincoln C	34	0
1996–97	Lincoln C	36	0
1997–98	Lincoln C	26	0
1998–99	Lincoln C	13	0
Total:		**255**	**0**

RICHARDSON, Craig — Defender

b.Newham 8-10-79

Source: Trainee.

1997–98	Leyton Orient	1	0
1998–99	Leyton Orient	0	0
Total:		**1**	**0**

RICHARDSON, Ian — Midfield

H: 5 11 W: 11 01 b.Barking 22-10-70

Source: Dagenham & Redbridge.

1995–96	Birmingham C	7	0
1995–96	Notts Co	15	0
1996–97	Notts Co	19	1
1997–98	Notts Co	30	2
1998–99	Notts Co	23	7
Total:		**94**	**10**

RICHARDSON, Jay — Midfield

H: 5 9 W: 11 00 b.Keston 14-11-79

Source: Trainee.

1997–98	Chelsea	0	0
1998–99	Chelsea	0	0

RICHARDSON, Jon — Defender

H: 6 1 W: 12 05 b.Nottingham 29-8-75

Source: Trainee.

1993–94	Exeter C	7	0
1994–95	Exeter C	38	1
1995–96	Exeter C	43	1
1996–97	Exeter C	43	1
1997–98	Exeter C	41	2
1998–99	Exeter C	40	2
Total:		**212**	**7**

RICHARDSON, Kevin — Midfield

H: 5 9 W: 11 08 b.Newcastle 4-12-62

Source: Apprentice. *Honours:* England 1 full cap.

1980–81	Everton	0	0
1981–82	Everton	18	2
1982–83	Everton	29	3
1983–84	Everton	28	4
1984–85	Everton	15	4
1985–86	Everton	18	3

1986–87	Everton	1	0
1986–87	Watford	39	2
1987–88	Arsenal	29	4
1988–89	Arsenal	34	1
1989–90	Arsenal	33	0
1990–91	Real Sociedad	37	0
1991–92	Aston Villa	42	6
1992–93	Aston Villa	42	2
1993–94	Aston Villa	40	5
1994–95	Aston Villa	19	0
1994–95	Coventry C	14	0
1995–96	Coventry C	33	0
1996–97	Coventry C	28	0
1997–98	Coventry C	3	0
1997–98	Southampton	28	0
1998–99	Barnsley	26	0
Total:		**556**	**36**

RICHARDSON, Leam — Defender

b.Leeds 19-11-79

Source: Trainee.

1997–98	Blackburn R	0	0
1998–99	Blackburn R	0	0

RICHARDSON, Lee J — Midfield

H: 5 10 W: 12 07 b.Halifax 12-3-69

1986–87	Halifax T	1	0
1987–88	Halifax T	30	1
1988–89	Halifax T	25	1
1988–89	Watford	9	0
1989–90	Watford	32	1
1990–91	Blackburn R	38	2
1991–92	Blackburn R	24	1
1992–93	Blackburn R	0	0
1992–93	Aberdeen	29	2
1993–94	Aberdeen	35	4
1994–95	Oldham Ath	30	6
1995–96	Oldham Ath	27	11
1996–97	Oldham Ath	31	4
1997–98	Oldham Ath	0	0
1997–98	Stockport Co (loan)	6	0
1997–98	Huddersfield T	21	3
1998–99	Huddersfield T	15	0
Total:		**353**	**36**

RICHARDSON, Neil — Defender

H: 6 0 W: 13 00 b.Sunderland 3-3-68

Source: Brandon U.

1989–90	Rotherham U	2	0
1990–91	Rotherham U	16	2
1991–92	Rotherham U	18	2
1992–93	Rotherham U	14	0
1993–94	Rotherham U	27	0
1994–95	Rotherham U	25	0
1995–96	Rotherham U	25	2
1996–97	Rotherham U	14	1
1996–97	Exeter C (loan)	14	0
1997–98	Rotherham U	38	2
1998–99	Rotherham U	5	0
Total:		**198**	**9**

RICHARDSON, Nick — Midfield

H: 6 1 W: 12 06 b.Halifax 11-4-67

Source: Local.

1988–89	Halifax T	7	0
1989–90	Halifax T	27	6
1990–91	Halifax T	26	3
1991–92	Halifax T	41	8
1992–93	Cardiff C	39	4
1993–94	Cardiff C	39	5
1994–95	Cardiff C	33	4
1994–95	Wrexham (loan)	4	2
1994–95	Chester C (loan)	6	1
1995–96	Bury	5	0
1995–96	Chester C	37	4
1996–97	Chester C	9	0
1997–98	Chester C	44	2
1998–99	Chester C	43	3
Total:		**360**	**42**

RICKERS, Paul — Midfield

H: 5 10 W: 10 07 b.Dewsbury 9-5-75

Source: Trainee.

1993–94	Oldham Ath	0	0
1994–95	Oldham Ath	4	1
1995–96	Oldham Ath	23	0
1996–97	Oldham Ath	46	4
1997–98	Oldham Ath	40	4
1998–99	Oldham Ath	45	4
Total:		**158**	**13**

RICKETTS, Michael — Forward

H: 6 1 W: 12 05 b.Birmingham 4-12-78

Source: Trainee.

1995–96	Walsall	1	1
1996–97	Walsall	11	1
1997–98	Walsall	24	1
1998–99	Walsall	8	0
Total:		**44**	**3**

RIDLER, Dave — Defender

H: 6 0 W: 12 02 b.Liverpool 12-3-76

Source: Prescot T.

1996–97	Wrexham	11	0
1997–98	Wrexham	20	0
1998–99	Wrexham	36	1
Total:		**67**	**1**

RIDLEY, Martin — Defender

H: 6 0 W: 11 09 b.Leicester 30-3-80

Source: Trainee.

1998–99	Aston Villa	0	0

RIEDLE, Karlheinz — Forward

H: 5 11 W: 12 00 b.Weiler 16-9-65

Source: Augsburg. *Honours:* Germany 42 full caps, 16 goals.

1986–87	Blau-Weiss 90	34	10
1987–88	Werder Bremen	33	17
1988–89	Werder Bremen	33	13
1989–90	Werder Bremen	20	8
1990–91	Lazio	33	9
1991–92	Lazio	29	13
1992–93	Lazio	22	8
1993–94	Borussia Dortmund	22	4
1994–95	Borussia Dortmund	29	6
1995–96	Borussia Dortmund	18	7
1996–97	Borussia Dortmund	18	7
1997–98	Liverpool	25	6
1998–99	Liverpool	34	5
Total:		**350**	**113**

RIEPER, Marc — Defender

H: 6 3 W: 13 10 b.Denmark 5-6-68

Source: Aarhus. *Honours:* Denmark 58 full caps, 2 goal.

1992–93	Brondby	32	2
1993–94	Brondby	31	0
1994–95	Brondby	18	1
1994–95	West Ham U	21	1
1995–96	West Ham U	36	2
1996–97	West Ham U	28	1
1997–98	West Ham U	5	1
1997–98	Celtic	30	2
1998–99	Celtic	7	0
Total:		**208**	**10**

RIGBY, Tony — Midfield

H: 5 10 W: 13 12 b.Ormskirk 10-8-72

Source: Barrow.

1992–93	Bury	21	2
1993–94	Bury	33	7
1994–95	Bury	30	2
1995–96	Bury	41	7
1996–97	Bury	15	0
1996–97	Scarborough (loan)	5	1
1997–98	Bury	24	1
1998–99	Bury	2	0
Total:		**171**	**20**

RIGGOTT, Chris — Defender

b.Derby 1-9-80

Source: Trainee. *Honours:* England Youth.

1998–99	Derby Co	0	0

RIMMER, Stephen — Defender

H: 6 3 W: 13 02 b.Liverpool 23-5-79

Source: Trainee.

1996–97	Manchester C	0	0
1997–98	Manchester C	0	0
1998–99	Manchester C	0	0

RIOCH, Greg — Defender

H: 5 11 W: 12 10 b.Sutton Coldfield 24-6-75

Source: Trainee.

1993–94	Luton T	0	0
1993–94	Barnet (loan)	3	0
1994–95	Luton T	0	0
1995–96	Peterborough U	18	0
1996–97	Hull C	39	1
1997–98	Hull C	39	5
1998–99	Hull C	13	0
Total:		**112**	**6**

RIPLEY, Stuart — Forward

H: 5 11 W: 13 05 b.Middlesbrough 20-11-67

Source: Apprentice. *Honours:* England Youth, Under-21, 2 full caps.

1984–85	Middlesbrough	1	0
1985–86	Middlesbrough	8	0
1985–86	Bolton W (loan)	5	1
1986–87	Middlesbrough	44	4
1987–88	Middlesbrough	43	8
1988–89	Middlesbrough	36	4
1989–90	Middlesbrough	39	1
1990–91	Middlesbrough	39	6
1991–92	Middlesbrough	39	3
1992–93	Blackburn R	40	7
1993–94	Blackburn R	40	4
1994–95	Blackburn R	37	0
1995–96	Blackburn R	28	0
1996–97	Blackburn R	13	0
1997–98	Blackburn R	29	2
1998–99	Southampton	22	0
Total:		**463**	**40**

RISETH, Vidar — Forward

H: 6 2 W: 12 06 b.Levanger 21-4-72

Honours: Norway 12 full caps, 2 goals.

1992	Rosenborg	1	0
1993	Rosenborg	10	2

1994	Kongsvinger	18	3
1995	Kongsvinger	24	12
1996	Kongsvinger	14	5
1996–97	LASK Linz	33	7
1997–98	LASK Linz	29	4
1998–99	Celtic	27	3
Total:		**156**	**36**

RISHWORTH, Steve — Midfield

H: 5 11 W: 11 09 b.Chester 8-6-80

Source: Schoolboy.

1998–99	Wrexham	4	0
Total:		**4**	**0**

RITCHIE, Andy — Forward

H: 5 11 W: 11 09 b.Manchester 28-11-60

Source: Apprentice. *Honours:* England Schools, Youth, Under-21.

1977–78	Manchester U	4	0
1978–79	Manchester U	17	10
1979–80	Manchester U	8	3
1980–81	Manchester U	4	0
1980–81	Brighton & HA	26	5
1981–82	Brighton & HA	39	13
1982–83	Brighton & HA	24	5
1982–83	Leeds U	10	3
1983–84	Leeds U	38	7
1984–85	Leeds U	28	12
1985–86	Leeds U	29	11
1986–87	Leeds U	31	7
1987–88	Oldham Ath	36	19
1988–89	Oldham Ath	31	14
1989–90	Oldham Ath	38	15
1990–91	Oldham Ath	31	15
1991–92	Oldham Ath	14	3
1992–93	Oldham Ath	12	3
1993–94	Oldham Ath	22	1
1994–95	Oldham Ath	33	12
1995–96	Scarborough	37	8
1996–97	Scarborough	31	9
1996–97	Oldham Ath	10	0
1997–98	Oldham Ath	15	2
1998–99	Oldham Ath	1	0
Total:		**569**	**177**

RITCHIE, Paul — Defender

H: 5 11 W: 12 00 b.Kirkcaldy 21-8-75

Source: Links U. *Honours:* Scotland Under-21, B, 2 full caps, 1 goal.

1992–93	Hearts	0	0
1993–94	Hearts	0	0
1994–95	Hearts	0	0
1995–96	Hearts	28	1
1996–97	Hearts	28	1
1997–98	Hearts	34	0
1998–99	Hearts	29	1
Total:		**119**	**3**

RIVERS, Mark — Forward

H: 5 10 W: 11 00 b.Crewe 26-11-75

Source: Trainee.

1993–94	Crewe Alex	0	0
1994–95	Crewe Alex	0	0
1995–96	Crewe Alex	33	10
1996–97	Crewe Alex	27	6
1997–98	Crewe Alex	35	6
1998–99	Crewe Alex	43	7
Total:		**138**	**29**

RIZA, Omer — Forward

b.Edmonton 8-11-79

Source: Trainee.

1998–99	Arsenal	0	0

RIZZO, Nicky — Midfield

H: 5 10 W: 12 00 b.Sydney 9-6-79

Source: Sydney Olympic.

1996–97	Liverpool	0	0
1997–98	Liverpool	0	0
1998–99	Crystal Palace	19	1
Total:		**19**	**1**

ROACH, Neville — Forward

H: 5 10 W: 11 12 b.Reading 29-9-78

Source: Trainee.

1996–97	Reading	3	1
1997–98	Reading	8	0
1998–99	Reading	5	0
1998–99	Southend U	8	1
Total:		**24**	**2**

ROBERTS, Andy — Midfield

H: 5 10 W: 13 00 b.Dartford 20-3-74

Source: Trainee. *Honours:* England Under-21.

1991–92	Millwall	7	0
1992–93	Millwall	45	0
1993–94	Millwall	42	2
1994–95	Millwall	44	3
1995–96	Crystal Palace	38	0
1996–97	Crystal Palace	45	2
1997–98	Crystal Palace	25	0
1997–98	Wimbledon	12	1
1998–99	Wimbledon	28	2
Total:		**286**	**10**

ROBERTS, Ben — Goalkeeper

H: 6 1 W: 12 11 b.Bishop Auckland 2-5-75

Source: Trainee. *Honours:* England Under-21.

1992–93	Middlesbrough	0	0
1993–94	Middlesbrough	0	0
1994–95	Middlesbrough	0	0
1995–96	Middlesbrough	0	0
1995–96	Hartlepool U (loan)	4	0
1995–96	Wycombe W (loan)	15	0
1996–97	Middlesbrough	10	0
1996–97	Bradford C (loan)	2	0
1997–98	Middlesbrough	6	0
1998–99	Middlesbrough	0	0
1998–99	Millwall (loan)	11	0
Total:		**48**	**0**

ROBERTS, Chris — Forward

H: 5 10 W: 12 03 b.Cardiff 22-10-79

Source: Trainee. *Honours:* Wales Under-21.

1997–98	Cardiff C	11	3
1998–99	Cardiff C	4	0
Total:		**15**	**3**

ROBERTS, Darren — Forward

H: 6 0 W: 12 04 b.Birmingham 12-10-69

Source: Burton Alb.

1991–92	Wolverhampton W	0	0
1992–93	Wolverhampton W	21	5
1993–94	Wolverhampton W	0	0
1993–94	Hereford U (loan)	6	5
1994–95	Doncaster R	0	0
1994–95	Chesterfield	11	1
1995–96	Chesterfield	14	0
1996–97	Darlington	44	16
1997–98	Darlington	28	12
1997–98	Peterborough U (loan)	3	0
1998–99	Darlington	24	5
1998–99	Scarborough	18	3
Total:		**169**	**47**

ROBERTS, Gareth — Defender

H: 5 8 W: 11 00 b.Wrexham 6-2-78

Source: Trainee. *Honours:* Wales Under-21, B.

1995–96	Liverpool	0	0
1996–97	Liverpool	0	0
1997–98	Liverpool	0	0
1998–99	Liverpool	0	0

ROBERTS, Iwan — Forward

H: 6 3 W: 13 06 b.Bangor 26-6-68

Source: Trainee. *Honours:* Wales Youth, 7 full caps.

1985–86	Watford	4	0
1986–87	Watford	3	1
1987–88	Watford	25	2
1988–89	Watford	22	6
1989–90	Watford	9	0
1990–91	Huddersfield T	44	13
1991–92	Huddersfield T	46	24
1992–93	Huddersfield T	37	9
1993–94	Huddersfield T	15	4
1993–94	Leicester C	26	13
1994–95	Leicester C	37	9
1995–96	Leicester C	37	19
1996–97	Wolverhampton W	33	12
1997–98	Norwich C	31	5
1998–99	Norwich C	45	19
Total:		**414**	**136**

ROBERTS, Jason — Forward

H: 6 1 W: 13 06 b.Park Royal 25-1-78

Source: Hayes.

1997–98	Wolverhampton W	0	0
1997–98	Torquay U (loan)	14	6
1997–98	Bristol C (loan)	3	1
1998–99	Bristol R	37	16
Total:		**54**	**23**

ROBERTS, Mark — Forward

H: 5 9 W: 9 10 b.Irvine 29-10-75

Source: Bellfield BC.

1991–92	Kilmarnock	1	0
1992–93	Kilmarnock	5	0
1993–94	Kilmarnock	13	2
1994–95	Kilmarnock	4	1
1995–96	Kilmarnock	11	0
1996–97	Kilmarnock	10	2
1997–98	Kilmarnock	31	7
1998–99	Kilmarnock	22	3
Total:		**97**	**15**

ROBERTS, Neil — Forward

H: 5 10 W: 11 02 b.Wrexham 7-4-78

Source: Trainee. *Honours:* Wales Under-21.

1996–97	Wrexham	0	0
1997–98	Wrexham	34	8
1998–99	Wrexham	22	3
Total:		**56**	**11**

ROBERTS, Paul — Forward

H: 5 11 W: 11 09 b.Bangor 29-7-77

Source: Porthmadog.

1996–97	Wrexham	1	0
1997–98	Wrexham	0	0
1998–99	Wrexham	0	0
Total:		**1**	**0**

ROBERTS, Steve — Defender

H: 6 2 W: 11 06 b.Wrexham 24-2-80

Source: Trainee.

1997–98	Wrexham	0	0
1998–99	Wrexham	0	0

ROBERTS, Stuart — Midfield

H: 5 6 W: 9 8 b.Carmarthen 22-7-80

Source: Trainee. *Honours:* Wales Under-21.

1998–99	Swansea C	32	3
Total:		**32**	**3**

ROBERTS, Tony — Goalkeeper

H: 6 0 W: 13 11 b.Holyhead 4-8-69

Source: Trainee. *Honours:* Wales Under-21, 2 full caps.

1987–88	QPR	1	0
1988–89	QPR	0	0
1989–90	QPR	5	0
1990–91	QPR	12	0
1991–92	QPR	1	0
1992–93	QPR	28	0
1993–94	QPR	16	0
1994–95	QPR	31	0
1995–96	QPR	5	0
1996–97	QPR	13	0
1997–98	QPR	10	0
1998–99	Millwall	8	0
Total:		**130**	**0**

ROBERTSON, David — Defender

H: 5 11 W: 13 01 b.Aberdeen 17-10-68

Source: Deeside BC. *Honours:* Scotland Under-21, 3 full caps.

1986–87	Aberdeen	34	0
1987–88	Aberdeen	23	0
1988–89	Aberdeen	23	0
1989–90	Aberdeen	20	1
1990–91	Aberdeen	35	1
1991–92	Rangers	42	1
1992–93	Rangers	39	3
1993–94	Rangers	32	1
1994–95	Rangers	23	3
1995–96	Rangers	25	3
1996–97	Rangers	22	4
1997–98	Leeds U	26	0
1998–99	Leeds U	0	0
Total:		**344**	**17**

ROBERTSON, Graham — Midfield

H: 5 10 W: 11 11 b.Edinburgh 12-11-76

Source: Balgorie Colts.

1993–94	Raith R	0	0
1994–95	Raith R	0	0
1995–96	Raith R	0	0
1996–97	Millwall	1	0
1997–98	Millwall	1	0
1998–99	Millwall	0	0
Total:		**2**	**0**

ROBERTSON, Hugh — Defender

H: 5 9 W: 12 07 b.Aberdeen 19-3-75

Source: Lewis U. *Honours:* Scotland Under-21.

1993–94	Aberdeen	8	0
1994–95	Aberdeen	3	2
1995–96	Aberdeen	11	0
1996–97	Aberdeen	0	0
1996–97	Dundee	15	1
1997–98	Dundee	0	0
1997–98	Brechin C (loan)	7	0
1998–99	Dundee	10	0
Total:		**54**	**3**

ROBERTSON, Mark — Midfield

H: 5 9 W: 11 09 b.Sydney 6-4-77

Source: Marconi.

1997–98	Burnley	11	0
1998–99	Burnley	24	1
Total:		**35**	**1**

ROBERTSON, Stephen — Goalkeeper

H: 5 10 W: 11 13 b.Glasgow 16-3-77

Source: Ashfield J.

1994–95	St Johnstone	0	0
1995–96	St Johnstone	2	0
1996–97	St Johnstone	2	0
1997–98	St Johnstone	2	0
1998–99	St Johnstone	0	0
Total:		**6**	**0**

ROBINS, Mark — Forward

H: 5 8 W: 11 11 b.Ashton-under-Lyne 22-12-69

Source: Apprentice. *Honours:* England Under-21.

1986–87	Manchester U	0	0
1987–88	Manchester U	0	0
1988–89	Manchester U	10	0
1989–90	Manchester U	17	7
1990–91	Manchester U	19	4
1991–92	Manchester U	2	0
1992–93	Norwich C	37	15
1993–94	Norwich C	13	1
1994–95	Norwich C	17	4
1994–95	Leicester C	17	5
1995–96	Leicester C	31	6
1996–97	Leicester C	8	1
1997–98	Leicester C	0	0
1997–98	Reading (loan)	5	0

From Panionios.

1998–99	Manchester C	2	0
Total:		**178**	**43**

ROBINSON, Carl — Midfield

H: 5 10 W: 11 10 b.Llandrindod Wells 13-10-76

Source: Trainee. *Honours:* Wales Under-21, B.

1995–96	Wolverhampton W	0	0
1995–96	Shrewsbury T (loan)	4	0
1996–97	Wolverhampton W	2	0
1997–98	Wolverhampton W	32	3
1998–99	Wolverhampton W	34	8
Total:		**72**	**11**

ROBINSON, Jamie — Defender

H: 6 1 W: 12 08 b.Liverpool 26-2-72

Source: Trainee.

1991–92	Liverpool	0	0
1992–93	Barnsley	8	0
1993–94	Barnsley	1	0
1993–94	Carlisle U	16	1
1994–95	Carlisle U	14	1
1995–96	Carlisle U	20	2
1996–97	Carlisle U	7	0
1997–98	Torquay U	46	0
1998–99	Torquay U	29	1
Total:		**141**	**5**

ROBINSON, John — Forward

H: 5 10 W: 11 02 b.Bulawayo 29-8-71

Source: Apprentice. *Honours:* Wales Under-21, 16 full caps, 2 goals.

1989–90	Brighton & HA	5	0
1990–91	Brighton & HA	15	0
1991–92	Brighton & HA	36	6
1992–93	Brighton & HA	6	0
1992–93	Charlton Ath	15	2
1993–94	Charlton Ath	27	1
1994–95	Charlton Ath	21	3
1995–96	Charlton Ath	44	6
1996–97	Charlton Ath	42	3
1997–98	Charlton Ath	38	8
1998–99	Charlton Ath	30	2
Total:		**279**	**31**

ROBINSON, Les — Defender

H: 5 9 W: 12 02 b.Shirebrook 1-3-67

Source: Local.

1984–85	Mansfield T	6	0
1985–86	Mansfield T	7	0
1986–87	Mansfield T	2	0
1986–87	Stockport Co	30	1
1987–88	Stockport Co	37	2
1987–88	Doncaster R	7	1
1988–89	Doncaster R	43	3
1989–90	Doncaster R	32	8
1989–90	Oxford U	1	0
1990–91	Oxford U	43	0
1991–92	Oxford U	27	0
1992–93	Oxford U	16	0
1993–94	Oxford U	36	2
1994–95	Oxford U	46	0
1995–96	Oxford U	41	0
1996–97	Oxford U	38	0
1997–98	Oxford U	46	1
1998–99	Oxford U	44	0
Total:		**502**	**18**

ROBINSON, Liam — Forward

H: 5 7 W: 12 07 b.Bradford 29-12-65

Source: Nottingham F Schoolboy.

1983–84	Huddersfield T	5	1
1984–85	Huddersfield T	15	1
1985–86	Huddersfield T	1	0
1985–86	Tranmere R (loan)	4	3
1986–87	Bury	33	13
1987–88	Bury	43	19
1988–89	Bury	43	20
1989–90	Bury	45	17
1990–91	Bury	43	4
1991–92	Bury	41	10
1992–93	Bury	14	6
1993–94	Bristol C	41	4
1994–95	Burnley	39	7
1995–96	Burnley	16	2
1996–97	Burnley	8	0
1997–98	Scarborough	36	4
1998–99	Scarborough	29	3
Total:		**456**	**114**

ROBINSON, Mark — Defender

H: 5 9 W: 12 04 b.Rochdale 21-11-68

Source: Trainee.

1985–86	WBA	1	0
1986–87	WBA	1	0
1987–88	Barnsley	3	0
1988–89	Barnsley	18	2
1989–90	Barnsley	24	0
1990–91	Barnsley	22	1
1991–92	Barnsley	41	2
1992–93	Barnsley	29	1
1992–93	Newcastle U	9	0
1993–94	Newcastle U	16	0
1994–95	Swindon T	40	0
1995–96	Swindon T	46	1
1996–97	Swindon T	43	1
1997–98	Swindon T	27	1
1998–99	Swindon T	29	0
Total:		**349**	**9**

ROBINSON, Marvin — Forward

H: 5 11 W: 12 09 b.Crewe 11-4-80

Source: Trainee.

1998–99	Derby Co	1	0
Total:		**1**	**0**

ROBINSON, Matthew — Defender

H: 5 11 W: 11 04 b.Exeter 23-12-74

Source: Trainee.

1993–94	Southampton	0	0
1994–95	Southampton	1	0
1995–96	Southampton	5	0
1996–97	Southampton	7	0
1997–98	Southampton	1	0
1997–98	Portsmouth	15	0
1998–99	Portsmouth	29	1
Total:		**58**	**1**

ROBINSON, Paul — Forward

H: 5 10 W: 10 12 b.Sunderland 20-11-78

Source: Trainee.

1995–96	Darlington	4	0
1996–97	Darlington	3	0
1997–98	Darlington	19	3
1997–98	Newcastle U	0	0
1998–99	Newcastle U	0	0
Total:		**26**	**3**

ROBINSON, Paul — Defender

H: 5 9 W: 11 10 b.Watford 14-12-78

Source: Trainee. *Honours:* England Under-21.

1996–97	Watford	12	0
1997–98	Watford	22	2
1998–99	Watford	29	0
Total:		**63**	**2**

ROBINSON, Paul — Goalkeeper

H: 6 4 W: 14 04 b.Beverley 15-10-79

Source: Trainee.

1996–97	Leeds U	0	0
1997–98	Leeds U	0	0
1998–99	Leeds U	5	0
Total:		**5**	**0**

ROBINSON, Phil — Midfield

H: 5 10 W: 11 06 b.Stafford 6-1-67

Source: Apprentice.

1984–85	Aston Villa	0	0
1985–86	Aston Villa	0	0
1986–87	Aston Villa	3	1
1987–88	Wolverhampton W	41	5
1988–89	Wolverhampton W	30	3
1989–90	Notts Co	46	2
1990–91	Notts Co	19	3
1990–91	Birmingham C (loan)	9	0
1991–92	Notts Co	1	0
1992–93	Notts Co	0	0
1992–93	Huddersfield T	36	4
1993–94	Huddersfield T	39	1
1994–95	Huddersfield T	0	0
1994–95	Northampton T (loan)	14	0
1994–95	Chesterfield	22	8
1995–96	Chesterfield	39	9
1996–97	Notts Co	37	2
1997–98	Notts Co	40	3
1998–99	Stoke C	40	1
Total:		**416**	**42**

ROBINSON, Phil — Defender

H: 5 9 W: 11 00 b.Manchester 28-9-80

Source: Trainee.

1998–99	Blackpool	5	0
Total:		**5**	**0**

ROBINSON, Steve — Forward

H: 5 9 W: 11 02 b.Crumlin 10-12-74

Source: Trainee. *Honours:* Northern Ireland Under-21, 3 full caps.

1992–93	Tottenham H	0	0
1993–94	Tottenham H	2	0
1994–95	Tottenham H	0	0
1994–95	Leyton Orient (loan)	0	0
1994–95	Bournemouth	32	5
1995–96	Bournemouth	41	7
1996–97	Bournemouth	40	7
1997–98	Bournemouth	45	10
1998–99	Bournemouth	42	13
Total:		**202**	**42**

ROBINSON, Steve — Midfield

H: 5 9 W: 11 00 b.Nottingham 17-10-75

Source: Trainee.

1993–94	Birmingham C	0	0
1994–95	Birmingham C	6	0
1995–96	Birmingham C	0	0
1995–96	Peterborough U (loan)	5	0
1996–97	Birmingham C	9	0
1997–98	Birmingham C	25	0
1998–99	Birmingham C	31	0
Total:		**76**	**0**

ROBSON, Glen — Forward

H: 5 10 W: 10 04 b.Sunderland 25-9-77

Source: Murton.

1996–97	Rochdale	3	0
1997–98	Rochdale	7	0
1998–99	Rochdale	0	0
Total:		**10**	**0**

ROBSON, Mark — Forward

H: 5 7 W: 10 02 b.Newham 22-5-69

Source: Trainee.

1986–87	Exeter C	26	7
1987–88	Tottenham H	0	0
1987–88	Reading (loan)	7	0
1988–89	Tottenham H	5	0
1989–90	Tottenham H	3	0
1989–90	Watford (loan)	1	0
1989–90	Plymouth Arg (loan)	7	0
1990–91	Tottenham H	0	0
1991–92	Tottenham H	0	0
1991–92	Exeter C (loan)	8	1
1992–93	West Ham U	44	8
1993–94	West Ham U	3	0
1993–94	Charlton Ath	23	2
1994–95	Charlton Ath	40	3
1995–96	Charlton Ath	27	1
1996–97	Charlton Ath	15	3
1997–98	Notts Co	28	4
1998–99	Notts Co	2	0
1998–99	Wycombe W (loan)	4	0
Total:		**243**	**29**

ROCHE, Lee — Defender

H: 5 10 W: 10 11 b.Bolton 28-10-80

Source: Trainee. *Honours:* England Youth.

1998–99	Manchester U	0	0

ROCHE, Stephen — Defender

H: 5 11 W: 11 02 b.Dublin 2-10-78

Source: Belvedere.

1995–96	Millwall	0	0
1996–97	Millwall	7	0
1997–98	Millwall	1	0
1998–99	Millwall	3	0
Total:		**11**	**0**

ROCKETT, Jason — Defender

H: 6 1 W: 13 04 b.London 26-9-69

1992–93	Rotherham U	0	0
1992–93	Rotherham U	0	0
1993–94	Scarborough	34	0
1994–95	Scarborough	27	0
1995–96	Scarborough	39	4
1996–97	Scarborough	40	5
1997–98	Scarborough	32	2
1998–99	Scarborough	0	0
Total:		**172**	**11**

RODGER, Simon — Midfield

H: 5 9 W: 11 09 b.Shoreham 3-10-71

Source: Trainee.

1989–90	Crystal Palace	0	0
1990–91	Crystal Palace	0	0
1991–92	Crystal Palace	22	0
1992–93	Crystal Palace	23	2
1993–94	Crystal Palace	42	3
1994–95	Crystal Palace	4	0
1995–96	Crystal Palace	24	0
1996–97	Crystal Palace	11	0
1996–97	Manchester C (loan)	8	1
1996–97	Stoke C (loan)	5	0
1997–98	Crystal Palace	29	2
1998–99	Crystal Palace	18	1
Total:		**186**	**9**

RODOSTHENOUS, Michael — Forward

H: 5 11 W: 11 02 b.Islington 25-8-76

Source: Trainee.

1995–96	WBA	0	0
1996–97	WBA	1	0
1997–98	WBA	0	0
1997–98	Cambridge U	2	0
1998–99	Plymouth Arg	0	0
Total:		**3**	**0**

RODRIGUES, Danny — Forward

H: 5 10 W: 11 07 b.Madeira 3-3-80

Source: Farense.

1998–99	Bournemouth	5	0
1998–99	Southampton	0	0
Total:		**5**	**0**

ROGAN, Anton — Defender

H: 6 0 W: 13 00 b.Belfast 25-3-66

Source: Distillery. *Honours:* Northern Ireland 18 full caps.

1986–87	Celtic	10	1
1987–88	Celtic	33	1
1988–89	Celtic	34	1
1989–90	Celtic	18	0
1990–91	Celtic	27	1
1991–92	Celtic	5	0
1991–92	Sunderland	33	1
1992–93	Sunderland	13	0
1993–94	Oxford U	29	2
1994–95	Oxford U	29	1

1995–96	Millwall	8	0
1996–97	Millwall	28	8
1997–98	Blackpool	1	0
1998–99	Blackpool	14	0
Total:		**282**	**16**

ROGERS, Alan — Defender

H: 5 10 W: 12 08 b.Liverpool 3-1-77

Source: Trainee.

1995–96	Tranmere R	26	2
1996–97	Tranmere R	31	0
1997–98	Nottingham F	46	1
1998–99	Nottingham F	34	4
Total:		**137**	**7**

ROGERS, Dave — Defender

H: 6 1 W: 12 00 b.Liverpool 25-8-75

Source: Trainee.

1994–95	Tranmere R	0	0
1995–96	Chester C	20	1
1996–97	Chester C	5	0
From Southport.			
1997–98	Dundee	32	1
1998–99	Dundee	11	0
Total:		**68**	**2**

ROGERS, Joel — Forward

b.Wimbledon 7-1-80

Source: Trainee.

1998–99	Colchester U	0	0

ROGERS, Mark — Defender

H: 6 1 W: 12 12 b.Geulph 3-11-75

1998–99	Wycombe W	0	0

ROGERS, Paul — Midfield

H: 6 0 W: 13 02 b.Portsmouth 21-3-65

Source: Sutton U.

1991–92	Sheffield U	13	0
1992–93	Sheffield U	27	3
1993–94	Sheffield U	25	3
1994–95	Sheffield U	44	4
1995–96	Sheffield U	16	0
1995–96	Notts Co	21	2
1996–97	Notts Co	1	0
1996–97	Wigan Ath	20	3
1997–98	Wigan Ath	38	0
1998–99	Wigan Ath	42	2
Total:		**247**	**17**

ROGET, Leo — Defender

H: 6 1 W: 12 02 b.Ilford 1-8-77

Source: Trainee.

1995–96	Southend U	8	1
1996–97	Southend U	25	0
1997–98	Southend U	11	0
1998–99	Southend U	14	0
Total:		**58**	**1**

ROLLING, Frank — Defender

H: 6 2 W: 13 00 b.Colmar 23-8-68

Source: FC Pau.

1994–95	Ayr U	33	2
1995–96	Ayr U	2	0
1995–96	Leicester C	17	0
1996–97	Leicester C	1	0
1997–98	Bournemouth	30	4
1998–99	Bournemouth	0	0
1998–99	Gillingham	1	0
Total:		**84**	**6**

ROPER, Ian — Defender

H: 6 3 W: 13 09 b.Nuneaton 20-6-77

Source: Trainee.

1994–95	Walsall	0	0
1995–96	Walsall	5	0
1996–97	Walsall	11	0
1997–98	Walsall	21	0
1998–99	Walsall	32	1
Total:		**69**	**1**

ROSCOE, Andy — Midfield

H: 5 10 W: 11 08 b.Liverpool 4-6-73

Source: Trainee.

1991–92	Liverpool	0	0
1992–93	Bolton W	0	0
1993–94	Bolton W	3	0
1994–95	Bolton W	0	0
1994–95	Rotherham U	31	4
1995–96	Rotherham U	45	2
1996–97	Rotherham U	43	0
1997–98	Rotherham U	45	7
1998–99	Rotherham U	38	5
Total:		**205**	**18**

ROSE, Andrew — Defender

H: 5 9 W: 10 13 b.Ascot 9-8-78

Source: Trainee.

1997–98	Oxford U	1	0
1998–99	Oxford U	4	0
Total:		**5**	**0**

ROSE, Karl — Forward

H: 5 10 W: 11 00 b.Barnsley 12-10-78

1995–96	Barnsley	0	0
1996–97	Barnsley	0	0
1997–98	Barnsley	0	0
1998–99	Barnsley	4	0
1998–99	Mansfield T (loan)	1	0
Total:		**5**	**0**

ROSE, Matthew — Defender

H: 5 11 W: 11 01 b.Dartford 24-9-75

Source: Trainee. *Honours:* England Under-21.

1994–95	Arsenal	0	0
1995–96	Arsenal	4	0
1996–97	Arsenal	1	0
1997–98	QPR	16	0
1998–99	QPR	29	0
Total:		**50**	**0**

ROSENTHAL, Ronny — Forward

H: 5 11 W: 13 04 b.Haifa 4-10-63

Source: Maccabi Haifa, FC Brugge, Standard Liege. *Honours:* Israel 60 full caps, 11 goals.

1989–90	Luton T (loan)	0	0
1989–90	Liverpool (loan)	8	7
1990–91	Liverpool	16	5
1991–92	Liverpool	20	3
1992–93	Liverpool	27	6
1993–94	Liverpool	3	0
1993–94	Tottenham H	15	2
1994–95	Tottenham H	20	0
1995–96	Tottenham H	33	1
1996–97	Tottenham H	20	1
1997–98	Watford	25	8
1998–99	Watford	5	0
Total:		**192**	**33**

ROSS, Ian — Midfield

H: 5 10 W: 10 07 b.Broxburn 27-8-74

Source: Bathgate Th.

1993–94	Motherwell	0	0
1994–95	Motherwell	0	0
1995–96	Motherwell	1	0
1996–97	Motherwell	30	2
1997–98	Motherwell	22	1
1998–99	Motherwell	12	0
Total:		**65**	**3**

ROUGIER, Tony — Forward

H: 5 10 W: 14 07 b.Trinidad 17-7-71

Source: Trinity Pros.

1994–95	Raith R	4	0
1995–96	Raith R	22	1
1996–97	Raith R	30	1
1997–98	Hibernian	20	3
1998–99	Hibernian	15	1
1998–99	Port Vale	13	0
Total:		**104**	**6**

ROUSSET, Gilles — Goalkeeper

H: 6 5 W: 14 07 b.Hyeres 22-8-63

Source: Sochaux, Lyon, Marseille, Rennes. *Honours:* France 2 full caps.

1995–96	Hearts	25	0
1996–97	Hearts	33	0
1997–98	Hearts	32	0
1998–99	Hearts	26	0
Total:		**116**	**0**

ROWBOTHAM, Darren — Forward

H: 5 10 W: 12 13 b.Cardiff 22-10-66

Source: Trainee.

1984–85	Plymouth Arg	7	0
1985–86	Plymouth Arg	14	1
1986–87	Plymouth Arg	16	1
1987–88	Plymouth Arg	9	0
1987–88	Exeter C	23	2
1988–89	Exeter C	45	20
1989–90	Exeter C	32	21
1990–91	Exeter C	13	3
1991–92	Exeter C	5	1
1991–92	Torquay U	14	3
1991–92	Birmingham C	22	4
1992–93	Birmingham C	14	2
1992–93	Hereford U (loan)	8	2
1992–93	Mansfield T (loan)	4	0
1993–94	Crewe Alex	40	15
1994–95	Crewe Alex	21	6
1995–96	Shrewsbury T	26	8
1996–97	Shrewsbury T	14	1
1996–97	Exeter C	25	9
1997–98	Exeter C	43	20
1998–99	Exeter C	32	6
Total:		**427**	**125**

ROWBOTHAM, Jason — Defender

H: 5 9 W: 11 09 b.Cardiff 3-1-69

Source: Trainee.

1987–88	Plymouth Arg	4	0
1988–89	Plymouth Arg	5	0

1989–90	Plymouth Arg	0	0
1990–91	Plymouth Arg	0	0
1991–92	Shrewsbury T	0	0
1992–93	Hereford U	5	1
1993–94	Raith R	36	1
1994–95	Raith R	20	0
1995–96	Wycombe W	27	0
1996–97	Wycombe W	0	0
1996–97	Plymouth Arg	15	0
1997–98	Plymouth Arg	25	0
1998–99	Plymouth Arg	0	0
Total:		**137**	**2**

ROWE, Rodney — Forward

H: 5 8 W: 12 08 b.Plymouth 30-7-75

Source: Trainee.

1993–94	Huddersfield T	13	1
1994–95	Huddersfield T	0	0
1994–95	Scarborough (loan)	14	1
1994–95	Bury (loan)	3	0
1995–96	Huddersfield T	14	1
1996–97	Huddersfield T	7	0
1996–97	York C	10	3
1997–98	York C	41	10
1998–99	York C	39	7
Total:		**141**	**23**

ROWE, Zeke — Forward

H: 5 10 W: 11 08 b.Stoke Newington 30-10-73

Source: Trainee.

1992–93	Chelsea	0	0
1993–94	Chelsea	0	0
1993–94	Barnet (loan)	10	2
1994–95	Chelsea	0	0
1995–96	Chelsea	0	0
1995–96	Brighton & HA (loan)	9	3
1996–97	Peterborough U	22	3
1997–98	Peterborough U	6	0
1997–98	Doncaster R (loan)	6	2
1998–99	Peterborough U	7	0
Total:		**60**	**10**

ROWETT, Gary — Defender

H: 6 0 W: 12 10 b.Bromsgrove 6-3-74

Source: Trainee.

1991–92	Cambridge U	13	2
1992–93	Cambridge U	21	2
1993–94	Cambridge U	29	5
1993–94	Everton	2	0
1994–95	Everton	2	0
1994–95	Blackpool (loan)	17	0
1995–96	Derby Co	35	0
1996–97	Derby Co	35	1
1997–98	Derby Co	35	1
1998–99	Derby Co	0	0
1998–99	Birmingham C	42	5
Total:		**231**	**16**

ROWLAND, Keith — Defender

H: 5 10 W: 10 00 b.Portadown 1-9-71

Source: Trainee. *Honours:* Northern Ireland 19 full caps, 1 goal.

1990–91	Bournemouth	0	0
1991–92	Bournemouth	37	0
1992–93	Bournemouth	35	2
1992–93	Coventry C (loan)	2	0
1993–94	West Ham U	23	0
1994–95	West Ham U	12	0
1995–96	West Ham U	23	0
1996–97	West Ham U	15	1
1997–98	West Ham U	7	0
1997–98	QPR	7	0
1998–99	QPR	30	3
Total:		**191**	**6**

ROWLANDS, Martin — Midfield

b.Ealing 8-2-79

Source: Farnborough T. *Honours:* Eire Under-21.

1998–99	Brentford	36	4
Total:		**36**	**4**

ROWSON, David — Midfield

H: 5 10 W: 11 10 b.Aberdeen 14-9-76

Source: FC Stoneywood. *Honours:* Scotland Under-21.

1994–95	Aberdeen	0	0
1995–96	Aberdeen	9	0
1996–97	Aberdeen	34	2
1997–98	Aberdeen	30	5
1998–99	Aberdeen	22	0
Total:		**95**	**7**

ROYCE, Simon — Goalkeeper

H: 6 2 W: 12 10 b.Forest Gate 9-9-71

Source: Heybridge Swifts. *Honours:*

1991–92	Southend U	1	0
1992–93	Southend U	3	0
1993–94	Southend U	6	0
1994–95	Southend U	13	0
1995–96	Southend U	46	0
1996–97	Southend U	43	0
1997–98	Southend U	37	0
1998–99	Charlton Ath	8	0
Total:		**157**	**0**

ROZENTAL, Sebastian — Forward

H: 5 10 W: 12 13 b.Santiago 1-9-76

Source: Univ Catolica, Chile. *Honours:* Chile full caps.

1996–97	Rangers	1	0
1997–98	Rangers	2	0
1998–99	Rangers	3	0
Total:		**6**	**0**

RUDDOCK, Neil — Defender

H: 6 2 W: 12 12 b.South London 9-5-68

Source: Apprentice. *Honours:* England Youth, Under-21, B, 1 full cap.

1985–86	Millwall	0	0
1985–86	Tottenham H	0	0
1986–87	Tottenham H	4	0
1987–88	Tottenham H	5	0
1988–89	Millwall	2	1
1988–89	Southampton	13	3
1989–90	Southampton	29	3
1990–91	Southampton	35	3
1991–92	Southampton	30	0
1992–93	Tottenham H	38	3
1993–94	Liverpool	39	3
1994–95	Liverpool	37	2
1995–96	Liverpool	20	5
1996–97	Liverpool	17	1
1997–98	Liverpool	2	0
1997–98	QPR (loan)	7	0
1998–99	West Ham U	27	2
Total:		**305**	**26**

RUDI, Petter — Defender

H: 6 3 W: 12 11 b.Kristiansund 17-9-73

Honours: Norway 25 full caps, 3 goals.

1991	Molde	12	0
1992	Molde	20	2
1993	Molde	22	3
1994	Molde	0	0
1995	Molde	25	1
1996	Molde	26	0
1997	Molde	11	1
1997–98	Sheffield W	22	0
1998–99	Sheffield W	34	6
Total:		**172**	**13**

RUFUS, Richard — Defender

H: 6 1 W: 10 05 b.Lewisham 12-1-75

Source: Trainee. *Honours:* England Under-21.

1993–94	Charlton Ath	0	0
1994–95	Charlton Ath	28	0
1995–96	Charlton Ath	41	0
1996–97	Charlton Ath	34	0
1997–98	Charlton Ath	42	0
1998–99	Charlton Ath	27	1
Total:		**172**	**1**

RUSH, David — Forward

H: 5 9 W: 11 02 b.Sunderland 15-5-71

Source: Trainee.

1989–90	Sunderland	0	0
1990–91	Sunderland	11	2
1991–92	Sunderland	25	4
1991–92	Hartlepool U (loan)	8	2
1992–93	Sunderland	18	6
1993–94	Sunderland	5	0
1993–94	Peterborough U (loan)	4	1
1994–95	Sunderland	0	0
1994–95	Cambridge U (loan)	2	0
1994–95	Oxford U	34	9
1995–96	Oxford U	43	11
1996–97	Oxford U	15	1
1996–97	York C	2	0
1997–98	York C	3	0
1998–99	York C	0	0
1998–99	Hartlepool U	10	0
Total:		**180**	**36**

RUSH, Ian — Forward

H: 6 0 W: 12 06 b.St Asaph 20-10-61

Source: Apprentice. *Honours:* Wales Schools, Under-21, 73 full caps, 28 goals.

1978–79	Chester C	1	0
1979–80	Chester C	33	14
1979–80	Liverpool	0	0
1980–81	Liverpool	7	0
1981–82	Liverpool	32	17
1982–83	Liverpool	34	24
1983–84	Liverpool	41	32
1984–85	Liverpool	28	14
1985–86	Liverpool	40	22
1986–87	Liverpool	42	30
1987–88	Juventus	29	7
1988–89	Liverpool	24	7
1989–90	Liverpool	36	18
1990–91	Liverpool	37	16
1991–92	Liverpool	18	4
1992–93	Liverpool	32	14
1993–94	Liverpool	42	14
1994–95	Liverpool	36	12
1995–96	Liverpool	20	5
1995–96	Leeds U	0	0
1996–97	Leeds U	36	3
1997–98	Leeds U	0	0
1997–98	Newcastle U	10	0
1997–98	Sheffield U (loan)	4	0
1998–99	Wrexham	17	0
Total:		**599**	**253**

RUSH, Matthew — Forward

H: 5 11 W: 12 05 b.Dalston 6-8-71

Source: Trainee. *Honours:* Eire Under-21.

1990–91	West Ham U	5	0
1991–92	West Ham U	10	2
1992–93	West Ham U	0	0
1992–93	Cambridge U (loan)	10	0
1993–94	West Ham U	10	1
1993–94	Swansea C (loan)	13	0
1994–95	West Ham U	23	2
1995–96	Norwich C	1	0
1996–97	Norwich C	2	0
1996–97	Northampton T (loan)	14	3
1996–97	Oldham Ath	8	2
1997–98	Oldham Ath	16	1
1998–99	Oldham Ath	0	0
Total:		**112**	**11**

RUSSELL, Alex — Midfield

H: 5 8 W: 11 10 b.Crosby 17-3-73

Source: Burscough.

1994–95	Rochdale	7	1
1995–96	Rochdale	25	0
1996–97	Rochdale	39	9
1997–98	Rochdale	31	4
1998–99	Cambridge U	37	6
Total:		**139**	**20**

RUSSELL, Craig — Forward

H: 5 10 W: 12 07 b.Jarrow 4-2-74

Source: Trainee.

1991–92	Sunderland	4	0
1992–93	Sunderland	0	0
1993–94	Sunderland	35	9
1994–95	Sunderland	38	5
1995–96	Sunderland	41	13
1996–97	Sunderland	29	4
1997–98	Sunderland	3	0
1997–98	Manchester C	24	1
1998–99	Manchester C	7	1
1998–99	Tranmere R (loan)	4	0
1998–99	Port Vale (loan)	8	1
Total:		**193**	**34**

RUSSELL, Darel — Midfield

H: 6 0 W: 12 00 b.Mile End 22-10-80

Source: Trainee. *Honours:* England Youth.

1997–98	Norwich C	1	0
1998–99	Norwich C	13	1
Total:		**14**	**1**

RUSSELL, Kevin — Midfield

H: 5 9 W: 10 12 b.Portsmouth 6-12-66

Source: Brighton & HA Apprentice. *Honours:* England Youth.

1984–85	Portsmouth	0	0
1985–86	Portsmouth	1	0
1986–87	Portsmouth	3	1
1987–88	Wrexham	38	21
1988–89	Wrexham	46	22
1989–90	Leicester C	10	0
1990–91	Leicester C	13	5
1990–91	Peterborough U (loan)	7	3
1990–91	Cardiff C (loan)	3	0
1991–92	Leicester C	20	5
1991–92	Hereford U (loan)	3	1
1991–92	Stoke C (loan)	5	1
1992–93	Stoke C	40	5
1993–94	Burnley	28	6
1993–94	Bournemouth	17	1
1994–95	Bournemouth	13	0
1994–95	Notts Co	11	0
1995–96	Wrexham	40	7
1996–97	Wrexham	41	0
1997–98	Wrexham	16	0
1998–99	Wrexham	31	2
Total:		**386**	**80**

RUSSELL, Lee — Defender

H: 5 10 W: 11 09 b.Southampton 3-9-69

Source: Trainee.

1988–89	Portsmouth	2	0
1989–90	Portsmouth	3	0
1990–91	Portsmouth	19	1
1991–92	Portsmouth	9	0
1992–93	Portsmouth	14	0
1993–94	Portsmouth	10	0
1994–95	Portsmouth	19	0
1994–95	Bournemouth (loan)	3	0
1995–96	Portsmouth	19	0
1996–97	Portsmouth	20	2
1997–98	Portsmouth	8	0
1998–99	Portsmouth	0	0
1998–99	Torquay U (loan)	9	0
Total:		**135**	**3**

RUSSELL, Matthew — Midfield

H: 6 0 W: 11 05 b.Leeds 17-1-78

Source: Trainee.

1996–97	Scarborough	5	0
1997–98	Scarborough	2	0
1997–98	Doncaster R (loan)	5	0
1998–99	Scarborough	37	3
Total:		**49**	**3**

RUST, Nicky — Goalkeeper

H: 6 1 W: 13 01 b.Ely 25-9-74

Source: Arsenal Trainee.

1993–94	Brighton & HA	46	0
1994–95	Brighton & HA	44	0
1995–96	Brighton & HA	46	0
1996–97	Brighton & HA	25	0
1997–98	Brighton & HA	16	0
1998–99	Barnet	2	0
Total:		**179**	**0**

RUTHERFORD, Mark — Forward

b.Birmingham 25-3-72

1989–90	Birmingham C	2	0
1990–91	Birmingham C	3	0
1991–92	Birmingham C	0	0
From Shelbourne			
1998–99	Shrewsbury T	3	0
Total:		**8**	**0**

RYAN, Ciaran — Defender

H: 5 8 W: 11 00 b.Dublin 3-9-79

Source: Trainee.

1996–97	Blackburn R	0	0
1997–98	Blackburn R	0	0
1998–99	Blackburn R	0	0

RYAN, Darragh — Forward

H: 5 10 W: 10 10 b.Cuckfield 21-5-80

Source: Trainee.

1997–98	Brighton & HA	4	1
1998–99	Brighton & HA	5	1
Total:		**9**	**2**

RYAN, Keith — Midfield

H: 5 11 W: 12 06 b.Northampton 25-6-70

Source: Berkhamsted T.

1993–94	Wycombe W	42	1
1994–95	Wycombe W	24	4
1995–96	Wycombe W	23	4
1996–97	Wycombe W	0	0
1997–98	Wycombe W	40	3
1998–99	Wycombe W	28	1
Total:		**157**	**13**

RYAN, Michael — Defender

H: 5 9 W: 11 00 b.Stockport 3-10-79

Source: Trainee.

1998–99	Manchester U	0	0
1998–99	Wrexham	0	0

RYAN, Robbie — Defender

H: 5 10 W: 12 00 b.Dublin 16-5-77

Source: Belvedere. *Honours:* Eire Youth, Under-21.

1994–95	Huddersfield T	0	0
1995–96	Huddersfield T	0	0
1996–97	Huddersfield T	5	0
1997–98	Huddersfield T	10	0
1997–98	Millwall	16	0
1998–99	Millwall	26	0
Total:		**57**	**0**

RYDER, Stuart — Defender

H: 6 0 W: 12 09 b.Sutton Coldfield 6-11-73

Source: Trainee. *Honours:* England Under-21.

1992–93	Walsall	22	0
1993–94	Walsall	26	0
1994–95	Walsall	36	5
1995–96	Walsall	3	0
1996–97	Walsall	1	0
1997–98	Walsall	13	0
1998–99	Mansfield T	22	2
Total:		**123**	**7**

SADLER, Adam — Goalkeeper

H: 5 11 W: 12 01 b.North Shields 9-1-80

Source: Manchester U Trainee.

1998–99	Barnsley	0	0

SADLIER, Richard — Forward

H: 6 2 W: 12 10 b.Dublin 14-1-79

Source: Belvedere. *Honours:* Eire Youth.

1996–97	Millwall	10	0
1997–98	Millwall	4	3
1998–99	Millwall	31	5
Total:		**45**	**8**

SAHA, Louis — Forward

H: 5 11 W: 11 06 b.Paris 8-8-78

1997–98	Metz	21	1
1998–99	Metz	3	0
1998–99	Newcastle U	11	1
Total:		**35**	**2**

SAIB, Moussa — Midfield

H: 5 9 W: 11 08 b.Theniet-El-Had 5-3-69

1992–93	Auxerre	9	1
1993–94	Auxerre	33	2
1994–95	Auxerre	26	6
1995–96	Auxerre	33	6
1996–97	Auxerre	33	8
1997–98	Valencia	14	0
1997–98	Tottenham H	9	1
1998–99	Tottenham H	4	0
Total:		**161**	**24**

SALAKO, John — Forward

H: 5 9 W: 11 10 b.Nigeria 11-2-69

Source: Trainee. *Honours:* England 5 full caps.

1986–87	Crystal Palace	4	0
1987–88	Crystal Palace	31	0
1988–89	Crystal Palace	28	0
1989–90	Crystal Palace	17	2
1989–90	Swansea C (loan)	13	3
1990–91	Crystal Palace	35	6
1991–92	Crystal Palace	10	2
1992–93	Crystal Palace	13	0
1993–94	Crystal Palace	38	8
1994–95	Crystal Palace	39	4
1995–96	Coventry C	37	3
1996–97	Coventry C	24	1
1997–98	Coventry C	11	0
1997–98	Bolton W	7	0
1998–99	Fulham	10	1
Total:		**317**	**30**

SALE, Mark — Forward

H: 6 5 W: 14 09 b.Burton-on-Trent 27-2-72

Source: Trainee.

1989–90	Stoke C	2	0
1990–91	Stoke C	0	0
1991–92	Cambridge U	0	0
1991–92	Birmingham C	6	0
1992–93	Birmingham C	15	0
1992–93	Torquay U	11	2
1993–94	Torquay U	33	6
1994–95	Preston NE	13	7
1995–96	Mansfield T	27	7
1996–97	Mansfield T	18	5
1996–97	Colchester U	10	3
1997–98	Colchester U	39	7
1998–99	Colchester U	31	2
1998–99	Plymouth Arg (loan)	8	1
Total:		**213**	**40**

SALMON, Mick — Goalkeeper

H: 6 2 W: 12 12 b.Leyland 14-6-64

Source: Local.

1981–82	Blackburn R	1	0
1982–83	Blackburn R	0	0
1982–83	Chester C (loan)	16	0
1983–84	Stockport Co	46	0
1984–85	Stockport Co	46	0
1985–86	Stockport Co	26	0
1986–87	Bolton W	26	0
1986–87	Wrexham (loan)	17	0
1987–88	Wrexham	40	0
1988–89	Wrexham	43	0
1989–90	Charlton Ath	0	0
1990–91	Charlton Ath	7	0
1991–92	Charlton Ath	0	0
1992–93	Charlton Ath	19	0
1993–94	Charlton Ath	41	0
1994–95	Charlton Ath	20	0
1995–96	Charlton Ath	27	0
1996–97	Charlton Ath	25	0
1997–98	Charlton Ath	9	0
1998–99	Charlton Ath	0	0
1998–99	Oxford U (loan)	1	0
Total:		**410**	**0**

SALT, Philip — Midfield

H: 5 10 W: 11 02 b.Huddersfield 2-3-79

Source: Trainee.

1997–98	Oldham Ath	2	0
1998–99	Oldham Ath	9	0
Total:		**11**	**0**

SALVATORI, Stefano — Midfield

H: 5 10 W: 12 03 b.Rome 29-12-67

1986–87	AC Milan	0	0
1987–88	Virescit	32	0
1988–89	Parma	7	0
1988–89	Fiorentina	23	1
1989–90	AC Milan	10	0
1990–91	AC Milan	0	0
1990–91	Fiorentina	18	1
1991–92	Fiorentina	27	0
1992–93	Fiorentina	0	0
1992–93	Spal	22	0
1993–94	Spal	8	0
1994–95	Atalanta	23	0
1995–96	Atalanta	22	0
1996–97	Hearts	14	0
1997–98	Hearts	32	1
1998–99	Hearts	12	0
Total:		**250**	**3**

SAMPSON, Ian — Defender

H: 6 2 W: 13 03 b.Wakefield 14-11-68

Source: Goole T.

1990–91	Sunderland	0	0
1991–92	Sunderland	8	0
1992–93	Sunderland	5	1
1993–94	Sunderland	4	0
1993–94	Northampton T (loan)	8	0
1994–95	Northampton T	42	2
1995–96	Northampton T	33	4
1996–97	Northampton T	43	5
1997–98	Northampton T	39	3
1998–99	Northampton T	42	1
Total:		**224**	**16**

SAMUEL, J Lloyd — Defender

H: 5 11 W: 11 04 b.Trinidad 29-3-81

Source: Charlton Ath Trainee.

1998–99	Aston Villa	0	0

SAMUELS, Dean — Forward

H: 6 2 W: 12 06 b.Hackney 29-3-73

Source: Boreham Wood.

1996–97	Barnet	17	1
1997–98	Barnet	22	3
1998–99	Barnet	0	0
Total:		**39**	**4**

SAMUELS, Jerome — Midfield

b.Jamaica 8-3-76

1998–99	Notts Co	0	0

SAMWAYS, Mark — Goalkeeper

H: 6 2 W: 14 01 b.Doncaster 11-11-68

Source: Trainee.

1987–88	Doncaster R	11	0
1988–89	Doncaster R	12	0
1989–90	Doncaster R	46	0
1990–91	Doncaster R	26	0
1991–92	Doncaster R	26	0
1991–92	Scunthorpe U (loan)	8	0
1992–93	Scunthorpe U	31	0
1993–94	Scunthorpe U	41	0
1994–95	Scunthorpe U	42	0
1995–96	Scunthorpe U	33	0
1996–97	Scunthorpe U	25	0
1996–97	York C (loan)	0	0
1997–98	York C	29	0
1998–99	Darlington	0	0
Total:		**330**	**0**

SANDFORD, Lee — Defender

H: 6 0 W: 13 07 b.Basingstoke 22-4-68

Source: Apprentice. *Honours:* England Youth.

1985–86	Portsmouth	7	0
1986–87	Portsmouth	0	0
1987–88	Portsmouth	21	1
1988–89	Portsmouth	31	0
1989–90	Portsmouth	13	0
1989–90	Stoke C	23	2
1990–91	Stoke C	32	2
1991–92	Stoke C	38	0
1992–93	Stoke C	42	2
1993–94	Stoke C	42	1
1994–95	Stoke C	35	1
1995–96	Stoke C	46	0
1996–97	Sheffield U	30	2
1997–98	Sheffield U	15	0
1997–98	Reading (loan)	5	0
1998–99	Sheffield U	35	0
Total:		**415**	**11**

SANDWITH, Kevin — Defender

H: 5 11 W: 12 05 b.Workington 30-4-78

Source: Trainee.

1996–97	Carlisle U	0	0
1997–98	Carlisle U	3	0
1998–99	Carlisle U	0	0
Total:		**3**	**0**

SANETTI, Francesco — Forward

H: 5 11 W: 12 07 b.Rome 11-1-79

Source: Genoa.

1997–98	Sheffield W	2	1
1998–99	Sheffield W	3	0
Total:		**5**	**1**

SANTOS, Georges — Defender

H: 6 3 W: 14 08 b.Marseille 15-8-70

Source: Toulon.

1998–99	Tranmere R	37	1
Total:		**37**	**1**

SANTOS, Nuno — Goalkeeper

H: 6 1 W: 13 00 b.Setubal 20-4-73

1996–97	Setubal	8	0
1997–98	Setubal	34	0
1998–99	Leeds U	0	0
Total:		**42**	**0**

SARLI, Cosimo — Forward

H: 5 10 W: 12 07 b.Conigliano Calabro 13-3-79

1997–98	Torino	0	0
1997–98	Southampton	0	0
1998–99	Southampton	0	0

SARR, Mass — Forward

H: 5 8 W: 11 13 b.Monrovia 6-2-73

1995–96	Hajduk Split	24	9
1996–97	Hajduk Split	18	6
1997–98	Hajduk Split	17	2
1998–99	Reading	28	3
Total:		**87**	**20**

SAUNDERS, Dean — Forward

H: 5 8 W: 10 06 b.Swansea 21-6-64

Source: Apprentice. *Honours:* Wales 69 full caps, 21 goals.

1982–83	Swansea C	0	0
1983–84	Swansea C	19	3
1984–85	Swansea C	30	9
1984–85	Cardiff C (loan)	4	0
1985–86	Brighton & HA	42	15
1986–87	Brighton & HA	30	6
1986–87	Oxford U	12	6
1987–88	Oxford U	37	12
1988–89	Oxford U	10	4
1988–89	Derby Co	30	14
1989–90	Derby Co	38	11
1990–91	Derby Co	38	17
1991–92	Liverpool	36	10
1992–93	Liverpool	6	1
1992–93	Aston Villa	35	12
1993–94	Aston Villa	38	10
1994–95	Aston Villa	39	15
1995–96	Galatasaray	27	15
1996–97	Nottingham F	34	3
1997–98	Nottingham F	9	2
1997–98	Sheffield U	24	10
1998–99	Sheffield U	19	7
Total:		**557**	**182**

SAUNDERS, Mark — Midfield

H: 5 11 W: 11 12 b.Reading 23-7-71

Source: Tiverton.

1995–96	Plymouth Arg	10	1
1996–97	Plymouth Arg	25	3
1997–98	Plymouth Arg	37	7
1998–99	Gillingham	34	4
Total:		**106**	**15**

SAUZEE, Franck — Defender

H: 6 2 W: 13 06 b.Aubenas 28-10-65

Source: Montelimar. *Honours:* France 39 full caps, 9 goals.

1983–84	Sochaux	19	1
1984–85	Sochaux	37	8
1985–86	Sochaux	27	7
1986–87	Sochaux	37	8
1987–88	Sochaux	30	16
1988–89	Marseille	32	4
1989–90	Marseille	36	5
1990–91	Monaco	28	7
1991–92	Marseille	22	2
1992–93	Marseille	35	12
1993–94	Atalanta	16	1
1994–95	Strasbourg	30	5
1995–96	Strasbourg	27	4
1996–97	Montpellier	27	7
1997–98	Montpellier	12	0
1998–99	Hibernian	9	2
Total:		**424**	**89**

SAVAGE, Dave — Midfield

H: 6 1 W: 12 07 b.Dublin 30-7-73

Source: Longford T. *Honours:* Eire Under-21, 5 full caps.

1994–95	Millwall	37	2
1995–96	Millwall	27	0
1996–97	Millwall	35	3
1997–98	Millwall	31	1
1998–99	Millwall	2	0
1998–99	Northampton T	27	5
Total:		**159**	**11**

SAVAGE, Robbie — Midfield

H: 5 11 W: 10 07 b.Wrexham 18-10-74

Source: Trainee. *Honours:* Wales Under-21, 13 full caps, 1 goal.

1993–94	Manchester U	0	0
1994–95	Crewe Alex	6	2
1995–96	Crewe Alex	30	7
1996–97	Crewe Alex	41	1
1997–98	Leicester C	35	2
1998–99	Leicester C	34	1
Total:		**146**	**13**

SAVILLE, Andy — Forward

H: 6 0 W: 12 09 b.Hull 12-12-64

Source: Local.

1983–84	Hull C	1	0
1984–85	Hull C	4	1
1985–86	Hull C	9	1
1986–87	Hull C	35	9
1987–88	Hull C	32	6
1988–89	Hull C	20	1

1988–89	Walsall	12	4
1989–90	Walsall	26	1
1989–90	Barnsley	15	3
1990–91	Barnsley	45	12
1991–92	Barnsley	22	6
1991–92	Hartlepool U	1	0
1992–93	Hartlepool U	36	13
1992–93	Birmingham C	10	7
1993–94	Birmingham C	39	10
1994–95	Birmingham C	10	0
1994–95	Burnley (loan)	4	1
1995–96	Preston NE	44	29
1996–97	Preston NE	12	1
1996–97	Wigan Ath	20	4
1997–98	Wigan Ath	5	0
1997–98	Cardiff C	33	11
1998–99	Cardiff C	2	1
1998–99	Hull C (loan)	3	0
1998–99	Scarborough	9	0
Total:		**449**	**121**

SAWYERS, Robert — Defender

H: 5 10 W: 11 03 b.Dudley 20-11-78

Source: Wolverhampton W Trainee.

1997–98	Barnet	1	0
1998–99	Barnet	22	0
Total:		**23**	**0**

SCALES, John — Defender

H: 6 2 W: 13 05 b.Harrogate 4-7-66

Honours: England B, 3 full caps.

1984–85	Leeds U	0	0
1985–86	Bristol R	29	1
1986–87	Bristol R	43	1
1987–88	Wimbledon	25	1
1988–89	Wimbledon	38	5
1989–90	Wimbledon	28	2
1990–91	Wimbledon	36	2
1991–92	Wimbledon	41	0
1992–93	Wimbledon	32	1
1993–94	Wimbledon	37	0
1994–95	Wimbledon	3	0
1994–95	Liverpool	35	2
1995–96	Liverpool	27	0
1996–97	Liverpool	3	0
1996–97	Tottenham H	12	0
1997–98	Tottenham H	10	0
1998–99	Tottenham H	7	0
Total:		**406**	**15**

SCARLETT, Andre — Midfield

H: 5 4 W: 9 12 b.Brent 11-1-80

Source: Trainee.

1998–99	Luton T	6	1
Total:		**6**	**1**

SCATES, Garth — Midfield

b.Dundonald 27-8-79

Source: Trainee.

1997–98	Blackburn R	0	0
1998–99	Blackburn R	0	0

SCHEUBER, Stuart — Midfield

b.Rhuddlan 3-4-81

Source: Trainee.

1997–98	Stoke C	0	0
1998–99	Stoke C	0	0

SCHMEICHEL, Peter — Goalkeeper

H: 6 4 W: 16 00 b.Gladsaxe 18-11-63

Honours: Denmark 112 full caps.

1984	Hvidovre	30	0
1985	Hvidovre	28	6
1986	Hvidovre	30	0
1987	Brondby	23	2
1988	Brondby	26	0
1989	Brondby	26	0
1990	Brondby	26	0
1991	Brondby	18	0
1991–92	Manchester U	40	0
1992–93	Manchester U	42	0
1993–94	Manchester U	40	0
1994–95	Manchester U	32	0
1995–96	Manchester U	36	0
1996–97	Manchester U	36	0
1997–98	Manchester U	32	0
1998–99	Manchester U	34	0
Total:		**499**	**8**

SCHNOOR, Stefan — Defender

H: 6 1 W: 12 04 b.Neumunster 24-4-71

1991–92	Hamburg	5	0
1992–93	Hamburg	19	1
1993–94	Hamburg	12	0
1994–95	Hamburg	28	3
1995–96	Hamburg	23	2
1996–97	Hamburg	21	0
1997–98	Hamburg	23	2
1998–99	Derby Co	23	2
Total:		**154**	**10**

SCHOFIELD, Danny — Forward

H: 5 10 W: 11 02 b.Doncaster 10-4-80

1998–99	Huddersfield T	1	0
Total:		**1**	**0**

SCHOFIELD, Jon — Defender

H: 5 10 W: 11 03 b.Barnsley 16-5-65

Source: Gainsborough T.

1988–89	Lincoln C	29	2
1989–90	Lincoln C	29	2
1990–91	Lincoln C	42	3
1991–92	Lincoln C	39	1
1992–93	Lincoln C	40	0
1993–94	Lincoln C	40	2
1994–95	Lincoln C	12	1
1994–95	Doncaster R	27	1
1995–96	Doncaster R	41	4
1996–97	Doncaster R	42	7
1997–98	Mansfield T	44	0
1998–99	Mansfield T	42	0
Total:		**427**	**23**

SCHOLES, Paul — Midfield

H: 5 7 W: 11 08 b.Salford 16-11-74

Source: Trainee. *Honours:* England Youth, 17 full caps, 7 goals.

1992–93	Manchester U	0	0
1993–94	Manchester U	0	0
1994–95	Manchester U	17	5
1995–96	Manchester U	26	10
1996–97	Manchester U	24	3
1997–98	Manchester U	31	8
1998–99	Manchester U	31	6
Total:		**129**	**32**

SCHWARZER, Mark — Goalkeeper

H: 6 5 W: 15 01 b.Sydney 6-10-72

Source: Blacktown Assoc, Marconi Sydney, Dynamo Dresden. *Honours:* Australia full caps.

1995–96	Kaiserslautern	4	0
1996–97	Kaiserslautern	0	0
1996–97	Bradford C	13	0
1996–97	Middlesbrough	7	0
1997–98	Middlesbrough	35	0
1998–99	Middlesbrough	34	0
Total:		**93**	**0**

SCIMECA, Riccardo — Defender

H: 6 0 W: 13 11 b.Leamington Spa 13-6-75

Source: Trainee. *Honours:* England Under-21, B.

1993–94	Aston Villa	0	0
1994–95	Aston Villa	0	0
1995–96	Aston Villa	17	0
1996–97	Aston Villa	17	0
1997–98	Aston Villa	21	0
1998–99	Aston Villa	18	2
Total:		**73**	**2**

SCOPE, Tynan — Goalkeeper

H: 6 2 W: 13 09 b.Sydney 30-7-79

1997–98	Coventry C	0	0
1998–99	Coventry C	0	0

SCOTT, Andy — Forward

H: 6 1 W: 11 05 b.Epsom 2-8-72

Source: Sutton U.

1992–93	Sheffield U	2	1
1993–94	Sheffield U	15	0
1994–95	Sheffield U	37	4
1995–96	Sheffield U	7	0
1996–97	Sheffield U	8	1
1996–97	Chesterfield (loan)	5	3
1996–97	Bury (loan)	8	0
1997–98	Sheffield U	6	0
1997–98	Brentford	26	5
1998–99	Brentford	34	7
Total:		**148**	**21**

SCOTT, Christopher — Defender

H: 5 11 W: 12 05 b.Burnley 12-2-80

Source: Trainee.

1998–99	Burnley	14	0
Total:		**14**	**0**

SCOTT, Gary — Defender

H: 5 8 W: 10 09 b.Liverpool 2-3-78

Source: Trainee.

1995–96	Tranmere R	0	0
1996–97	Tranmere R	0	0
1997–98	Rotherham U	7	0
1998–99	Rotherham U	13	0
Total:		**20**	**0**

SCOTT, Keith — Forward

H: 6 2 W: 14 07 b.Westminster 9-6-67

Source: Leicester U.

1989–90	Lincoln C	10	2
1990–91	Lincoln C	6	0
From Wycombe W			
1993–94	Wycombe W	15	10
1993–94	Swindon T	27	4
1994–95	Swindon T	24	8
1994–95	Stoke C	18	3
1995–96	Stoke C	7	0
1995–96	Norwich C	12	2
1995–96	Bournemouth (loan)	8	1
1996–97	Norwich C	13	3
1996–97	Watford (loan)	6	2
1996–97	Wycombe W (loan)	9	3

1997–98	Wycombe W	29	11
1998–99	Wycombe W	25	6
1998–99	Reading	9	2
Total:		**218**	**57**

SCOTT, Kevin — Defender

H: 6 3 W: 14 03 b.Easington 17-12-66

Source: Middlesbrough.

1984–85	Newcastle U	0	0
1985–86	Newcastle U	0	0
1986–87	Newcastle U	3	1
1987–88	Newcastle U	4	1
1988–89	Newcastle U	29	0
1989–90	Newcastle U	42	3
1990–91	Newcastle U	42	0
1991–92	Newcastle U	44	1
1992–93	Newcastle U	45	2
1993–94	Newcastle U	18	0
1993–94	Tottenham H	12	1
1994–95	Tottenham H	4	0
1994–95	Port Vale (loan)	17	1
1995–96	Tottenham H	2	0
1996–97	Tottenham H	0	0
1996–97	Charlton Ath (loan)	4	0
1996–97	Norwich C	9	0
1997–98	Norwich C	24	0
1998–99	Norwich C	0	0
1998–99	Darlington (loan)	4	0
Total:		**303**	**10**

SCOTT, Martin — Defender

H: 5 9 W: 11 00 b.Sheffield 7-1-68

Source: Apprentice.

1984–85	Rotherham U	3	0
1985–86	Rotherham U	0	0
1986–87	Rotherham U	12	0
1987–88	Rotherham U	19	0
1987–88	Nottingham F (loan)	0	0
1988–89	Rotherham U	19	1
1989–90	Rotherham U	28	1
1990–91	Rotherham U	13	1
1990–91	Bristol C	27	1
1991–92	Bristol C	46	3
1992–93	Bristol C	35	3
1993–94	Bristol C	45	5
1994–95	Bristol C	18	2
1994–95	Sunderland	24	0
1995–96	Sunderland	43	6
1996–97	Sunderland	15	1
1997–98	Sunderland	8	0
1998–99	Sunderland	16	2
Total:		**371**	**26**

SCOTT, Paul — Defender

H: 6 0 W: 11 11 b.Wakefield 5-11-79

Source: Trainee.

1998–99	Huddersfield T	0	0

SCOTT, Philip — Midfield

H: 5 9 W: 11 01 b.Perth 14-11-74

Source: Scone Thistle. *Honours:* Scotland Under-21.

1991–92	St Johnstone	0	0
1992–93	St Johnstone	3	0
1993–94	St Johnstone	24	3
1994–95	St Johnstone	12	1
1995–96	St Johnstone	28	8
1996–97	St Johnstone	29	12
1997–98	St Johnstone	22	1
1998–99	St Johnstone	16	2
1998–99	Sheffield W	4	1
Total:		**138**	**28**

SCOTT, Richard — Midfield

H: 5 9 W: 10 10 b.Dudley 29-9-74

Source: Trainee.

1992–93	Birmingham C	1	0
1993–94	Birmingham C	6	0
1994–95	Birmingham C	5	0
1994–95	Shrewsbury T	8	1
1995–96	Shrewsbury T	36	6
1996–97	Shrewsbury T	27	1
1997–98	Shrewsbury T	34	10
1998–99	Peterborough U	27	4
Total:		**144**	**22**

SCOTT, Rob — Forward

H: 6 1 W: 12 04 b.Epsom 15-8-73

Source: Sutton U.

1993–94	Sheffield U	0	0
1994–95	Sheffield U	1	0
1994–95	Scarborough (loan)	8	3
1995–96	Sheffield U	5	1
1995–96	Northampton T (loan)	5	0
1995–96	Fulham	21	5
1996–97	Fulham	43	9
1997–98	Fulham	17	3
1998–99	Fulham	3	0
1998–99	Carlisle U (loan)	7	3
1998–99	Rotherham U	6	1
Total:		**116**	**25**

SCOWCROFT, James — Forward

H: 6 2 W: 14 02 b.Bury St Edmunds 15-11-75

Source: Trainee. *Honours:* England Under-21.

1994–95	Ipswich T	0	0

1995–96	Ipswich T	23	2
1996–97	Ipswich T	41	9
1997–98	Ipswich T	31	6
1998–99	Ipswich T	32	13
Total:		**127**	**30**

SCULLY, Tony — Forward

H: 5 7 W: 11 05 b.Dublin 12-6-76

Source: Trainee. *Honours:* Eire Under-21.

1993–94	Crystal Palace	0	0
1994–95	Crystal Palace	0	0
1994–95	Bournemouth (loan)	10	0
1995–96	Crystal Palace	2	0
1995–96	Cardiff C (loan)	14	0
1996–97	Crystal Palace	1	0
1997–98	Crystal Palace	0	0
1997–98	Manchester C	9	0
1997–98	Stoke C (loan)	7	0
1997–98	QPR	7	0
1998–99	QPR	23	2
Total:		**73**	**2**

SEABURY, Kevin — Midfield

H: 5 9 W: 11 06 b.Shrewsbury 24-11-73

Source: Trainee.

1992–93	Shrewsbury T	1	0
1993–94	Shrewsbury T	0	0
1994–95	Shrewsbury T	30	0
1995–96	Shrewsbury T	34	0
1996–97	Shrewsbury T	38	0
1997–98	Shrewsbury T	39	2
1998–99	Shrewsbury T	44	5
Total:		**186**	**7**

SEAL, David — Forward

H: 5 11 W: 12 04 b.Penrith 26-1-72

Source: Aalst.

1994–95	Bristol C	9	0
1995–96	Bristol C	30	10
1996–97	Bristol C	12	0
1997–98	Northampton T	37	12
1998–99	Northampton T	6	0
Total:		**94**	**22**

SEALEY, Les — Goalkeeper

H: 6 1 W: 13 06 b.Bethnal Green 29-11-57

Source: Apprentice.

1975–76	Coventry C	0	0
1976–77	Coventry C	11	0
1977–78	Coventry C	2	0
1978–79	Coventry C	36	0
1979–80	Coventry C	20	0
1980–81	Coventry C	35	0
1981–82	Coventry C	15	0
1982–83	Coventry C	39	0
1983–84	Luton T	42	0
1984–85	Luton T	26	0
1984–85	Plymouth Arg (loan)	6	0
1985–86	Luton T	35	0
1986–87	Luton T	41	0
1987–88	Luton T	31	0
1988–89	Luton T	32	0
1989–90	Luton T	0	0
1989–90	Manchester U (loan)	2	0
1990–91	Manchester U	31	0
1991–92	Aston Villa	18	0
1991–92	Coventry C (loan)	2	0
1992–93	Aston Villa	0	0
1992–93	Birmingham C (loan)	12	0
1992–93	Manchester U	0	0
1993–94	Manchester U	0	0
1994–95	Blackpool	7	0
1994–95	West Ham U	0	0
1995–96	West Ham U	2	0
1996–97	Leyton Orient	12	0
1996–97	West Ham U	2	0
1997–98	West Ham U	0	0
1997–98	Bury (loan)	0	0
1998–99	West Ham U	0	0
Total:		**459**	**0**

SEAMAN, David — Goalkeeper

H: 6 4 W: 14 10 b.Rotherham 19-9-63

Source: Apprentice. *Honours:* England Under-21, B, 52 full caps.

1981–82	Leeds U	0	0
1982–83	Peterborough U	38	0
1983–84	Peterborough U	45	0
1984–85	Peterborough U	8	0
1984–85	Birmingham C	33	0
1985–86	Birmingham C	42	0
1986–87	QPR	41	0
1987–88	QPR	32	0
1988–89	QPR	35	0
1989–90	QPR	33	0
1990–91	Arsenal	38	0
1991–92	Arsenal	42	0
1992–93	Arsenal	39	0
1993–94	Arsenal	39	0
1994–95	Arsenal	31	0
1995–96	Arsenal	38	0
1996–97	Arsenal	22	0
1997–98	Arsenal	31	0
1998–99	Arsenal	32	0
Total:		**619**	**0**

SEARLE, Damon — Midfield

H: 5 10 W: 11 00 b.Cardiff 26-10-71

Source: Trainee. *Honours:* Wales Schools, Youth, Under-21.

1990–91	Cardiff C	35	0
1991–92	Cardiff C	42	1

1992–93	Cardiff C	42	1
1993–94	Cardiff C	42	0
1994–95	Cardiff C	32	0
1995–96	Cardiff C	41	1
1996–97	Stockport Co	10	0
1997–98	Stockport Co	31	0
1998–99	Carlisle U	45	2
Total:		**320**	**5**

SEARLE, Stevie — Midfield

H: 5 10 W: 11 08 b.Lambeth 7-3-77

Source: Sittingbourne.

1997–98	Barnet	30	2
1998–99	Barnet	35	3
Total:		**65**	**5**

SEBOK, Vilmos — Defender

b.Hungary 13-6-73

Source: Ujpesti. *Honours:* Hungary 26 full caps, 4 goals.

1998–99	Bristol C	12	0
Total:		**12**	**0**

SEDGEMORE, Ben — Midfield

H: 6 0 W: 12 08 b.Wolverhampton 5-8-75

Source: Trainee. *Honours:* England Schools.

1993–94	Birmingham C	0	0
1994–95	Birmingham C	0	0
1994–95	Northampton T (loan)	1	0
1995–96	Birmingham C	0	0
1995–96	Mansfield T (loan)	9	0
1995–96	Peterborough U	17	0
1996–97	Peterborough U	0	0
1996–97	Mansfield T	39	4
1997–98	Mansfield T	28	2
1997–98	Macclesfield T	5	0
1998–99	Macclesfield T	35	2
Total:		**134**	**8**

SEDGLEY, Steve — Defender

H: 6 1 W: 13 13 b.Enfield 26-5-68

Source: Apprentice. *Honours:* England Under-21.

1986–87	Coventry C	26	0
1987–88	Coventry C	27	2
1988–89	Coventry C	31	1
1989–90	Tottenham H	32	0
1990–91	Tottenham H	34	0
1991–92	Tottenham H	34	0
1992–93	Tottenham H	22	3
1993–94	Tottenham H	42	6
1994–95	Ipswich T	26	4
1995–96	Ipswich T	40	4
1996–97	Ipswich T	39	7
1997–98	Wolverhampton W	19	0
1998–99	Wolverhampton W	44	3
Total:		**416**	**30**

SEDGWICK, Chris — Forward

H: 5 11 W: 10 10 b.Sheffield 28-4-80

Source: Trainee.

1997–98	Rotherham U	4	0
1998–99	Rotherham U	33	4
Total:		**37**	**4**

SEDLAN, Jason — Midfield

H: 5 10 W: 10 11 b.Peterborough 5-8-79

Source: Trainee.

1997–98	Mansfield T	1	0
1998–99	Mansfield T	5	0
Total:		**6**	**0**

SEDLOSKI, Goce — Defender

H: 6 2 W: 13 00 b.Golemo Konjari 10-4-74

Source: Hajduk Split. *Honours:* Macedonia 14 full caps.

1997–98	Sheffield W	4	0
1998–99	Sheffield W	0	0
Total:		**4**	**0**

SEGERS, Hans — Goalkeeper

H: 5 11 W: 12 12 b.Eindhoven 30-10-61

Source: PSV Eindhoven.

1984–85	Nottingham F	28	0
1985–86	Nottingham F	11	0
1986–87	Nottingham F	14	0
1986–87	Stoke C (loan)	1	0
1987–88	Nottingham F	5	0
1987–88	Sheffield U (loan)	10	0
1987–88	Dunfermline Ath (loan)	4	0
1988–89	Nottingham F	0	0
1988–89	Wimbledon	33	0
1989–90	Wimbledon	38	0
1990–91	Wimbledon	37	0
1991–92	Wimbledon	41	0
1992–93	Wimbledon	41	0
1993–94	Wimbledon	41	0
1994–95	Wimbledon	32	0
1995–96	Wimbledon	4	0
1996–97	Wolverhampton W	0	0
1997–98	Wolverhampton W	11	0
1998–99	Tottenham H	1	0
Total:		**352**	**0**

SEGURA, Victor — Defender

H: 6 0 W: 12 00 b.Zaragoza 13-3-73

Source: Lleida.

1997–98	Norwich C	25	0
1998–99	Norwich C	4	0
Total:		**29**	**0**

SELFE, Oliver — Midfield

H: 5 9 W: 10 02 b.Warrington 1-10-79

Source: Trainee.

1997–98	Oldham Ath	0	0
1998–99	Oldham Ath	0	0

SELLARS, Scott — Midfield

H: 5 8 W: 10 00 b.Sheffield 27-11-65

Source: Apprentice. *Honours:* England Under-21.

1982–83	Leeds U	1	0
1983–84	Leeds U	19	3
1984–85	Leeds U	39	7
1985–86	Leeds U	17	2
1986–87	Blackburn R	32	4
1987–88	Blackburn R	42	7
1988–89	Blackburn R	46	2
1989–90	Blackburn R	43	14
1990–91	Blackburn R	9	1
1991–92	Blackburn R	30	7
1992–93	Leeds U	7	0
1992–93	Newcastle U	13	2
1993–94	Newcastle U	30	3
1994–95	Newcastle U	12	0
1995–96	Newcastle U	6	0
1995–96	Bolton W	22	3
1996–97	Bolton W	42	8
1997–98	Bolton W	22	2
1998–99	Bolton W	25	2
Total:		**457**	**67**

SELLEY, Ian — Midfield

H: 5 9 W: 11 05 b.Chertsey 14-6-74

Source: Trainee. *Honours:* England Youth, Under-21.

1992–93	Arsenal	9	0
1993–94	Arsenal	18	0
1994–95	Arsenal	13	0
1995–96	Arsenal	0	0
1996–97	Arsenal	1	0
1996–97	Southend U (loan)	4	0
1997–98	Arsenal	0	0
1997–98	Fulham	3	0
1998–99	Fulham	0	0
Total:		**48**	**0**

SENDA, Daniel — Forward

H: 5 9 W: 10 02 b.Harrow 17-4-81

Source: Southampton Trainee. *Honours:* England Youth.

1998–99	Wycombe W	6	0
Total:		**6**	**0**

SERRANT, Carl — Defender

H: 5 11 W: 11 02 b.Bradford 12-9-75

Source: Trainee. *Honours:* England Under-21, B.

1994–95	Oldham Ath	0	0
1995–96	Oldham Ath	20	1
1996–97	Oldham Ath	40	0
1997–98	Oldham Ath	30	0
1998–99	Newcastle U	4	0
1998–99	Bury (loan)	15	0
Total:		**109**	**1**

SERTORI, Mark — Defender

H: 6 2 W: 14 02 b.Manchester 1-9-67

1986–87	Stockport Co	3	0
1987–88	Stockport Co	1	0
1987–88	Lincoln C	0	0
1988–89	Lincoln C	26	4
1989–90	Lincoln C	24	5
1989–90	Wrexham	18	2
1990–91	Wrexham	29	0
1991–92	Wrexham	36	0
1992–93	Wrexham	12	0
1993–94	Wrexham	15	1
1994–95	Bury	2	0
1995–96	Bury	11	1
1996–97	Scunthorpe U	42	1
1997–98	Scunthorpe U	41	1
1998–99	Halifax T	40	0
Total:		**300**	**15**

SEVERIN, Scott — Midfield

H: 5 11 W: 12 07 b.Stirling 15-2-79

Source: Musselburgh Ath.

1996–97	Hearts	0	0
1997–98	Hearts	0	0
1998–99	Hearts	7	0
Total:		**7**	**0**

SEYDI, Elhadji — Defender

H: 6 3 W: 13 04 b.Dakar 25-12-75

Source: Le Mans.

1998–99	Bournemouth	0	0

SHAIL, Mark — Defender

H: 6 1 W: 12 06 b.Sweden 15-10-66

Source: Yeovil T.

1992–93	Bristol C	4	0
1993–94	Bristol C	36	2
1994–95	Bristol C	38	2
1995–96	Bristol C	12	0
1996–97	Bristol C	11	0
1997–98	Bristol C	2	0

1998–99	Bristol C	24	0
Total:		**127**	**4**

SHAKESPEARE, Craig — Midfield

H: 5 10 W: 13 06 b.Birmingham 26-10-63

Source: Apprentice.

1981–82	Walsall	0	0
1982–83	Walsall	31	4
1983–84	Walsall	46	6
1984–85	Walsall	41	9
1985–86	Walsall	32	4
1986–87	Walsall	44	11
1987–88	Walsall	45	8
1988–89	Walsall	45	3
1989–90	Sheffield W	17	0
1989–90	WBA	18	1
1990–91	WBA	36	1
1991–92	WBA	44	8
1992–93	WBA	14	2
1993–94	Grimsby T	33	3
1994–95	Grimsby T	19	3
1995–96	Grimsby T	28	2
1996–97	Grimsby T	26	2
1997–98	Scunthorpe U	4	0
1998–99	Scunthorpe U	0	0
Total:		**523**	**67**

SHANNON, Greg — Goalkeeper

H: 6 0 W: 11 00 b.Maghreafelt 15-2-81

Source: Trainee.

1997–98	Sunderland	0	0
1998–99	Sunderland	0	0

SHANNON, Rab — Defender

H: 5 11 W: 11 08 b.Bellshill 20-4-66

Source: St Columba's BC. *Honours:* Scotland Youth, Under-21.

1982–83	Dundee	0	0
1983–84	Dundee	6	0
1984–85	Dundee	3	0
1985–86	Dundee	33	0
1986–87	Dundee	39	5
1987–88	Dundee	41	0
1988–89	Dundee	29	1
1989–90	Dundee	36	1
1990–91	Dundee	37	2
1991–92	Middlesbrough (loan)	1	0
1991–92	Dundee	3	0
1991–92	Dunfermline Ath	27	0
1992–93	Dunfermline Ath	42	0
1993–94	Motherwell	43	0
1994–95	Motherwell	25	3
1995–96	Dundee U	26	1
1996–97	Dundee U	9	0
1996–97	Hibernian	5	0
1997–98	Hibernian	0	0
1998–99	Hibernian	1	0
Total:		**406**	**13**

SHARMAN, Sam — Defender

H: 5 10 W: 12 01 b.Hull 7-11-77

Source: Sheffield W Trainee.

1996–97	Hull C	4	0
1997–98	Hull C	0	0
1998–99	Hull C	0	0
Total:		**4**	**0**

SHARP, Kevin — Defender

H: 5 9 W: 11 04 b.Ontario 19-9-74

Source: Auxerre. *Honours:* England Schools, Youth.

1992–93	Leeds U	4	0
1993–94	Leeds U	10	0
1994–95	Leeds U	2	0
1995–96	Leeds U	1	0
1995–96	Wigan Ath	20	6
1996–97	Wigan Ath	35	2
1997–98	Wigan Ath	38	0
1998–99	Wigan Ath	31	2
Total:		**141**	**10**

SHARP, Lee — Defender

H: 5 8 W: 11 07 b.Glasgow 22-5-75

Source: Ashfield Juniors. *Honours:*

1995–96	Dumbarton	15	1
1996–97	Dumbarton	35	5
1997–98	Dumbarton	34	7
1998–99	Dundee	6	1
Total:		**90**	**14**

SHARPE, Lee — Forward

H: 6 0 W: 12 10 b.Halesowen 27-5-71

Source: Trainee. *Honours:* England Under-21, B, 8 full caps.

1987–88	Torquay U	14	3
1988–89	Manchester U	22	0
1989–90	Manchester U	18	1
1990–91	Manchester U	23	2
1991–92	Manchester U	14	1
1992–93	Manchester U	27	1
1993–94	Manchester U	30	9
1994–95	Manchester U	28	3
1995–96	Manchester U	31	4
1996–97	Leeds U	26	5
1997–98	Leeds U	0	0
1998–99	Leeds U	4	0
1998–99	Bradford C (loan)	9	2
1998–99	Sampdoria	3	0
Total:		**249**	**31**

SHARPLES, John — Defender

H: 6 0 W: 11 03 b.Bury 26-1-73

Source: Manchester U Trainee.

1991–92	Hearts	0	0
1992–93	Hearts	0	0
1993–94	Hearts	0	0
1994–95	Ayr U	27	0
1995–96	Ayr U	26	4
1995–96	York C	10	0
1996–97	York C	28	1
1997–98	York C	0	0
1998–99	York C	0	0
Total:		**91**	**5**

SHARPLING, Christopher — Forward

b.Bromley 21-4-81

Source: Trainee.

1998–99	Crystal Palace	0	0

SHARPS, Ian — Midfield

H: 6 3 W: 13 05 b.Warrington 23-10-80

Source: Trainee.

1998–99	Tranmere R	1	0
Total:		**1**	**0**

SHAW, George — Forward

H: 5 7 W: 10 09 b.Glasgow 10-2-69

Source: Ayresome N.

1987–88	St Mirren	2	0
1988–89	St Mirren	10	1
1989–90	St Mirren	23	2
1990–91	St Mirren	33	1
1991–92	Partick T	43	9
1992–93	Partick T	31	10
1993–94	Partick T	17	2
1993–94	Dundee	17	6
1994–95	Dundee	34	16
1995–96	Dundee	36	7
1996–97	Dundee	8	3
From Home Farm			
1996–97	Dundee	13	2
1997–98	Dunfermline Ath	23	2
1998–99	Dunfermline Ath	18	2
Total:		**308**	**63**

SHAW, Paul — Forward

H: 5 11 W: 12 04 b.Burnham 4-9-73

Source: Trainee.

1991–92	Arsenal	0	0
1992–93	Arsenal	0	0
1993–94	Arsenal	0	0
1994–95	Arsenal	1	0
1994–95	Burnley (loan)	9	4
1995–96	Arsenal	3	0
1995–96	Cardiff C (loan)	6	0
1995–96	Peterborough U (loan)	12	5
1996–97	Arsenal	8	2
1997–98	Arsenal	0	0
1997–98	Millwall	40	11
1998–99	Millwall	34	10
Total:		**113**	**32**

SHAW, Richard — Defender

H: 5 9 W: 12 08 b.Brentford 11-9-68

Source: Apprentice.

1986–87	Crystal Palace	0	0
1987–88	Crystal Palace	3	0
1988–89	Crystal Palace	14	0
1989–90	Crystal Palace	21	0
1989–90	Hull C (loan)	4	0
1990–91	Crystal Palace	36	1
1991–92	Crystal Palace	10	0
1992–93	Crystal Palace	33	0
1993–94	Crystal Palace	34	2
1994–95	Crystal Palace	41	0
1995–96	Crystal Palace	15	0
1995–96	Coventry C	21	0
1996–97	Coventry C	35	0
1997–98	Coventry C	33	0
1998–99	Coventry C	37	0
Total:		**337**	**3**

SHEARER, Alan — Forward

H: 5 11 W: 12 06 b.Newcastle 13-8-70

Source: Trainee. *Honours:* England Youth, Under-21, B, 51 full caps, 24 goals.

1987–88	Southampton	5	3
1988–89	Southampton	10	0
1989–90	Southampton	26	3
1990–91	Southampton	36	4
1991–92	Southampton	41	13
1992–93	Blackburn R	21	16
1993–94	Blackburn R	40	31
1994–95	Blackburn R	42	34
1995–96	Blackburn R	35	31
1996–97	Newcastle U	31	25
1997–98	Newcastle U	17	2
1998–99	Newcastle U	30	14
Total:		**334**	**176**

SHEARER, Peter — Midfield

H: 6 0 W: 11 00 b.Birmingham 4-2-67

Source: Apprentice.

1984–85	Birmingham C	4	0
1985–86	Birmingham C	0	0
1986–87	Rochdale	1	0
From Cheltenham T			

1988–89	Bournemouth	4	1
1989–90	Bournemouth	34	4
1990–91	Bournemouth	5	0
1991–92	Bournemouth	8	1
1992–93	Bournemouth	34	4
1993–94	Bournemouth	0	0
1993–94	Birmingham C	2	0
1994–95	Birmingham C	23	7
1995–96	Birmingham C	0	0
1996–97	Birmingham C	0	0
1997–98	Peterborough U	0	0
1998–99	Peterborough U	0	0
Total:		**115**	**17**

SHEERIN, Joe — Forward

H: 6 1 W: 13 09 b.Hammersmith 1-2-79

Source: Trainee.

1996–97	Chelsea	1	0
1997–98	Chelsea	0	0
1998–99	Chelsea	0	0
Total:		**1**	**0**

SHEFFIELD, Jon — Goalkeeper

H: 5 11 W: 11 06 b.Bedworth 1-2-69

Source: Apprentice.

1986–87	Norwich C	0	0
1987–88	Norwich C	0	0
1988–89	Norwich C	1	0
1989–90	Norwich C	0	0
1989–90	Aldershot (loan)	11	0
1989–90	Ipswich T (loan)	0	0
1990–91	Norwich C	0	0
1990–91	Aldershot (loan)	15	0
1990–91	Cambridge U (loan)	2	0
1991–92	Cambridge U	13	0
1992–93	Cambridge U	13	0
1993–94	Cambridge U	0	0
1993–94	Colchester U (loan)	6	0
1993–94	Swindon T (loan)	2	0
1994–95	Cambridge U	28	0
1994–95	Hereford U (loan)	8	0
1995–96	Peterborough U	46	0
1996–97	Peterborough U	16	0
1996–97	Watford (loan)	0	0
1996–97	Oldham Ath (loan)	0	0
1997–98	Plymouth Arg	46	0
1998–99	Plymouth Arg	39	0
Total:		**246**	**0**

SHELDON, Gareth — Forward

H: 5 11 W: 11 10 b.Birmingham 31-1-80

Source: Trainee.

1997–98	Scunthorpe U	1	0
1998–99	Scunthorpe U	11	1
Total:		**12**	**1**

SHELIA, Murtaz — Defender

H: 6 0 W: 13 02 b.Georgia 7-9-68

Honours: Georgia 29 full caps.

1994–95	Dynamo Tbilisi	10	2
1995	Alania	22	4
1996	Alania	27	5
1997	Alania	13	0
1997–98	Manchester C	12	2
1998–99	Manchester C	3	0
Total:		**87**	**13**

SHELTON, Andy — Midfield

H: 5 10 W: 12 00 b.Sutton Coldfield 19-6-80

Source: Trainee.

1997–98	Chester C	2	0
1998–99	Chester C	22	1
Total:		**24**	**1**

SHELTON, Gary — Midfield

H: 5 7 W: 11 02 b.Nottingham 21-3-58

Source: Apprentice. *Honours:* England Under-21.

1975–76	Walsall	2	0
1976–77	Walsall	10	0
1977–78	Walsall	12	0
1977–78	Aston Villa	0	0
1978–79	Aston Villa	19	7
1979–80	Aston Villa	4	0
1979–80	Notts Co (loan)	8	0
1980–81	Aston Villa	0	0
1981–82	Aston Villa	1	0
1981–82	Sheffield W	9	1
1982–83	Sheffield W	40	4
1983–84	Sheffield W	40	5
1984–85	Sheffield W	41	4
1985–86	Sheffield W	31	1
1986–87	Sheffield W	37	3
1987–88	Oxford U	32	0
1988–89	Oxford U	33	1
1989–90	Bristol C	43	9
1990–91	Bristol C	43	8
1991–92	Bristol C	19	3
1992–93	Bristol C	42	4
1993–94	Bristol C	3	0
1993–94	Rochdale (loan)	3	0
1994–95	Chester C	33	2
1995–96	Chester C	11	1
1996–97	Chester C	22	3
1997–98	Chester C	3	0
1998–99	Chester C	0	0
Total:		**541**	**56**

SHEPHERD, Paul — Defender

H: 5 11 W: 12 00 b.Leeds 17-11-77

Source: Trainee. *Honours:* England Youth.

1995–96	Leeds U	0	0
1996–97	Leeds U	1	0
1997–98	Leeds U	0	0
1997–98	Ayr U (loan)	6	1
1998–99	Leeds U	0	0
1998–99	Tranmere R (loan)	1	0
Total:		**8**	**1**

SHERIDAN, Darren — Midfield

H: 5 6 W: 11 03 b.Manchester 8-12-67

Source: Winsford U.

1993–94	Barnsley	3	0
1994–95	Barnsley	35	2
1995–96	Barnsley	41	0
1996–97	Barnsley	41	2
1997–98	Barnsley	26	0
1998–99	Barnsley	25	1
Total:		**171**	**5**

SHERIDAN, John — Midfield

H: 5 10 W: 12 01 b.Stretford 1-10-64

Source: Local. *Honours:* Eire Youth, Under-21, Under-23, B, 34 full caps, 5 goals.

1981–82	Leeds U	0	0
1982–83	Leeds U	27	2
1983–84	Leeds U	11	1
1984–85	Leeds U	42	6
1985–86	Leeds U	32	4
1986–87	Leeds U	40	15
1987–88	Leeds U	38	12
1988–89	Leeds U	40	7
1989–90	Nottingham F	0	0
1989–90	Sheffield W	27	2
1990–91	Sheffield W	46	10
1991–92	Sheffield W	24	6
1992–93	Sheffield W	25	3
1993–94	Sheffield W	20	3
1994–95	Sheffield W	36	1
1995–96	Sheffield W	17	0
1995–96	Birmingham C (loan)	2	0
1996–97	Sheffield W	2	0
1996–97	Bolton W	20	2
1997–98	Bolton W	12	0
From Doncaster R			
1998–99	Oldham Ath	30	2
Total:		**491**	**76**

SHERINGHAM, Teddy — Forward

H: 6 0 W: 13 00 b.Highams Park 2-4-66

Source: Apprentice. *Honours:* England Youth, 38 full caps, 9 goals.

1983–84	Millwall	7	1
1984–85	Millwall	0	0
1984–85	Aldershot (loan)	5	0
1985–86	Millwall	18	4
1986–87	Millwall	42	13
1987–88	Millwall	43	22
1988–89	Millwall	33	11
1989–90	Millwall	31	9
1990–91	Millwall	46	33
1991–92	Nottingham F	39	13
1992–93	Nottingham F	3	1
1992–93	Tottenham H	38	21
1993–94	Tottenham H	19	13
1994–95	Tottenham H	42	18
1995–96	Tottenham H	38	16
1996–97	Tottenham H	29	7
1997–98	Manchester U	31	9
1998–99	Manchester U	17	2
Total:		**481**	**193**

SHERON, Mike — Forward

H: 5 10 W: 12 07 b.Liverpool 11-1-72

Source: Trainee. *Honours:* England Under-21.

1990–91	Manchester C	0	0
1990–91	Bury (loan)	5	1
1991–92	Manchester C	29	7
1992–93	Manchester C	38	11
1993–94	Manchester C	33	6
1994–95	Norwich C	21	1
1995–96	Norwich C	7	1
1995–96	Stoke C	28	15
1996–97	Stoke C	41	19
1997–98	QPR	40	11
1998–99	QPR	23	8
1998–99	Barnsley	15	2
Total:		**280**	**82**

SHERWOOD, Tim — Midfield

H: 6 1 W: 12 09 b.St Albans 2-2-69

Source: Trainee. *Honours:* England Under-21, B, 3 full caps.

1986–87	Watford	0	0
1987–88	Watford	13	0
1988–89	Watford	19	2
1989–90	Norwich C	27	3
1990–91	Norwich C	37	7
1991–92	Norwich C	7	0
1991–92	Blackburn R	11	0
1992–93	Blackburn R	39	3
1993–94	Blackburn R	38	2
1994–95	Blackburn R	38	6
1995–96	Blackburn R	33	3

Shields, Greg

1996–97	Blackburn R	37	3
1997–98	Blackburn R	31	5
1998–99	Blackburn R	19	3
1998–99	Tottenham H	14	2
Total:		**363**	**39**

SHIELDS, Greg — Defender

H: 5 9 W: 10 10 b.Falkirk 21-8-76

Source: Rangers BC. *Honours:* Scotland Under-21.

1994–95	Rangers	0	0
1995–96	Rangers	1	0
1996–97	Rangers	6	0
1997–98	Dunfermline Ath	36	0
1998–99	Dunfermline Ath	36	0
Total:		**79**	**0**

SHIELDS, Tony — Midfield

H: 5 8 W: 10 01 b.Derry 4-6-80

Source: Trainee.

1997–98	Peterborough U	1	0
1998–99	Peterborough U	9	0
Total:		**10**	**0**

SHILTON, Sam — Midfield

H: 5 11 W: 11 06 b.Nottingham 21-7-78

Source: School.

1994–95	Plymouth Arg	2	0
1995–96	Plymouth Arg	1	0
1995–96	Coventry C	0	0
1996–97	Coventry C	0	0
1997–98	Coventry C	2	0
1998–99	Coventry C	5	0
Total:		**10**	**0**

SHIPPERLEY, Neil — Forward

H: 6 1 W: 14 01 b.Chatham 30-10-74

Source: Trainee. *Honours:* England Under-21.

1992–93	Chelsea	3	1
1993–94	Chelsea	24	4
1994–95	Chelsea	10	2
1994–95	Watford (loan)	6	1
1994–95	Southampton	19	4
1995–96	Southampton	37	7
1996–97	Southampton	10	1
1996–97	Crystal Palace	32	12
1997–98	Crystal Palace	26	7
1998–99	Crystal Palace	3	1
1998–99	Nottingham F	20	1
Total:		**190**	**41**

SHIVUTE, Eliphas — Forward

H: 5 11 W: 11 04 b.Windhoek 27-9-74

Source: Eleven Arrows.

1997–98	Motherwell	23	3
1998–99	Motherwell	1	0
Total:		**24**	**3**

SHORE, Jamie — Midfield

H: 5 9 W: 12 05 b.Bristol 1-9-77

Source: Trainee. *Honours:* England Youth.

1994–95	Norwich C	0	0
1995–96	Norwich C	0	0
1996–97	Norwich C	0	0
1997–98	Norwich C	0	0
1998–99	Bristol R	24	2
Total:		**24**	**2**

SHORT, Chris — Defender

H: 5 10 W: 12 03 b.Munster 9-5-70

Source: Pickering T.

1988–89	Scarborough	2	0
1989–90	Scarborough	41	1
1990–91	Scarborough	0	0
1990–91	Manchester U (loan)	0	0
1990–91	Notts Co	15	1
1991–92	Notts Co	27	0
1992–93	Notts Co	31	1
1993–94	Notts Co	6	0
1994–95	Notts Co	13	0
1994–95	Huddersfield T (loan)	6	0
1995–96	Notts Co	2	0
1995–96	Sheffield U	15	0
1996–97	Sheffield U	24	0
1997–98	Sheffield U	5	0
1998–99	Stoke C	21	0
Total:		**208**	**3**

SHORT, Craig — Defender

H: 6 0 W: 14 01 b.Bridlington 25-6-68

Source: Pickering T. *Honours:* England Schools.

1987–88	Scarborough	21	2
1988–89	Scarborough	42	5
1989–90	Notts Co	44	2
1990–91	Notts Co	0	0
1990–91	Notts Co	43	0
1991–92	Notts Co	38	3
1992–93	Notts Co	3	1
1992–93	Derby Co	38	3
1993–94	Derby Co	43	3
1994–95	Derby Co	37	3
1995–96	Everton	23	2
1996–97	Everton	23	2

1997–98	Everton	31	0
1998–99	Everton	22	0
Total:		**408**	**26**

SHOWLER, Paul — Midfield

H: 5 10 W: 11 00 b.Doncaster 10-10-66

Source: Sheffield W, Sunderland, Colne Dynamoes, Altrincham.

1991–92	Barnet	39	7
1992–93	Barnet	32	5
1993–94	Bradford C	32	5
1994–95	Bradford C	23	2
1995–96	Bradford C	33	8
1996–97	Luton T	23	6
1997–98	Luton T	1	0
1998–99	Luton T	3	0
Total:		**186**	**33**

SHUTT, Carl — Forward

H: 5 10 W: 12 10 b.Sheffield 10-10-61

Source: Spalding U.

1984–85	Sheffield W	0	0
1985–86	Sheffield W	19	9
1986–87	Sheffield W	20	7
1987–88	Sheffield W	1	0
1987–88	Bristol C	22	9
1988–89	Bristol C	24	1
1988–89	Leeds U	3	4
1989–90	Leeds U	20	2
1990–91	Leeds U	28	10
1991–92	Leeds U	14	1
1992–93	Leeds U	14	0
1993–94	Leeds U	0	0
1993–94	Birmingham C	26	4
1993–94	Manchester C (loan)	6	0
1994–95	Bradford C	32	4
1995–96	Bradford C	34	8
1996–97	Bradford C	22	3
1996–97	Darlington	6	2
1997–98	Darlington	33	5
1998–99	Darlington	14	2
Total:		**338**	**71**

SHUTTLEWORTH, Barry — Defender

H: 5 8 W: 11 00 b.Accrington 9-7-77

Source: Trainee.

1995–96	Bury	0	0
1996–97	Bury	0	0
1997–98	Rotherham U	0	0
1998–99	Blackpool	14	1
Total:		**14**	**1**

SIDDALL, Christopher — Defender

H: 5 10 W: 11 05 b.Sheffield 11-12-79

Source: Trainee.

1998–99	Sheffield W	0	0

SIDDALL, Richard — Goalkeeper

H: 6 1 W: 11 06 b.Sheffield 24-1-82

Source: Scholarship.

1998–99	Barnsley	0	0

SIDHU, Amrit — Forward

b.Coventry 16-12-81

Source: Trainee.

1998–99	Derby Co	0	0

SIGURDSSON, Kris — Defender

H: 5 11 W: 11 11 b.Akureyri 7-10-80

1997	KA	15	0
1997–98	Stoke C	0	0
1998–99	Stoke C	0	0
Total:		**15**	**0**

SIGURDSSON, Larus — Defender

H: 6 0 W: 13 11 b.Akureyri 4-6-73

Source: Thor. *Honours:* Iceland 25 full caps, 1 goal.

1994–95	Stoke C	23	1
1995–96	Stoke C	46	0
1996–97	Stoke C	45	0
1997–98	Stoke C	43	1
1998–99	Stoke C	38	4
Total:		**195**	**6**

SIMAO, Miguel — Midfield

H: 5 8 W: 11 04 b.Oporto 26-2-73

Source: Desportivo Aves.

1998–99	St Johnstone	26	4
Total:		**26**	**4**

SIMB, Jean-Pierre — Forward

H: 6 1 W: 11 05 b.Paris 4-9-74

Source: FC Paris.

1998–99	Torquay U	9	1
Total:		**9**	**1**

SIMBA, Amara — Forward

H: 6 1 W: 13 00 b.Paris 23-12-61

Source: Jeanne D'Arc, Houdan, Versailles. *Honours:* France 3 full caps, 2 goals.

1988–89	Paris St Germain	8	1
1989–90	Paris St Germain	27	6
1990–91	Paris St Germain	5	0
1990–91	Cannes	28	10
1991–92	Paris St Germain	25	6
1992–93	Paris St Germain	13	4
1993–94	Monaco	32	4
1994–95	Caen	37	12
1995–96	Lille	34	4
1996–97	Lille	5	0
From Lyon			
1998–99	Leyton Orient	24	10
Total:		**238**	**57**

SIMMS, Gordon — Defender

H: 6 1 W: 12 06 b.Larne 23-3-81

Source: Trainee.

1997–98	Wolverhampton W	0	0
1998–99	Wolverhampton W	0	0

SIMONSEN, Steve — Goalkeeper

H: 6 3 W: 13 02 b.South Shields 3-4-79

Source: Trainee. *Honours:* England Youth, Under-21.

1996–97	Tranmere R	0	0
1997–98	Tranmere R	30	0
1998–99	Tranmere R	5	0
1998–99	Everton	0	0
Total:		**35**	**0**

SIMPKINS, James — Midfield

H: 6 0 W: 11 11 b.Sheffield 28-11-78

Source: Trainee.

1997–98	Sheffield W	0	0
1997–98	Chesterfield	0	0
1998–99	Chesterfield	0	0

SIMPKINS, Mike — Defender

H: 6 0 W: 11 11 b.Sheffield 28-11-78

Source: Trainee.

1997–98	Sheffield W	0	0
1997–98	Chesterfield	0	0
1998–99	Chesterfield	1	0
Total:		**1**	**0**

SIMPSON, Colin — Forward

H: 6 1 W: 11 05 b.Oxford 30-4-76

Source: Trainee.

1994–95	Watford	0	0
1995–96	Watford	1	0
1996–97	Watford	0	0
1997–98	Watford	0	0
From Hendon			
1997–98	Leyton Orient	14	3
1998–99	Leyton Orient	0	0
Total:		**15**	**3**

SIMPSON, Fitzroy — Midfield

H: 5 8 W: 12 00 b.Trowbridge 26-2-70

Source: Trainee. *Honours:* Jamaica 27 full caps, 1 goal.

1988–89	Swindon T	7	0
1989–90	Swindon T	30	2
1990–91	Swindon T	38	3
1991–92	Swindon T	30	4
1991–92	Manchester C	11	1
1992–93	Manchester C	29	1
1993–94	Manchester C	15	0
1994–95	Manchester C	16	2
1994–95	Bristol C (loan)	4	0
1995–96	Manchester C	0	0
1995–96	Portsmouth	30	5
1996–97	Portsmouth	41	4
1997–98	Portsmouth	19	0
1998–99	Portsmouth	41	1
Total:		**311**	**23**

SIMPSON, Michael — Midfield

H: 5 6 W: 11 07 b.Nottingham 28-2-74

Source: Trainee.

1992–93	Notts Co	0	0
1993–94	Notts Co	6	1
1994–95	Notts Co	19	2
1995–96	Notts Co	23	0
1996–97	Notts Co	1	0
1996–97	Plymouth Arg (loan)	12	0
1996–97	Wycombe W	20	1
1997–98	Wycombe W	21	0
1998–99	Wycombe W	33	4
Total:		**135**	**8**

SIMPSON, Paul — Midfield

H: 5 8 W: 11 11 b.Carlisle 26-7-66

Source: Apprentice. *Honours:* England Youth, Under-21.

1982–83	Manchester C	3	0
1983–84	Manchester C	0	0
1984–85	Manchester C	10	6
1985–86	Manchester C	37	8
1986–87	Manchester C	32	3

1987–88	Manchester C	38	1
1988–89	Manchester C	1	0
1988–89	Oxford U	25	8
1989–90	Oxford U	42	9
1990–91	Oxford U	46	17
1991–92	Oxford U	31	9
1991–92	Derby Co	16	7
1992–93	Derby Co	35	12
1993–94	Derby Co	34	9
1994–95	Derby Co	42	8
1995–96	Derby Co	39	10
1996–97	Derby Co	19	2
1996–97	Sheffield U (loan)	6	0
1997–98	Derby Co	1	0
1997–98	Wolverhampton W	28	4
1998–99	Wolverhampton W	11	2
1998–99	Walsall (loan)	10	1
Total:		**506**	**116**

SIMPSON, Phil — Midfield

H: 5 8 W: 11 12 b.Lambeth 19-10-69

Source: Stevenage Bor.

1995–96	Barnet	24	1
1996–97	Barnet	32	2
1997–98	Barnet	31	4
1998–99	Barnet	13	0
Total:		**100**	**7**

SIMPSON, Robbie — Forward

H: 5 10 W: 11 06 b.Luton 3-3-76

Source: Trainee. *Honours:* England Youth.

1993–94	Tottenham H	0	0
1994–95	Tottenham H	0	0
1995–96	Tottenham H	0	0
1996–97	Portsmouth	0	0
1997–98	Portsmouth	2	0
1998–99	Portsmouth	0	0
Total:		**2**	**0**

SINCLAIR, Frank — Defender

H: 5 10 W: 12 07 b.Lambeth 3-12-71

Source: Trainee. *Honours:* Jamaica 8 full caps.

1989–90	Chelsea	0	0
1990–91	Chelsea	4	0
1991–92	Chelsea	8	1
1991–92	WBA (loan)	6	1
1992–93	Chelsea	32	0
1993–94	Chelsea	35	0
1994–95	Chelsea	35	3
1995–96	Chelsea	13	1
1996–97	Chelsea	20	1
1997–98	Chelsea	22	1
1998–99	Leicester C	31	1
Total:		**206**	**9**

SINCLAIR, Ronnie — Goalkeeper

H: 5 11 W: 12 09 b.Stirling 19-11-64

Source: Apprentice. *Honours:* Scotland Schools, Youth.

1982–83	Nottingham F	0	0
1983–84	Nottingham F	0	0
1983–84	Wrexham (loan)	11	0
1984–85	Nottingham F	0	0
1984–85	Derby Co (loan)	0	0
1985–86	Nottingham F	0	0
1985–86	Sheffield U (loan)	0	0
1985–86	Leeds U (loan)	0	0
1986–87	Leeds U	8	0
1986–87	Halifax T (loan)	4	0
1987–88	Leeds U	0	0
1988–89	Leeds U	0	0
1988–89	Halifax T (loan)	10	0
1989–90	Leeds U	0	0
1989–90	Bristol C	27	0
1990–91	Bristol C	17	0
1991–92	Bristol C	0	0
1991–92	Walsall (loan)	10	0
1991–92	Stoke C	26	0
1992–93	Stoke C	29	0
1993–94	Stoke C	0	0
1994–95	Stoke C	24	0
1994–95	Bradford C (loan)	0	0
1995–96	Stoke C	1	0
1996–97	Chester C	37	0
1997–98	Chester C	33	0
1998–99	Cardiff C	0	0
1998–99	Stoke C	0	0
Total:		**237**	**0**

SINCLAIR, Trevor — Forward

H: 5 10 W: 12 05 b.Dulwich 2-3-72

Source: Trainee. *Honours:* England Youth, Under-21, B.

1989–90	Blackpool	9	0
1990–91	Blackpool	31	1
1991–92	Blackpool	27	3
1992–93	Blackpool	45	11
1993–94	QPR	32	4
1994–95	QPR	33	4
1995–96	QPR	37	2
1996–97	QPR	39	3
1997–98	QPR	26	3
1997–98	West Ham U	14	7
1998–99	West Ham U	36	7
Total:		**329**	**45**

SINGH, Harpal — Forward

H: 5 7 W: 10 02 b.Bradford 15-9-81

Source: Trainee.

1998–99	Leeds U	0	0

SINNOTT, Lee — Defender

H: 6 1 W: 13 01 b.Pelsall 12-7-65

Source: Apprentice. *Honours:* England Youth, Under-21.

1981–82	Walsall	4	0
1982–83	Walsall	32	2
1983–84	Walsall	4	0
1983–84	Watford	20	0
1984–85	Watford	30	0
1985–86	Watford	18	2
1986–87	Watford	10	0
1987–88	Bradford C	42	1
1988–89	Bradford C	42	2
1989–90	Bradford C	45	2
1990–91	Bradford C	44	1
1991–92	Crystal Palace	36	0
1992–93	Crystal Palace	19	0
1993–94	Crystal Palace	0	0
1993–94	Bradford C	18	0
1994–95	Bradford C	16	1
1994–95	Huddersfield T	25	1
1995–96	Huddersfield T	32	0
1996–97	Huddersfield T	30	0
1997–98	Oldham Ath	13	0
1997–98	Bradford C (loan)	7	0
1998–99	Oldham Ath	18	0
Total:		**505**	**12**

SINTON, Andy — Midfield

H: 5 8 W: 11 01 b.Newcastle 19-3-66

Source: Apprentice. *Honours:* England Schools, B, 12 full caps.

1982–83	Cambridge U	13	5
1983–84	Cambridge U	34	6
1984–85	Cambridge U	26	2
1985–86	Cambridge U	20	0
1985–86	Brentford	26	3
1986–87	Brentford	46	5
1987–88	Brentford	46	11
1988–89	Brentford	31	9
1988–89	QPR	10	3
1989–90	QPR	38	6
1990–91	QPR	38	3
1991–92	QPR	38	3
1992–93	QPR	36	7
1993–94	Sheffield W	25	3
1994–95	Sheffield W	25	0
1995–96	Sheffield W	10	0
1995–96	Tottenham H	9	0
1996–97	Tottenham H	33	6
1997–98	Tottenham H	19	0
1998–99	Tottenham H	22	0
Total:		**545**	**72**

SISSON, Michael — Midfield

H: 5 9 W: 10 11 b.Sutton-in-Ashfield 24-11-78

Source: Trainee.

1997–98	Mansfield T	1	0
1998–99	Mansfield T	1	0
Total:		**2**	**0**

SKELTON, Aaron — Midfield

H: 6 0 W: 12 08 b.Welwyn 22-11-74

Source: Trainee.

1992–93	Luton T	0	0
1993–94	Luton T	0	0
1994–95	Luton T	5	0
1995–96	Luton T	0	0
1996–97	Luton T	3	0
1997–98	Colchester U	39	7
1998–99	Colchester U	9	0
Total:		**56**	**7**

SKINNER, Craig — Midfield

H: 5 8 W: 11 00 b.Bury 21-10-70

Source: Trainee.

1989–90	Blackburn R	0	0
1990–91	Blackburn R	7	0
1991–92	Blackburn R	9	0
1992–93	Plymouth Arg	13	1
1993–94	Plymouth Arg	16	0
1994–95	Plymouth Arg	24	3
1995–96	Wrexham	23	3
1996–97	Wrexham	27	4
1997–98	Wrexham	25	1
1998–99	Wrexham	12	2
1998–99	York C	5	0
Total:		**161**	**14**

SKINNER, Justin — Midfield

H: 6 0 W: 11 03 b.Hounslow 30-1-69

Source: Apprentice.

1986–87	Fulham	3	0
1987–88	Fulham	32	6
1988–89	Fulham	38	8
1989–90	Fulham	30	4
1990–91	Fulham	32	5
1991–92	Bristol R	42	3
1992–93	Bristol R	12	0
1993–94	Bristol R	29	5
1994–95	Bristol R	38	2
1995–96	Bristol R	28	0
1996–97	Bristol R	34	2
1997–98	Bristol R	4	0
1997–98	Walsall (loan)	10	0
1997–98	Hibernian	6	0
1998–99	Hibernian	24	2
Total:		**362**	**37**

SKOLDMARK, Magnus — Defender

H: 6 1 W: 12 00 b.Langsele 22-9-68

Source: Dalian Wanda.

1997–98	Dundee U	19	0
1998–99	Dundee U	25	0
Total:		**44**	**0**

SLADE, Steve — Forward

H: 6 0 W: 10 13 b.Hackney 6-10-75

Source: Trainee. *Honours:* England Under-21.

1994–95	Tottenham H	0	0
1995–96	Tottenham H	5	0
1996–97	QPR	17	4
1996–97	Brentford (loan)	4	0
1997–98	QPR	22	0
1998–99	QPR	20	1
Total:		**68**	**5**

SLATER, Robbie — Defender

H: 5 10 W: 13 03 b.Ormskirk 22-11-64

Source: Anderlecht. *Honours:* Australia full caps.

1991–92	Lens	34	2
1992–93	Lens	25	0
1993–94	Lens	22	2
1994–95	Blackburn R	18	0
1995–96	West Ham U	22	2
1996–97	West Ham U	3	0
1996–97	Southampton	30	2
1997–98	Southampton	11	0
1997–98	Wolverhampton W	6	0
1998–99	Wolverhampton W	0	0
Total:		**171**	**8**

SLATER, Stuart — Midfield

H: 5 9 W: 10 13 b.Sudbury 27-3-69

Source: Apprentice. *Honours:* England Under-21, B.

1986–87	West Ham U	0	0
1987–88	West Ham U	2	0
1988–89	West Ham U	18	1
1989–90	West Ham U	40	7
1990–91	West Ham U	40	3
1991–92	West Ham U	41	0
1992–93	Celtic	39	2
1993–94	Celtic	4	1
1993–94	Ipswich T	28	1
1994–95	Ipswich T	27	1
1995–96	Ipswich T	17	2
1996–97	Ipswich T	0	0
1996–97	Leicester C	0	0
1996–97	Watford	16	1
1997–98	Watford	14	0
1998–99	Watford	0	0
Total:		**286**	**19**

SLATTER, Danny — Midfield

H: 5 8 W: 11 01 b.Cardiff 15-11-80

Source: Trainee.

1998–99	Chelsea	0	0

SLOAN, Christopher — Midfield

b.Gillingham 21-2-80

Source: Trainee.

1998–99	Bristol C	0	0

SMALL, Bryan — Defender

H: 5 9 W: 11 09 b.Birmingham 15-11-71

Source: Trainee. *Honours:* England Under-21.

1989–90	Aston Villa	0	0
1990–91	Aston Villa	0	0
1991–92	Aston Villa	8	0
1992–93	Aston Villa	14	0
1993–94	Aston Villa	9	0
1994–95	Aston Villa	5	0
1994–95	Birmingham C (loan)	3	0
1995–96	Aston Villa	0	0
1995–96	Bolton W	1	0
1996–97	Bolton W	11	0
1997–98	Bolton W	0	0
1997–98	Luton T (loan)	15	0
1997–98	Bradford C (loan)	5	0
1997–98	Bury	18	1
1998–99	Stoke C	37	0
Total:		**126**	**1**

SMART, Allan — Forward

H: 6 2 W: 12 11 b.Perth 8-7-74

1994–95	Caledonian Th	4	0
1994–95	Preston NE	19	6
1995–96	Preston NE	2	0
1995–96	Carlisle U (loan)	4	0
1996–97	Preston NE	0	0
1996–97	Northampton T (loan)	1	0
1996–97	Carlisle U	28	10
1997–98	Carlisle U	16	6
1998–99	Watford	35	7
Total:		**109**	**29**

SMEETS, Jorg — Forward

H: 5 6 W: 10 04 b.Bussum 5-11-70

1997–98	Heracles	8	2
1997–98	Wigan Ath	23	3
1998–99	Wigan Ath	1	0
1998–99	Chester C (loan)	3	0
Total:		**35**	**5**

SMITH, Alan — Forward

H: 5 9 W: 10 13 b.Leeds 28-10-80

Source: Trainee. *Honours:* England Youth.

1997–98	Leeds U	0	0
1998–99	Leeds U	22	7
Total:		**22**	**7**

SMITH, Alex — Midfield

H: 5 9 W: 9 09 b.Liverpool 15-2-76

Source: Trainee.

1994–95	Everton	0	0
1995–96	Everton	0	0
1995–96	Swindon T	8	0
1996–97	Swindon T	18	1
1997–98	Swindon T	5	0
1998–99	Chester C	32	2
1998–99	Port Vale	8	0
Total:		**71**	**3**

SMITH, Andrew — Midfield

H: 5 5 W: 11 08 b.Blackpool 13-1-80

Source: Trainee.

1998–99	Barnsley	0	0

SMITH, Andy — Forward

H: 6 1 W: 12 07 b.Aberdeen 22-11-68

Source: Peterhead. *Honours:* Scotland B.

1990–91	Airdrieonians	28	3
1991–92	Airdrieonians	29	4
1992–93	Airdrieonians	34	4
1993–94	Airdrieonians	38	7
1994–95	Airdrieonians	36	12
1995–96	Dunfermline Ath	19	9
1996–97	Dunfermline Ath	35	10
1997–98	Dunfermline Ath	33	16
1998–99	Dunfermline Ath	35	8
Total:		**287**	**73**

SMITH, Barry — Defender

H: 5 10 W: 12 00 b.Paisley 19-2-74

Source: Giffnock N. *Honours:* Scotland Under-21.

1991–92	Celtic	3	0
1992–93	Celtic	6	0
1993–94	Celtic	7	0
1994–95	Celtic	3	0
1995–96	Celtic	0	0
1995–96	Dundee	20	0
1996–97	Dundee	36	0
1997–98	Dundee	34	1
1998–99	Dundee	33	0
Total:		**142**	**1**

SMITH, Carl — Defender

H: 5 8 W: 11 00 b.Sheffield 15-1-79

Source: Trainee.

1997–98	Burnley	1	0
1998–99	Burnley	10	0
Total:		**11**	**0**

SMITH, David — Midfield

H: 5 10 W: 12 11 b.Liverpool 26-12-70

Source: Trainee.

1989–90	Norwich C	1	0
1990–91	Norwich C	3	0
1991–92	Norwich C	1	0
1992–93	Norwich C	6	0
1993–94	Norwich C	7	0
1994–95	Oxford U	42	0
1995–96	Oxford U	45	1
1996–97	Oxford U	45	0
1997–98	Oxford U	44	1
1998–99	Oxford U	22	0
1998–99	Stockport Co	17	1
Total:		**233**	**3**

SMITH, David — Midfield

H: 5 8 W: 11 04 b.Stonehouse 29-3-68

Honours: England Under-21.

1986–87	Coventry C	0	0
1987–88	Coventry C	16	4
1988–89	Coventry C	35	3
1989–90	Coventry C	37	6
1990–91	Coventry C	36	1
1991–92	Coventry C	24	4
1992–93	Coventry C	6	1
1992–93	Bournemouth (loan)	1	0
1992–93	Birmingham C	13	1
1993–94	Birmingham C	25	2
1993–94	WBA	18	0
1994–95	WBA	22	0
1995–96	WBA	16	0
1996–97	WBA	24	2
1997–98	WBA	22	0
1997–98	Grimsby T	17	1
1998–99	Grimsby T	31	5
Total:		**343**	**30**

SMITH, Dean — Defender

H: 6 0 W: 13 00 b.West Bromwich 19-3-71

Source: Trainee.

1988–89	Walsall	15	0
1989–90	Walsall	7	0
1990–91	Walsall	33	0
1991–92	Walsall	9	0
1992–93	Walsall	42	1

1993–94	Walsall	36	1
1994–95	Hereford U	35	3
1995–96	Hereford U	40	8
1996–97	Hereford U	42	8
1997–98	Leyton Orient	43	9
1998–99	Leyton Orient	37	9
Total:		**339**	**39**

SMITH, Gary
Defender

H: 6 0 W: 12 03 b.Glasgow 25-3-71

Source: Duntocher BC.

1988–89	Falkirk	3	0
1989–90	Falkirk	36	0
1990–91	Falkirk	31	0
1991–92	Aberdeen	16	1
1992–93	Aberdeen	40	0
1993–94	Aberdeen	21	0
1994–95	Aberdeen	31	0
1995–96	Aberdeen	33	0
1996–97	Rennes	14	0
1997–98	Aberdeen	31	1
1998–99	Aberdeen	30	0
Total:		**286**	**2**

SMITH, Gordon
Midfield

b.Glasgow 18-12-80

Source: Trainee.

1997–98	Bolton W	0	0
1998–99	Bolton W	0	0

SMITH, Grant
Midfield

b.Irvine 5-5-80

1998–99	Reading	0	0

SMITH, Jamie
Defender

H: 5 8 W: 11 02 b.Birmingham 17-9-74

Source: Trainee.

1993–94	Wolverhampton W	0	0
1994–95	Wolverhampton W	25	0
1995–96	Wolverhampton W	13	0
1996–97	Wolverhampton W	38	0
1997–98	Wolverhampton W	11	0
1997–98	Crystal Palace	18	0
1998–99	Crystal Palace	26	0
1998–99	Fulham (loan)	9	1
Total:		**140**	**1**

SMITH, Jason
Defender

H: 6 1 W: 13 06 b.Bromsgrove 6-9-74

Source: Tiverton. *Honours:* England Schools.

1993–94	Coventry C	0	0
1994–95	Coventry C	0	0
1995–96	Coventry C	0	0
1996–97	Coventry C	0	0
1997–98	Coventry C	0	0
From Tiverton T			
1998–99	Swansea C	42	4
Total:		**42**	**4**

SMITH, Jeff
Midfield

H: 5 10 W: 11 01 b.Middlesbrough 28-6-80

Source: Trainee.

1998–99	Hartlepool U	3	0
Total:		**3**	**0**

SMITH, Mark
Defender

H: 6 0 W: 13 07 b.Bristol 13-9-79

Source: Trainee.

1998–99	Bristol R	14	0
Total:		**14**	**0**

SMITH, Martin
Forward

H: 5 11 W: 12 00 b.Sunderland 13-11-74

Source: Trainee. *Honours:* England Schools, Under-21.

1992–93	Sunderland	0	0
1993–94	Sunderland	29	8
1994–95	Sunderland	35	10
1995–96	Sunderland	20	2
1996–97	Sunderland	11	0
1997–98	Sunderland	16	2
1998–99	Sunderland	8	3
Total:		**119**	**25**

SMITH, Neil
Midfield

H: 5 8 W: 12 02 b.Lambeth 30-9-71

Source: Trainee.

1990–91	Tottenham H	0	0
1991–92	Tottenham H	0	0
1991–92	Gillingham	26	2
1992–93	Gillingham	39	3
1993–94	Gillingham	35	2
1994–95	Gillingham	33	1
1995–96	Gillingham	37	1
1996–97	Gillingham	42	1
1997–98	Fulham	44	0
1998–99	Fulham	29	1
Total:		**285**	**11**

SMITH, Paul — Midfield

H: 5 11 W: 12 08 b.East Ham 18-9-71

Source: Trainee.

1989–90	Southend U	10	1
1990–91	Southend U	2	0
1991–92	Southend U	0	0
1992–93	Southend U	8	0
1993–94	Brentford	32	3
1994–95	Brentford	35	3
1995–96	Brentford	46	4
1996–97	Brentford	46	1
1997–98	Gillingham	46	3
1998–99	Gillingham	45	6
Total:		**270**	**21**

SMITH, Paul — Midfield

H: 5 11 W: 11 07 b.Hastings 25-1-76

Source: Hastings T.

1994–95	Nottingham F	0	0
1995–96	Nottingham F	0	0
1996–97	Nottingham F	0	0
1997–98	Nottingham F	0	0
1997–98	Lincoln C (loan)	17	3
1998–99	Lincoln C	28	2
Total:		**45**	**5**

SMITH, Paul — Midfield

H: 6 0 W: 13 03 b.Leeds 22-7-76

Source: Trainee.

1993–94	Burnley	1	0
1994–95	Burnley	0	0
1995–96	Burnley	10	0
1996–97	Burnley	37	4
1997–98	Burnley	14	0
1998–99	Burnley	12	0
Total:		**74**	**4**

SMITH, Paul — Goalkeeper

H: 6 3 W: 12 04 b.Epsom 17-12-79

1998–99	Charlton Ath	0	0
1998–99	Brentford (loan)	0	0

SMITH, Peter — Defender

H: 6 2 W: 12 10 b.Stone 12-7-69

Source: Alma Swanley.

1994–95	Brighton & HA	38	1
1995–96	Brighton & HA	31	1
1996–97	Brighton & HA	30	1
1997–98	Brighton & HA	27	2
1998–99	Brighton & HA	14	0
Total:		**140**	**5**

SMITH, Peter — Forward

H: 5 10 W: 10 00 b.Rhuddlan 15-9-78

Source: Trainee.

1996–97	Crewe Alex	1	0
1997–98	Crewe Alex	6	0
1998–99	Crewe Alex	4	0
1998–99	Macclesfield T (loan)	12	3
Total:		**23**	**3**

SMITH, Peter — Midfield

b.Skemsdale 31-10-80

Source: Trainee.

1998–99	Exeter C	1	0
Total:		**1**	**0**

SMITH, Phil — Goalkeeper

H: 6 1 W: 13 00 b.Harrow 14-12-79

Source: Trainee.

1997–98	Millwall	0	0
1998–99	Millwall	5	0
Total:		**5**	**0**

SMITH, Richard — Defender

H: 6 0 W: 13 07 b.Lutterworth 3-10-70

Source: Trainee.

1988–89	Leicester C	0	0
1989–90	Leicester C	4	0
1989–90	Cambridge U (loan)	4	0
1990–91	Leicester C	4	0
1991–92	Leicester C	25	1
1992–93	Leicester C	44	0
1993–94	Leicester C	8	0
1994–95	Leicester C	12	0
1995–96	Leicester C	1	0
1995–96	Grimsby T	18	0
1996–97	Grimsby T	14	0
1997–98	Grimsby T	0	0
1998–99	Grimsby T	30	0
Total:		**164**	**1**

SMITH, Shaun — Defender

H: 5 10 W: 11 00 b.Leeds 9-4-71

Source: Trainee.

1988–89	Halifax T	1	0

1989–90	Halifax T	6	0
1990–91	Halifax T	0	0
1991–92	Crewe Alex	10	0
1992–93	Crewe Alex	36	4
1993–94	Crewe Alex	37	7
1994–95	Crewe Alex	45	8
1995–96	Crewe Alex	29	1
1996–97	Crewe Alex	38	4
1997–98	Crewe Alex	43	6
1998–99	Crewe Alex	46	4
Total:		**291**	**34**

SMITH, Thomas — Midfield

H: 5 8 W: 11 07 b.Glasgow 12-10-73

Source: 'S' Form.

1990–91	Partick T	1	0
1991–92	Partick T	0	0
1992–93	Cork City	1	0
1992–93	Partick T	2	0
1993–94	Partick T	8	1
1994–95	Portadown	4	0
1994–95	Partick T	14	1
1995–96	Partick T	25	2
1996–97	Partick T	1	0
1996–97	Ayr U	21	4
1997–98	Ayr U	18	1
1998–99	Clydebank	21	3
1998–99	Hibernian	5	0
Total:		**121**	**12**

SMITH, Tommy — Midfield

H: 5 9 W: 13 00 b.Northampton 25-11-77

Source: Trainee.

1994–95	Manchester U	0	0
1995–96	Manchester U	0	0
1996–97	Manchester U	0	0
1997–98	Manchester U	0	0
1997–98	Cambridge U	1	0
1998–99	Cambridge U	0	0
Total:		**1**	**0**

SMITH, Tommy — Forward

H: 5 9 W: 10 11 b.Hemel Hempstead 22-5-80

Source: Trainee. *Honours:* England Youth.

1997–98	Watford	1	0
1998–99	Watford	8	2
Total:		**9**	**2**

SNEEKES, Richard — Midfield

H: 5 11 W: 12 03 b.Amsterdam 30-10-68

Honours: Holland Under-21.

1985–86	Ajax	1	0
1986–87	Ajax	1	0
1987–88	Ajax	1	0
1988–89	Volendam	31	7
1989–90	Fortuna Sittard	32	2
1990–91	Fortuna Sittard	32	7
1991–92	Fortuna Sittard	33	5
1992–93	Fortuna Sittard	29	6
From Locarno, Fortuna Sittard.			
1994–95	Bolton W	38	6
1995–96	Bolton W	17	1
1995–96	WBA	13	10
1996–97	WBA	45	8
1997–98	WBA	42	3
1998–99	WBA	40	4
Total:		**355**	**59**

SNIJDERS, Mark — Defender

H: 6 2 W: 14 04 b.Alkmaar 12-3-72

1997–98	Port Vale	24	2
1998–99	Port Vale	10	0
Total:		**34**	**2**

SNORRASON, Olafur — Forward

b.Reykjavik 22-4-82

1998–99	Bolton W	0	0

SODJE, Efetobar — Defender

H: 6 1 W: 12 00 b.Greenwich 5-10-72

Source: Delta Steel Pioneer, Stevenage Bor.

1997–98	Macclesfield T	41	3
1998–99	Macclesfield T	42	3
Total:		**83**	**6**

SOLANO, Norberto — Midfield

H: 5 9 W: 11 06 b.Callao 12-12-74

1994–95	Sporting Cristal	38	12
1995–96	Sporting Cristal	26	13
1996–97	Sporting Cristal	11	7
1997–98	Boca Juniors	32	5
1998–99	Newcastle U	29	6
Total:		**136**	**43**

SOLEY, Steve — Midfield

H: 5 11 W: 12 08 b.Widnes 22-4-71

Source: Warrington, Leek T.

1998–99	Portsmouth	8	0
1998–99	Macclesfield T (loan)	10	0
Total:		**18**	**0**

SOLIS, Mauricio — Midfield

H: 5 8 W: 12 00 b.Costa Rica 13-12-72

Source: Herediano. *Honours:* Costa Rica full caps.

1996–97	Derby Co	2	0
1997–98	Derby Co	9	0
1998–99	Derby Co	0	0
Total:		**11**	**0**

SOLSKJAER, Ole Gunnar — Forward

H: 5 10 W: 11 06 b.Kristiansund 26-2-73

Honours: Norway Under-21, 22 full caps, 11 goals.

1995	Molde	26	20
1996	Molde	16	11
1996–97	Manchester U	33	17
1997–98	Manchester U	22	6
1998–99	Manchester U	19	12
Total:		**116**	**66**

SOLTVEDT, Trond Egil — Midfield

H: 6 1 W: 12 08 b.Voss 15-2-67

Source: Dale, Ny-Krohnborg. *Honours:* Norway 4 full caps.

1988	Viking	21	3
1989	Viking	11	3
1990	Viking	20	3
1991	Viking	13	1
1992	Brann	22	6
1993	Brann	21	16
1994	Brann	21	12
1995	Rosenborg	25	4
1996	Rosenborg	26	10
1997	Rosenborg	9	4
1997–98	Coventry C	30	1
1998–99	Coventry C	27	2
Total:		**246**	**65**

SONG, Rigobert — Defender

H: 6 0 W: 13 00 b.Nkanglicock 1-7-76

Source: Tonnerre. *Honours:* Cameroon 30 full caps, 1 goal.

1994–95	Metz	24	2
1995–96	Metz	37	0
1996–97	Metz	34	0
1997–98	Metz	28	1
1998–99	Salernitana	4	1
1998–99	Liverpool	13	0
Total:		**140**	**4**

SONNER, Danny — Midfield

H: 6 0 W: 12 08 b.Wigan 9-1-72

Source: Wigan Ath. *Honours:* Northern Ireland B, 3 full caps.

1990–91	Burnley	2	0
1991–92	Burnley	3	0
1992–93	Burnley	1	0
1992–93	Bury (loan)	5	3
From Erzgebirge Aue			
1996–97	Ipswich T	29	2
1997–98	Ipswich T	23	1
1998–99	Ipswich T	4	0
1998–99	Sheffield W	26	3
Total:		**93**	**9**

SORENSEN, Thomas — Goalkeeper

H: 6 3 W: 12 05 b.Fredericia 12-6-76

Source: Odense.

1998–99	Sunderland	45	0
Total:		**45**	**0**

SORVEL, Neil — Midfield

H: 6 0 W: 12 09 b.Whiston 2-3-73

Source: Trainee.

1991–92	Crewe Alex	9	0
1992–93	Crewe Alex	0	0
1997–98	Macclesfield T	45	3
1998–99	Macclesfield T	41	4
Total:		**95**	**7**

SOUTER, Ryan — Midfield

H: 5 10 W: 12 00 b.Bedford 5-2-78

Source: Weston-Super-Mare.

1998–99	Bury	1	0
Total:		**1**	**0**

SOUTHALL, Neville — Goalkeeper

H: 6 1 W: 13 00 b.Llandudno 16-9-58

Source: Winsford U. *Honours:* Wales Under-21, 92 full caps.

1980–81	Bury	39	0
1981–82	Everton	26	0
1982–83	Everton	17	0
1982–83	Port Vale (loan)	9	0
1983–84	Everton	35	0
1984–85	Everton	42	0
1985–86	Everton	32	0

1986–87	Everton	31	0
1987–88	Everton	32	0
1988–89	Everton	38	0
1989–90	Everton	38	0
1990–91	Everton	38	0
1991–92	Everton	42	0
1992–93	Everton	40	0
1993–94	Everton	42	0
1994–95	Everton	41	0
1995–96	Everton	38	0
1996–97	Everton	34	0
1997–98	Everton	12	0
1997–98	Southend U (loan)	9	0
1997–98	Stoke C	12	0
From Doncaster R.			
1998–99	Torquay U	25	0
Total:		**672**	**0**

SOUTHALL, Nicky — Midfield

H: 5 10 W: 12 12 b.Middlesbrough 28-1-72

Source: Trainee.

1990–91	Hartlepool U	0	0
1991–92	Hartlepool U	22	3
1992–93	Hartlepool U	39	6
1993–94	Hartlepool U	40	9
1994–95	Hartlepool U	37	6
1995–96	Grimsby T	33	2
1996–97	Grimsby T	34	3
1997–98	Grimsby T	5	0
1997–98	Gillingham	23	2
1998–99	Gillingham	42	4
Total:		**275**	**35**

SOUTHERN, Keith — Midfield

b.Gateshead 24-4-81

Source: Trainee.

1998–99	Everton	0	0

SOUTHGATE, Gareth — Midfield

H: 6 0 W: 12 06 b.Watford 3-9-70

Source: Trainee. *Honours:* England 31 full caps, 1 goal.

1988–89	Crystal Palace	0	0
1989–90	Crystal Palace	0	0
1990–91	Crystal Palace	1	0
1991–92	Crystal Palace	30	0
1992–93	Crystal Palace	33	3
1993–94	Crystal Palace	46	9
1994–95	Crystal Palace	42	3
1995–96	Aston Villa	31	1
1996–97	Aston Villa	28	1
1997–98	Aston Villa	32	0
1998–99	Aston Villa	38	1
Total:		**281**	**18**

SPARROW, Paul — Defender

H: 6 0 W: 11 00 b.London 24-3-75

Source: Trainee.

1993–94	Crystal Palace	0	0
1994–95	Crystal Palace	0	0
1995–96	Crystal Palace	1	0
1995–96	Preston NE	13	0
1996–97	Preston NE	6	0
1997–98	Preston NE	1	0
1998–99	Rochdale	25	2
Total:		**46**	**2**

SPEAKMAN, Robert — Defender

b.Swansea 5-12-80

Source: Trainee.

1998–99	Exeter C	1	0
Total:		**1**	**0**

SPEDDING, Duncan — Defender

H: 6 1 W: 11 01 b.Frimley 7-9-77

Source: Trainee.

1996–97	Southampton	0	0
1997–98	Southampton	7	0
1998–99	Northampton T	24	1
Total:		**31**	**1**

SPEED, Gary — Midfield

H: 5 10 W: 10 12 b.Mancot 8-9-69

Source: Trainee. *Honours:* Wales Under-21, 52 full caps, 3 goals.

1988–89	Leeds U	1	0
1989–90	Leeds U	25	3
1990–91	Leeds U	38	7
1991–92	Leeds U	41	7
1992–93	Leeds U	39	7
1993–94	Leeds U	36	10
1994–95	Leeds U	39	3
1995–96	Leeds U	29	2
1996–97	Everton	37	9
1997–98	Everton	21	7
1997–98	Newcastle U	13	1
1998–99	Newcastle U	38	4
Total:		**357**	**60**

SPENCER, John — Forward

H: 5 6 W: 11 11 b.Glasgow 11-9-70

Source: Rangers BC. *Honours:* Scotland Under-21, 14 full caps.

1986–87	Rangers	0	0
1987–88	Rangers	0	0
1988–89	Rangers	0	0
1988–89	Morton (loan)	4	1

From Lai Sun			
1990–91	Rangers	5	1
1991–92	Rangers	8	1
1992–93	Chelsea	23	7
1993–94	Chelsea	19	5
1994–95	Chelsea	29	11
1995–96	Chelsea	28	13
1996–97	Chelsea	4	0
1996–97	QPR	25	17
1997–98	QPR	23	5
1997–98	Everton	6	0
1998–99	Everton	3	0
1998–99	Motherwell	21	7
Total:		**198**	**68**

SPENCER, Ryan — Midfield

b.Harrow 3-1-79

Source: Trainee.

1997–98	Tottenham H	0	0
1998–99	Tottenham H	0	0

SPILLER, Richard — Midfield

b.Enfield 5-9-79

Source: Trainee.

1998–99	Bristol C	0	0

SPINK, Dean — Defender

H: 6 1 W: 12 12 b.Halesowen 22-1-67

Source: Halesowen T.

1989–90	Aston Villa	0	0
1989–90	Scarborough (loan)	3	2
1989–90	Bury (loan)	6	1
1989–90	Shrewsbury T	13	5
1990–91	Shrewsbury T	43	6
1991–92	Shrewsbury T	40	1
1992–93	Shrewsbury T	23	1
1993–94	Shrewsbury T	40	18
1994–95	Shrewsbury T	39	11
1995–96	Shrewsbury T	34	6
1996–97	Shrewsbury T	41	4
1997–98	Wrexham	36	6
1998–99	Wrexham	34	3
Total:		**352**	**64**

SPINK, Nigel — Goalkeeper

H: 6 2 W: 14 06 b.Chelmsford 8-8-58

Source: Chelmsford C. *Honours:* England B, 1 full cap.

1976–77	Aston Villa	0	0
1977–78	Aston Villa	0	0
1978–79	Aston Villa	0	0
1979–80	Aston Villa	1	0
1980–81	Aston Villa	0	0
1981–82	Aston Villa	0	0
1982–83	Aston Villa	22	0
1983–84	Aston Villa	28	0
1984–85	Aston Villa	19	0
1985–86	Aston Villa	31	0
1986–87	Aston Villa	32	0
1987–88	Aston Villa	44	0
1988–89	Aston Villa	34	0
1989–90	Aston Villa	38	0
1990–91	Aston Villa	34	0
1991–92	Aston Villa	23	0
1992–93	Aston Villa	25	0
1993–94	Aston Villa	15	0
1994–95	Aston Villa	13	0
1995–96	Aston Villa	2	0
1995–96	WBA	15	0
1996–97	WBA	4	0
1997–98	WBA	0	0
1997–98	Millwall	21	0
1998–99	Millwall	22	0
Total:		**423**	**0**

SPOONER, Nicky — Defender

H: 5 10 W: 11 09 b.Manchester 5-6-71

Source: Trainee.

1990–91	Bolton W	0	0
1991–92	Bolton W	15	1
1992–93	Bolton W	6	1
1993–94	Bolton W	1	0
1994–95	Bolton W	1	0
1995–96	Bolton W	0	0
1996–97	Bolton W	0	0
1997–98	Bolton W	0	0
1998–99	Bolton W	0	0
1998–99	Oldham Ath (loan)	2	0
Total:		**25**	**2**

SPRING, Matthew — Midfield

H: 5 11 W: 11 07 b.Harlow 17-11-79

Source: Trainee.

1997–98	Luton T	12	0
1998–99	Luton T	45	3
Total:		**57**	**3**

SQUIRES, Jamie — Defender

H: 6 2 W: 13 03 b.Preston 15-11-75

Source: Trainee.

1993–94	Preston NE	4	0
1994–95	Preston NE	11	0
1995–96	Preston NE	7	0
1996–97	Preston NE	9	0
1997–98	Preston NE	0	0
1997–98	Mansfield T (loan)	1	0
1997–98	Dunfermline Ath	5	0
1998–99	Dunfermline Ath	21	2
Total:		**58**	**2**

SQUIRES, Oliver — Midfield

H: 5 9 W: 12 09 b.Harrow 15-9-80

Source: Trainee.

1997–98	Watford	0	0
1998–99	Watford	0	0

SRNICEK, Pavel — Goalkeeper

H: 6 2 W: 14 07 b.Bohumin 10-3-68

Source: Banik Ostrava. *Honours:* Czech Republic 24 full caps.

1990–91	Newcastle U	7	0
1991–92	Newcastle U	13	0
1992–93	Newcastle U	32	0
1993–94	Newcastle U	21	0
1994–95	Newcastle U	38	0
1995–96	Newcastle U	15	0
1996–97	Newcastle U	22	0
1997–98	Newcastle U	1	0
From Banik Ostrava			
1998–99	Sheffield W	24	0
Total:		**173**	**0**

STALLARD, Mark — Forward

H: 6 0 W: 12 10 b.Derby 24-10-74

Source: Trainee.

1991–92	Derby Co	3	0
1992–93	Derby Co	5	0
1993–94	Derby Co	0	0
1994–95	Derby Co	16	2
1994–95	Fulham (loan)	4	3
1995–96	Derby Co	3	0
1995–96	Bradford C	21	9
1996–97	Bradford C	22	1
1996–97	Preston NE (loan)	4	1
1996–97	Wycombe W	12	4
1997–98	Wycombe W	43	17
1998–99	Wycombe W	15	2
1998–99	Notts Co	14	4
Total:		**162**	**43**

STAM, Jaap — Defender

H: 6 3 W: 13 09 b.Kampen 17-7-72

Honours: Holland 25 full caps, 2 goals.

1992–93	Zwolle	32	1
1993–94	Cambuur	33	1
1994–95	Cambuur	33	2
1995–96	Willem II	19	1
1995–96	PSV Eindhoven	14	1
1996–97	PSV Eindhoven	33	7
1997–98	PSV Eindhoven	29	4
1998–99	Manchester U	30	1
Total:		**223**	**18**

STAMP, Darryn — Forward

H: 6 1 W: 11 10 b.Beverley 21-9-78

1997–98	Scunthorpe U	10	1
1998–99	Scunthorpe U	25	4
Total:		**35**	**5**

STAMP, Neville — Defender

H: 5 10 W: 11 08 b.Reading 7-7-81

Source: Trainee.

1998–99	Reading	1	0
Total:		**1**	**0**

STAMP, Phil — Midfield

H: 5 11 W: 14 09 b.Middlesbrough 12-12-75

Source: Trainee. *Honours:* England Youth.

1992–93	Middlesbrough	0	0
1993–94	Middlesbrough	10	0
1994–95	Middlesbrough	3	0
1995–96	Middlesbrough	12	2
1996–97	Middlesbrough	24	1
1997–98	Middlesbrough	10	0
1998–99	Middlesbrough	16	2
Total:		**75**	**5**

STAMPS, Scott — Defender

H: 5 11 W: 11 09 b.Edgbaston 20-3-75

Source: Trainee.

1992–93	Torquay U	2	0
1993–94	Torquay U	6	0
1994–95	Torquay U	25	1
1995–96	Torquay U	23	1
1996–97	Torquay U	30	3
1996–97	Colchester U	8	0
1997–98	Colchester U	27	1
1998–99	Colchester U	21	0
Total:		**142**	**6**

STANDING, Michael — Midfield

H: 5 10 W: 10 05 b.Shoreham 20-3-81

Source: Trainee. *Honours:* England Schools.

1997–98	Aston Villa	0	0
1998–99	Aston Villa	0	0

STANIFORTH, Thomas — Midfield

b.Carlisle 15-12-80

Source: Trainee.

1998–99	Sheffield W	0	0

STANNARD, Jim — Goalkeeper

H: 6 2 W: 16 00 b.London 16-10-62

Source: Local.

1980–81	Fulham	17	0
1981–82	Fulham	2	0
1982–83	Fulham	0	0
1983–84	Fulham	15	0
1984–85	Fulham	7	0
1984–85	Charlton Ath (loan)	1	0
1984–85	Southend U (loan)	17	0
1985–86	Southend U	46	0
1986–87	Southend U	46	0
1987–88	Fulham	46	0
1988–89	Fulham	45	0
1989–90	Fulham	44	1
1990–91	Fulham	42	0
1991–92	Fulham	46	0
1992–93	Fulham	43	0
1993–94	Fulham	46	0
1994–95	Fulham	36	0
1995–96	Gillingham	46	0
1996–97	Gillingham	38	0
1997–98	Gillingham	20	0
1998–99	Gillingham	2	0
Total:		**605**	**1**

STANSFIELD, James — Defender

H: 6 1 W: 13 06 b.Dewsbury 18-9-78

Source: Trainee.

1997–98	Huddersfield T	0	0
1998–99	Halifax T	12	1
Total:		**12**	**1**

STANT, Phil — Forward

H: 6 1 W: 12 07 b.Bolton 13-10-62

Source: Camberley.

1982–83	Reading	4	2
From Army			
1986–87	Hereford U	9	1
1987–88	Hereford U	39	9
1988–89	Hereford U	41	28
1989–90	Notts Co	22	6
1990–91	Notts Co	0	0
1990–91	Blackpool (loan)	12	5
1990–91	Lincoln C (loan)	4	0
1990–91	Huddersfield T (loan)	5	1
1990–91	Fulham	19	5
1991–92	Mansfield T	40	26
1992–93	Mansfield T	17	6
1992–93	Cardiff C	24	11
1993–94	Cardiff C	36	10
1993–94	Mansfield T (loan)	4	1
1994–95	Cardiff C	19	13
1994–95	Bury	20	13
1995–96	Bury	34	9
1996–97	Bury	8	1
1996–97	Northampton T (loan)	5	2
1996–97	Lincoln C	22	15
1997–98	Lincoln C	21	2
1998–99	Lincoln C	3	0
Total:		**408**	**166**

STANTON, Nathan — Defender

H: 5 11 W: 12 00 b.Nottingham 6-5-81

Source: Trainee. *Honours:* England Youth.

1997–98	Scunthorpe U	1	0
1998–99	Scunthorpe U	4	0
Total:		**5**	**0**

STATHAM, Brian — Defender

H: 5 7 W: 11 06 b.Zimbabwe 21-5-69

Source: Apprentice. *Honours:* England Youth, Under-21.

1987–88	Tottenham H	18	0
1988–89	Tottenham H	6	0
1989–90	Tottenham H	0	0
1990–91	Tottenham H	0	0
1990–91	Reading (loan)	8	0
1991–92	Tottenham H	0	0
1991–92	Bournemouth (loan)	2	0
1991–92	Brentford (loan)	18	0
1992–93	Brentford	45	0
1993–94	Brentford	31	1
1994–95	Brentford	36	0
1995–96	Brentford	17	0
1996–97	Brentford	19	0
1997–98	Gillingham	20	0
1998–99	Gillingham	0	0
Total:		**220**	**1**

STATON, Luke — Midfield

H: 5 7 W: 10 07 b.Doncaster 10-3-79

Source: Trainee. *Honours:* England Schools, Youth.

1995–96	Blackburn R	0	0
1996–97	Blackburn R	0	0
1997–98	Blackburn R	0	0
1998–99	Blackburn R	0	0
1998–99	Bolton W	0	0

STAUNTON, Steve — Defender

H: 6 1 W: 12 11 b.Drogheda 19-1-69

Source: Dundalk. *Honours:* Eire Under-21, 78 full caps, 5 goals.

1986–87	Liverpool	0	0
1987–88	Liverpool	0	0
1987–88	Bradford C (loan)	8	0
1988–89	Liverpool	21	0
1989–90	Liverpool	20	0
1990–91	Liverpool	24	0
1991–92	Aston Villa	37	4

1992–93	Aston Villa	42	2
1993–94	Aston Villa	24	2
1994–95	Aston Villa	35	5
1995–96	Aston Villa	13	0
1996–97	Aston Villa	30	2
1997–98	Aston Villa	27	1
1998–99	Liverpool	31	0
Total:		**312**	**16**

STEELE, Lee — Forward

H: 5 8 W: 12 05 b.Liverpool 7-12-73

Source: Bootle, Northwich V.

1997–98	Shrewsbury T	38	13
1998–99	Shrewsbury T	38	13
Total:		**76**	**26**

STEFANOVIC, Dejan — Defender

H: 6 2 W: 13 00 b.Yugoslavia 28-10-74

Honours: Yugoslavia 10 full caps.

1995–96	Sheffield W	6	0
1996–97	Sheffield W	29	2
1997–98	Sheffield W	20	2
1998–99	Sheffield W	11	0
Total:		**66**	**4**

STEIN, Mark — Forward

H: 5 6 W: 11 07 b.Cupetown 29-1-66

Honours: England Youth.

1983–84	Luton T	1	0
1984–85	Luton T	1	0
1985–86	Luton T	6	0
1985–86	Aldershot (loan)	2	1
1986–87	Luton T	21	8
1987–88	Luton T	25	11
1988–89	QPR	31	4
1989–90	QPR	2	0
1989–90	Oxford U	41	9
1990–91	Oxford U	34	8
1991–92	Oxford U	7	1
1991–92	Stoke C	36	16
1992–93	Stoke C	46	26
1993–94	Stoke C	12	8
1993–94	Chelsea	18	13
1994–95	Chelsea	24	8
1995–96	Chelsea	8	0
1996–97	Chelsea	0	0
1996–97	Stoke C (loan)	11	4
1997–98	Chelsea	0	0
1997–98	Ipswich T (loan)	7	2
1997–98	Bournemouth (loan)	11	4
1998–99	Bournemouth	43	15
Total:		**387**	**138**

STEINER, Rob — Forward

H: 6 2 W: 13 00 b.Finsprong 20-6-73

Honours: Sweden 4 full caps, 1 goal.

1995	Norrkoping	16	2
1996	Norrkoping	25	12
1996–97	Bradford C	15	4
1997	Norrkoping	6	1
1997–98	Bradford C	37	10
1998–99	Bradford C	0	0
1998–99	QPR (loan)	12	3
1998–99	Walsall (loan)	10	3
Total:		**121**	**35**

STENSAAS, Stale — Defender

H: 5 11 W: 12 01 b.Trondheim 7-7-71

1992	Rosenburg	1	0
1993	Rosenborg	6	0
1994	Rosenborg	20	0
1995	Rosenburg	24	1
1996	Rosenborg	25	1
1997	Rosenborg	9	0
1997–98	Rangers	20	1
1998–99	Rangers	1	0
1998–99	Nottingham F (loan)	7	0
Total:		**113**	**3**

STENSGAARD, Michael — Goalkeeper

H: 6 2 W: 13 11 b.Denmark 1-9-74

Source: Hvidovre. *Honours:* Denmark Under-21.

1994–95	Liverpool	0	0
1995–96	Liverpool	0	0
1996–97	Liverpool	0	0
1997–98	Liverpool	0	0
1998–99	FC Copenhagen	17	0
1998–99	Southampton	0	0
Total:		**17**	**0**

STEPHENSON, Ashlyn — Goalkeeper

H: 6 2 W: 11 05 b.Manchester 6-7-74

1995–96	Birmingham C	0	0
1995–96	Darlington	1	0
1996–97	Darlington	0	0
From Kilkenny			
1997–98	Darlington	0	0
1998–99	Darlington	0	0
Total:		**1**	**0**

STEPHENSON, Paul — Forward

H: 5 10 W: 12 07 b.Wallsend 2-1-68

Source: Apprentice. *Honours:* England Youth.

1985–86	Newcastle U	22	1
1986–87	Newcastle U	24	0
1987–88	Newcastle U	7	0
1988–89	Newcastle U	8	0
1989–90	Millwall	12	1
1989–90	Millwall	23	2
1990–91	Millwall	30	1
1991–92	Millwall	28	2
1992–93	Millwall	5	0
1992–93	Gillingham (loan)	12	2
1992–93	Brentford	11	0
1993–94	Brentford	25	0
1994–95	Brentford	34	2
1995–96	York C	27	2
1996–97	York C	35	1
1997–98	York C	35	5
1997–98	Hartlepool U	3	0
1998–99	Hartlepool U	27	2
Total:		**368**	**21**

STEVENS, Ian — Forward

H: 5 10 W: 12 07 b.Malta 21-10-69

Source: Trainee.

1984–85	Preston NE	4	1
1985–86	Preston NE	7	1
1986–87	Stockport Co	2	0
From Lancaster C			
1986–87	Bolton W	8	2
1987–88	Bolton W	9	0
1988–89	Bolton W	21	5
1989–90	Bolton W	4	0
1990–91	Bolton W	5	0
1991–92	Bury	45	17
1992–93	Bury	32	14
1993–94	Bury	33	7
1994–95	Shrewsbury T	38	8
1995–96	Shrewsbury T	32	12
1996–97	Shrewsbury T	41	17
1996–97	Carlisle U	0	0
1997–98	Carlisle U	37	17
1998–99	Carlisle U	41	9
Total:		**359**	**110**

STEVENS, Keith — Defender

H: 6 0 W: 12 12 b.Merton 21-6-64

Source: Apprentice.

1980–81	Millwall	1	0
1981–82	Millwall	7	0
1982–83	Millwall	26	0
1983–84	Millwall	17	0
1984–85	Millwall	41	0
1985–86	Millwall	33	1
1986–87	Millwall	35	1
1987–88	Millwall	35	1
1988–89	Millwall	23	0
1989–90	Millwall	28	0
1990–91	Millwall	42	1
1991–92	Millwall	27	0
1992–93	Millwall	31	2
1993–94	Millwall	44	1
1994–95	Millwall	20	0
1995–96	Millwall	39	2
1996–97	Millwall	6	0
1997–98	Millwall	4	0
1998–99	Millwall	3	0
Total:		**462**	**9**

STEWART, Colin — Goalkeeper

H: 6 3 W: 12 07 b.Cleveland 10-1-80

Source: Trainee.

1998–99	Ipswich T	0	0

STEWART, Gareth — Goalkeeper

H: 6 0 W: 12 08 b.Preston 3-2-80

Source: Trainee. *Honours:* England Schools, Youth.

1996–97	Blackburn R	0	0
1997–98	Blackburn R	0	0
1998–99	Blackburn R	0	0

STEWART, Marcus — Forward

H: 5 10 W: 11 08 b.Bristol 7-11-72

Source: Trainee. *Honours:* England Schools, Football League.

1991–92	Bristol R	33	5
1992–93	Bristol R	38	11
1993–94	Bristol R	29	5
1994–95	Bristol R	27	15
1995–96	Bristol R	44	21
1996–97	Huddersfield T	20	7
1997–98	Huddersfield T	41	15
1998–99	Huddersfield T	43	22
Total:		**275**	**101**

STEWART, Michael — Midfield

H: 5 11 W: 11 06 b.Edinburgh 26-2-81

Source: Trainee.

1997–98	Manchester U	0	0
1998–99	Manchester U	0	0

STEWART, Paul — Forward

H: 6 0 W: 14 01 b.Manchester 7-10-64

Source: Apprentice. *Honours:* England Youth, Under-21, B, 3 full caps.

1981–82	Blackpool	14	3
1982–83	Blackpool	38	7

1983–84	Blackpool	44	10
1984–85	Blackpool	31	7
1985–86	Blackpool	42	8
1986–87	Blackpool	32	21
1986–87	Manchester C	11	2
1987–88	Manchester C	40	24
1988–89	Tottenham H	30	12
1989–90	Tottenham H	28	8
1990–91	Tottenham H	35	3
1991–92	Tottenham H	38	5
1992–93	Liverpool	24	1
1993–94	Liverpool	8	0
1993–94	Crystal Palace (loan)	18	3
1994–95	Liverpool	0	0
1994–95	Wolverhampton W (loan)	8	2
1994–95	Burnley (loan)	6	0
1995–96	Liverpool	0	0
1995–96	Sunderland	12	1
1996–97	Sunderland	24	4
1997–98	Stoke C	22	3
1998–99	Stoke C	0	0
Total:		**505**	**124**

STILLIE, Derek — Goalkeeper

H: 6 0 W: 12 00 b.Irvine 3-12-73

Source: Notts Co. *Honours:* Scotland Under-21.

1991–92	Aberdeen	0	0
1992–93	Aberdeen	0	0
1993–94	Aberdeen	5	0
1994–95	Aberdeen	0	0
1995–96	Aberdeen	0	0
1996–97	Aberdeen	8	0
1997–98	Aberdeen	2	0
1998–99	Aberdeen	8	0
Total:		**23**	**0**

STIMAC, Igor — Defender

H: 6 2 W: 13 00 b.Metkovic 6-9-67

Source: Cibalia Vinkovci, Hajduk Split. *Honours:* Yugoslavia Youth. Croatia 40 full caps, 2 goals.

1992–93	Cadiz	32	0
1993–94	Cadiz	30	4
1994–95	Hajduk Split	21	2
1995–96	Derby Co	27	1
1996–97	Derby Co	21	1
1997–98	Derby Co	22	1
1998–99	Derby Co	14	0
Total:		**167**	**9**

STIMSON, Mark — Defender

H: 5 10 W: 12 02 b.Plaistow 27-12-67

Source: Trainee.

1984–85	Tottenham H	0	0
1985–86	Tottenham H	0	0
1986–87	Tottenham H	1	0
1987–88	Tottenham H	0	0
1987–88	Leyton Orient (loan)	10	0
1988–89	Tottenham H	1	0
1988–89	Gillingham (loan)	18	0
1989–90	Newcastle U	37	1
1990–91	Newcastle U	23	1
1991–92	Newcastle U	24	0
1992–93	Newcastle U	2	0
1992–93	Portsmouth (loan)	4	0
1993–94	Portsmouth	29	1
1994–95	Portsmouth	15	0
1995–96	Portsmouth	14	1
1995–96	Barnet (loan)	5	0
1995–96	Southend U	10	0
1996–97	Southend U	9	0
1997–98	Southend U	20	0
1998–99	Southend U	17	0
1998–99	Leyton Orient	2	0
Total:		**241**	**4**

STIRLING, Jered — Defender

H: 6 0 W: 11 06 b.Stirling 13-10-76

Honours: Croatia 31 full caps, 3 goals.

1993–94	Partick T	0	0
1994–95	Partick T	0	0
1995–96	Partick T	2	0
1996–97	Partick T	34	7
1997–98	Partick T	22	6
1998–99	Motherwell	5	1
Total:		**63**	**14**

STOCKDALE, Robbie — Defender

H: 6 0 W: 12 03 b.Redcar 30-11-79

Source: Trainee.

1997–98	Middlesbrough	1	0
1998–99	Middlesbrough	19	0
Total:		**20**	**0**

STOCKLEY, Sam — Defender

H: 6 0 W: 12 00 b.Tiverton 5-9-77

Source: Trainee.

1996–97	Southampton	0	0
1996–97	Barnet	21	0
1997–98	Barnet	41	0
1998–99	Barnet	41	0
Total:		**103**	**0**

STOCKWELL, Mick — Midfield

H: 5 7 W: 11 07 b.Chelmsford 14-2-65

Source: Apprentice.

1982–83	Ipswich T	0	0
1983–84	Ipswich T	0	0
1984–85	Ipswich T	0	0
1985–86	Ipswich T	8	0

1986–87	Ipswich T	21	1
1987–88	Ipswich T	43	1
1988–89	Ipswich T	23	2
1989–90	Ipswich T	34	3
1990–91	Ipswich T	44	6
1991–92	Ipswich T	46	2
1992–93	Ipswich T	39	4
1993–94	Ipswich T	42	1
1994–95	Ipswich T	15	0
1995–96	Ipswich T	37	1
1996–97	Ipswich T	43	7
1997–98	Ipswich T	46	3
1998–99	Ipswich T	30	2
Total:		**471**	**33**

STOKER, Gareth — Midfield

H: 5 9 W: 11 04 b.Bishop Auckland 22-2-73

Source: Leeds U Trainee.

1991–92	Hull C	24	2
1992–93	Hull C	6	0
1993–94	Hull C	0	0
1994–95	Hereford U	10	0
1995–96	Hereford U	33	3
1996–97	Hereford U	27	3
1996–97	Cardiff C	17	3
1997–98	Cardiff C	20	1
1998–99	Cardiff C	0	0
1998–99	Rochdale	12	1
Total:		**149**	**13**

STOKES, Dean — Defender

H: 5 8 W: 11 02 b.Birmingham 23-5-70

Source: Halesowen T.

1992–93	Port Vale	0	0
1993–94	Port Vale	21	0
1994–95	Port Vale	3	0
1995–96	Port Vale	18	0
1996–97	Port Vale	10	0
1997–98	Port Vale	8	0
1998–99	Rochdale	11	0
Total:		**71**	**0**

STOKOE, Graham — Midfield

H: 6 0 W: 13 03 b.Newcastle-under-Lyme 17-12-75

Source: Birmingham C.

1994–95	Stoke C	0	0
1995–96	Stoke C	0	0
1995–96	Hartlepool U (loan)	8	0
1996–97	Stoke C	2	0
1997–98	Stoke C	0	0
1998–99	Hartlepool U	20	0
Total:		**30**	**0**

STONE, Gavin — Midfield

b.Staffordshire 9-1-80

1998–99	Tottenham H	0	0

STONE, Steve — Midfield

H: 5 8 W: 12 02 b.Gateshead 20-8-71

Source: Trainee. *Honours:* England 9 full caps, 2 goals.

1989–90	Nottingham F	0	0
1990–91	Nottingham F	0	0
1991–92	Nottingham F	1	0
1992–93	Nottingham F	12	1
1993–94	Nottingham F	45	5
1994–95	Nottingham F	41	5
1995–96	Nottingham F	34	7
1996–97	Nottingham F	5	0
1997–98	Nottingham F	29	2
1998–99	Nottingham F	26	3
1998–99	Aston Villa	10	0
Total:		**203**	**23**

STONEMAN, Paul — Defender

H: 6 0 W: 12 07 b.Whitley Bay 26-2-73

Source: Trainee.

1991–92	Blackpool	19	0
1992–93	Blackpool	10	0
1993–94	Blackpool	10	0
1994–95	Blackpool	4	0
1994–95	Colchester U (loan)	3	1
1998–99	Halifax T	40	4
Total:		**86**	**5**

STONES, Craig — Midfield

b.Scunthorpe 31-5-80

Source: Trainee.

1996–97	Lincoln C	2	0
1997–98	Lincoln C	15	0
1998–99	Lincoln C	1	0
Total:		**18**	**0**

STORER, Stuart — Forward

H: 5 11 W: 12 12 b.Rugby 16-1-67

Source: Local.

1983–84	Mansfield T	1	0
1984–85	Birmingham C	0	0
1985–86	Birmingham C	2	0
1986–87	Birmingham C	6	0
1986–87	Everton	0	0
1987–88	Everton	0	0
1987–88	Wigan Ath (loan)	12	0
1987–88	Bolton W	15	1
1988–89	Bolton W	23	2
1989–90	Bolton W	38	4

1990–91	Bolton W	35	5
1991–92	Bolton W	9	0
1992–93	Bolton W	3	0
1992–93	Exeter C	10	4
1993–94	Exeter C	44	2
1994–95	Exeter C	23	2
1994–95	Brighton & HA	2	1
1995–96	Brighton & HA	38	2
1996–97	Brighton & HA	42	6
1997–98	Brighton & HA	37	2
1998–99	Brighton & HA	23	0
Total:		**363**	**31**

STOWELL, Matt — Defender

H: 5 10 W: 11 06 b.Reading 1-3-77

Source: Trainee.

1995–96	Reading	0	0
1996–97	Reading	0	0
1997–98	Reading	0	0
From Slough T			
1998–99	Bristol C	0	0

STOWELL, Mike — Goalkeeper

H: 6 2 W: 13 10 b.Portsmouth 19-4-65

Source: Leyland Motors.

1984–85	Preston NE	0	0
1985–86	Preston NE	0	0
1985–86	Everton	0	0
1986–87	Everton	0	0
1987–88	Chester C (loan)	14	0
1987–88	York C (loan)	6	0
1987–88	Manchester C (loan)	14	0
1988–89	Everton	0	0
1988–89	Port Vale (loan)	7	0
1988–89	Wolverhampton W (loan)	7	0
1989–90	Everton	0	0
1989–90	Preston NE (loan)	2	0
1990–91	Wolverhampton W	39	0
1991–92	Wolverhampton W	46	0
1992–93	Wolverhampton W	26	0
1993–94	Wolverhampton W	46	0
1994–95	Wolverhampton W	37	0
1995–96	Wolverhampton W	38	0
1996–97	Wolverhampton W	46	0
1997–98	Wolverhampton W	35	0
1998–99	Wolverhampton W	46	0
Total:		**409**	**0**

STRACHAN, Gavin — Midfield

H: 5 10 W: 11 07 b.Aberdeen 23-12-78

Source: Trainee. *Honours:* Scotland Under-21.

1996–97	Coventry C	0	0
1997–98	Coventry C	9	0
1998–99	Coventry C	0	0
1998–99	Dundee (loan)	6	0
Total:		**15**	**0**

STRANGE, Gareth — Midfield

H: 5 9 W: 10 09 b.Bolton 3-10-81

Source: Trainee. *Honours:* England Schools.

1998–99	Manchester U	0	0

STREET, Kevin — Midfield

H: 5 10 W: 10 08 b.Crewe 25-11-77

Source: Trainee.

1996–97	Crewe Alex	0	0
1997–98	Crewe Alex	32	4
1998–99	Crewe Alex	23	2
Total:		**55**	**6**

STREETER, Terry — Midfield

b.Brighton 26-10-79

Source: Trainee.

1997–98	Brighton & HA	2	0
1998–99	Brighton & HA	0	0
Total:		**2**	**0**

STREVENS, Ben — Midfield

b.Edgware 24-5-80

1998–99	Barnet	0	0

STRODDER, Gary — Defender

H: 6 2 W: 13 04 b.Mirfield 1-4-65

Source: Apprentice.

1982–83	Lincoln C	8	0
1983–84	Lincoln C	22	1
1984–85	Lincoln C	26	2
1985–86	Lincoln C	43	1
1986–87	Lincoln C	33	2
1986–87	West Ham U	12	0
1987–88	West Ham U	30	1
1988–89	West Ham U	7	0
1989–90	West Ham U	16	1
1990–91	WBA	34	1
1991–92	WBA	37	3
1992–93	WBA	29	1
1993–94	WBA	21	2
1994–95	WBA	19	1
1995–96	Notts Co	43	3
1996–97	Notts Co	28	2
1997–98	Notts Co	39	4
1998–99	Notts Co	11	1
1998–99	Rotherham U (loan)	3	0
1998–99	Hartlepool U	13	0
Total:		**474**	**26**

STRONG, Greg — Defender

H: 6 2 W: 11 12 b.Bolton 5-9-75

Source: Trainee. *Honours:* England Schools, Youth.

1992–93	Wigan Ath	0	0
1993–94	Wigan Ath	18	1
1994–95	Wigan Ath	17	2
1995–96	Bolton W	1	0
1996–97	Bolton W	0	0
1997–98	Bolton W	0	0
1997–98	Blackpool (loan)	11	1
1998–99	Bolton W	5	1
1998–99	Stoke C (loan)	5	1
Total:		**57**	**6**

STUART, Graham — Midfield

H: 5 8 W: 11 11 b.Tooting 24-10-70

Source: Trainee. *Honours:* FA Schools, England Under-21.

1989–90	Chelsea	2	1
1990–91	Chelsea	19	4
1991–92	Chelsea	27	0
1992–93	Chelsea	39	9
1993–94	Everton	30	3
1994–95	Everton	28	3
1995–96	Everton	29	9
1996–97	Everton	35	5
1997–98	Everton	14	2
1997–98	Sheffield U	28	5
1998–99	Sheffield U	25	6
1998–99	Charlton Ath	9	4
Total:		**285**	**51**

STUART, Jamie — Defender

H: 5 10 W: 11 00 b.Southwark 15-10-76

Source: Trainee. *Honours:* England Youth, Under-21.

1994–95	Charlton Ath	12	0
1995–96	Charlton Ath	27	2
1996–97	Charlton Ath	10	1
1997–98	Charlton Ath	1	0
1998–99	Millwall	35	0
Total:		**85**	**3**

STUART, Mark — Midfield

H: 5 11 W: 11 12 b.Hammersmith 15-12-66

Source: QPR Schoolboy.

1984–85	Charlton Ath	6	1
1985–86	Charlton Ath	30	12
1986–87	Charlton Ath	36	9
1987–88	Charlton Ath	31	6
1988–89	Charlton Ath	4	0
1988–89	Plymouth Arg	32	5
1989–90	Plymouth Arg	25	6
1989–90	Ipswich T (loan)	5	2
1990–91	Bradford C	13	2
1991–92	Bradford C	16	3
1992–93	Bradford C	0	0
1992–93	Huddersfield T	15	3
1993–94	Rochdale	42	13
1994–95	Rochdale	31	2
1995–96	Rochdale	34	13
1996–97	Rochdale	31	7
1997–98	Rochdale	45	6
1998–99	Rochdale	19	0
Total:		**415**	**90**

STUBBS, Alan — Defender

H: 6 2 W: 13 10 b.Kirkby 6-10-71

Source: Trainee.

1990–91	Bolton W	23	0
1991–92	Bolton W	32	1
1992–93	Bolton W	42	2
1993–94	Bolton W	41	1
1994–95	Bolton W	39	1
1995–96	Bolton W	25	4
1996–97	Celtic	20	0
1997–98	Celtic	29	1
1998–99	Celtic	23	1
Total:		**274**	**11**

STURGESS, Paul — Defender

H: 5 11 W: 12 05 b.Dartford 4-8-75

Source: Trainee.

1992–93	Charlton Ath	4	0
1993–94	Charlton Ath	8	0
1994–95	Charlton Ath	23	0
1995–96	Charlton Ath	13	0
1996–97	Charlton Ath	3	0
1997–98	Millwall	14	0
1998–99	Millwall	0	0
1998–99	Brighton & HA	30	0
Total:		**95**	**0**

STURRIDGE, Dean — Forward

H: 5 8 W: 12 06 b.Birmingham 27-7-73

Source: Trainee.

1991–92	Derby Co	1	0
1992–93	Derby Co	10	0
1993–94	Derby Co	0	0
1994–95	Derby Co	12	1
1994–95	Torquay U (loan)	10	5
1995–96	Derby Co	39	20
1996–97	Derby Co	30	11
1997–98	Derby Co	30	9
1998–99	Derby Co	29	5
Total:		**161**	**51**

STURRIDGE, Simon — Forward

H: 5 6 W: 11 10 b.Birmingham 9-12-69

Source: Trainee.

1988–89	Birmingham C	21	3
1989–90	Birmingham C	31	10
1990–91	Birmingham C	38	6
1991–92	Birmingham C	40	10
1992–93	Birmingham C	20	1
1993–94	Birmingham C	0	0
1993–94	Stoke C	13	0
1994–95	Stoke C	8	1
1995–96	Stoke C	41	13
1996–97	Stoke C	5	0
1997–98	Stoke C	1	0
1998–99	Stoke C	3	0
1998–99	Blackpool (loan)	5	1
Total:		**226**	**45**

SUGDEN, Ryan — Midfield

b.Bradford 26-12-80

1998–99	Oldham Ath	2	0
Total:		**2**	**0**

SULLIVAN, Neil — Goalkeeper

H: 6 0 W: 12 01 b.Sutton 24-2-70

Source: Trainee. *Honours:* Scotland 8 full caps.

1988–89	Wimbledon	0	0
1989–90	Wimbledon	0	0
1990–91	Wimbledon	1	0
1991–92	Wimbledon	1	0
1991–92	Crystal Palace (loan)	1	0
1992–93	Wimbledon	1	0
1993–94	Wimbledon	2	0
1994–95	Wimbledon	11	0
1995–96	Wimbledon	16	0
1996–97	Wimbledon	36	0
1997–98	Wimbledon	38	0
1998–99	Wimbledon	38	0
Total:		**145**	**0**

SULLIVAN, Wayne — Forward

H: 5 7 W: 11 01 b.Hartlepool 20-5-80

Source: Trainee.

1998–99	Hartlepool U	0	0

SUMMERBEE, Nicky — Forward

H: 5 8 W: 11 08 b.Altrincham 26-8-71

Source: Trainee. *Honours:* England Under-21.

1989–90	Swindon T	1	0
1990–91	Swindon T	7	0
1991–92	Swindon T	27	0
1992–93	Swindon T	39	3
1993–94	Swindon T	38	3
1994–95	Manchester C	41	1
1995–96	Manchester C	37	1
1996–97	Manchester C	44	4
1997–98	Manchester C	9	0
1997–98	Sunderland	25	3
1998–99	Sunderland	36	3
Total:		**304**	**18**

SUMMERBELL, Mark — Midfield

H: 5 9 W: 11 01 b.Durham 30-10-76

Source: Trainee.

1995–96	Middlesbrough	1	0
1996–97	Middlesbrough	2	0
1997–98	Middlesbrough	11	0
1998–99	Middlesbrough	11	0
Total:		**25**	**0**

SUTCH, Daryl — Defender

H: 5 11 W: 12 09 b.Lowestoft 11-9-71

Source: Trainee. *Honours:* England Youth, Under-21.

1989–90	Norwich C	0	0
1990–91	Norwich C	4	0
1991–92	Norwich C	9	0
1992–93	Norwich C	22	2
1993–94	Norwich C	3	0
1994–95	Norwich C	30	1
1995–96	Norwich C	13	0
1996–97	Norwich C	44	3
1997–98	Norwich C	40	1
1998–99	Norwich C	36	0
Total:		**201**	**7**

SUTTON, Chris — Forward

H: 6 3 W: 13 07 b.Nottingham 10-3-73

Source: Trainee. *Honours:* England Under-21, B, 1 full cap.

1990–91	Norwich C	2	0
1991–92	Norwich C	21	2
1992–93	Norwich C	38	8
1993–94	Norwich C	41	25
1994–95	Blackburn R	40	15
1995–96	Blackburn R	13	0
1996–97	Blackburn R	25	11
1997–98	Blackburn R	35	18
1998–99	Blackburn R	17	3
Total:		**232**	**82**

SVENSSON, Mathias — Forward

H: 6 0 W: 12 06 b.Boras 24-9-74

Honours: Sweden 2 full caps.

1996	Elfsborg	22	15
1996–97	Portsmouth	19	6
1997–98	Portsmouth	26	4

From Tirol.

1998–99	Crystal Palace	8	1
Total:		**75**	**26**

SWAILES, Chris — Defender

H: 6 2 W: 13 07 b.Gateshead 19-10-70

Source: Ipswich T Trainee, Peterborough U, Boston U, Birmingham C, Bridlington T.

1993–94	Doncaster R	17	0
1994–95	Doncaster R	32	0
1995–96	Ipswich T	5	0
1996–97	Ipswich T	23	1
1997–98	Ipswich T	5	0
1997–98	Bury	13	1
1998–99	Bury	43	3
Total:		**138**	**5**

SWAILES, Danny — Defender

H: 6 3 W: 12 06 b.Bolton 1-4-79

Source: Trainee.

1997–98	Bury	0	0
1998–99	Bury	0	0

SWALES, Steve — Defender

H: 5 9 W: 10 03 b.Scarborough 26-12-73

Source: Trainee.

1991–92	Scarborough	4	0
1992–93	Scarborough	3	0
1993–94	Scarborough	26	0
1994–95	Scarborough	21	1
1995–96	Reading	9	0
1996–97	Reading	3	0
1997–98	Reading	31	1
1998–99	Reading	0	0
1998–99	Hull C	22	0
Total:		**119**	**2**

SWALWELL, Andrew — Midfield

H: 5 9 W: 10 06 b.Middlesbrough 29-3-79

Source: Trainee.

1995–96	Middlesbrough	0	0
1996–97	Middlesbrough	0	0
1997–98	Middlesbrough	0	0
1998–99	Middlesbrough	0	0

SWAN, Iain — Defender

H: 6 2 W: 11 03 b.Glasgow 4-7-80

Source: Trainee.

1996–97	Oldham Ath	0	0
1997–98	Oldham Ath	0	0
1998–99	Oldham Ath	1	0
Total:		**1**	**0**

SWAN, Peter — Defender

H: 6 2 W: 14 02 b.Leeds 28-9-66

Source: Local.

1984–85	Leeds U	0	0
1985–86	Leeds U	16	3
1986–87	Leeds U	7	0
1987–88	Leeds U	25	8
1988–89	Leeds U	1	0
1988–89	Hull C	11	1
1989–90	Hull C	31	11
1990–91	Hull C	38	12
1991–92	Port Vale	33	3
1992–93	Port Vale	38	2
1993–94	Port Vale	40	0
1994–95	Plymouth Arg	27	2
1995–96	Plymouth Arg	0	0
1995–96	Burnley	32	5
1996–97	Burnley	17	2
1997–98	Bury	37	6
1998–99	Burnley	17	0
Total:		**370**	**55**

SWEENEY, Terry — Midfield

H: 5 9 W: 11 10 b.Paisley 26-1-79

Source: Trainee.

1996–97	Luton T	0	0
1997–98	Luton T	0	0
1998–99	Luton T	0	0
1998–99	Plymouth Arg	13	1
Total:		**13**	**1**

SYMONS, Kit — Defender

H: 6 1 W: 13 07 b.Basingstoke 8-3-71

Source: Trainee. *Honours:* Wales Under-21, 31 full caps, 2 goals.

1988–89	Portsmouth	2	0
1989–90	Portsmouth	1	0
1990–91	Portsmouth	1	0
1991–92	Portsmouth	46	1
1992–93	Portsmouth	41	2
1993–94	Portsmouth	29	3
1994–95	Portsmouth	40	4
1995–96	Portsmouth	1	0
1995–96	Manchester C	38	2
1996–97	Manchester C	44	0
1997–98	Manchester C	42	2
1998–99	Fulham	45	11
Total:		**330**	**25**

TAAFFE, Steven — Forward

H: 5 5 W: 9 08 b.Stoke 10-9-79

Source: Trainee.

1996–97	Stoke C	0	0

1997–98	Stoke C	3	0
1998–99	Stoke C	3	0
Total:		**6**	**0**

TAGGART, Gerry — Defender

H: 6 2 W: 14 00 b.Belfast 18-10-70

Source: Trainee. *Honours:* Northern Ireland Under-23, 45 full caps, 7 goals.

1988–89	Manchester C	11	1
1989–90	Manchester C	1	0
1989–90	Barnsley	21	2
1990–91	Barnsley	30	2
1991–92	Barnsley	38	3
1992–93	Barnsley	44	4
1993–94	Barnsley	38	2
1994–95	Barnsley	41	3
1995–96	Bolton W	11	1
1996–97	Bolton W	43	3
1997–98	Bolton W	15	0
1998–99	Leicester C	15	0
Total:		**308**	**21**

TAIT, Jordan — Defender

b.Berwick 27-9-79

Source: Trainee.

1998–99	Newcastle U	0	0

TAIT, Mick — Defender

H: 5 11 W: 14 05 b.Wallsend 30-9-56

Source: Apprentice.

1974–75	Oxford U	4	0
1975–76	Oxford U	37	12
1976–77	Oxford U	23	11
1976–77	Carlisle U	13	3
1977–78	Carlisle U	43	10
1978–79	Carlisle U	46	7
1979–80	Carlisle U	4	0
1979–80	Hull C	33	3
1980–81	Portsmouth	38	8
1981–82	Portsmouth	35	9
1982–83	Portsmouth	44	6
1983–84	Portsmouth	36	3
1984–85	Portsmouth	33	1
1985–86	Portsmouth	26	2
1986–87	Portsmouth	28	1
1987–88	Portsmouth	0	0
1987–88	Reading	35	2
1988–89	Reading	36	4
1989–90	Reading	28	3
1990–91	Darlington	45	2
1991–92	Darlington	34	0
1992–93	Hartlepool U	35	1
1993–94	Hartlepool U	26	0
From Gretna			
1994–95	Hartlepool U	20	0
1995–96	Hartlepool U	39	2
1996–97	Hartlepool U	19	0
1997–98	Hartlepool U	0	0
1998–99	Hartlepool U	0	0
Total:		**760**	**90**

TAIT, Paul — Midfield

H: 5 11 W: 11 10 b.Sutton Coldfield 31-7-71

Source: Trainee.

1987–88	Birmingham C	1	0
1988–89	Birmingham C	10	0
1989–90	Birmingham C	14	2
1990–91	Birmingham C	17	3
1991–92	Birmingham C	12	0
1992–93	Birmingham C	28	2
1993–94	Birmingham C	10	0
1993–94	Millwall (loan)	0	0
1994–95	Birmingham C	25	4
1995–96	Birmingham C	27	3
1996–97	Birmingham C	26	0
1997–98	Birmingham C	0	0
1997–98	Northampton T (loan)	3	0
1998–99	Birmingham C	0	0
1998–99	Oxford U	17	0
Total:		**190**	**14**

TALBOT, Paul — Defender

H: 5 10 W: 10 09 b.Gateshead 11-8-79

Source: Trainee.

1997–98	Newcastle U	0	0
1998–99	Newcastle U	0	0

TALBOT, Stuart — Midfield

H: 5 11 W: 13 07 b.Birmingham 14-6-73

Source: Doncaster R, Moor Green.

1994–95	Port Vale	2	0
1995–96	Port Vale	20	0
1996–97	Port Vale	34	4
1997–98	Port Vale	42	6
1998–99	Port Vale	33	0
Total:		**131**	**10**

TALIA, Frank — Goalkeeper

H: 6 1 W: 13 06 b.Melbourne 20-7-72

Source: Sunshine GC.

1992–93	Blackburn R	0	0
1992–93	Hartlepool U (loan)	14	0
1993–94	Blackburn R	0	0
1994–95	Blackburn R	0	0
1995–96	Blackburn R	0	0
1995–96	Swindon T	16	0
1996–97	Swindon T	15	0
1997–98	Swindon T	2	0
1998–99	Swindon T	43	0
Total:		**90**	**0**

TALLON, Gary — Midfield

H: 5 9 W: 12 09 b.Drogheda 5-9-73

Honours: Trainee.

1991–92	Blackburn R	0	0
1992–93	Blackburn R	0	0
1993–94	Blackburn R	0	0
1994–95	Blackburn R	0	0
1995–96	Blackburn R	0	0
1996–97	Kilmarnock	4	0
1996–97	Chester C (loan)	1	0
1997–98	Kilmarnock	0	0
1997–98	Mansfield T	26	1
1998–99	Mansfield T	36	1
Total:		**67**	**2**

TANKARD, Allen — Defender

H: 5 10 W: 13 04 b.Fleet 21-5-69

Source: Trainee. *Honours:* England Youth.

1985–86	Southampton	3	0
1986–87	Southampton	2	0
1987–88	Southampton	0	0
1988–89	Wigan Ath	33	1
1989–90	Wigan Ath	45	1
1990–91	Wigan Ath	46	1
1991–92	Wigan Ath	44	0
1992–93	Wigan Ath	41	1
1993–94	Port Vale	26	0
1994–95	Port Vale	39	1
1995–96	Port Vale	29	0
1996–97	Port Vale	37	1
1997–98	Port Vale	39	0
1998–99	Port Vale	37	4
Total:		**421**	**10**

TANNER, Adam — Midfield

H: 6 0 W: 13 00 b.Maldon 25-10-73

Source: Trainee.

1992–93	Ipswich T	0	0
1993–94	Ipswich T	0	0
1994–95	Ipswich T	10	2
1995–96	Ipswich T	10	0
1996–97	Ipswich T	16	4
1997–98	Ipswich T	18	1
1998–99	Ipswich T	19	0
Total:		**73**	**7**

TARDIF, Chris — Goalkeeper

H: 6 0 W: 12 05 b.Guernsey 19-9-79

Source: Trainee.

1998–99	Portsmouth	0	0

TARICCO, Mauricio — Defender

H: 5 8 W: 11 05 b.Buenos Aires 10-3-73

Honours: Argentina Under-23.

1993–94	Argentinos Juniors	21	0
1994–95	Ipswich T	0	0
1995–96	Ipswich T	39	0
1996–97	Ipswich T	41	3
1997–98	Ipswich T	41	0
1998–99	Ipswich T	16	1
1998–99	Tottenham H	13	0
Total:		**171**	**4**

TARRANT, Neil — Midfield

H: 6 0 W: 12 00 b.Darlington 24-6-79

Honours: Scotland Under-21.

1997–98	Darlington	0	0
1997–98	Shamrock R	2	0
1997–98	Ross Co	11	3
1998–99	Ross Co	33	17
1998–99	Aston Villa	0	0
Total:		**46**	**20**

TATE, Chris — Forward

H: 6 0 W: 12 00 b.York 27-12-77

Source: York C Trainee.

1996–97	Sunderland	0	0
1997–98	Scarborough	24	1
1998–99	Scarborough	25	12
Total:		**49**	**13**

TATE, Daniel — Goalkeeper

H: 5 11 W: 11 12 b.Bedford 12-11-80

Source: Trainee.

1998–99	Luton T	0	0

TAYLOR, Bob — Forward

H: 5 11 W: 11 09 b.Easington 3-2-67

Source: Horden CW.

1985–86	Leeds U	2	0
1986–87	Leeds U	2	0
1987–88	Leeds U	32	9
1988–89	Leeds U	6	0
1988–89	Bristol C	12	8
1989–90	Bristol C	37	27
1990–91	Bristol C	39	11
1991–92	Bristol C	18	4
1991–92	WBA	19	8
1992–93	WBA	46	30
1993–94	WBA	42	18
1994–95	WBA	42	11
1995–96	WBA	42	17
1996–97	WBA	32	10

1997–98	WBA	15	2
1997–98	Bolton W (loan)	12	3
1998–99	Bolton W	38	15
Total:		**436**	**173**

TAYLOR, Craig — Defender

H: 6 1 W: 12 03 b.Plymouth 24-1-74

Source: Dorchester T.

1996–97	Swindon T	0	0
1997–98	Swindon T	32	2
1998–99	Swindon T	21	0
1998–99	Plymouth Arg (loan)	6	1
Total:		**59**	**3**

TAYLOR, Gareth — Forward

H: 6 1 W: 12 02 b.Weston-Super-Mare 25-2-73

Source: Southampton Trainee. *Honours:* Wales Under-21, 8 full caps.

1991–92	Bristol R	1	0
1992–93	Bristol R	0	0
1993–94	Bristol R	0	0
1994–95	Bristol R	39	12
1995–96	Bristol R	7	4
1995–96	Crystal Palace	20	1
1995–96	Sheffield U	10	2
1996–97	Sheffield U	34	12
1997–98	Sheffield U	28	10
1998–99	Sheffield U	12	1
1998–99	Manchester C	26	4
Total:		**177**	**46**

TAYLOR, Ian — Midfield

H: 6 1 W: 12 00 b.Birmingham 4-6-68

Source: Moor Green.

1992–93	Port Vale	41	15
1993–94	Port Vale	42	13
1994–95	Sheffield W	14	1
1994–95	Aston Villa	22	1
1995–96	Aston Villa	25	3
1996–97	Aston Villa	34	2
1997–98	Aston Villa	32	6
1998–99	Aston Villa	33	4
Total:		**243**	**45**

TAYLOR, John — Forward

H: 6 2 W: 14 00 b.Norwich 24-10-64

Source: Local.

1982–83	Colchester U	0	0
1983–84	Colchester U	0	0
1984–85	Colchester U	0	0
From Sudbury T			
1988–89	Cambridge U	40	12
1989–90	Cambridge U	45	15
1990–91	Cambridge U	40	14
1991–92	Cambridge U	35	5
1991–92	Bristol R	8	7
1992–93	Bristol R	42	14
1993–94	Bristol R	45	23
1994–95	Bradford C	36	11
1994–95	Luton T	9	3
1995–96	Luton T	28	0
1996–97	Luton T	0	0
1996–97	Lincoln C (loan)	5	2
1996–97	Colchester U (loan)	8	5
1996–97	Cambridge U	21	4
1997–98	Cambridge U	34	10
1998–99	Cambridge U	40	17
Total:		**436**	**142**

TAYLOR, Maik — Goalkeeper

H: 6 3 W: 13 09 b.Hildeshein 4-9-71

Source: Farnborough T. *Honours:* Northern Ireland Under-21, 4 full caps.

1995–96	Barnet	45	0
1996–97	Barnet	25	0
1996–97	Southampton	18	0
1997–98	Southampton	0	0
1997–98	Fulham	28	0
1998–99	Fulham	46	0
Total:		**162**	**0**

TAYLOR, Martin — Goalkeeper

H: 5 11 W: 13 11 b.Tamworth 9-12-66

Source: Mile Oak R.

1986–87	Derby Co	0	0
1987–88	Derby Co	0	0
1987–88	Carlisle U (loan)	10	0
1987–88	Scunthorpe U (loan)	8	0
1988–89	Derby Co	0	0
1989–90	Derby Co	3	0
1990–91	Derby Co	7	0
1991–92	Derby Co	5	0
1992–93	Derby Co	21	0
1993–94	Derby Co	46	0
1994–95	Derby Co	12	0
1995–96	Derby Co	0	0
1996–97	Derby Co	3	0
1996–97	Crewe Alex (loan)	6	0
1996–97	Wycombe W (loan)	4	0
1997–98	Wycombe W	45	0
1998–99	Wycombe W	44	0
Total:		**214**	**0**

TAYLOR, Martin — Defender

H: 6 4 W: 14 00 b.Ashington 9-11-79

Source: Trainee. *Honours:* England Youth.

1997–98	Blackburn R	0	0
1998–99	Blackburn R	3	0
Total:		**3**	**0**

TAYLOR, Matthew — Defender

H: 5 10 W: 11 08 b.Oxford 27-11-81

Source: Trainee.

1998–99	Luton T	0	0

TAYLOR, Perry — Midfield

H: 5 11 W: 12 02 b.Birkenhead 29-1-81

Source: Trainee. *Honours:* England Schools.

1998–99	Tranmere R	0	0

TAYLOR, Robert — Forward

H: 6 1 W: 13 08 b.Norwich 30-4-71

Source: Trainee.

1989–90	Norwich C	0	0
1990–91	Norwich C	0	0
1990–91	Leyton Orient (loan)	3	1
1991–92	Birmingham C	0	0
1991–92	Leyton Orient	11	1
1992–93	Leyton Orient	39	18
1993–94	Leyton Orient	23	1
1993–94	Brentford	5	2
1994–95	Brentford	43	23
1995–96	Brentford	42	11
1996–97	Brentford	43	7
1997–98	Brentford	40	13
1998–99	Gillingham	43	16
Total:		**292**	**93**

TAYLOR, Scott — Forward

H: 5 10 W: 11 06 b.Chertsey 5-5-76

Source: Staines T.

1994–95	Millwall	6	0
1995–96	Millwall	22	0
1995–96	Bolton W	1	0
1996–97	Bolton W	11	1
1997–98	Bolton W	0	0
1997–98	Rotherham U (loan)	10	3
1997–98	Blackpool (loan)	5	1
1998–99	Bolton W	0	0
1998–99	Tranmere R	36	9
Total:		**91**	**14**

TAYLOR, Scott — Midfield

H: 5 9 W: 11 05 b.Portsmouth 23-11-70

Source: Trainee.

1988–89	Reading	3	0
1989–90	Reading	29	2
1990–91	Reading	32	1
1991–92	Reading	29	2
1992–93	Reading	32	5
1993–94	Reading	38	6
1994–95	Reading	44	8
1995–96	Leicester C	39	6
1996–97	Leicester C	25	0
1997–98	Leicester C	0	0
1998–99	Leicester C	0	0
Total:		**271**	**30**

TAYLOR, Shaun — Defender

H: 6 1 W: 12 10 b.Plymouth 26-2-63

Source: Bideford.

1986–87	Exeter C	23	0
1987–88	Exeter C	41	1
1988–89	Exeter C	46	6
1989–90	Exeter C	45	5
1990–91	Exeter C	45	4
1991–92	Swindon T	42	4
1992–93	Swindon T	46	11
1993–94	Swindon T	42	4
1994–95	Swindon T	37	4
1995–96	Swindon T	43	7
1996–97	Swindon T	2	0
1996–97	Bristol C	29	1
1997–98	Bristol C	43	2
1998–99	Bristol C	8	0
Total:		**492**	**49**

TAYLOR, Stuart — Goalkeeper

b.Romford 28-11-80

Source: Trainee. *Honours:* FA Schools, England Youth.

1998–99	Arsenal	0	0

TEALE, Shaun — Defender

H: 6 0 W: 13 07 b.Southport 10-3-64

Source: Southport, Northwich Vic, Weymouth.

1988–89	Bournemouth	20	0
1989–90	Bournemouth	34	0
1990–91	Bournemouth	46	4
1991–92	Aston Villa	42	0
1992–93	Aston Villa	39	1
1993–94	Aston Villa	38	1
1994–95	Aston Villa	28	0
1995–96	Tranmere R	29	0
1996–97	Tranmere R	25	0
1996–97	Preston NE (loan)	5	0
From Happy Valley.			
1998–99	Motherwell	29	1
Total:		**335**	**7**

TEATHER, Paul — Defender

H: 6 0 W: 11 08 b.Rotherham 28-12-77

Source: Trainee. *Honours:* England Schools, Youth.

1994–95	Manchester U	0	0
1995–96	Manchester U	0	0
1996–97	Manchester U	0	0
1997–98	Manchester U	0	0

1997–98	Bournemouth (loan)	10	0
1998–99	Manchester U	0	0
Total:		**10**	**0**

TEBILY, Oliver — Defender

H: 6 0 W: 13 00 b.Abidjan 19-12-75

Source: Chateauroux.

1998–99	Sheffield U	8	0
Total:		**8**	**0**

TEDALDI, Domenico — Midfield

H: 5 11 W: 12 00 b.Aberystwyth 22-10-80

Source: Trainee.

1997–98	Doncaster R	2	1
1998–99	Bury	0	0
Total:		**2**	**1**

TELFER, Paul — Midfield

H: 5 9 W: 11 06 b.Edinburgh 21-10-71

Source: Trainee. *Honours:* Scotland Under-21.

1988–89	Luton T	0	0
1989–90	Luton T	0	0
1990–91	Luton T	1	0
1991–92	Luton T	20	1
1992–93	Luton T	32	2
1993–94	Luton T	45	7
1994–95	Luton T	46	9
1995–96	Coventry C	31	1
1996–97	Coventry C	34	0
1997–98	Coventry C	33	3
1998–99	Coventry C	32	2
Total:		**274**	**25**

TEMPLEMAN, Christopher — Forward

H: 6 4 W: 13 02 b.Kirkcaldy 12-1-80

Source: Rosyth Rec.

1997–98	Dunfermline Ath	0	0
1998–99	Dunfermline Ath	12	0
Total:		**12**	**0**

TERRY, John — Defender

H: 6 0 W: 11 11 b.Barking 7-12-80

Source: Trainee.

1997–98	Chelsea	0	0
1998–99	Chelsea	2	0
Total:		**2**	**0**

TESTIMITANU, Ivan — Midfield

b.Moldova 27-4-74

1995–96	Zimbru Chisinau	28	11
1996–97	Zimbru Chisinau	25	4
1997–98	Zimbru Chisinau	26	9
1998–99	Bristol C	8	0
Total:		**87**	**24**

THACKERAY, Andy — Defender

H: 5 9 W: 11 00 b.Huddersfield 13-2-68

Source: School.

1985–86	Manchester C	0	0
1986–87	Huddersfield T	2	0
1986–87	Newport Co	11	3
1987–88	Newport Co	43	1
1988–89	Wrexham	35	2
1989–90	Wrexham	34	7
1990–91	Wrexham	41	2
1991–92	Wrexham	42	3
1992–93	Rochdale	41	6
1993–94	Rochdale	37	4
1994–95	Rochdale	41	3
1995–96	Rochdale	29	0
1996–97	Rochdale	17	0
1997–98	Rochdale	0	0
1998–99	Halifax T	38	5
Total:		**411**	**36**

THATCHER, Ben — Defender

H: 5 11 W: 12 07 b.Swindon 30-11-75

Source: Trainee. *Honours:* England Youth, Under-21.

1992–93	Millwall	0	0
1993–94	Millwall	8	0
1994–95	Millwall	40	1
1995–96	Millwall	42	0
1996–97	Wimbledon	9	0
1997–98	Wimbledon	26	0
1998–99	Wimbledon	31	0
Total:		**156**	**1**

THELWELL, Alton — Defender

b.London 5-9-80

Source: Trainee.

1998–99	Tottenham H	0	0

THEOBALD, David — Defender

H: 6 3 W: 11 00 b.Cambridge 15-12-78

Source: Trainee.

1997–98	Ipswich T	0	0
1998–99	Ipswich T	0	0

THERN, Jonas — Midfield

H: 5 11 W: 13 03 b.Falkoping 20-3-67

Honours: Sweden 75 full caps, 6 goals.

1985	Malmo	1	0
1986	Malmo	16	2
1987	Malmo	20	3
1987–88	Zurich	0	0
1988	Malmo	22	4
1989	Malmo	13	1
1989–90	Benfica	21	2
1990–91	Benfica	24	4
1991–92	Benfica	27	2
1992–93	Napoli	27	0
1993–94	Napoli	21	1
1994–95	Roma	12	0
1995–96	Roma	22	1
1996–97	Roma	25	2
1997–98	Rangers	22	5
1998–99	Rangers	1	0
Total:		**274**	**27**

THETIS, Manuel — Defender

H: 6 3 W: 14 13 b.France 5-11-71

Source: Sevilla.

1998–99	Ipswich T	31	2
Total:		**31**	**2**

THIRLWELL, Paul — Midfield

H: 5 11 W: 11 04 b.Newcastle 13-2-79

Source: Trainee.

1996–97	Sunderland	0	0
1997–98	Sunderland	0	0
1998–99	Sunderland	2	0
Total:		**2**	**0**

THOGERSEN, Thomas — Defender

H: 6 1 W: 13 00 b.Copenhagen 2-4-68

1989	Frem	2	0
1990	Frem	17	0
1991–92	Frem	20	5
1992–93	Frem	18	2
1993–94	Brondby	32	11
1994–95	Brondby	26	7
1995–96	Brondby	21	1
1996–97	Brondby	21	2
1997–98	Brondby	11	1
1998–99	Portsmouth	34	0
Total:		**202**	**29**

THOLOT, Didier — Forward

b.Feurs 2-4-64

Source: INF Vichy, Toulon, Niort, Reims, St Etienne, Martigues, Bordeaux, Sion.

1997–98	Walsall	14	4
1998–99	Walsall	0	0
Total:		**14**	**4**

THOM, Stuart — Defender

H: 6 2 W: 11 10 b.Dewsbury 27-12-76

Source: Trainee.

1993–94	Nottingham F	0	0
1994–95	Nottingham F	0	0
1995–96	Nottingham F	0	0
1996–97	Nottingham F	0	0
1997–98	Nottingham F	0	0
1997–98	Mansfield T (loan)	5	0
1998–99	Nottingham F	0	0
1998–99	Oldham Ath	25	1
Total:		**30**	**1**

THOMAS, Dai — Forward

H: 5 11 W: 13 07 b.Caerphilly 26-9-75

Source: Trainee.

1994–95	Swansea C	4	0
1995–96	Swansea C	16	1
1996–97	Swansea C	36	9
1997–98	Watford	16	3
1998–99	Cardiff C	24	4
Total:		**96**	**17**

THOMAS, Danny — Defender

H: 5 7 W: 10 07 b.Leamington Spa 1-5-81

Source: Trainee.

1997–98	Nottingham F	0	0
1997–98	Leicester C	0	0
1998–99	Leicester C	0	0

THOMAS, Geoff — Midfield

H: 6 1 W: 13 07 b.Manchester 5-8-64

Source: Local. *Honours:* England B, 9 full caps.

1981–82	Rochdale	0	0
1982–83	Rochdale	1	0
1983–84	Rochdale	10	1
1983–84	Crewe Alex	8	1
1984–85	Crewe Alex	40	4
1985–86	Crewe Alex	37	6
1986–87	Crewe Alex	40	9
1987–88	Crystal Palace	41	6
1988–89	Crystal Palace	22	5
1989–90	Crystal Palace	35	1
1990–91	Crystal Palace	38	6

1991–92	Crystal Palace	30	6
1992–93	Crystal Palace	29	2
1993–94	Wolverhampton W	8	4
1994–95	Wolverhampton W	14	1
1995–96	Wolverhampton W	2	0
1996–97	Wolverhampton W	22	3
1997–98	Nottingham F	20	3
1998–99	Nottingham F	5	1
Total:		**402**	**59**

THOMAS, Glen — Defender

H: 6 0 W: 14 00 b.Hackney 6-10-67

Source: Apprentice.

1985–86	Fulham	0	0
1986–87	Fulham	1	0
1987–88	Fulham	27	0
1988–89	Fulham	40	1
1989–90	Fulham	17	1
1990–91	Fulham	34	1
1991–92	Fulham	45	3
1992–93	Fulham	43	0
1993–94	Fulham	37	0
1994–95	Fulham	7	0
1994–95	Peterborough U	8	0
1994–95	Barnet	7	0
1995–96	Barnet	16	0
1995–96	Gillingham	15	0
1996–97	Gillingham	10	0
1997–98	Gillingham	3	0
1998–99	Brighton & HA	3	0
Total:		**313**	**6**

THOMAS, James — Forward

H: 6 0 W: 13 00 b.Swansea 16-1-79

Source: Trainee. *Honours:* Wales Under-21.

1996–97	Blackburn R	0	0
1997–98	Blackburn R	0	0
1997–98	WBA (loan)	3	0
1998–99	Blackburn R	0	0
Total:		**3**	**0**

THOMAS, Martin — Midfield

H: 5 8 W: 11 06 b.Lyndhurst 12-9-73

Source: Trainee.

1992–93	Southampton	0	0
1993–94	Southampton	0	0
1993–94	Leyton Orient	5	2
1994–95	Fulham	23	3
1995–96	Fulham	37	5
1996–97	Fulham	26	0
1997–98	Fulham	4	0
1998–99	Swansea C	30	3
Total:		**125**	**13**

THOMAS, Michael — Midfield

H: 5 9 W: 12 06 b.Lambeth 24-8-67

Source: Apprentice. *Honours:* England Schools, Youth, Under-21, B, 2 full caps.

1985–86	Arsenal	0	0
1986–87	Arsenal	12	0
1986–87	Portsmouth (loan)	3	0
1987–88	Arsenal	37	9
1988–89	Arsenal	37	7
1989–90	Arsenal	36	5
1990–91	Arsenal	31	2
1991–92	Arsenal	10	1
1991–92	Liverpool	17	3
1992–93	Liverpool	8	1
1993–94	Liverpool	7	0
1994–95	Liverpool	23	0
1995–96	Liverpool	27	1
1996–97	Liverpool	31	3
1997–98	Liverpool	11	1
1997–98	Middlesbrough (loan)	10	0
1998–99	Liverpool	0	0
Total:		**300**	**33**

THOMAS, Mitchell — Defender

H: 6 2 W: 14 00 b.Luton 2-10-64

Source: Apprentice. *Honours:* England Youth, Under-21, B.

1982–83	Luton T	4	0
1983–84	Luton T	26	0
1984–85	Luton T	36	0
1985–86	Luton T	41	1
1986–87	Tottenham H	39	4
1987–88	Tottenham H	36	0
1988–89	Tottenham H	25	1
1989–90	Tottenham H	26	1
1990–91	Tottenham H	31	0
1991–92	West Ham U	35	3
1992–93	West Ham U	3	0
1993–94	West Ham U	0	0
1993–94	Luton T	20	1
1994–95	Luton T	36	0
1995–96	Luton T	27	0
1996–97	Luton T	42	3
1997–98	Luton T	28	1
1998–99	Luton T	32	0
Total:		**487**	**15**

THOMAS, Rod — Forward

H: 5 6 W: 11 11 b.London 10-10-70

Source: Trainee. *Honours:* England Schools, Youth, Under-21.

1987–88	Watford	4	0
1988–89	Watford	18	2
1989–90	Watford	32	6
1990–91	Watford	24	1
1991–92	Watford	5	0
1991–92	Gillingham (loan)	8	1

1992–93	Watford	1	0
1993–94	Carlisle U	38	9
1994–95	Carlisle U	36	6
1995–96	Carlisle U	36	1
1996–97	Carlisle U	36	0
1997–98	Chester C	38	4
1998–99	Chester C	6	3
1998–99	Brighton & HA	12	3
Total:		**294**	**36**

THOMAS, Steve — Midfield

H: 5 10 W: 11 07 b.Hartlepool 23-6-79

Source: Trainee.

1997–98	Wrexham	0	0
1998–99	Wrexham	4	0
Total:		**4**	**0**

THOMAS, Tony — Defender

H: 5 11 W: 13 00 b.Liverpool 12-7-71

Source: Trainee.

1988–89	Tranmere R	9	2
1989–90	Tranmere R	42	2
1990–91	Tranmere R	33	3
1991–92	Tranmere R	30	3
1992–93	Tranmere R	16	0
1993–94	Tranmere R	40	2
1994–95	Tranmere R	26	0
1995–96	Tranmere R	31	0
1996–97	Tranmere R	30	0
1997–98	Everton	7	0
1998–99	Everton	1	0
1998–99	Motherwell	10	0
Total:		**275**	**12**

THOMAS, Wayne — Defender

H: 5 11 W: 11 02 b.Gloucester 17-5-79

Source: Trainee.

1995–96	Torquay U	6	0
1996–97	Torquay U	12	0
1997–98	Torquay U	21	1
1998–99	Torquay U	44	1
Total:		**83**	**2**

THOMAS, Wayne — Midfield

H: 5 8 W: 12 02 b.Walsall 28-8-78

Source: Trainee.

1996–97	Walsall	20	0
1997–98	Walsall	5	0
1998–99	Walsall	12	0
Total:		**37**	**0**

THOMPSON, Alan — Midfield

H: 6 0 W: 13 11 b.Newcastle 22-12-73

Source: Trainee. *Honours:* England Youth, Under-21.

1990–91	Newcastle U	0	0
1991–92	Newcastle U	14	0
1992–93	Newcastle U	2	0
1993–94	Bolton W	27	6
1994–95	Bolton W	37	7
1995–96	Bolton W	26	1
1996–97	Bolton W	34	10
1997–98	Bolton W	33	9
1998–99	Aston Villa	25	2
Total:		**198**	**35**

THOMPSON, Andy — Defender

H: 5 5 W: 10 06 b.Cannock 9-11-67

Source: Apprentice.

1985–86	WBA	15	1
1986–87	WBA	9	0
1986–87	Wolverhampton W	29	8
1987–88	Wolverhampton W	42	2
1988–89	Wolverhampton W	46	6
1989–90	Wolverhampton W	33	4
1990–91	Wolverhampton W	44	3
1991–92	Wolverhampton W	17	0
1992–93	Wolverhampton W	20	0
1993–94	Wolverhampton W	37	3
1994–95	Wolverhampton W	31	9
1995–96	Wolverhampton W	45	6
1996–97	Wolverhampton W	32	2
1997–98	Tranmere R	44	3
1998–99	Tranmere R	37	1
Total:		**481**	**48**

THOMPSON, David — Midfield

H: 5 7 W: 10 00 b.Birkenhead 12-9-77

Source: Trainee. *Honours:* England Youth, Under-21.

1994–95	Liverpool	0	0
1995–96	Liverpool	0	0
1996–97	Liverpool	2	0
1997–98	Liverpool	5	1
1997–98	Swindon T (loan)	10	0
1998–99	Liverpool	14	1
Total:		**31**	**2**

THOMPSON, Garry — Forward

H: 6 1 W: 14 07 b.Birmingham 7-10-59

Source: Apprentice. *Honours:* England Under-21.

1977–78	Coventry C	6	2
1978–79	Coventry C	20	8
1979–80	Coventry C	17	6
1980–81	Coventry C	35	8
1981–82	Coventry C	36	10

1982–83	Coventry C	20	4
1982–83	WBA	12	7
1983–84	WBA	37	13
1984–85	WBA	42	19
1985–86	Sheffield W	36	7
1986–87	Aston Villa	31	6
1987–88	Aston Villa	24	11
1988–89	Aston Villa	5	0
1988–89	Watford	21	7
1989–90	Watford	13	1
1989–90	Crystal Palace	9	2
1990–91	Crystal Palace	11	1
1991–92	QPR	15	1
1992–93	QPR	4	0
1993–94	Cardiff C	30	5
1994–95	Cardiff C	13	0
1994–95	Northampton T	15	4
1995–96	Northampton T	34	2
1996–97	Northampton T	1	0
1997–98	Northampton T	0	0
1998–99	Northampton T	0	0
1998–99	Bristol R	0	0
Total:		**487**	**124**

THOMPSON, Glyn — Goalkeeper

H: 6 3 W: 11 03 b.Shrewsbury 24-2-81

Source: Trainee.

1998–99	Shrewsbury T	1	0
Total:		**1**	**0**

THOMPSON, Neil — Defender

H: 6 0 W: 13 08 b.Beverley 2-10-63

Source: Nottingham F Apprentice.

1981–82	Hull C	23	0
1982–83	Hull C	8	0
From Scarborough			
1987–88	Scarborough	41	6
1988–89	Scarborough	46	9
1989–90	Ipswich T	45	3
1990–91	Ipswich T	38	6
1991–92	Ipswich T	45	6
1992–93	Ipswich T	31	3
1993–94	Ipswich T	32	0
1994–95	Ipswich T	10	0
1995–96	Ipswich T	5	1
1996–97	Barnsley	24	5
1997–98	Barnsley	3	0
1997–98	Oldham Ath (loan)	8	0
1997–98	York C	12	2
1998–99	York C	24	6
Total:		**395**	**47**

THOMPSON, Niall — Forward

H: 5 11 W: 11 00 b.Birmingham 16-4-74

Source: Trainee.

1992–93	Crystal Palace	0	0
1993–94	Crystal Palace	0	0
1994–95	Colchester U	13	5
From Zulte VV.			
1997–98	Brentford	8	0
1998–99	Brentford	0	0
Total:		**21**	**5**

THOMPSON, Phil — Defender

H: 5 11 W: 12 00 b.Blackpool 1-4-81

Source: Trainee.

1997–98	Blackpool	1	0
1998–99	Blackpool	22	2
Total:		**23**	**2**

THOMPSON, Richard — Forward

H: 5 7 W: 12 02 b.Lambeth 2 5-74

Source: Crawley T.

1998–99	Wycombe W	0	0

THOMPSON, Scott — Defender

H: 6 3 W: 13 00 b.Warrington 28-6-80

Source: Trainee.

1998–99	Chester C	0	0

THOMPSON, Steve — Midfield

H: 5 11 W: 13 00 b.Oldham 2-11-64

Source: Apprentice.

1982–83	Bolton W	3	0
1983–84	Bolton W	40	3
1984–85	Bolton W	34	4
1985–86	Bolton W	35	8
1986–87	Bolton W	44	7
1987–88	Bolton W	44	7
1988–89	Bolton W	43	9
1989–90	Bolton W	45	6
1990–91	Bolton W	45	5
1991–92	Bolton W	2	0
1991–92	Luton T	5	0
1991–92	Leicester C	34	3
1992–93	Leicester C	44	8
1993–94	Leicester C	30	7
1994–95	Leicester C	19	0
1994–95	Burnley	12	0
1995–96	Burnley	18	0
1996–97	Burnley	19	1
1997–98	Rotherham U	39	3
1998–99	Rotherham U	33	5
Total:		**588**	**76**

THOMPSON, Steven — Forward

H: 6 2 W: 12 05 b.Paisley 14-10-78

Source: Dundee U BC. *Honours:* Scotland Under-21.

1996–97	Dundee U	1	0
1997–98	Dundee U	8	0
1998–99	Dundee U	15	1
Total:		**24**	**1**

THOMSON, Andy — Defender

H: 6 3 W: 14 03 b.Swindon 28-3-74

Source: Trainee.

1992–93	Swindon T	0	0
1993–94	Swindon T	1	0
1994–95	Swindon T	21	0
1995–96	Swindon T	0	0
1995–96	Portsmouth	16	0
1996–97	Portsmouth	28	1
1997–98	Portsmouth	35	2
1998–99	Portsmouth	14	0
1998–99	Bristol R	21	1
Total:		**136**	**4**

THOMSON, Andy — Forward

H: 5 10 W: 11 05 b.Motherwell 1-4-71

Source: Jerviston BC.

1989–90	Q of S	26	6
1990–91	Q of S	37	11
1991–92	Q of S	39	26
1992–93	Q of S	38	21
1993–94	Q of S	35	29
1994–95	Southend U	39	11
1995–96	Southend U	33	6
1996–97	Southend U	17	5
1997–98	Southend U	33	6
1998–99	Oxford U	38	7
Total:		**335**	**128**

THOMSON, Scott M — Midfield

H: 5 10 W: 11 10 b.Aberdeen 29-1-72

Source: Shrewsbury T Trainee.

1990–91	Brechin C	30	3
1991–92	Brechin C	11	3
1991–92	Aberdeen	0	0
1992–93	Aberdeen	2	0
1993–94	Aberdeen	3	0
1994–95	Aberdeen	10	1
1995–96	Aberdeen	4	0
1995–96	Raith R	9	1
1996–97	Raith R	22	2
1997–98	Raith R	31	1
1998–99	Dunfermline Ath	21	2
Total:		**143**	**13**

THOMSON, Scott Y — Goalkeeper

H: 6 0 W: 11 09 b.Edinburgh 8-11-66

Source: Hutchison Vale BC.

1986–87	Dundee U	3	0
1987–88	Dundee U	0	0
1988–89	Dundee U	1	0
1989–90	Dundee U	2	0
1990–91	Dundee U	0	0
1991–92	Forfar Ath	44	0
1992–93	Forfar Ath	39	0
1993–94	Forfar Ath	5	0
1993–94	Raith R	34	0
1994–95	Raith R	35	0
1995–96	Raith R	26	0
1996–97	Raith R	28	0
1997–98	Hull C	9	0
1997–98	Motherwell	1	0
1998–99	Hull C	0	0
Total:		**227**	**0**

THOMSON, Steve — Midfield

H: 5 8 W: 10 04 b.Glasgow 23-1-78

Source: Trainee.

1995–96	Crystal Palace	0	0
1996–97	Crystal Palace	0	0
1997–98	Crystal Palace	0	0
1998–99	Crystal Palace	16	0
Total:		**16**	**0**

THORNE, Peter — Forward

H: 6 0 W: 13 07 b.Manchester 21-6-73

Source: Trainee.

1991–92	Blackburn R	0	0
1992–93	Blackburn R	0	0
1993–94	Blackburn R	0	0
1993–94	Wigan Ath (loan)	11	0
1994–95	Blackburn R	0	0
1994–95	Swindon T	20	9
1995–96	Swindon T	26	10
1996–97	Swindon T	31	8
1997–98	Stoke C	36	12
1998–99	Stoke C	34	9
Total:		**158**	**48**

THORNLEY, Ben — Forward

H: 5 7 W: 11 07 b.Bury 21-4-75

Source: Trainee. *Honours:* England Schools, Under-21.

1992–93	Manchester U	0	0
1993–94	Manchester U	1	0
1994–95	Manchester U	0	0
1995–96	Manchester U	1	0
1995–96	Stockport Co (loan)	10	1
1995–96	Huddersfield T (loan)	12	2

1996–97	Manchester U	2	0
1997–98	Manchester U	5	0
1998–99	Huddersfield T	35	4
Total:		**66**	**7**

THORPE, Jeff — Midfield

H: 5 11 W: 12 08 b.Cockermouth 17-11-72

Source: Trainee.

1990–91	Carlisle U	13	0
1991–92	Carlisle U	28	1
1992–93	Carlisle U	28	0
1993–94	Carlisle U	0	0
1994–95	Carlisle U	28	4
1995–96	Carlisle U	34	1
1996–97	Carlisle U	5	0
1997–98	Carlisle U	14	0
1998–99	Carlisle U	13	0
Total:		**163**	**6**

THORPE, Lee — Forward

H: 6 0 W: 11 06 b.Wolverhampton 14-12-75

Source: Trainee.

1993–94	Blackpool	1	0
1994–95	Blackpool	1	0
1995–96	Blackpool	1	0
1996–97	Blackpool	9	0
1997–98	Lincoln C	44	14
1998–99	Lincoln C	38	8
Total:		**94**	**22**

THORPE, Tony — Forward

H: 5 8 W: 12 06 b.Leicester 10-4-74

Source: Leicester C.

1992–93	Luton T	0	0
1993–94	Luton T	14	1
1994–95	Luton T	4	0
1995–96	Luton T	33	7
1996–97	Luton T	41	28
1997–98	Luton T	28	14
1997–98	Fulham	13	3
1998–99	Bristol C	16	2
1998–99	Reading (loan)	6	1
1998–99	Luton T (loan)	8	4
Total:		**163**	**60**

THORRINGTON, John — Forward

H: 5 7 W: 10 05 b.Johannesburg 17-10-79

Source: US College.

1997–98	Manchester U	0	0
1998–99	Manchester U	0	0

THURGOOD, Sean — Defender

H: 6 2 W: 12 09 b.Hayling Island 11-2-80

Source: Alton T.

1998–99	Wimbledon	0	0

THURSTON, Mark — Midfield

H: 6 2 W: 11 08 b.Carlisle 10-2-80

Source: Trainee.

1998–99	Carlisle U	0	0

TIATTO, Danny — Defender

H: 5 8 W: 11 01 b.Melbourne 22-5-73

Source: Baden.

1997–98	Stoke C	15	1
1998–99	Manchester C	17	0
Total:		**32**	**1**

TIERNEY, Fran — Midfield

H: 5 10 W: 11 00 b.Liverpool 9-10-75

Source: Trainee.

1992–93	Crewe Alex	1	0
1993–94	Crewe Alex	8	1
1994–95	Crewe Alex	20	4
1995–96	Crewe Alex	22	2
1996–97	Crewe Alex	32	3
1997–98	Crewe Alex	4	0
1998–99	Crewe Alex	0	0
1998–99	Notts Co	20	3
Total:		**107**	**13**

TILER, Carl — Defender

H: 6 2 W: 13 10 b.Sheffield 11-2-70

Source: Trainee. *Honours:* England Under-21.

1987–88	Barnsley	1	0
1988–89	Barnsley	4	0
1989–90	Barnsley	21	1
1990–91	Barnsley	45	2
1991–92	Nottingham F	26	1
1992–93	Nottingham F	37	0
1993–94	Nottingham F	3	0
1994–95	Nottingham F	3	0
1994–95	Swindon T (loan)	2	0
1995–96	Nottingham F	0	0
1995–96	Aston Villa	1	0
1996–97	Aston Villa	11	1
1996–97	Sheffield U	6	1
1997–98	Sheffield U	17	1
1997–98	Everton	19	1
1998–99	Everton	2	0
1998–99	Charlton Ath	27	1
Total:		**225**	**9**

TILLSON, Andy — Defender

H: 6 2 W: 13 05 b.Huntingdon 30-6-66

Source: Kettering T.

1988–89	Grimsby T	45	2
1989–90	Grimsby T	42	3
1990–91	Grimsby T	18	0
1990–91	QPR	19	2
1991–92	QPR	10	0
1992–93	QPR	0	0
1992–93	Grimsby T (loan)	4	0
1992–93	Bristol R	29	0
1993–94	Bristol R	13	0
1994–95	Bristol R	40	2
1995–96	Bristol R	38	1
1996–97	Bristol R	38	2
1997–98	Bristol R	33	3
1998–99	Bristol R	19	2
Total:		**348**	**17**

TIMMONS, Darren — Midfield

H: 6 1 W: 11 02 b.North Shields 3-2-80

Source: Trainee.

1998–99	Hartlepool U	0	0

TINDALL, Jason — Midfield

H: 6 1 W: 12 01 b.Stepney 15-11-77

Source: Trainee.

1996–97	Charlton Ath	0	0
1997–98	Charlton Ath	0	0
1998–99	Bournemouth	17	1
Total:		**17**	**1**

TINKLER, Eric — Midfield

H: 6 2 W: 12 06 b.Roodepoort 30-7-70

Honours: South Africa 5 full caps.

1993–94	Vitoria Setubal	21	0
1994–95	Vitoria Setubal	17	1
1995–96	Vitoria Setubal	19	0
1996–97	Cagliari	20	0
1997–98	Barnsley	25	2
1998–99	Barnsley	25	3
Total:		**127**	**6**

TINKLER, Mark — Midfield

H: 5 11 W: 11 04 b.Bishop Auckland 21-10-74

Source: Trainee. *Honours:* England Schools, Youth.

1991–92	Leeds U	0	0
1992–93	Leeds U	7	0
1993–94	Leeds U	3	0
1994–95	Leeds U	3	0
1995–96	Leeds U	9	0
1996–97	Leeds U	3	0
1996–97	York C	9	1
1997–98	York C	44	5
1998–99	York C	37	2
Total:		**115**	**8**

TINNION, Brian — Midfield

H: 5 11 W: 12 13 b.Stanley 23-3-68

Source: Apprentice.

1985–86	Newcastle U	0	0
1986–87	Newcastle U	3	0
1987–88	Newcastle U	16	1
1988–89	Newcastle U	13	1
1988–89	Bradford C	14	1
1989–90	Bradford C	37	5
1990–91	Bradford C	41	5
1991–92	Bradford C	26	8
1992–93	Bradford C	27	3
1992–93	Bristol C	11	2
1993–94	Bristol C	41	5
1994–95	Bristol C	35	2
1995–96	Bristol C	30	3
1996–97	Bristol C	32	1
1997–98	Bristol C	44	3
1998–99	Bristol C	35	1
Total:		**405**	**41**

TINSON, Darren — Defender

H: 6 0 W: 14 04 b.Birmingham 15-11-69

Source: Northwich V.

1997–98	Macclesfield T	44	0
1998–99	Macclesfield T	37	0
Total:		**81**	**0**

TIPTON, Matthew — Forward

H: 5 10 W: 11 02 b.Bridgend 29-6-80

Source: Trainee. *Honours:* Wales Under-21.

1997–98	Oldham Ath	3	0
1998–99	Oldham Ath	28	2
Total:		**31**	**2**

TISDALE, Paul — Midfield

H: 5 9 W: 10 09 b.Malta 14-1-73

Source: School. *Honours:* England Schools.

1991–92	Southampton	0	0
1992–93	Southampton	0	0
1992–93	Northampton T (loan)	5	0
1993–94	Southampton	0	0
1994–95	Southampton	7	0
1995–96	Southampton	9	1
1996–97	Southampton	0	0
1996–97	Huddersfield T (loan)	2	0
1997–98	Bristol C	5	0
1997–98	Exeter C (loan)	10	1
1998–99	Bristol C	0	0
Total:		**38**	**2**

TOD, Andrew — Defender

H: 6 3 W: 12 00 b.Dunfermline 4-11-71

Source: Kelty Hearts.

1993–94	Dunfermline Ath	22	11
1994–95	Dunfermline Ath	35	6
1995–96	Dunfermline Ath	36	5
1996–97	Dunfermline Ath	35	4
1997–98	Dunfermline Ath	35	6
1998–99	Dunfermline Ath	25	1
Total:		**188**	**33**

TODD, Andrew — Midfield

H: 6 0 W: 11 03 b.Nottingham 22-2-79

Source: Eastwood T.

1995–96	Nottingham F	0	0
1996–97	Nottingham F	0	0
1997–98	Nottingham F	0	0
1998–99	Nottingham F	0	0
1998–99	Scarborough	1	0
Total:		**1**	**0**

TODD, Andy — Defender

H: 5 10 W: 10 11 b.Derby 21-9-74

Source: Trainee.

1991–92	Middlesbrough	0	0
1992–93	Middlesbrough	0	0
1993–94	Middlesbrough	3	0
1994–95	Middlesbrough	5	0
1994–95	Swindon T (loan)	13	0
1995–96	Bolton W	12	2
1996–97	Bolton W	15	0
1997–98	Bolton W	25	0
1998–99	Bolton W	20	0
Total:		**93**	**2**

TODD, Lee — Defender

H: 5 7 W: 11 01 b.Hartlepool 7-3-72

Source: Hartlepool U Trainee.

1990–91	Stockport Co	14	0
1991–92	Stockport Co	19	0
1992–93	Stockport Co	39	0
1993–94	Stockport Co	33	0
1994–95	Stockport Co	37	2
1995–96	Stockport Co	42	0
1996–97	Stockport Co	41	0
1997–98	Southampton	10	0
1998–99	Bradford C	15	0
Total:		**250**	**2**

TOLSON, Neil — Forward

H: 6 3 W: 11 05 b.Wordley 25-10-73

Source: Trainee.

1991–92	Walsall	9	1
1991–92	Oldham Ath	0	0
1992–93	Oldham Ath	3	0
1993–94	Oldham Ath	0	0
1993–94	Bradford C	22	2
1994–95	Bradford C	10	2
1994–95	Chester C (loan)	4	0
1995–96	Bradford C	31	8
1996–97	York C	40	12
1997–98	York C	16	3
1998–99	York C	28	3
Total:		**163**	**31**

TOMASSON, Jon Dahl — Forward

H: 6 0 W: 11 02 b.Copenhagen 29-8-76

Source: Koge. *Honours:* Denmark 4 full caps.

1994–95	Heerenveen	16	5
1995–96	Heerenveen	30	14
1996–97	Heerenveen	32	18
1997–98	Newcastle U	23	3
1998–99	Newcastle U	0	0
Total:		**101**	**40**

TOMLINSON, Graeme — Forward

H: 5 10 W: 12 04 b.Watford 10-12-75

Source: Trainee.

1993–94	Bradford C	17	6
1994–95	Manchester U	0	0
1995–96	Manchester U	0	0
1995–96	Luton T (loan)	7	0
1996–97	Manchester U	0	0
1997–98	Manchester U	0	0
1997–98	Bournemouth (loan)	7	1
1997–98	Millwall (loan)	3	1
1998–99	Macclesfield T	28	4
Total:		**62**	**12**

TOMS, Frazer — Midfield

H: 6 1 W: 11 00 b.Ealing 13-9-79

Source: Trainee.

1998–99	Charlton Ath	0	0

TOPLEY, Jonathan — Forward

b.Craigavon 12-7-80

Source: Trainee.

1997–98	Blackburn R	0	0
1998–99	Blackburn R	0	0

TORPEY, Steve — Forward

H: 6 3 W: 13 06 b.Islington 8-12-70

Source: Trainee.

1988–89	Millwall	0	0
1989–90	Millwall	7	0
1990–91	Millwall	0	0
1990–91	Bradford C	29	7
1991–92	Bradford C	43	10
1992–93	Bradford C	24	5
1993–94	Swansea C	40	9
1994–95	Swansea C	41	11
1995–96	Swansea C	42	15
1996–97	Swansea C	39	9
1997–98	Bristol C	29	8
1998–99	Bristol C	21	4
1998–99	Notts Co (loan)	6	1
Total:		**321**	**79**

TORPEY, Steve — Midfield

b.Fazackerley 16-9-81

Source: Trainee. *Honours:* England Youth.

1998–99	Liverpool	0	0

TOSH, Paul — Forward

H: 6 0 W: 11 10 b.Arbroath 18-10-73

Source: Arbroath Lads.

1991–92	Arbroath	8	1
1992–93	Arbroath	34	12
1993–94	Dundee	26	1
1994–95	Dundee	27	5
1995–96	Dundee	30	9
1996–97	Dundee	23	4
1996–97	Hibernian	6	1
1997–98	Hibernain	15	1
1998–99	Hibernain	1	0
1998–99	Exeter C (loan)	10	2
Total:		**180**	**36**

TOWN, David — Forward

H: 5 7 W: 11 13 b.Bournemouth 9-12-76

Source: Trainee.

1993–94	Bournemouth	1	0
1994–95	Bournemouth	5	0
1995–96	Bournemouth	7	0
1996–97	Bournemouth	26	2
1997–98	Bournemouth	7	0
1998–99	Bournemouth	10	0
Total:		**56**	**2**

TOWNLEY, Leon — Defender

H: 6 2 W: 13 06 b.Loughton 16-2-76

Source: Trainee.

1994–95	Tottenham H	0	0
1995–96	Tottenham H	0	0
1996–97	Tottenham H	0	0
1997–98	Tottenham H	0	0
1997–98	Brentford	16	2
1998–99	Brentford	0	0
Total:		**16**	**2**

TOWNSEND, Andy — Midfield

H: 6 0 W: 13 05 b.Maidstone 27-7-63

Source: Welling U, Weymouth. *Honours:* Eire B, 70 full caps, 7 goals.

1984–85	Southampton	5	0
1985–86	Southampton	27	1
1986–87	Southampton	14	1
1987–88	Southampton	37	3
1988–89	Norwich C	36	5
1989–90	Norwich C	35	3
1990–91	Chelsea	34	2
1991–92	Chelsea	35	6
1992–93	Chelsea	41	4
1993–94	Aston Villa	32	3
1994–95	Aston Villa	32	1
1995–96	Aston Villa	33	2
1996–97	Aston Villa	34	2
1997–98	Aston Villa	3	0
1997–98	Middlesbrough	37	2
1998–99	Middlesbrough	35	1
Total:		**470**	**36**

TRACEY, Richard — Forward

H: 5 11 W: 12 04 b.Muirfield 9-7-79

Source: Trainee.

1997–98	Sheffield U	0	0
1997–98	Rotherham U	0	0
1998–99	Rotherham U	3	0
1998–99	Carlisle U	11	3
Total:		**14**	**3**

TRACEY, Simon — Goalkeeper

H: 6 0 W: 13 12 b.Woolwich 9-12-67

Source: Apprentice.

1985–86	Wimbledon	0	0
1986–87	Wimbledon	0	0
1987–88	Wimbledon	0	0
1988–89	Wimbledon	1	0
1988–89	Sheffield U	7	0
1989–90	Sheffield U	46	0
1990–91	Sheffield U	31	0
1991–92	Sheffield U	29	0

1992–93	Sheffield U	10	0
1993–94	Sheffield U	15	0
1994–95	Sheffield U	5	0
1994–95	Manchester C (loan)	3	0
1994–95	Norwich C (loan)	1	0
1995–96	Sheffield U	11	0
1995–96	Wimbledon (loan)	1	0
1996–97	Sheffield U	7	0
1997–98	Sheffield U	27	0
1998–99	Sheffield U	18	0
Total:		**212**	**0**

TRAMEZZANI, Paolo — Defender

H: 6 1 W: 13 06 b.Reggio-Emilia 30-7-70

1989–90	Internazionale	0	0
1989–90	Prato	29	0
1990–91	Cosenza	15	0
1991–92	Lucchese	30	1
1992–93	Internazionale	13	0
1993–94	Internazionale	13	0
1994–95	Internazionale	0	0
1994–95	Venezia	15	0
1995–96	Venezia	10	0
1995–96	Cesena	19	2
1996–97	Piacenza	25	1
1997–98	Piacenza	32	1
1998–99	Tottenham H	6	0
Total:		**207**	**5**

TRANTER, Carl — Midfield

b.Sandwell 4-10-78

Source: Trainee.

1997–98	WBA	0	0
1998–99	WBA	0	0

TRAORE, Djimi — Defender

H: 6 3 W: 13 10 b.Saint Ouen 1-3-80

Source: Laval.

1998–99	Liverpool	0	0

TRAVIS, Simon — Defender

H: 5 7 W: 10 00 b.Preston 22-3-77

Source: Trainee.

1995–96	Torquay U	8	0
1996–97	Torquay U	0	0
From Holywell T.			
1997–98	Stockport Co	13	2
1998–99	Stockport Co	9	0
Total:		**30**	**2**

TREES, Robert — Midfield

H: 5 10 W: 12 07 b.Manchester 18-12-77

Source: Trainee.

1996–97	Manchester U	0	0
From Witton Alb.			
1998–99	Bristol R	36	0
Total:		**36**	**0**

TRETTON, Andrew — Defender

H: 6 0 W: 12 08 b.Derby 9-10-76

Source: Trainee.

1993–94	Derby Co	0	0
1994–95	Derby Co	0	0
1995–96	Derby Co	0	0
1996–97	Derby Co	0	0
1997–98	Chesterfield	0	0
1997–98	Shrewsbury T	14	1
1998–99	Shrewsbury T	23	0
Total:		**37**	**1**

TREVOR, Kris — Forward

H: 5 9 W: 11 08 b.South Shields 15-5-79

Source: Trainee.

1997–98	Middlesbrough	0	0
1998–99	Middlesbrough	0	0

TROLLOPE, Paul — Midfield

H: 6 0 W: 12 01 b.Swindon 3-6-72

Source: Trainee. *Honours:* Wales 5 full caps.

1989–90	Swindon T	0	0
1990–91	Swindon T	0	0
1991–92	Swindon T	0	0
1991–92	Torquay U (loan)	10	0
1992–93	Torquay U	36	2
1993–94	Torquay U	42	10
1994–95	Torquay U	18	4
1994–95	Derby Co	24	4
1995–96	Derby Co	17	0
1996–97	Derby Co	14	1
1996–97	Grimsby T (loan)	7	1
1996–97	Crystal Palace (loan)	9	0
1997–98	Derby Co	10	0
1997–98	Fulham	24	3
1998–99	Fulham	20	2
Total:		**231**	**27**

TROUGHT, Michael — Defender

H: 6 2 W: 14 03 b.Bristol 19-10-80

Source: Trainee.

1998–99	Bristol R	9	0
Total:		**9**	**0**

TRUEMAN, Kevin — Forward

H: 5 6 W: 10 11 b.Downpatrick 8-8-79

Source: Trainee.

1998–99	Bolton W	0	0

TSKHADADZE, Kakhabor — Defender

H: 6 1 W: 12 04 b.Rustavi 7-9-68

Honours: Georgia 25 full caps, 1 goal.

1988	Dynamo Tbilisi	14	1
1989	Dynamo Tbilisi	27	0
1990	Sundsvall*	0	0
1991	Sundsvall	4	0
1992	Spartak Moscow	7	0
1992–93	Eintracht Frankfurt	17	0
1993–94	Eintracht Frankfurt	29	0
1994–95	Eintracht Frankfurt	15	1
1995–96	Eintracht Frankfurt	3	0
1996–97	Eintracht Frankfurt*	0	0
1997	Alania	17	1
1997–98	Manchester C	10	1
1998–99	Manchester C	2	1
Total:		**145**	**5**

TUCK, Stuart — Defender

H: 5 10 W: 11 10 b.Brighton 1-10-74

Source: Trainee.

1993–94	Brighton & HA	11	0
1994–95	Brighton & HA	23	0
1995–96	Brighton & HA	8	0
1996–97	Brighton & HA	27	0
1997–98	Brighton & HA	22	1
1998–99	Brighton & HA	2	0
Total:		**93**	**1**

TUCKER, Dexter — Forward

H: 6 1 W: 12 02 b.Pontefract 22-9-79

Source: Trainee.

1997–98	Hull C	7	0
1998–99	Hull C	0	0
Total:		**7**	**0**

TULLY, Stephen — Midfield

H: 5 7 W: 10 04 b.Paignton 10-2-80

Source: Trainee.

1997–98	Torquay U	9	0
1998–99	Torquay U	37	2
Total:		**46**	**2**

TURKINGTON, Eddie — Midfield

H: 6 1 W: 13 00 b.Merseyside 15-5-78

Source: Trainee.

1995–96	Liverpool	0	0
1996–97	Liverpool	0	0
1997–98	Liverpool	0	0
1998–99	Stockport Co	0	0

TURLEY, Billy — Goalkeeper

H: 6 4 W: 14 10 b.Wolverhampton 15-7-73

Source: Evesham U.

1995–96	Northampton T	2	0
1996–97	Northampton T	1	0
1997–98	Northampton T	0	0
1997–98	Leyton Orient (loan)	14	0
1998–99	Northampton T	25	0
Total:		**42**	**0**

TURNER, Andy — Forward

H: 5 10 W: 11 10 b.Woolwich 23-3-75

Source: Trainee. *Honours:* England Schools, Eire Under-21.

1991–92	Tottenham H	0	0
1992–93	Tottenham H	18	3
1993–94	Tottenham H	1	0
1994–95	Tottenham H	1	0
1994–95	Wycombe W (loan)	4	0
1994–95	Doncaster R (loan)	4	1
1995–96	Tottenham H	0	0
1995–96	Huddersfield T (loan)	5	1
1995–96	Southend U (loan)	6	0
1996–97	Tottenham H	0	0
1996–97	Portsmouth	24	2
1997–98	Portsmouth	16	1
1998–99	Portsmouth	0	0
1998–99	Crystal Palace	2	0
1998–99	Wolverhampton W	0	0
Total:		**81**	**8**

TURNER, John — Goalkeeper

H: 6 1 W: 12 05 b.Pontypool 9-9-80

Source: Trainee.

1998–99	Charlton Ath	0	0

TURNER, Matthew — Forward

H: 5 9 W: 10 00 b.Nottingham 29-12-81

Source: Trainee. *Honours:* England Youth.

1998–99	Nottingham F	0	0

TURNER, Mike — Forward

H: 6 2 W: 13 03 b.Stoke 2-4-76

Source: Bilston T.

1998–99	Barnsley	13	1
Total:		**13**	**1**

TUTILL, Steve — Defender

H: 5 10 W: 12 06 b.Derwent 1-10-69

Source: Trainee. *Honours:* England Schools.

1987–88	York C	21	0
1988–89	York C	22	1
1989–90	York C	42	0
1990–91	York C	42	0
1991–92	York C	39	1
1992–93	York C	8	0
1993–94	York C	46	4
1994–95	York C	39	0
1995–96	York C	25	0
1996–97	York C	15	0
1997–98	York C	2	0
1997–98	Darlington	7	0
1998–99	Darlington	36	0
Total:		**344**	**6**

TUTTLE, David — Defender

H: 6 2 W: 12 10 b.Reading 6-2-72

Source: Trainee. *Honours:* England Youth.

1989–90	Tottenham H	0	0
1990–91	Tottenham H	6	0
1991–92	Tottenham H	2	0
1992–93	Tottenham H	5	0
1992–93	Peterborough U (loan)	7	0
1993–94	Sheffield U	31	0
1994–95	Sheffield U	6	0
1995–96	Sheffield U	26	1
1995–96	Crystal Palace	10	1
1996–97	Crystal Palace	39	2
1997–98	Crystal Palace	9	0
1998–99	Crystal Palace	22	2
Total:		**163**	**6**

TWEED, Steven — Defender

H: 6 3 W: 13 02 b.Edinburgh 8-8-72

Source: Hutchison Vale. *Honours:* Scotland Under-21.

1991–92	Hibernian	1	0
1992–93	Hibernian	14	0
1993–94	Hibernian	29	3
1994–95	Hibernian	33	0
1995–96	Hibernian	31	0
1996–97	Ionikos	2	0
1997–98	Stoke C	38	0
1998–99	Stoke C	1	0
1998–99	Dundee	10	1
Total:		**159**	**4**

TWISS, Michael — Midfield

H: 5 11 W: 12 00 b.Salford 18-12-77

Source: Trainee.

1996–97	Manchester U	0	0
1997–98	Manchester U	0	0
1998–99	Sheffield U (loan)	12	1
Total:		**12**	**1**

TYLER, Mark — Goalkeeper

H: 5 11 W: 12 00 b.Norwich 2-4-77

Source: Trainee. *Honours:* England Youth.

1994–95	Peterborough U	5	0
1995–96	Peterborough U	0	0
1996–97	Peterborough U	3	0
1997–98	Peterborough U	46	0
1998–99	Peterborough U	27	0
Total:		**81**	**0**

TYNAN, Robert — Midfield

H: 5 9 W: 11 00 b.Birkenhead 13-1-78

Source: Trainee.

1996–97	Everton	0	0
1997–98	Everton	0	0
1998–99	Everton	0	0

TYNE, Thomas — Forward

b.Lambeth 2-3-81

1998–99	Millwall	0	0

UHLENBEEK, Gus — Midfield

H: 5 10 W: 12 06 b.Paramaribo 20-8-70

1990–91	Ajax	2	0
1991–92	Ajax	0	0
1992–93	Cambuur	24	0
1993–94	Cambuur	15	0
1994–95	TOPS SV	22	3
1995–96	Ipswich T	40	4
1996–97	Ipswich T	38	0
1997–98	Ipswich T	11	0
1998–99	Fulham	23	1
Total:		**175**	**8**

ULLATHORNE, Robert — Defender

H: 5 8 W: 10 10 b.Wakefield 11-10-71

Source: Trainee.

1989–90	Norwich C	0	0
1990–91	Norwich C	2	0
1991–92	Norwich C	20	3

1992–93	Norwich C	0	0
1993–94	Norwich C	16	2
1994–95	Norwich C	27	2
1995–96	Norwich C	29	0
1996–97	Osasuna	18	0
1996–97	Leicester C	0	0
1997–98	Leicester C	6	1
1998–99	Leicester C	25	0
Total:		**143**	**8**

UNGER, Lars — Midfield

H: 6 2 W: 13 09 b.Eutin 30-9-72

1998–99	Southend U	14	0
Total:		**14**	**0**

UNSWORTH, Dave — Defender

H: 6 0 W: 15 00 b.Chorley 16-10-73

Source: Trainee. *Honours:* England Youth, Under-21, 1 full cap.

1991–92	Everton	2	1
1992–93	Everton	3	0
1993–94	Everton	8	0
1994–95	Everton	38	3
1995–96	Everton	31	2
1996–97	Everton	34	5
1997–98	West Ham U	32	2
1998–99	Aston Villa	0	0
1998–99	Everton	34	1
Total:		**182**	**14**

UNSWORTH, Lee — Defender

H: 5 11 W: 11 02 b.Eccles 25-2-73

Source: Ashton U.

1994–95	Crewe Alex	0	0
1995–96	Crewe Alex	29	0
1996–97	Crewe Alex	29	0
1997–98	Crewe Alex	36	0
1998–99	Crewe Alex	24	0
Total:		**118**	**0**

UPSON, Matthew — Defender

H: 6 1 W: 11 05 b.Eye 18-4-79

Source: Trainee. *Honours:* England Youth, Under-21.

1995–96	Luton T	0	0
1996–97	Luton T	1	0
1996–97	Arsenal	0	0
1997–98	Arsenal	5	0
1998–99	Arsenal	5	0
Total:		**11**	**0**

VAESEN, Nico — Goalkeeper

H: 6 4 W: 13 01 b.Hasselt 28-9-69

Source: Tongeren.

1993–94	CS Brugge	13	0
1994–95	CS Brugge	3	0
1995–96	Aalst	20	0
1996–97	Aalst	0	0
1997–98	Aalst	14	0
1998–99	Huddersfield T	43	0
Total:		**93**	**0**

VALAKARI, Simo — Midfield

H: 5 10 W: 11 11 b.Helsinki 28-4-73

Honours: Finland 3 full caps.

1995	Finn PA	22	3
1996	Finn PA	26	2
1996–97	Motherwell	11	0
1997–98	Motherwell	28	0
1998–99	Motherwell	35	0
Total:		**122**	**5**

VALERIANI, Jose — Midfield

b. 0-0-0

1998–99	Dundee U	1	0
Total:		**1**	**0**

VALERY, Patrick — Defender

H: 5 8 W: 13 04 b.Brignoles 3-7-69

Source: AS Brignoles.

1988–89	Monaco	28	0
1989–90	Monaco	19	0
1990–91	Monaco	32	0
1991–92	Monaco	14	0
1992–93	Monaco	29	0
1993–94	Monaco	32	0
1994–95	Monaco	23	0
1995–96	Monaco	3	0
1996–97	Monaco	30	0
1997–98	Blackburn R	15	0
1998–99	Blackburn R	0	0
Total:		**225**	**0**

VAN BLERK, Jason — Defender

H: 6 1 W: 13 00 b.Sydney 16-3-68

Source: Go Ahead. *Honours:* Australia full caps.

1994–95	Millwall	27	1
1995–96	Millwall	42	1
1996–97	Millwall	4	0
1997–98	Manchester C	19	0
1997–98	WBA	8	0
1998–99	WBA	30	0
Total:		**130**	**2**

VAN BRONCKHORST, Giovanni
Midfield

H: 5 10 W: 11 10 b.Rotterdam 5-2-75

Source: LMO, SC Feyenoord. *Honours:* Holland 8 full caps, 1 goal.

1993–94	Feyenoord	0	0
1993–94	RKC	12	2
1994–95	Feyenoord	10	1
1995–96	Feyenoord	27	9
1996–97	Feyenoord	34	4
1997–98	Feyenoord	32	8
1998–99	Rangers	35	7
Total:		**150**	**31**

VAN HEUSDEN, Arjan
Goalkeeper

H: 6 4 W: 14 07 b.Alphen 11-12-72

Source: Noordwijk.

1994–95	Port Vale	2	0
1995–96	Port Vale	7	0
1996–97	Port Vale	13	0
1997–98	Port Vale	5	0
1997–98	Oxford U (loan)	11	0
1998–99	Cambridge U	27	0
Total:		**65**	**0**

VAN HOOIJDONK, Pierre
Forward

H: 6 4 W: 13 07 b.Steenbergen 29-11-69

Source: NAC Breda. *Honours:* Holland Under-21, 16 full caps, 7 goals.

1989–90	RBC	32	6
1990–91	RBC	37	27
1991–92	NAC	35	20
1992–93	NAC	33	26
1993–94	NAC	31	25
1994–95	Celtic	14	4
1995–96	Celtic	34	26
1996–97	Celtic	21	14
1996–97	Nottingham F	8	1
1997–98	Nottingham F	42	29
1998–99	Nottingham F	21	6
Total:		**308**	**184**

VAN DER GOUW, Raimond
Goalkeeper

H: 6 3 W: 13 07 b.Oldenzaal 24-3-63

1985–86	Go Ahead	28	0
1986–87	Go Ahead	34	0
1987–88	Go Ahead	35	0
1988–89	Vitesse	36	0
1989–90	Vitesse	34	0
1990–91	Vitesse	31	0
1991–92	Vitesse	34	0
1992–93	Vitesse	34	0
1993–94	Vitesse	34	0
1994–95	Vitesse	34	0
1995–96	Vitesse	21	0
1996–97	Manchester U	2	0
1997–98	Manchester U	5	0
1998–99	Manchester U	5	0
Total:		**367**	**0**

VAN DER KWAAK, Peter
Goalkeeper

H: 6 4 W: 13 12 b.Haarlem 12-10-68

Source: EDO, RCH, Stormvogels, Ajax.

1994–95	Dordrecht	2	0
1995–96	Dordrecht	19	0
1996–97	Dordrecht	29	0
1998–99	Reading	3	0
Total:		**53**	**0**

VAN DER LAAN, Robin
Midfield

H: 5 11 W: 13 08 b.Schiedam 5-9-68

Source: Wageningen.

1990–91	Port Vale	18	4
1991–92	Port Vale	43	5
1992–93	Port Vale	38	6
1993–94	Port Vale	33	4
1994–95	Port Vale	44	5
1995–96	Derby Co	39	6
1996–97	Derby Co	16	2
1996–97	Wolverhampton W (loan)	7	0
1997–98	Derby Co	10	0
1998–99	Barnsley	17	1
Total:		**265**	**33**

VAREILLE, Jerome
Forward

H: 5 11 W: 12 12 b.Vernoux 1-6-74

Source: Mulhouse.

1997–98	Kilmarnock	34	4
1998–99	Kilmarnock	23	5
Total:		**57**	**9**

VARTY, Will
Defender

H: 6 0 W: 12 00 b.Workington 1-10-76

Source: Trainee.

1995–96	Carlisle U	0	0
1996–97	Carlisle U	32	0
1997–98	Carlisle U	44	1
1998–99	Carlisle U	6	0
1998–99	Rotherham U (loan)	14	0
Total:		**96**	**1**

VASSELL, Darius — Forward

H: 5 7 W: 12 00 b.Birmingham 13-6-80

Source: Trainee. *Honours:* England Youth, Under-21.

1998–99	Aston Villa	6	0
Total:		**6**	**0**

VAUGHAN, Francis — Midfield

H: 5 10 W: 11 00 b.Salford 8-9-79

Source: Trainee.

1997–98	Stockport Co	0	0
1998–99	Stockport Co	0	0

VAUGHAN, John — Goalkeeper

H: 5 10 W: 13 01 b.Isleworth 26-6-64

Source: Apprentice.

1981–82	West Ham U	0	0
1982–83	West Ham U	0	0
1983–84	West Ham U	0	0
1984–85	West Ham U	0	0
1984–85	Charlton Ath (loan)	6	0
1985–86	West Ham U	0	0
1985–86	Bristol R (loan)	6	0
1985–86	Wrexham (loan)	4	0
1985–86	Bristol C (loan)	2	0
1986–87	Fulham	44	0
1987–88	Fulham	0	0
1987–88	Bristol C (loan)	3	0
1988–89	Cambridge U	29	0
1989–90	Cambridge U	46	0
1990–91	Cambridge U	43	0
1991–92	Cambridge U	33	0
1992–93	Cambridge U	27	0
1993–94	Charlton Ath	6	0
1994–95	Preston NE	26	0
1995–96	Preston NE	40	0
1996–97	Lincoln C	10	0
1996–97	Colchester U (loan)	5	0
1997–98	Lincoln C	19	0
1998–99	Lincoln C	31	0
Total:		**380**	**0**

VAUGHAN, Tony — Defender

H: 6 1 W: 12 10 b.Manchester 11-10-75

Source: Trainee. *Honours:* England Schools.

1994–95	Ipswich T	10	0
1995–96	Ipswich T	25	1
1996–97	Ipswich T	32	2
1997–98	Manchester C	19	1
1998–99	Manchester C	38	1
Total:		**124**	**5**

VAUGHAN, Wayne — Midfield

b.Barking 18-2-80

Source: Trainee.

1997–98	Tottenham H	0	0
1998–99	Tottenham H	0	0

VEART, Carl — Midfield

H: 5 10 W: 11 05 b.Whyalla 21-5-70

Source: Adelaide C. *Honours:* Australia full caps.

1994–95	Sheffield U	39	10
1995–96	Sheffield U	27	5
1995–96	Crystal Palace	12	0
1996–97	Crystal Palace	39	6
1997–98	Crystal Palace	6	0
1997–98	Millwall	8	1
1998–99	Millwall	0	0
Total:		**131**	**22**

VEGA, Ramon — Defender

H: 6 3 W: 13 00 b.Olten 14-6-71

Source: Trimbach. *Honours:* Switzerland 21 full caps, 2 goals.

1990–91	Grasshoppers	3	0
1991–92	Grasshoppers	34	2
1992–93	Grasshoppers	20	2
1993–94	Grasshoppers	36	2
1994–95	Grasshoppers	33	3
1995–96	Grasshoppers	30	4
1996–97	Cagliari	14	0
1996–97	Tottenham H	8	1
1997–98	Tottenham H	25	3
1998–99	Tottenham H	16	2
Total:		**219**	**19**

VELLA, Simon — Defender

H: 6 2 W: 11 11 b.Westminster 19-9-79

Source: Trainee.

1998–99	Wimbledon	0	0

VENUS, Mark — Defender

H: 6 1 W: 12 12 b.Hartlepool 6-4-67

1984–85	Hartlepool U	4	0
1985–86	Leicester C	1	0
1986–87	Leicester C	39	0
1987–88	Leicester C	21	1
1987–88	Wolverhampton W	4	0
1988–89	Wolverhampton W	35	0
1989–90	Wolverhampton W	44	2
1990–91	Wolverhampton W	6	0
1991–92	Wolverhampton W	46	1
1992–93	Wolverhampton W	12	0
1993–94	Wolverhampton W	39	1
1994–95	Wolverhampton W	39	3

1995–96	Wolverhampton W	22	0
1996–97	Wolverhampton W	40	0
1997–98	Ipswich T	14	1
1998–99	Ipswich T	44	9
Total:		**410**	**18**

VERITY, Daniel — Defender

H: 5 11 W: 10 12 b.Bradford 19-4-80

Source: Trainee.

1997–98	Bradford C	1	0
1998–99	Bradford C	0	0
Total:		**1**	**0**

VERNAZZA, Paulo — Midfield

b.Islington 1-11-79

Source: Trainee. *Honours:* England Youth.

1997–98	Arsenal	1	0
1998–99	Arsenal	0	0
1998–99	Ipswich T (loan)	2	0
Total:		**3**	**0**

VEYSEY, Kenneth — Goalkeeper

H: 5 11 W: 12 07 b.Hackney 8-6-67

1987–88	Torquay U	0	0
1988–89	Torquay U	25	0
1989–90	Torquay U	46	0
1990–91	Torquay U	1	0
1990–91	Oxford U	25	0
1991–92	Oxford U	32	0
1992–93	Oxford U	0	0
1992–93	Sheffield U (loan)	0	0
1993–94	Exeter C	12	0
From Dorchester T.			
1997–98	Torquay U	27	0
1998–99	Torquay U	10	0
Total:		**178**	**0**

VIALLI, Gianluca — Forward

H: 5 10 W: 13 06 b.Cremona 9-7-64

Honours: Italy Youth, Under-21, 59 full caps, 16 goals.

1980–81	Cremonese	2	0
1981–82	Cremonese	31	5
1982–83	Cremonese	35	8
1983–84	Cremonese	37	10
1984–85	Sampdoria	28	3
1985–86	Sampdoria	28	6
1986–87	Sampdoria	28	12
1987–88	Sampdoria	30	10
1988–89	Sampdoria	30	14
1989–90	Sampdoria	22	10
1990–91	Sampdoria	26	19
1991–92	Sampdoria	31	11
1992–93	Juventus	32	6
1993–94	Juventus	10	4
1994–95	Juventus	30	17
1995–96	Juventus	30	11
1996–97	Chelsea	28	9
1997–98	Chelsea	21	11
1998–99	Chelsea	9	1
Total:		**488**	**167**

VICKERS, Ashley — Defender

H: 6 3 W: 13 10 b.Sheffield 14-6-72

Source: Heybridge S.

1997–98	Peterborough U	1	0
1998–99	Peterborough U	0	0
Total:		**1**	**0**

VICKERS, Steve — Defender

H: 6 2 W: 13 01 b.Bishop Auckland 13-10-67

Source: Spennymoor U.

1985–86	Tranmere R	3	0
1986–87	Tranmere R	36	2
1987–88	Tranmere R	46	1
1988–89	Tranmere R	46	3
1989–90	Tranmere R	42	3
1990–91	Tranmere R	42	1
1991–92	Tranmere R	43	1
1992–93	Tranmere R	42	0
1993–94	Tranmere R	11	0
1993–94	Middlesbrough	26	3
1994–95	Middlesbrough	44	3
1995–96	Middlesbrough	32	1
1996–97	Middlesbrough	29	0
1997–98	Middlesbrough	33	0
1998–99	Middlesbrough	31	1
Total:		**506**	**19**

VIDMAR, Tony — Defender

H: 6 1 W: 12 13 b.Adelaide 4-7-70

Source: Adelaide C. *Honours:* Australia full caps.

1992–93	Ekeren	9	1
From Adelaide C			
1995–96	NAC	30	2
1996–97	NAC	31	2
1997–97	Rangers	12	0
1998–99	Rangers	28	1
Total:		**110**	**6**

VIDUKA, Marko — Forward

H: 6 2 W: 13 09 b.Australia 9-10-75

Source: Croatia Zagreb. *Honours:* Australia full caps.

1998–99	Celtic	9	5
Total:		**9**	**5**

VIEIRA, Patrick — Midfield

H: 6 4 W: 13 00 b.Dakar 23-6-76

Honours: France Under-21, 14 full caps.

1993–94	Cannes	5	0
1994–95	Cannes	31	2
1995–96	Cannes	13	0
1995–96	AC Milan	2	0
1996–97	Arsenal	31	2
1997–98	Arsenal	33	2
1998–99	Arsenal	34	3
Total:		**149**	**9**

VINCENT, Jamie — Defender

H: 5 10 W: 11 09 b.London 18-6-75

Source: Trainee.

1993–94	Crystal Palace	0	0
1994–95	Crystal Palace	0	0
1994–95	Bournemouth (loan)	8	0
1995–96	Crystal Palace	25	0
1996–97	Crystal Palace	0	0
1996–97	Bournemouth	29	0
1997–98	Bournemouth	44	3
1998–99	Bournemouth	32	2
1998–99	Huddersfield T	7	0
Total:		**145**	**5**

VINDHEIM, Rune — Defender

H: 5 11 W: 12 04 b.Hoyancuer 18-5-72

1998–99	Burnley	8	2
Total:		**8**	**2**

VINNICOMBE, Chris — Defender

H: 5 8 W: 10 12 b.Exeter 20-10-70

Honours: England Under-21.

1988–89	Exeter C	25	0
1989–90	Exeter C	14	1
1989–90	Rangers	7	0
1990–91	Rangers	10	1
1991–92	Rangers	2	0
1992–93	Rangers	0	0
1993–94	Rangers	4	0
1994–95	Burnley	29	1
1995–96	Burnley	35	2
1996–97	Burnley	8	0
1997–98	Burnley	23	0
1998–99	Wycombe W	41	0
Total:		**198**	**5**

VINNICOMBE, Luke — Defender

H: 6 1 W: 11 07 b.Paignton 7-3-80

Source: Trainee.

1998–99	Exeter C	0	0

VIVAS, Nelson — Defender

b.San Nicolas 18-10-69

Source: Quilmes, Boca Juniors, Lugano. *Honours:* Argentina 16 full caps, 1 goal.

1998–99	Arsenal	23	0
Total:		**23**	**0**

VIVEASH, Adrian — Defender

H: 6 1 W: 13 05 b.Swindon 30-9-69

Source: Trainee.

1988–89	Swindon T	0	0
1989–90	Swindon T	0	0
1990–91	Swindon T	25	1
1991–92	Swindon T	10	0
1992–93	Swindon T	5	0
1992–93	Reading (loan)	5	0
1993–94	Swindon T	0	0
1994–95	Swindon T	14	1
1994–95	Reading (loan)	6	0
1995–96	Swindon T	0	0
1995–96	Barnsley (loan)	2	1
1995–96	Walsall	31	0
1996–97	Walsall	46	9
1997–98	Walsall	42	3
1998–99	Walsall	40	0
Total:		**226**	**15**

VLACHOS, Michalis — Defender

H: 5 11 W: 12 08 b.Athens 20-9-67

Honours: Greece 10 full caps.

1988–89	Apollon	22	4
1989–90	Apollon	29	6
1990–91	Apollon	29	0
1991–92	Olympiakos	27	1
1992–93	Olympiakos	20	1
1993–94	AEK Athens	26	1
1994–95	AEK Athens	20	1
1995–96	AEK Athens	24	0
1996–97	AEK Athens	25	1
1997–98	AEK Athens	10	0
1997–98	Portsmouth	15	0
1998–99	Portsmouth	30	0
Total:		**277**	**15**

VONK, Michael — Defender

H: 6 3 W: 13 03 b.Alkmaar 28-10-68

1986–87	AZ	19	3

1987–88	AZ	25	1
1988–89	AZ	35	4
1989–90	AZ	33	0
1990–91	SVV/Dordrecht	29	1
1991–92	Manchester C	9	0
1992–93	Manchester C	26	2
1993–94	Manchester C	35	1
1994–95	Manchester C	21	0
1995–96	Manchester C	0	0
1995–96	Oldham Ath (loan)	5	1
1995–96	Sheffield U	17	0
1996–97	Sheffield U	17	2
1997–98	Sheffield U	3	0
1998–99	Sheffield U	0	0
Total:		**274**	**15**

WADDLE, Chris — Midfield

H: 6 0 W: 13 07 b.Hedworth 14-12-60

Source: Tow Law T. *Honours:* England Under-21, 62 full caps, 6 goals. Football League.

1980–81	Newcastle U	13	1
1981–82	Newcastle U	42	7
1982–83	Newcastle U	37	7
1983–84	Newcastle U	42	18
1984–85	Newcastle U	36	13
1985–86	Tottenham H	39	11
1986–87	Tottenham H	39	6
1987–88	Tottenham H	22	2
1988–89	Tottenham H	38	14
1989–90	Marseille	37	9
1990–91	Marseille	35	6
1991–92	Marseille	35	7
1992–93	Sheffield W	33	1
1993–94	Sheffield W	19	3
1994–95	Sheffield W	25	4
1995–96	Sheffield W	32	2
1996–97	Sheffield W	0	0
1996–97	Falkirk	4	1
1996–97	Bradford C	25	5
1996–97	Sunderland	7	1
1997–98	Burnley	31	1
1998–99	Torquay U	7	0
Total:		**598**	**119**

WAINWRIGHT, Jody — Goalkeeper

H: 6 1 W: 14 07 b.Dewsbury 22-2-80

Source: Trainee.

1998–99	Sheffield W	0	0

WAINWRIGHT, Neil — Forward

H: 5 10 W: 10 02 b.Warrington 4-11-77

Source: Trainee.

1996–97	Wrexham	0	0
1997–98	Wrexham	11	3
1998–99	Sunderland	2	0
Total:		**13**	**3**

WALKER, Andrew — Midfield

b.Salford 2-1-81

Source: Trainee.

1998–99	Newcastle U	0	0

WALKER, Andrew — Midfield

b.Eastbourne 20-4-80

1998–99	Brentford	0	0

WALKER, Andy — Forward

H: 5 8 W: 11 05 b.Glasgow 6-4-65

Source: Baillieston Jun. *Honours:* Scotland Under-21, 3 full caps.

1984–85	Motherwell	11	3
1985–86	Motherwell	22	4
1986–87	Motherwell	43	10
1987–88	Celtic	42	16
1988–89	Celtic	22	8
1989–90	Celtic	32	6
1990–91	Celtic	11	0
1991–92	Celtic	1	0
1991–92	Newcastle U (loan)	2	0
1991–92	Bolton W	24	15
1992–93	Bolton W	32	26
1993–94	Bolton W	11	3
1994–95	Celtic	26	6
1995–96	Celtic	16	3
1995–96	Sheffield U	14	8
1996–97	Sheffield U	37	12
1997–98	Sheffield U	1	0
1997–98	Hibernian (loan)	8	3
1997–98	Raith R (loan)	7	2
1998–99	Sheffield U	0	0
Total:		**362**	**125**

WALKER, Andy — Goalkeeper

b.Bexley 30-9-81

1998–99	Colchester U	1	0
Total:		**1**	**0**

WALKER, Des

Defender

H: 5 11 W: 11 12 b.Hackney 26-11-65

Source: Apprentice. *Honours:* England Under-21, 59 full caps.

1983–84	Nottingham F	4	0
1984–85	Nottingham F	3	0
1985–86	Nottingham F	39	0
1986–87	Nottingham F	41	0
1987–88	Nottingham F	35	0
1988–89	Nottingham F	34	0
1989–90	Nottingham F	38	0
1990–91	Nottingham F	37	0
1991–92	Nottingham F	33	1
1992–93	Sampdoria	30	0
1993–94	Sheffield W	42	0
1994–95	Sheffield W	38	0
1995–96	Sheffield W	36	0
1996–97	Sheffield W	36	0
1997–98	Sheffield W	38	0
1998–99	Sheffield W	37	0
Total:		**521**	**1**

WALKER, Ian

Goalkeeper

H: 6 2 W: 13 01 b.Watford 31-10-71

Source: Trainee. *Honours:* England Youth, Under-21, B, 3 full caps.

1989–90	Tottenham H	0	0
1990–91	Tottenham H	1	0
1990–91	Oxford U (loan)	2	0
1990–91	Ipswich T (loan)	0	0
1991–92	Tottenham H	18	0
1992–93	Tottenham H	17	0
1993–94	Tottenham H	11	0
1994–95	Tottenham H	41	0
1995–96	Tottenham H	38	0
1996–97	Tottenham H	37	0
1997–98	Tottenham H	29	0
1998–99	Tottenham H	25	0
Total:		**219**	**0**

WALKER, James

Goalkeeper

H: 5 10 W: 13 01 b.Sutton-in-Ashfield 9-7-73

Source: Trainee.

1991–92	Notts Co	0	0
1992–93	Notts Co	0	0
1993–94	Walsall	31	0
1994–95	Walsall	4	0
1995–96	Walsall	26	0
1996–97	Walsall	36	0
1997–98	Walsall	46	0
1998–99	Walsall	46	0
Total:		**189**	**0**

WALKER, John

Midfield

H: 5 7 W: 11 00 b.Glasgow 12-12-73

Source: Clydebank BC.

1990–91	Rangers	0	0
1991–92	Rangers	0	0
1992–93	Rangers	0	0
1993–94	Clydebank	6	2
1994–95	Clydebank	21	0
1995–96	Clydebank	0	0
1995–96	Grimsby T	2	1
1996–97	Grimsby T	1	0
1996–97	Mansfield T	36	3
1997–98	Mansfield T	1	0
1998–99	Mansfield T	37	1
Total:		**104**	**7**

WALKER, Justin

Midfield

H: 6 0 W: 13 03 b.Nottingham 6-9-75

Source: Trainee. *Honours:* England Schools, Youth.

1992–93	Nottingham F	0	0
1993–94	Nottingham F	0	0
1994–95	Nottingham F	0	0
1995–96	Nottingham F	0	0
1996–97	Nottingham F	0	0
1996–97	Scunthorpe U	9	0
1997–98	Scunthorpe U	40	1
1998–99	Scunthorpe U	41	1
Total:		**90**	**2**

WALKER, Keith

Defender

H: 6 0 W: 12 08 b.Edinburgh 17-4-66

Source: ICI Juveniles.

1984–85	Stirling Albion	38	6
1985–86	Stirling Albion	32	5
1986–87	Stirling Albion	21	6
1987–88	St Mirren	19	3
1988–89	St Mirren	14	1
1989–90	St Mirren	10	2
1989–90	Swansea C	13	0
1990–91	Swansea C	24	0
1991–92	Swansea C	32	1
1992–93	Swansea C	42	2
1993–94	Swansea C	27	2
1994–95	Swansea C	28	0
1995–96	Swansea C	33	0
1996–97	Swansea C	31	1
1997–98	Swansea C	39	3
1998–99	Swansea C	1	0
Total:		**404**	**32**

WALKER, Richard — Forward

H: 6 0 W: 12 04 b.Sutton Coldfield 8-11-77

Source: Trainee.

1995–96	Aston Villa	0	0
1996–97	Aston Villa	0	0
1997–98	Aston Villa	1	0
1998–99	Aston Villa	0	0
1998–99	Cambridge U (loan)	21	3
Total:		**22**	**3**

WALKER, Scott — Midfield

H: 5 8 W: 11 00 b.Exeter 17-3-80

Source: Trainee.

1998–99	Exeter C	0	0

WALKLATE, Steve — Midfield

H: 5 11 W: 12 00 b.Durham 27-9-79

Source: Trainee.

1998–99	Middlesbrough	0	0

WALL, James — Defender

b.Carshalton 21-3-80

Source: Trainee.

1998–99	Derby Co	0	0

WALLACE, Ray — Midfield

H: 5 7 W: 11 05 b.Lewisham 2-10-69

Source: Trainee. *Honours:* England Under-21.

1987–88	Southampton	0	0
1988–89	Southampton	26	0
1989–90	Southampton	9	0
1990–91	Southampton	0	0
1991–92	Leeds U	0	0
1991–92	Swansea C (loan)	2	0
1992–93	Leeds U	6	0
1993–94	Leeds U	1	0
1993–94	Reading (loan)	3	0
1994–95	Stoke C	20	1
1994–95	Hull C (loan)	7	0
1995–96	Stoke C	44	6
1996–97	Stoke C	45	2
1997–98	Stoke C	39	3
1998–99	Stoke C	31	3
Total:		**233**	**15**

WALLACE, Rod — Forward

H: 5 7 W: 11 03 b.Lewisham 2-10-69

Source: Trainee. *Honours:* England Under-21, B.

1987–88	Southampton	15	1
1988–89	Southampton	38	12
1989–90	Southampton	38	18
1990–91	Southampton	37	14
1991–92	Leeds U	34	11
1992–93	Leeds U	32	7
1993–94	Leeds U	37	17
1994–95	Leeds U	32	4
1995–96	Leeds U	24	1
1996–97	Leeds U	22	3
1997–98	Leeds U	31	10
1998–99	Rangers	34	18
Total:		**374**	**116**

WALLEMME, Jean-Guy — Defender

H: 6 0 W: 13 00 b.Naubeuge 10-8-67

1986–87	Lens	19	0
1987–88	Lens	32	0
1988–89	Lens	36	1
1989–90	Lens	31	2
1990–91	Lens	30	1
1991–92	Lens	33	0
1992–93	Lens	34	1
1993–94	Lens	36	3
1994–95	Lens	38	2
1995–96	Lens	35	1
1996–97	Lens	26	1
1997–98	Lens	28	0
1998–99	Coventry C	6	0
Total:		**384**	**12**

WALLING, Dean — Defender

H: 6 0 W: 10 00 b.Leeds 17-4-69

Source: Apprentice.

1986–87	Leeds U	0	0
1987–88	Rochdale	12	2
1988–89	Rochdale	34	3
1989–90	Rochdale	19	3
From Guiseley			
1991–92	Carlisle U	37	5
1992–93	Carlisle U	23	0
1993–94	Carlisle U	40	5
1994–95	Carlisle U	41	7
1995–96	Carlisle U	43	2
1996–97	Carlisle U	46	3
1997–98	Carlisle U	6	0
1997–98	Lincoln C	35	5
1998–99	Lincoln C	3	0
Total:		**339**	**35**

WALLWORK, Ronnie — Defender

H: 5 10 W: 12 12 b.Manchester 10-9-77

Source: Trainee. *Honours:* England Youth.

1994–95	Manchester U	0	0
1995–96	Manchester U	0	0
1996–97	Manchester U	0	0

1997–98	Manchester U	1	0
1997–98	Carlisle U (loan)	10	1
1997–98	Stockport Co (loan)	7	0
1998–99	Manchester U	0	0
Total:		**18**	**1**

WALSCHAERTS, Wim — Midfield

H: 5 11 W: 12 00 b.Antwerp 5-11-72

Source: FC Tielen.

1998–99	Leyton Orient	44	3
Total:		**44**	**3**

WALSH, Danny — Defender

H: 5 9 W: 12 03 b.Manchester 16-9-78

Source: Trainee.

1998–99	Oldham Ath	1	0
Total:		**1**	**0**

WALSH, Dave — Goalkeeper

H: 6 1 W: 12 05 b.Wrexham 29-4-79

Source: Trainee.

1997–98	Wrexham	0	0
1998–99	Wrexham	0	0

WALSH, Gary — Goalkeeper

H: 6 3 W: 14 11 b.Wigan 21-3-68

Source: Apprentice. *Honours:* England Under-21.

1984–85	Manchester U	0	0
1985–86	Manchester U	0	0
1986–87	Manchester U	14	0
1987–88	Manchester U	16	0
1988–89	Manchester U	0	0
1988–89	Airdrieonians (loan)	3	0
1989–90	Manchester U	0	0
1990–91	Manchester U	5	0
1991–92	Manchester U	2	0
1992–93	Manchester U	0	0
1993–94	Manchester U	3	0
1993–94	Oldham Ath (loan)	6	0
1994–95	Manchester U	10	0
1995–96	Middlesbrough	32	0
1996–97	Middlesbrough	12	0
1997–98	Middlesbrough	0	0
1997–98	Bradford C	35	0
1998–99	Bradford C	46	0
Total:		**184**	**0**

WALSH, Michael — Defender

H: 6 0 W: 12 08 b.Rotherham 5-8-77

Source: Trainee.

1994–95	Scunthorpe U	3	0
1995–96	Scunthorpe U	25	0
1996–97	Scunthorpe U	36	0
1997–98	Scunthorpe U	39	1
1998–99	Port Vale	19	1
Total:		**122**	**2**

WALSH, Steve — Defender

H: 6 3 W: 14 09 b.Fulwood 3-11-64

Source: Local.

1982–83	Wigan Ath	31	0
1983–84	Wigan Ath	42	1
1984–85	Wigan Ath	40	2
1985–86	Wigan Ath	13	1
1986–87	Leicester C	21	0
1987–88	Leicester C	32	7
1988–89	Leicester C	30	2
1989–90	Leicester C	34	3
1990–91	Leicester C	35	3
1991–92	Leicester C	43	7
1992–93	Leicester C	40	15
1993–94	Leicester C	10	4
1994–95	Leicester C	5	0
1995–96	Leicester C	37	4
1996–97	Leicester C	22	2
1997–98	Leicester C	26	3
1998–99	Leicester C	22	3
Total:		**483**	**57**

WALTERS, Mark — Midfield

H: 5 9 W: 11 05 b.Birmingham 2-6-64

Source: Apprentice. *Honours:* England Schools, Youth, Under-21, B, 1 full cap.

1981–82	Aston Villa	1	0
1982–83	Aston Villa	22	1
1983–84	Aston Villa	37	8
1984–85	Aston Villa	36	10
1985–86	Aston Villa	40	10
1986–87	Aston Villa	21	3
1987–88	Aston Villa	24	7
1987–88	Rangers	18	7
1988–89	Rangers	31	8
1989–90	Rangers	27	5
1990–91	Rangers	30	12
1991–92	Liverpool	25	3
1992–93	Liverpool	34	11
1993–94	Liverpool	17	0
1993–94	Stoke C (loan)	9	2
1994–95	Liverpool	18	0
1994–95	Wolverhampton W (loan)	11	3
1995–96	Liverpool	0	0
1995–96	Southampton	5	0
1996–97	Swindon T	27	7
1997–98	Swindon T	34	6
1998–99	Swindon T	38	10
Total:		**505**	**113**

WALTON, David — Defender

H: 6 2 W: 14 07 b.Bellingham 10-4-73

Source: Trainee.

1991–92	Sheffield U	0	0
1992–93	Sheffield U	0	0
1993–94	Sheffield U	0	0
1993–94	Shrewsbury T	27	5
1994–95	Shrewsbury T	36	3
1995–96	Shrewsbury T	35	0
1996–97	Shrewsbury T	24	1
1997–98	Shrewsbury T	6	1
1997–98	Crewe Alex	27	0
1998–99	Crewe Alex	38	1
Total:		**193**	**11**

WALTON, Mark — Goalkeeper

H: 6 4 W: 15 08 b.Merthyr 1-6-69

Source: Swansea C. *Honours:* Wales Under-21.

1986–87	Luton T	0	0
1987–88	Luton T	0	0
1987–88	Colchester U	17	0
1988–89	Colchester U	23	0
1989–90	Norwich C	1	0
1990–91	Norwich C	4	0
1991–92	Norwich C	17	0
1992–93	Norwich C	0	0
1993–94	Norwich C	0	0
1993–94	Wrexham (loan)	6	0
1993–94	Dundee	0	0
1993–94	Bolton W	3	0
From Fakenham T.			
1996–97	Fulham	28	0
1997–98	Fulham	12	0
1997–98	Gillingham (loan)	1	0
1997–98	Norwich C (loan)	0	0
1998–99	Brighton & HA	19	0
Total:		**131**	**0**

WANCHOPE, Paulo — Forward

H: 6 3 W: 12 05 b.Heredia 31-7-76

Source: Herediano. *Honours:* Costa Rica full caps.

1996–97	Derby Co	5	1
1997–98	Derby Co	32	13
1998–99	Derby Co	35	9
Total:		**72**	**23**

WANLESS, Paul — Midfield

H: 6 1 W: 13 11 b.Banbury 14-12-73

Source: Trainee.

1991–92	Oxford U	6	0
1992–93	Oxford U	7	0
1993–94	Oxford U	9	0
1994–95	Oxford U	10	0
1995–96	Lincoln C	8	0
1995–96	Cambridge U (loan)	14	1
1996–97	Cambridge U	30	3
1997–98	Cambridge U	42	8
1998–99	Cambridge U	45	8
Total:		**171**	**20**

WARBURTON, Ray — Defender

H: 6 0 W: 12 13 b.Rotherham 7-10-67

Source: Apprentice.

1984–85	Rotherham U	1	0
1985–86	Rotherham U	0	0
1986–87	Rotherham U	3	0
1987–88	Rotherham U	0	0
1988–89	Rotherham U	0	0
1989–90	York C	43	2
1990–91	York C	22	4
1991–92	York C	9	0
1992–93	York C	10	3
1993–94	York C	6	0
1993–94	Northampton T (loan)	17	1
1994–95	Northampton T	39	3
1995–96	Northampton T	44	3
1996–97	Northampton T	35	4
1997–98	Northampton T	39	0
1998–99	Northampton T	12	1
Total:		**280**	**21**

WARD, Ashley — Forward

H: 6 1 W: 12 02 b.Manchester 24-11-70

Source. Trainee.

1989–90	Manchester C	1	0
1990–91	Manchester C	0	0
1990–91	Wrexham (loan)	4	2
1991–92	Leicester C	10	0
1992–93	Leicester C	0	0
1992–93	Blackpool (loan)	2	1
1992–93	Crewe Alex	20	4
1993–94	Crewe Alex	25	13
1994–95	Crewe Alex	16	8
1994–95	Norwich C	25	8
1995–96	Norwich C	28	10
1995–96	Derby Co	7	1
1996–97	Derby Co	30	8
1997–98	Derby Co	3	0
1997–98	Barnsley	29	8
1998–99	Barnsley	17	12
1998–99	Blackburn R	17	5
Total:		**234**	**80**

WARD, Darran — Defender

H: 6 0 W: 14 02 b.Kenton 13-9-78

Source: Trainee.

1995–96	Watford	1	0
1996–97	Watford	7	0

Ward, Darren

1997–98	Watford	0	0
1998–99	Watford	1	0
Total:		**9**	**0**

WARD, Darren — Goalkeeper

H: 5 11 W: 12 09 b.Worksop 11-5-74

Source: Trainee. *Honours:* Wales Under-21.

1992–93	Mansfield T	13	0
1993–94	Mansfield T	33	0
1994–95	Mansfield T	35	0
1995–96	Notts Co	46	0
1996–97	Notts Co	38	0
1997–98	Notts Co	44	0
1998–99	Notts Co	43	0
Total:		**252**	**0**

WARD, Gavin — Goalkeeper

H: 6 2 W: 13 06 b.Sutton Coldfield 30-6-70

Source: Aston Villa Trainee.

1988–89	Shrewsbury T	0	0
1989–90	WBA	0	0
1989–90	Cardiff C	2	0
1990–91	Cardiff C	1	0
1991–92	Cardiff C	24	0
1992–93	Cardiff C	32	0
1993–94	Leicester C	32	0
1994–95	Leicester C	6	0
1995–96	Bradford C	36	0
1995–96	Bolton W	5	0
1996–97	Bolton W	11	0
1997–98	Bolton W	6	0
1998–99	Bolton W	0	0
1998–99	Burnley (loan)	17	0
1998–99	Stoke C	6	0
Total:		**178**	**0**

WARD, Mitch — Midfield

H: 5 8 W: 11 13 b.Sheffield 19-6-71

Source: Trainee.

1989–90	Sheffield U	0	0
1990–91	Sheffield U	4	0
1990–91	Crewe Alex (loan)	4	1
1991–92	Sheffield U	6	2
1992–93	Sheffield U	26	0
1993–94	Sheffield U	22	1
1994–95	Sheffield U	14	2
1995–96	Sheffield U	42	1
1996–97	Sheffield U	34	4
1997–98	Sheffield U	6	1
1997–98	Everton	8	0
1998–99	Everton	6	0
Total:		**172**	**12**

WARD, Peter — Midfield

H: 6 0 W: 12 01 b.Durham 15-10-64

Source: Chester-le-Street.

1986–87	Huddersfield T	7	0
1987–88	Huddersfield T	26	2
1988–89	Huddersfield T	4	0
1989–90	Rochdale	40	5
1990–91	Rochdale	44	5
1991–92	Stockport Co	44	1
1992–93	Stockport Co	35	3
1993–94	Stockport Co	35	3
1994–95	Stockport Co	28	3
1995–96	Wrexham	34	5
1996–97	Wrexham	24	1
1997–98	Wrexham	37	6
1998–99	Wrexham	25	2
Total:		**383**	**36**

WARD, Scott — Goalkeeper

H: 6 2 W: 13 00 b.Brent 5-10-81

Source: Trainee.

1998–99	Luton T	0	0

WARHURST, Paul — Defender

H: 6 1 W: 12 01 b.Stockport 26-9-69

Source: Trainee. *Honours:* England Under-21.

1987–88	Manchester C	0	0
1988–89	Oldham Ath	4	0
1989–90	Oldham Ath	30	1
1990–91	Oldham Ath	33	1
1991–92	Sheffield W	33	0
1992–93	Sheffield W	29	6
1993–94	Sheffield W	4	0
1993–94	Blackburn R	9	0
1994–95	Blackburn R	27	2
1995–96	Blackburn R	10	0
1996–97	Blackburn R	11	2
1997–98	Crystal Palace	22	3
1998–99	Crystal Palace	5	1
1998–99	Bolton W	20	0
Total:		**237**	**16**

WARNE, Paul — Forward

H: 5 8 W: 11 01 b.Norwich 8-5-73

Source: Wroxham.

1997–98	Wigan Ath	25	2
1998–99	Wigan Ath	11	1
1998–99	Rotherham U	19	8
Total:		**55**	**11**

WARNER, Michael — Midfield

H: 5 9 W: 10 10 b.Harrogate 17-1-74

Source: Tamworth.

1995–96	Northampton T	0	0
1996–97	Northampton T	9	0
1997–98	Northampton T	10	0
1998–99	Northampton T	9	0
Total:		**28**	**0**

WARNER, Phil — Defender

H: 5 10 W: 11 09 b.Southampton 2-2-79

Source: Trainee.

1997–98	Southampton	1	0
1998–99	Southampton	5	0
Total:		**6**	**0**

WARNER, Tony — Goalkeeper

H: 6 4 W: 13 09 b.Liverpool 11-5-74

Source: School.

1993–94	Liverpool	0	0
1994–95	Liverpool	0	0
1995–96	Liverpool	0	0
1996–97	Liverpool	0	0
1997–98	Liverpool	0	0
1997–98	Swindon T (loan)	2	0
1998–99	Liverpool	0	0
1998–99	Celtic (loan)	3	0
1998–99	Aberdeen (loan)	6	0
Total:		**11**	**0**

WARNER, Vance — Defender

H: 6 0 W: 13 04 b.Leeds 3-9-74

Source: Trainee.

1991–92	Nottingham F	0	0
1992–93	Nottingham F	0	0
1993–94	Nottingham F	1	0
1994–95	Nottingham F	1	0
1995–96	Nottingham F	0	0
1995–96	Grimsby T (loan)	3	0
1996–97	Nottingham F	3	0
1997–98	Nottingham F	0	0
1997–98	Rotherham U	21	0
1998–99	Rotherham U	23	1
Total:		**52**	**1**

WARNOCK, Stephen — Midfield

b.Ormskirk 12-12-81

Source: Trainee. *Honours:* England Schools, Youth.

1998–99	Liverpool	0	0

WARREN, Christer — Forward

H: 5 10 W: 11 12 b.Poole 10-10-74

Source: Cheltenham T.

1994–95	Southampton	0	0
1995–96	Southampton	7	0
1996–97	Southampton	1	0
1996–97	Brighton & HA (loan)	3	0
1996–97	Fulham (loan)	11	1
1997–98	Southampton	0	0
1997–98	Bournemouth	30	6
1998–99	Bournemouth	32	5
Total:		**84**	**12**

WARREN, Mark — Defender

H: 6 0 W: 12 02 b.Clapton 12-11-74

Source: Trainee.

1991–92	Leyton Orient	1	0
1992–93	Leyton Orient	14	0
1993–94	Leyton Orient	6	0
1993–94	West Ham U (loan)	0	0
1994–95	Leyton Orient	31	3
1995–96	Leyton Orient	22	1
1996–97	Leyton Orient	27	1
1997–98	Leyton Orient	41	0
1998–99	Leyton Orient	10	0
1998–99	Oxford U (loan)	4	0
1998–99	Notts Co	18	0
Total:		**174**	**5**

WARRINGTON, Andy — Goalkeeper

H: 6 3 W: 12 13 b.Sheffield 10-6-76

Source: Trainee.

1994–95	York C	0	0
1995–96	York C	6	0
1996–97	York C	27	0
1997–98	York C	17	0
1998–99	York C	11	0
Total:		**61**	**0**

WASSALL, Darren — Defender

H: 6 0 W: 12 07 b.Edgbaston 27-6-68

1987–88	Nottingham F	3	0
1987–88	Hereford U (loan)	5	0
1988–89	Nottingham F	0	0
1988–89	Bury (loan)	7	1
1989–90	Nottingham F	3	0
1990–91	Nottingham F	7	0
1991–92	Nottingham F	14	0
1992–93	Derby Co	24	0
1993–94	Derby Co	25	0
1994–95	Derby Co	32	0
1995–96	Derby Co	17	0

1996–97	Derby Co	0	0
1996–97	Manchester C (loan)	15	0
1996–97	Birmingham C (loan)	8	0
1997–98	Birmingham C	14	0
1998–99	Birmingham C	3	0
Total:		**177**	**1**

WATERMAN, David — Defender

H: 5 10 W: 13 02 b.Guernsey 16-5-77

Source: Trainee. *Honours:* Northern Ireland Under-21.

1995–96	Portsmouth	0	0
1996–97	Portsmouth	4	0
1997–98	Portsmouth	15	0
1998–99	Portsmouth	10	0
Total:		**29**	**0**

WATKIN, Steve — Forward

H: 5 10 W: 11 10 b.Wrexham 16-6-71

Source: School.

1989–90	Wrexham	0	0
1990–91	Wrexham	9	1
1991–92	Wrexham	28	8
1992–93	Wrexham	33	18
1993–94	Wrexham	40	9
1994–95	Wrexham	32	4
1995–96	Wrexham	29	7
1996–97	Wrexham	26	7
1997–98	Wrexham	3	1
1997–98	Swansea C	32	3
1998–99	Swansea C	43	17
Total:		**275**	**75**

WATKISS, Stuart — Defender

H: 6 2 W: 13 06 b.Wolverhampton 8-5-66

Source: Apprentice.

1983–84	Wolverhampton W	2	0
From Rushall Olympic			
1993–94	Walsall	39	2
1994–95	Walsall	8	0
1995–96	Walsall	15	0
1995–96	Hereford U	19	0
1996–97	Mansfield T	31	1
1997–98	Mansfield T	10	0
1998–99	Mansfield T	0	0
Total:		**124**	**3**

WATSON, Alex — Defender

H: 6 1 W: 12 00 b.Liverpool 5-4-68

Source: Apprentice. *Honours:* England Youth.

1984–85	Liverpool	0	0
1985–86	Liverpool	0	0
1986–87	Liverpool	0	0
1987–88	Liverpool	2	0
1988–89	Liverpool	2	0
1989–90	Liverpool	0	0
1990–91	Liverpool	0	0
1990–91	Derby Co (loan)	5	0
1990–91	Bournemouth	23	3
1991–92	Bournemouth	15	0
1992–93	Bournemouth	46	1
1993–94	Bournemouth	45	1
1994–95	Bournemouth	22	0
1995–96	Bournemouth	0	0
1995–96	Gillingham (loan)	10	1
1995–96	Torquay U	29	2
1996–97	Torquay U	46	1
1997–98	Torquay U	46	1
1998–99	Torquay U	8	0
Total:		**299**	**10**

WATSON, Andy — Forward

H: 5 8 W: 12 06 b.Leeds 1-4-67

Source: Harrogate T.

1988–89	Halifax T	45	5
1989–90	Halifax T	38	10
1990–91	Swansea C	14	1
1991–92	Swansea C	0	0
1991–92	Carlisle U	35	14
1992–93	Carlisle U	21	8
1992–93	Blackpool	15	2
1993–94	Blackpool	40	20
1994–95	Blackpool	33	15
1995–96	Blackpool	27	6
1996–97	Blackpool	0	0
1996–97	Walsall	36	5
1997–98	Walsall	27	7
1998–99	Walsall	21	3
Total:		**352**	**96**

WATSON, Dave — Defender

H: 5 11 W: 11 12 b.Liverpool 20-11-61

Source: Amateur. *Honours:* England Under-21, 12 full caps.

1979–80	Liverpool	0	0
1980–81	Liverpool	0	0
1980–81	Norwich C	18	3
1981–82	Norwich C	38	3
1982–83	Norwich C	35	1
1983–84	Norwich C	40	1
1984–85	Norwich C	39	0
1985–86	Norwich C	42	3
1986–87	Everton	35	4
1987–88	Everton	37	4
1988–89	Everton	32	3
1989–90	Everton	29	1
1990–91	Everton	32	2
1991–92	Everton	35	3
1992–93	Everton	40	1
1993–94	Everton	28	1
1994–95	Everton	38	2
1995–96	Everton	34	1
1996–97	Everton	29	1

1997–98	Everton	26	0
1998–99	Everton	22	0
Total:		**629**	**34**

WATSON, David — Goalkeeper

H: 6 0 W: 12 09 b.Barnsley 10-11-73

Source: Trainee. *Honours:* England Youth, Under-21.

1992–93	Barnsley	5	0
1993–94	Barnsley	9	0
1994–95	Barnsley	37	0
1995–96	Barnsley	45	0
1996–97	Barnsley	46	0
1997–98	Barnsley	30	0
1998–99	Barnsley	6	0
Total:		**178**	**0**

WATSON, Gordon — Forward

H: 5 10 W: 12 08 b.Sidcup 20-3-71

Source: Trainee. *Honours:* England Under-21.

1988–89	Charlton Ath	0	0
1989–90	Charlton Ath	9	0
1990–91	Charlton Ath	22	7
1990–91	Sheffield W	5	0
1991–92	Sheffield W	4	0
1992–93	Sheffield W	11	1
1993–94	Sheffield W	23	12
1994–95	Sheffield W	23	2
1994–95	Southampton	12	3
1995–96	Southampton	25	3
1996–97	Southampton	15	2
1996–97	Bradford C	3	1
1997–98	Bradford C	0	0
1998–99	Bradford C	18	4
Total:		**170**	**35**

WATSON, Kevin — Midfield

H: 5 9 W: 12 08 b.Hackney 3-1-74

Source: Trainee.

1991–92	Tottenham H	0	0
1992–93	Tottenham H	5	0
1993–94	Tottenham H	0	0
1993–94	Brentford (loan)	3	0
1994–95	Tottenham H	0	0
1994–95	Bristol C (loan)	2	0
1994–95	Barnet (loan)	13	0
1995–96	Tottenham H	0	0
1996–97	Swindon T	27	1
1997–98	Swindon T	18	0
1998–99	Swindon T	18	0
Total:		**86**	**1**

WATSON, Mark — Defender

H: 6 0 W: 12 04 b.Vancouver 8-9-70

Honours: Canada full caps.

1993–94	Watford	17	0
1994–95	Watford	1	0
1995–96	Watford	0	0
1997	Osters	4	0
1998	Osters	20	0
1998–99	Oxford U	23	0
Total:		**65**	**0**

WATSON, Paul — Defender

H: 5 8 W: 10 10 b.Hastings 4-1-75

Source: Trainee.

1992–93	Gillingham	1	0
1993–94	Gillingham	14	0
1994–95	Gillingham	39	2
1995–96	Gillingham	8	0
1996–97	Fulham	44	3
1997–98	Fulham	6	1
1997–98	Brentford	25	0
1998–99	Brentford	12	0
Total:		**149**	**6**

WATSON, Richard — Midfield

b.Salford 2-11-78

Source: Waterford.

1998–99	Bury	0	0

WATSON, Simon — Midfield

H: 5 9 W: 10 00 b.Strabane 22-9-80

Source: Trainee.

1997–98	Leeds U	0	0
1998–99	Leeds U	0	0

WATSON, Steve — Defender

H: 6 1 W: 12 07 b.North Shields 1-4-74

Source: Trainee. *Honours:* England Youth, Under-21, B.

1990–91	Newcastle U	24	0
1991–92	Newcastle U	28	1
1992–93	Newcastle U	2	0
1993–94	Newcastle U	32	2
1994–95	Newcastle U	27	4
1995–96	Newcastle U	23	3
1996–97	Newcastle U	36	1
1997–98	Newcastle U	29	1
1998–99	Newcastle U	7	0
1998–99	Aston Villa	27	0
Total:		**235**	**12**

WATT, Michael — Goalkeeper

H: 6 2 W: 13 05 b.Aberdeen 27-11-70

Source: Cove Rangers. *Honours:* Scotland Under-21.

1989–90	Aberdeen	7	0
1990–91	Aberdeen	10	0
1991–92	Aberdeen	2	0
1992–93	Aberdeen	3	0
1993–94	Aberdeen	4	0
1994–95	Aberdeen	14	0
1995–96	Aberdeen	30	0
1996–97	Aberdeen	9	0
1997–98	Blackburn R	0	0
1998–99	Norwich C	8	0
Total:		**87**	**0**

WATTS, Julian — Defender

H: 6 2 W: 13 06 b.Sheffield 17-3-71

Source: Trainee.

1990–91	Rotherham U	10	0
1991–92	Rotherham U	10	1
1991–92	Sheffield W	0	0
1992–93	Sheffield W	4	0
1992–93	Shrewsbury T (loan)	9	0
1993–94	Sheffield W	1	0
1994–95	Sheffield W	0	0
1995–96	Sheffield W	11	1
1995–96	Leicester C	9	0
1996–97	Leicester C	26	1
1997–98	Leicester C	3	0
1997–98	Crewe Alex (loan)	5	0
1997–98	Huddersfield T (loan)	8	0
1998–99	Bristol C	17	1
1998–99	Lincoln C (loan)	2	0
1998–99	Blackpool (loan)	9	0
Total:		**124**	**4**

WATTS, Steve — Forward

H: 6 1 W: 13 00 b.Lambeth 11-7-76

Source: Fisher Ath.

1998–99	Leyton Orient	28	6
Total:		**28**	**6**

WAUGH, Warren — Forward

H: 6 0 W: 12 02 b.Harlesden 9-10-80

Source: Trainee.

1998–99	Exeter C	7	0
Total:		**7**	**0**

WAY, Darren — Midfield

H: 5 6 W: 10 09 b.Plymouth 21-11-79

Source: Trainee.

1998–99	Norwich C	0	0

WEARE, Ross — Forward

H: 6 2 W: 13 05 b.Perivale 19-3-77

Source: East Ham U.

1998–99	QPR	0	0

WEATHERSTONE, Simon — Forward

H: 5 10 W: 12 04 b.Reading 26-1-80

Source: Trainee.

1996–97	Oxford U	1	0
1997–98	Oxford U	11	1
1998–99	Oxford U	12	1
Total:		**24**	**2**

WEAVER, Luke — Goalkeeper

H: 6 2 W: 13 02 b.Woolwich 26-6-79

Source: Trainee. *Honours:* England Schools, Youth.

1996–97	Leyton Orient	9	0
1996–97	West Ham U (loan)	0	0
1997–98	Leyton Orient	0	0
1997–98	Sunderland	0	0
1998–99	Sunderland	0	0
1998–99	Scarborough (loan)	6	0
Total:		**15**	**0**

WEAVER, Nick — Goalkeeper

H: 6 3 W: 13 01 b.Sheffield 2-3-79

Source: Trainee.

1995–96	Mansfield T	1	0
1996–97	Mansfield T	0	0
1996–97	Manchester C	0	0
1997–98	Manchester C	0	0
1998–99	Manchester C	45	0
Total:		**46**	**0**

WEBB, Darren — Midfield

H: 5 9 W: 11 00 b.Brighton 24-10-79

Source: Trainee.

1998–99	Cambridge U	0	0

WEBB, Simon — Midfield

H: 5 11 W: 12 03 b.Castle Bar 19-1-78

Source: Trainee.

1994–95	Tottenham H	0	0
1995–96	Tottenham H	0	0
1996–97	Tottenham H	0	0
1997–98	Tottenham H	0	0
1998–99	Tottenham H	0	0

WEBBER, Danny — Forward

H: 5 9 W: 10 03 b.Manchester 28-12-81

Source: Trainee. *Honours:* England Youth.

1998–99	Manchester U	0	0

WEBSTER, Adam — Midfield

b.Leicester 3-7-80

1998–99	Notts Co	0	0

WEBSTER, Colin — Midfield

b.Chester 10-9-79

Source: Trainee.

1998–99	Crewe Alex	0	0

WEIR, David — Defender

H: 6 2 W: 13 07 b.Falkirk 10-5-70

Source: Celtic BC. *Honours:* Scotland 13 full caps.

1992–93	Falkirk	30	1
1993–94	Falkirk	37	3
1994–95	Falkirk	32	1
1995–96	Falkirk	34	3
1996–97	Hearts	34	6
1997–98	Hearts	35	1
1998–99	Hearts	23	1
1998–99	Everton	14	0
Total:		**239**	**16**

WEIR, James — Defender

H: 6 1 W: 12 05 b.Motherwell 15-6-69

Source: Motherwell Orbiston BC.

1987–88	Hamilton A	6	0
1988–89	Hamilton A	29	0
1989–90	Hamilton A	30	1
1990–91	Hamilton A	39	2
1991–92	Hamilton A	40	1
1992–93	Hamilton A	37	1
1993–94	Hamilton A	2	0
1993–94	Hearts	26	0
1994–95	Hearts	2	0
1994–95	St Johnstone	17	0
1995–96	St Johnstone	29	0
1996–97	St Johnstone	32	3
1997–98	St Johnstone	25	0
1998–99	St Johnstone	7	1
Total:		**321**	**9**

WELCH, Keith — Goalkeeper

H: 6 2 W: 13 13 b.Bolton 3-10-68

Source: Trainee.

1986–87	Bolton W	0	0
1986–87	Rochdale	24	0
1987–88	Rochdale	46	0
1988–89	Rochdale	46	0
1989–90	Rochdale	46	0
1990–91	Rochdale	43	0
1991–92	Bristol C	26	0
1992–93	Bristol C	45	0
1993–94	Bristol C	45	0
1994–95	Bristol C	44	0
1995–96	Bristol C	35	0
1996–97	Bristol C	11	0
1997–98	Bristol C	44	0
1998–99	Bristol C	21	0
Total:		**476**	**0**

WELLENS, Richard — Midfield

H: 5 9 W: 11 05 b.Manchester 26-3-80

Source: Trainee. *Honours:* England Youth.

1996–97	Manchester U	0	0
1997–98	Manchester U	0	0
1998–99	Manchester U	0	0

WELLER, Paul — Midfield

H: 5 8 W: 11 02 b.Brighton 6-3-75

Source: Trainee.

1993–94	Burnley	0	0
1994–95	Burnley	0	0
1995–96	Burnley	25	1
1996–97	Burnley	31	2
1997–98	Burnley	39	2
1998–99	Burnley	1	0
Total:		**96**	**5**

WELSBY, Kevin — Goalkeeper

H: 6 0 W: 10 06 b.Crewe 27-8-80

Source: Trainee.

1998–99	Crewe Alex	0	0

WENLOCK, Steve — Defender

H: 5 7 W: 11 01 b.Peterborough 11-3-78

Source: Trainee.

1996–97	Leicester C	0	0
1997–98	Leicester C	0	0
1998–99	Leicester C	0	0

WEST, Dean — Defender

H: 5 10 W: 11 07 b.Wakefield 5-12-72

Source: Leeds U Schoolboy.

1990–91	Lincoln C	1	1
1991–92	Lincoln C	32	3
1992–93	Lincoln C	19	3
1993–94	Lincoln C	18	6
1994–95	Lincoln C	41	6
1995–96	Lincoln C	8	1
1995–96	Bury	37	1
1996–97	Bury	46	4
1997–98	Bury	4	0
1998–99	Bury	23	2
Total:		**229**	**27**

WEST, Gareth — Defender

H: 6 1 W: 11 10 b.Oldham 1-8-78

Source: Trainee.

1996–97	Burnley	0	0
1997–98	Burnley	0	0
1998–99	Burnley	0	0

WESTCOTT, John — Forward

H: 5 9 W: 10 03 b.Eastbourne 31-5-79

Source: Trainee.

1997–98	Brighton & HA	34	0
1998–99	Brighton & HA	4	0
Total:		**38**	**0**

WESTHEAD, Mark — Goalkeeper

H: 6 2 W: 14 05 b.Blackpool 19-7-75

1996–97	Bolton W	0	0
1997–98	Bolton W	0	0
From Telford U.			
1998–99	Wycombe W	2	0
Total:		**2**	**0**

WESTWATER, Ian — Goalkeeper

H: 6 0 W: 13 00 b.Loughborough 8-11-63

Source: Salvesen BC.

1980–81	Hearts	2	0
1981–82	Hearts	0	0
1982–83	Hearts	0	0
1983–84	Hearts	0	0
1984–85	Dunfermline Ath	8	0
1985–86	Dunfermline Ath	38	0
1986–87	Dunfermline Ath	42	0
1987–88	Dunfermline Ath	28	0
1988–89	Dunfermline Ath	39	0
1989–90	Dunfermline Ath	36	0
1990–91	Dunfermline Ath	1	0
1991–92	Falkirk	40	0
1992–93	Falkirk	24	0
1993–94	Falkirk	3	0
1993–94	Dunfermline Ath	9	0
1994–95	Dunfermline Ath	17	0
1995–96	Dunfermline Ath	11	0
1996–97	Dunfermline Ath	29	0
1997–98	Dunfermline Ath	36	0
1998–99	Dunfermline Ath	1	0
Total:		**364**	**0**

WESTWOOD, Ashley — Defender

H: 5 11 W: 11 02 b.Bridgnorth 31-8-76

Source: Trainee. *Honours:* England Youth.

1994–95	Manchester U	0	0
1995–96	Crewe Alex	33	4
1996–97	Crewe Alex	44	2
1997–98	Crewe Alex	21	3
1998–99	Bradford C	19	2
Total:		**117**	**11**

WESTWOOD, Chris — Defender

H: 5 11 W: 12 10 b.Dudley 13-2-77

Source: Trainee.

1995–96	Wolverhampton W	0	0
1996–97	Wolverhampton W	0	0
1997–98	Wolverhampton W	4	1
1998–99	Wolverhampton W	0	0
1998–99	Hartlepool U	4	0
Total:		**8**	**1**

WETHERALL, David — Defender

H: 6 4 W: 13 05 b.Sheffield 14-3-71

Source: School. *Honours:* England Schools.

1989–90	Sheffield W	0	0
1990–91	Sheffield W	0	0
1991–92	Leeds U	1	0
1992–93	Leeds U	13	1
1993–94	Leeds U	32	1
1994–95	Leeds U	38	3
1995–96	Leeds U	34	4
1996–97	Leeds U	29	0
1997–98	Leeds U	34	3
1998–99	Leeds U	21	0
Total:		**202**	**12**

WHALLEY, Gareth — Midfield

H: 5 10 W: 11 06 b.Manchester 19-12-73

Source: Trainee.

1992–93	Crewe Alex	25	1
1993–94	Crewe Alex	15	1
1994–95	Crewe Alex	40	1
1995–96	Crewe Alex	44	2
1996–97	Crewe Alex	38	3

1997–98	Crewe Alex	18	1
1998–99	Bradford C	45	2
Total:		**225**	**11**

WHEATCROFT, Paul — Forward

H: 5 8 W: 9 09 b.Manchester 22-11-80

Source: Trainee. *Honours:* England Schools, Youth.

1998–99	Manchester U	0	0

WHELAN, Noel — Forward

H: 6 2 W: 12 03 b.Leeds 30-12-74

Source: Trainee. *Honours:* England Under-21.

1992–93	Leeds U	1	0
1993–94	Leeds U	16	0
1994–95	Leeds U	23	7
1995–96	Leeds U	8	0
1995–96	Coventry C	21	8
1996–97	Coventry C	35	6
1997–98	Coventry C	21	6
1998–99	Coventry C	31	10
Total:		**156**	**37**

WHELAN, Phil — Defender

H: 6 3 W: 13 05 b.Stockport 7-3-72

Honours: England Under-21.

1989–90	Ipswich T	0	0
1990–91	Ipswich T	0	0
1991–92	Ipswich T	8	2
1992–93	Ipswich T	32	0
1993–94	Ipswich T	29	0
1994–95	Ipswich T	13	0
1994–95	Middlesbrough	0	0
1995–96	Middlesbrough	13	1
1996–97	Middlesbrough	9	0
1997–98	Oxford U	8	0
1998–99	Oxford U	15	0
1998–99	Rotherham U (loan)	13	4
Total:		**140**	**7**

WHELAN, Spencer — Defender

H: 6 2 W: 13 00 b.Liverpool 17-9-71

Source: Liverpool.

1990–91	Chester C	11	0
1991–92	Chester C	32	0
1992–93	Chester C	28	0
1993–94	Chester C	22	0
1994–95	Chester C	23	1
1995–96	Chester C	39	2
1996–97	Chester C	25	1
1997–98	Chester C	35	4
1998–99	Chester C	0	0
1998–99	Shrewsbury T	9	0
Total:		**224**	**8**

WHITBREAD, Adrian — Defender

H: 6 1 W: 13 00 b.Epping 22-10-71

Source: Trainee.

1989–90	Leyton Orient	8	0
1990–91	Leyton Orient	38	0
1991–92	Leyton Orient	43	1
1992–93	Leyton Orient	36	1
1993–94	Swindon T	35	1
1994–95	Swindon T	1	0
1994–95	West Ham U	8	0
1995–96	West Ham U	2	0
1995–96	Portsmouth (loan)	13	0
1996–97	West Ham U	0	0
1996–97	Portsmouth	24	0
1997–98	Portsmouth	38	1
1998–99	Portsmouth	33	0
Total:		**279**	**4**

WHITE, Alan — Defender

H: 6 1 W: 13 07 b.Darlington 22-3-76

Source: Derby Co Schoolboy.

1994–95	Middlesbrough	0	0
1995–96	Middlesbrough	0	0
1996–97	Middlesbrough	0	0
1997–98	Middlesbrough	0	0
1997–98	Luton T	28	1
1998–99	Luton T	33	1
Total:		**61**	**2**

WHITE, David — Midfield

H: 6 1 W: 13 09 b.Manchester 30-10-67

Honours: England Youth, Under-21, B, 1 full cap.

1985–86	Manchester C	0	0
1986–87	Manchester C	24	1
1987–88	Manchester C	44	13
1988–89	Manchester C	45	6
1989–90	Manchester C	37	8
1990–91	Manchester C	38	16
1991–92	Manchester C	39	18
1992–93	Manchester C	42	16
1993–94	Manchester C	16	1
1993–94	Leeds U	15	5
1994–95	Leeds U	23	3
1995–96	Leeds U	4	1
1995–96	Sheffield U	28	7
1996–97	Sheffield U	37	6
1997–98	Sheffield U	1	0
1998–99	Sheffield U	0	0
Total:		**393**	**101**

WHITE, Devon — Forward

H: 6 3 W: 14 00 b.Nottingham 2-3-64

Source: Arnold T.

1984–85	Lincoln C	7	1
1985–86	Lincoln C	22	3
1986–87	Lincoln C	0	0
From Boston U			
1987–88	Bristol R	39	15
1988–89	Bristol R	40	5
1989–90	Bristol R	43	12
1990–91	Bristol R	45	11
1991–92	Bristol R	35	10
1991–92	Cambridge U	2	0
1992–93	Cambridge U	20	4
1992–93	QPR	7	2
1993–94	QPR	18	7
1994–95	QPR	1	0
1994–95	Notts Co	20	7
1995–96	Notts Co	20	8
1995–96	Watford	16	5
1996–97	Watford	22	2
1996–97	Notts Co	9	2
1997–98	Notts Co	6	2
1997–98	Shrewsbury T	32	10
1998–99	Shrewsbury T	11	0
Total:		**415**	**106**

WHITE, Jason — Forward

H: 6 1 W: 12 12 b.Meriden 19-10-71

Source: Derby Co Trainee. *Honours:*

1991–92	Scunthorpe U	22	11
1992–93	Scunthorpe U	37	5
1993–94	Scunthorpe U	9	0
1993–94	Darlington (loan)	4	1
1993–94	Scarborough	24	9
1994–95	Scarborough	39	11
1995–96	Northampton T	45	16
1996–97	Northampton T	32	2
1997–98	Northampton T	0	0
1997–98	Rotherham U	27	13
1998–99	Rotherham U	26	5
Total:		**265**	**73**

WHITE, Tom — Defender

H: 5 11 W: 14 03 b.Bristol 26-1-76

Source: Trainee.

1994–95	Bristol R	4	0
1995–96	Bristol R	2	0
1996–97	Bristol R	21	0
1997–98	Bristol R	24	1
1998–99	Bristol R	0	0
Total:		**51**	**1**

WHITEFORD, Andrew — Defender

H: 5 10 W: 11 04 b.Bellshill 22-8-77

Source: Possil YMCA. *Honours:* Scotland Under-21, Under-18.

1994–95	St Johnstone	0	0
1995–96	St Johnstone	4	0
1996–97	St Johnstone	11	0
1997–98	St Johnstone	1	0
1998–99	St Johnstone	1	0
Total:		**17**	**0**

WHITEHALL, Steve — Forward

H: 5 11 W: 11 07 b.Bromborough 8-12-66

Source: Southport.

1991–92	Rochdale	34	8
1992–93	Rochdale	42	14
1993–94	Rochdale	39	14
1994–95	Rochdale	42	10
1995–96	Rochdale	46	20
1996–97	Rochdale	35	9
1997–98	Mansfield T	43	24
1998–99	Oldham Ath	36	4
Total:		**317**	**103**

WHITEHEAD, Phil — Goalkeeper

H: 6 3 W: 15 04 b.Halifax 17-12-69

Source: Trainee.

1986–87	Halifax T	12	0
1987–88	Halifax T	0	0
1988–89	Halifax T	11	0
1989–90	Halifax T	19	0
1989–90	Barnsley	0	0
1990–91	Barnsley	0	0
1990–91	Halifax T (loan)	9	0
1991–92	Barnsley	3	0
1991–92	Scunthorpe U (loan)	8	0
1992–93	Barnsley	13	0
1992–93	Scunthorpe U (loan)	8	0
1992–93	Bradford C (loan)	6	0
1993–94	Barnsley	0	0
1993–94	Oxford U	39	0
1994–95	Oxford U	38	0
1995–96	Oxford U	34	0
1996–97	Oxford U	43	0
1997–98	Oxford U	32	0
1998–99	Oxford U	21	0
1998–99	WBA	26	0
Total:		**322**	**0**

WHITEHEAD, Stuart — Defender

H: 6 0 W: 12 02 b.Bromsgrove 17-7-76

Source: Bromsgrove R.

1995–96	Bolton W	0	0
1996–97	Bolton W	0	0

1997–98	Bolton W	0	0
1998–99	Carlisle U	37	0
Total:		**37**	**0**

WHITEHOUSE, Dane — Midfield

H: 5 10 W: 12 08 b.Sheffield 14-10-70

Source: Trainee.

1988–89	Sheffield U	5	0
1989–90	Sheffield U	12	1
1990–91	Sheffield U	4	0
1991–92	Sheffield U	34	7
1992–93	Sheffield U	14	5
1993–94	Sheffield U	38	5
1994–95	Sheffield U	39	8
1995–96	Sheffield U	38	4
1996–97	Sheffield U	30	6
1997–98	Sheffield U	17	3
1998–99	Sheffield U	0	0
Total:		**231**	**39**

WHITLEY, Jeff — Midfield

H: 5 9 W: 10 10 b.Zambia 28-1-79

Source: Trainee. *Honours:* Northern Ireland Under-21, 3 full caps.

1995–96	Manchester C	0	0
1996–97	Manchester C	23	1
1997–98	Manchester C	17	1
1998–99	Manchester C	8	1
1998–99	Wrexham (loan)	9	2
Total:		**57**	**5**

WHITLEY, Jim — Midfield

H: 5 9 W: 10 12 b.Zambia 14-4-75

Source: Trainee. *Honours:* Northern Ireland 2 full caps.

1993–94	Manchester C	0	0
1994–95	Manchester C	0	0
1995–96	Manchester C	0	0
1996–97	Manchester C	0	0
1997–98	Manchester C	19	0
1998–99	Manchester C	18	0
Total:		**37**	**0**

WHITLOW, Mike — Defender

H: 6 1 W: 11 06 b.Northwich 13-1-68

Source: Witton Alb.

1988–89	Leeds U	20	1
1989–90	Leeds U	29	1
1990–91	Leeds U	18	1
1991–92	Leeds U	10	1
1991–92	Leicester C	5	0
1992–93	Leicester C	24	1
1993–94	Leicester C	31	2
1994–95	Leicester C	28	2
1995–96	Leicester C	42	3
1996–97	Leicester C	17	0
1997–98	Leicester C	0	0
1997–98	Bolton W	13	0
1998–99	Bolton W	28	0
Total:		**265**	**12**

WHITNEY, Jon — Defender

H: 5 10 W: 13 08 b.Nantwich 23-12-70

Source: Winsford U.

1993–94	Huddersfield T	14	0
1994–95	Huddersfield T	0	0
1994–95	Wigan Ath (loan)	12	0
1995–96	Huddersfield T	4	0
1995–96	Lincoln C	26	2
1996–97	Lincoln C	18	3
1997–98	Lincoln C	44	1
1998–99	Lincoln C	13	2
1998–99	Hull C	21	1
Total:		**152**	**9**

WHITTAKER, David — Midfield

b.Stockport 13-8-78

Source: Trainee.

1997–98	Crewe Alex	0	0
1998–99	Crewe Alex	0	0

WHITTAKER, Stuart — Midfield

H: 5 7 W: 10 06 b.Liverpool 2-1-75

Source: Liverpool Trainee.

1993–94	Bolton W	2	0
1994–95	Bolton W	1	0
1995–96	Bolton W	0	0
1996–97	Bolton W	0	0
1996–97	Wigan Ath (loan)	3	0
1997–98	Macclesfield T	31	4
1998–99	Macclesfield T	27	1
Total:		**64**	**5**

WHITTINGHAM, Guy — Forward

H: 5 8 W: 12 02 b.Evesham 10-11-64

Source: Yeovil T, Army.

1989–90	Portsmouth	42	23
1990–91	Portsmouth	37	12
1991–92	Portsmouth	35	11
1992–93	Portsmouth	46	42
1993–94	Aston Villa	18	3
1993–94	Wolverhampton W (loan)	13	8
1994–95	Aston Villa	7	2
1994–95	Sheffield W	21	9
1995–96	Sheffield W	29	6
1996–97	Sheffield W	33	3
1997–98	Sheffield W	28	4
1998–99	Sheffield W	2	0
1998–99	Wolverhampton W (loan)	10	1

1998–99	Portsmouth (loan)	9	7
1998–99	Watford (loan)	5	0
Total:		**335**	**131**

WHITTLE, Christopher — Midfield

b.Preston 31-7-80

Source: Trainee.

1998–99	Blackburn R	0	0

WHITTLE, David — Midfield

H: 5 10 W: 12 07 b.Waterford 2-12-78

Source: Trainee.

1996–97	QPR	0	0
1997–98	QPR	0	0
1998–99	QPR	0	0

WHITTLE, Justin — Defender

H: 6 1 W: 13 09 b.Derby 18-3-71

Source: Celtic.

1994–95	Stoke C	0	0
1995–96	Stoke C	8	0
1996–97	Stoke C	37	0
1997–98	Stoke C	20	0
1998–99	Stoke C	14	1
1998–99	Hull C	24	1
Total:		**103**	**2**

WHITWORTH, Neil — Defender

H: 6 0 W: 12 13 b.Ince 12-4-72

Source: Trainee. *Honours:* England Youth.

1989–90	Wigan Ath	2	0
1990–91	Manchester U	1	0
1991–92	Manchester U	0	0
1991–92	Preston NE (loan)	6	0
1991–92	Barnsley (loan)	11	0
1992–93	Manchester U	0	0
1993–94	Manchester U	0	0
1993–94	Rotherham U (loan)	8	1
1993–94	Blackpool (loan)	3	0
1994–95	Kilmarnock	30	3
1995–96	Kilmarnock	28	0
1996–97	Kilmarnock	7	0
1997–98	Kilmarnock	11	0
1997–98	Wigan Ath	4	0
1998–99	Hull C	18	2
Total:		**129**	**6**

WHYTE, David — Forward

H: 5 8 W: 12 00 b.Greenwich 20-4-71

Source: Greenwich Bor.

1988–89	Crystal Palace	0	0
1989–90	Crystal Palace	0	0
1990–91	Crystal Palace	0	0
1991–92	Crystal Palace	11	1
1991–92	Charlton Ath (loan)	8	2
1992–93	Crystal Palace	0	0
1993–94	Crystal Palace	16	3
1994–95	Charlton Ath	38	19
1995–96	Charlton Ath	25	2
1996–97	Charlton Ath	22	7
1997–98	Ipswich T	2	0
1997–98	Bristol R	4	0
1997–98	Southend U	8	1
1998–99	Southend U	18	2
Total:		**152**	**37**

WHYTE, Derek — Defender

H: 5 11 W: 12 13 b.Glasgow 31-8-68

Source: Celtic BC. *Honours:* Scotland Schools, Youth, Under-21, B, 12 full caps.

1985–86	Celtic	11	0
1986–87	Celtic	42	0
1987–88	Celtic	41	3
1988–89	Celtic	22	0
1989–90	Celtic	35	1
1990–91	Celtic	24	2
1991–92	Celtic	40	1
1992–93	Celtic	1	0
1992–93	Middlesbrough	35	0
1993–94	Middlesbrough	42	1
1994–95	Middlesbrough	36	1
1995–96	Middlesbrough	25	0
1996–97	Middlesbrough	21	0
1997–98	Middlesbrough	8	0
1997–98	Aberdeen	19	0
1998–99	Aberdeen	35	0
Total:		**437**	**9**

WICKS, Matthew — Defender

H: 6 2 W: 13 05 b.Reading 8-9-78

Source: Manchester U Trainee. *Honours:* England Youth.

1995–96	Arsenal	0	0
1996–97	Arsenal	0	0
1997–98	Arsenal	0	0
1998–99	Crewe Alex	6	0
1998–99	Peterborough U	11	0
Total:		**17**	**0**

WIDDRINGTON, Tommy — Midfield

H: 5 8 W: 11 00 b.Newcastle 1-10-71

Source: Trainee.

1989–90	Southampton	0	0
1990–91	Southampton	0	0
1991–92	Southampton	3	0
1991–92	Wigan Ath (loan)	6	0
1992–93	Southampton	12	0
1993–94	Southampton	11	1

1994–95	Southampton	28	0
1995–96	Southampton	21	2
1996–97	Grimsby T	42	4
1997–98	Grimsby T	21	3
1998–99	Grimsby T	26	1
1998–99	Port Vale (loan)	9	1
Total:		**179**	**12**

WIEGHORST, Morten — Midfield

H: 6 3 W: 14 00 b.Glostrup 25-2-71

Source: Lyngby. *Honours:* Denmark 14 full caps, 2 goals.

1992–93	Dundee	23	2
1993–94	Dundee	24	2
1994–95	Dundee	29	3
1995–96	Dundee	14	4
1995–96	Celtic	11	1
1996–97	Celtic	17	2
1997–98	Celtic	31	4
1998–99	Celtic	7	0
Total:		**156**	**18**

WIEKENS, Gerard — Defender

H: 6 0 W: 12 06 b.Tolhuiswyk 25-2-73

1996–97	Veendam	33	1
1997–98	Manchester C	37	5
1998–99	Manchester C	42	2
Total:		**112**	**8**

WIJNHARD, Clyde — Forward

H: 5 11 W: 13 06 b.Paramaribo 9-11-73

1992–93	Ajax	4	2
1993–94	Groningen	23	3
1994–95	Ajax	0	0
1995–96	RKC	33	8
1996–97	RKC	17	10
1997–98	Willem II	29	14
1998–99	Leeds U	18	3
Total:		**124**	**40**

WILBRAHAM, Aaron — Forward

H: 6 3 W: 12 04 b.Knutsford 21-10-79

Source: Trainee.

1997–98	Stockport Co	7	1
1998–99	Stockport Co	26	0
Total:		**33**	**1**

WILCOX, Jason — Forward

H: 6 0 W: 11 00 b.Bolton 15-7-71

Source: Trainee. *Honours:* England B, 2 full caps.

1989–90	Blackburn R	1	0
1990–91	Blackburn R	18	0
1991–92	Blackburn R	38	4
1992–93	Blackburn R	33	4
1993–94	Blackburn R	33	6
1994–95	Blackburn R	27	5
1995–96	Blackburn R	10	3
1996–97	Blackburn R	28	2
1997–98	Blackburn R	31	4
1998–99	Blackburn R	30	3
Total:		**249**	**31**

WILCOX, Rob — Midfield

H: 5 9 W: 12 06 b.Bury 7-11-79

Source: Trainee.

1998–99	Bury	0	0

WILCOX, Russ — Defender

H: 6 0 W: 12 13 b.Hemsworth 25-3-64

Source: Apprentice.

1980–81	Doncaster R	1	0
From Cambridge U, Frickley Ath			
1986–87	Northampton T	35	1
1987–88	Northampton T	46	4
1988–89	Northampton T	11	1
1989–90	Northampton T	46	3
1990–91	Hull C	31	1
1991–92	Hull C	40	4
1992–93	Hull C	29	2
1993–94	Doncaster R	40	2
1994–95	Doncaster R	37	4
1995–96	Doncaster R	4	0
1995–96	Preston NE	27	1
1996–97	Preston NE	35	0
1997–98	Scunthorpe U	31	2
1998–99	Scunthorpe U	28	1
Total:		**441**	**26**

WILDE, Adam — Midfield

H: 5 9 W: 11 11 b.Southampton 22-5-79

Source: Trainee.

1996–97	Cambridge U	1	0
1997–98	Cambridge U	2	0
1998–99	Cambridge U	1	0
Total:		**4**	**0**

WILDER, Chris — Defender

H: 5 11 W: 12 07 b.Stocksbridge 23-9-67

Source: Apprentice.

1985–86	Southampton	0	0
1986–87	Sheffield U	11	0
1987–88	Sheffield U	25	0
1988–89	Sheffield U	29	1
1989–90	Sheffield U	8	0
1989–90	Walsall (loan)	4	0

1990–91	Sheffield U	16	0
1990–91	Charlton Ath (loan)	1	0
1991–92	Sheffield U	4	0
1991–92	Charlton Ath (loan)	2	0
1991–92	Leyton Orient (loan)	16	1
1992–93	Rotherham U	32	8
1993–94	Rotherham U	37	2
1994–95	Rotherham U	45	1
1995–96	Rotherham U	18	0
1995–96	Notts Co	9	0
1996–97	Notts Co	37	0
1996–97	Bradford C	7	0
1997–98	Bradford C	35	0
1997–98	Sheffield U	8	0
1998–99	Sheffield U	4	0
1998–99	Northampton T (loan)	1	0
1998–99	Lincoln C (loan)	3	0
Total:		**352**	**13**

WILDING, Peter — Defender

H: 6 1 W: 12 09 b.Shrewsbury 28-11-68

Source: Telford U.

1997–98	Shrewsbury T	34	1
1998–99	Shrewsbury T	42	0
Total:		**76**	**1**

WILES, Ian — Defender

H: 6 0 W: 11 13 b.Epping 28-4-80

Source: Trainee.

1998–99	Colchester U	1	0
Total:		**1**	**0**

WILKINS, Christopher — Defender

H: 5 6 W: 11 00 b.Walsall 25-2-80

Source: Trainee.

1998–99	Mansfield T	0	0

WILKINS, Ian — Defender

b.Lincoln 3-4-80

Source: Trainee.

1997–98	Lincoln C	2	0
1998–99	Lincoln C	0	0
Total:		**2**	**0**

WILKINS, Richard — Midfield

H: 6 0 W: 12 04 b.Streatham 25-5-65

Source: Haverhill R.

1986–87	Colchester U	23	2
1987–88	Colchester U	46	9
1988–89	Colchester U	40	7
1989–90	Colchester U	43	4
1990–91	Cambridge U	41	3
1991–92	Cambridge U	32	4
1992–93	Cambridge U	1	0
1993–94	Cambridge U	7	0
1994–95	Hereford U	35	2
1995–96	Hereford U	42	3
1996–97	Colchester U	40	2
1997–98	Colchester U	37	5
1998–99	Colchester U	26	2
Total:		**413**	**43**

WILKINSON, John — Midfield

H: 5 8 W: 10 12 b.Exeter 24-8-79

Source: Trainee.

1997–98	Exeter C	1	0
1998–99	Exeter C	18	2
Total:		**19**	**2**

WILKINSON, Paul — Forward

H: 6 1 W: 12 04 b.Louth 30-10-64

Source: Apprentice. *Honours:* England Under-21.

1982–83	Grimsby T	4	1
1983–84	Grimsby T	37	12
1984–85	Grimsby T	30	14
1984–85	Everton	5	2
1985–86	Everton	4	1
1986–87	Everton	22	4
1986–87	Nottingham F	8	0
1987–88	Nottingham F	26	5
1988–89	Watford	45	19
1989–90	Watford	43	15
1990–91	Watford	46	18
1991–92	Middlesbrough	46	15
1992–93	Middlesbrough	41	13
1993–94	Middlesbrough	45	15
1994–95	Middlesbrough	31	6
1995–96	Middlesbrough	3	0
1995–96	Oldham Ath (loan)	4	1
1995–96	Watford (loan)	4	0
1995–96	Luton T (loan)	3	0
1996–97	Barnsley	45	9
1997–98	Barnsley	4	0
1997–98	Millwall	30	3
1998–99	Northampton T	15	1
Total:		**541**	**154**

WILKINSON, Steve — Forward

H: 5 11 W: 11 11 b.Lincoln 1-9-68

Source: Apprentice.

1986–87	Leicester C	1	0
1987–88	Leicester C	5	1
1988–89	Leicester C	1	0
1988–89	Rochdale (loan)	0	0
1988–89	Crewe Alex (loan)	5	2
1989–90	Leicester C	2	0
1989–90	Mansfield T	37	15

1990–91	Mansfield T	39	11
1991–92	Mansfield T	30	14
1992–93	Mansfield T	43	11
1993–94	Mansfield T	42	10
1994–95	Mansfield T	41	22
1995–96	Preston NE	42	10
1996–97	Preston NE	10	3
1997–98	Chesterfield	30	6
1998–99	Chesterfield	23	6
Total:		**351**	**111**

WILKINSON, Steve — Midfield

H: 6 1 W: 13 05 b.Rochdale 7-12-79

Source: Trainee.

1998–99	Bury	0	0

WILLEMS, Ron — Forward

H: 6 1 W: 12 05 b.Epe 20-9-66

1983–84	PEC Zwolle	14	1
1984–85	PEC Zwolle	29	6
1985–86	Twente	22	0
1986–87	Twente	31	5
1987–88	Twente	32	11
1988–89	Ajax	1	0
1989–90	Ajax	19	7
1990–91	Ajax	22	6
1991–92	Ajax	3	0
1992–93	Ajax	2	2
1993–94	Grasshoppers	27	9
1994–95	Grasshoppers	29	9
1995–96	Derby Co	33	11
1996–97	Derby Co	16	2
1997–98	Derby Co	10	0
1998–99	Derby Co	0	0
Total:		**290**	**69**

WILLIAMS, Adam — Midfield

H: 6 0 W: 11 13 b.West Sussex 4-10-78

Source: Trainee.

1997–98	Portsmouth	0	0
1998–99	Portsmouth	0	0

WILLIAMS, Adrian — Defender

H: 6 2 W: 12 06 b.Reading 16-8-71

Source: Trainee. *Honours:* Wales 12 full caps, 1 goal.

1988–89	Reading	8	0
1989–90	Reading	16	2
1990–91	Reading	7	0
1991–92	Reading	40	4
1992–93	Reading	31	4
1993–94	Reading	41	0
1994–95	Reading	22	1
1995–96	Reading	31	3
1996–97	Wolverhampton W	6	0
1997–98	Wolverhampton W	20	0
1998–99	Wolverhampton W	0	0
Total:		**222**	**14**

WILLIAMS, Andy — Forward

H: 5 9 W: 10 12 b.Bristol 8-10-77

Source: Trainee. *Honours:* Wales Under-21, 2 full caps.

1996–97	Southampton	0	0
1997–98	Southampton	20	0
1998–99	Southampton	1	0
Total:		**21**	**0**

WILLIAMS, Anthony — Goalkeeper

H: 6 1 W: 13 08 b.Ogwr 20-9-77

Source: Trainee. *Honours:* Wales Under-21.

1996–97	Blackburn R	0	0
1997–98	Blackburn R	0	0
1997–98	QPR (loan)	0	0
1998–99	Blackburn R	0	0
1998–99	Macclesfield T (loan)	4	0
1998–99	Huddersfield T (loan)	0	0
1998–99	Bristol R (loan)	9	0
Total:		**13**	**0**

WILLIAMS, Danny — Midfield

H: 6 1 W: 13 00 b.Wrexham 12-7-79

Source: Trainee. *Honours:* Wales Under-21.

1996–97	Liverpool	0	0
1997–98	Liverpool	0	0
1998–99	Liverpool	0	0
1998–99	Wrexham	0	0

WILLIAMS, Darren — Defender

H: 5 9 W: 11 00 b.Middlebrough 28-4-77

Source: Trainee. *Honours:* England Under-21, B.

1994–95	York C	1	0
1995–96	York C	18	0
1996–97	York C	1	0
1996–97	Sunderland	11	2
1997–98	Sunderland	36	2
1998–99	Sunderland	25	0
Total:		**92**	**4**

WILLIAMS, Eifion — Forward

H: 5 11 W: 11 00 b.Bangor 15-11-75

Source: Barry T.

1998–99	Torquay U	7	5
Total:		**7**	**5**

WILLIAMS, Gareth — Midfield

H: 6 0 W: 12 02 b.Newport (IW) 12-3-67

Source: Gosport Bor.

1987–88	Aston Villa	1	0
1988–89	Aston Villa	1	0
1989–90	Aston Villa	10	0
1990–91	Aston Villa	0	0
1991–92	Barnsley	17	0
1992–93	Barnsley	8	5
1992–93	Hull C (loan)	4	0
1993–94	Barnsley	9	1
1993–94	Hull C (loan)	16	2
1994–95	Barnsley	0	0
1994–95	Bournemouth	1	0
1994–95	Northampton T	15	0
1995–96	Northampton T	35	1
1996–97	Scarborough	45	10
1997–98	Scarborough	43	15
1998–99	Scarborough	17	2
1998–99	Hull C	25	1
Total:		**247**	**37**

WILLIAMS, Gareth — Midfield

H: 5 11 W: 11 08 b.Glasgow 16-12-81

Source: Trainee.

1998–99	Nottingham F	0	0

WILLIAMS, Geraint — Midfield

H: 5 8 W: 13 00 b.Cwmpare 5-1-62

Source: Apprentice. *Honours:* Wales Youth, Under-21, 13 full caps.

1979–80	Bristol R	0	0
1980–81	Bristol R	28	1
1981–82	Bristol R	16	0
1982–83	Bristol R	35	3
1983–84	Bristol R	34	4
1984–85	Bristol R	28	0
1984–85	Derby Co	12	0
1985–86	Derby Co	40	4
1986–87	Derby Co	40	1
1987–88	Derby Co	40	1
1988–89	Derby Co	37	1
1989–90	Derby Co	38	0
1990–91	Derby Co	31	0
1991–92	Derby Co	39	2
1992–93	Ipswich T	37	0
1993–94	Ipswich T	34	0
1994–95	Ipswich T	38	1
1995–96	Ipswich T	42	1
1996–97	Ipswich T	43	1
1997–98	Ipswich T	23	0
1998–99	Colchester U	39	0
Total:		**674**	**20**

WILLIAMS, James — Midfield

b.Liverpool 15-7-82

Source: Trainee.

1998–99	Swindon T	3	0
Total:		**3**	**0**

WILLIAMS, Jamie — Defender

H: 5 9 W: 12 00 b.Bedworth 3-1-80

Source: Trainee.

1997–98	Coventry C	0	0
1998–99	Coventry C	0	0

WILLIAMS, John — Forward

H: 6 2 W: 13 08 b.Birmingham 11-5-68

Source: Cradley T.

1991–92	Swansea C	39	11
1992–93	Coventry C	41	8
1993–94	Coventry C	32	3
1994–95	Coventry C	7	0
1994–95	Notts Co (loan)	5	2
1994–95	Stoke C (loan)	4	0
1994–95	Swansea C (loan)	7	2
1995–96	Coventry C	0	0
1995–96	Wycombe W	29	8
1996–97	Wycombe W	19	1
1996–97	Hereford U	11	3
1997–98	Walsall	1	0
1997–98	Exeter C	36	4
1998–99	Cardiff C	43	12
Total:		**274**	**54**

WILLIAMS, Lee — Defender

H: 5 8 W: 11 13 b.Edgbaston 3-2-73

Source: Trainee.

1991–92	Aston Villa	0	0
1992–93	Aston Villa	0	0
1992–93	Shrewsbury T (loan)	3	0
1993–94	Aston Villa	0	0
1993–94	Peterborough U	18	0
1994–95	Peterborough U	40	1
1995–96	Peterborough U	33	0
1996–97	Tranmere R	0	0
1996–97	Mansfield T	6	0
1997–98	Mansfield T	38	3
1998–99	Mansfield T	44	2
Total:		**182**	**6**

WILLIAMS, Marc — Forward

H: 5 9 W: 11 07 b.Bangor 8-2-73

Source: Bangor C.

1994–95	Stockport Co	1	0
1995–96	Stockport Co	17	1

1996–97	Stockport Co	0	0
1997–98	Stockport Co	0	0
1998–99	Stockport Co	0	0
1998–99	Halifax T	24	6
1998–99	York C	11	4
Total:		**53**	**11**

WILLIAMS, Mark — Defender

H: 6 0 W: 12 04 b.Stalybridge 28-9-70

Source: Newtown. *Honours:* Northern Ireland 4 full caps.

1991–92	Shrewsbury T	3	0
1992–93	Shrewsbury T	28	1
1993–94	Shrewsbury T	36	1
1994–95	Shrewsbury T	35	1
1995–96	Chesterfield	42	3
1996–97	Chesterfield	42	3
1997–98	Chesterfield	44	3
1998–99	Chesterfield	40	3
Total:		**270**	**15**

WILLIAMS, Mark — Forward

H: 5 11 W: 12 07 b.Bangor 10-12-73

1991–92	Shrewsbury T	1	0
1992–93	Shrewsbury T	2	0
1997–98	Shrewsbury T	5	0
1998–99	Shrewsbury T	0	0
Total:		**8**	**0**

WILLIAMS, Mark — Defender

H: 6 0 W: 11 02 b.Liverpool 10-11-78

Source: Tranmere Trainee. *Honours:*

1998–99	Rochdale	14	1
1998–99	Rotherham U	11	0
Total:		**25**	**1**

WILLIAMS, Martin — Forward

H: 5 9 W: 11 12 b.Luton 12-7-73

Source: Leicester C Trainee.

1991–92	Luton T	1	0
1992–93	Luton T	22	1
1993–94	Luton T	15	1
1994–95	Luton T	2	0
1994–95	Colchester U (loan)	3	0
1995–96	Reading	15	1
1996–97	Reading	29	3
1997–98	Reading	29	6
1998–99	Reading	26	11
Total:		**142**	**23**

WILLIAMS, Michael — Midfield

H: 5 10 W: 12 00 b.Bradford 21-11-69

Source: Maltby MW.

1991–92	Sheffield W	0	0
1992–93	Sheffield W	3	0
1992–93	Halifax T (loan)	9	1
1993–94	Sheffield W	4	0
1994–95	Sheffield W	10	1
1995–96	Sheffield W	5	0
1996–97	Sheffield W	1	0
1996–97	Huddersfield T (loan)	2	0
1996–97	Peterborough U (loan)	6	0
1997–98	Burnley	14	1
1998–99	Burnley	2	0
1998–99	Oxford U	2	0
Total:		**58**	**3**

WILLIAMS, Paul — Midfield

H: 5 7 W: 11 07 b.Leicester 11-9-69

Source: Trainee.

1988–89	Leicester C	0	0
1989–90	Stockport Co	7	0
1990–91	Stockport Co	24	2
1991–92	Stockport Co	13	1
1992–93	Stockport Co	26	1
1993–94	Coventry C	9	0
1993–94	WBA (loan)	5	0
1994–95	Coventry C	5	0
1994–95	Huddersfield T (loan)	9	0
1995–96	Plymouth Arg	46	2
1996–97	Plymouth Arg	46	2
1997–98	Plymouth Arg	39	0
1998–99	Gillingham	10	1
1998–99	Bury	15	1
Total:		**254**	**10**

WILLIAMS, Paul — Defender

H: 5 11 W: 12 10 b.Burton 26-3-71

Source: Trainee. *Honours:* England Under-21.

1989–90	Derby Co	10	1
1989–90	Lincoln C (loan)	3	0
1990–91	Derby Co	19	4
1991–92	Derby Co	41	13
1992–93	Derby Co	19	4
1993–94	Derby Co	34	1
1994–95	Derby Co	37	3
1995–96	Coventry C	32	2
1996–97	Coventry C	32	2
1997–98	Coventry C	20	0
1998–99	Coventry C	22	0
Total:		**269**	**30**

WILLIAMS, Ryan — Forward

H: 5 4 W: 11 02 b.Chesterfield 31-8-78

Source: Trainee. *Honours:* England Youth.

1995–96	Mansfield T	10	3
1996–97	Mansfield T	16	0
1997–98	Tranmere R	0	0
1998–99	Tranmere R	5	0
Total:		**31**	**3**

WILLIAMS, Scott — Midfield

H: 6 0 W: 12 05 b.Bangor 7-8-74

Source: Trainee. *Honours:* Wales Under-21.

1992–93	Wrexham	1	0
1993–94	Wrexham	14	0
1994–95	Wrexham	10	0
1995–96	Wrexham	0	0
1996–97	Wrexham	4	0
1997–98	Wrexham	3	0
1998–99	Rochdale	0	0
Total:		**32**	**0**

WILLIAMSON, Danny — Midfield

H: 5 11 W: 13 13 b.West Ham 5-12-73

Source: Trainee.

1992–93	West Ham U	0	0
1993–94	West Ham U	3	1
1993–94	Doncaster R (loan)	13	1
1994–95	West Ham U	4	0
1995–96	West Ham U	29	4
1996–97	West Ham U	15	0
1997–98	West Ham U	0	0
1997–98	Everton	15	0
1998–99	Everton	0	0
Total:		**79**	**6**

WILLIAMSON, John

b.Derby 3-3-81

Source: Trainee.

1998–99	Burnley	1	0
Total:		**1**	**0**

WILLIAMSON, Michael — Midfield

b.Liverpool 29-12-78

1997–98	Crewe Alex	0	0
1998–99	Crewe Alex	0	0

WILLIAMSON, Russell — Defender

H: 5 4 W: 8 10 b.Epping 17-3-80

Source: Trainee.

1998–99	Wimbledon	0	0

WILLIS, Adam — Defender

H: 6 1 W: 13 02 b.Nuneaton 21-9-76

Source: Trainee.

1995–96	Coventry C	0	0
1996–97	Coventry C	0	0
1997–98	Coventry C	0	0
1997–98	Swindon T	0	0
1998–99	Swindon T	11	0
1998–99	Mansfield T (loan)	10	0
Total:		**21**	**0**

WILLIS, Roger — Midfield

H: 6 0 W: 12 00 b.Islington 17-6-67

1989–90	Grimsby T	9	0
From Barnet			
1991–92	Barnet	38	12
1992–93	Barnet	6	1
1992–93	Watford	32	2
1993–94	Watford	4	0
1993–94	Birmingham C	16	5
1994–95	Birmingham C	3	0
1994–95	Southend U	21	4
1995–96	Southend U	10	3
1996–97	Peterborough U	40	6
1997–98	Chesterfield	34	8
1998–99	Chesterfield	17	0
Total:		**230**	**41**

WILLMOTT, Chris — Defender

H: 6 2 W: 11 13 b.Bedford 30-9-77

Source: Trainee.

1995–96	Luton T	0	0
1996–97	Luton T	0	0
1997–98	Luton T	0	0
1998–99	Luton T	14	0
Total:		**14**	**0**

WILLS, David — Forward

H: 5 5 W: 9 04 b.Manchester 9-3-79

Source: Trainee.

1996–97	Manchester C	0	0
1997–98	Manchester C	0	0
1998–99	Halifax T	0	0

WILLS, Kevin — Forward

H: 5 7 W: 10 04 b.Torbay 15-10-80

Source: Trainee.

1998–99	Plymouth Arg	2	0
Total:		**2**	**0**

WILLY, Mark — Midfield

H: 5 11 W: 12 00 b.Sidcup 5-8-80

Source: Trainee.

1998–99	Wimbledon	0	0

WILMOT, Ellis — Midfield

b.Bournemouth 2-11-79

Source: Trainee.

1998–99	Bristol C	0	0

WILNIS, Fabian — Defender

H: 5 8 W: 12 06 b.Paramaribo 23-8-70

Source: Het Noorden, NOC, De Zwervers, Sparta.

1990–91	NAC	7	3
1991–92	NAC	30	0
1992–93	NAC	32	0
1993–94	NAC	34	0
1994–95	NAC	31	0
1995–96	De Graafschap	32	0
1996–97	De Graafschap	23	0
1997–98	De Graafschap	33	1
1998–99	De Graafschap	19	0
1998–99	Ipswich T	18	1
Total:		**259**	**5**

WILSON, Che — Defender

H: 5 11 W: 11 04 b.Ely 17-1-79

Source: Trainee.

1997–98	Norwich C	0	0
1998–99	Norwich C	17	0
Total:		**17**	**0**

WILSON, Clive — Defender

H: 5 7 W: 11 04 b.Manchester 13-11-61

Source: Local.

1979–80	Manchester C	0	0
1980–81	Manchester C	0	0
1981–82	Manchester C	4	0
1982–83	Manchester C	0	0
1982–83	Chester (loan)	21	2
1983–84	Manchester C	11	0
1984–85	Manchester C	27	4
1985–86	Manchester C	25	5
1986–87	Manchester C	31	0
1986–87	Chelsea	0	0
1986–87	Manchester C (loan)	11	0
1987–88	Chelsea	31	2
1988–89	Chelsea	32	3
1989–90	Chelsea	18	0
1990–91	QPR	13	1
1991–92	QPR	40	3
1992–93	QPR	41	3
1993–94	QPR	42	3
1994–95	QPR	36	2
1995–96	Tottenham H	28	0
1996–97	Tottenham H	26	1
1997–98	Tottenham H	16	0
1998–99	Tottenham H	0	0
Total:		**453**	**29**

WILSON, Kevin — Forward

H: 5 8 W: 11 04 b.Banbury 18-4-61

Source: Banbury U. *Honours:* Northern Ireland 42 full caps, 6 goals.

1979–80	Derby Co	4	0
1980–81	Derby Co	27	7
1981–82	Derby Co	24	9
1982–83	Derby Co	22	4
1983–84	Derby Co	32	2
1984–85	Derby Co	13	8
1984–85	Ipswich T	17	7
1985–86	Ipswich T	39	7
1986–87	Ipswich T	42	20
1987–88	Chelsea	25	5
1988–89	Chelsea	46	13
1989–90	Chelsea	37	14
1990–91	Chelsea	22	7
1991–92	Chelsea	22	3
1991–92	Notts Co	8	1
1992–93	Notts Co	32	1
1993–94	Notts Co	29	1
1993–94	Bradford C (loan)	5	0
1994–95	Walsall	42	16
1995–96	Walsall	46	15
1996–97	Walsall	37	7
1997–98	Northampton T	9	0
1998–99	Northampton T	8	1
Total:		**588**	**148**

WILSON, Mark — Midfield

H: 6 0 W: 13 02 b.Scunthorpe 9-2-79

Source: Trainee. *Honours:* England Schools.

1995–96	Manchester U	0	0
1996–97	Manchester U	0	0
1997–98	Manchester U	0	0
1997–98	Wrexham (loan)	13	4
1998–99	Manchester U	0	0
Total:		**13**	**4**

WILSON, Paul — Midfield

H: 5 9 W: 12 00 b.Forest Gate 26-9-64

Source: West Ham U, Billericay, Barking.

1991–92	Barnet	25	1
1992–93	Barnet	9	0
1993–94	Barnet	34	3
1994–95	Barnet	36	3
1995–96	Barnet	33	4
1996–97	Barnet	37	5
1997–98	Barnet	39	5
1998–99	Barnet	31	2
Total:		**244**	**23**

WILSON, Scott — Defender

H: 6 1 W: 11 04 b.Edinburgh 19-3-77

Source: Rangers BC. *Honours:* Scotland Under-21.

1996–97	Rangers	1	0
1997–98	Rangers	0	0
1998–99	Rangers	12	1
Total:		**13**	**1**

WILSON, Steve — Goalkeeper

H: 5 10 W: 10 12 b.Hull 24-4-74

Source: Trainee.

1990–91	Hull C	2	0
1991–92	Hull C	3	0
1992–93	Hull C	26	0
1993–94	Hull C	9	0
1994–95	Hull C	20	0
1995–96	Hull C	19	0
1996–97	Hull C	15	0
1997–98	Hull C	37	0
1998–99	Hull C	23	0
Total:		**154**	**0**

WILSON, Stuart — Forward

H: 5 8 W: 9 12 b.Leicester 16-9-77

Source: Trainee.

1996–97	Leicester C	2	1
1997–98	Leicester C	11	2
1998–99	Leicester C	9	0
Total:		**22**	**3**

WILSTERMAN, Brian — Defender

H: 6 1 W: 13 03 b.Surinam 19-11-66

Source: Beerschot.

1996–97	Oxford U	1	0
1997–98	Oxford U	24	0
1998–99	Oxford U	17	2
Total:		**42**	**2**

WILTSHIRE, Luke — Midfield

b.Australia 2-10-81

1998–99	Middlesbrough	0	0

WINDASS, Dean — Forward

H: 5 10 W: 12 06 b.Hull 1-4-69

Source: N Ferriby U.

1991–92	Hull C	32	6
1992–93	Hull C	41	7
1993–94	Hull C	43	23
1994–95	Hull C	44	17
1995–96	Hull C	16	4
1995–96	Aberdeen	20	6
1996–97	Aberdeen	29	10
1997–98	Aberdeen	24	5
1998–99	Oxford U	33	15
1998–99	Bradford C	12	3
Total:		**294**	**96**

WINSTANLEY, Mark — Defender

H: 6 1 W: 12 08 b.St Helens 22-1-68

Source: Trainee.

1984–85	Bolton W	0	0
1985–86	Bolton W	3	0
1986–87	Bolton W	13	0
1987–88	Bolton W	8	1
1988–89	Bolton W	44	0
1989–90	Bolton W	43	1
1990–91	Bolton W	32	0
1991–92	Bolton W	27	0
1992–93	Bolton W	29	1
1993–94	Bolton W	21	0
1994–95	Burnley	44	2
1995–96	Burnley	45	3
1996–97	Burnley	35	0
1997–98	Burnley	27	0
1998–99	Burnley	1	0
1998–99	Shrewsbury T (loan)	8	0
Total:		**380**	**8**

WINTERBURN, Nigel — Defender

H: 5 8 W: 11 04 b.Coventry 11-12-63

Source: Local. *Honours:* England Youth, Under-21, B, 2 full caps.

1981–82	Birmingham C	0	0
1982–83	Birmingham C	0	0
1983–84	Oxford U	0	0
1983–84	Wimbledon	43	1
1984–85	Wimbledon	41	4
1985–86	Wimbledon	39	1
1986–87	Wimbledon	42	2
1987–88	Arsenal	17	0
1988–89	Arsenal	38	3
1989–90	Arsenal	36	0
1990–91	Arsenal	38	0
1991–92	Arsenal	41	1
1992–93	Arsenal	29	1
1993–94	Arsenal	34	0
1994–95	Arsenal	39	0
1995–96	Arsenal	36	2
1996–97	Arsenal	38	0
1997–98	Arsenal	36	1
1998–99	Arsenal	30	0
Total:		**577**	**16**

WINTERS, Robert — Forward

H: 5 10 W: 11 06 b.East Kilbride 4-11-74

Source: Muirend Amateur. *Honours:* Scotland 1 full cap.

1993–94	Dundee U	0	0
1994–95	Dundee U	13	2
1995–96	Dundee U	35	7
1996–97	Dundee U	36	8
1997–98	Dundee U	30	8
1998–99	Dundee U	3	1
1998–99	Aberdeen	28	12
Total:		**145**	**38**

WISE, Dennis — Forward

H: 5 6 W: 10 11 b.Kensington 16-12-66

Source: Southampton Apprentice. *Honours:* England Under-21, B, 12 full caps, 1 goal.

1984–85	Wimbledon	1	0
1985–86	Wimbledon	4	0
1986–87	Wimbledon	28	4
1987–88	Wimbledon	30	10
1988–89	Wimbledon	37	5
1989–90	Wimbledon	35	8
1990–91	Chelsea	33	10
1991–92	Chelsea	38	10
1992–93	Chelsea	27	3
1993–94	Chelsea	35	4
1994–95	Chelsea	19	6
1995–96	Chelsea	35	7
1996–97	Chelsea	31	3
1997–98	Chelsea	26	3
1998–99	Chelsea	22	0
Total:		**401**	**73**

WITTER, Tony — Defender

H: 6 1 W: 13 00 b.London 12-8-65

Source: Grays Ath.

1990–91	Crystal Palace	0	0
1991–92	QPR	0	0
1991–92	Millwall (loan)	0	0
1991–92	Plymouth Arg (loan)	3	1
1992–93	QPR	0	0
1993–94	QPR	1	0
1993–94	Reading (loan)	4	0
1994–95	QPR	0	0
1994–95	Millwall	27	1
1995–96	Millwall	31	1
1996–97	Millwall	33	0
1997–98	Millwall	11	0
1998–99	Northampton T	4	0
1998–99	Torquay U	4	0
From Welling U.			
1998–99	Scunthorpe U	14	0
Total:		**132**	**3**

WOAN, Ian — Forward

H: 5 10 W: 12 07 b.Wirrall 14-12-67

Source: Runcorn.

1989–90	Nottingham F	0	0
1990–91	Nottingham F	12	3
1991–92	Nottingham F	21	5
1992–93	Nottingham F	28	3
1993–94	Nottingham F	24	5
1994–95	Nottingham F	37	5
1995–96	Nottingham F	33	8
1996–97	Nottingham F	32	1
1997–98	Nottingham F	21	1
1998–99	Nottingham F	2	0
Total:		**210**	**31**

WOLLEASTON, Robert — Forward

H: 5 11 W: 11 10 b.Perivale 21-12-79

Source: Trainee.

1998–99	Chelsea	0	0

WOOD, Jamie — Forward

H: 5 10 W: 12 11 b.Salford 21-9-78

Source: Trainee.

1997–98	Manchester U	0	0
1998–99	Manchester U	0	0

WOOD, Steve — Midfield

H: 5 9 W: 10 10 b.Oldham 23-6-63

Source: Ashton U.

1997–98	Macclesfield T	43	13
1998–99	Macclesfield T	42	4
Total:		**85**	**17**

WOODCOCK, Chris — Forward

H: 5 7 W: 10 08 b.Bradford 7-5-80

Source: Trainee.

1997–98	Newcastle U	0	0
1998–99	Newcastle U	0	0

WOODFIELD, Craig — Midfield

b.Coventry 4-9-79

Source: Trainee.

1998–99	Blackburn R	0	0

WOODGATE, Jonathan — Defender

H: 6 2 W: 12 09 b.Middlesbrough 22-1-80

Source: Trainee. *Honours:* England Youth, 1 full cap.

1996–97	Leeds U	0	0

1997–98	Leeds U	0	0
1998–99	Leeds U	25	2
Total:		**25**	**2**

WOODHOUSE, Curtis — Midfield

H: 5 8 W: 11 00 b.Driffield 17-4-80

Source: Trainee. *Honours:* England Youth, Under-21.

1997–98	Sheffield U	9	0
1998–99	Sheffield U	33	3
Total:		**42**	**3**

WOODMAN, Andy — Goalkeeper

H: 6 3 W: 13 07 b.Camberwell 11-8-71

Source: Apprentice.

1989–90	Crystal Palace	0	0
1990–91	Crystal Palace	0	0
1991–92	Crystal Palace	0	0
1992–93	Crystal Palace	0	0
1993–94	Crystal Palace	0	0
1994–95	Exeter C	6	0
1994–95	Northampton T	10	0
1995–96	Northampton T	44	0
1996–97	Northampton T	45	0
1997–98	Northampton T	46	0
1998–99	Northampton T	18	0
1998–99	Brentford	22	0
Total:		**191**	**0**

WOODS, Matt — Defender

H: 6 1 W: 12 03 b.Gosport 9-9-76

Source: Trainee.

1995–96	Everton	0	0
1996–97	Chester C	21	1
1997–98	Chester C	29	2
1998–99	Chester C	43	1
Total:		**93**	**4**

WOODS, Neil — Forward

H: 6 0 W: 12 11 b.York 30-7-66

Source: Apprentice.

1982–83	Doncaster R	4	0
1983–84	Doncaster R	7	1
1984–85	Doncaster R	6	2
1985–86	Doncaster R	30	7
1986–87	Doncaster R	18	6
1986–87	Rangers	3	0
1987–88	Ipswich T	19	4
1988–89	Ipswich T	1	0
1989–90	Ipswich T	7	1
1989–90	Bradford C	14	2
1990–91	Bradford C	0	0
1990–91	Grimsby T	44	12
1991–92	Grimsby T	37	8
1992–93	Grimsby T	30	4
1993–94	Grimsby T	11	0
1994–95	Grimsby T	37	14
1995–96	Grimsby T	33	3
1996–97	Grimsby T	24	1
1997–98	Grimsby T	10	0
1997–98	Wigan Ath (loan)	1	0
1997–98	Scunthorpe U (loan)	2	0
1997–98	Mansfield T (loan)	6	0
1998–99	York C	8	0
Total:		**352**	**65**

WOODS, Stephen — Defender

H: 5 11 W: 11 13 b.Davenham 15-12-76

Source: Trainee.

1995–96	Stoke C	0	0
1996–97	Stoke C	0	0
1997–98	Stoke C	1	0
1997–98	Plymouth Arg (loan)	5	0
1998–99	Stoke C	33	0
Total:		**39**	**0**

WOODS, Stephen — Goalkeeper

H: 6 2 W: 12 00 b.Glasgow 23-2-70

Source: Kilpatrick BC.

1989–90	Hibernian	0	0
1990–91	Hibernian	0	0
1991–92	Hibernian	0	0
1991–92	Clydebank	5	0
1992–93	Clydebank	42	0
1993–94	Preston NE	20	0
1994–95	Motherwell	33	0
1995–96	Motherwell	0	0
1996–97	Motherwell	6	0
1997–98	Motherwell	35	0
1998–99	Motherwell	7	0
Total:		**148**	**0**

WOODTHORPE, Colin — Defender

H: 6 0 W: 11 08 b.Ellesmere Pt 13-1-69

Source: Apprentice.

1986–87	Chester C	30	2
1987–88	Chester C	35	0
1988–89	Chester C	44	3
1989–90	Chester C	46	1
1990–91	Norwich C	1	0
1991–92	Norwich C	15	1
1992–93	Norwich C	7	0
1993–94	Norwich C	20	0
1994–95	Aberdeen	14	0
1995–96	Aberdeen	15	1
1996–97	Aberdeen	19	0
1997–98	Stockport Co	32	1
1998–99	Stockport Co	37	2
Total:		**315**	**11**

WOODWARD, Andy — Defender

H: 6 0 W: 13 06 b.Stockport 23-9-73

Source: Trainee.

1992–93	Crewe Alex	6	0
1993–94	Crewe Alex	12	0
1994–95	Crewe Alex	2	0
1994–95	Bury	8	0
1995–96	Bury	1	0
1996–97	Bury	23	0
1997–98	Bury	32	0
1998–99	Bury	37	1
Total:		**121**	**1**

WOODWARD, Jonathan — Goalkeeper

b.Sheffield 16-6-79

Source: Trainee.

1997–98	Sheffield W	0	0
1998–99	Sheffield W	0	0

WOOLISCROFT, Ashley — Defender

H: 5 10 W: 11 02 b.Stoke 28-12-79

Source: Trainee.

1996–97	Stoke C	0	0
1997–98	Stoke C	0	0
1998–99	Stoke C	1	0
Total:		**1**	**0**

WOOLSEY, Jeff — Defender

H: 5 11 W: 12 03 b.Upminster 0-11-77

Source: Trainee.

1995–96	Arsenal	0	0
1996–97	Arsenal	0	0
1997–98	QPR	0	0
1997–98	Brighton & HA	3	0
1998–99	Brighton & HA	0	0
Total:		**3**	**0**

WOOZLEY, David — Defender

H: 6 0 W: 12 10 b.Berkshire 6-12-79

Source: Trainee.

1997–98	Crystal Palace	0	0
1998–99	Crystal Palace	7	0
Total:		**7**	**0**

WORMULL, Simon — Midfield

H: 5 10 W: 12 03 b.Crawley 1-12-76

Source: Trainee.

1995–96	Tottenham H	0	0
1996–97	Tottenham H	0	0
1997–98	Brentford	5	0
1997–98	Brighton & HA	0	0
1998–99	Brentford	0	0
Total:		**5**	**0**

WORRALL, Ben — Midfield

H: 5 5 W: 10 00 b.Swindon 7-12-75

Source: Trainee. *Honours:* England Youth.

1994–95	Swindon T	3	0
1995–96	Swindon T	0	0
1996–97	Scarborough	15	1
1997–98	Scarborough	21	2
1998–99	Scarborough	31	0
Total:		**70**	**3**

WORRELL, David — Defender

H: 5 11 W: 12 04 b.Dublin 12-1-78

Source: Trainee. *Honours:* Eire Youth, Under-21.

1994–95	Blackburn R	0	0
1995–96	Blackburn R	0	0
1996–97	Blackburn R	0	0
1997–98	Blackburn R	0	0
1998–99	Blackburn R	0	0
1998–99	Dundee U	4	0
Total:		**4**	**0**

WORTHINGTON, Martin — Forward

H: 5 10 W: 11 11 b.Torquay 25-1-81

Source: Trainee.

1998–99	Torquay U	1	0
Total:		**1**	**0**

WORTHINGTON, Nigel — Defender

H: 5 11 W: 12 06 b.Ballymena 4-11-61

Source: Ballymena U. *Honours:* Northern Ireland Youth, 66 full caps.

1981–82	Notts Co	2	0
1982–83	Notts Co	41	3
1983–84	Notts Co	24	1
1983–84	Sheffield W	14	1
1984–85	Sheffield W	38	1
1985–86	Sheffield W	15	0
1986–87	Sheffield W	35	0
1987–88	Sheffield W	38	0
1988–89	Sheffield W	28	0
1989–90	Sheffield W	32	2
1990–91	Sheffield W	33	1
1991–92	Sheffield W	34	5
1992–93	Sheffield W	40	1
1993–94	Sheffield W	31	1
1994–95	Leeds U	27	1
1995–96	Leeds U	16	0
1996–97	Stoke C	12	0

1997–98	Blackpool	9	0
1998–99	Blackpool	0	0
Total:		**469**	**17**

WOTTON, Paul — Midfield

H: 5 11 W: 11 08 b.Plymouth 17-8-77

Source: Trainee.

1994–95	Plymouth Arg	7	0
1995–96	Plymouth Arg	1	0
1996–97	Plymouth Arg	9	1
1997–98	Plymouth Arg	34	1
1998–99	Plymouth Arg	36	1
Total:		**87**	**3**

WRACK, Darren — Midfield

H: 5 10 W: 12 02 b.Cleethorpes 5-5-76

Source: Trainee.

1994–95	Derby Co	16	1
1995–96	Derby Co	10	0
1996–97	Grimsby T	12	1
1996–97	Shrewsbury T (loan)	4	0
1997–98	Grimsby T	1	0
1998–99	Walsall	46	13
Total:		**89**	**15**

WRAIGHT, Gary — Defender

H: 5 9 W: 11 13 b.Epping 5-3-79

Source: Trainee.

1997–98	Wycombe W	1	0
1998–99	Wycombe W	6	0
Total:		**7**	**0**

WREH, Christopher — Forward

H: 5 8 W: 11 13 b.Liberia 14-5-75

1995–96	Monaco	13	3
1996–97	Guincamp	33	10
1997–98	Arsenal	16	3
1998–99	Arsenal	12	0
Total:		**74**	**16**

WRIGHT-PHILLIPS, Shaun — Forward

H: 5 6 W: 10 01 b.London 25-10-81

1998–99	Manchester C	0	0

WRIGHT, Alan — Defender

H: 5 4 W: 9 09 b.Ashton-under-Lyme 28-9-71

Source: Trainee. *Honours:* England Schools, Youth, Under-21.

1987–88	Blackpool	1	0
1988–89	Blackpool	16	0
1989–90	Blackpool	24	0
1990–91	Blackpool	45	0
1991–92	Blackpool	12	0
1991–92	Blackburn R	33	1
1992–93	Blackburn R	24	0
1993–94	Blackburn R	12	0
1994–95	Blackburn R	5	0
1994–95	Aston Villa	8	0
1995–96	Aston Villa	38	2
1996–97	Aston Villa	38	1
1997–98	Aston Villa	37	0
1998–99	Aston Villa	38	0
Total:		**331**	**4**

WRIGHT, Andy — Midfield

H: 5 8 W: 9 06 b.Leeds 21-10-78

Source: Trainee.

1995–96	Leeds U	0	0
1996–97	Leeds U	0	0
1997–98	Leeds U	0	0
1998–99	Leeds U	0	0
1998–99	Reading (loan)	2	0
Total:		**2**	**0**

WRIGHT, Andy — Forward

H: 6 0 W: 11 04 b.Bristol 12-9-79

1998–99	Macclesfield T	0	0

WRIGHT, Ben — Midfield

b.Munster 1-7-80

1998–99	Bristol C	0	0

WRIGHT, Daniel — Forward

H: 5 8 W: 10 06 b.London 24-9-81

Source: Trainee.

1998–99	QPR	0	0

WRIGHT, Darren — Forward

H: 5 6 W: 10 00 b.Warrington 7-9-79

Source: Trainee.

1997–98	Chester C	5	0
1998–99	Chester C	18	1
Total:		**23**	**1**

WRIGHT, David — Defender

H: 5 11 W: 10 09 b.Warrington 1-5-80

Source: Trainee. *Honours:* England Youth.

1997–98	Crewe Alex	3	0
1998–99	Crewe Alex	20	1
Total:		**23**	**1**

WRIGHT, David — Midfield

b.Portsmouth 24-11-79

Source: Portsmouth Trainee.

1998–99	Crystal Palace	0	0

WRIGHT, Ian — Forward

H: 5 10 W: 11 08 b.Woolwich 3-11-63

Source: Greenwich Bor. *Honours:* England B, 33 full caps, 9 goals.

1985–86	Crystal Palace	32	9
1986–87	Crystal Palace	38	8
1987–88	Crystal Palace	41	20
1988–89	Crystal Palace	42	24
1989–90	Crystal Palace	26	8
1990–91	Crystal Palace	38	15
1991–92	Crystal Palace	8	5
1991–92	Arsenal	30	24
1992–93	Arsenal	31	15
1993–94	Arsenal	39	23
1994–95	Arsenal	31	18
1995–96	Arsenal	31	15
1996–97	Arsenal	35	23
1997–98	Arsenal	24	10
1998–99	West Ham U	22	9
Total:		**468**	**226**

WRIGHT, Ian — Defender

H: 6 1 W: 13 04 b.Lichfield 10-3-72

Source: Trainee.

1989–90	Stoke C	1	0
1990–91	Stoke C	1	0
1991–92	Stoke C	3	0
1992–93	Stoke C	1	0
1993–94	Stoke C	0	0
1993–94	Bristol R	29	0
1994–95	Bristol R	7	1
1995–96	Bristol R	18	0
1996–97	Hull C	40	0
1997–98	Hull C	33	2
1998–99	Hull C	0	0
Total:		**133**	**3**

WRIGHT, Jermaine — Midfield

H: 5 10 W: 11 09 b.Greenwich 21-10-75

Source: Trainee. *Honours:* England Youth.

1992–93	Millwall	0	0
1993–94	Millwall	0	0
1994–95	Millwall	0	0
1994–95	Wolverhampton W	6	0
1995–96	Wolverhampton W	7	0
1995–96	Doncaster R (loan)	13	0
1996–97	Wolverhampton W	3	0
1997–98	Wolverhampton W	4	0
1997–98	Crewe Alex	5	0
1998–99	Crewe Alex	44	5
Total:		**82**	**5**

WRIGHT, Mark — Defender

H: 6 2 W: 13 03 b.Dorchester 1-8-63

Source: Amateur. *Honours:* England Under-21, 45 full caps, 1 goal.

1980–81	Oxford U	0	0
1981–82	Oxford U	10	0
1981–82	Southampton	3	0
1982–83	Southampton	39	2
1983–84	Southampton	29	1
1984–85	Southampton	36	0
1985–86	Southampton	33	3
1986–87	Southampton	30	1
1987–88	Southampton	0	0
1987–88	Derby Co	38	3
1988–89	Derby Co	33	1
1989–90	Derby Co	36	6
1990–91	Derby Co	37	0
1991–92	Liverpool	21	0
1992–93	Liverpool	33	2
1993–94	Liverpool	31	1
1994–95	Liverpool	6	0
1995–96	Liverpool	28	2
1996–97	Liverpool	33	0
1997–98	Liverpool	6	0
1998–99	Liverpool	0	0
Total:		**482**	**22**

WRIGHT, Mark — Forward

H: 5 10 W: 11 04 b.Chorley 4-9-81

Source: Schoolboy.

1998–99	Preston NE	1	0
Total:		**1**	**0**

WRIGHT, Nick — Forward

H: 5 9 W: 11 13 b.Derby 15-10-75

Source: Trainee.

1994–95	Derby Co	0	0
1995–96	Derby Co	0	0
1996–97	Derby Co	0	0
1997–98	Derby Co	0	0
1997–98	Carlisle U	25	5
1998–99	Watford	33	6
Total:		**58**	**11**

WRIGHT, Paul — Forward

H: 5 8 W: 10 08 b.East Kilbride 17-8-67

Source: 'S' Form. *Honours:* Scotland Youth, Under-21, B.

1983–84	Aberdeen	1	0
1984–85	Aberdeen	0	0
1985–86	Aberdeen	10	2

1986–87	Aberdeen	25	4
1987–88	Aberdeen	9	4
1988–89	Aberdeen	23	6
1989–90	QPR	15	5
1989–90	Hibernian	3	1
1990–91	Hibernian	33	6
1991–92	St Johnstone	41	18
1992–93	St Johnstone	42	14
1993–94	St Johnstone	17	7
1994–95	St Johnstone	12	1
1994–95	Kilmarnock	7	1
1995–96	Kilmarnock	36	13
1996–97	Kilmarnock	31	14
1997–98	Kilmarnock	28	10
1998–99	Kilmarnock	33	6
Total:		**366**	**112**

WRIGHT, Richard — Goalkeeper

H: 6 2 W: 13 07 b.Ipswich 5-11-77

Source: Trainee. *Honours:* England Schools, Youth, Under-21.

1994–95	Ipswich T	3	0
1995–96	Ipswich T	23	0
1996–97	Ipswich T	40	0
1997–98	Ipswich T	46	0
1998–99	Ipswich T	46	0
Total:		**158**	**0**

WRIGHT, Stephen — Defender

H: 5 10 W: 11 09 b.Bellshill 27-8-71

Source: Aberdeen Lads. *Honours:* Scotland Under-21, 2 full caps.

1987–88	Aberdeen	0	0
1988–89	Aberdeen	0	0
1989–90	Aberdeen	1	0
1990–91	Aberdeen	17	1
1991–92	Aberdeen	23	0
1992–93	Aberdeen	36	0
1993–94	Aberdeen	36	0
1994–95	Aberdeen	34	1
1995–96	Rangers	6	0
1996–97	Rangers	1	0
1997–98	Rangers	0	0
1997–98	Wolverhampton W (loan)	3	0
1998–99	Bradford C	22	0
Total:		**179**	**2**

WRIGHT, Stephen — Defender

b.Liverpool 8-2-80

Source: Trainee. *Honours:* England Youth.

1997–98	Liverpool	0	0
1998–99	Liverpool	0	0

WRIGHT, Tommy — Goalkeeper

H: 6 1 W: 14 05 b.Belfast 29-8-63

Source: Linfield. *Honours:* Northern Ireland 30 full caps. Football League.

1987–88	Newcastle U	0	0
1988–89	Newcastle U	9	0
1989–90	Newcastle U	14	0
1990–91	Newcastle U	0	0
1990–91	Hull C (loan)	6	0
1991–92	Newcastle U	33	0
1992–93	Newcastle U	14	0
1993–94	Newcastle U	3	0
1993–94	Nottingham F	10	0
1994–95	Nottingham F	0	0
1995–96	Nottingham F	0	0
1996–97	Nottingham F	1	0
1996–97	Reading (loan)	17	0
1996–97	Manchester C	13	0
1997–98	Manchester C	18	0
1998–99	Manchester C	1	0
1998–99	Wrexham (loan)	16	0
Total:		**155**	**0**

WRIGHT, Tony — Midfield

H: 5 7 W: 11 01 b.Swansea 1-9-79

Source: Trainee. *Honours:* Wales Under-21.

1997–98	Oxford U	1	0
1998–99	Oxford U	6	0
Total:		**7**	**0**

WYATT, Nicky — Forward

H: 5 6 W: 10 00 b.Portsmouth 22-10-79

Source: Trainee.

1998–99	Portsmouth	0	0

WYNESS, Dennis — Midfield

H: 5 10 W: 11 04 b.Aberdeen 22-3-77

Source: FC Stoneywood.

1996–97	Aberdeen	7	0
1997–98	Aberdeen	0	0
1998–99	Aberdeen	14	1
Total:		**21**	**1**

XIOUROUPPA, Costas — Forward

H: 5 11 W: 11 00 b.Dudley 11-9-79

Source: Trainee.

1996–97	Bolton W	0	0
1997–98	Bolton W	0	0
1998–99	Bolton W	0	0

YATES, Dean — Defender

H: 6 2 W: 12 06 b.Leicester 26-10-67

Source: Apprentice. *Honours:* England Under-21.

1984–85	Notts Co	8	0
1985–86	Notts Co	44	4
1986–87	Notts Co	42	9
1987–88	Notts Co	46	2
1988–89	Notts Co	41	6
1989–90	Notts Co	45	6
1990–91	Notts Co	41	4
1991–92	Notts Co	25	2
1992–93	Notts Co	0	0
1993–94	Notts Co	1	0
1994–95	Notts Co	21	0
1994–95	Derby Co	11	1
1995–96	Derby Co	38	2
1996–97	Derby Co	10	0
1997–98	Derby Co	9	0
1998–99	Watford	9	1
Total:		**391**	**37**

YATES, Steve — Defender

H: 5 10 W: 12 02 b.Bristol 29-1-70

Source: Trainee.

1986–87	Bristol R	2	0
1987–88	Bristol R	0	0
1988–89	Bristol R	35	0
1989–90	Bristol R	42	0
1990–91	Bristol R	34	0
1991–92	Bristol R	39	0
1992–93	Bristol R	44	0
1993–94	Bristol R	1	0
1993–94	QPR	29	0
1994–95	QPR	23	1
1995–96	QPR	30	0
1996–97	QPR	16	1
1997–98	QPR	30	0
1998–99	QPR	6	0
Total:		**331**	**2**

YORKE, Dwight — Forward

H: 5 10 W: 12 04 b.Canaan 3-11-71

Source: St Clair's, Tobago. *Honours:* Trinidad & Tobago 10 full caps.

1989–90	Aston Villa	2	0
1990–91	Aston Villa	18	2
1991–92	Aston Villa	32	11
1992–93	Aston Villa	27	6
1993–94	Aston Villa	12	2
1994–95	Aston Villa	37	6
1995–96	Aston Villa	35	17
1996–97	Aston Villa	37	17
1997–98	Aston Villa	30	12
1998–99	Aston Villa	1	0
1998–99	Manchester U	32	18
Total:		**263**	**91**

YOUDS, Eddie — Defender

H: 6 1 W: 13 00 b.Liverpool 3-5-70

Source: Trainee.

1988–89	Everton	0	0
1989–90	Everton	0	0
1989–90	Cardiff C (loan)	1	0
1989–90	Wrexham (loan)	20	2
1990–91	Everton	8	0
1991–92	Everton	0	0
1991–92	Ipswich T	1	0
1992–93	Ipswich T	16	0
1993–94	Ipswich T	23	1
1994–95	Ipswich T	10	0
1994–95	Bradford C	17	3
1995–96	Bradford C	30	4
1996–97	Bradford C	0	0
1997–98	Bradford C	38	1
1997–98	Charlton Ath	8	0
1998–99	Charlton Ath	22	2
Total:		**194**	**13**

YOUNG, Darren — Forward

H: 5 8 W: 10 03 b.Glasgow 13-10-78

Source: Crombie Sports. *Honours:* Scotland Under-17, Under-21.

1995–96	Aberdeen	0	0
1996–97	Aberdeen	26	1
1997–98	Aberdeen	5	0
1998–99	Aberdeen	11	0
Total:		**42**	**1**

YOUNG, Derek — Forward

H: 5 8 W: 10 10 b.Glasgow 27-5-80

Source: Lewis U.

1996–97	Aberdeen	0	0
1997–98	Aberdeen	0	0
1998–99	Aberdeen	4	0
Total:		**4**	**0**

YOUNG, Luke — Midfield

b.Harlow 19-7-79

Source: Trainee. *Honours:* England Youth, Under-21.

1997–98	Tottenham H	0	0
1998–99	Tottenham H	15	0
Total:		**15**	**0**

YOUNG, Neil — Defender

H: 5 9 W: 12 00 b.Harlow 31-8-73

Source: Trainee.

1991–92	Tottenham H	0	0
1992–93	Tottenham H	0	0
1993–94	Tottenham H	0	0

1994–95	Bournemouth	32	0
1995–96	Bournemouth	41	0
1996–97	Bournemouth	44	0
1997–98	Bournemouth	44	2
1998–99	Bournemouth	44	1
Total:		**205**	**3**

YOUNG, Scott — Defender

H: 6 1 W: 13 02 b.Llywnypia 14-1-76

Source: Trainee. *Honours:* Wales Under-21.

1993–94	Cardiff C	6	0
1994–95	Cardiff C	22	0
1995–96	Cardiff C	41	0
1996–97	Cardiff C	32	1
1997–98	Cardiff C	31	3
1998–99	Cardiff C	33	1
Total:		**165**	**5**

YOUNGS, Tom — Forward

H: 5 9 W: 10 07 b.Bury St Edmunds 31-8-79

Source: Trainee.

1997–98	Cambridge U	4	0
1998–99	Cambridge U	10	0
Total:		**14**	**0**

ZABEK, Lee — Midfield

H: 6 0 W: 13 08 b.Bristol 13-10-78

Source: Trainee.

1996–97	Bristol R	1	0
1997–98	Bristol R	13	1
1998–99	Bristol R	11	0
Total:		**25**	**1**

ZAGORAKIS, Theo — Midfield

H: 5 9 W: 11 08 b.Kavala 27-10-71

Source: PAOK Salonika. *Honours:* Greece 43 full caps.

1997–98	Leicester C	14	1
1998–99	Leicester C	19	1
Total:		**33**	**2**

ZAHANA-ONI, Landry — Midfield

H: 5 9 W: 10 09 b.Ivory Coast 8-8-76

Source: Bromley.

1998–99	Luton T	8	0
Total:		**8**	**0**

ZETTERLUND, Lars — Midfield

H: 6 2 W: 11 13 b.HÑrnîsand, Sweden 11-2-64

1987	IFK Gothenburg	18	1
1988	IFK Gothenburg	22	5
1989	IFK Gothenburg	13	1
1990	Orebro	24	2
1991	Orebro	10	0
1992	Orebro	1	0
1993	Orebro	26	1
1994	Orebro	26	2
1995	Orebro	24	2
1996	Orebro	26	4
1996–97	Dundee U	25	1
1997–98	Dundee U	33	2
1998–99	Dundee U	21	1
Total:		**269**	**22**

ZHIYI, Fan — Midfield

H: 6 0 W: 12 01 b.Shanghai 22-1-70

Source: Shanghai Shenhua. *Honours:* China full caps.

1998–99	Crystal Palace	29	2
Total:		**29**	**2**

ZOLA, Gianfranco — Forward

H: 5 6 W: 10 10 b.Oliena 5-7-66

Honours: Italy 34 full caps, 9 goals.

1984–85	Nuorese	4	0
1985–86	Nuorese	27	10
1986–87	Torres	30	8
1987–88	Torres	24	2
1988–89	Torres	34	11
1989–90	Napoli	18	2
1990–91	Napoli	20	6
1991–92	Napoli	34	12
1992–93	Napoli	33	12
1993–94	Parma	33	18
1994–95	Parma	32	19
1995–96	Parma	29	10
1996–97	Parma	8	2
1996–97	Chelsea	23	8
1997–98	Chelsea	27	8
1998–99	Chelsea	37	13
Total:		**413**	**141**

ZWIJNENBERG, Clemens — Midfield

b.Enschede 18-5-70

Source: Aalborg.

1998–99	Bristol C	3	0
Total:		**3**	**0**

STOP PRESS

Summer transfers included the following:

May:

Daniel Brown, Leyton Orient to Barnet; Sagi Burton, Crystal Palace to Colchester United; Matthew Hocking, Hull City to York City; Seth Johnson, Crewe Alexandra to Derby County; Dean Kiely, Bury to Charlton Athletic; Joshua Low, Bristol Rovers to Leyton Orient; Dean Walling, Lincoln City to Doncaster Rovers.

June:

Paul Dalglish, Newcastle United to Norwich City; Adam Eaton, Everton to Preston North End; Martin Gray, Oxford United to Darlington; Gunnar Halle, Leeds United to Bradford City; Christopher Lucketti, Bury to Huddersfield Town; Andrew Oakes, Hull City to Derby County; John Varty, Carlisle United to Rotherham United.

July:

Ibrahima Bakayoko, Everton to Marseille; Darren Bazeley, Watford to Wolverhampton Wanderers; Eyal Berkovic, West Ham United to Celtic; Steve Bould, Arsenal to Sunderland; Mark Bosnich, Aston Villa to Manchester United; Titi Camara, Marseille to Liverpool; Lee Clark, Sunderland to Fulham; Philippe Clement, Coventry City to FC Brugge; Jason Crowe, Arsenal to Portsmouth; Olivier Dacourt, Everton to Lens; Didier Deschamps, Juventus to Chelsea; Simon Donnelly, Celtic to Sheffield Wednesday; Nicky Forster, Birmingham City to Reading; Carsten Fredgaard, Lyngby to Sunderland; George Georgiadis, Newcastle United to PAOK Salonika; Alain Goma, Paris St Germain to Newcastle United; Neil Heaney, Manchester City to Darlington; Dirk Heinen, Leverkusen to Liverpool; Thomas Helmer, Bayern Munich to Sunderland; Stephane Henchoz, Blackburn Rovers to Liverpool; Sami Hyypia, Willem II to Liverpool; Kenny Irons, Tranmere Rovers to Huddersfield Town; David James, Liverpool to Aston Villa; Dmitri Kharine, Chelsea to Celtic; William Korsten, Leeds United to Tottenham Hotspur; Des Lyttle, Nottingham Forest to Watford; Mario Malchiot, Ajax to Chelsea; Elena Marcelino, Mallorca to Newcastle United; Marco Materazzi, Everton to Perugia; Erik Meijer, Leverkusen to Liverpool; Danny Mills, Charlton Athletic to Leeds United; Andy Myers, Chelsea to Bradford City; Phil O'Donnell, Celtic to Sheffield Wednesday; Eddie Newton, Chelsea to Birmingham City; Kevin Nicholls, Charlton Athletic to Wigan Athletic; Tore Pedersen, Eintracht Frankfurt to Wimbledon; Chris Perry, Wimbledon to Tottenham Hotspur; Peter Schmeichel, Manchester United to Sporting Lisbon; Scott Sellars, Bolton Wanderers to Huddersfield Town; Andy Sinton, Tottenham Hotspur to Wolverhampton Wanderers; Lee Sharpe, Leeds United to Bradford City; Neil Shipperley, Nottingham Forest to Barnsley; Silvinho, Corinthians to Arsenal; Vladimir Smicer, Lens to Liverpool; Chris Sutton, Blackburn Rovers to Chelsea; Pierre Van Hooijdonk, Nottingham Forest to Vitesse; Sander Westerveld, Vitesse to Liverpool; David Wetherall, Leeds United to Bradford City; Mark Williams, Chesterfield to Watford; Chris Willmott, Luton Town to Wimbledon.

The Football League welcome Cheltenham Town, whose appearances and goals in the Nationwide Conference for the 1998-99 season were as follows:

Conference Appearances: Bailey, D. 7(1); Banks, C. 34(1); Bloomer, B. 15(13); Brough, J. 34(6); Book, S. 42; Duff, M. 41; Eaton, J. 27(7); Freeman, M. 36(1); Grayson, N. 39(2); Howarth, N. 5(3); Howells, L. 37(1); Jackson, M. (1); Knight, K. 8(15); Milton, R. 6(11); Norton, D. 35(1); Smith, J. 2(5); Victory, J. 42; Walker, C. 17(7); Walker, R. 14(2); Watkins, D. 9(10); Yates, M. 12.
Goals (71): Grayson 17, Eaton 9, Howells 6, Watkins 6, Freeman 5, Brough 4, Victory 4, Walker C 4, Duff 3, Knight 3, Norton 3, Bailey 2, Banks 1, Smith 1, og 3.